SAMUEL JOHNSON SELECTED ESSAYS

SAMUEL JOHNSON was born in Lichfield in 1709, the son of a bookseller, and was educated at Lichfield Grammar School and, for a short time at Pembroke College, Oxford. He taught for a while, after which he worked for a Birmingham printer, for whom he translated Lobo's *A Voyage to Abyssinia*. In 1735 he married Elizabeth Jervis Porter and with her money opened a boarding academy. The school was a failure and in 1737 Johnson left for London. There, he became a regular contributor to the *Gentleman's Magazine* and struggled to earn a living from writing. But it was not until the award of a government pension in 1762 that Johnson gained financial security. His *London: A Poem in Imitation of the Third Satire of Juvenal* was published anonymously in 1738 and attracted some attention. *The Vanity of Human Wishes: The Tenth Satire of Juvenal Imitated* appeared under his own name in 1749. From 1750 to 1752 he issued the *Rambler*, a periodical written almost entirely by himself, and consolidated his position as a notable moral essayist with some twenty-five essays in the *Adventurer*. The *Idler* essays, lighter in tone, appeared weekly between 1758 and 1760. When his *Dictionary of the English Language* was published in 1755, Johnson took on the proportions of a literary monarch in the London of his day. In need of money to visit his sick mother, he wrote *Rasselas* (1759) reportedly in the evenings of one week, finishing a couple of days after his mother's death. In 1763 Boswell became his faithful follower and it is mainly to his *Life* that we owe our intimate knowledge of Johnson. Founded in 1764, 'The Club' (of literary men) was the perfect forum for the exercise of Johnson's great conversational art. His edition of Shakespeare's plays appeared in 1765. From August to November 1773 he and Boswell toured Scotland and in 1775 his *Journey to the Western Islands of Scotland* appeared. His last major work was *Lives of the Poets*. He died in December 1784.

DAVID WOMERSLEY is Thomas Warton Professor of English Literature at the University of Oxford and a Fellow of St Catherine's College. His book *The Transformation of The*

Decline and Fall of the Roman Empire was published by Cambridge University Press in 1988. He has also edited *Augustan Critical Writing*, a three-volume complete edition of Gibbon's *The History of the Decline and Fall of the Roman Empire* and Edmund Burke's *A Philosophical Enquiry into the Sublime and Beautiful and Other Pre-Revolutionary Writings*, all for Penguin Classics.

SAMUEL JOHNSON

Selected Essays

Edited with an Introduction and Notes by
DAVID WOMERSLEY

PENGUIN BOOKS

PENGUIN BOOKS

Published by the Penguin Group
Penguin Books Ltd, 80 Strand, London WC2R ORL, England
Penguin Putnam Inc., 375 Hudson Street, New York, New York 10014, USA
Penguin Books Australia Ltd, 250 Camberwell Road, Camberwell, Victoria 3124, Australia
Penguin Books Canada Ltd, 10 Alcorn Avenue, Toronto, Ontario, Canada M4V 3B2
Penguin Books India (P) Ltd, 11, Community Centre, Panchsheel Park, New Delhi – 110 017, India
Penguin Books (NZ) Ltd, Cnr Rosedale and Airborne Roads, Albany, Auckland, New Zealand
Penguin Books (South Africa) (Pty) Ltd, 24 Sturdee Avenue, Rosebank 2196, South Africa

Penguin Books Ltd, Registered Offices: 80 Strand, London WC2R ORL, England

www.penguin.com

Essays published 1739–61
This selection first published 2003

015

Set in 10.25/12.25 pt PostScript Adobe Sabon
Typeset by Rowland Phototypesetting Ltd, Bury St Edmunds, Suffolk
Printed in Great Britain by Clays Ltd, St Ives plc

www.greenpenguin.co.uk

MIX
Paper from
responsible sources
FSC FSC® C018179
www.fsc.org

Penguin Books is committed to a sustainable
future for our business, our readers and our planet.
This book is made from Forest Stewardship
Council™ certified paper.

Contents

MISCELLANEOUS ESSAYS

A Chronology of Samuel Johnson

1709 Born on 18 September in Lichfield; son of Michael and Sarah Johnson.

1712 Touched for the king's evil (scrofula) by Queen Anne.

1717–25 Attends Lichfield Grammar School.

1728 Enters Pembroke College, Oxford, in October.

1729 Leaves Oxford in December.

1731 Death of his father, Michael Johnson.

1732 Works as an usher at Market Bosworth school.

1733 Translates Lobo's *Voyage to Abyssinia*; contributes essays to the *Birmingham Journal*.

1735 Marries Elizabeth Porter; takes out lease on school at Edial.

1737 Leaves for London in March, accompanied by one of his pupils, David Garrick; begins working for the publisher Edward Cave, and contributes to *The Gentleman's Magazine*.

1738 Publication of *London: A Poem in Imitation of the Third Satire of Juvenal*.

1739 Publication of *A Compleat Vindication of the Licensers of the Stage*.

1744 Publication of *Life of Mr. Richard Savage*, and *Harleian Miscellany*.

1746 Contract signed for *Dictionary*.

1747 Publication of the 'Plan' of the *Dictionary*.

1749 Publication of *The Vanity of Human Wishes*; Garrick produces *Irene*.

1750 Begins *The Rambler*.

1752 Death of Elizabeth Johnson; *The Rambler* concludes.

1753 Begins contributing to *The Adventurer* in March.

1754 Ceases to contribute to *The Adventurer* in March; publishes biography of Cave.

1755 Publication of the *Dictionary*; awarded honorary MA, Oxford.

1758 Begins *The Idler*, published in *The Universal Chronicle*.

1759 Death of his mother, Sarah Johnson; publication of *Rasselas: The Prince of Abyssinia*.

1760 *The Idler* concludes.

1762 Receives pension of £300 per annum from George III.

1763 Meets James Boswell.

1764 Founding of 'The Club' (an informal group founded at suggestion of Joshua Reynolds).

1765 Awarded LL D, Dublin; publication of *The Dramatic Works of William Shakespeare* (8 vols.). Meets Henry and Hester Thrale.

1770 Publication of *The False Alarm*.

1771 Publication of *Thoughts on the late Transactions Respecting Falkland's Islands*.

1773 Tour of the highlands of Scotland and the Hebrides.

1774 Publication of *The Patriot*; tour of Wales with the Thrales.

1775 Awarded DCL, Oxford; visits Paris with the Thrales; publication of *A Journey to the Western Islands of Scotland* and *Taxation No Tyranny*.

1777 Begins work on the *Lives of the Poets*.

1779 Publication of first instalment of the *Lives of the Poets*.

1781 Publication of second instalment of the *Lives of the Poets*.

1783 Founding of the Essex Head Club.

1784 Dies on 13 December.

Introduction

When Samuel Johnson died in 1784, William Hamilton saw the event as an irreparable calamity: 'He has made a chasm, which not only nothing can fill up, but which nothing has a tendency to fill up. – Johnson is dead. – Let us go to the next best: – there is nobody; no man can be said to put you in mind of Johnson.'[1] This is not just testimony to the warmth of Johnson's friendships, for his death had also made a rent in the literary life of the nation. Ever since 1759, when the novelist and man of letters Tobias Smollett had referred to Johnson as 'that great CHAM of literature', Johnson had contended for a station at the centre of English literature.[2] His claims were not everywhere acknowledged – in 1770, for instance, Gilbert Cowper had dismissed him as 'the Caliban of literature'.[3] But Joseph Towers, writing in 1786, two years after Johnson's death, believed that he had in the end prevailed:

His works, with all their defects, are a most valuable and important accession to the literature of England ... his *Dictionary*, his moral essays, and his productions in polite literature, will convey useful instruction, and elegant entertainment, as long as the language in which they are written shall be understood; and give him a just claim to a distinguished rank among the best and ablest writers that England has produced.[4]

For the quarter of a century before he died, Johnson's output as a poet, a novelist, a critic, a lexicographer, a biographer, an editor and (as we shall see) perhaps primarily as an essayist had made him a dominant figure in English literary life.

However, no one is born to such a position. It has to be attained. And Johnson seems to have taken the first, crucial steps towards that position in the early 1750s, when he composed a series of periodical essays published twice weekly as *The Rambler*. It was here that he created the literary character, identified the distinctive preoccupations, and forged the prose style, which established him in the mind of the reading public. As Johnson's friend, Arthur Murphy, said in his *Essay on the Life and Genius of Johnson* (1792), *The Rambler* 'may be considered as Johnson's great work. It was the basis of that high reputation which went on increasing to the end of his days.'[5] Therefore this selection from Johnson's journalism includes a generous proportion of essays from *The Rambler*, and a conscious attempt has been made to include examples of all the different kinds of essay Johnson composed for that paper. Furthermore, and to throw into relief how marked an innovation *The Rambler* was for Johnson, a number of his earlier essays and short pamphlets are also included. Finally, also included is the best of Johnson's later journalism, whether published as separate items or in the two successors to *The Rambler*, namely *The Idler* and *The Adventurer*. Aside from their intrinsic interest, in these later works we can see Johnson at moments struggling within and even against the persona and literary style which he had so successfully created for himself in *The Rambler*.

What was that persona, and what was the style Johnson forged in order to express and give body to it? In his *Life of Johnson*, James Boswell records a conversation with Johnson on the subject of death which is of help here. Boswell had deliberately introduced this subject, and had provocatively cited instances of those who professed to be untroubled by their mortality, in order to draw Johnson out. It was a ploy which later caused him some remorse:

Here I am sensible I was in the wrong, to bring before his view what he ever looked upon with horrour; for although when in a celestial frame, in his 'Vanity of human Wishes', he has supposed death to be 'kind Nature's signal for retreat,' from this state of being to 'a happier seat', his thoughts upon this aweful change were in general full of dismal apprehensions. His mind resembled the vast amphitheatre, the Colisæum at Rome. In the centre stood his judgement, which, like a mighty gladiator, combated those apprehensions that, like the wild beasts of the Arena, were all around in cells, ready to be let out upon him. After a conflict, he drove them back into their dens; but not killing them, they were still assailing him.[6]

This image of Johnson's mind as a place of interminable, endlessly renewed and never concluded struggle helps us to appreciate his prose style. In conversation Johnson tended to the simple and vigorous: 'He uttered his short, weighty, and pointed sentences with a power of voice, and a justness and energy of emphasis.'[7] But on paper his prose was marked by the ebb and flow of contrary qualities, as satire succeeded compassion, and inspiration was checked by reflection. In his *Lectures on the English Comic Writers* (1819) William Hazlitt was sensitive to this quality in Johnson's style, although he did not care for it:

Dr. Johnson was also a complete balance-master in the topics of morality. He never encourages hope, but he counteracts it by fear; he never elicits a truth, but he suggests some objection in answer to it. He seizes and alternately quits the clue of reason, lest it should involve him in the labyrinths of endless error: he wants confidence in himself and his fellows.[8]

A more sympathetic analysis of the dynamics of Johnson's style will be offered below. The restlessness of Johnson's prose is the signature of a moral wisdom which is always alert to the vanity of dogmatizing, and which therefore speaks to us most powerfully, not so much in what it says as in what it implies. Arthur Murphy sensed in Johnson's essays the powerful presence of what is either left unsaid or unable to be said, when he reflected on how in *The Rambler* the powers of language seem to be exhausted: 'the language seems to fall short of his ideas'.[9] This falling short is not a defect, still less (as Hazlitt seems to imply) a case of fence-sitting. It is instead a means of dispelling what George Gleig, writing in the *Encyclopedia Britannica* (1793), referred to as 'that inattention by which known truths are suffered to lie neglected'.[10] As we attend to it, we discover a Johnson who can speak to our condition with a surprising directness, either when writing about, for instance, lotteries,[11] or when reflecting with more sombreness on the permanent features of our moral existence.

One of the moments in Johnson's life which still has the power to move the sympathetic reader of today arose out of his composition of *The Rambler*. In the *Life of Johnson* Boswell records Johnson's memory that, some time early in 1750 and after the publication of a few *Ramblers*, his wife Tetty had confessed that these most recent writings had transformed her understanding of her husband. They had revealed in him unsuspected powers: 'I thought very well of you before; but I did not imagine you could have written any thing equal to this.'[12] Some two years later, on 13 March 1752, Johnson presented his wife with the four duodecimo volumes of the collected *Rambler*. A few days later she was dead. As Allen Reddick has said with compassionate insight of this episode: 'The timing of her epiphanic comment – the discovery of the extent of her husband's genius just as her own decline began to hasten – and Johnson's touching and desperate attempt to reach her through a gift of his own work that she had valued are simply further sad and ironical elements characteristic of the Johnsons' marriage.'[13] The common view of Tetty – that she was a slothful woman of unleavenable ordinariness, who took no interest in the work of the literary genius to whom she was married, and who killed herself with drink and opium[14] – might encourage us to see her surprise at *The Rambler* as just another instance of her inability to understand her own experience. But would anyone have guessed in the early months of 1750 that Johnson would be able to write, not only anything as good as *The Rambler*, but even anything like it?

Even those who in 1750 knew Johnson well might have seen few clues. He had been born on 18 September 1709, the son of Michael Johnson, a bookseller in Lichfield. In 1717 he entered Lichfield Grammar School, proceeding in 1728 to Pembroke College, Oxford. However, Johnson remained in Oxford for barely a year, leaving in December 1729. After the death of his father in 1731 he spent the early 1730s teaching and pursuing a literary career in the Midlands; for instance, in 1733 he had translated Lobo's *Voyage to Abyssinia*, a work eventually published in 1735. This was also the year in which Johnson married Elizabeth (or Tetty) Jervis, a widow with three children. In the following year he opened his own school at Edial near Lichfield, and began work on *Irene*, a moral tragedy set in Constantinople after its fall to the Turks (although the play was not to be performed until January 1749). Meanwhile, the school at Edial seems never to have flourished. It closed in 1737, and in March of that year Johnson, accompanied by David Garrick, moved to London and committed himself to a career as a man of letters. The late 1730s and early 1740s were accordingly for Johnson a period of Grub-Street hackery,[15] interspersed with some brighter triumphs, such as the publication in 1738 of his Juvenalian imitation, *London*.[16] He began writing for *The Gentleman's Magazine*, contributing the 'Debates in the Senate of Lilliput' which, in a period when it was forbidden to report the debates in the House of Commons directly, were a mock-Swiftian vehicle for disseminating awareness of what was happening in Parliament. It was at this time, too, that Johnson composed two anti-government pamphlets, the anti-Walpolean *Marmor Norfolciense* and *A Compleat Vindication of the Licensers of the Stage* (the second of which is reprinted below, pp. 495–509); in both these works he revealed his antipathy to Whiggism, as well as a streak of literary inventiveness.

The other literary form Johnson pursued during these years was biography. He composed lives of his friend the poet Richard Savage, of the historian Paolo Sarpi and of the physician Herman Boerhaave, as well as a series of shorter biographical sketches which he contributed to *The Gentleman's Magazine*. Now, too, he began to frame larger literary projects. He contributed to the *Harleian Miscellany* (writing the 'Introduction', which is reprinted below on pp. 517–23), and compiled the catalogue of the Harleian library. He proposed an edition of Shakespeare, and in 1746 signed the contract for the *Dictionary* (finally to be published in 1755). In 1747 he published the *Plan of an English*

Dictionary, dedicated to Lord Chesterfield, and in 1749 there appeared a second Juvenalian imitation, *The Vanity of Human Wishes*. So when the first *Rambler* appeared anonymously in 1750, even had its readers known that the author was Samuel Johnson, that name would have identified a jobbing journalist and political pamphleteer, who was also an accomplished if not prolific poet, and who had recently branched out into lexicography, textual editing and antiquarianism. It would not have suggested a master of moral wisdom. Yet in a few years, it would be these moral essays which formed Johnson's surest claim to regard. When in 1755 the Earl of Arran wrote to the Vice-Chancellor of Oxford to request that the degree of MA be conferred on Johnson, he emphasized that Johnson had 'very eminently distinguished himself by the publication of a series of essays, excellently calculated to form the manners of the people, and in which the cause of religion and morality is every where maintained by the strongest powers of argument and language'.[17] It was a judgement endorsed towards the end of the century by Arthur Murphy: 'In this collection [*The Rambler*] Johnson is the great moral teacher of his countrymen; his essays form a body of ethics; the observations on life and manners are acute and instructive; and the essays, professedly critical, serve to promote the cause of literature.'[18]

The periodical essay was a well-established form before Johnson wrote *The Rambler*, and towards the end of his life, when writing on Addison, he explained what he saw as its particular strengths. In his view, the periodical essay derived from conduct books such as Giovanni della Casa's *Il Galatheo*, Castiglione's *Il libro del cortegiano* and La Bruyère's *Les caractères, ou les moeurs de ce siècle*. These works, according to Johnson, had set themselves to 'teach the minuter decencies and inferior duties, to regulate the practice of daily conversation, to correct those depravities which are rather ridiculous than criminal, and remove those grievances which, if they produce no lasting calamities, impress hourly vexation'.[19] But, in Johnson's opinion, before the publication of *The Tatler* and *The Spectator* in 1709–11 and 1711–12 respectively, 'England had no masters of common life':

No writers had yet undertaken to reform either the savageness of neglect or the impertinence of civility; to shew when to speak, or to be silent; how to refuse, or how to comply. We had many books to teach us our more important duties, and to settle opinions in philosophy or politicks; but an *Arbiter elegantiarum*, a judge of propriety, was yet wanting, who should survey the track of daily conversation and free it from thorns and prickles, which teaze the passer, though they do not wound him.[20]

Yet this important function is discharged by nothing so well as 'the frequent publication of short papers, which we read not as study, but amusement. If the subject be slight, the treatise is short. The busy may find time, and the idle may find patience.'[21] Johnson was, in fact, wrong when he suggested that *The Tatler* and *The Spectator* had been first in the field. The periodical format went back as far as the 1660s and Henry Muddiman's *Oxford Gazette*, while (as Angus Ross has pointed out) 'it is no exaggeration to say that every form of writing, every topic of discussion or method of circulation (save the issue of collected papers by subscription) characteristic of *The Tatler* and *The Spectator* had been seen in some periodical or other before they appeared'.[22] Moreover, when Johnson came to write *The Rambler*, he aspired to a much graver character than that of an 'arbiter elegantiarum'. Instead, he chose to move the periodical form back towards those 'more important duties' which in the 'Life of Addison' he considered were already adequately covered. Johnson wished 'to reach the same audience the *Spectator* had so successfully entertained, but to encourage in it a more rigorously *critical* kind of thinking'.[23] What nudged him in this direction?

It was perhaps the work on the *Dictionary of the English Language*, on which Johnson had embarked during the later 1740s, which both made the periodical essay an attractive form, and impelled him to give that form a graver moral turn. At one level, the composition of brief essays must have seemed a relief after the unremitting reading required by the *Dictionary*. At the same time, that very reading may have suggested to Johnson both the perennial moral topics which form the heart of *The*

Rambler, and how to treat them. In part, that was because work
on the *Dictionary* was gradually equipping Johnson with a
philosophical vocabulary in which he could give weighty
expression to his judgements on the topics of common life.[24]
The programme of reading which Johnson had set himself in
order to assemble his illustrative quotations was in itself an
education, involving as it did 'incessant reading' of 'the best
authors in our language'.[25] Johnson fortified himself for his
labours by drinking deeply from what in the Preface to the
Dictionary he called '*the wells of English undefiled* . . . the pure
sources of genuine diction': namely, the best English writers
between the last years of Elizabeth I and the Restoration, when
the language had purged itself of barbarity, but before it had
succumbed to the French influence which had entered the kingdom with Charles II.[26] Even if those draughts were drained for
lexicographical ends, it is inconceivable that Johnson's mind
would not have received from them a wider irrigation.

But there was perhaps another way in which the effort of
compiling the *Dictionary* fertilized Johnson's other writings.
The broad consideration which compiling the *Dictionary*
obliged Johnson to give to questions of language and grammar
also alerted him to the possibility that the affective strengths of
the English language might be found in what at a first and
formal glance might look like its deficiencies. If we consider
some of Johnson's pronouncements on language, and then compare them with a poem he wrote towards the end of his life –
the verses 'On the Death of Dr. Robert Levet' – we will be in a
better position to appreciate how his grapplings with language
in the making of the *Dictionary* may have influenced his ideas
about the possibilities and pitfalls involved in what he was
undertaking in *The Rambler*: that is, imbuing language with
moral content.

Just as Johnson was politically an internal exile (a stubborn
Tory obliged to live under Hanoverian monarchs and in a world
of which the politics, irrespective of which particular party
happened to be in or out, were fundamentally shaped by the
Revolution Principles of 1688) so, too, he was estranged from
the most fashionable ethical theories of his time, the spokesman

for a conscious ethics of the will at a time when a contrary theory of morals was dominant. The two positions were elegantly formulated by David Hume, in his *Enquiry Concerning the Principles of Morals* (1751):

There has been a controversy started of late . . . concerning the general foundation of Morals; whether they be derived from Reason, or from Sentiment; whether we attain the knowledge of them by a chain of argument and induction, or by an immediate feeling and finer internal sense; whether, like all sound judgement of truth and falsehood, they should be the same to every rational intelligent being; or whether, like the perception of beauty and deformity, they be founded entirely on the particular fabric and constitution of the human species.[27]

Johnson, of course, was, in the terms of this opposition, an opponent of affective theories of ethics; that is to say, theories which located the origin of moral discriminations in involuntary sentiments, rather than conscious and reasoned judgements. The very holders of such views were probably enough to blacken them irredeemably in Johnson's eyes: Shaftesbury, the arch-Whig and free-thinker; Hume, the religious sceptic against whom Johnson repeatedly ranged and defined himself; Adam Smith, leading figure of that Scottish Enlightenment which Johnson emphatically slighted in his *Journey to the Western Islands*.

In conversation with Boswell, however, Johnson expanded on his opposition to the ethical theories of Shaftesbury, Hume and Smith, and made clear that his suspicion of those theories was not simply transferred suspicion of the men who disseminated them:

We can have no dependence upon that instinctive, that constitutional goodness which is not founded upon principle. I grant you that such a man may be a very amiable member of society. I can conceive him placed in such a situation that he is not much tempted to deviate from what is right; and as every man prefers virtue, when there is not some strong incitement to transgress its precepts, I can conceive him doing nothing wrong. But if such a man stood in need of money, I should not like to trust him; and I should certainly not trust him with young ladies, for *there* there is always temptation.[28]

This conviction, that a morality based upon the affections might not serve to support us in those hard cases which are the test of any morality, led Johnson also to oppose speculative theories which tended to diminish man's responsibility for his moral health – for example, fashionable theories which related morals to climate, or which located the cause of moral degeneration in broad social phenomena such as luxury. A good example of Johnson's resistance to anything which suggested that moral judgements were not peculiarly human, and rooted in the conscious will, is his refusal even to entertain one of Boswell's experiences while on the Grand Tour:

I told him that I had several times, when in Italy, seen the experiment of placing a scorpion within a circle of burning coals; that it ran round and round in extreme pain; and finding no way to escape, retired to the centre, and like a true Stoick philosopher, darted its sting into its head, and thus at once freed itself from its woes. . . . I said, this was a curious fact, as it shewed deliberate suicide in a reptile.[29]

Johnson refused point blank to accept the possibility of a reptile's committing suicide, because he could admit neither that animals possess a moral sense, nor that an authentically ethical act could be a reflex, without sacrificing the essence of his moral position; namely, that our moral sense is the product of our waking judgement.

Given that Johnson was such an advocate for an ethics of conscious principle, one would expect his ethical language to be overt and declaratory; that is to say, conscious, stated and argued for. But the experience of reading Johnson is, I think, not like that. Sir John Hawkins caught well how the impact of Johnson's writing is not one of propositional clarity:

In all Johnson's disquisitions, whether argumentative or critical, there is a certain even-handed justice that leaves the mind in a strange perplexity.

'A strange perplexity': it is precisely that sense of being moved at a level beyond or beneath the level of language which, I think, characterizes the experience of reading Johnson's best moral writing. To understand why this should be so, we need to consider the theory of language which exerted the greatest influence over Johnson, that elaborated by John Locke in Book III of *An Essay Concerning Human Understanding*.

The importance of language for Locke was that, since words represent ideas, not objects, they can form the conduit of knowledge:

> . . . it was further necessary that he [man] should be *able to use these sounds as signs of internal conceptions*, and to make them stand as marks for the *ideas* within his own mind, whereby they might be made known to others, and the thoughts of men's minds be conveyed from one to another.[30]

The ideas that language could convey are of two kinds, simple and complex. An example of a simple idea would be 'goat'. Simple ideas, Locke insisted, cannot be defined. However, in practice this is not a great problem since they can be demonstrated or pointed out. An example of a complex idea (or 'mixed mode', as Locke more often calls it) would be 'ingratitude' (and indeed the ideas represented by all ethical language fall into this category of mixed modes). For mixed modes, the reverse holds true. They cannot be demonstrated, because, in Locke's words, 'they are the creatures of the understanding rather than the works of nature'.[31] However, the compensation for this is that they can be *defined* with perfect precision:

> . . . the signification of their names [those of mixed modes] cannot be made known, as those of simple *ideas*, by any showing, but, in recompense thereof, may be perfectly and exactly *defined*. For they being combinations of several *ideas* that the mind of man has arbitrarily put together, without reference to any archetypes [i.e. things existing in nature which form the original patterns of those ideas], men may, if they please, exactly know the *ideas* that go to each composition, and so both use these words in a certain and undoubted

signification, and perfectly declare, when there is occasion, what they stand for.[32]

For Locke, this is a source of great comfort, because from it he deduces that moral language can be made more precise than any other kind of language:

This, if well considered, would lay great blame on those who make not their discourses about moral things very clear and distinct. For since the precise signification of the names of mixed modes ... is to be known, they being not of nature's but man's making, it is a great negligence and perverseness to discourse of moral things with uncertainty and obscurity ... Upon this ground it is that I am bold to think that *morality is capable of demonstration*, as well as mathematics: since the precise real essence of the things moral words stand for may be perfectly known, and so the congruity or incongruity of the things themselves be certainly discovered, in which consists perfect knowledge.[33]

Johnson's famous comment – 'words are the daughters of earth, and ... things are the sons of heaven. Language is only the instrument of science and words are but the signs of ideas' – shows his affinity with Locke's theory of language.[34] But on this point of the demonstrability of morality, he is at the opposite pole from his philosophical predecessor. What Locke saw as a source of encouragement – that moral terms are susceptible of exact definition – Johnson, as a practical rather than a speculative moralist, found a cause of disquiet. It may be that such moral *terms* can be precisely defined. But those precise definitions may not help in the practical business of grasping the substantive essence of moral *ideas*.

The point can be clarified if we compare definitions from the *Dictionary* of what Locke would have called simple ideas with mixed modes. First, two definitions of simple ideas:

Horse: A neighing quadruped, used in war, in draught, and in carriage.

Ink: The black liquor with which men write.

These definitions follow on from Locke's insistence on the demonstrability of a simple idea, in that they take the form of a set of instructions as to where to look. If you want to know what ink is, you find a man who is writing, and look at the black liquor he is using. Johnson's definitions of mixed modes are quite different:

Virtue: Moral goodness: opposed to vice.

Vice: The course of action opposite to virtue.

Good: Not bad; not ill.

Ill: Not well.

It is quite clear that, considered purely as *definitions*, these have a precision which the definitions of 'horse' and 'ink' lack; but it is hard to see what use they are to someone who wishes to lead a moral life, and therefore needs to know the content of the ideas these terms represent. Locke had assumed that, because these words could be precisely defined, we could have exact knowledge of the essence of the idea. But for Johnson, it is possible to have a precision of moral language, but nothing else, as he shows in the character of the philosopher in chapter twenty-two of *Rasselas*:

To live according to nature, is to act always with due regard to the fitness arising from the relations and qualities of causes and effects; to concur with the great and unchangeable scheme of universal felicity; to co-operate with the general disposition and tendency of the present system of things.[35]

For Johnson, to live a moral life was less a question of possessing a vocabulary than of performing actions. In *Rambler* No. 14 he acknowledged the power of moral theory: 'in moral discussions it is to be remembered that many impediments obstruct our practice, which very easily give way to theory'.[36] But that power will be only a snare and a delusion unless it be also remembered that 'human experience, which is constantly contradicting theory, is the great test of truth'.[37] How can language lay hold on the substance of morality, instead of shadowing the world of moral action with a self-regarding and futile precision?[38]

It is here that Johnson's notion of the special virtue of poetic language is important. In *Idler* No. 60 Johnson amusingly mocked Dick Minim's enactment theory of poetic language. He was obliged to do so in order to distinguish that crassness from a notion of poetic language which he took very seriously: namely, that 'the force of poetry' 'calls new powers into being', which powers are capable of 'embod[ying] sentiment', including moral sentiment.[39] If we turn now to his poem on Robert Levet, we can see an example of that force and of those powers at work.

Boswell gave a disdainful sketch of Levet: 'he was of a strange grotesque appearance, stiff and formal in his manner, and seldom said a word while any company was present.'[40] From this unpromising material, Johnson made a moral poem of extraordinary force. In his 'Essay on Epitaphs', he wrote:

The best Subject for EPITAPHS is private Virtue; Virtue exerted in the same Circumstances in which the Bulk of Mankind are placed, and which, therefore, may admit of many Imitators ... he that has repelled the Temptations of Poverty, and disdained to free himself from Distress, at the Expence of his Virtue, may animate Multitudes, by his Example, to the same Firmness of Heart and Steadiness of Resolution.[41]

It takes no very profound reading of 'On the Death of Dr. Robert Levet' to see that its surface meaning is very much concerned with rectifying the neglect of society, and of paying due accord to the virtues of the obscure and the petty.

But, beneath that, there is also a more profound moral level to the poem, where it engages with the consideration that Johnson felt should always inform a person's moral conduct; that is to say, the certainty of death. *Rambler* No. 78 states the principle:

... the remembrance of death ought to predominate in our minds, as an habitual and settled principle, always operating, though not always

perceived . . . [for] the great incentive to virtue is the reflection that we
must die.

Yet the fact of our own eventual death, as Johnson conceded in
that same paper, is a certainty from which the repetitious nature
of daily life, its common round, perpetually distracts us. In the
poem on Levet, Johnson employed what he had, as a grammarian, considered a flaw in the English language, to penetrate
the reader afresh with the knowledge that, while virtually everything else can happen to us many times, or may not happen to
us at all, we will certainly encounter death, and will encounter
it only once.

On the Death of Dr. Robert Levet

Condemn'd to hope's delusive mine,
 As on we toil from day to day,
By sudden blasts, or slow decline,
 Our social comforts drop away.

Well tried through many a varying year,
 See LEVET to the grave descend;
Officious, innocent, sincere,
 Of ev'ry friendless name the friend.

Yet still he fills affection's eye,
 Obscurely wise, and coarsely kind;
Nor, letter'd arrogance, deny
 Thy praise to merit unrefin'd.

When fainting nature call'd for aid,
 And hov'ring death prepar'd the blow,
His vig'rous remedy display'd
 The power of art without the show.

In misery's darkest caverns known,
 His useful care was ever nigh,
Where hopeless anguish pour'd his groan,
 And lonely want retir'd to die.

No summons mock'd by chill delay,
　　No petty gain disdain'd by pride,
The modest wants of ev'ry day
　　The toil of ev'ry day supplied.

His virtues walked their narrow round,
　　Nor made a pause, nor left a void;
And sure th'Eternal Master found
　　The single talent well employed.

The busy day, the peaceful night,
　　Unfelt, uncounted, glided by;
His frame was firm, his powers were bright,
　　Tho' now his eightieth year was nigh.

Then with no throbbing fiery pain,
　　No cold gradations of decay,
Death broke at once the vital chain,
　　And freed his soul the nearest way.

For the first eight stanzas of this poem, Johnson is concerned
with repeated actions: our daily toil in hope's delusive mine,
Levet's toil of every day which met the needs of every day, the
narrow round of his habitual exercise of his single talent. And
in the penultimate stanza Johnson also alludes to the inattention
engendered by the repetitive nature of our quotidian existence:

The busy day, the peaceful night,
　　Unfelt, uncounted, glided by;

But in the last stanza the verbs do not describe repeated actions.
They become instead true preterites, referring to single, accomplished actions:

Death broke at once the vital chain,
　　And freed his soul the nearest way.

It is a feature of 'the anomalous preterites of verbs' in English
that these two functions of the past tense (that of referring to

repeated action in the past, and also to single, accomplished past actions) are not distinguished by the suffix. Had, for instance, Johnson decided to write this poem in Latin (as he was well capable of doing), the suffixes of the verbs would clearly have distinguished the separate kinds of past event to which they refer. 'Glided' might have been rendered by 'surrepebant'; 'broke' and 'freed' by 'fregit' and 'liberavit'. This hypothetical Latin poem, by virtue of the more regular and intricate formation of past tenses in the Latin language, would have discriminated the two types of past event which lie behind the poem more scrupulously than does, or could, the English poem we possess. But this hypothetical Latin poem would also, I believe, be a lesser poem. For it is in the 'strange perplexity' (to return to Hawkins's phrase) which every reader must, for a moment, feel as we move, without preparation or warning, from imperfect to perfect tense in the final stanza, that the poem achieves its moral impact. The irregular identity of imperfect and perfect tenses in English, deplored by Johnson the grammarian as an irregularity, is here made the vehicle for the reflection which Johnson the moralist wished to place in the foundations of our ethical existence: namely, the 'reflection that we must die'. The tenses of our hypothetical Latin poem could register vividly and directly the different event which is death. It could shock us with it. It could not, as Johnson's English poem does, *ambush* us with it. For the moral impact of this poem is more subtle, and more profound because more subtle, than that of any translation could be, except a translation into a language as casual as is English in forming its past tenses. Only in such a language could what Johnson does in this poem be duplicated. Surprised by death at the end of the poem, we are forced to acknowledge, before our habitual distractedness resumes, that we too will die, and to reflect, albeit momentarily, on whether or not death will be for us an emancipation, as it was for Levet. In the strange perplexity of that final moment, Johnson's poem achieves its moral stature, triumphs over the solipsism which lies in wait for moral language, and administers to its reader an impetus to moral reformation. At the same time, Johnson comes close to his subject: he, too, displays 'the power of art without the show'.

In *Idler* No. 41 Johnson, recently smitten by the death of his mother, had already reflected on the paradoxes arising from our distracted awareness of the inevitability of death:

That it is vain to shrink from what cannot be avoided, and to hide that from ourselves which must some time be found, is a truth which we all know, but which all neglect . . . Nothing is more evident than that the decays of age must terminate in death; yet there is no man, says *Tully*, who does not believe that he may yet live another year.[42]

The purpose of moral writing is forcibly to awaken us from this condition of impotent awareness. It is therefore a kind of assault upon us – in just the way that Johnson reported to Boswell that he himself had been assaulted and awakened, when a young man, from an unexpected quarter. The 'religious progress' of the young Johnson had, it seems, been fitful and uneven:

I fell into an inattention to religion, or an indifference about it, in my ninth year. The church at Lichfield, in which we had a seat, wanted reparation, so I was to go and find a seat in other churches; and having bad eyes, and being awkward about this, I used to go and read in the fields on Sunday. This habit continued till my fourteenth year; and still I find a great reluctance to go to church. I then became a sort of lax *talker* against religion, for I did not much *think* against it; and this lasted till I went to Oxford, where it would not be *suffered*. When at Oxford, I took up Law's 'Serious Call to a Holy Life', expecting to find it a dull book, (as such books generally are), and perhaps to laugh at it. But I found Law quite an overmatch for me; and this was the first occasion of my thinking in earnest of religion, after I became capable of rational enquiry.[43]

When Johnson says that Law was an 'overmatch' for him, he draws a metaphor from wrestling, which hints to us that the benefit which flowed from Johnson's reading of Law's *Serious Call* arose precisely from the energy of its attack upon the dullness of his spiritual apprehension. Such writing is like ethical sandpaper. By means of literary surprise it out-manoeuvres expectation, and re-sensitizes us to the moral realities from which the carapace of quotidian life will effectively separate us unless it is vigorously challenged. It is a kind of writing which Johnson himself could achieve in *The Rambler*, as the conclusion of the second essay shows:

But, though it should happen that an author is capable of excelling, yet his merit may pass without notice, huddled in the variety of things, and thrown into the general miscellany of life. He that endeavours after fame by writing, solicits the regard of a multitude fluctuating in pleasures, or immersed in business, without time for intellectual amusements; he appeals to judges prepossessed by passions, or corrupted by prejudices, which preclude their approbation of any new performance. Some are too indolent to read any thing, till its reputation is established; others too envious to promote that fame, which gives them pain by its increase. What is new is opposed, because most are unwilling to be taught; and what is known is rejected, because it is not sufficiently considered, that men more frequently require to be reminded than informed. The learned are afraid to declare their opinion early, lest they should put their reputation in hazard; the ignorant always imagine themselves giving some proof of delicacy, when they refuse to be pleased: and he that finds his way to reputation, through all these obstructions, must acknowledge that he is indebted to other causes besides his industry, his learning, or his wit.[44]

The paragraph opens with the proposition that fame is elusive, and then goes on to offer a series of particular reasons why this is so. At this point, then, Johnson seems to be offering consolation to the obscure. However, the final limb of the concluding sentence springs the mine: 'and he that finds his way to reputation, through all these obstructions, must acknowledge that he is indebted to other causes besides his industry, his learning, or his wit'. The shift in perspective, from consoling the obscure to mortifying the proud, is abrupt and complete, and arises from Johnson's astute perception of the further implication hidden within the instances explaining the elusiveness of fame: for what is balm to the overlooked may be wormwood to the celebrated. The startling pivot jolts the complacent, and reminds us that the conditions of our moral life are more surprising and reticulated than we slackly suppose them to be. As a result, all readers should be unsettled by this writing: the lowly should feel less securely tethered to their lowliness, the eminent more precarious in their elevation. In *Adventurer* No. 111 Johnson revealingly misremembers one of Robert South's sermons.[45] South had proposed that men would find 'a Continuall un-intermitted Pleasure' intolerable. Johnson characteristically substitutes idleness for South's pleasure. Notwithstanding – indeed, perhaps because of – all his temptations to sloth, Johnson recognized that for men work was a condition of happiness. The resistances of his own moral style create for his reader an opportunity of healthily laborious struggle, in which they may find Johnson an overmatch for them, just as William Law had been for Johnson. For, as Arthur Murphy understood, 'Johnson is always profound, and of course gives the fatigue of thinking.'[46]

The Rambler did not sell well (though unless we recall that it was widely reprinted in provincial newspapers we are likely seriously to underestimate the contemporary readership of these essays).[47] This may have been due to the unexpected seriousness of its moral appeal. However, there is also evidence to suggest that Johnson's style was difficult for some readers, even repugnant for others. Like any literary manner, it could be guyed. 'The ludicrous imitators of Johnson's style are innumerable,' as Boswell pointed out.[48] Bonnell Thornton's parody shows that imitation could be done with affection.[49] A sharper emotion, however, seems to have prompted Horace Walpole's strictures on Johnson's style. The *Journey to the Western Islands* he dismissed as verbose: 'What a heap of words to express very little! and though it is the least cumbrous of any style he ever used, how far from easy and natural!'[50] But the much more cumbrous style of *The Rambler* inspired Walpole to a freak of satiric imagination. Writing to the Countess of Ossory on 1 February 1779, he began by distancing himself from the popular mania for David Garrick, before moving on to Johnson himself:

. . . I have always thought that he [Garrick] was just the counterpart of Shakespeare; this, the first of writers, and an indifferent actor; that, the first of actors, and a woeful author. Posterity would believe me, who will see only his writings; and who will see those of another modern idol, far less deservedly enshrined, Dr. Johnson. I have been saying this morning, that the latter deals so much in triple tautology, or the fault of repeating the same sense in three different phrases, that I believe it would be possible, taking the ground-work for all three, to make one of his 'Ramblers' into three different papers, that should all have exactly the same purport and meaning, but in different phrases. It would be a good trick for somebody to produce one and read it; a second would say, "Bless me, I have this very paper in my pocket, but in quite another diction"; and so a third . . .[51]

If one recollects the conclusion of *Rambler* 2 quoted above, it is easy to see what prompted this Walpolean fantasy. The very premise of Johnson's moral essays, that men more often require to be reminded than informed, perhaps by itself drives their author towards an iterative style.[52] Moreover, it may be that Johnson himself after a while found the character of the 'Rambler' constricting. If, when he first forged that character, it offered release by allowing him to give voice to the fund of information and reflection which he had accumulated as a result of earlier study and the labours of the *Dictionary*, it was also a character he found it increasingly hard to shake off. Certainly towards the end of his life Johnson was troubled by thoughts of the path not taken:

Johnson, however, had a noble ambition floating in his mind, and had, undoubtedly, often speculated on the possibility of his supereminent powers being rewarded in this great and liberal country by the highest honours of the state. Sir William Scott informs me, that upon the death of the late Lord Lichfield, who was Chancellor of the University of Oxford, he said to Johnson, 'What a pity it is, Sir, that you did not follow the profession of the law. You might have been Lord Chancellor of Great Britain, and attained to the dignity of the peerage; and now that the title of Lichfield, your native city, is extinct, you might have had it.' Johnson, upon this, seemed much agitated; and, in an angry tone, exclaimed, 'Why will you vex me by suggesting this, when it is too late?'[53]

This reluctance to contemplate possibilities not grasped surely accompanies a measure of restiveness – an agitation even – concerning the life that has been lived. Certainly the literary personae that Johnson created for himself in *The Idler* and *The Adventurer* seem partly to have been chosen to contrast with that of *The Rambler* by trimming back some of the moral seriousness associated with Johnson's first set of periodical essays. And as *The Rambler* itself progressed, it sometimes seems as if the author is attempting to increase the tonal range and formal variety of the papers. In addition to the moral disquisitions, we have a series of moral case studies (sometimes amounting almost to a compressed novel, as in the story of 'Misella' in *Rambler*s 170 and 171), stories continued over some distance, as with *Rambler*s 132 and 194, and also the *contes* set in the Orient and even Greenland.

But to step away from the character of the 'Rambler' was for Johnson a difficult task. Once he was dead, and when the advent of the French Revolution had turned Johnson from a recently deceased author to the embodiment of a resistant Englishness and a bulwark against the democratical principles then ravaging France, it was impossible for that character to be laid aside. In the 'Advertisement' to the second edition of the *Life of Johnson*, published after the execution of Louis XVI in 1793, Boswell presented his dead friend to a new group of readers in precisely these terms:

His strong, clear, and animated enforcement of religion, morality, loyalty, and subordination, while it delights and improves the wise and the good, will, I trust, prove an effectual antidote to that detestable sophistry which has been lately imported from France, under the false name of *Philosophy*, and with a malignant industry has been employed against the peace, good order, and happiness of society, in our free and prosperous country; but thanks be to GOD, without producing the pernicious effects which were hoped for by its propagators.[54]

This Johnson seems distant from the exuberant political ventriloquist of *A Compleat Vindication of the Licensers of the Stage*, or the mordant author of the essays critical of the government's conduct of the Seven Years' War, or the bleak satire of the suppressed *Idler* 22. Therefore, one of the principles of selection in the present volume has been in a modest way to begin to restore what has come to be comparatively neglected. I have thus included alongside the moral 'Rambler' some evidence of Johnson's other literary characters, from both earlier and later in his career, and sought thereby to place before today's readers evidence of Johnson's diversity, as well as of his centrality.

Oxford, 2001

NOTES

1. James Boswell, *The Life of Johnson*, ed. R. W. Chapman, corr. J. D. Fleeman (Oxford: Oxford University Press, 1976), pp. 1394–95.

2. Boswell, *Life of Johnson*, p. 247.

3. Boswell, *Life of Johnson*, p. 445.

4. Joseph Towers, *An Essay on the Life, Character, and Writings of Dr. Samuel Johnson* (1786), reprinted in *Johnson: The Critical Heritage*, ed. James T. Boulton (London: Routledge & Kegan Paul, 1971), p. 382.

5. Arthur Murphy, *Essay on the Life and Genius of Johnson* (1792), reprinted in *Johnson: The Critical Heritage*, p. 69.

6. Boswell, *Life of Johnson*, p. 427.

7. Thomas Babington Macaulay, 'Samuel Johnson', in *Miscellaneous Writings*, 2 vols (1860), vol. ii, p. 288.

8. William Hazlitt, *Lectures on the English Comic Writers* (1819), reprinted in *Johnson: The Critical Heritage*, p. 88.

9. Murphy, *Essay on the Life and Genius of Johnson* (1792), reprinted in *Johnson: The Critical Heritage*, p. 71.

10. George Gleig, *Encyclopedia Britannica* (1793), reprinted in *Johnson: The Critical Heritage*, p. 73.

11. See below, *Rambler* No. 181.

12. Boswell, *Life of Johnson*, p. 149.

13. Allen Reddick, *The Making of Johnson's Dictionary 1746–1773*, revised edition (Cambridge: Cambridge University Press, 1996), p. 68.

14. See the clipped and unsympathetic judgement of Robert Levet; *Thraliana*, ed. K. C. Balderston, second edition, 2 vols. (Oxford: Clarendon Press, 1951), vol. i, p. 178.

15. In 1739 Lord Gower, in the course of supplying a testimonial to assist Johnson in his candidacy for the headmastership of Appleby School, reported that Johnson would prefer 'to die upon the road, *than be starved to death in translating for booksellers*; which has been his only subsistence for some time past' (Boswell, *Life of Johnson*, p. 96).

16. For Pope's 'candid and liberal' praise of the poem, see Boswell, *Life of Johnson*, p. 92.

17. Boswell, *Life of Johnson*, p. 199.

18. Murphy, *Essay on the Life and Genius of Johnson* (1792), reprinted in *Johnson: The Critical Heritage*, p. 69.

19. 'Addison', in *Lives of the English Poets*, ed. G. B. Hill, 3 vols. (Oxford: Clarendon Press, 1905), vol. ii, p. 92.

20. Ibid., p. 93.

21. Ibid.

22. *Selections from The Tatler and The Spectator*, ed. A. Ross (Harmondsworth: Penguin Books, 1982), p. 22.

23. Leo Damrosch, 'Johnson's Manner of Proceeding in the *Rambler*', *English Literary History* (*ELH*), 40 (1973), p. 72.

24. W. K. Wimsatt, *Philosophic Words: A Study of Style and Meaning in the Rambler and Dictionary of Samuel Johnson* (New Haven: Yale University Press, 1948). Reddick, *Making of Johnson's Dictionary 1746–1773*. See, too, the following passage from the coda to *Rambler* No. 208: 'Whatever shall be the final sentence of mankind, I have at least endeavoured to deserve their kindness. I have laboured to refine our language to grammatical purity, and to clear it from colloquial barbarisms, licentious idioms, and irregular combinations. Something, perhaps, I have added to the elegance of its construction, and something to the harmony of its cadence. When common words were less pleasing to the ear, or less distinct in their signification, I have familiarized the terms of philosophy by applying them to popular ideas ...' (below, p. 325). Arthur Murphy also reflected on how *The Rambler* might have been influenced by the *Dictionary*: 'It is remarkable, that the pomp of diction, which has been objected to Johnson, was first assumed in the *Rambler*. His *Dictionary* was going on at the same time, and, in the course of that work, as he grew familiar with technical and scholastic words he thought the bulk of his readers were equally learned ...' (*Essay on the Life and Genius of Johnson* (1792), reprinted in *Johnson: The Critical Heritage*, p. 70).

25. Sir John Hawkins, *The Life of Samuel Johnson, LL.D.*, second edition (London, 1787), p. 175. Although Thomas Percy dissents from Hawkins's account of the physical process whereby the illustrative

quotations for the *Dictionary* were assembled and collated, he endorses what Hawkins says about the trawl of reading which underpropped the whole enterprise: 'He began his task by devoting his first care to a diligent perusal of all such English writers as were most correct in their language' (*Johnsonian Miscellanies*, ed. G. Birkbeck Hill (Oxford: Clarendon Press, 1897), vol. ii, p. 214). For the manner in which the *Dictionary* was compiled, see Reddick, *Making of Johnson's Dictionary*, esp. pp. 27–41.

26. The whole passage from the 'Preface' bears repetition:

So far have I been from any care to grace my pages with modern decorations, that I have studiously endeavoured to collect examples and authorities from the writers before the restoration, whose works I regard as *the wells of English undefiled*, as the pure sources of genuine diction. Our language, for almost a century, has, by the concurrence of many causes, been gradually departing from its original *Teutonick* character, and deviating towards a *Gallick* structure and phraseology, from which it ought to be our endeavour to recal it, by making our ancient volumes the ground-work of style, admitting among the additions of later times, only such as may supply real deficiencies, such as are readily adopted by the genius of our tongue, and incorporate easily with our native idioms.

But as every language has a time of rudeness antecedent to perfection, as well as of false refinement and declension, I have been cautious lest my zeal for antiquity might drive me into times too remote, and crowd my book with words now no longer understood. I have fixed *Sidney*'s work for the boundary, beyond which I make few excursions. From the authors which rose in the time of *Elizabeth*, a speech might be formed adequate to all the purposes of use and elegance. If the language of theology were extracted from *Hooker* and the translation of the bible; the terms of natural knowledge from *Bacon*; the phrases of policy, war, and navigation from *Raleigh*; the dialect of poetry and fiction from *Spenser* and *Sidney*; and the diction of common life from *Shakespeare*, few ideas would be lost to mankind, for want of *English* words, in which they might be expressed.

This was not the period of English literature which all Johnson's contemporaries would have selected as best representative of the language. For example, at the end of the 1750s, when Gibbon returned to England from nearly five years speaking French in Lausanne, David Mallet encouraged him to regain fluency in English by reading 'the prose of Swift and Addison', in which could be found 'the purity, the grace, the idiom, of the English style' (Edward Gibbon, *The Autobiographies of Edward Gibbon*, ed. John Murray (London, 1896), p. 251).

The diverse choices made by Mallet (whom Johnson despised) and Johnson himself may flow from and reflect their ideological and religious differences.

27. David Hume, *Enquiry Concerning the Principles of Morals* (London, 1751), Section 1, para. 134.

28. Boswell, *Life of Johnson*, p. 314.

29. Ibid., pp. 392–3.

30. John Locke, *An Essay Concerning Human Understanding*, III, 1.2.

31. Ibid., III, 5.12.

32. Ibid., III, 11.15.

33. Ibid., III, 11.15–16.

34. Samuel Johnson, *Dictionary*, 'Preface'.

35. Samuel Johnson, *Rasselas*, ed. G. J. Kolb (New Haven: Yale University Press, 1990), p. 88.

36. See *Rambler* No. 14.

37. Boswell, *Life of Johnson*, pp. 320–21.

38. Cf. the remark of Leo Damrosch, that 'the heart of Johnson's mission as a moralist is to make us stop parroting the precepts of moralists and start thinking for ourselves' ('Johnson's Manner of Proceeding in the *Rambler*', *ELH*, 40 (1973), p. 81).

39. From *Rambler* No. 168, below, p. 282.

40. Boswell, *Life of Johnson*, p. 172.

41. See 'An Essay on Epitaphs', below, p. 515.

42. See *Idler* No. 41.

43. Boswell, *Life of Johnson*, pp. 50–51.

44. See *Rambler* No. 2.

45. See pp. 580–81 for the relevant quotation from South's sermon.

46. Murphy, *Essay on the Life and Genius of Johnson* (1792), reprinted in *Johnson: The Critical Heritage*, p. 72.

47. R. M. Wiles, 'The Contemporary Distribution of Johnson's *Rambler*', *Eighteenth-Century Studies* (*ECS*), 2 (1968), pp. 155–71.

48. Boswell, *Life of Johnson*, p. 1369. An interesting and neglected instance of such imitation is to be found in Philip Parsons, *Dialogues of the Dead with the Living* (1779), in which dialogue VII is between Johnson and Addison.

49. See Appendix III.

50. To the Countess of Ossory, 19 January 1775; *The Yale Edition of Horace Walpole's Correspondence*, ed. W. S. Lewis, vol. 32 (London: Oxford University Press, and New Haven: Yale University Press, 1965), p. 225.

51. To the Countess of Ossory, 1 February 1779; *Yale Edition of Horace Walpole's Correspondence*, vol. 33, pp. 88–9.

52. See *Rambler* No. 2.

53. Boswell, *Life of Johnson*, p. 961.

54. Boswell, *Life of Johnson*, p. 7.

Further Reading

1. BIBLIOGRAPHY

Clifford, J. L. and D. J. Greene, *Samuel Johnson: A Survey and Bibliography of Critical Studies* (Minneapolis: University of Minnesota Press, 1970).

Courtney, W. P., *A Bibliography of Samuel Johnson* (Oxford: Oxford University Press, 1915).

Greene, D. J. and J. A. Vance, *A Bibliography of Johnson Studies, 1970–1985* (Victoria, BC: University of Victoria, BC, 1987).

2. BIOGRAPHY

Bate, W. J., *Samuel Johnson* (New York: Harcourt Brace Jovanovich, 1977).

Boswell, James, *The Life of Johnson*, ed. G. B. Hill, revised by L. F. Powell, 6 vols. (Oxford: Oxford University Press, 1934–64).

Clifford, J. L., *Young Sam Johnson* (London: Heinemann, 1955).

—, *Dictionary Johnson* (London: Heinemann, 1979).

De Maria, Robert, *The Life of Samuel Johnson* (Oxford: Blackwell Publishers, 1993).

Kaminski, T., *The Early Career of Samuel Johnson* (Oxford: Oxford University Press, 1987).

Kelly, R. E. and O. M. Brack, *Samuel Johnson's Early Biographers* (Iowa: University of Iowa Press, 1971).

Lipking, L., *Samuel Johnson: The Life of an Author* (Cambridge, Mass. and London: Harvard University Press, 1998).

3. EDITIONS

a) Complete editions

Works, 11 vols. (Oxford, 1825).

The Yale Edition of the Works of Samuel Johnson (New Haven: Yale University Press, 1958–).

The Letters of Samuel Johnson, ed. Bruce Redford, 5 vols. (Oxford: Clarendon Press, 1992–94).

b) Editions of the periodical essays

The Idler and The Adventurer, ed. W. J. Bate, J. M. Bullitt and L. F. Powell (New Haven and London: Yale University Press, 1963).

The Rambler, ed. W. J. Bate and A. B. Strauss, 3 vols. (New Haven and London: Yale University Press, 1969).

Essays from the Rambler, Adventurer and Idler, ed. W. J. Bate (New Haven and London: Yale University Press, 1968).

4. CRITICAL AND SCHOLARLY STUDIES

a) General studies

Bate, W. J., *The Achievement of Samuel Johnson* (New York: Oxford University Press, 1955).

Boulton, J. T., *Johnson: The Critical Heritage* (London: Routledge and Kegan Paul, 1971).

De Maria Jr., R., *Johnson's Dictionary and the Language of Learning* (Oxford: Clarendon Press, 1986).

—, *Samuel Johnson and the Life of Reading* (Baltimore and London: The Johns Hopkins University Press, 1997).

Engell, James (ed.), *Johnson and his Age* (Cambridge, Mass. and London: Harvard University Press, 1984).

Fussell, P., *Samuel Johnson and the Life of Writing* (London: Chatto and Windus, 1972).

Greene, D. (ed.), *Samuel Johnson: A Collection of Critical Essays* (Englewood Cliffs, NJ: Prentice-Hall, 1965).

Reddick, A., *The Making of Johnson's Dictionary 1746–1773* (Cambridge: Cambridge University Press, 1990; rev. edn. 1996).

Reinert, T., *Regulating Confusion: Samuel Johnson and the Crowd* (Durham, NC and London: Duke University Press, 1996).

Voitle, R., *Samuel Johnson the Moralist* (Cambridge, Mass.: Harvard University Press, 1961).

Wimsatt, W. K., *The Prose Style of Samuel Johnson* (New Haven and London: Yale University Press, 1941).

b) Studies focusing on the periodical essay

Bond, R. P. (ed.), *Contemporaries of the Tatler and Spectator* (Los Angeles: William Andrews Clark Memorial Library, 1954).

—, *Studies in the Early English Periodical* (Chapel Hill: University of North Carolina Press, 1957).

Graham, W., *The Beginnings of the English Literary Periodicals: A Study of Periodical Literature, 1665–1715* (New York: Oxford University Press, 1926).

—, *English Literary Periodicals* (New York: T. Nelson and Sons, 1930).

Habermas, J., *Strukturwandel der Öffentlichkeit* (Darmstadt and Neuwied: Hermann Luchterhand Verlag, 1962).

Hanson, L., *The Government and the Press, 1695–1763* (London: Oxford University Press, 1936).

Marr, G. S., *The Periodical Essayists of the Eighteenth Century* (New York: Augustus M. Kelley, 1971).

Parks, S., 'John Dunton and *The Works of the Learned*', *The Library*, 23 (1968), pp. 13–24.

Snyder, H. L., 'The Circulation of Newspapers in the Reign of Queen Anne', *The Library*, 23 (1968), pp. 206–35.

Spector, R. D., *English Literary Periodicals and the Climate of*

Opinion during the Seven Years' War (The Hague: Mouton, 1966).

Sutherland, J. R., 'The Circulation of Newspapers and Literary Periodicals, 1700–1730', *The Library*, 15 (1934), pp. 110–24.

c) Studies focusing on Johnson's essays

Bloom, E. A., 'Symbolic Names in Johnson's Periodical Essays', *Modern Language Quarterly (MLQ)*, 13 (1952), pp. 333–52.

Cunningham, J. S., 'The Essayist, "Our Present State", and "The Passions"', in *Samuel Johnson: New Critical Essays*, ed. I. Grundy (London and Totowa, NJ: Vision and Barnes and Noble, 1984), pp. 137–57.

Damrosch, L., 'Johnson's Manner of Proceeding in the *Rambler*', *ELH*, 40 (1973), pp. 70–89.

Davis, P., *In Mind of Johnson: A Study of Johnson the Rambler* (Athens, GA: University of Georgia Press, 1989).

Elder, A. T., 'Thematic Patterning and Development in Johnson's Essays', *Studies in Philology (SP)*, 62 (1965), pp. 610–32.

Kenney, W., 'Parodies and Imitations of Johnson in the Eighteenth Century', *Studies in Eighteenth-Century Culture*, 6 (1977), pp. 157–81.

Lynn, S., *Samuel Johnson after Deconstruction* (Carbondale and Edwardsville: Southern Illinois University Press, 1992).

O'Flaherty, P., 'Towards an Understanding of Johnson's *Rambler*', *Studies in English Literature (SEL)*, 18 (1978), pp. 523–36.

Olson, R. L., *Motto, Context, Essay: The Classical Background of Samuel Johnson's 'Rambler' and 'Adventurer' Essays* (New York: University Press of America, 1984).

Riely, J. C., 'The Pattern of Imagery in Johnson's Periodical Essays', *ECS*, 3 (1970), pp. 384–97.

Schwartz, R. B., 'Johnson's "Mr. Rambler" and the Periodical Tradition', *Genre*, 7 (1974), pp. 196–204.

Spector, R. D., *Samuel Johnson and the Essay* (Westport, CT and London: Greenwood Press, 1997).

Trowbridge, H., 'The Language of Reasoned Rhetoric in *The Rambler*', in *Greene Centennial Studies*, ed. P. J. Korshin and R. R. Allen (Charlottesville: University Press of Virginia, 1984).

Van Tassel, M. M., 'Johnson's Elephant: The Reader of the *Rambler*', *SEL*, 28 (1988), pp. 461–69.

Wiles, R. M., 'The Contemporary Distribution of Johnson's *Rambler*', *ECS*, 2 (1968), pp. 155–71.

Wimsatt, W. K., *Philosophic Words: A Study of Style and Meaning in the Rambler and Dictionary of Samuel Johnson* (New Haven and London: Yale University Press, 1948).

A Note on the Texts

The following texts have served as copy-texts for the works reprinted in this edition:

The Rambler: the fourth edition of 1756.
The Adventurer: the second edition of 1754.
The Idler: the second edition of 1761 (except that the text for the original *Idler* 22 is taken from *Payne's Universal Chronicle*, 23, 1758).
A Compleat Vindication of the Licensers of the Stage: first edition of 1739.
'An Essay on Epitaphs': *The Gentleman's Magazine*, December 1740.
'Introduction' to the *Harleian Miscellany*: *The Harleian Miscellany*, 1744.
'Observations on the Present State of Affairs': *The Literary Magazine*, iv, 15 July – 15 August 1756.
'Of the Duty of a Journalist': *Payne's Universal Chronicle*, 1, 1758.
'The Bravery of the *English* Common Soldiers': *The British Magazine*, 1, January 1760.

The texts as printed in this edition are unmodernized transcriptions of the copy-texts, save that slips have been silently corrected, and Greek quotations have been furnished with accents and breathings in line with modern scholarly editions. No attempt has been made to bring eighteenth-century printers' conventions into line with modern usage, apart from the deletion of the use of small capitals for the initial words of paragraphs.

THE RAMBLER
(1750–52)

No. 1. Tuesday, 20 March 1750.

Cur tamen hoc libeat potius decurrere campo,
Per quem magnus equos Auruncæ flexit alumnus,
Si vacat, et placidi rationem admittitis, edam.

JUV.[1]

Why to expatiate in this beaten field,
Why arms, oft us'd in vain, I mean to wield;
If time permit, and candour will attend,
Some satisfaction this essay may lend.

ELPHINSTON.*

The difficulty of the first address on any new occasion, is felt by every man in his transactions with the world, and confessed by the settled and regular forms of salutation which necessity has introduced into all languages. Judgment was wearied with the perplexity of being forced upon choice, where there was no motive to preference; and it was found convenient that some easy method of introduction should be established, which, if it wanted the allurement of novelty, might enjoy the security of prescription.

Perhaps few authors have presented themselves before the public, without wishing that such ceremonial modes of entrance had been anciently established, as might have freed them from those dangers which the desire of pleasing is certain to produce, and precluded the vain expedients of softening censure by apologies, or rousing attention by abruptness.

The epic writers have found the proemial part of the poem such an addition to their undertaking, that they have almost unanimously adopted the first lines of Homer, and the reader needs only be informed of the subject to know in what manner the poem will begin.

* Mr. ELPHINSTON, to whom the author of these papers is indebted for many elegant translations of the mottos which are inserted from the Edinburgh edition, now keeps an academy for young gentlemen, at Brompton, near Kensington.

But this solemn repetition is hitherto the peculiar distinction of heroic poetry; it has never been legally extended to the lower orders of literature, but seems to be considered as an hereditary privilege, to be enjoyed only by those who claim it from their alliance to the genius of Homer.

The rules which the injudicious use of this prerogative suggested to Horace,[2] may indeed be applied to the direction of candidates for inferior fame; it may be proper for all to remember, that they ought not to raise expectation which it is not in their power to satisfy, and that it is more pleasing to see smoke brightening into flame, than flame sinking into smoke.

This precept has been long received both from regard to the authority of Horace and its conformity to the general opinion of the world, yet there have been always some, that thought it no deviation from modesty to recommend their own labours, and imagined themselves entitled by indisputable merit to an exemption from general restraints, and to elevations not allowed in common life. They, perhaps, believed that when, like Thucydides, they bequeathed to mankind κτῆμα ἐς ἀεὶ, *an estate for ever*,[3] it was an additional favour to inform them of its value.

It may, indeed, be no less dangerous to claim, on certain occasions, too little than too much. There is something captivating in spirit and intrepidity, to which we often yield, as to a resistless power; nor can he reasonably expect the confidence of others, who too apparently distrusts himself.

Plutarch, in his enumeration of the various occasions, on which a man may without just offence proclaim his own excellencies, has omitted the case of an author entering the world; unless it may be comprehended under his general position, that a man may lawfully praise himself for those qualities which cannot be known but from his own mouth; as when he is among strangers, and can have no opportunity of an actual exertion of his powers.[4] That the case of an author is parallel will scarcely be granted, because he necessarily discovers the degree of his merit to his judges, when he appears at his trial. But it should be remembered, that unless his judges are inclined to favour him, they will hardly be persuaded to hear the cause.

In love, the state which fills the heart with a degree of solicitude next that of an author, it has been held a maxim, that success is most easily obtained by indirect and unperceived approaches; he who too soon professes himself a lover, raises obstacles to his own wishes, and those whom disappointments have taught experience, endeavour to conceal their passion till they believe their mistress wishes for the discovery. The same method, if it were practicable to writers, would save many complaints of the severity of the age, and the caprices of criticism. If a man could glide imperceptibly into the favour of the publick, and only proclaim his pretensions to literary honours when he is sure of not being rejected, he might commence author with better hopes, as his failings might escape contempt, though he shall never attain much regard.

But since the world supposes every man that writes ambitious of applause, as some ladies have taught themselves to believe that every man intends love, who expresses civility, the miscarriage of any endeavour in learning raises an unbounded contempt, indulged by most minds without scruple, as an honest triumph over unjust claims, and exorbitant expectations. The artifices of those who put themselves in this hazardous state, have therefore been multiplied in proportion to their fear as well as their ambition; and are to be looked upon with more indulgence, as they are incited at once by the two great movers of the human mind, the desire of good, and the fear of evil. For who can wonder that, allured on one side, and frightned on the other, some should endeavour to gain favour by bribing the judge with an appearance of respect which they do not feel, to excite compassion by confessing weakness of which they are not convinced, and others to attract regard by a shew of openness and magnanimity, by a daring profession of their own deserts, and a publick challenge of honours and rewards.

The ostentatious and haughty display of themselves has been the usual refuge of diurnal writers, in vindication of whose practice it may be said, that what it wants in prudence is supplied by sincerity, and who at least may plead, that if their boasts deceive any into the perusal of their performances, they defraud them of but little time.

——Quid enim? Concurritur—horae
Momento cita mors venit, aut victoria laeta.[5]

The battle joins, and, in a moment's flight,
Death, or a joyful conquest, ends the fight.

FRANCIS.

The question concerning the merit of the day is soon decided, and we are not condemned to toil thro' half a folio, to be convinced that the writer has broke his promise.

It is one among many reasons for which I purpose to endeavour the entertainment of my countrymen by a short essay on Tuesday and Saturday, that I hope not much to tire those whom I shall not happen to please; and if I am not commended for the beauty of my works, to be at least pardoned for their brevity. But whether my expectations are most fixed on pardon or praise, I think it not necessary to discover; for having accurately weighed the reasons for arrogance and submission, I find them so nearly equiponderant, that my impatience to try the event of my first performance will not suffer me to attend any longer the trepidations of the balance.

There are, indeed, many conveniencies almost peculiar to this method of publication, which may naturally flatter the author, whether he be confident or timorous. The man to whom the extent of his knowledge, or the sprightliness of his imagination, has, in his own opinion, already secured the praises of the world, willingly takes that way of displaying his abilities which will soonest give him an opportunity of hearing the voice of fame; it heightens his alacrity to think in how many places he shall hear what he is now writing, read with ecstasies to morrow. He will often please himself with reflecting, that the author of a large treatise must proceed with anxiety, lest, before the completion of his work, the attention of the publick may have changed its object; but that he who is confined to no single topick, may follow the national taste through all its variations, and catch the *Aura popularis*,[6] the gale of favour, from what point soever it shall blow.

Nor is the prospect less likely to ease the doubts of the

cautious, and the terrours of the fearful, for to such the shortness of every single paper is a powerful encouragement. He that questions his abilities to arrange the dissimilar parts of an extensive plan, or fears to be lost in a complicated system, may yet hope to adjust a few pages without perplexity; and if, when he turns over the repositories of his memory, he finds his collection too small for a volume, he may yet have enough to furnish out an essay. He that would fear to lay out too much time upon an experiment of which he knows not the event, persuades himself that a few days will shew him what he is to expect from his learning and his genius. If he thinks his own judgment not sufficiently enlightned, he may, by attending the remarks which every paper will produce, rectify his opinions. If he should with too little premeditation encumber himself by an unwieldly subject, he can quit it without confessing his ignorance, and pass to other topicks less dangerous, or more tractable. And if he finds, with all his industry, and all his artifices, that he cannot deserve regard, or cannot attain it, he may let the design fall at once, and, without injury to others or himself, retire to amusements of greater pleasure, or to studies of better prospect.

No. 2. Saturday, 24 March 1750.

Stare loco nescit, pereunt vestigia mille
Ante fugam, absentemque ferit gravis ungula campum.
STATIUS.[1]

Th'impatient courser pants in ev'ry vein,
And pawing seems to beat the distant plain;
Hills, vales, and floods, appear already crost,
And, ere he starts, a thousand steps are lost.
POPE.[2]

That the mind of man is never satisfied with the objects immediately before it, but is always breaking away from the present moment, and losing itself in schemes of future felicity; and that we forget the proper use of the time now in our power, to provide for the enjoyment of that which, perhaps, may never be granted us, has been frequently remarked; and as this practice is a commodious subject of raillery to the gay, and of declamation to the serious, it has been ridiculed with all the pleasantry of wit, and exaggerated with all the amplifications of rhetoric. Every instance, by which its absurdity might appear most flagrant, has been studiously collected; it has been marked with every epithet of contempt, and all the tropes and figures have been called forth against it.

Censure is willingly indulged, because it always implies some superiority; men please themselves with imagining that they have made a deeper search, or wider survey, than others, and detected faults and follies, which escape vulgar observation. And the pleasure of wantoning in common topicks is so tempting to a writer, that he cannot easily resign it; a train of sentiments generally received enables him to shine without labour, and to conquer without a contest. It is so easy to laugh at the folly of him who lives only in idea, refuses immediate ease for distant pleasures, and, instead of enjoying the blessings of life, lets life glide away in preparations to enjoy them. It affords such opportunities of triumphant exultation, to exemplify the uncertainty of the human state, to rouse mortals from their dream, and inform them of the silent celerity of time, that we may believe authors willing rather to transmit than examine so advantageous a principle, and more inclined to pursue a track so smooth and so flowery, than attentively to consider whether it leads to truth.

This quality of looking forward into futurity seems the unavoidable condition of a being, whose motions are gradual, and whose life is progressive: as his powers are limited, he must use means for the attainment of his ends, and intend first what he performs last; as, by continual advances from his first stage of existence, he is perpetually varying the horizon of his prospects, he must always discover new motives of action, new excitements of fear, and allurements of desire.

The end therefore which at present calls forth our efforts will be found, when it is once gained, to be only one of the means to some remoter end. The natural flights of the human mind are not from pleasure to pleasure, but from hope to hope.[3]

He that directs his steps to a certain point, must frequently turn his eyes to that place which he strives to reach; he that undergoes the fatigue of labour, must solace his weariness with the contemplation of its reward. In agriculture, one of the most simple and necessary employments, no man turns up the ground but because he thinks of the harvest, that harvest which blights may intercept, which inundations may sweep away, or which death or calamity may hinder him from reaping.

Yet as few maxims are widely received or long retained but for some conformity with truth and nature, it must be confessed, that this caution against keeping our view too intent upon remote advantages is not without its propriety or usefulness, though it may have been recited with too much levity, or enforced with too little distinction: for, not to speak of that vehemence of desire which presses through right and wrong to its gratification, or that anxious inquietude which is justly chargeable with distrust of heaven, subjects too solemn for my present purpose; it frequently happens that, by indulging early the raptures of success, we forget the measures necessary to secure it, and suffer the imagination to riot in the fruition of some possible good, till the time of obtaining it has slipped away.

There would however be few enterprises of great labour or hazard undertaken, if we had not the power of magnifying the advantages which we persuade ourselves to expect from them. When the knight of La Mancha gravely recounts to his companion the adventures by which he is to signalize himself in such a manner that he shall be summoned to the support of empires, solicited to accept the heiress of the crown which he has preserved, have honours and riches to scatter about him, and an island to bestow on his worthy squire, very few readers, amidst their mirth or pity, can deny that they have admitted visions of the same kind; though they have not, perhaps, expected events equally strange, or by means equally inadequate.[4] When we pity him, we reflect on our own disappointments; and when we laugh, our hearts inform us that he is not more ridiculous than ourselves, except that he tells what we have only thought.

The understanding of a man, naturally sanguine, may, indeed, be easily vitiated by the luxurious indulgence of hope,

however necessary to the production of every thing great or
excellent, as some plants are destroyed by too open exposure to
that sun which gives life and beauty to the vegetable world.

Perhaps no class of the human species requires more to be
cautioned against this anticipation of happiness, than those that
aspire to the name of authors. A man of lively fancy no sooner
finds a hint moving in his mind, than he makes momentaneous
excursions to the press, and to the world, and, with a little
encouragement from flattery, pushes forward into future ages,
and prognosticates the honours to be paid him, when envy is
extinct, and faction forgotten, and those, whom partiality now
suffers to obscure him, shall have given way to other triflers of
as short duration as themselves.

Those, who have proceeded so far as to appeal to the tribunal
of succeeding times, are not likely to be cured of their infatuation; but all endeavours ought to be used for the prevention of
a disease, for which, when it has attained its height, perhaps no
remedy will be found in the gardens of philosophy, however she
may boast her physick of the mind, her catharticks of vice, or
lenitives of passion.

I shall, therefore, while I am yet but lightly touched with the
symptoms of the writer's malady, endeavour to fortify myself
against the infection, not without some weak hope, that my
preservatives may extend their virtue to others, whose employment exposes them to the same danger:

> *Laudis amore tumes? Sunt certa piacula, quæ te*
> *Ter pure lecto poterunt recreare libello.*[5]

> Is fame your passion? Wisdom's pow'rful charm,
> If thrice read over, shall its force disarm.
>
>   FRANCIS.

It is the sage advice of Epictetus,[6] that a man should accustom
himself often to think of what is most shocking and terrible, that
by such reflexions he may be preserved from too ardent wishes
for seeming good, and from too much dejection in real evil.

There is nothing more dreadful to an author than neglect,

compared with which reproach, hatred, and opposition, are names of happiness; yet this worst, this meanest fate every man who dares to write has reason to fear.

I nunc, et versus tecum meditare canoros.[7]

Go now, and meditate thy tuneful lays.
ELPHINSTON.

It may not be unfit for him who makes a new entrance into the lettered world, so far to suspect his own powers as to believe that he possibly may deserve neglect; that nature may not have qualified him much to enlarge or embellish knowledge, nor sent him forth entitled by indisputable superiority to regulate the conduct of the rest of mankind; that, though the world must be granted to be yet in ignorance, he is not destined to dispel the cloud, nor to shine out as one of the luminaries of life. For this suspicion, every catalogue of a library will furnish sufficient reason, as he will find it crouded with names of men, who, though now forgotten, were once no less enterprising or confident than himself, equally pleased with their own productions, equally caressed by their patrons, and flattered by their friends.

But, though it should happen that an author is capable of excelling, yet his merit may pass without notice, huddled in the variety of things, and thrown into the general miscellany of life. He that endeavours after fame by writing, solicits the regard of a multitude fluctuating in pleasures, or immersed in business, without time for intellectual amusements; he appeals to judges prepossessed by passions, or corrupted by prejudices, which preclude their approbation of any new performance. Some are too indolent to read any thing, till its reputation is established; others too envious to promote that fame, which gives them pain by its increase. What is new is opposed, because most are unwilling to be taught; and what is known is rejected, because it is not sufficiently considered, that men more frequently require to be reminded than informed. The learned are afraid to declare their opinion early, lest they should put their reputation in hazard; the ignorant always imagine themselves giving some proof of delicacy, when they refuse to be pleased: and he that finds his way to reputation, through all these obstructions, must acknowledge that he is indebted to other causes besides his industry, his learning, or his wit.

No. 4. Saturday, 31 March 1750.

Simul et jucunda et idonea dicere Vitæ.[1]
HOR.

And join both profit and delight in one.
CREECH.[2]

The works of fiction,[3] with which the present generation seems more particularly delighted, are such as exhibit life in its true state, diversified only by accidents that daily happen in the world, and influenced by passions and qualities which are really to be found in conversing with mankind.

This kind of writing may be termed not improperly the comedy of romance, and is to be conducted nearly by the rules of comic poetry. Its province is to bring about natural events by easy means, and to keep up curiosity without the help of wonder: it is therefore precluded from the machines and expedients of the heroic romance, and can neither employ giants to snatch away a lady from the nuptial rites, nor knights to bring her back from captivity; it can neither bewilder its personages in desarts, nor lodge them in imaginary castles.

I remember a remark made by Scaliger upon Pontanus,[4] that all his writings are filled with the same images; and that if you take from him his lillies and his roses, his satyrs and his dryads, he will have nothing left that can be called poetry. In like manner, almost all the fictions of the last age will vanish, if you deprive them of a hermit and a wood, a battle and a shipwreck.

Why this wild strain of imagination found reception so long, in polite and learned ages, it is not easy to conceive; but we cannot wonder that, while readers could be procured, the authors were willing to continue it: for when a man had by practice gained some fluency of language, he had no further care than to retire to his closet, let loose his invention, and heat his mind with incredibilities; a book was thus produced without fear of criticism, without the toil of study, without knowledge of nature, or acquaintance with life.

The task of our present writers is very different; it requires, together with that learning which is to be gained from books, that experience which can never be attained by solitary diligence, but must arise from general converse, and accurate observation of the living world. Their performances have, as Horace expresses it, *plus oneris quantum veniæ minus*,[5] little indulgence, and therefore more difficulty. They are engaged in portraits of which every one knows the original, and can detect any deviation from exactness of resemblance. Other writings are safe, except from the malice of learning, but these are in danger from every common reader; as the slipper ill executed was censured by a shoemaker who happened to stop in his way at the Venus of Apelles.[6]

But the fear of not being approved as just copyers of human manners, is not the most important concern that an author of this sort ought to have before him. These books are written chiefly to the young, the ignorant, and the idle, to whom they serve as lectures of conduct, and introductions into life. They are the entertainment of minds unfurnished with ideas, and therefore easily susceptible of impressions; not fixed by principles, and therefore easily following the current of fancy; not informed by experience, and consequently open to every false suggestion and partial account.

That the highest degree of reverence should be paid to youth, and that nothing indecent should be suffered to approach their eyes or ears; are precepts extorted by sense and virtue from an ancient writer, by no means eminent for chastity of thought.[7] The same kind, tho' not the same degree of caution, is required to every thing which is laid before them, to secure them from unjust prejudices, perverse opinions, and incongruous combinations of images.

In the romances formerly written, every transaction and sentiment was so remote from all that passes among men, that the reader was in very little danger of making any applications to himself; the virtues and crimes were equally beyond his sphere of activity; and he amused himself with heroes and with traitors, deliverers and persecutors, as with beings of another species, whose actions were regulated upon motives of their own, and who had neither faults nor excellencies in common with himself.

But when an adventurer is levelled with the rest of the world, and acts in such scenes of the universal drama, as may be the lot of any other man; young spectators fix their eyes upon him with closer attention, and hope by observing his behaviour and success to regulate their own practices, when they shall be engaged in the like part.

For this reason these familiar histories may perhaps be made of greater use than the solemnities of professed morality and convey the knowledge of vice and virtue with more efficacy than axioms and definitions. But if the power of example is so great, as to take possession of the memory by a kind of violence, and produce effects almost without the intervention of the will, care ought to be taken that, when the choice is unrestrained, the best examples only should be exhibited; and that which is likely to operate so strongly, should not be mischievous or uncertain in its effects.[8]

The chief advantage which these fictions have over real life is, that their authors are at liberty, tho' not to invent, yet to select objects, and to cull from the mass of mankind, those individuals upon which the attention ought most to be employ'd; as a diamond, though it cannot be made, may be polished by art, and placed in such a situation, as to display that lustre which before was buried among common stones.

It is justly considered as the greatest excellency of art, to imitate nature; but it is necessary to distinguish those parts of nature, which are most proper for imitation: greater care is still required in representing life, which is so often discoloured by passion, or deformed by wickedness. If the world be promiscuously described, I cannot see of what use it can be to read the account; or why it may not be as safe to turn the eye immediately upon mankind, as upon a mirror which shows all that presents itself without discrimination.

It is therefore not a sufficient vindication of a character, that it is drawn as it appears, for many characters ought never to be drawn; nor of a narrative, that the train of events is agreeable to observation and experience, for that observation which is called knowledge of the world, will be found much more frequently to make men cunning than good. The purpose of these writings is surely not only to show mankind, but to provide that they may be seen hereafter with less hazard; to teach the means of avoiding the snares which are laid by TREACHERY for INNOCENCE, without infusing any wish for that superiority with which the betrayer flatters his vanity; to give the power of counteracting fraud, without the temptation to practise it; to initiate youth by mock encounters in the art of necessary defence, and to increase prudence without impairing virtue.

Many writers, for the sake of following nature, so mingle good and bad qualities in their principal personages, that they are both equally conspicuous; and as we accompany them through their adventures with delight, and are led by degrees to interest ourselves in their favour, we lose the abhorrence of their faults, because they do not hinder our pleasure, or, perhaps, regard them with some kindness for being united with so much merit.

There have been men indeed splendidly wicked, whose endowments threw a brightness on their crimes, and whom scarce any villainy made perfectly detestable, because they never could be wholly divested of their excellencies; but such have been in all ages the great corrupters of the world, and their resemblance ought no more to be preserved, than the art of murdering without pain.

Some have advanced, without due attention to the consequences of this notion, that certain virtues have their correspondent faults, and therefore that to exhibit either apart is to deviate from probability. Thus men are observed by Swift to be "grateful in the same degree as they are resentful."[9] This principle, with others of the same kind, supposes man to act from a brute impulse, and persue a certain degree of inclination, without any choice of the object; for, otherwise, though it should be allowed that gratitude and resentment arise from the same constitution of the passions, it follows not that they will be equally indulged when reason is consulted; yet unless that consequence be admit-

ted, this sagacious maxim becomes an empty sound, without
any relation to practice or to life.

Nor is it evident, that even the first motions to these effects
are always in the same proportion. For pride, which produces
quickness of resentment, will obstruct gratitude, by unwillingness to admit that inferiority which obligation implies; and it is
very unlikely, that he who cannot think he receives a favour will
acknowledge or repay it.

It is of the utmost importance to mankind, that positions of
this tendency should be laid open and confuted; for while men
consider good and evil as springing from the same root, they
will spare the one for the sake of the other, and in judging, if
not of others at least of themselves, will be apt to estimate their
virtues by their vices. To this fatal error all those will contribute,
who confound the colours of right and wrong, and instead of
helping to settle their boundaries, mix them with so much art,
that no common mind is able to disunite them.

In narratives, where historical veracity has no place, I cannot
discover why there should not be exhibited the most perfect
idea of virtue; of virtue not angelical, nor above probability, for
what we cannot credit we shall never imitate, but the highest
and purest that humanity can reach, which, exercised in such
trials as the various revolutions of things shall bring upon it,
may, by conquering some calamities, and enduring others, teach
us what we may hope, and what we can perform. Vice, for vice
is necessary to be shewn, should always disgust; nor should the
graces of gaiety, or the dignity of courage, be so united with it,
as to reconcile it to the mind. Wherever it appears, it should
raise hatred by the malignity of its practices, and contempt by
the meanness of its stratagems; for while it is supported by either
parts or spirit, it will be seldom heartily abhorred. The Roman
tyrant was content to be hated, if he was but feared;[10] and there
are thousands of the readers of romances willing to be thought
wicked, if they may be allowed to be wits. It is therefore to be
steadily inculcated, that virtue is the highest proof of understanding, and the only solid basis of greatness; and that vice is
the natural consequence of narrow thoughts, that it begins in
mistake, and ends in ignominy.

No. 6. Saturday, 7 April 1750.

Strenua nos exercet inertia, navibus atque
Quadrigis petimus bene vivere: quod petis, hic est;
Est Ulubris, animus si te non deficit æquus.

HOR.[1]

Active in indolence, abroad we roam
In quest of happiness, which dwells at home:
With vain persuits fatigu'd, at length you'll find,
No place excludes it from an equal mind.

ELPHINSTON.

That man should never suffer his happiness to depend upon external circumstances, is one of the chief precepts of the Stoical philosophy; a precept, indeed, which that lofty sect has extended beyond the condition of human life, and in which some of them seem to have comprised an utter exclusion of all corporal pain and pleasure, from the regard or attention of a wise man.

Such *sapientia insaniens*,[2] as Horace calls the doctrine of another sect, such extravagance of philosophy, can want neither authority nor argument for its confutation; it is overthrown by the experience of every hour, and the powers of nature rise up against it. But we may very properly enquire, how near to this exalted state it is in our power to approach, how far we can exempt ourselves from outward influences, and secure to our minds a state of tranquillity: For, though the boast of absolute independence is ridiculous and vain, yet a mean flexibility to every impulse, and a patient submission to the tyranny of casual troubles, is below the dignity of that mind, which, however depraved or weakened, boasts its derivation from a celestial original, and hopes for an union with infinite goodness, and unvariable felicity.

Ni vitiis pejora fovens
Proprium deserat ortum.[3]

Unless the soul, to vice a thrall,
Desert her own original.

The necessity of erecting ourselves to some degree of intellectual dignity, and of preserving resources of pleasure, which may not be wholly at the mercy of accident, is never more apparent than when we turn our eyes upon those whom fortune has let loose to their own conduct; who not being chained down by their condition to a regular and stated allotment of their hours, are obliged to find themselves business or diversion, and having nothing within that can entertain or employ them, are compelled to try all the arts of destroying time.

The numberless expedients practised by this class of mortals to alleviate the burthen of life, is not less shameful, nor, perhaps, much less pitiable, than those to which a trader on the edge of bankruptcy is reduced. I have seen melancholy overspread a whole family at the disappointment of a party for cards; and when, after the proposal of a thousand schemes, and the dispatch of the footman upon a hundred messages, they have submitted, with gloomy resignation, to the misfortune of passing one evening in conversation with each other, on a sudden, such are the revolutions of the world, an unexpected visiter has brought them relief, acceptable as provision to a starving city, and enabled them to hold out till the next day.

The general remedy of those, who are uneasy without knowing the cause, is change of place; they are willing to imagine that their pain is the consequence of some local inconvenience, and endeavour to fly from it, as children from their shadows; always hoping for more satisfactory delight from every new scene, and always returning home with disappointment and complaints.

Who can look upon this kind of infatuation, without reflecting on those that suffer under the dreadful symptom of canine madness,[4] termed by physicians the "dread of water"? These miserable wretches, unable to drink, though burning with thirst, are sometimes known to try various contortions, or inclinations of the body, flattering themselves that they can swallow in one posture that liquor, which they find in another to repel their lips.

Yet such folly is not peculiar to the thoughtless or ignorant, but sometimes seizes those minds which seem most exempted from it, by the variety of attainments, quickness of penetration, or severity of judgment; and, indeed, the pride of wit and knowledge is often mortified by finding, that they confer no security against the common errors, which mislead the weakest and meanest of mankind.

These reflexions arose in my mind upon the remembrance of a passage in Cowley's preface to his poems, where, however exalted by genius, and enlarged by study, he informs us of a scheme of happiness to which the imagination of a girl, upon the loss of her first lover, could have scarcely given way; but which he seems to have indulged till he had totally forgotten its absurdity, and would probably have put in execution, had he been hindered only by his reason.

"My desire," says he, "has been for some years past, though the execution has been accidentally diverted, and does still vehemently continue, to retire myself to some of our American plantations, not to seek for gold, or enrich myself with the traffic of those parts, which is the end of most men that travel thither; but to forsake this world for ever, with all the vanities and vexations of it, and to bury myself there in some obscure retreat, but not without the consolation of letters and philosophy."[5]

Such was the chimerical provision which Cowley had made, in his own mind, for the quiet of his remaining life, and which he seems to recommend to posterity, since there is no other reason for disclosing it. Surely no stronger instance can be given of a persuasion that content was the inhabitant of particular regions, and that a man might set sail with a fair wind, and leave behind him all his cares, incumbrances, and calamities.

If he travelled so far with no other purpose than to "bury himself in some obscure retreat," he might have found, in his own country, innumerable coverts sufficiently dark to have concealed the genius of Cowley; for, whatever might be his opinion of the importunity with which he should be summoned back into publick life, a short experience would have convinced him, that privation is easier than acquisition, and that it would require little continuance to free himself from the intrusion of the world. There is pride enough in the human heart to prevent much desire of acquaintance with a man by whom we are sure to be neglected, however his reputation for science or virtue may excite our curiosity or esteem; so that the lover of retirement needs not be afraid lest the respect of strangers should overwhelm him with visits. Even those to whom he has formerly been known will very patiently support his absence, when they have tried a little to live without him, and found new diversions for those moments which his company contributed to exhilarate.

It was, perhaps, ordained by providence, to hinder us from tyrannising over one another, that no individual should be of such importance, as to cause, by his retirement or death, any chasm in the world. And Cowley had conversed to little purpose with mankind, if he had never remarked, how soon the useful friend, the gay companion, and the favoured lover, when once they are removed from before the sight, give way to the succession of new objects.

The privacy, therefore, of his hermitage might have been safe enough from violation, though he had chosen it within the limits of his native island; he might have found here preservatives against the *vanities* and *vexations* of the world, not less efficacious than those which the woods or fields of America could afford him: but having once his mind imbittered with disgust, he conceived it impossible to be far enough from the cause of his uneasiness; and was posting away with the expedition of a coward, who, for want of venturing to look behind him, thinks the enemy perpetually at his heels.

When he was interrupted by company, or fatigued with business, he so strongly imaged to himself the happiness of leisure and retreat, that he determined to enjoy them for the future without interruption, and to exclude for ever all that could deprive him of his darling satisfaction. He forgot, in the vehemence of desire, that solitude and quiet owe their pleasures to those miseries, which he was so studious to obviate; for such are the vicissitudes of the world, through all its parts, that day and night, labour and rest, hurry and retirement, endear each other; such are the changes that keep the mind in action; we desire, we pursue, we obtain, we are satiated; we desire something else, and begin a new persuit.[6]

If he had proceeded in his project, and fixed his habitation in the most delightful part of the new world, it may be doubted, whether his distance from the *vanities* of life would have enabled him to keep away the *vexations*. It is common for a man, who feels pain, to fancy that he could bear it better in any other part. Cowley having known the troubles and perplexities of a particular condition, readily persuaded himself that nothing worse was to be found, and that every alteration would bring some improvement; he never suspected that the cause of his unhappiness was within, that his own passions were not sufficiently regulated, and that he was harrassed by his own impatience, which could never be without something to awaken it, would accompany him over the sea, and find its way to his American elysium. He would, upon the tryal, have been soon convinced, that the fountain of content must spring up in the mind; and that he, who has so little knowledge of human nature, as to seek happiness by changing any thing, but his own dispositions, will waste his life in fruitless efforts, and multiply the griefs which he purposes to remove.

No. 7. Tuesday, 10 April 1750.

O qui perpetuâ mundum ratione gubernas,
Terrarum cœlique sator!——
Disjice terrenæ nebulas & pondera molis,
Atque tuo splendore mica! Tu namque serenum,
Tu requies tranquilla piis. Te cernere, finis,
Principium, vector, dux, semita, terminus, idem.
BOETHIUS.[1]

O Thou whose pow'r o'er moving worlds presides,
Whose voice created, and whose wisdom guides,
On darkling man in pure effulgence shine,
And chear the clouded mind with light divine.
'Tis thine alone to calm the pious breast
With silent confidence and holy rest;
From thee, great God, we spring, to thee we tend,
Path, motive, guide, original and end.

The love of RETIREMENT has, in all ages, adhered closely to those minds, which have been most enlarged by knowledge, or elevated by genius. Those who enjoyed every thing generally supposed to confer happiness, have been forced to seek it in the shades of privacy. Though they possessed both power and riches, and were, therefore, surrounded by men, who considered it as their chief interest to remove from them every thing that might offend their ease, or interrupt their pleasure, they have soon felt the languors of satiety, and found themselves unable to pursue the race of life without frequent respirations of inter-mediate solitude.

To produce this disposition nothing appears requisite but quick sensibility, and active imagination; for, though not devoted to virtue, or science, the man, whose faculties enable him to make ready comparisons of the present with the past, will find such a constant recurrence of the same pleasures, and troubles, the same expectations, and disappointments, that he will gladly snatch an hour of retreat, to let his thoughts expatiate at large, and seek for that variety in his own ideas, which the objects of sense cannot afford him.

Nor will greatness, or abundance, exempt him from the importunities of this desire, since, if he is born to think, he cannot restrain himself from a thousand enquiries and specu-lations, which he must persue by his own reason, and which the splendour of his condition can only hinder; for those who are most exalted above dependance or controul, are yet condemned to pay so large a tribute of their time to custom, ceremony, and popularity, that, according to the *Greek* proverb, no man in the house is more a slave than the master.[2]

When a king asked Euclid the mathematician, whether he could not explain his art to him in a more compendious manner, he was answered, that there was no royal way to geometry.[3] Other things may be seized by might, or purchased with money, but knowledge is to be gained only by study, and study to be prosecuted only in retirement.

These are some of the motives which have had power to sequester kings and heroes from the crouds that soothed them with flatteries, or inspirited them with acclamations; but their efficacy seems confined to the higher mind, and to operate little upon the common classes of mankind, to whose conceptions the present assemblage of things is adequate, and who seldom range beyond those entertainments and vexations, which solicit their attention by pressing on their senses.

But there is an universal reason for some stated intervals of solitude, which the institutions of the church call upon me, now especially,[4] to mention; a reason, which extends as wide as moral duty, or the hopes of divine favour in a future state; and which ought to influence all ranks of life, and all degrees of intellect; since none can imagine themselves not comprehended in its obligation, but such as determine to set their maker at defiance by obstinate wickedness, or whose enthusiastick security of his approbation places them above external ordinances, and all human means of improvement.

The great task of him, who conducts his life by the precepts of religion, is to make the future predominate over the present, to impress upon his mind so strong a sense of the importance of obedience to the divine will, of the value of the reward promised to virtue, and the terrors of the punishment denounced against crimes, as may overbear all the temptations which temporal hope or fear can bring in his way, and enable him to bid equal defiance to joy and sorrow, to turn away at one time from the allurements of ambition, and push forward at another against the threats of calamity.

It is not without reason that the apostle represents our passage through this stage of our existence by images drawn from the alarms and solicitude of a military life; for we are placed in such a state, that almost every thing about us conspires against our chief interest. We are in danger from whatever can get possession of our thoughts; all that can excite in us either pain or pleasure has a tendency to obstruct the way that leads to happiness, and either to turn us aside, or retard our progress.

Our senses, our appetites, and our passions, are our lawful and faithful guides, in most things that relate solely to this life; and, therefore, by the hourly necessity of consulting them, we gradually sink into an implicit submission, and habitual confidence. Every act of compliance with their motions facilitates a second compliance, every new step towards depravity is made with less reluctance than the former, and thus the descent to life merely sensual is perpetually accelerated.

The senses have not only that advantage over conscience, which things necessary must always have over things chosen, but they have likewise a kind of prescription in their favour. We feared pain much earlier than we apprehended guilt, and were delighted with the sensations of pleasure, before we had capacities to be charmed with the beauty of rectitude. To this power, thus early established, and incessantly increasing, it must be remembered, that almost every man has, in some part of his life, added new strength by a voluntary or negligent subjection of himself; for who is there that has not instigated his appetites by indulgence, or suffered them by an unresisting neutrality to enlarge their dominion, and multiply their demands?

From the necessity of dispossessing the sensitive faculties of the influence which they must naturally gain by this preoccupation of the soul, arises that conflict between opposite desires, in the first endeavours after a religious life; which, however enthusiastically it may have been described, or however contemptuously ridiculed, will naturally be felt in some degree, though varied without end, by different tempers of mind, and innumerable circumstances of health or condition, greater or less fervour, more or fewer temptations to relapse.

From the perpetual necessity of consulting the animal faculties, in our provision for the present life, arises the difficulty of withstanding their impulses, even in cases where they ought to be of no weight; for the motions of sense are instantaneous, its objects strike unsought, we are accustomed to follow its directions, and therefore often submit to the sentence without examining the authority of the judge.

Thus it appears, upon a philosophical estimate, that, supposing the mind, at any certain time, in an equipoise between the pleasures of this life, and the hopes of futurity, present objects falling more frequently into the scale would in time preponderate, and that our regard for an invisible state would grow every moment weaker, till at last it would lose all its activity, and become absolutely without effect.

To prevent this dreadful event, the balance is put into our own hands, and we have power to transfer the weight to either side. The motives to a life of holiness are infinite, not less than the favour or anger of omnipotence, not less than eternity of happiness or misery. But these can only influence our conduct as they gain our attention, which the business, or diversions, of the world are always calling off by contrary attractions.

The great art therefore of piety, and the end for which all the rites of religion seem to be instituted, is the perpetual renovation of the motives to virtue, by a voluntary employment of our mind in the contemplation of its excellence, its importance, and its necessity, which, in proportion as they are more frequently and more willingly revolved, gain a more forcible and permanent influence, 'till in time they become the reigning ideas, the standing principles of action, and the test by which every thing proposed to the judgment is rejected or approved.

To facilitate this change of our affections, it is necessary that we weaken the temptations of the world, by retiring at certain seasons from it; for its influence arising only from its presence, is much lessened when it becomes the object of solitary meditation. A constant residence amidst noise and pleasure inevitably obliterates the impressions of piety, and a frequent abstraction of ourselves into a state, where this life, like the next, operates only upon the reason, will reinstate religion in its just authority, even without those irradiations from above, the hope of which I have yet no intention to withdraw from the sincere and the diligent.

This is that conquest of the world and of ourselves, which has been always considered as the perfection of human nature; and this is only to be obtained by fervent prayer, steady resolutions, and frequent retirement from folly and vanity, from the cares of avarice, and the joys of intemperance, from the lulling sounds of deceitful flattery, and the tempting sight of prosperous wickedness.

No. 8. Saturday, 14 April 1750.

——*Patitur poenas peccandi sola voluntas;*
Nam scelus intra se tacitum qui cogitat ullum,
Facti crimen habet.

JUV.[1]

For he that but conceives a crime in thought,
Contracts the danger of an actual fault.

CREECH.

If the most active and industrious of mankind was able, at the close of life, to recollect distinctly his past moments, and distribute them, in a regular account, according to the manner in which they have been spent, it is scarcely to be imagined how few would be marked out to the mind, by any permanent or visible effects, how small a proportion his real action would bear to his seeming possibilities of action, how many chasms he would find of wide and continued vacuity, and how many interstitial spaces unfilled, even in the most tumultuous hurries of business, and the most eager vehemence of persuit.

It is said by modern philosophers, that not only the great globes of matter are thinly scattered thro' the universe, but the hardest bodies are so porous, that, if all matter were compressed to perfect solidity, it might be contained in a cube of a few feet. In like manner, if all the employment of life were crowded into the time which it really occupied, perhaps a few weeks, days, or hours, would be sufficient for its accomplishment, so far as the mind was engaged in the performance. For such is the inequality of our corporeal to our intellectual faculties, that we contrive in minutes what we execute in years, and the soul often stands an idle spectator of the labour of the hands, and expedition of the feet.

For this reason, the antient generals often found themselves at leisure to persue the study of philosophy in the camp; and Lucan, with historical veracity, makes Cæsar relate of himself, that he noted the revolutions of the stars in the midst of preparations for battle.

————*Media inter prœlia semper*
Sideribus, cœlique plagis, superisque vacavi.[2]

Amid the storms of war, with curious eyes
I trace the planets and survey the skies.

That the soul always exerts her peculiar powers, with greater or less force, is very probable, though the common occasions of our present condition require but a small part of that incessant cogitation; and by the natural frame of our bodies, and general combination of the world, we are so frequently condemned to inactivity, that as through all our time we are thinking, so for a great part of our time we can only think.

Lest a power so restless should be either unprofitably, or hurtfully employed, and the superfluities of intellect run to waste, it is no vain speculation to consider how we may govern our thoughts, restrain them from irregular motions, or confine them from boundless dissipation.

How the understanding is best conducted to the knowledge of science, by what steps it is to be led forwards in its persuit, how it is to be cured of its defects, and habituated to new studies, has been the inquiry of many acute and learned men, whose observations I shall not either adopt or censure; my purpose being to consider the moral discipline of the mind, and to promote the increase of virtue rather than of learning.

This inquiry seems to have been neglected for want of remembering that all action has its origin in the mind, and that therefore to suffer the thoughts to be vitiated, is to poison the fountains of morality: Irregular desires will produce licentious practices; what men allow themselves to wish they will soon believe, and will be at last incited to execute what they please themselves with contriving.

For this reason the casuists of the Romish church, who gain, by confession, great opportunities of knowing human nature, have generally determined that what it is a crime to do, it is a crime to think.[3] Since by revolving with pleasure, the facility, safety or advantage of a wicked deed, a man soon begins to find his constancy relax, and his detestation soften; the happiness of success glittering before him, withdraws his attention from the atrociousness of the guilt, and acts are at last confidently perpetrated, of which the first conception only crept into the mind, disguised in pleasing complications, and permitted rather than invited.

No man has ever been drawn to crimes, by love or jealousy, envy or hatred, but he can tell how easily he might at first have repelled the temptation, how readily his mind would have obeyed a call to any other object, and how weak his passion has been after some casual avocation, 'till he has recalled it again to his heart, and revived the viper by too warm a fondness.

Such, therefore, is the importance of keeping reason a constant guard over imagination, that we have otherwise no security for our own virtue, but may corrupt our hearts in the most recluse solitude, with more pernicious and tyrannical appetites and wishes, than the commerce of the world will generally produce; for we are easily shocked by crimes which appear at once in their full magnitude, but the gradual growth of our own wickedness, endeared by interest, and palliated by all the artifices of self-deceit, gives us time to form distinctions in our own favour, and reason by degrees submits to absurdity, as the eye is in time accommodated to darkness.

In this disease of the soul, it is of the utmost importance to apply remedies at the beginning; and, therefore, I shall endeavour to shew what thoughts are to be rejected or improved, as they regard the past, present, or future; in hopes that some may be awakened to caution and vigilance, who, perhaps, indulge themselves in dangerous dreams, so much the more dangerous, because being yet only dreams they are concluded innocent.

The recollection of the past is only useful by way of provision for the future; and therefore, in reviewing all occurrences that fall under a religious consideration, it is proper that a man stop at the first thoughts, to remark how he was led thither, and why he continues the reflexion. If he is dwelling with delight upon a stratagem of successful fraud, a night of licentious riot, or an intrigue of guilty pleasure, let him summon off his imagination as from an unlawful persuit, expel those passages from his remembrance, of which, though he cannot seriously approve them, the pleasure overpowers the guilt, and refer them to a future hour, when they may be considered with greater safety. Such an hour will certainly come; for the impressions of past pleasure are always lessening, but the sense of guilt, which respects futurity, continues the same.

The serious and impartial retrospect of our conduct is indisputably necessary to the confirmation or recovery of virtue, and is, therefore, recommended under the name of self-examination, by divines, as the first act previous to repentance. It is, indeed, of so great use, that without it we should always be to begin life, be seduced for ever by the same allurements, and misled by the same fallacies. But in order that we may not lose the advantage of our experience, we must endeavour to see every thing in its proper form, and excite in ourselves those sentiments which the great author of nature has decreed the concomitants or followers of good or bad actions.

> Μηδ' ὕπνον μαλακοῖσιν ἐπ' ὄμμασι προσδέξασθαι,
> Πρὶν τῶν ἡμερινῶν ἔργων τρὶς ἕκαστον ἐπελθεῖν·
> Πῇ παρέβην; τί δ'ἔρεξα; τί μοὶ δέον οὐκ ἐτελέσθη;
> 'Αρξάμενος δ' ἀπὸ πρώτου ἐπέξιθι· καὶ μετέπειτα,
> Δειλὰ μὲν ἐκπρήξας, ἐπιπλήσσεο, χρηστὰ δὲ, τέρπου.[4]

Let not sleep, says Pythagoras, *fall upon thy eyes till thou hast thrice reviewed the transactions of the past day. Where have I turned aside from rectitude? What have I been doing? What have I left undone, which I ought to have done? Begin thus from the first act, and proceed; and in conclusion, at the ill which thou hast done be troubled, and rejoice for the good.*

Our thoughts on present things being determined by the objects before us, fall not under those indulgences, or excursions, which I am now considering. But I cannot forbear, under this head, to caution pious and tender minds, that are disturbed by the irruptions of wicked imaginations, against too great dejection, and too anxious alarms; for thoughts are only criminal, when they are first chosen, and then voluntarily continued.

Evil into the mind of god or man
May come and go, so unapprov'd, and leave
No spot or stain behind.

MILTON.[5]

In futurity chiefly are the snares lodged, by which the imagination is intangled. Futurity is the proper abode of hope and fear, with all their train and progeny of subordinate apprehensions and desires. In futurity events and chances are yet floating at large, without apparent connexion with their causes, and we therefore easily indulge the liberty of gratifying ourselves with a pleasing choice. To pick and cull among possible advantages is, as the civil law terms it, *in vacuum venire,* to take what belongs to nobody; but it has this hazard in it, that we shall be unwilling to quit what we have seized, though an owner should be found. It is easy to think on that which may be gained, till at last we resolve to gain it, and to image the happiness of particular conditions till we can be easy in no other. We ought, at least, to let our desires fix upon nothing in another's power for the sake of our quiet, or in another's possession for the sake of our innocence. When a man finds himself led, though by a train of honest sentiments, to a wish for that to which he has no right, he should start back as from a pitfal covered with flowers. He that fancies he should benefit the publick more in a great station than the man that fills it, will in time imagine it an act of virtue to supplant him; and, as opposition readily kindles into hatred, his eagerness to do that good, to which he is not called, will betray him to crimes, which in his original scheme were never purposed.

He therefore that would govern his actions by the laws of virtue, must regulate his thoughts by those of reason; he must keep guilt from the recesses of his heart, and remember that the pleasures of fancy, and the emotions of desire are more dangerous as they are more hidden, since they escape the awe of observation, and operate equally in every situation, without the concurrence of external opportunities.

No. 9. Tuesday, 17 April 1750.

Quod sis esse velis, nihilque malis.
MART.[1]

Chuse what you are; no other state prefer.
ELPHINSTON.

It is justly remarked by Horace, that, howsoever every man may complain occasionally of the hardships of his condition, he is seldom willing to change it for any other on the same level: for whether it be that he, who follows an employment, made choice of it at first on account of its suitableness to his inclination; or that when accident, or the determination of others, have placed him in a particular station, he, by endeavouring to reconcile himself to it, gets the custom of viewing it only on the fairest side; or whether every man thinks that class to which he belongs the most illustrious, merely because he has honoured it with his name; it is certain that, whatever be the reason, most men have a very strong and active prejudice in favour of their own vocation, always working upon their minds, and influencing their behaviour.

This partiality is sufficiently visible in every rank of the human species; but it exerts itself more frequently and with greater force among those who have never learned to conceal their sentiments for reasons of policy, or to model their expressions by the laws of politeness; and therefore the chief contests of wit among artificers and handicraftsmen arise from a mutual endeavour to exalt one trade by depreciating another.

From the same principle are derived many consolations to alleviate the inconveniences to which every calling is peculiarly exposed. A blacksmith was lately pleasing himself at his anvil, with observing that, though his trade was hot and sooty, laborious and unhealthy, yet he had the honour of living by his hammer, he got his bread like a man, and if his son should rise in the world, and keep his coach, no body could reproach him that his father was a taylor.

A man, truly zealous for his fraternity, is never so irresistibly flattered, as when some rival calling is mentioned with contempt. Upon this principle a linen-draper boasted that he had got a new customer, whom he could safely trust, for he could have no doubt of his honesty, since it was known, from unquestionable authority, that he was now filing a bill in chancery to delay payment for the cloaths which he had worn the last seven years; and he himself had heard him declare, in a publick coffee-house, that he looked upon the whole generation of woollen-drapers to be such despicable wretches, that no gentleman ought to pay them.

It has been observed that physicians and lawyers are no friends to religion; and many conjectures have been formed to discover the reason of such a combination between men who agree in nothing else, and who seem less to be affected, in their own provinces, by religious opinions, than any other part of the community. The truth is, very few of them have thought about religion; but they have all seen a parson, seen him in a habit different from their own, and therefore declared war against him. A young student from the inns of court, who has often attacked the curate of his father's parish with such arguments as his acquaintances could furnish, and returned to town without success, is now gone down with a resolution to destroy him; for he has learned at last how to manage a prig, and if he pretends to hold him again to syllogism, he has a catch in reserve, which neither logic nor metaphysics can resist.

> *I laugh to think how your unshaken* Cato
> *Will look aghast, when unforeseen destruction*
> *Pours in upon him thus.*[2]

The malignity of soldiers and sailors against each other has been often experienced at the cost of their country; and, perhaps, no orders of men have an enmity of more acrimony, or longer continuance. When, upon our late successes at sea,[3] some new regulations were concerted for establishing the rank of the naval commanders, a captain of foot very acutely remarked, that nothing was more absurd than to give any honorary rewards to seamen, "for honour," says he, "ought only to be won by bravery, and all the world knows that in a sea-fight there is no danger, and therefore no evidence of courage."

But although this general desire of aggrandizing themselves by raising their profession, betrays men to a thousand ridiculous and mischievous acts of supplantation and detraction, yet as almost all passions have their good as well as bad effects, it likewise excites ingenuity, and sometimes raises an honest and useful emulation of diligence. It may be observed in general that no trade had ever reached the excellence to which it is now improved, had its professors looked upon it with the eyes of indifferent spectators; the advances, from the first rude essays, must have been made by men who valued themselves for performances, for which scarce any other would be persuaded to esteem them.

It is pleasing to contemplate a manufacture rising gradually from its first mean state by the successive labours of innumerable minds; to consider the first hollow trunk of an oak, in which, perhaps, the shepherd could scarce venture to cross a brook swelled with a shower, enlarged at last into a ship of war, attacking fortresses, terrifying nations, setting storms and billows at defiance, and visiting the remotest parts of the globe. And it might contribute to dispose us to a kinder regard for the labours of one another, if we were to consider from what unpromising beginnings the most useful productions of art have probably arisen. Who, when he saw the first sand or ashes, by a casual intenseness of heat melted into a metalline form, rugged with excrescences, and clouded with impurities, would have imagined, that in this shapeless lump lay concealed so many conveniencies of life, as would in time constitute a great part of the happiness of the world? Yet by some such fortuitous liquefaction was mankind taught to procure a body at once in a high degree solid and transparent, which might admit the light of the sun, and exclude the violence of the wind; which might extend the sight of the philosopher to new ranges of existence, and charm him at one time with the unbounded extent of the material creation, and at another with the endless subordination of animal life; and, what is yet of more importance, might supply the decays of nature, and succour old age with subsidiary sight. Thus was the first artificer in glass employed, though without his own knowledge or expectation. He was facilitating and prolonging the enjoyment of light, enlarging the avenues of science, and conferring the highest and most lasting pleasures; he was enabling the student to contemplate nature, and the beauty to behold herself.

This passion for the honour of a profession, like that for the grandeur of our own country, is to be regulated not extinguished. Every man, from the highest to the lowest station, ought to warm his heart and animate his endeavours with the hopes of being useful to the world, by advancing the art which it is his lot to exercise; and for that end he must necessarily consider the whole extent of its application, and the whole weight of its importance. But let him not too readily imagine that another is ill employed, because, for want of fuller knowledge of his business, he is not able to comprehend its dignity. Every man ought to endeavour at eminence, not by pulling others down, but by raising himself, and enjoy the pleasure of his own superiority, whether imaginary or real, without interrupting others in the same felicity. The philosopher may very justly be delighted with the extent of his views, and the artificer with the readiness of his hands; but let the one remember, that, without mechanical performances, refined speculation is an empty dream, and the other, that, without theoretical reasoning, dexterity is little more than a brute instinct.

No. 13. Tuesday, 1 May 1750.

Commissumque teges & vino tortus & irâ.

HOR.[1]

And let not wine or anger wrest
Th' intrusted secret from your breast.

FRANCIS.

It is related by Quintus Curtius, that the Persians always conceived an invincible contempt of a man, who had violated the laws of secrecy; for they thought, that, however he might be deficient in the qualities requisite to actual excellence, the negative virtues at least were in his power, and though he perhaps could not speak well if he was to try, it was still easy for him not to speak.[2]

In forming this opinion of the easiness of secrecy, they seem to have consider'd it as opposed, not to treachery, but loquacity, and to have conceived the man, whom they thus censured, not frighted by menaces to reveal, or bribed by promises to betray, but incited by the mere pleasure of talking, or some other motive equally trifling, to lay open his heart without reflection, and to let whatever he knew slip from him, only for want of power to retain it. Whether, by their settled and avowed scorn of thoughtless talkers, the Persians were able to diffuse to any great extent the virtue of taciturnity, we are hindered by the distance of those times from being able to discover, there being very few memoirs remaining of the court of Persepolis, nor any distinct accounts handed down to us of their office clerks, their ladies of the bed-chamber, their attorneys, their chamber-maids, or their footmen.

In these latter ages, though the old animosity against a prattler is still retained, it appears wholly to have lost its effects upon the conduct of mankind; for secrets are so seldom kept, that it may with some reason be doubted, whether the antients were not mistaken in their first postulate, whether the quality of retention be so generally bestowed, and whether a secret has not some subtle volatility, by which it escapes imperceptibly at the smallest vent, or some power of fermentation, by which it expands itself so as to burst the heart that will not give it way.

Those that study either the body or the mind of man, very often find the most specious and pleasing theory falling under the weight of contrary experience; and instead of gratifying their vanity by inferring effects from causes, they are always reduced at last to conjecture causes from effects. That it is easy to be secret the speculatist can demonstrate in his retreat, and therefore thinks himself justified in placing confidence; the man of the world knows, that, whether difficult or not, it is uncommon, and therefore finds himself rather inclined to search after the reason of this universal failure in one of the most important duties of society.

The vanity of being known to be trusted with a secret is generally one of the chief motives to disclose it; for however absurd it may be thought to boast an honour by an act which shews that it was conferred without merit, yet most men seem rather inclined to confess the want of virtue than of importance, and more willingly shew their influence, though at the expense of their probity, than glide through life with no other pleasure than the private consciousness of fidelity; which, while it is preserved, must be without praise, except from the single person who tries and knows it.

There are many ways of telling a secret, by which a man exempts himself from the reproaches of his conscience, and gratifies his pride without suffering himself to believe that he impairs his virtue. He tells the private affairs of his patron, or his friend, only to those from whom he would not conceal his own; he tells them to those, who have no temptation to betray the trust, or with a denunciation of a certain forfeiture of his friendship, if he discovers that they become public.

Secrets are very frequently told in the first ardour of kindness, or of love, for the sake of proving, by so important a sacrifice, sincerity, or tenderness; but with this motive, though it be strong in itself, vanity concurs, since every man desires to be most esteemed by those whom he loves, or with whom he converses, with whom he passes his hours of pleasure, and to whom he retires from business and from care.

When the discovery of secrets is under consideration, there is always a distinction carefully to be made between our own and those of another; those of which we are fully masters as they affect only our own interest, and those which are reposited with us in trust, and involve the happiness or convenience of such as we have no right to expose to hazard. To tell our own secrets is generally folly, but that folly is without guilt; to communicate those with which we are intrusted is always treachery, and treachery for the most part combined with folly.

There have, indeed, been some enthusiastick and irrational zealots for friendship, who have maintained, and perhaps believed, that one friend has a right to all that is in possession of another; and that therefore it is a violation of kindness to exempt any secret from this boundless confidence. Accordingly a late female minister of state has been shameless enough to inform the world, that she used, when she wanted to extract any thing from her sovereign, to remind her of Montaigne's reasoning, who has determined, that to tell a secret to a friend is no breach of fidelity, because the number of persons trusted is not multiplied, a man and his friend being virtually the same.[3]

That such a fallacy could be imposed upon any human understanding, or that an author could have advanced a position so remote from truth and reason, any otherwise than as a declaimer, to shew to what extent he could stretch his imagination, and with what strength he could press his principle, would scarcely have been credible, had not this lady kindly shewn us how far weakness may be deluded, or indolence amused. But since it appears, that even this sophistry has been able, with the help of a strong desire to repose in quiet upon the understanding of another, to mislead honest intentions, and an understanding not contemptible, it may not be superfluous to remark, that those things which are common among friends are only such as either possesses in his own right, and can alienate or destroy without injury to any other person. Without this limitation, confidence must run on without end, the second person may tell the secret to the third upon the same principle as he received it from the first, and the third may hand it forward to a fourth, till at last it is told in the round of friendship to them from whom it was the first intention chiefly to conceal it.

The confidence which Caius has of the faithfulness of Titius is nothing more than an opinion which himself cannot know to be true, and which Claudius, who first tells his secret to Caius may know to be false; and therefore the trust is transferred by Caius, if he reveal what has been told him, to one from whom the person originally concerned would have withheld it; and, whatever may be the event, Caius has hazarded the happiness of his friend, without necessity and without permission, and has put that trust in the hand of fortune which was given only to virtue.

All the arguments upon which a man who is telling the private affairs of another may ground his confidence of security, he must upon reflection know to be uncertain, because he finds them without effect upon himself. When he is imagining that Titius will be cautious from a regard to his interest, his reputation, or his duty, he ought to reflect that he is himself at that instant acting in opposition to all these reasons, and revealing what interest, reputation, and duty direct him to conceal.

Every one feels that in his own case he should consider the man incapable of trust, who believed himself at liberty to tell whatever he knew to the first whom he should conclude deserving of his confidence; therefore Caius, in admitting Titius to the affairs imparted only to himself, must know that he violates his faith, since he acts contrary to the intention of Claudius, to whom that faith was given. For promises of friendship are, like all others, useless and vain, unless they are made in some known sense, adjusted and acknowledged by both parties.

I am not ignorant that many questions may be started relating to the duty of secrecy, where the affairs are of publick concern; where subsequent reasons may arise to alter the appearance and nature of the trust; that the manner in which the secret was told may change the degree of obligation; and that the principles upon which a man is chosen for a confident may not always equally constrain him. But these scruples, if not too intricate, are of too extensive consideration for my present purpose, nor are they such as generally occur in common life; and though casuistical knowledge be useful in proper hands, yet it ought by no means to be carelessly exposed, since most will use it rather to lull than awaken their own consciences; and the threads of reasoning, on which truth is suspended, are frequently drawn to such subtility, that common eyes cannot perceive, and common sensibility cannot feel them.

The whole doctrine as well as practice of secrecy, is so perplexing and dangerous, that, next to him who is compelled to trust, I think him unhappy who is chosen to be trusted; for he is often involved in scruples without the liberty of calling in the help of any other understanding; he is frequently drawn into guilt, under the appearance of friendship and honesty; and sometimes subjected to suspicion by the treachery of others, who are engaged without his knowledge in the same schemes;

for he that has one confident has generally more, and when he is at last betrayed, is in doubt on whom he shall fix the crime.

The rules therefore that I shall propose concerning secrecy, and from which I think it not safe to deviate, without long and exact deliberation, are—Never to solicit the knowledge of a secret. Not willingly, nor without many limitations, to accept such confidence when it is offered. When a secret is once admitted, to consider the trust as of a very high nature, important as society, and sacred as truth, and therefore not to be violated for any incidental convenience, or slight appearance of contrary fitness.

No. 14. Saturday, 5 May 1750.

———————————————— *Nil fuit unquam*

Sic dispar sibi ————————————————

HOR.[1]

Sure such a various creature ne'er was known.

FRANCIS.

Among the many inconsistencies which folly produces, or infirmity suffers in the human mind, there has often been observed a manifest and striking contrariety between the life of an author and his writings; and Milton, in a letter to a learned stranger, by whom he had been visited, with great reason congratulates himself upon the consciousness of being found equal to his own character, and having preserved in a private and familiar interview that reputation which his works had procured him.[2]

Those whom the appearance of virtue, or the evidence of genius, have tempted to a nearer knowledge of the writer in whose performances they may be found, have indeed had frequent reason to repent their curiosity; the bubble that sparkled before them has become common water at the touch; the phantom of perfection has vanished when they wished to press it to their bosom. They have lost the pleasure of imagining how far humanity may be exalted, and, perhaps, felt themselves less inclined to toil up the steeps of virtue, when they observe those who seem best able to point the way, loitering below, as either afraid of the labour, or doubtful of the reward.

It has been long the custom of the oriental monarchs to hide themselves in gardens and palaces, to avoid the conversation of mankind, and to be known to their subjects only by their edicts. The same policy is no less necessary to him that writes, than to him that governs; for men would not more patiently submit to be taught, than commanded, by one known to have the same follies and weaknesses with themselves. A sudden intruder into the closet of an author would perhaps feel equal indignation with the officer, who having long solicited admission into the presence of Sardanapalus, saw him not consulting upon laws, enquiring into grievances, or modelling armies, but employed in feminine amusements, and directing the ladies in their work.[3]

It is not difficult to conceive, however, that for many reasons a man writes much better than he lives. For, without entering into refined speculations, it may be shown much easier to design than to perform. A man proposes his schemes of life in a state of abstraction and disengagement, exempt from the enticements of hope, the solicitations of affection, the importunities of appetite, or the depressions of fear, and is in the same state with him that teaches upon land the art of navigation, to whom the sea is always smooth, and the wind always prosperous.

The mathematicians are well acquainted with the difference between pure science, which has to do only with ideas, and the application of its laws to the use of life, in which they are constrained to submit to the imperfection of matter and the influence of accidents. Thus, in moral discussions it is to be remembred that many impediments obstruct our practice, which very easily give way to theory. The speculatist is only in danger of erroneous reasoning, but the man involved in life has his own passions, and those of others, to encounter, and is embarrassed with a thousand inconveniences, which confound him with variety of impulse, and either perplex or obstruct his way. He is forced to act without deliberation, and obliged to choose before he can examine; he is surprised by sudden alterations of the state of things, and changes his measures according to superficial appearances; he is led by others, either because he is indolent, or because he is timorous; he is sometimes afraid to know what is right, and sometimes finds friends or enemies diligent to deceive him.

We are, therefore, not to wonder that most fail, amidst tumult, and snares, and danger, in the observance of those precepts, which they laid down in solitude, safety, and tranquillity, with a mind unbiassed, and with liberty unobstructed. It is the condition of our present state to see more than we can attain, the exactest vigilance and caution can never maintain a single day of unmingled innocence, much less can the utmost efforts of incorporated mind reach the summits of speculative virtue.

It is, however, necessary for the idea of perfection to be proposed, that we may have some object to which our endeavours are to be directed; and he that is most deficient in the duties of life, makes some atonement for his faults, if he warns others against his own failings, and hinders, by the salubrity of his admonitions, the contagion of his example.

Nothing is more unjust, however common, than to charge with hypocrisy him that expresses zeal for those virtues, which he neglects to practise; since he may be sincerely convinced of the advantages of conquering his passions, without having yet obtained the victory, as a man may be confident of the advantages of a voyage, or a journey, without having courage or industry to undertake it, and may honestly recommend to others, those attempts which he neglects himself.

The interest which the corrupt part of mankind have in hardening themselves against every motive to amendment, has disposed them to give to these contradictions, when they can be produced against the cause of virtue, that weight which they will not allow them in any other case. They see men act in opposition to their interest, without supposing, that they do not know it; those who give way to the sudden violence of passion, and forsake the most important persuits for petty pleasures, are not supposed to have changed their opinions, or to approve their own conduct. In moral or religious questions alone, they determine the sentiments by the actions, and charge every man with endeavouring to impose upon the world, whose writings are not confirmed by his life. They never consider that they themselves neglect, or practise something every day, inconsistently with their own settled judgment, nor discover that the conduct of the advocates for virtue can little increase, or lessen, the obligations of their dictates; argument is to be invalidated only by argument, and is in itself of the same force, whether or not it convinces him by whom it is proposed.

Yet since this prejudice, however unreasonable, is always likely to have some prevalence, it is the duty of every man to take care lest he should hinder the efficacy of his own instructions. When he desires to gain the belief of others, he should shew that he believes himself; and when he teaches the fitness of virtue by his reasonings, he should, by his example, prove its possibility: Thus much at least may be required of him, that he shall not act worse than others because he writes better, nor imagine that, by the merit of his genius, he may claim indulgence beyond mortals of the lower classes, and be excused for want of prudence, or neglect of virtue.

BACON, in his History of the winds, after having offered something to the imagination as desirable, often proposes lower advantages in its place to the reason as attainable.[4] The same method may be sometimes pursued in moral endeavours, which this philosopher has observed in natural enquiries; having first set positive and absolute excellence before us, we may be pardoned though we sink down to humbler virtue, trying, however, to keep our point always in view, and struggling not to lose ground, though we cannot gain it.

It is recorded of Sir Matthew Hale, that he, for a long time, concealed the consecration of himself to the stricter duties of religion, lest, by some flagitious and shameful action, he should bring piety into disgrace.[5] For the same reason, it may be prudent for a writer, who apprehends that he shall not inforce his own maxims by his domestic character, to conceal his name that he may not injure them.

There are, indeed, a greater number whose curiosity to gain a more familiar knowledge of successful writers, is not so much prompted by an opinion of their power to improve as to delight, and who expect from them not arguments against vice, or dissertations on temperance or justice, but flights of wit, and sallies of pleasantry, or, at least, acute remarks, nice distinctions, justness of sentiment, and elegance of diction.

This expectation is, indeed, specious and probable, and yet, such is the fate of all human hopes, that it is very often frustrated, and those who raise admiration by their books, disgust by their company. A man of letters for the most part spends, in the privacies of study, that season of life in which the manners are to be softened into ease, and polished into elegance, and, when he has gained knowledge enough to be respected, has neglected the minuter acts by which he might have pleased. When he enters life, if his temper be soft and timorous, he is diffident and bashful, from the knowledge of his defects; or if he was born with spirit and resolution, he is ferocious and arrogant from the consciousness of his merit: he is either dissipated by the awe of company, and unable to recollect his reading, and arrange his arguments; or he is hot, and dogmatical, quick in opposition, and tenacious in defence, disabled by his own violence, and confused by his haste to triumph.

The graces of writing and conversation are of different kinds, and though he who excels in one might have been with opportunities and application equally successful in the other, yet as many please by extemporary talk, though utterly unacquainted with the more accurate method, and more laboured beauties, which composition requires; so it is very possible that men, wholly accustomed to works of study, may be without that readiness of conception, and affluence of language, always necessary to colloquial entertainment. They may want address to watch the hints which conversation offers for the display of their particular attainments, or they may be so much unfurnished with matter on common subjects, that discourse not professedly literary glides over them as heterogeneous bodies, without admitting their conceptions to mix in the circulation.

A transition from an author's books to his conversation, is too often like an entrance into a large city, after a distant prospect. Remotely, we see nothing but spires of temples, and turrets of palaces, and imagine it the residence of splendor, grandeur, and magnificence; but, when we have passed the gates, we find it perplexed with narrow passages, disgraced with despicable cottages, embarrassed with obstructions, and clouded with smoke.

No. 16. Saturday, 12 May 1750.

——— *Multis dicendi copia torrens,*
Et sua mortifera est facundia ———
JUV.[1]

Some who the depths of eloquence have found,
In that unnavigable stream were drown'd.

DRYDEN.

SIR,

I am the modest young man whom you favoured with your advice, in a late paper;[2] and, as I am very far from suspecting that you foresaw the numberless inconveniences which I have, by following it, brought upon myself, I will lay my condition open before you, for you seem bound to extricate me from the perplexities, in which your counsel, however innocent in the intention, has contributed to involve me.

You told me, as you thought, to my comfort, that a writer might easily find means of introducing his genius to the world, for the *presses of England were open*. This I have now fatally experienced; the press is, indeed, open.

——— *Facilis descensus Averni,*
Noctes atque dies patet atri janua Ditis.[3]

The gates of hell are open night and day;
Smooth the descent, and easy is the way.

DRYDEN.

The means of doing hurt to ourselves are always at hand. I immediately sent to a printer, and contracted with him for an impression of several thousands of my pamphlet. While it was at the press, I was seldom absent from the printing-house, and continually urged the workmen to haste, by solicitations, promises, and rewards. From the day all other pleasures were excluded, by the delightful employment of correcting the sheets; and from the night sleep was generally banished, by anticipations of the happiness, which every hour was bringing nearer.

At last the time of publication approached, and my heart beat with the raptures of an author. I was above all little precautions, and, in defiance of envy or of criticism, set my name upon the title, without sufficiently considering, that what has once passed the press is irrevocable, and that though the printing-house may properly be compared to the infernal regions, for the facility of its entrance, and the difficulty with which authors return from it; yet there is this difference, that a great genius can never return to his former state, by a happy draught of the waters of oblivion.

I am now, Mr. Rambler, known to be an author, and am condemned, irreversibly condemned, to all the miseries of high reputation. The first morning after publication my friends assembled about me; I presented each, as is usual, with a copy of my book. They looked into the first pages, but were hindered, by their admiration, from reading farther. The first pages are, indeed, very elaborate. Some passages they particularly dwelt upon, as more eminently beautiful than the rest; and some delicate strokes, and secret elegancies, I pointed out to them, which had escaped their observation. I then begged of them to forbear their compliments, and invited them, I could not do less, to dine with me at a tavern. After dinner, the book was resumed; but their praises very often so much overpowered my modesty, that I was forced to put about the glass, and had often no means of repressing the clamours of their admiration, but by thundering to the drawer for another bottle.

Next morning another set of my acquaintance congratulated me upon my performance, with such importunity of praise, that I was again forced to obviate their civilities by a treat. On the third day I had yet a greater number of applauders to put to silence in the same manner; and, on the fourth, those whom I had entertained the first day came again, having, in the perusal of the remaining part of the book, discovered so many forcible

sentences and masterly touches, that it was impossible for me
to bear the repetition of their commendations. I, therefore,
persuaded them once more to adjourn to the tavern, and choose
some other subject, on which I might share in the conversation.
But it was not in their power to withold their attention from my
performance, which had so entirely taken possession of their
minds, that no intreaties of mine could change their topick, and
I was obliged to stifle, with claret, that praise, which neither my
modesty could hinder, nor my uneasiness repress.

The whole week was thus spent in a kind of literary revel,
and I have now found that nothing is so expensive as great
abilities, unless there is join'd with them an insatiable eagerness
of praise; for to escape from the pain of hearing myself exalted
above the greatest names dead and living of the learned world,
it has already cost me two hogsheads of port, fifteen gallons
of arrack, ten dozen of claret, and five and forty bottles of
champagne.

I was resolved to stay at home no longer, and, therefore, rose
early and went to the coffee-house; but found that I had now
made myself too eminent for happiness, and that I was no longer
to enjoy the pleasure of mixing, upon equal terms, with the rest
of the world. As soon as I enter the room, I see part of the
company raging with envy, which they endeavour to conceal,
sometimes with the appearance of laughter, and sometimes with
that of contempt; but the disguise is such, that I can discover
the secret rancour of their hearts, and as envy is deservedly its
own punishment, I frequently indulge myself in tormenting them
with my presence.

But, though there may be some slight satisfaction received
from the mortification of my enemies, yet my benevolence will
not suffer me to take any pleasure in the terrors of my friends. I
have been cautious, since the appearance of my work, not to
give myself more premeditated airs of superiority, than the most
rigid humility might allow. It is, indeed, not impossible that I
may sometimes have laid down my opinion, in a manner that
shewed a consciousness of my ability to maintain it, or interrupted the conversation, when I saw its tendency, without suffering the speaker to waste his time in explaining his sentiments;

and, indeed, I did indulge myself for two days in a custom of drumming with my fingers, when the company began to lose themselves in absurdities, or to encroach upon subjects which I knew them unqualified to discuss. But I generally acted with great appearance of respect, even to those whose stupidity I pitied in my heart. Yet, notwithstanding this exemplary moderation, so universal is the dread of uncommon powers, and such the unwillingness of mankind to be made wiser, that I have now for some days found myself shunned by all my acquaintance. If I knock at a door, no body is at home; if I enter a coffee-house, I have the box to myself. I live in the town like a lion in his desart, or an eagle on his rock, too great for friendship or society, and condemned to solitude, by unhappy elevation, and dreaded ascendency.

Nor is my character only formidable to others, but burdensome to myself. I naturally love to talk without much thinking, to scatter my merriment at random, and to relax my thoughts with ludicrous remarks and fanciful images; but such is now the importance of my opinion, that I am afraid to offer it, lest, by being established too hastily into a maxim, it should be the occasion of error to half the nation; and such is the expectation with which I am attended, when I am going to speak, that I frequently pause to reflect whether what I am about to utter is worthy of myself.

This, Sir, is sufficiently miserable, but there are still greater calamities behind. You must have read in Pope and Swift how men of parts have had their closets rifled, and their cabinets broke open at the instigation of piratical booksellers, for the profit of their works;[4] and it is apparent, that there are many prints now sold in the shops, of men whom you cannot suspect of sitting for that purpose, and whose likenesses must have been certainly stolen when their names made their faces vendible. These considerations at first put me on my guard, and I have, indeed, found sufficient reason for my caution, for I have discovered many people examining my countenance, with a curiosity that shewed their intention to draw it; I immediately left the house, but find the same behaviour in another.

Others may be persecuted, but I am haunted; I have good

reason to believe that eleven painters are now dogging me, for they know that he who can get my face first will make his fortune. I often change my wig, and wear my hat over my eyes, by which I hope somewhat to confound them; for you know it is not fair to sell my face, without admitting me to share the profit.

I am, however, not so much in pain for my face as for my papers, which I dare neither carry with me nor leave behind. I have, indeed, taken some measures for their preservation, having put them in an iron chest, and fixed a padlock upon my closet. I change my lodgings five times a week, and always remove at the dead of night.

Thus I live, in consequence of having given too great proofs of a predominant genius, in the solitude of a hermit, with the anxiety of a miser, and the caution of an outlaw; afraid to shew my face, lest it should be copied; afraid to speak, lest I should injure my character, and to write lest my correspondents should publish my letters; always uneasy lest my servants should steal my papers for the sake of money, or my friends for that of the publick. This it is to soar above the rest of mankind; and this representation I lay before you, that I may be informed how to divest myself of the laurels which are so cumbersome to the wearer, and descend to the enjoyment of that quiet from which I find a writer of the first class so fatally debarred.

MISELLUS.

No. 17. Tuesday, 15 May 1750.

—————*Me non oracula certum,*
Sed mors certa facit.

LUCAN.[1]

Let those weak minds, who live in doubt and fear,
To juggling priests for oracles repair;
One certain hour of death to each decreed,
My fixt, my certain soul from doubt has freed.

ROWE.[2]

It is recorded of some eastern monarch, that he kept an officer in his house, whose employment it was to remind him of his mortality, by calling out every morning, at a stated hour: *Remember, prince, that thou shalt die.*[3] And the contemplation of the frailness and uncertainty of our present state appeared of so much importance to Solon of Athens, that he left this precept to future ages: *Keep thine eye fixed upon the end of life.*[4]

A frequent and attentive prospect of that moment, which must put a period to all our schemes, and deprive us of all our acquisitions, is, indeed, of the utmost efficacy to the just and rational regulation of our lives; nor would ever any thing wicked, or often any thing absurd, be undertaken or prosecuted by him who should begin every day with a serious reflection, that he is born to die.

The disturbers of our happiness, in this world, are our desires, our griefs, and our fears, and to all these, the consideration of mortality is a certain and adequate remedy. Think, says Epictetus, frequently on poverty, banishment, and death, and thou wilt then never indulge violent desires, or give up thy heart to mean sentiments, οὐδὲν οὐδέποτε ταπεινὸν ἐνθυμήσῃ, οὔτε ἄγαν ἐπιθυμήσεις τινός.[5]

That the maxim of Epictetus is founded on just observation will easily be granted, when we reflect, how that vehemence of eagerness after the common objects of persuit is kindled in our minds. We represent to ourselves the pleasures of some future possession, and suffer our thoughts to dwell attentively upon it, till it has wholly ingrossed the imagination, and permits us not to conceive any happiness but its attainment, or any misery but its loss; every other satisfaction which the bounty of providence has scattered over life is neglected as inconsiderable, in comparison of the great object which we have placed before us, and is thrown from us as incumbering our activity, or trampled under foot as standing in our way.

Every man has experienced, how much of this ardour has been remitted, when a sharp or tedious sickness has set death before his eyes. The extensive influence of greatness, the glitter of wealth, the praises of admirers, and the attendance of supplicants, have appeared vain and empty things, when the last hour seemed to be approaching; and the same appearance they would always have, if the same thought was always predominant. We should then find the absurdity of stretching out our arms incessantly to grasp that which we cannot keep, and wearing out our lives in endeavours to add new turrets to the fabrick of ambition, when the foundation itself is shaking, and the ground on which it stands is mouldering away.

All envy is proportionate to desire; we are uneasy at the attainments of another, according as we think our own happiness would be advanced by the addition of that which he witholds from us; and, therefore, whatever depresses immoderate wishes, will, at the same time, set the heart free from the corrosion of envy, and exempt us from that vice which is, above most others, tormenting to ourselves, hateful to the world, and productive of mean artifices, and sordid projects. He that considers how soon he must close his life, will find nothing of so much importance as to close it well; and will, therefore, look with indifference upon whatever is useless to that purpose. Whoever reflects frequently upon the uncertainty of his own duration, will find out, that the state of others is not more permanent, and that what can confer nothing on himself very desirable, cannot so much improve the condition of a rival, as to make him much superior to those from whom he has carried the prize, a prize too mean to deserve a very obstinate opposition.

Even grief, that passion to which the virtuous and tender mind is particularly subject, will be obviated, or alleviated, by the same thoughts. It will be obviated, if all the blessings of our condition are enjoyed with a constant sense of this uncertain tenure. If we remember, that whatever we possess is to be in our hands but a very little time, and that the little, which our most lively hopes can promise us, may be made less, by ten thousand accidents; we shall not much repine at a loss, of which we cannot estimate the value, but of which, though we are not able to tell the least amount, we know, with sufficient certainty, the greatest, and are convinced that the greatest is not much to be regretted.

But, if any passion has so much usurped our understanding, as not to suffer us to enjoy advantages with the moderation prescribed by reason, it is not too late to apply this remedy, when we find ourselves sinking under sorrow, and inclined to pine for that which is irrecoverably vanished. We may then usefully revolve the uncertainty of our own condition, and the folly of lamenting that from which, if it had stayed a little longer, we should ourselves have been taken away.

With regard to the sharpest and most melting sorrow, that which arises from the loss of those whom we have loved with tenderness, it may be observed, that friendship between mortals can be contracted on no other terms, than that one must sometime mourn for the other's death: And this grief will always yield to the surviver one consolation proportionate to his affliction; for the pain, whatever it be, that he himself feels, his friend has escaped.

Nor is fear, the most overbearing and resistless of all our passions, less to be temperated by this universal medicine of the mind. The frequent contemplation of death, as it shows the vanity of all human good, discovers likewise the lightness of all terrestrial evil, which, certainly, can last no longer than the subject upon which it acts, and, according to the old observation, must be shorter, as it is more violent. The most cruel calamity, which misfortune can produce, must, by the necessity of nature, be quickly at an end. The soul cannot long be held in prison, but will fly away, and leave a lifeless body to human malice.

—————— *Ridetque sui ludibria trunci.*[6]

And soaring mocks the broken frame below.

The utmost that we can threaten to one another is that death, which, indeed, we may precipitate, but cannot retard, and from which, therefore, it cannot become a wise man to buy a reprieve at the expence of virtue, since he knows not how small a portion of time he can purchase, but knows that, whether short or long, it will be made less valuable by the remembrance of the price at which it has been obtained. He is sure that he destroys his happiness, but is not sure that he lengthens his life.

The known shortness of life, as it ought to moderate our passions, may likewise, with equal propriety, contract our designs. There is not time for the most forcible genius, and most active industry, to extend its effects beyond a certain sphere. To project the conquest of the world, is the madness of mighty princes; to hope for excellence in every science, has been the folly of literary heroes; and both have found, at last, that they have panted for a height of eminence denied to humanity, and have lost many opportunities of making themselves useful and happy, by a vain ambition of obtaining a species of honour, which the eternal laws of providence have placed beyond the reach of man.

The miscarriages of the great designs of princes are recorded in the histories of the world, but are of little use to the bulk of mankind, who seem very little interested in admonitions against errors which they cannot commit. But the fate of learned ambition is a proper subject for every scholar to consider; for who has not had occasion to regret the dissipation of great abilities in a boundless multiplicity of persuits, to lament the sudden desertion of excellent designs, upon the offer of some other subject, made inviting by its novelty, and to observe the inaccuracy and deficiencies of works left unfinished by too great an extension of the plan?

It is always pleasing to observe, how much more our minds can conceive, than our bodies can perform; yet it is our duty, while we continue in this complicated state, to regulate one part of our composition by some regard to the other. We are not to indulge our corporeal appetites with pleasures that impair our intellectual vigour, nor gratify our minds with schemes which we know our lives must fail in attempting to execute. The uncertainty of our duration ought at once to set bounds to our designs, and add incitements to our industry; and when we find ourselves inclined either to immensity in our schemes, or sluggishness in our endeavours, we may either check, or animate, ourselves, by recollecting, with the father of physic, *that art is long, and life is short.*[7]

No. 18. Saturday, 19 May 1750.

Illic matre carentibus
Privignis mulier temperat innocens,
Nec dotata regit virum
Conjux, nec nitido fidit adultero:
Dos est magna parentium
Virtus, et metuens alterius tori
Certo fœdere castitas.

HOR.[1]

Not there the guiltless step-dame knows
The baleful draught for orphans to compose;
No wife high-portion'd rules her spouse,
Or trusts her essenc'd lover's faithless vows:
The lovers there for dowr'y claim,
The father's virtue, and the spotless fame,
Which dares not break the nuptial tie.

FRANCIS.

There is no observation more frequently made by such as employ themselves in surveying the conduct of mankind, than that marriage, though the dictate of nature, and the institution of providence, is yet very often the cause of misery, and that those who enter into that state can seldom forbear to express their repentance, and their envy of those whom either chance or caution has witheld from it.

This general unhappiness has given occasion to many sage maxims among the serious, and smart remarks among the gay; the moralist and the writer of epigrams have equally shown their abilities upon it; some have lamented, and some have ridiculed it; but as the faculty of writing has been chiefly a masculine endowment, the reproach of making the world miserable has been always thrown upon the women, and the grave and the merry have equally thought themselves at liberty to conclude either with declamatory complaints, or satirical censures, of female folly or fickleness, ambition or cruelty, extravagance or lust.

Led by such a number of examples, and incited by my share in the common interest, I sometimes venture to consider this universal grievance, having endeavoured to divest my heart of all partiality, and place myself as a kind of neutral being between the sexes, whose clamours, being equally vented on both sides with all the vehemence of distress, all the apparent confidence of justice, and all the indignation of injured virtue, seem entitled to equal regard. The men have, indeed, by their superiority of writing, been able to collect the evidence of many ages, and raise prejudices in their favour by the venerable testimonies of philosophers, historians and poets; but the pleas of the ladies appeal to passions of more forcible operation than the reverence of antiquity. If they have not so great names on their side, they have stronger arguments; it is to little purpose that Socrates, or Euripides, are produced against the sighs of softness, and the tears of beauty. The most frigid and inexorable judge would, at least, stand suspended between equal powers, as Lucan was perplexed in the determination of the cause, where the deities were on one side, and Cato on the other.[2]

But I, who have long studied the severest and most abstracted philosophy, have now, in the cool maturity of life, arrived to such command over my passions, that I can hear the vociferations of either sex without catching any of the fire from those that utter them. For I have found, by long experience, that a man will sometimes rage at his wife, when in reality his mistress has offended him; and a lady complain of the cruelty of her husband, when she has no other enemy than bad cards. I do not suffer myself to be any longer imposed upon by oaths on one side, or fits on the other; nor when the husband hastens to the tavern, and the lady retires to her closet, am I always confident that they are driven by their miseries; since I have sometimes reason to believe, that they purpose not so much to sooth their sorrows, as to animate their fury. But how little credit soever may be given to particular accusations, the general accumulation of the charge shews, with too much evidence, that married persons are not very often advanced in felicity; and, therefore, it may be proper to examine at what avenues so many evils have made their way into the world. With this purpose, I have reviewed the lives of my friends, who have been least successful in connubial contracts, and attentively considered by what motives they were incited to marry, and by what principles they regulated their choice.

One of the first of my acquaintances that resolved to quit the unsettled thoughtless condition of a batchelor, was Prudentius, a man of slow parts, but not without knowledge or judgment in things which he had leisure to consider gradually before he determined them. Whenever we met at a tavern, it was his province to settle the scheme of our entertainment, contract with the cook, and inform us when we had called for wine to the sum originally proposed. This grave considerer found by deep meditation that a man was no loser by marrying early, even though he contented himself with a less fortune; for estimating the exact worth of annuities, he found that, considering the constant diminution of the value of life, with the probable fall of the interest of money, it was not worse to have ten thousand pounds at the age of two and twenty years, than a much larger fortune at thirty; for many opportunities, says he, occur of improving money, which if a man misses, he may not afterwards recover.

Full of these reflections, he threw his eyes about him, not in search of beauty, or elegance, dignity, or understanding, but of a woman with ten thousand pounds. Such a woman, in a wealthy part of the kingdom, it was not very difficult to find; and by artful management with her father, whose ambition was to make his daughter a gentlewoman, my friend got her, as he boasted to us in confidence two days after his marriage, for a settlement of seventy three pounds a year less than her fortune might have claimed, and less than he would himself have given, if the fools had been but wise enough to delay the bargain.

Thus, at once delighted with the superiority of his parts, and the augmentation of his fortune, he carried Furia to his own house, in which he never afterwards enjoyed one hour of happiness. For Furia was a wretch of mean intellects, violent passions, a strong voice, and low education, without any sense of happiness but that which consisted in eating, and counting money. Furia was a scold. They agreed in the desire of wealth, but with this difference, that Prudentius was for growing rich by gain, Furia by parsimony. Prudentius would venture his money with chances

very much in his favour; but Furia very wisely observing that what
they had was, while they had it, *their own*, thought all traffick too
great a hazard, and was for putting it out at low interest, upon
good security. Prudentius ventured, however, to insure a ship, at
a very unreasonable price, but happening to lose his money, was
so tormented with the clamours of his wife, that he never durst
try a second experiment. He has now grovelled seven and forty
years under Furia's direction, who never once mentioned him,
since his bad luck, by any other name than that of *the insurer*.

The next that married from our society was Florentius. He
happened to see Zephyretta in a chariot at a horse-race, danced
with her at night, was confirmed in his first ardour, waited on
her next morning, and declared himself her lover. Florentius
had not knowledge enough of the world, to distinguish between
the flutter of coquetry, and the sprightliness of wit, or between
the smile of allurement, and that of chearfulness. He was soon
waked from his rapture by conviction that his pleasure was but
the pleasure of a day. Zephyretta had in four and twenty hours
spent her stock of repartee, gone round the circle of her airs,
and had nothing remaining for him but childish insipidity, or
for herself, but the practice of the same artifices upon new men.

Melissus was a man of parts, capable of enjoying, and of
improving life. He had passed through the various scenes of
gayety with that indifference and possession of himself, natural
to men who have something higher and nobler in their prospect.
Retiring to spend the summer in a village little frequented, he
happened to lodge in the same house with Ianthe, and was
unavoidably drawn to some acquaintance, which her wit and
politeness soon invited him to improve. Having no opportunity
of any other company, they were always together; and, as they
owed their pleasures to each other, they began to forget that
any pleasure was enjoyed before their meeting. Melissus, from
being delighted with her company, quickly began to be uneasy
in her absence, and being sufficiently convinced of the force of
her understanding, and finding, as he imagined, such a conformity of temper as declared them formed for each other, addressed
her as a lover, after no very long courtship obtained her for his
wife, and brought her next winter to town in triumph.

Now began their infelicity. Melissus had only seen her in one scene, where there was no variety of objects, to produce the proper excitements to contrary desires. They had both loved solitude and reflection, where there was nothing but solitude and reflection to be loved; but when they came into publick life, Ianthe discovered those passions which accident rather than hypocrisy had hitherto concealed. She was, indeed, not without the power of thinking, but was wholly without the exertion of that power, when either gayety, or splendour, played on her imagination. She was expensive in her diversions, vehement in her passions, insatiate of pleasure however dangerous to her reputation, and eager of applause by whomsoever it might be given. This was the wife which Melissus the philosopher found in his retirement, and from whom he expected an associate in his studies, and an assistant to his virtues.

Prosapius, upon the death of his younger brother, that the family might not be extinct, married his housekeeper, and has ever since been complaining to his friends that mean notions are instilled into his children, that he is ashamed to sit at his own table, and that his house is uneasy to him for want of suitable companions.

Avaro, master of a very large estate, took a woman of bad reputation, recommended to him by a rich uncle, who made that marriage the condition on which he should be his heir. Avaro now wonders to perceive his own fortune, his wife's, and his uncle's, insufficient to give him that happiness which is to be found only with a woman of virtue.

I intend to treat in more papers on this important article of life, and shall, therefore, make no reflexion upon these histories, except that all whom I have mentioned failed to obtain happiness, for want of considering that marriage is the strictest tye of perpetual friendship; that there can be no friendship without confidence, and no confidence without integrity; and that he must expect to be wretched, who pays to beauty, riches, or politeness, that regard which only virtue and piety can claim.

No. 22. Saturday, 2 June 1750.

—*Ego nec studium sine divite venâ,*
Nec rude quid prosit video ingenium, alterius sic
Altera poscit opem res, & conjurat amice.

HOR.[1]

Without a genius learning soars in vain;
And without learning genius sinks again:
Their force united crowns the sprightly reign.

ELPHINSTON.

WIT and LEARNING were the children of Apollo, by different mothers; WIT was the offspring of EUPHROSYNE, and resembled her in chearfulness and vivacity; LEARNING was born of SOPHIA, and retained her seriousness and caution. As their mothers were rivals, they were bred up by them, from their birth, in habitual opposition, and all means were so incessantly employed to impress upon them a hatred and contempt of each other, that though Apollo, who foresaw the ill effects of their discord, endeavoured to soften them, by dividing his regard equally between them, yet his impartiality and kindness were without effect; the maternal animosity was deeply rooted, having been intermingled with their first ideas, and was confirmed every hour, as fresh opportunities occurred of exerting it. No sooner were they of age to be received into the apartments of the other celestials, than WIT began to entertain Venus at her toilet, by aping the solemnity of LEARNING, and LEARNING to divert Minerva at her loom, by exposing the blunders and ignorance of WIT.

Thus they grew up, with malice perpetually increasing, by the encouragement which each received from those whom their mothers had persuaded to patronise and support them; and longed to be admitted to the table of Jupiter, not so much for the hope of gaining honour, as of excluding a rival from all pretensions to regard, and of putting an everlasting stop to the progress of that influence which either believed the other to have obtained by mean arts and false appearances.

At last the day came, when they were both, with the usual solemnities, received into the class of superior deities, and allowed to take nectar from the hand of Hebe. But from that hour CONCORD lost her authority at the table of Jupiter. The rivals, animated by their new dignity, and incited by the alternate applauses of the associate powers, harrassed each other by incessant contests, with such a regular vicissitude of victory, that neither was depressed.

It was observable, that at the beginning of every debate, the advantage was on the side of WIT; and that, at the first sallies, the whole assembly sparkled, according to Homer's expression, with unextinguishable merriment.[2] But LEARNING would reserve her strength till the burst of applause was over, and the languor with which the violence of joy is always succeeded, began to promise more calm and patient attention. She then attempted her defence, and, by comparing one part of her antagonist's objections with another, commonly made him confute himself; or, by shewing how small a part of the question he had taken into his view, proved that his opinion could have no weight. The audience began gradually to lay aside their prepossessions, and rose, at last, with great veneration for LEARNING, but with greater kindness for WIT.

Their conduct was, whenever they desired to recommend themselves to distinction, entirely opposite. WIT was daring and adventurous; LEARNING cautious and deliberate. WIT thought nothing reproachful but dulness; LEARNING was afraid of no imputation, but that of error. WIT answered before he understood, lest his quickness of apprehension should be questioned; LEARNING paused, where there was no difficulty, lest any insidious sophism should lie undiscovered. WIT perplexed every debate by rapidity and confusion; LEARNING tired the hearers with endless distinctions, and prolonged the dispute without advantage, by proving that which never was denied. WIT, in hopes of shining, would venture to produce what he had not considered, and often succeeded beyond his own expectation, by following the train of a lucky thought; LEARNING would reject every new notion, for fear of being intangled in consequences which she could not foresee, and was often hindered, by her caution, from pressing her advantages, and subduing her opponent.

Both had prejudices, which in some degree hindered their progress towards perfection, and left them open to attacks. Novelty was the darling of WIT, and antiquity of LEARNING. To WIT, all that was new, was specious; to LEARNING, whatever was antient, was venerable. WIT, however, seldom failed to divert those whom he could not convince, and to convince was not often his ambition; LEARNING always supported her opinion with so many collateral truths, that, when the cause was decided against her, her arguments were remembered with admiration.

Nothing was more common, on either side, than to quit their proper characters, and to hope for a compleat conquest by the use of the weapons which had been employed against them. WIT would sometimes labour a syllogism, and LEARNING distort her features with a jest; but they always suffered by the experiment, and betrayed themselves to confutation or contempt. The seriousness of WIT was without dignity, and the merriment of LEARNING without vivacity.

Their contests, by long continuance, grew at last important, and the divinities broke into parties. WIT was taken into the protection of the laughter-loving Venus, had a retinue allowed him of SMILES and JESTS, and was often permitted to dance among the GRACES. LEARNING still continued the favourite of Minerva, and seldom went out of her palace, without a train of the severer virtues, CHASTITY, TEMPERANCE, FORTITUDE, and LABOUR. WIT, cohabiting with MALICE, had a son named SATYR, who followed him, carrying a quiver filled with poisoned arrows, which, where they once drew blood, could by no skill ever be extracted. These arrows he frequently shot at LEARNING, when she was most earnestly or usefully employed, engaged in abstruse inquiries, or giving instructions to her followers. Minerva, therefore, deputed CRITICISM to her aid, who generally broke the point of SATYR's arrows, turned them aside, or retorted them on himself.

Jupiter was at last angry, that the peace of the heavenly regions should be in perpetual danger of violation, and resolved to dismiss these troublesome antagonists to the lower world. Hither therefore they came, and carried on their antient quarrel among mortals, nor was either long without zealous votaries. WIT, by his gaiety, captivated the young; and LEARNING, by her authority, influenced the old. Their power quickly appeared by very eminent effects, theatres were built for the reception of WIT, and colleges endowed for the residence of LEARNING. Each party endeavoured to outvy the other in cost and magnificence, and to propagate an opinion, that it was necessary, from the first entrance into life, to enlist in one of the factions; and that none could hope for the regard of either divinity, who had once entered the temple of the rival power.

There were indeed a class of mortals, by whom WIT and LEARNING were equally disregarded: These were the devotees of Plutus, the god of riches; among these it seldom happened that the gaiety of WIT could raise a smile, or the eloquence of LEARNING procure attention. In revenge of this contempt, they agreed to incite their followers against them; but the forces that were sent on those expeditions frequently betrayed their trust; and, in contempt of the orders which they had received, flattered the rich in public, while they scorned them in their hearts; and when, by this treachery, they had obtained the favour of Plutus, affected to look with an air of superiority on those who still remained in the service of WIT and LEARNING.

Disgusted with these desertions, the two rivals, at the same time, petitioned Jupiter for re-admission to their native habitations, Jupiter thundered on the right hand, and they prepared to obey the happy summons. WIT readily spread his wings, and soared aloft, but not being able to see far, was bewildered in the pathless immensity of the ethereal spaces. LEARNING, who knew the way, shook her pinions; but for want of natural vigour could only take short flights: so, after many efforts, they both sunk again to the ground, and learned, from their mutual distress, the necessity of union. They therefore joined their hands, and renewed their flight: LEARNING was borne up by the vigour of WIT, and WIT guided by the perspicacity of LEARNING. They soon reached the dwellings of Jupiter, and were so endeared to each other, that they lived afterwards in perpetual concord.

WIT persuaded LEARNING to converse with the GRACES, and LEARNING engaged WIT in the service of the VIRTUES. They were now the favourites of all the powers of heaven, and gladdened every banquet by their presence. They soon after married, at the command of Jupiter, and had a numerous progeny of ARTS and SCIENCES.

No. 23. Tuesday, 5 June 1750.

Tres mihi convivæ prope dissentire videntur;
Poscentur vario multum diversa palato.

HOR.[1]

Three guests I have, dissenting at my feast,
Requiring each to gratify his taste
With different food.

FRANCIS.

That every man should regulate his actions by his own conscience, without any regard to the opinions of the rest of the world, is one of the first precepts of moral prudence; justified not only by the suffrage of reason, which declares that none of the gifts of heaven are to lie useless, but by the voice likewise of experience, which will soon inform us that, if we make the praise or blame of others the rule of our conduct, we shall be distracted by a boundless variety of irreconcileable judgments, be held in perpetual suspense between contrary impulses, and consult for ever without determination.

I know not whether, for the same reason, it is not necessary for an author to place some confidence in his own skill, and to satisfy himself in the knowledge that he has not deviated from the established law of composition, without submitting his works to frequent examinations before he gives them to the publick, or endeavouring to secure success by a solicitous conformity to advice and criticism.

It is, indeed, quickly discoverable, that consultation and compliance can conduce little to the perfection of any literary performance; for whoever is so doubtful of his own abilities as to encourage the remarks of others, will find himself every day embarrassed with new difficulties, and will harrass his mind, in vain, with the hopeless labour of uniting heterogeneous ideas, digesting independent hints, and collecting into one point the several rays of borrowed light, emitted often with contrary directions.

Of all authors, those who retail their labours in periodical sheets would be most unhappy, if they were much to regard the censures or the admonitions of their readers; for, as their works are not sent into the world at once, but by small parts in gradual succession, it is always imagined, by those who think themselves qualified to give instructions, that they may yet redeem their former failings by hearkening to better judges, and supply the deficiencies of their plan, by the help of the criticisms which are so liberally afforded.

I have had occasion to observe, sometimes with vexation, and sometimes with merriment, the different temper with which the same man reads a printed and manuscript performance. When a book is once in the hands of the public, it is considered as permanent and unalterable; and the reader, if he be free from personal prejudices, takes it up with no other intention than of pleasing or instructing himself; he accommodates his mind to the author's design; and, having no interest in refusing the amusement that is offered him, never interrupts his own tranquillity by studied cavils, or destroys his satisfaction in that which is already well, by an anxious enquiry how it might be better; but is often contented without pleasure, and pleased without perfection.

But if the same man be called to consider the merit of a production yet unpublished, he brings an imagination heated with objections to passages, which he has yet never heard; he invokes all the powers of criticism, and stores his memory with Taste and Grace, Purity and Delicacy, Manners and Unities, sounds which, having been once uttered by those that understood them, have been since re-echoed without meaning, and kept up to the disturbance of the world, by a constant repercussion from one coxcomb to another. He considers himself as obliged to shew, by some proof of his abilities, that he is not consulted to no purpose, and, therefore, watches every opening for objection, and looks round for every opportunity to propose some specious alteration. Such opportunities a very small degree of sagacity will enable him to find; for, in every work of imagination, the disposition of parts, the insertion of incidents, and use of decorations, may be varied a thousand ways with equal propriety; and as, in things nearly equal, that will always seem best to every man which he himself produces, the critic, whose business is only to propose, without the care of execution, can never want the satisfaction of believing that he has suggested very important improvements, nor the power of enforcing his advice by arguments, which, as they appear convincing to himself, either his kindness, or his vanity, will press obstinately and importunately, without suspicion that he may possibly judge too hastily in favour of his own advice, or enquiry whether the advantage of the new scheme be proportionate to the labour.

It is observed, by the younger Pliny,[2] that an orator ought not so much to select the strongest arguments which his cause admits, as to employ all which his imagination can afford; for, in pleading, those reasons are of most value, which will most affect the judges; and the judges, says he, will be always most touched with that which they had before conceived. Every man, who is called to give his opinion of a performance, decides upon the same principle; he first suffers himself to form expectations, and then is angry at his disappointment. He lets his imagination rove at large, and wonders that another, equally unconfined in the boundless ocean of possibility, takes a different course.

But, though the rule of Pliny be judiciously laid down, it is not applicable to the writer's cause, because there always lies an appeal from domestick criticism to a higher judicature, and the publick, which is never corrupted, nor often deceived, is to pass the last sentence upon literary claims.

Of the great force of preconceived opinions I had many proofs, when I first entered upon this weekly labour. My readers having, from the performances of my predecessors, established an idea of unconnected essays, to which they believed all future authors under a necessity of conforming, were impatient of the least deviation from their system, and numerous remonstrances were accordingly made by each, as he found his favourite subject omitted or delayed. Some were angry that the RAMBLER did not, like the SPECTATOR, introduce himself to the acquaintance of the publick, by an account of his own birth and studies, an enumeration of his adventures, and a description of his physiognomy.[3] Others soon began to remark that he was a solemn, serious, dictatorial writer, without sprightliness or gaiety, and called out with vehemence for mirth and humour. Another admonished him to have a special eye upon the various clubs of this great city, and informed him that much of the Spectator's vivacity was laid out upon such assemblies. He has been censured for not imitating the politeness of his predecessors, having hitherto neglected to take the ladies under his protection, and give them rules for the just opposition of colours, and the proper dimensions of ruffles and pinners. He has been required by one to fix a particular censure upon those matrons who play at cards with spectacles. And another is very much offended whenever he meets with a speculation, in which naked precepts are comprised, without the illustration of examples and characters.

I make not the least question that all these monitors intend the promotion of my design, and the instruction of my readers; but they do not know, or do not reflect that an author has a rule of choice peculiar to himself; and selects those subjects which he is best qualified to treat, by the course of his studies, or the accidents of his life; that some topicks of amusement have been already treated with too much success to invite a competition; and that he who endeavours to gain many readers, must try various arts of invitation, essay every avenue of pleasure, and make frequent changes in his methods of approach.

I cannot but consider myself amidst this tumult of criticism, as a ship in a poetical tempest, impelled at the same time by opposite winds, and dashed by the waves from every quarter, but held upright by the contrariety of the assailants, and secured, in some measure, by multiplicity of distress. Had the opinion of my censurers been unanimous, it might, perhaps, have overset my resolution; but since I find them at variance with each other,

I can, without scruple, neglect them, and endeavour to gain the favour of the publick, by following the direction of my own reason, and indulging the sallies of my own imagination.

No. 24. Saturday, 9 June 1750.

Nemo in sese tentat descendere.
PERSIUS.[1]

None, none descends into himself.
DRYDEN.

Among the precepts, or aphorisms, admitted by general consent, and inculcated by frequent repetition, there is none more famous among the masters of antient wisdom, than that compendious lesson, Γνῶθι σεαυτὸν, *Be acquainted with thyself*; ascribed by some to an oracle, and by others to Chilo of Lacedemon.[2]

This is, indeed, a dictate, which, in the whole extent of its meaning, may be said to comprise all the speculation requisite to a moral agent. For what more can be necessary to the regulation of life, than the knowledge of our original, our end, our duties, and our relation to other beings?

It is however very improbable that the first author, whoever he was, intended to be understood in this unlimited and complicated sense; for of the inquiries, which, in so large an acceptation, it would seem to recommend, some are too extensive for the powers of man, and some require light from above, which was not yet indulged to the heathen world.

We might have had more satisfaction concerning the original import of this celebrated sentence, if history had informed us, whether it was uttered as a general instruction to mankind, or as a particular caution to some private inquirer; whether it was applied to some single occasion, or laid down as the universal rule of life.

There will occur, upon the slightest consideration, many possible circumstances, in which this monition might very properly be inforced; for every error in human conduct must arise from ignorance in ourselves, either perpetual or temporary; and happen either because we do not know what is best and fittest, or because our knowledge is at the time of action not present to the mind.

When a man employs himself upon remote and unnecessary subjects, and wastes his life upon questions, which cannot be resolved, and of which the solution would conduce very little to the advancement of happiness; he, when he lavishes his hours in calculating the weight of the terraqueous globe, or in adjusting successive systems of worlds beyond the reach of the telescope; he may be very properly recalled from his excursions by this precept, and reminded that there is a nearer being with which it is his duty to be more acquainted; and from which, his attention has hitherto been witheld, by studies, to which he has no other motive, than vanity or curiosity.

The great praise of Socrates is, that he drew the wits of Greece, by his instruction and example, from the vain persuit of natural philosophy to moral inquiries, and turned their thoughts from stars and tides, and matter and motion, upon the various modes of virtue, and relations of life. All his lectures were but commentaries upon this saying; if we suppose the knowledge of ourselves recommended by Chilo, in opposition to other inquiries less suitable to the state of man.

The great fault of men of learning is still, that they offend against this rule, and appear willing to study any thing rather than themselves; for which reason they are often despised by those, with whom they imagine themselves above comparison; despised, as useless to common purposes, as unable to conduct the most trivial affairs, and unqualified to perform those offices by which the concatenation of society is preserved, and mutual tenderness excited and maintained.

Gelidus is a man of great penetration, and deep researches.[3] Having a mind naturally formed for the abstruser sciences, he can comprehend intricate combinations without confusion, and being of a temper naturally cool and equal, he is seldom interrupted by his passions in the persuit of the longest chain of unexpected consequences. He has, therefore, a long time indulged hopes, that the solution of some problems, by which the professors of science have been hitherto baffled, is reserved for his genius and industry. He spends his time in the highest room of his house, into which none of his family are suffered to enter; and when he comes down to his dinner, or his rest, he walks about like a stranger that is there only for a day, without any tokens of regard or tenderness. He has totally divested himself of all human sensations; he has neither eye for beauty, nor ear for complaint; he neither rejoices at the good fortune of his nearest friend, nor mourns for any publick or private calamity. Having once received a letter, and given it his servant to read, he was informed, that it was written by his brother, who, being shipwrecked, had swam naked to land, and was destitute of necessaries in a foreign country. Naked and destitute! says Gelidus, reach down the last volume of meteorological observations, extract an exact account of the wind, and note it carefully in the diary of the weather.

The family of Gelidus once broke into his study, to shew him that a town at a small distance was on fire, and in a few moments a servant came up to tell him, that the flame had caught so many houses on both sides, that the inhabitants were confounded, and began to think rather of escaping with their lives, than saving their dwellings. What you tell me, says Gelidus, is very probable, for fire naturally acts in a circle.

Thus lives this great philosopher, insensible to every spectacle of distress, and unmoved by the loudest call of social nature, for want of considering that men are designed for the succour and comfort of each other; that, though there are hours which may be laudably spent upon knowledge not immediately useful, yet the first attention is due to practical virtue; and that he may be justly driven out from the commerce of mankind, who has so far abstracted himself from the species, as to partake neither of the joys nor griefs of others, but neglects the endearments of his wife, and the caresses of his children, to count the drops of rain, note the changes of the wind, and calculate the eclipses of the moons of Jupiter.

I shall reserve to some future paper the religious and important meaning of this epitome of wisdom, and only remark, that it may be applied to the gay and light, as well as to the grave and solemn parts of life; and that not only the philosopher may forfeit his pretences to real learning, but the wit, and the beauty, may miscarry in their schemes, by the want of this universal requisite, the knowledge of themselves.

It is surely for no other reason, that we see such numbers resolutely struggling against nature, and contending for that which they never can attain, endeavouring to unite contradictions, and determined to excel in characters inconsistent with each other; that stock-jobbers affect dress, gaiety, and elegance, and mathematicians labour to be wits; that the soldier teazes his acquaintance with questions in theology, and the academick hopes to divert the ladies by a recital of his gallantries. That absurdity of pride could proceed only from ignorance of themselves, by which Garth attempted criticism, and Congreve waved his title to dramatick reputation,[4] and desired to be considered only as a gentleman.

Euphues, with great parts, and extensive knowledge, has a clouded aspect, and ungracious form; yet it has been his ambition, from his first entrance into life, to distinguish himself by particularities in his dress, to outvie beaus in embroidery, to import new trimmings, and to be foremost in the fashion. Euphues has turned on his exterior appearance, that attention, which would always have produced esteem had it been fixed upon his mind; and, though his virtues, and abilities, have preserved him from the contempt which he has so diligently solicited, he has, at least, raised one impediment to his reputation; since all can judge of his dress, but few of his understanding; and many who discern that he is a fop, are unwilling to believe that he can be wise.

There is one instance in which the ladies are particularly unwilling to observe the rule of Chilo. They are desirous to hide from themselves the advances of age, and endeavour too frequently to supply the sprightliness and bloom of youth by artificial beauty, and forced vivacity. They hope to inflame the heart by glances which have lost their fire, or melt it by languor which is no longer delicate; they play over the airs which pleased at a time when they were expected only to please, and forget that airs ought in time to give place to virtues. They continue to trifle, because they could once trifle agreeably, till those who shared their early pleasures are withdrawn to more serious engagements; and are scarcely awakened from their dream of perpetual youth, but by the scorn of those whom they endeavour to rival.

No. 25. Tuesday, 12 June 1750.

Possunt quia posse videntur.
VIRGIL.[1]

For they can conquer who believe they can.
DRYDEN.

There are some vices and errors, which, though often fatal to those in whom they are found, have yet, by the universal consent of mankind, been considered as entitled to some degree of respect, or have, at least, been exempted from contemptuous infamy, and condemned by the severest moralists with pity rather than detestation.

A constant and invariable example of this general partiality will be found in the different regard which has always been shown to rashness and cowardice, two vices, of which, though they may be conceived equally distant from the middle point, where true fortitude is placed, and may equally injure any publick or private interest, yet the one is never mentioned without some kind of veneration, and the other always considered as a topick of unlimited and licentious censure, on which all the virulence of reproach may be lawfully exerted.

The same distinction is made, by the common suffrage, between profusion and avarice, and, perhaps, between many other opposite vices: and, as I have found reason to pay great regard to the voice of the people, in cases where knowledge has been forced upon them by experience, without long deductions or deep researches, I am inclined to believe that this distribution of respect, is not without some agreement with the nature of things; and that in the faults, which are thus invested with extraordinary privileges, there are generally some latent principles of merit, some possibilities of future virtue, which may, by degrees, break from obstruction, and by time and opportunity be brought into act.

It may be laid down as an axiom, that it is more easy to take away superfluities than to supply defects; and, therefore, he that is culpable, because he has passed the middle point of virtue, is always accounted a fairer object of hope, than he who fails by falling short. The one has all that perfection requires, and more, but the excess may be easily retrenched; the other wants the qualities requisite to excellence, and who can tell how he shall obtain them? We are certain that the horse may be taught to keep pace with his fellows, whose fault is that he leaves them behind. We know that a few strokes of the axe will lop a cedar; but what arts of cultivation can elevate a shrub?

To walk with circumspection and steadiness in the right path,[2] at an equal distance between the extremes of error, ought to be the constant endeavour of every reasonable being; nor can I think those teachers of moral wisdom much to be honoured as benefactors to mankind, who are always enlarging upon the difficulty of our duties, and providing rather excuses for vice, than incentives to virtue.

But, since to most it will happen often, and to all sometimes, that there will be a deviation towards one side or the other, we ought always to employ our vigilance, with most attention, on that enemy from which there is greatest danger, and to stray, if we must stray, towards those parts from whence we may quickly and easily return.

Among other opposite qualities of the mind, which may become dangerous, though in different degrees, I have often had occasion to consider the contrary effects of presumption and despondency; of heady confidence, which promises victory without contest, and heartless pusillanimity, which shrinks back from the thought of great undertakings, confounds difficulty with impossibility, and considers all advancement towards any new attainment as irreversibly prohibited.

Presumption will be easily corrected. Every experiment will teach caution, and miscarriages will hourly shew, that attempts are not always rewarded with success. The most precipitate ardour will, in time, be taught the necessity of methodical gradation, and preparatory measures; and the most daring confidence be convinced that neither merit, nor abilities, can command events.

It is the advantage of vehemence and activity, that they are always hastening to their own reformation; because they incite us to try whether our expectations are well grounded, and therefore detect the deceits which they are apt to occasion. But timidity is a disease of the mind more obstinate and fatal; for a man once persuaded, that any impediment is insuperable, has given it, with respect to himself, that strength and weight which it had not before. He can scarcely strive with vigour and perseverance, when he has no hope of gaining the victory; and since he never will try his strength, can never discover the unreasonableness of his fears.

There is often to be found in men devoted to literature, a kind of intellectual cowardice, which whoever converses much among them, may observe frequently to depress the alacrity of enterprise, and, by consequence, to retard the improvement of science. They have annexed to every species of knowledge some chimerical character of terror and inhibition, which they transmit, without much reflexion, from one to another; they first fright themselves, and then propagate the panic to their scholars and acquaintance. One study is inconsistent with a lively imagination, another with a solid judgment; one is improper in the early parts of life, another requires so much time, that it is not to be attempted at an advanced age; one is dry and contracts the sentiments, another is diffuse and overburdens the memory; one is insufferable to taste and delicacy, and another wears out life in the study of words, and is useless to a wise man, who desires only the knowledge of things.

But of all the bugbears by which the *Infantes barbati*,[3] boys both young and old, have been hitherto frighted from digressing into new tracts of learning, none has been more mischievously efficacious than an opinion that every kind of knowledge requires a peculiar genius, or mental constitution, framed for the reception of some ideas, and the exclusion of others; and that to him whose genius is not adapted to the study which he prosecutes, all labour shall be vain and fruitless, vain as an endeavour to mingle oil and water, or, in the language of chemistry, to amalgamate bodies of heterogeneous principles.

This opinion we may reasonably suspect to have been propagated, by vanity, beyond the truth. It is natural for those who have raised a reputation by any science, to exalt themselves as endowed by heaven with peculiar powers, or marked out by an extraordinary designation for their profession; and to fright competitors away by representing the difficulties with which they must contend, and the necessity of qualities which are supposed to be not generally conferred, and which no man can know, but by experience, whether he enjoys.

To this discouragement it may be possibly answered, that since a genius, whatever it be, is like fire in the flint, only to be produced by collision with a proper subject, it is the business of every man to try whether his faculties may not happily co-operate with his desires; and since they whose proficiency he admires, knew their own force only by the event, he needs but engage in the same undertaking, with equal spirit, and may reasonably hope for equal success.

There is another species of false intelligence, given by those who profess to shew the way to the summit of knowledge, of equal tendency to depress the mind with false distrust of itself, and weaken it by needless solicitude and dejection. When a scholar, whom they desire to animate, consults them at his entrance on some new study, it is common to make flattering representations of its pleasantness and facility. Thus they generally attain one of two ends almost equally desirable; they either incite his industry by elevating his hopes, or produce a high opinion of their own abilities, since they are supposed to relate only what they have found, and to have proceeded with no less ease than they promise to their followers.

The student, inflamed by this encouragement, sets forward in the new path, and proceeds a few steps with great alacrity, but he soon finds asperities and intricacies of which he has not been forewarned, and imagining that none ever were so entangled or fatigued before him, sinks suddenly into despair, and desists as from an expedition in which fate opposes him. Thus his terrors are multiplied by his hopes, and he is defeated without resistance, because he had no expectation of an enemy.

Of these treacherous instructors, the one destroys industry, by declaring that industry is vain, the other by representing it as needless; the one cuts away the root of hope, the other raises it only to be blasted. The one confines his pupil to the shore, by telling him that his wreck is certain, the other sends him to sea, without preparing him for tempests.

False hopes and false terrors are equally to be avoided. Every man, who proposes to grow eminent by learning, should carry in his mind, at once, the difficulty of excellence, and the force of industry; and remember that fame is not conferred but as the recompense of labour, and that labour, vigorously continued, has not often failed of its reward.

No. 28. Saturday, 23 June 1750.

Illi mors gravis incubat,
Qui, notus nimis omnibus,
Ignotus moritur sibi.
SENECA.[1]

To him, alas, to him, I fear,
The face of death will terrible appear,
Who in his life, flatt'ring his senseless pride,
By being known to all the world beside,
Does not himself, when he is dying know,
Nor what he is, nor whither he's to go.
COWLEY.[2]

I have shewn, in a late essay,[3] to what errors men are hourly betrayed by a mistaken opinion of their own powers, and a negligent inspection of their own character. But as I then confined my observations to common occurrences, and familiar scenes, I think it proper to enquire how far a nearer acquaintance with ourselves is necessary to our preservation from crimes as well as follies, and how much the attentive study of our own minds may contribute to secure to us the approbation of that being, to whom we are accountable for our thoughts and our actions, and whose favour must finally constitute our total happiness.

If it be reasonable to estimate the difficulty of any enterprise by frequent miscarriages, it may justly be concluded that it is not easy for a man to know himself; for wheresoever we turn our view, we shall find almost all with whom we converse so nearly as to judge of their sentiments, indulging more favourable conceptions of their own virtue than they have been able to impress upon others, and congratulating themselves upon degrees of excellence, which their fondest admirers cannot allow them to have attained.

Those representations of imaginary virtue are generally considered as arts of hypocrisy, and as snares laid for confidence and praise. But I believe the suspicion often unjust; those who thus propagate their own reputation, only extend the fraud by which they have been themselves deceived; for this failing is incident to numbers, who seem to live without designs, competitions, or persuits; it appears on occasions which promise no accession of honour or of profit, and to persons from whom very little is to be hoped or feared. It is, indeed, not easy to tell how far we may be blinded by the love of ourselves, when we reflect how much a secondary passion can cloud our judgment, and how few faults a man, in the first raptures of love, can discover in the person or conduct of his mistress.

To lay open all the sources from which error flows in upon him who contemplates his own character, would require more exact knowledge of the human heart, than, perhaps, the most acute and laborious observers have acquired. And, since falsehood may be diversified without end, it is not unlikely that every man admits an imposture in some respect peculiar to himself, as his views have been accidentally directed, or his ideas particularly combined.

Some fallacies, however, there are, more frequently insidious, which it may, perhaps, not be useless to detect, because though they are gross they may be fatal, and because nothing but attention is necessary to defeat them.

One sophism by which men persuade themselves that they have those virtues which they really want, is formed by the substitution of single acts for habits. A miser who once relieved a friend from the danger of a prison, suffers his imagination to dwell for ever upon his own heroick generosity; he yields his heart up to indignation at those who are blind to merit, or insensible to misery, and who can please themselves with the enjoyment of that wealth, which they never permit others to partake. From any censures of the world, or reproaches of his conscience, he has an appeal to action and to knowledge; and though his whole life is a course of rapacity and avarice, he concludes himself to be tender and liberal, because he has once performed an act of liberality and tenderness.

As a glass which magnifies objects by the approach of one end to the eye, lessens them by the application of the other, so vices are extenuated by the inversion of that fallacy, by which virtues are augmented. Those faults which we cannot conceal from our own notice, are considered, however frequent, not as habitual corruptions, or settled practices, but as casual failures, and single lapses. A man who has, from year to year, set his country to sale, either for the gratification of his ambition or resentment, confesses that the heat of party now and then betrays the severest virtue to measures that cannot be seriously defended. He that spends his days and nights in riot and debauchery, owns that his passions oftentimes overpower his resolution. But each comforts himself that his faults are not without precedent, for the best and the wisest men have given way to the violence of sudden temptations.

There are men who always confound the praise of goodness with the practice, and who believe themselves mild and moderate, charitable and faithful, because they have exerted their eloquence in commendation of mildness, fidelity, and other virtues. This is an error almost universal among those that converse much with dependents, with such whose fear or interest disposes them to a seeming reverence for any declamation, however enthusiastick, and submission to any boast, however arrogant. Having none to recall their attention to their lives, they rate themselves by the goodness of their opinions, and forget how much more easily men may shew their virtue in their talk than in their actions.

The tribe is likewise very numerous of those who regulate their lives, not by the standard of religion, but the measure of other men's virtue; who lull their own remorse with the remembrance of crimes more atrocious than their own, and seem to believe that they are not bad while another can be found worse.

For escaping these and a thousand other deceits, many expedients have been proposed. Some have recommended the frequent consultation of a wise friend, admitted to intimacy, and encouraged to sincerity.[4] But this appears a remedy by no means adapted to general use: for in order to secure the virtue of one, it presupposes more virtue in two than will generally be found. In the first, such a desire of rectitude and amendment, as may incline him to hear his own accusation from the mouth of him whom he esteems, and by whom, therefore, he will always hope that his faults are not discovered; and in the second such zeal and honesty, as will make him content for his friend's advantage to lose his kindness.

A long life may be passed without finding a friend in whose understanding and virtue we can equally confide, and whose opinion we can value at once for its justness and sincerity. A weak man, however honest, is not qualified to judge. A man of the world, however penetrating, is not fit to counsel. Friends are often chosen for similitude of manners, and therefore each palliates the other's failings, because they are his own. Friends are tender and unwilling to give pain, or they are interested, and fearful to offend.

These objections have inclined others to advise, that he who would know himself, should consult his enemies, remember the reproaches that are vented to his face, and listen for the censures that are uttered in private. For his great business is to know his faults, and those malignity will discover, and resentment will reveal. But this precept may be often frustrated; for it seldom happens that rivals or opponents are suffered to come near enough to know our conduct with so much exactness as that conscience should allow and reflect the accusation. The charge of an enemy is often totally false, and commonly so mingled with falsehood, that the mind takes advantage from the failure of one part to discredit the rest, and never suffers any disturbance afterward from such partial reports.

Yet it seems that enemies have been always found by experience the most faithful monitors; for adversity has ever been considered as the state in which a man most easily becomes acquainted with himself, and this effect it must produce by withdrawing flatterers, whose business it is to hide our weaknesses from us, or by giving loose to malice, and licence to reproach; or at least by cutting off those pleasures which called us away from meditation on our conduct, and repressing that pride which too easily persuades us, that we merit whatever we enjoy.

Part of these benefits it is in every man's power to procure to himself, by assigning proper portions of his life to the examination of the rest, and by putting himself frequently in such a situation by retirement and abstraction, as may weaken the influence of external objects. By this practice he may obtain the solitude of adversity without its melancholy, its instructions without its censures, and its sensibility without its perturbations.

The necessity of setting the world at a distance from us, when we are to take a survey of ourselves, has sent many from high stations to the severities of a monastick life; and indeed, every man deeply engaged in business, if all regard to another state be not extinguished, must have the conviction, tho', perhaps, not the resolution of Valdesso, who, when he solicited Charles the fifth to dismiss him, being asked, whether he retired upon disgust, answered that he laid down his commission, for no other reason but because *there ought to be some time for sober reflection between the life of a soldier and his death*.[5]

There are few conditions which do not entangle us with sublunary hopes and fears, from which it is necessary to be at intervals disencumbered, that we may place ourselves in his presence who views effects in their causes, and actions in their motives; that we may, as Chillingworth expresses it, consider things as if there were no other beings in the world but God and ourselves;[6] or, to use language yet more awful, *may commune with our own hearts, and be still.*[7]

Death, says Seneca, falls heavy upon him who is too much known to others, and too little to himself;[8] and Pontanus,[9] a man celebrated among the early restorers of literature, thought the study of our own hearts of so much importance, that he has recommended it from his tomb. *Sum* Joannes Jovianus Pontanus, *quem amaverunt bonæ musæ, suspexerunt viri probi, honestaverunt reges domini; jam scis qui sim, vel qui potius fuerim; ego vero te, hospes, noscere in tenebris nequeo, sed teipsum ut noscas rogo.* "I am Pontanus, beloved by the powers of literature, admired by men of worth, and dignified by the monarchs of the world. Thou knowest now who I am, or more properly who I was. For thee, stranger, I who am in darkness cannot know thee, but I intreat thee to know thyself."

I hope every reader of this paper will consider himself as engaged to the observation of a precept, which the wisdom and virtue of all ages have concurred to enforce, a precept dictated by philosophers, inculcated by poets, and ratified by saints.

No. 29. Tuesday, 26 June 1750.

Prudens futuri temporis exitum
Caliginosa nocte premit deus,
   Ridetque si mortalis ultra
      Fas trepidet——

                                        HOR.[1]

But God has wisely hid from human sight
   The dark decrees of future fate,
And sown their seeds in depth of night;
   He laughs at all the giddy turns of state,
When mortals search too soon, and fear too late.
                                        DRYDEN.

There is nothing recommended with greater frequency among the gayer poets of antiquity, than the secure possession of the present hour, and the dismission[2] of all the cares which intrude upon our quiet, or hinder, by importunate perturbations, the enjoyment of those delights which our condition happens to set before us.

The antient poets are, indeed, by no means unexceptionable teachers of morality; their precepts are to be always considered as the sallies of a genius, intent rather upon giving pleasure than instruction, eager to take every advantage of insinuation, and provided the passions can be engaged on its side, very little solicitous about the suffrage of reason.

The darkness and uncertainty through which the heathens were compelled to wander in the persuit of happiness, may, indeed, be alleged as an excuse for many of their seducing invitations to immediate enjoyment, which the moderns, by whom they have been imitated, have not to plead. It is no wonder that such as had no promise of another state should eagerly turn their thoughts upon the improvement of that which was before them; but surely those who are acquainted with the hopes and fears of eternity, might think it necessary to put some restraint upon their imagination, and reflect that by echoing the songs of the ancient bacchanals, and transmitting the maxims of past debauchery, they not only prove that they want invention, but virtue, and submit to the servility of imitation only to copy that of which the writer, if he was to live now, would often be ashamed.

Yet as the errors and follies of a great genius are seldom without some radiations of understanding, by which meaner minds may be enlightened, the incitements to pleasure are, in these authors, generally mingled with such reflections upon life, as well deserve to be considered distinctly from the purposes for which they are produced, and to be treasured up as the settled conclusions of extensive observation, acute sagacity, and mature experience.

It is not without true judgment that on these occasions they often warn their readers against enquiries into futurity, and solicitude about events which lie hid in causes yet unactive, and which time has not brought forward into the view of reason. An idle and thoughtless resignation to chance, without any struggle against calamity, or endeavour after advantage, is indeed below the dignity of a reasonable being, in whose power providence has put a great part even of his present happiness; but it shews an equal ignorance of our proper sphere, to harrass our thoughts with conjectures about things not yet in being. How can we regulate events, of which we yet know not whether they will ever happen? And why should we think, with painful anxiety, about that on which our thoughts can have no influence?

It is a maxim commonly received, that a wise man is never surprised;[3] and perhaps, this exemption from astonishment may be imagined to proceed from such a prospect into futurity, as gave previous intimation of those evils which often fall unexpected upon others that have less foresight. But the truth is, that things to come, except when they approach very nearly, are equally hidden from men of all degrees of understanding; and if a wise man is not amazed at sudden occurrences, it is not that he has thought more, but less upon futurity. He never considered things not yet existing as the proper objects of his attention; he never indulged dreams till he was deceived by their phantoms, nor ever realized nonentities to his mind. He is not surprised because he is not disappointed, and he escapes disappointment because he never forms any expectations.

The concern about things to come, that is so justly censured, is not the result of those general reflections on the variableness of fortune, the uncertainty of life, and the universal insecurity of all human acquisitions, which must always be suggested by the view of the world; but such a desponding anticipation of misfortune, as fixes the mind upon scenes of gloom and melancholy, and makes fear predominate in every imagination.

Anxiety of this kind is nearly of the same nature with jealousy in love, and suspicion in the general commerce of life; a temper which keeps the man always in alarms, disposes him to judge of every thing in a manner that least favours his own quiet, fills him with perpetual stratagems of counteraction, wears him out in schemes to obviate evils which never threatened him, and at length, perhaps, contributes to the production of those mischiefs of which it had raised such dreadful apprehensions.

It has been usual in all ages for moralists to repress the swellings of vain hope by representations of the innumerable casualties to which life is subject, and by instances of the unexpected defeat of the wisest schemes of policy, and sudden subversions of the highest eminences of greatness. It has, perhaps, not been equally observed, that all these examples afford the proper antidote to fear as well as to hope, and may be applied with no less efficacy as consolations to the timorous, than as restraints to the proud.

Evil is uncertain in the same degree as good, and for the reason that we ought not to hope too securely, we ought not to fear with too much dejection. The state of the world is continually changing, and none can tell the result of the next vicissitude. Whatever is afloat in the stream of time, may, when it is very near us, be driven away by an accidental blast, which shall happen to cross the general course of the current. The sudden accidents by which the powerful are depressed, may fall upon those whose malice we fear; and the greatness by which we expect to be overborn, may become another proof of the false flatteries of fortune. Our enemies may become weak, or we grow strong before our encounter, or we may advance against each other without ever meeting. There are, indeed, natural evils which we can flatter ourselves with no hopes of escaping, and with little of delaying; but of the ills which are apprehended from human malignity, or the opposition of rival interests, we may always alleviate the terror by considering that our persecutors are weak and ignorant, and mortal like ourselves.

The misfortunes which arise from the concurrence of unhappy incidents should never be suffered to disturb us before they happen; because, if the breast be once laid open to the dread of mere possibilities of misery, life must be given a prey to dismal solicitude, and quiet must be lost for ever.

It is remarked by old Cornaro,[4] that it is absurd to be afraid of the natural dissolution of the body; because it must certainly happen, and can, by no caution or artifice, be avoided. Whether this sentiment be entirely just, I shall not examine; but certainly, if it be improper to fear events which must happen, it is yet more evidently contrary to right reason to fear those which may never happen, and which, if they should come upon us, we cannot resist.

As we ought not to give way to fear any more than indulgence to hope, because the objects both of fear and hope are yet uncertain, so we ought not to trust the representations of one more than of the other, because they are both equally fallacious; as hope enlarges happiness, fear aggravates calamity. It is generally allowed, that no man ever found the happiness of possession proportionate to that expectation which incited his desire, and invigorated his pursuit; nor has any man found the evils of life so formidable in reality, as they were described to him by his own imagination; every species of distress brings with it some peculiar supports, some unforeseen means of resisting, or power of enduring. Taylor justly blames some pious persons, who indulge their fancies too much, set themselves, by the force of imagination, in the place of the ancient martyrs and confessors, and question the validity of their own faith because they shrink at the thoughts of flames and tortures. It is, says he, sufficient that you are able to encounter the temptations which now assault you; when God sends trials, he may send strength.[5]

All fear is in itself painful, and when it conduces not to safety is painful without use. Every consideration, therefore, by which groundless terrors may be removed, adds something to human happiness. It is likewise not unworthy of remark, that in proportion as our cares are imployed upon the future, they are abstracted from the present, from the only time which we can call our own, and of which if we neglect the duties, to make provision against visionary attacks, we shall certainly counteract our own purpose; for he, doubtless, mistakes his true interest, who thinks that he can increase his safety, when he impairs his virtue.

No. 31. Tuesday, 3 July 1750.

Non ego mendosos ausim defendere mores,
Falsaque pro vitiis arma tenere meis.
                                                    OVID.[1]

Corrupted manners I shall ne'er defend,
Nor, falsely witty, for my faults contend.
                                                    ELPHINSTON.

Though the fallibility of man's reason, and the narrowness of
his knowledge, are very liberally confessed, yet the conduct of
those who so willingly admit the weakness of human nature,
seems to discern that this acknowledgement is not altogether
sincere; at least, that most make it with a tacit reserve in favour
of themselves, and that with whatever ease they give up the
claims of their neighbours, they are desirous of being thought
exempt from faults in their own conduct, and from error in their
opinions.

The certain and obstinate opposition, which we may observe
made to confutation, however clear, and to reproof however
tender, is an undoubted argument, that some dormant privilege
is thought to be attacked; for as no man can lose what he neither
possesses, nor imagines himself to possess, or be defrauded of
that to which he has no right, it is reasonable to suppose that
those who break out into fury at the softest contradiction, or
the slightest censure, since they apparently conclude themselves
injured, must fancy some antient immunity violated, or some
natural prerogative invaded. To be mistaken, if they thought
themselves liable to mistake, could not be considered as either
shameful or wonderful, and they would not receive with so
much emotion intelligence which only informed them of what
they knew before, nor struggle with such earnestness against
an attack that deprived them of nothing to which they held
themselves entitled.

It is related of one of the philosophers,[2] that when an account
was brought him of his son's death, he received it only with this

reflexion, *I knew that my son was mortal.* He that is convinced of an error, if he had the same knowledge of his own weakness, would, instead of straining for artifices, and brooding malignity, only regard such oversights as the appendages of humanity, and pacify himself with considering that he had always known man to be a fallible being.

If it be true that most of our passions are excited by the novelty of objects, there is little reason for doubting that to be considered as subject to fallacies of ratiocination, or imperfection of knowledge, is to a great part of mankind entirely new; for it is impossible to fall into any company where there is not some regular and established subordination, without finding rage and vehemence produced only by difference of sentiments about things in which neither of the disputants have any other interest than what proceeds from their mutual unwillingness to give way to any opinion that may bring upon them the disgrace of being wrong.

I have heard of one that, having advanced some erroneous doctrines in philosophy, refused to see the experiments by which they were confuted:[3] and the observation of every day will give new proofs with how much industry subterfuges and evasions are sought to decline the pressure of resistless arguments, how often the state of the question is altered, how often the antagonist is wilfully misrepresented, and in how much perplexity the clearest positions are involved by those whom they happen to oppose.

Of all mortals none seem to have been more infected with this species of vanity, than the race of writers, whose reputation arising solely from their understanding, gives them a very delicate sensibility of any violence attempted on their literary honour. It is not unpleasing to remark with what solicitude men of acknowledged abilities will endeavour to palliate absurdities and reconcile contradictions, only to obviate criticisms to which all human performances must ever be exposed, and from which they can never suffer, but when they teach the world by a vain and ridiculous impatience to think them of importance.

DRYDEN, whose warmth of fancy, and haste of composition very frequently hurried him into inaccuracies, heard himself sometimes exposed to ridicule for having said in one of his tragedies,

I follow fate, which does too fast persue.[4]

That no man could at once follow and be followed was, it may be thought, too plain to be long disputed; and the truth is, that DRYDEN was apparently betrayed into the blunder by the double meaning of the word FATE, to which in the former part of the verse he had annexed the idea of FORTUNE, and in the latter that of DEATH; so that the sense only was, *though persued by* DEATH, *I will not resign myself to despair, but will follow* FORTUNE, *and do and suffer what is appointed*. This however was not completely expressed, and DRYDEN being determined not to give way to his critics, never confessed that he had been surprised by an ambiguity; but finding luckily in *Virgil* an account of a man moving in a circle, with this expression, *Et se sequiturque fugitque,*[5] "Here, says he, is the passage in imitation of which I wrote the line that my critics were pleased to condemn as nonsense; not but I may sometimes write nonsense, though they have not the fortune to find it."[6]

Every one sees the folly of such mean doublings to escape the persuit of criticism; nor is there a single reader of this poet, who would not have paid him greater veneration, had he shewn consciousness enough of his own superiority to set such cavils at defiance, and owned that he sometimes slipped into errors by the tumult of his imagination, and the multitude of his ideas.

It is happy when this temper discovers itself only in little things, which may be right or wrong without any influence on the virtue or happiness of mankind. We may, with very little inquietude, see a man persist in a project, which he has found to be impracticable, live in an inconvenient house because it was contrived by himself, or wear a coat of a particular cut, in hopes by perseverance to bring it into fashion. These are indeed follies, but they are only follies, and, however wild or ridiculous, can very little affect others.

But such pride, once indulged, too frequently operates upon more important objects, and inclines men not only to vindicate their errors, but their vices; to persist in practices which their own hearts condemn, only lest they should seem to feel reproaches, or be made wiser by the advice of others; or to search for sophisms tending to the confusion of all principles, and the evacuation of all duties, that they may not appear to act what they are not able to defend.

Let every man, who finds vanity so far predominant, as to betray him to the danger of this last degree of corruption, pause a moment to consider what will be the consequences of the plea which he is about to offer for a practice to which he knows himself not led at first by reason, but impelled by the violence of desire, surprized by the suddenness of passion, or seduced by the soft approaches of temptation, and by imperceptible gradations of guilt. Let him consider what he is going to commit by forcing his understanding to patronise those appetites, which it is its chief business to hinder and reform.

The cause of virtue requires so little art to defend it, and good and evil, when they have been once shewn, are so easily distinguished, that such apologists seldom gain proselytes to their party, nor have their fallacies power to deceive any but those whose desires have clouded their discernment. All that the best faculties thus employed can perform is, to persuade the hearers that the man is hopeless whom they only thought vitious, that corruption has passed from his manners to his principles, that all endeavours for his recovery are without prospect of success, and that nothing remains but to avoid him as infectious, or hunt him down as destructive.

But if it be supposed that he may impose on his audience by partial representations of consequences, intricate deductions of remote causes, or perplexed combinations of ideas, which having various relations appear different as viewed on different sides; that he may sometimes puzzle the weak and well-meaning, and now and then seduce, by the admiration of his abilities, a young mind still fluctuating in unsettled notions, and neither fortified by instruction nor enlightened by experience; yet what must be the event of such a triumph? A man cannot spend all this life in frolick: age, or disease, or solitude will bring some hours of serious consideration, and it will then afford no comfort to think, that he has extended the dominion of vice, that he has loaded himself with the crimes of others, and can never know the extent of his own wickedness, or make reparation for the mischief that he has caused. There is not perhaps in all the stores of ideal anguish, a thought more painful, than the consciousness of having propagated corruption by vitiating principles, of having not only drawn others from the paths of virtue, but blocked up the way by which they should return, of having blinded them to every beauty but the paint of pleasure, and deafened them to every call but the alluring voice of the syrens of destruction.

There is yet another danger in this practice: men who cannot deceive others, are very often successful in deceiving themselves; they weave their sophistry till their own reason is entangled, and repeat their positions till they are credited by themselves; by often contending they grow sincere in the cause, and by long wishing for demonstrative arguments they at last bring themselves to fancy that they have found them. They are then at the uttermost verge of wickedness, and may die without having that light rekindled in their minds, which their own pride and contumacy have extinguished.

The men who can be charged with fewest failings, either with respect to abilities or virtue, are generally most ready to allow them; for not to dwell on things of solemn and awful consideration, the humility of confessors, the tears of saints, and the dying terrors of persons eminent for piety and innocence, it is well known that Caesar wrote an account of the errors committed by him in his wars of Gaul, and that Hippocrates, whose name is perhaps in rational estimation greater than Caesar's, warned posterity against a mistake into which he had fallen. *So much*, says Celsus, *does the open and artless confession of an error become a man conscious that he has enough remaining to support his character*.[7]

As all error is meanness, it is incumbent on every man who consults his own dignity, to retract it as soon as he discovers it, without fearing any censure so much as that of his own mind. As justice requires that all injuries should be repaired, it is the duty of him who has seduced others by bad practices, or false notions, to endeavour that such as have adopted his errors should know his retraction, and that those who have learned vice by his example, should by his example be taught amendment.

No. 32. Saturday, 7 July 1750.

Ὅσσά τε δαιμονίῃσι τύχαις βροτοὶ ἄλγε' ἔχουσιν,
Ὧν ἂν μοῖραν ἔχῃς, πρᾴως φέρε, μηδ' ἀγανάκτει·
Ἰᾶσθαι δὲ πρέπει κάθοσον δύνῃ.

PYTHAG.[1]

Of all the woes that load the mortal state,
Whate'er thy portion, mildly meet thy fate;
But ease it as thou can'st——

ELPHINSTON.

So large a part of human life passes in a state contrary to our natural desires, that one of the principal topics of moral instruction is the art of bearing calamities. And such is the certainty of evil, that it is the duty of every man to furnish his mind with those principles that may enable him to act under it with decency and propriety.

The sect of ancient philosophers, that boasted to have carried this necessary science to the highest perfection, were the stoics, or scholars of Zeno,[2] whose wild enthusiastick virtue pretended to an exemption from the sensibilities of unenlightened mortals, and who proclaimed themselves exalted, by the doctrines of their sect, above the reach of those miseries, which embitter life to the rest of the world. They therefore removed pain, poverty, loss of friends, exile, and violent death, from the catalogue of evils; and passed, in their haughty stile, a kind of irreversible decree, by which they forbad them to be counted any longer among the objects of terror or anxiety, or to give any disturbance to the tranquillity of a wise man.

This edict was, I think, not universally observed, for though one of the more resolute, when he was tortured by a violent disease, cried out, that let pain harrass him to its utmost power, it should never force him to consider it as other than indifferent and neutral; yet all had not stubbornness to hold out against their senses: for a weaker pupil of *Zeno* is recorded to have confessed in the anguish of the gout, that *he now found pain to be an evil*.[3]

It may however be questioned, whether these philosophers can be very properly numbered among the teachers of patience; for if pain be not an evil, there seems no instruction requisite how it may be borne; and therefore when they endeavour to arm their followers with arguments against it, they may be thought to have given up their first position. But such inconsistencies are to be expected from the greatest understandings, when they endeavour to grow eminent by singularity, and employ their strength in establishing opinions opposite to nature.

The controversy about the reality of external evils is now at an end. That life has many miseries, and that those miseries are, sometimes at least, equal to all the powers of fortitude, is now universally confessed; and therefore it is useful to consider not only how we may escape them, but by what means those which either the accidents of affairs, or the infirmities of nature must bring upon us, may be mitigated and lightened; and how we may make those hours less wretched, which the condition of our present existence will not allow to be very happy.

The cure for the greatest part of human miseries is not radical, but palliative. Infelicity is involved in corporeal nature, and interwoven with our being; all attempts therefore to decline it wholly are useless and vain: the armies of pain send their arrows against us on every side, the choice is only between those which are more or less sharp, or tinged with poison of greater or less malignity; and the strongest armour which reason can supply, will only blunt their points, but cannot repel them.

The great remedy which heaven has put in our hands is patience, by which, though we cannot lessen the torments of the body, we can in a great measure preserve the peace of the mind, and shall suffer only the natural and genuine force of an evil, without heightening its acrimony, or prolonging its effects.

There is indeed nothing more unsuitable to the nature of

man in any calamity than rage and turbulence, which, without examining whether they are not sometimes impious, are at least always offensive, and incline others rather to hate and despise than to pity and assist us. If what we suffer has been brought upon us by ourselves, it is observed by an ancient poet, that patience is eminently our duty, since no one should be angry at feeling that which he has deserved.

> *Leniter ex merito quicquid patiare ferendum est.*[4]

> Let pain deserv'd without complaint be borne.

And surely, if we are conscious that we have not contributed to our own sufferings, if punishment fall upon innocence, or disappointment happens to industry and prudence, patience, whether more necessary or not, is much easier, since our pain is then without aggravation, and we have not the bitterness of remorse to add to the asperity of misfortune.

In those evils which are allotted to us by providence, such as deformity, privation of any of the senses, or old age, it is always to be remembred, that impatience can have no present effect, but to deprive us of the consolations which our condition admits, by driving away from us those by whose conversation or advice we might be amused or helped; and that with regard to futurity it is yet less to be justified, since, without lessening the pain, it cuts off the hope of that reward, which he by whom it is inflicted will confer upon them that bear it well.

In all evils which admit a remedy, impatience is to be avoided, because it wastes that time and attention in complaints, that, if properly applied, might remove the cause. Turenne, among the acknowledgments which he used to pay in conversation to the memory of those by whom he had been instructed in the art of war, mentioned one with honour, who taught him not to spend his time in regretting any mistake which he had made, but to set himself immediately and vigorously to repair it.[5]

Patience and submission are very carefully to be distinguished from cowardice and indolence. We are not to repine, but we may lawfully struggle; for the calamities of life, like the necessities of nature, are calls to labour, and exercises of diligence. When we feel any pressure of distress, we are not to conclude that we can only obey the will of heaven by languishing under it, any more than when we perceive the pain of thirst we are to imagine that water is prohibited. Of misfortune it never can be certainly known whether, as proceeding from the hand of GOD, it is an act of favour, or of punishment: but since all the ordinary dispensations of providence are to be interpreted according to the general analogy of things, we may conclude, that we have a right to remove one inconvenience as well as another; that we are only to take care lest we purchase ease with guilt; and that our Maker's purpose, whether of reward or severity, will be answered by the labours which he lays us under the necessity of performing.

This duty is not more difficult in any state, than in diseases intensely painful, which may indeed suffer such exacerbations as seem to strain the powers of life to their utmost stretch, and leave very little of the attention vacant to precept or reproof. In this state the nature of man requires some indulgence, and every extravagance but impiety may be easily forgiven him. Yet, lest we should think ourselves too soon entitled to the mournful privileges of irresistible misery, it is proper to reflect that the utmost anguish which human wit can contrive, or human malice can inflict, has been borne with constancy; and that if the pains of disease be, as I believe they are, sometimes greater than those of artificial torture, they are therefore in their own nature shorter, the vital frame is quickly broken, or the union between soul and body is for a time suspended by insensibility, and we soon cease to feel our maladies when they once become too violent to be born. I think there is some reason for questioning whether the body and mind are not so proportioned, that the one can bear all which can be inflicted on the other, whether virtue cannot stand its ground as long as life, and whether a soul well principled will not be separated sooner than subdued.

In calamities which operate chiefly on our passions, such as diminution of fortune, loss of friends, or declension of character, the chief danger of impatience is upon the first attack, and many expedients have been contrived, by which the blow may be broken. Of these the most general precept is, not to take pleasure in any thing, of which it is not in our power to secure the possession to ourselves. This counsel, when we consider the enjoyment of any terrestrial advantage, as opposite to a constant and habitual solicitude for future felicity, is undoubtedly just, and delivered by that authority which cannot be disputed; but in any other sense, is it not like advice, not to walk lest we should stumble, or not to see lest our eyes should light upon deformity? It seems to me reasonable to enjoy blessings with confidence as well as to resign them with submission, and to hope for the continuance of good which we possess without insolence or voluptuousness, as for the restitution of that which we lose without despondency or murmurs.

The chief security against the fruitless anguish of impatience, must arise from frequent reflection on the wisdom and goodness of the GOD of nature, in whose hands are riches and poverty, honour and disgrace, pleasure and pain, and life and death. A settled conviction of the tendency of every thing to our good, and of the possibility of turning miseries into happiness, by receiving them rightly, will incline us to *bless the name of the* LORD, *whether he gives or takes away.*[6]

No. 33. Tuesday, 10 July 1750.

Quod caret alternâ requie durabile non est.
OVID.[1]

Alternate rest and labour long endure.

In the early ages of the world, as is well known to those who are versed in antient traditions, when innocence was yet untainted, and simplicity unadulterated, mankind was happy in the enjoyment of continual pleasure, and constant plenty, under the protection of REST; a gentle divinity, who required of her worshippers neither altars nor sacrifices, and whose rites were only performed by prostrations upon tufts of flowers in shades of jasmine and myrtle, or by dances on the banks of rivers flowing with milk and nectar.

Under this easy government the first generations breathed the fragrance of perpetual spring, eat the fruits, which, without culture, fell ripe into their hands, and slept under bowers arched by nature, with the birds singing over their heads, and the beasts sporting about them. But by degrees they began to lose their original integrity; each, though there was more than enough for all, was desirous of appropriating part to himself. Then entered violence and fraud, and theft and rapine. Soon after pride and envy broke into the world, and brought with them a new standard of wealth; for men, who till then thought themselves rich when they wanted nothing, now rated their demands, not by the calls of nature, but by the plenty of others; and began to consider themselves as poor when they beheld their own possessions exceeded by those of their neighbours. Now only one could be happy, because only one could have most, and that one was always in danger, lest the same arts by which he had supplanted others should be practised upon himself.

Amidst the prevalence of this corruption, the state of the earth was changed; the year was divided into seasons; part of the ground became barren, and the rest yielded only berries, acorns, and herbs. The summer and autumn indeed furnished a coarse and inelegant sufficiency, but winter was without any relief; FAMINE, with a thousand diseases, which the inclemency of the air invited into the upper regions, made havock among men, and there appeared to be danger lest they should be destroyed before they were reformed.

To oppose the devastations of FAMINE, who scattered the ground every where with carcases, LABOUR came down upon earth. LABOUR was the son of NECESSITY, the nurseling of HOPE, and the pupil of ART; he had the strength of his mother, the spirit of his nurse, and the dexterity of his governess. His face was wrinkled with the wind, and swarthy with the sun; he had the implements of husbandry in one hand, with which he turned up the earth; in the other he had the tools of architecture, and raised walls and towers at his pleasure. He called out with a rough voice, "Mortals! see here the power to whom you are

consigned, and from whom you are to hope for all your pleasures, and all your safety. You have long languished under
the dominion of REST, an impotent and deceitful goddess,
who can neither protect nor relieve you, but resigns you to the
first attacks of either FAMINE or DISEASE, and suffers her
shades to be invaded by every enemy, and destroyed by every
accident."

"Awake therefore to the call of LABOUR. I will teach you to
remedy the sterility of the earth, and the severity of the sky; I
will compel summer to find provisions for the winter; I will
force the waters to give you their fish, the air its fowls, and the
forest its beasts; I will teach you to pierce the bowels of the
earth, and bring out from the caverns of the mountains metals
which shall give strength to your hands, and security to your
bodies, by which you may be covered from the assaults of the
fiercest beasts, and with which you shall fell the oak, and divide
rocks, and subject all nature to your use and pleasure."

Encouraged by this magnificent invitation, the inhabitants of
the globe considered LABOUR as their only friend, and hasted
to his command. He led them out to the fields and mountains,
and shewed them how to open mines, to level hills, to drain
marshes, and change the course of rivers. The face of things was
immediately transformed; the land was covered with towns and
villages, encompassed with fields of corn, and plantations of
fruit-trees; and nothing was seen but heaps of grain, and baskets
of fruit, full tables, and crouded storehouses.

Thus LABOUR and his followers added every hour new acquisitions to their conquests, and saw FAMINE gradually dispos-
sessed of his dominions; till at last, amidst their jollity and
triumphs, they were depressed and amazed by the approach of
LASSITUDE, who was known by her sunk eyes, and dejected
countenance. She came forward trembling and groaning: at
every groan the hearts of all those that beheld her lost their
courage, their nerves slackened, their hands shook, and the
instruments of labour fell from their grasp.

Shocked with this horrid phantom they reflected with regret
on their easy compliance with the solicitations of LABOUR,
and began to wish again for the golden hours which they

remembered to have passed under the reign of REST, whom they resolved again to visit, and to whom they intended to dedicate the remaining part of their lives. REST had not left the world; they quickly found her, and to attone for their former desertion, invited her to the enjoyment of those acquisitions which LABOUR had procured them.

REST therefore took leave of the groves and vallies, which she had hitherto inhabited, and entered into palaces, reposed herself in alcoves, and slumbered away the winter upon beds of down, and the summer in artificial grottos with cascades playing before her. There was indeed always something wanting to complete her felicity, and she could never lull her returning fugitives to that serenity, which they knew before their engagements with LABOUR: Nor was her dominion entirely without controul, for she was obliged to share it with LUXURY, tho' she always looked upon her as a false friend, by whom her influence was in reality destroyed, while it seemed to be promoted.

The two soft associates, however, reigned for some time without visible disagreement, till at last LUXURY betrayed her charge, and let in DISEASE to seize upon her worshippers. REST then flew away, and left the place to the usurpers; who employed all their arts to fortify themselves in their possession, and to strengthen the interest of each other.

REST had not always the same enemy: in some places she escaped the incursions of DISEASE; but had her residence invaded by a more slow and subtle intruder, for very frequently when every thing was composed and quiet, when there was neither pain within, nor danger without, when every flower was in bloom, and every gale freighted with perfumes, SATIETY would enter with a languishing and repining look, and throw herself upon the couch placed and adorned for the accommodation of REST. No sooner was she seated than a general gloom spread itself on every side, the groves immediately lost their verdure, and their inhabitants desisted from their melody, the breeze sunk in sighs, and the flowers contracted their leaves and shut up their odours. Nothing was seen on every side but multitudes wandering about they knew not whither, in quest they knew not of what; no voice was heard but of complaints that mentioned no pain, and murmurs that could tell of no misfortune.

REST had now lost her authority. Her followers again began to treat her with contempt; some of them united themselves more closely to LUXURY, who promised by her arts to drive SATIETY away, and others that were more wise or had more fortitude, went back again to LABOUR, by whom they were indeed protected from SATIETY, but delivered up in time to LASSITUDE, and forced by her to the bowers of REST.

Thus REST and LABOUR equally perceived their reign of short duration and uncertain tenure, and their empire liable to inrodes from those who were alike enemies to both. They each found their subjects unfaithful, and ready to desert them upon every opportunity. LABOUR saw the riches which he had given always carried away as an offering to REST, and REST found her votaries in every exigence flying from her to beg help of LABOUR. They, therefore, at last determined upon an interview, in which they agreed to divide the world between them, and govern it alternately, allotting the dominion of the day to one, and that of the night to the other, and promised to guard the frontiers of each other, so that, whenever hostilities were attempted, SATIETY should be intercepted by LABOUR, and LASSITUDE expelled by REST. Thus the antient quarrel was appeased, and as hatred is often succeeded by its contrary, REST afterwards became pregnant by LABOUR, and was delivered of HEALTH, a benevolent goddess, who consolidated the union of her parents, and contributed to the regular vicissitudes of their reign, by dispensing her gifts to those only who shared their lives in just proportions between REST and LABOUR.

No. 36. Saturday, 21 July 1750.

"Ἀμ᾽ ἕποντο νομῆες
Τερπόμενοι σύριγξι· δόλον δ᾽ οὔτι προνόησαν.
                                               HOMER.[1]

——Piping on their reeds, the shepherds go,
Nor fear an ambush, nor suspect a foe.
                                               POPE.

There is scarcely any species of poetry, that has allured more readers, or excited more writers, than the pastoral. It is generally pleasing, because it entertains the mind with representations of scenes familiar to almost every imagination, and of which all can equally judge whether they are well described. It exhibits a life, to which we have been always accustomed to associate peace, and leisure, and innocence: and therefore we readily set open the heart, for the admission of its images, which contribute to drive away cares and perturbations, and suffer ourselves, without resistance, to be transported to elysian regions, where we are to meet with nothing but joy, and plenty, and content-ment; where every gale whispers pleasure, and every shade promises repose.

It has been maintained by some, who love to talk of what they do not know, that pastoral is the most antient poetry; and, indeed, since it is probable, that poetry is nearly of the same antiquity with rational nature, and since the life of the first men was certainly rural, we may reasonably conjecture, that, as their ideas would necessarily be borrowed from those objects with which they were acquainted, their composures, being filled chiefly with such thoughts on the visible creation as must occur to the first observers, were pastoral hymns like those which *Milton* introduces the original pair singing, in the day of inno-cence, to the praise of their Maker.[2]

For the same reason that pastoral poetry was the first employ-ment of the human imagination, it is generally the first literary amusement of our minds. We have seen fields, and meadows, and groves from the time that our eyes opened upon life; and are pleased with birds, and brooks, and breezes, much earlier than we engage among the actions and passions of mankind. We are therefore delighted with rural pictures, because we know the original at an age when our curiosity can be very little awakened, by descriptions of courts which we never beheld, or representations of passion which we never felt.

The satisfaction received from this kind of writing not only begins early, but lasts long; we do not, as we advance into the intellectual world, throw it away among other childish amusements and pastimes, but willingly return to it in any hour of indolence and relaxation. The images of true pastoral have always the power of exciting delight, because the works of nature, from which they are drawn, have always the same order and beauty, and continue to force themselves upon our thoughts, being at once obvious to the most careless regard, and more than adequate to the strongest reason, and severest contemplation. Our inclination to stillness and tranquillity is seldom much lessened by long knowledge of the busy and tumultuary part of the world. In childhood we turn our thoughts to the country, as to the region of pleasure, we recur to it in old age as a port of rest, and perhaps with that secondary and adventitious gladness, which every man feels on reviewing those places, or recollecting those occurrences, that contributed to his youthful enjoyments, and bring him back to the prime of life, when the world was gay with the bloom of novelty, when mirth wantoned at his side, and hope sparkled before him.

The sense of this universal pleasure has invited *numbers without number*[3] to try their skill in pastoral performances, in which they have generally succeeded after the manner of other imitators, transmitting the same images in the same combination from one to another, till he that reads the title of a poem, may guess at the whole series of the composition; nor will a man, after the perusal of thousands of these performances, find his knowledge enlarged with a single view of nature not produced before, or his imagination amused with any new application of those views to moral purposes.

The range of pastoral is indeed narrow, for though nature

itself, philosophically considered, be inexhaustible, yet its general effects on the eye and on the ear are uniform, and incapable of much variety of description. Poetry cannot dwell upon the minuter distinctions, by which one species differs from another, without departing from that simplicity of grandeur which fills the imagination; nor dissect the latent qualities of things, without losing its general power of gratifying every mind by recalling its conceptions. However, as each age makes some discoveries, and those discoveries are by degrees generally known, as new plants or modes of culture are introduced, and by little and little become common, pastoral might receive, from time to time, small augmentations, and exhibit once in a century a scene somewhat varied.

But pastoral subjects have been often, like others, taken into the hands of those that were not qualified to adorn them, men to whom the face of nature was so little known, that they have drawn it only after their own imagination, and changed or distorted her features, that their portraits might appear something more than servile copies from their predecessors.

Not only the images of rural life, but the occasions on which they can be properly produced, are few and general. The state of a man confined to the employments and pleasures of the country, is so little diversified, and exposed to so few of those accidents which produce perplexities, terrors and surprises, in more complicated transactions, that he can be shewn but seldom in such circumstances as attract curiosity. His ambition is without policy, and his love without intrigue. He has no complaints to make of his rival, but that he is richer than himself; nor any disasters to lament, but a cruel mistress, or a bad harvest.

The conviction of the necessity of some new source of pleasure induced *Sannazarius*[4] to remove the scene from the fields to the sea, to substitute fishermen for shepherds, and derive his sentiments from the piscatory life; for which he has been censured by succeeding criticks, because the sea is an object of terrour, and by no means proper to amuse the mind, and lay the passions asleep. Against this objection he might be defended by the established maxim, that the poet has a right to select his images, and is no more obliged to shew the sea in a storm, than the land under an inundation; but may display all the pleasures, and conceal the dangers of the water, as he may lay his shepherd under a shady beech, without giving him an ague, or letting a wild beast loose upon him.

There are however two defects in the piscatory eclogue, which perhaps cannot be supplied. The sea, though in hot countries it is considered by those who live, like *Sannazarius*, upon the coast, as a place of pleasure and diversion, has notwithstanding much less variety than the land, and therefore will be sooner exhausted by a descriptive writer. When he has once shewn the sun rising or setting upon it, curled its waters with the vernal breeze, rolled the waves in gentle succession to the shore, and enumerated the fish sporting in the shallows, he has nothing remaining but what is common to all other poetry, the complaint of a nymph for a drowned lover, or the indignation of a fisher that his oysters are refused, and Mycon's accepted.

Another obstacle to the general reception of this kind of poetry, is the ignorance of maritime pleasures, in which the greater part of mankind must always live. To all the inland inhabitants of every region, the sea is only known as an immense diffusion of waters, over which men pass from one country to another, and in which life is frequently lost. They have, therefore, no opportunity of tracing, in their own thoughts, the descriptions of winding shores, and calm bays, nor can look on the poem in which they are mentioned, with other sensations, than on a sea-chart, or the metrical geography of *Dionysius*.[5]

This defect *Sannazarius* was hindered from perceiving, by writing in a learned language to readers generally acquainted with the works of nature; but if he had made his attempt in any vulgar tongue, he would soon have discovered how vainly he had endeavoured to make that loved, which was not understood.

I am afraid it will not be found easy to improve the pastorals of antiquity, by any great additions or diversifications. Our descriptions may indeed differ from those of Virgil, as an English from an Italian summer, and, in some respects, as modern from ancient life; but as nature is in both countries nearly the same, and as poetry has to do rather with the passions of men, which are uniform, than their customs, which are changeable, the varieties, which time or place can furnish, will be inconsiderable: and I shall endeavour to shew, in the next paper, how little the latter ages have contributed to the improvement of the rustick muse.

No. 37. Tuesday, 24 July 1750.

> *Canto quæ solitus, si quando armenta vocabat,*
> *Amphion Dircæus.*
>   VIRG.[1]

> Such strains I sing as once *Amphion* play'd,
> When list'ning flocks the pow'rful call obey'd.
>   ELPHINSTON.

In writing or judging of pastoral poetry, neither the authors nor criticks of latter times seem to have paid sufficient regard to the originals left us by antiquity, but have entangled themselves with unnecessary difficulties, by advancing principles, which, having no foundation in the nature of things, are wholly to be rejected from a species of composition in which, above all others, mere nature is to be regarded.

It is, therefore, necessary to enquire after some more distinct and exact idea of this kind of writing. This may, I think, be easily found in the pastorals of Virgil, from whose opinion it will not appear very safe to depart, if we consider that every advantage of nature, and of fortune, concurred to complete his productions; that he was born with great accuracy and severity of judgment, enlightened with all the learning of one of the brightest ages, and embellished with the elegance of the Roman court; that he employed his powers rather in improving, than inventing, and therefore must have endeavoured to recompense the want of novelty by exactness; that taking Theocritus[2] for his original, he found pastoral far advanced towards perfection, and that having so great a rival, he must have proceeded with uncommon caution.

If we search the writings of Virgil, for the true definition of a pastoral, it will be found *a poem in which any action or passion is represented by its effects upon a country life*. Whatsoever therefore may, according to the common course of things, happen in the country, may afford a subject for a pastoral poet.

In this definition, it will immediately occur to those who are versed in the writings of the modern criticks, that there is no mention of the golden age. I cannot indeed easily discover why it is thought necessary to refer descriptions of a rural state to remote times, nor can I perceive that any writer has consistently preserved the Arcadian manners and sentiments. The only reason, that I have read, on which this rule has been founded, is, that, according to the customs of modern life, it is improbable that shepherds should be capable of harmonious numbers, or delicate sentiments; and therefore the reader must exalt his ideas of the pastoral character, by carrying his thoughts back to the age in which the care of herds and flocks was the employment of the wisest and greatest men.

These reasoners seem to have been led into their hypothesis, by considering pastoral, not in general, as a representation of rural nature, and consequently as exhibiting the ideas and sentiments of those, whoever they are, to whom the country affords pleasure or employment, but simply as a dialogue, or narrative of men actually tending sheep, and busied in the lowest and most laborious offices; from whence they very readily concluded, since characters must necessarily be preserved, that either the sentiments must sink to the level of the speakers, or the speakers must be raised to the height of the sentiments.

In consequence of these original errors, a thousand precepts have been given, which have only contributed to perplex and to confound. Some have thought it necessary that the imaginary manners of the golden age should be universally preserved, and have therefore believed, that nothing more could be admitted in pastoral, than lilies and roses, and rocks and streams, among which are heard the gentle whispers of chaste fondness, or the soft complaints of amorous impatience. In pastoral, as in other writings, chastity of sentiment ought doubtless to be observed, and purity of manners to be represented; not because the poet is confined to the images of the golden age, but because, having the subject in his own choice, he ought always to consult the interest of virtue.

These advocates for the golden age lay down other principles, not very consistent with their general plan; for they tell us, that, to support the character of the shepherd, it is proper that all refinement should be avoided, and that some slight instances of ignorance should be interspersed. Thus the shepherd in Virgil is supposed to have forgot the name of Anaximander, and in Pope the term Zodiack is too hard for a rustick apprehension.[3] But if we place our shepherds in their primitive condition, we may give them learning among their other qualifications; and if we suffer them to allude at all to things of later existence, which, perhaps, cannot with any great propriety be allowed, there can be no danger of making them speak with too much accuracy, since they conversed with divinities, and transmitted to succeeding ages the arts of life.

Other writers, having the mean and despicable condition of a shepherd always before them, conceive it necessary to degrade the language of pastoral, by obsolete terms and rustick words, which they very learnedly call Dorick, without reflecting, that they thus become authors of a mingled dialect, which no human being ever could have spoken, that they may as well refine the speech as the sentiments of their personages, and that none of the inconsistencies which they endeavour to avoid, is greater than that of joining elegance of thought with coarseness of diction. Spenser begins one of his pastorals with studied barbarity;

> Diggon Davie, *I bid her good-day:*
> Or, Diggon *her is, or I missay.*
> Dig. *Her was her while it was day-light,*
> *But now her is a most wretched wight.*[4]

What will the reader imagine to be the subject on which speakers like these exercise their eloquence? Will he not be somewhat disappointed, when he finds them met together to condemn the corruptions of the church of Rome? Surely, at the same time that a shepherd learns theology, he may gain some acquaintance with his native language.

Pastoral admits of all ranks of persons, because persons of all ranks inhabit the country. It excludes not, therefore, on account of the characters necessary to be introduced, any elevation or delicacy of sentiment; those ideas only are improper, which, not owing their original to rural objects, are not pastoral. Such is the exclamation in Virgil,

> Nunc scio quid sit Amor, duris in cautibus illum
> Ismarus, aut Rhodope, aut extremi Garamantes,
> Nec generis nostri puerum nec sanguinis, edunt;[5]

> I know thee, love, in desarts thou wert bred,
> And at the dugs of savage tygers fed:
> Alien of birth, usurper of the plains.
>
> DRYDEN.

which Pope endeavouring to copy, was carried to still greater impropriety.

> I know thee, Love, wild as the raging main,
> More fierce than tigers on the Libyan plain;
> Thou wert from Ætna's burning entrails torn,
> Begot in tempests, and in thunders born![6]

Sentiments like these, as they have no ground in nature, are indeed of little value in any poem, but in pastoral they are particularly liable to censure, because it wants that exaltation above common life, which in tragick or heroick writings often reconciles us to bold flights and daring figures.

Pastoral being the *representation of an action or passion, by its effects upon a country life*, has nothing peculiar but its confinement to rural imagery, without which it ceases to be pastoral. This is its true characteristick, and this it cannot lose by any dignity of sentiment, or beauty of diction. The Pollio[7] of Virgil, with all its elevation, is a composition truly bucolic, though rejected by the criticks; for all the images are either taken from the country, or from the religion of the age common to all parts of the empire.

The Silenus[8] is indeed of a more disputable kind, because though the scene lies in the country, the song being religious and historical, had been no less adapted to any other audience or place. Neither can it well be defended as a fiction, for the introduction of a god seems to imply the golden age, and yet he alludes to many subsequent transactions, and mentions Gallus,[9] the poet's contemporary.

It seems necessary, to the perfection of this poem, that the occasion which is supposed to produce it, be at least not inconsistent with a country life, or less likely to interest those who have retired into places of solitude and quiet, than the more busy part of mankind. It is therefore improper to give the title of a pastoral to verses, in which the speakers, after the slight mention of their flocks, fall to complaints of errors in the church, and corruptions in the government, or to lamentations of the death of some illustrious person, whom when once the poet has called a shepherd, he has no longer any labour upon his hands, but can make the clouds weep, and lilies wither, and the sheep hang their heads, without art or learning, genius or study.

It is part of Claudian's character of his rustick, that he computes his time not by the succession of consuls, but of harvests.[10] Those who pass their days in retreats distant from the theatres of business, are always least likely to hurry their imagination with publick affairs.

The facility of treating actions or events in the pastoral stile, has incited many writers, from whom more judgment might have been expected, to put the sorrow or the joy which the occasion required into the mouth of Daphne or of Thyrsis, and as one absurdity must naturally be expected to make way for another, they have written with an utter disregard both of life and nature, and filled their productions with mythological allusions, with incredible fictions, and with sentiments which neither passion nor reason could have dictated, since the change which religion has made in the whole system of the world.

No. 39. Tuesday, 31 July 1750.

Infelix——nulli bene nupta marito.
AUSONIUS.[1]

Unblest, still doom'd to wed with misery.

The condition of the female sex has been frequently the subject of compassion to medical writers, because their constitution of body is such, that every state of life brings its peculiar diseases: they are placed, according to the proverb, between Scylla and Charybdis, with no other choice than of dangers equally formidable; and whether they embrace marriage, or determine upon a single life, are exposed, in consequence of their choice, to sickness, misery, and death.

It were to be wished that so great a degree of natural infelicity might not be increased by adventitious and artificial miseries; and that beings whose beauty we cannot behold without admiration, and whose delicacy we cannot contemplate without tenderness, might be suffered to enjoy every alleviation of their sorrows. But, however it has happened, the custom of the world seems to have been formed in a kind of conspiracy against them, though it does not appear but they had themselves an equal share in its establishment; and prescriptions which, by whomsoever they were begun, are now of long continuance, and by consequence of great authority, seem to have almost excluded them from content, in whatsoever condition they shall pass their lives.

If they refuse the society of men, and continue in that state which is reasonably supposed to place happiness most in their own power, they seldom give those that frequent their conversation, any exalted notions of the blessing of liberty; for whether it be that they are angry to see with what inconsiderate eagerness other heedless females rush into slavery, or with what absurd vanity the married ladies boast the change of their condition, and condemn the heroines who endeavour to assert the natural dignity of their sex; whether they are conscious that like barren countries they are free, only because they were never thought to deserve the trouble of a conquest, or imagine that their sincerity is not always unsuspected, when they declare their contempt of men; it is certain, that they generally appear to have some great and incessant cause of uneasiness, and that many of them have at last been persuaded, by powerful rhetoricians, to try the life which they had so long contemned, and put on the bridal ornaments at a time when they least became them.

What are the real causes of the impatience which the ladies discover in a virgin state, I shall perhaps take some other occasion to examine. That it is not to be envied for its happiness, appears from the solicitude with which it is avoided; from the opinion universally prevalent among the sex, that no woman continues long in it but because she is not invited to forsake it; from the disposition always shewn to treat old maids as the refuse of the world; and from the willingness with which it is often quitted at last, by those whose experience has enabled them to judge at leisure, and decide with authority.

Yet such is life, that whatever is proposed, it is much easier to find reasons for rejecting than embracing. Marriage, though a certain security from the reproach and solitude of antiquated virginity, has yet, as it is usually conducted, many disadvantages, that take away much from the pleasure which society promises, and might afford, if pleasures and pains were honestly shared, and mutual confidence inviolably preserved.

The miseries, indeed, which many ladies suffer under conjugal vexations, are to be considered with great pity, because their husbands are often not taken by them as objects of affection, but forced upon them by authority and violence, or by persuasion and importunity, equally resistless when urged by those whom they have been always accustomed to reverence and obey; and it very seldom appears, that those who are thus despotick in the disposal of their children, pay any regard to their domestick and personal felicity, or think it so much to be enquired whether they will be happy, as whether they will be rich.

It may be urged, in extenuation of this crime, which parents, not in any other respect to be numbered with robbers and assassins, frequently commit, that, in their estimation, riches and happiness are equivalent terms. They have passed their lives with no other wish than that of adding acre to acre, and filling one bag after another, and imagine the advantage of a daughter sufficiently considered, when they have secured her a large jointure, and given her reasonable expectations of living in the midst of those pleasures, with which she had seen her father and mother solacing their age.

There is an oeconomical oracle received among the prudential part of the world, which advises fathers *to marry their daughters lest they should marry themselves*; by which I suppose it is implied that women left to their own conduct, generally unite themselves with such partners as can contribute very little to their felicity. Who was the author of this maxim, or with what intention it was originally uttered, I have not yet discovered; but imagine that however solemnly it may be transmitted, or however implicitly received, it can confer no authority which nature has denied; it cannot license Titius to be unjust, lest Caia should be imprudent; nor give right to imprison for life, lest liberty should be ill employed.

That the ladies have sometimes incurred imputations which might naturally produce edicts not much in their favour, must be confessed by their warmest advocates; and I have indeed seldom observed, that when the tenderness or virtue of their parents has preserved them from forced marriage, and left them at large to chuse their own path in the labyrinth of life, they have made any great advantage of their liberty: They commonly take the opportunity of independence to trifle away youth and lose their bloom in a hurry of diversions, recurring in a succession too quick to leave room for any settled reflection; they see the world without gaining experience, and at last regulate their choice by motives trifling as those of a girl, or mercenary as those of a miser.

Melanthia came to town upon the death of her father, with a very large fortune, and with the reputation of a much larger; she was therefore followed and caressed by many men of rank, and by some of understanding; but having an insatiable desire of pleasure, she was not at leisure, from the park, the gardens, the theatres, visits, assemblies, and masquerades, to attend seriously to any proposal, but was still impatient for a new flatterer, and neglected marriage as always in her power; till in time her admirers fell away, wearied with expence, disgusted at her folly, or offended by her inconstancy; she heard of concerts to which she was not invited, and was more than once forced to sit still at an assembly, for want of a partner. In this distress, chance threw in her way Philotryphus, a man vain, glittering, and thoughtless as herself, who had spent a small fortune in equipage and dress, and was shining in the last suit for which his taylor would give him credit. He had been long endeavouring to retrieve his extravagance by marriage, and therefore soon paid his court to Melanthia, who after some weeks of insensibility saw him at a ball, and was wholly overcome by his performance in a minuet. They married; but a man cannot always dance, and Philotryphus had no other method of pleasing; however, as neither was in any great degree vitious, they live together with no other unhappiness, than vacuity of mind, and that tastelessness of life, which proceeds from a satiety of juvenile pleasures, and an utter inability to fill their place by nobler employments. As they have known the fashionable world at the same time, they agree in their notions of all those subjects on which they ever speak, and being able to add nothing to the ideas of each other, are not much inclined to conversation, but very often join in one wish, "That they could sleep more, and think less."

Argyris, after having refused a thousand offers, at last consented to marry Cotylus, the younger brother of a duke, a man without elegance of mien, beauty of person, or force of understanding; who, while he courted her, could not always forbear allusions to her birth, and hints how cheaply she would purchase an alliance to so illustrious a family. His conduct from the hour of his marriage has been insufferably tyrannical, nor has he any other regard to her than what arises from his desire that her appearance may not disgrace him. Upon this principle, however, he always orders that she should be gaily dressed, and splendidly attended; and she has, among all her mortifications, the happiness to take place of her eldest sister.

No. 41. Tuesday, 7 August 1750.

Nulla recordanti lux est ingrata gravisque,
Nulla fuit cujus non meminisse velit.
Ampliat ætatis spatium sibi vir bonus, hoc est
Vivere bis, vitâ posse priore frui.

MART.[1]

No day's remembrance shall the good regret,
Nor wish one bitter moment to forget;
They stretch the limits of this narrow span,
And, by enjoying, live past life again.

F. LEWIS.

So few of the hours of life are filled up with objects adequate to the mind of man, and so frequently are we in want of present pleasure or employment, that we are forced to have recourse every moment to the past and future for supplemental satisfactions, and relieve the vacuities of our being, by recollection of former passages, or anticipation of events to come.

I cannot but consider this necessity of searching on every side for matter on which the attention may be employed, as a strong proof of the superior and celestial nature of the soul of man. We have no reason to believe that other creatures have higher faculties, or more extensive capacities, than the preservation of themselves, or their species, requires; they seem always to be fully employed, or to be completely at ease without employment, to feel few intellectual miseries or pleasures, and to have no exuberance of understanding to lay out upon curiosity or caprice, but to have their minds exactly adapted to their bodies, with few other ideas than such as corporal pain or pleasure impress upon them.

Of memory, which makes so large a part of the excellence of the human soul, and which has so much influence upon all its other powers, but a small portion has been allotted to the animal world. We do not find the grief, with which the dams lament the loss of their young, proportionate to the tenderness with which they caress, the assiduity with which they feed, or the vehemence with which they defend them. Their regard for their offspring, when it is before their eyes, is not, in appearance, less than that of a human parent; but when it is taken away, it is very soon forgotten, and, after a short absence, if brought again, wholly disregarded.

That they have very little remembrance of any thing once out of the reach of their senses, and scarce any power of comparing the present with the past, and regulating their conclusions from experience, may be gathered from this, that their intellects are produced in their full perfection. The sparrow that was hatched last spring makes her first nest the ensuing season, of the same materials, and with the same art, as in any following year; and the hen conducts and shelters her first brood of chickens with all the prudence that she ever attains.

It has been asked by men who love to perplex any thing that is plain to common understandings, how reason differs from instinct; and Prior has with no great propriety made Solomon himself declare, that, to distinguish them is *the fool's ignorance, and the pedant's pride.*[2] To give an accurate answer to a question, of which the terms are not compleatly understood, is impossible; we do not know in what either reason or instinct consist, and therefore cannot tell with exactness how they differ; but surely he that contemplates a ship and a bird's nest, will not be long without finding out, that the idea of the one was impressed at once, and continued through all the progressive descents of the species, without variation or improvement; and that the other is the result of experiments compared with experiments, has grown, by accumulated observation, from less to greater excellence, and exhibits the collective knowledge of different ages, and various professions.

Memory is the purveyor of reason, the power which places those images before the mind upon which the judgment is to be exercised, and which treasures up the determinations that are once passed, as the rules of future action, or grounds of subsequent conclusions.

It is, indeed, the faculty of remembrance, which may be said to place us in the class of moral agents. If we were to act only in consequence of some immediate impulse, and receive no direction from internal motives of choice, we should be pushed forward by an invincible fatality, without power or reason for the most part to prefer one thing to another, because we could make no comparison but of objects which might both happen to be present.

We owe to memory not only the increase of our knowledge, and our progress in rational enquiries, but many other intellectual pleasures. Indeed, almost all that we can be said to enjoy is past or future; the present is in perpetual motion, leaves us as soon as it arrives, ceases to be present before its presence is well perceived, and is only known to have existed by the effects which it leaves behind. The greatest part of our ideas arises, therefore, from the view before or behind us, and we are happy or miserable, according as we are affected by the survey of our life, or our prospect of future existence.

With regard to futurity, when events are at such a distance from us, that we cannot take the whole concatenation into our view, we have generally power enough over our imagination to turn it upon pleasing scenes, and can promise ourselves riches, honours, and delights, without intermingling those vexations and anxieties, with which all human enjoyments are polluted. If fear breaks in on one side, and alarms us with dangers and disappointments, we can call in hope on the other, to solace us with rewards, and escapes, and victories; so that we are seldom without means of palliating remote evils, and can generally sooth ourselves to tranquillity, whenever any troublesome presage happens to attack us.

It is therefore, I believe, much more common for the solitary and thoughtful, to amuse themselves with schemes of the future, than reviews of the past. For the future is pliant and ductile, and will be easily moulded by a strong fancy into any form. But the images which memory presents are of a stubborn and untractable nature, the objects of remembrance have already existed, and left their signature behind them impressed upon the mind, so as to defy all attempts of rasure,[3] or of change.

As the satisfactions, therefore, arising from memory are less arbitrary, they are more solid, and are, indeed, the only joys which we can call our own. Whatever we have once reposited, as Dryden expresses it, *in the sacred treasure of the past,*[4] is out of the reach of accident, or violence, nor can be lost either by our own weakness, or another's malice:

> ———— *Non tamen irritum*
> *Quodcunque retro est efficiet, neque*
> *Diffinget, infectumque reddet,*
> *Quod fugiens semel hora vexit.*[5]

> Be fair or foul or rain or shine,
> The joys I have possess'd in spite of fate are mine.
> Not heav'n itself upon the past has pow'r,
> But what has been has been, and I have had my hour.
>   DRYDEN.

There is certainly no greater happiness, than to be able to look back on a life usefully and virtuously employed, to trace our own progress in existence, by such tokens as excite neither shame nor sorrow. Life, in which nothing has been done or suffered to distinguish one day from another, is to him that has passed it, as if it had never been, except that he is conscious how ill he has husbanded the great deposit of his Creator. Life, made memorable by crimes, and diversified thro' its several periods by wickedness, is indeed easily reviewed, but reviewed only with horror and remorse.

The great consideration which ought to influence us in the use of the present moment, is to arise from the effect, which, as well or ill applied, it must have upon the time to come; for though its actual existence be inconceivably short, yet its effects are unlimited, and there is not the smallest point of time but may extend its consequences, either to our hurt or our advantage, through all eternity, and give us reason to remember it for ever, with anguish or exultation.

The time of life, in which memory seems particularly to claim predominance over the other faculties of the mind, is our declining age. It has been remarked by former writers, that old men are generally narrative, and fall easily into recitals of past transactions, and accounts of persons known to them in their youth. When we approach the verge of the grave it is more eminently true;

> *Vitæ summa brevis spem nos vetat inchoare longam.*[6]

> Life's span forbids thee to extend thy cares,
>   And stretch thy hopes beyond thy years.

CREECH.

We have no longer any possibility of great vicissitudes in our favour; the changes which are to happen in the world will come too late for our accommodation; and those who have no hope before them, and to whom their present state is painful and irksome, must of necessity turn their thoughts back to try what retrospect will afford. It ought, therefore, to be the care of those who wish to pass the last hours with comfort, to lay up such a treasure of pleasing ideas, as shall support the expences of that time, which is to depend wholly upon the fund already acquired.

> —— *Petite hinc juvenesque senesque*
> *Finem animo certum, miserisque viatica canis.*[7]

> Seek here, ye young, the anchor of your mind;
>   Here, suff'ring age, a bless'd provision find.

ELPHINSTON.

In youth, however unhappy, we solace ourselves with the hope of better fortune, and, however vicious, appease our consciences with intentions of repentance; but the time comes at last, in which life has no more to promise, in which happiness can be drawn only from recollection, and virtue will be all that we can recollect with pleasure.

No. 45. Tuesday, 21 August 1750.

Ἥπερ μεγίστη γίγνεται σωτηρία,
Ὅταν γύνη πρὸς ἄνδρα μὴ διχοστατῇ,
Νῦν δ' ἐχθρὰ πάντα.

EURIP.[1]

This is the chief felicity of life,
That concord smile on the connubial bed;
But now 'tis hatred all ——————

To the RAMBLER.

SIR,

Though, in the dissertations[2] which you have given us on marriage, very just cautions are laid down against the common causes of infelicity, and the necessity of having, in that important choice, the first regard to virtue is carefully inculcated; yet I cannot think the subject so much exhausted, but that a little reflection would present to the mind many questions in the discussion of which great numbers are interested, and many precepts which deserve to be more particularly and forcibly impressed.

You seem, like most of the writers that have gone before you, to have allowed, as an uncontested principle, that *Marriage is generally unhappy*: but I know not whether a man who professes to think for himself, and concludes from his own observations, does not depart from his character when he follows the crowd thus implicitly, and receives maxims without recalling them to a new examination, especially when they comprise so wide a circuit of life, and include such variety of circumstances. As I have an equal right with others to give my opinion of the objects about me, and a better title to determine concerning that state which I have tried, than many who talk of it without experience, I am unwilling to be restrained by mere authority from advancing what, I believe, an accurate view of the world will confirm, that marriage is not commonly unhappy, otherwise than as life is unhappy; and that most of those who complain of connubial miseries, have as much satisfaction as their nature would have admitted, or their conduct procured in any other condition.

It is, indeed, common to hear both sexes repine at their change, relate the happiness of their earlier years, blame the folly and rashness of their own choice, and warn those whom they see coming into the world against the same precipitance and infatuation. But it is to be remembred, that the days which they so much wish to call back, are the days not only of celibacy but of youth, the days of novelty and improvement, of ardour and of hope, of health and vigour of body, of gayety and lightness of heart. It is not easy to surround life with any circumstances in which youth will not be delightful; and I am afraid that whether married or unmarried, we shall find the vesture of terrestrial existence more heavy and cumbrous, the longer it is worn.

That they censure themselves for the indiscretion of their choice, is not a sufficient proof that they have chosen ill, since we see the same discontent at every other part of life which we cannot change. Converse with almost any man, grown old in a profession, and you will find him regretting that he did not enter into some different course, to which he too late finds his genius better adapted, or in which he discovers that wealth and honour are more easily attained. "The merchant," says Horace, "envies the soldier, and the soldier recounts the felicity of the merchant; the lawyer when his clients harrass him, calls out for the quiet of the countryman; and the countryman, when business calls him to town, proclaims that there is no happiness but amidst opulence and crouds."[3] Every man recounts the inconveniencies of his own station, and thinks those of any other less, because he has not felt them. Thus the married praise the ease and freedom of a single state, and the single fly to marriage from the weariness of solitude. From all our observations we may collect with certainty, that misery is the lot of man, but cannot discover in what particular condition it will find most alleviations; or whether all external appendages are not, as we use them, the causes either of good or ill.

Whoever feels great pain naturally hopes for ease from change of posture; he changes it, and finds himself equally tormented:

and of the same kind are the expedients by which we endeavour to obviate or elude those uneasinesses, to which mortality will always be subject. It is not likely that the married state is eminently miserable, since we see such numbers, whom the death of their partners has set free from it, entering it again.

Wives and husbands are, indeed, incessantly complaining of each other; and there would be reason for imagining that almost every house was infested with perverseness or oppression beyond human sufferance, did we not know upon how small occasions some minds burst out into lamentations and re-proaches, and how naturally every animal revenges his pain upon those who happen to be near, without any nice examin-ation of its cause. We are always willing to fancy ourselves within a little of happiness, and when, with repeated efforts, we cannot reach it, persuade ourselves that it is intercepted by an ill-paired mate, since, if we could find any other obstacle, it would be our own fault that it was not removed.

Anatomists have often remarked, that though our diseases are sufficiently numerous and severe, yet when we enquire into the structure of the body, the tenderness of some parts, the minuteness of others, and the immense multiplicity of animal functions that must concur to the healthful and vigorous exercise of all our powers, there appears reason to wonder rather that we are preserved so long, than that we perish so soon, and that our frame subsists for a single day, or hour, without disorder, rather than that it should be broken or obstructed by violence of accidents, or length of time.

The same reflection arises in my mind, upon observation of the manner in which marriage is frequently contracted. When I see the avaricious and crafty taking companions to their tables, and their beds, without any enquiry, but after farms and money; or the giddy and thoughtless uniting themselves for life to those whom they have only seen by the light of tapers at a ball; when parents make articles for their children, without enquiring after their consent; when some marry for heirs to disappoint their brothers, and others throw themselves into the arms of those whom they do not love, because they have found themselves rejected where they were more solicitous to please; when some marry because their servants cheat them, some because they squander their own money, some because their houses are pestered with company, some because they will live like other people, and some only because they are sick of themselves, I am not so much inclined to wonder that marriage is sometimes unhappy, as that it appears so little loaded with calamity; and cannot but conclude that society has something in itself eminently agreeable to human nature, when I find its pleasures so great that even the ill choice of a companion can hardly over-balance them.

By the ancient custom of the Muscovites the men and women never saw each other till they were joined beyond the power of parting. It may be suspected that by this method many unsuitable matches were produced, and many tempers associated that were not qualified to give pleasure to each other. Yet, perhaps, among a people so little delicate, where the paucity of gratifications, and the uniformity of life gave no opportunity for imagination to interpose its objections, there was not much danger of capricious dislike, and while they felt neither cold nor hunger they might live quietly together, without any thought of the defects of one another.

Amongst us, whom knowledge has made nice, and affluence wanton, there are, indeed, more cautions requisite to secure tranquillity; and yet if we observe the manner in which those converse, who have singled out each other for marriage, we shall, perhaps, not think that the Russians lost much by their restraint. For the whole endeavour of both parties, during the time of courtship, is to hinder themselves from being known, and to disguise their natural temper, and real desires, in hypocritical imitation, studied compliance, and continued affectation. From the time that their love is avowed, neither sees the other but in a mask, and the cheat is managed often on both sides with so much art, and discovered afterwards with so much abruptness, that each has reason to suspect that some transformation has happened on the wedding-night, and that by a strange imposture one has been courted, and another married.

I desire you, therefore, Mr. RAMBLER, to question all who shall hereafter come to you with matrimonial complaints, concerning their behaviour in the time of courtship, and inform them that they are neither to wonder nor repine, when a contract begun with fraud has ended in disappointment.

I AM, &c.

No. 47. Tuesday, 28 August 1750.

Quanquam his solatiis acquiescam, debilitor & frangor eadem illa humanitate quæ me, ut hoc ipsum permitterem, induxit, non ideo tamen velim durior fieri: nec ignoro alios hujusmodi casus nihil amplius vocare quam damnum; eoque sibi magnos homines & sapientes videri. Qui an magni sapientesque sint, nescio: homines non sunt. Hominis est enim affici dolore, sentire: resistere tamen, & solatia admittere; non solatiis non egere.

PLIN.[1]

These proceedings have afforded me some comfort in my distress; notwithstanding which, I am still dispirited, and unhinged by the same motives of humanity that induced me to grant such indulgences. However, I by no means wish to become less susceptible of tenderness. I know these kind of misfortunes would be estimated by other persons only as common losses, and from such sensations they would conceive themselves great and wise men. I shall not determine either their greatness or their wisdom; but I am certain they have no humanity. It is the part of a man to be affected with grief; to feel sorrow, at the same time, that he is to resist it, and to admit of comfort.

Earl of ORRERY.

Of the passions with which the mind of man is agitated, it may be observed, that they naturally hasten towards their own extinction by inciting and quickening the attainment of their objects. Thus fear urges our flight, and desire animates our progress; and if there are some which perhaps may be indulged till they out-grow the good appropriated to their satisfaction, as is frequently observed of avarice and ambition, yet their immediate tendency is to some means of happiness really existing, and generally within the prospect. The miser always imagines that there is a certain sum that will fill his heart to the brim; and every ambitious man, like king Pyrrhus, has an acquisition in his thoughts that is to terminate his labours, after which he shall pass the rest of his life in ease or gayety, in repose or devotion.[2]

Sorrow is perhaps the only affection of the breast that can be excepted from this general remark, and it therefore deserves the particular attention of those who have assumed the arduous province of preserving the balance of the mental constitution. The other passions are diseases indeed, but they necessarily direct us to their proper cure. A man at once feels the pain, and knows the medicine, to which he is carried with greater haste as the evil which requires it is more excruciating, and cures himself by unerring instinct, as the wounded stags of Crete are related by Ælian to have recourse to vulnerary herbs.[3] But for sorrow there is no remedy provided by nature; it is often occasioned by accidents irreparable, and dwells upon objects that have lost or changed their existence; it requires what it cannot hope, that the laws of the universe should be repealed; that the dead should return, or the past should be recalled.

Sorrow is not that regret for negligence or error which may animate us to future care or activity, or that repentance of crimes for which, however irrevocable, our Creator has promised to accept it as an attonement; the pain which arises from these causes has very salutary effects, and is every hour extenuating itself by the reparation of those miscarriages that produce it. Sorrow is properly that state of the mind in which our desires are fixed upon the past, without looking forward to the future, an incessant wish that something were otherwise than it has been, a tormenting and harrassing want of some enjoyment or possession which we have lost, and which no endeavours can possibly regain. Into such anguish many have sunk upon some sudden diminution of their fortune, an unexpected blast of their reputation, or the loss of children or of friends. They have suffered all sensibility of pleasure to be destroyed by a single blow, have given up for ever the hopes of substituting any other object in the room of that which they lament, resigned their lives to gloom and despondency, and worn themselves out in unavailing misery.

Yet so much is this passion the natural consequence of tenderness and endearment, that, however painful and however useless, it is justly reproachful not to feel it on some occasions; and so widely and constantly has it always prevailed, that the laws of some nations, and the customs of others, have limited a time for the external appearances of grief caused by the dissolution of close alliances, and the breach of domestic union.

It seems determined, by the general suffrage of mankind, that sorrow is to a certain point laudable, as the offspring of love, or at least pardonable as the effect of weakness; but that it ought not to be suffered to increase by indulgence, but must give way, after a stated time, to social duties, and the common avocations of life. It is at first unavoidable, and therefore must be allowed, whether with or without our choice; it may afterwards be admitted as a decent and affectionate testimony of kindness and esteem; something will be extorted by nature, and something may be given to the world. But all beyond the bursts of passion, or the forms of solemnity, is not only useless, but culpable; for we have no right to sacrifice, to the vain longings of affection, that time which providence allows us for the task of our station.

Yet it too often happens that sorrow, thus lawfully entering, gains such a firm possession of the mind, that it is not afterwards to be ejected; the mournful ideas, first violently impressed, and afterwards willingly received, so much engross the attention, as to predominate in every thought, to darken gayety, and perplex ratiocination. An habitual sadness seizes upon the soul, and the faculties are chained to a single object, which can never be contemplated but with hopeless uneasiness.

From this state of dejection it is very difficult to rise to chearfulness and alacrity, and therefore many who have laid down rules of intellectual health, think preservatives easier than remedies, and teach us not to trust ourselves with favourite enjoyments, not to indulge the luxury of fondness, but to keep our minds always suspended in such indifference, that we may change the objects about us without emotion.

An exact compliance with this rule might, perhaps, contribute to tranquillity, but surely it would never produce happiness. He that regards none so much as to be afraid of losing them, must live for ever without the gentle pleasures of sympathy and confidence; he must feel no melting fondness, no warmth of benevolence, nor any of those honest joys which nature annexes to the power of pleasing. And as no man can justly claim more tenderness than he pays, he must forfeit his share in that officious and watchful kindness which love only can dictate, and those lenient endearments by which love only can soften life. He may justly be overlooked and neglected by such as have more warmth in their heart; for who would be the friend of him, whom, with whatever assiduity he may be courted, and with whatever services obliged, his principles will not suffer to make equal returns, and who, when you have exhausted all the instances of good will, can only be prevailed on not to be an enemy?

An attempt to preserve life in a state of neutrality and indifference, is unreasonable and vain. If by excluding joy we could shut out grief, the scheme would deserve very serious attention; but since, however we may debar ourselves from happiness, misery will find its way at many inlets, and the assaults of pain will force our regard, though we may withhold it from the invitations of pleasure, we may surely endeavour to raise life above the middle point of apathy at one time, since it will necessarily sink below it at another.

But though it cannot be reasonable not to gain happiness for fear of losing it, yet it must be confessed, that in proportion to the pleasure of possession, will be for some time our sorrow for the loss; it is therefore the province of the moralist to enquire whether such pains may not quickly give way to mitigation. Some have thought, that the most certain way to clear the heart from its embarrassment is to drag it by force into scenes of merriment. Others imagine, that such a transition is too violent, and recommend rather to sooth it into tranquillity, by making it acquainted with miseries more dreadful and afflictive, and diverting to the calamities of others the regard which we are inclined to fix too closely upon our own misfortunes.

It may be doubted whether either of those remedies will be sufficiently powerful. The efficacy of mirth it is not always easy to try, and the indulgence of melancholy may be suspected to be one of those medicines, which will destroy, if it happens not to cure.

The safe and general antidote against sorrow, is employment. It is commonly observed, that among soldiers and seamen, though there is much kindness, there is little grief; they see their friend fall without any of that lamentation which is indulged in security and idleness, because they have no leisure to spare from the care of themselves; and whoever shall keep his thoughts equally busy, will find himself equally unaffected with irretrievable losses.

Time is observed generally to wear out sorrow, and its effects might doubtless be accelerated by quickening the succession, and enlarging the variety of objects.

> *Si tempore longo*
> *Leniri poterit luctus, tu sperne morari,*
> *Qui sapiet sibi tempus erit.* ——
>
> GROTIUS.[4]

> 'Tis long e'er time can mitigate your grief;
> To wisdom fly, she quickly brings relief.
>
> F. LEWIS.

Sorrow is a kind of rust of the soul, which every new idea contributes in its passage to scour away. It is the putrefaction of stagnant life, and is remedied by exercise and motion.

No. 49. Tuesday, 4 September 1750.

Non omnis moriar, multaque pars mei
Vitabit Libitinam, usque ego posterâ
Crescam laude recens.

HOR.[1]

Whole *Horace* shall not die; his songs shall save
The greatest portion from the greedy grave.

CREECH.

The first motives of human actions are those appetites which providence has given to man, in common with the rest of the inhabitants of the earth. Immediately after our birth, thirst and hunger incline us to the breast, which we draw by instinct, like other young creatures, and, when we are satisfied, we express our uneasiness by importunate and incessant cries, till we have obtained a place or posture proper for repose.

The next call that rouses us from a state of inactivity, is that of our passions; we quickly begin to be sensible of hope and fear, love and hatred, desire and aversion; these arising from the power of comparison and reflexion, extend their range wider, as our reason strengthens, and our knowledge enlarges. At first we have no thought of pain, but when we actually feel it; we afterwards begin to fear it, yet not before it approaches us very nearly; but by degrees we discover it at a greater distance, and find it lurking in remote consequences. Our terror in time improves into caution, and we learn to look round with vigilance and solicitude, to stop all the avenues at which misery can enter, and to perform or endure many things in themselves toilsome and unpleasing, because we know by reason, or by experience, that our labour will be overbalanced by the reward, that it will either procure some positive good, or avert some evil greater than itself.

But as the soul advances to a fuller exercise of its powers, the animal appetites, and the passions immediately arising from them, are not sufficient to find it employment; the wants of nature are soon supplied, the fear of their return is easily pre-cluded, and something more is necessary to relieve the long intervals of inactivity, and to give those faculties, which cannot lie wholly quiescent, some particular direction. For this reason, new desires, and artificial passions are by degrees produced; and, from having wishes only in consequence of our wants, we begin to feel wants in consequence of our wishes; we persuade ourselves to set a value upon things which are of no use, but because we have agreed to value them; things which can neither satisfy hunger, nor mitigate pain, nor secure us from any real calamity, and which, therefore, we find of no esteem among those nations whose artless and barbarous manners keep them always anxious for the necessaries of life.

This is the original of avarice, vanity, ambition, and generally of all those desires which arise from the comparison of our condition with that of others. He that thinks himself poor, because his neighbour is richer; he that, like Caesar, would rather be the first man of a village, than the second in the capital of the world,[2] has apparently kindled in himself desires which he never received from nature, and acts upon principles established only by the authority of custom.

Of those adscititious[3] passions, some, as avarice and envy, are universally condemned; some, as friendship and curiosity, generally praised; but there are others about which the suffrages of the wise are divided, and of which it is doubted, whether they tend most to promote the happiness, or increase the miseries of mankind.

Of this ambiguous and disputable kind is the love of fame, a desire of filling the minds of others with admiration, and of being celebrated by generations to come with praises which we shall not hear. This ardour has been considered by some, as nothing better than splendid madness, as a flame kindled by pride, and fanned by folly; for what, say they, can be more remote from wisdom, than to direct all our actions by the hope of that which is not to exist till we ourselves are in the grave? To pant after that which can never be possessed, and of which the value thus wildly put upon it, arises from this particular condition, that, during life, it is not to be obtained? To gain the favour, and hear the applauses of our contemporaries, is indeed equally desirable with any other prerogative of superiority, because fame may be of use to smooth the paths of life, to terrify opposition, and fortify tranquillity; but to what end shall we be the darlings of mankind, when we can no longer receive any benefits from their favour? It is more reasonable to wish for reputation, while it may yet be enjoyed, as Anacreon calls upon his companions to give him for present use the wine and garlands which they purpose to bestow upon his tomb.[4]

The advocates for the love of fame allege in its vindication, that it is a passion natural and universal; a flame lighted by heaven, and always burning with greatest vigour in the most enlarged and elevated minds. That the desire of being praised by posterity implies a resolution to deserve their praises, and that the folly charged upon it, is only a noble and disinterested generosity, which is not felt, and therefore not understood by those who have been always accustomed to refer every thing to themselves, and whose selfishness has contracted their understandings. That the soul of man, formed for eternal life, naturally springs forward beyond the limits of corporeal existence, and rejoices to consider herself as co-operating with future ages, and as co-extended with endless duration. That the reproach urged with so much petulance, the reproach of labouring for what cannot be enjoyed, is founded on an opinion which may with great probability be doubted; for since we suppose the powers of the soul to be enlarged by its separation, why should we conclude that its knowledge of sublunary transactions is contracted or extinguished?

Upon an attentive and impartial review of the argument, it will appear that the love of fame is to be regulated, rather than extinguished; and that men should be taught not to be wholly careless about their memory, but to endeavour that they may be remembered chiefly for their virtues, since no other reputation will be able to transmit any pleasure beyond the grave.

It is evident that fame, considered merely as the immortality of a name, is not less likely to be the reward of bad actions than of good; he therefore has no certain principle for the regulation of his conduct, whose single aim is not to be forgotten. And history will inform us, that this blind and undistinguishing appetite of renown has always been uncertain in its effects, and directed by accident or opportunity, indifferently to the benefit or devastation of the world. When Themistocles complained that the trophies of Miltiades hindered him from sleep, he was animated by them to perform the same services in the same cause.[5] But Cæsar, when he wept at the sight of Alexander's picture, having no honest opportunities of action, let his ambition break out to the ruin of his country.[6]

If, therefore, the love of fame is so far indulged by the mind as to become independent and predominant, it is dangerous and irregular; but it may be usefully employed as an inferior and secondary motive, and will serve sometimes to revive our activity, when we begin to languish and lose sight of that more certain, more valuable, and more durable reward, which ought always to be our first hope and our last. But it must be strongly impressed upon our minds, that virtue is not to be persued as one of the means to fame, but fame to be accepted as the only recompence which mortals can bestow on virtue; to be accepted with complacence, but not sought with eagerness. Simply to be remembered is no advantage; it is a privilege which satire as well as panegyric can confer, and is not more enjoyed by Titus or Constantine, than by Timocreon of Rhodes, of whom we only know from his epitaph, *that he had eaten many a meal, drank many a flaggon, and uttered many a reproach.*

Πολλὰ φαγὼν, καὶ πολλὰ πιὼν, καὶ πολλὰ κακ' εἰπὼν
Ἀνθρώπους, κεῖμαι Τιμοκρέων Ῥόδιος.[7]

The true satisfaction which is to be drawn from the consciousness that we shall share the attention of future times, must arise from the hope, that, with our name, our virtues will be propagated; and that those whom we cannot benefit in our lives, may receive instruction from our examples, and incitement from our renown.

No. 60. Saturday, 13 October 1750.

— *Quid sit pulchrum, quid turpe, quid utile, quid non,*
Plenius et melius Chrysippo et Crantore dicit.

HOR.[1]

Whose works the beautiful and base contain;
Of vice and virtue more instructive rules,
Than all the sober sages of the schools.

FRANCIS.

All joy or sorrow for the happiness or calamities of others is produced by an act of the imagination, that realises the event however fictitious, or approximates it however remote, by placing us, for a time, in the condition of him whose fortune we contemplate; so that we feel, while the deception lasts, whatever motions would be excited by the same good or evil happening to ourselves.

Our passions are therefore more strongly moved, in proportion as we can more readily adopt the pains or pleasure proposed to our minds, by recognising them as once our own, or considering them as naturally incident to our state of life. It is not easy for the most artful writer to give us an interest in happiness or misery, which we think ourselves never likely to feel, and with which we have never yet been made acquainted. Histories of the downfal of kingdoms, and revolutions of empires, are read with great tranquillity; the imperial tragedy pleases common auditors only by its pomp of ornament, and grandeur of ideas; and the man whose faculties have been engrossed by business, and whose heart never fluttered but at the rise or fall of stocks, wonders how the attention can be seized, or the affections agitated by a tale of love.

Those parallel circumstances, and kindred images, to which we readily conform our minds, are, above all other writings, to be found in narratives of the lives of particular persons; and therefore no species of writing seems more worthy of cultivation than biography, since none can be more delightful or more useful, none can more certainly enchain the heart by irresistible interest, or more widely diffuse instruction to every diversity of condition.

The general and rapid narratives of history, which involve a thousand fortunes in the business of a day, and complicate innumerable incidents in one great transaction, afford few lessons applicable to private life, which derives its comforts and its wretchedness from the right or wrong management of things which nothing but their frequency makes considerable, *Parva, si non fiunt quotidie*, says Pliny,[2] and which can have no place in those relations which never descend below the consultation of senates, the motions of armies, and the schemes of conspirators.

I have often thought that there has rarely passed a life of which a judicious and faithful narrative would not be useful. For, not only every man has, in the mighty mass of the world, great numbers in the same condition with himself, to whom his mistakes and miscarriages, escapes and expedients, would be of immediate and apparent use; but there is such an uniformity in the state of man, considered apart from adventitious and separable decorations and disguises, that there is scarce any possibility of good or ill, but is common to human kind. A great part of the time of those who are placed at the greatest distance by fortune, or by temper, must unavoidably pass in the same manner; and though, when the claims of nature are satisfied, caprice, and vanity, and accident, begin to produce discriminations and peculiarities, yet the eye is not very heedful, or quick, which cannot discover the same causes still terminating their influence in the same effects, though sometimes accelerated, sometimes retarded, or perplexed by multiplied combinations. We are all prompted by the same motives, all deceived by the same fallacies, all animated by hope, obstructed by danger, entangled by desire, and seduced by pleasure.

It is frequently objected to relations of particular lives, that they are not distinguished by any striking or wonderful vicissitudes. The scholar who passed his life among his books, the merchant who conducted only his own affairs, the priest, whose sphere of action was not extended beyond that of his duty, are considered as no proper objects of publick regard, however they might have excelled in their several stations, whatever might have been their learning, integrity, and piety. But this notion arises from false measures of excellence and dignity, and must be eradicated by considering, that, in the esteem of uncorrupted reason, what is of most use is of most value.

It is, indeed, not improper to take honest advantages of prejudice, and to gain attention by a celebrated name; but the business of the biographer is often to pass slightly over those performances and incidents, which produce vulgar greatness, to lead the thoughts into domestick privacies, and display the minute details of daily life, where exterior appendages are cast aside, and men excel each other only by prudence and by virtue. The account of Thuanus is, with great propriety, said by its author to have been written, that it might lay open to posterity the private and familiar character of that man, *cujus ingenium et candorem ex ipsius scriptis sunt olim semper miraturi*,[3] whose candour and genius will to the end of time be by his writings preserved in admiration.

There are many invisible circumstances which, whether we read as enquirers after natural or moral knowledge, whether we intend to enlarge our science, or increase our virtue, are more important than publick occurrences. Thus Salust, the great master of nature, has not forgot, in his account of Catiline, to remark that *his walk was now quick, and again slow*,[4] as an indication of a mind revolving something with violent commotion. Thus the story of Melancthon affords a striking lecture on the value of time, by informing us, that when he made an appointment, he expected not only the hour, but the minute to be fixed, that the day might not run out in the idleness of suspense;[5] and all the plans and enterprizes of De Wit are now of less importance to the world, than that part of his personal character which represents him as *careful of his health, and negligent of his life*.[6]

But biography has often been allotted to writers who seem very little acquainted with the nature of their task, or very negligent about the performance. They rarely afford any other account than might be collected from publick papers, but imagine themselves writing a life when they exhibit a chronological series of actions or preferments; and so little regard the manners or behaviour of their heroes, that more knowledge may be gained of a man's real character, by a short conversation with one of his servants, than from a formal and studied narrative, begun with his pedigree, and ended with his funeral.

If now and then they condescend to inform the world of particular facts, they are not always so happy as to select the most important. I know not well what advantage posterity can receive from the only circumstance by which Tickell has distinguished Addison from the rest of mankind, *the irregularity of his pulse*:[7] nor can I think myself overpaid for the time spent in reading the life of Malherb, by being enabled to relate, after the learned biographer, that Malherb had two predominant opinions; one, that the looseness of a single woman might destroy all her boast of ancient descent; the other, that the French beggars made use very improperly and barbarously of the phrase *noble Gentleman,* because either word included the sense of both.[8]

There are, indeed, some natural reasons why these narratives are often written by such as were not likely to give much instruction or delight, and why most accounts of particular persons are barren and useless. If a life be delayed till interest and envy are at an end, we may hope for impartiality, but must expect little intelligence; for the incidents which give excellence to biography are of a volatile and evanescent kind, such as soon escape the memory, and are rarely transmitted by tradition. We know how few can portray a living acquaintance, except by his most prominent and observable particularities, and the grosser features of his mind; and it may be easily imagined how much of this little knowledge may be lost in imparting it, and how soon a succession of copies will lose all resemblance of the original.

If the biographer writes from personal knowledge, and makes haste to gratify the publick curiosity, there is danger lest his interest, his fear, his gratitude, or his tenderness, overpower his fidelity, and tempt him to conceal, if not to invent. There are many who think it an act of piety to hide the faults or failings of their friends, even when they can no longer suffer by their detection; we therefore see whole ranks of characters adorned with uniform panegyrick, and not to be known from one another, but by extrinsick and casual circumstances. "Let me remember, says Hale, when I find myself inclined to pity a criminal, that there is likewise a pity due to the country."[9] If we owe regard to the memory of the dead, there is yet more respect to be paid to knowledge, to virtue, and to truth.

No. 63. Tuesday, 23 October 1750.

—— *Habebat sæpe ducentos,*
Sæpe decem servos; modò reges atque tetrarchas,
Omnia magna loquens: modò, sit mihi mensa tripes, et
Concha salis puri, et toga, quæ defendere frigus,
Quamvis crassa, queat.

HOR.[1]

Now with two hundred slaves he crowds his train;
Now walks with ten. In high and haughty strain
At morn, of kings and governors he prates:
At night —— "A frugal table, O ye fates,
A little shell the sacred salt to hold,
And clothes, tho' coarse, to keep me from the cold."

FRANCIS.

It has been remarked, perhaps, by every writer, who has left behind him observations upon life, that no man is pleased with his present state, which proves equally unsatisfactory, says Horace, whether fallen upon by chance or chosen with deliberation;[2] we are always disgusted with some circumstance or other of our situation, and imagine the condition of others more abundant in blessings, or less exposed to calamities.

This universal discontent has been generally mentioned with great severity of censure, as unreasonable in itself, since of two, equally envious of each other, both cannot have the larger share of happiness, and as tending to darken life with unnecessary gloom, by withdrawing our minds from the contemplation and enjoyment of that happiness which our state affords us, and fixing our atten-

tion upon foreign objects, which we only behold to depress ourselves, and increase our misery by injurious comparisons.

When this opinion of the felicity of others predominates in
the heart, so as to excite resolutions of obtaining, at whatever
price, the condition to which such transcendent privileges are
supposed to be annexed; when it bursts into action, and produces fraud, violence, and injustice, it is to be persued with all
the rigour of legal punishments. But while operating only upon
the thoughts, it disturbs none but him who has happened to
admit it, and, however it may interrupt content, makes no attack
on piety or virtue, I cannot think it so far criminal or ridiculous,
but that it may deserve some pity, and admit some excuse.

That all are equally happy, or miserable, I suppose none
is sufficiently enthusiastical to maintain; because, though we
cannot judge of the condition of others, yet every man has found
frequent vicissitudes in his own state, and must therefore be
convinced that life is susceptible of more or less felicity. What
then shall forbid us to endeavour the alteration of that which is
capable of being improved, and to grasp at augmentations of
good, when we know it possible to be increased, and believe
that any particular change of situation will increase it?

If he that finds himself uneasy may reasonably make efforts
to rid himself from vexation, all mankind have a sufficient plea
for some degree of restlessness, and the fault seems to be little
more than too much temerity of conclusion, in favour of something not yet experienced, and too much readiness to believe,
that the misery which our own passions and appetites produce,
is brought upon us by accidental causes, and external efficients.

It is, indeed, frequently discovered by us, that we complained
too hastily of peculiar hardships, and imagined ourselves distinguished by embarrassments, in which other classes of men are
equally entangled. We often change a lighter for a greater evil,
and wish ourselves restored again to the state from which we
thought it desirable to be delivered. But this knowledge, though
it is easily gained by the trial, is not always attainable any other
way; and that error cannot justly be reproached, which reason
could not obviate, nor prudence avoid.

To take a view at once distinct and comprehensive of human

life, with all its intricacies of combination, and varieties of connexion, is beyond the power of mortal intelligences. Of the state with which practice has not acquainted us, we snatch a glimpse, we discern a point, and regulate the rest by passion, and by fancy. In this enquiry every favourite prejudice, every innate desire, is busy to deceive us. We are unhappy, at least less happy than our nature seems to admit; we necessarily desire the melioration of our lot; what we desire, we very reasonably seek, and what we seek we are naturally eager to believe that we have found. Our confidence is often disappointed, but our reason is not convinced, and there is no man who does not hope for something which he has not, though perhaps his wishes lie unactive, because he foresees the difficulty of attainment. As among the numerous students of Hermetick philosophy,[3] not one appears to have desisted from the task of transmutation, from conviction of its impossibility, but from weariness of toil, or impatience of delay, a broken body, or exhausted fortune.

Irresolution and mutability are often the faults of men, whose views are wide, and whose imagination is vigorous and excursive, because they cannot confine their thoughts within their own boundaries of action, but are continually ranging over all the scenes of human existence, and consequently, are often apt to conceive that they fall upon new regions of pleasure, and start new possibilities of happiness. Thus they are busied with a perpetual succession of schemes, and pass their lives in alternate elation and sorrow, for want of that calm and immoveable acquiescence in their condition, by which men of slower understandings are fixed for ever to a certain point, or led on in the plain beaten track, which their fathers, and grandsires, have trod before them.

Of two conditions of life equally inviting to the prospect, that will always have the disadvantage which we have already tried; because the evils which we have felt we cannot extenuate; and tho' we have, perhaps from nature, the power as well of aggravating the calamity which we fear, as of heightening the blessing we expect, yet in those meditations which we indulge by choice, and which are not forced upon the mind by necessity, we have always the art of fixing our regard upon the more pleasing images, and suffer hope to dispose the lights by which we look upon futurity.

The good and ill of different modes of life are sometimes so equally opposed, that perhaps no man ever yet made his choice between them upon a full conviction, and adequate knowledge; and therefore fluctuation of will is not more wonderful, when they are proposed to the election, than oscillations of a beam charged with equal weights. The mind no sooner imagines itself determined by some prevalent advantage, than some convenience of equal weight is discovered on the other side, and the resolutions which are suggested by the nicest examination, are often repented as soon as they are taken.

Eumenes, a young man of great abilities, inherited a large estate from a father, long eminent in conspicuous employments. His father, harrassed with competitions, and perplexed with multiplicity of business, recommended the quiet of a private station with so much force, that Eumenes for some years resisted every motion of ambitious wishes; but being once provoked by the sight of oppression, which he could not redress, he began to think it the duty of an honest man to enable himself to protect others, and gradually felt a desire of greatness, excited by a thousand projects of advantage to his country. His fortune placed him in the senate, his knowledge and eloquence advanced him at court, and he possessed that authority and influence which he had resolved to exert for the happiness of mankind.

He now became acquainted with greatness, and was in a short time convinced, that in proportion as the power of doing well is enlarged, the temptations to do ill are multiplied and enforced. He felt himself every moment in danger of being either seduced or driven from his honest purposes. Sometimes a friend was to be gratified, and sometimes a rival to be crushed, by means which his conscience could not approve. Sometimes he was forced to comply with the prejudices of the publick, and sometimes with the schemes of the ministry. He was by degrees wearied with perpetual struggles to unite policy and virtue, and went back to retirement as the shelter of innocence, persuaded that he could only hope to benefit mankind by a blameless example of private virtue. Here he spent some years in tranquillity and beneficence; but finding that corruption increased, and false opinions in government prevailed, he thought himself again summoned to posts of publick trust, from which new evidence of his own weakness again determined him to retire.

Thus men may be made inconstant by virtue and by vice, by too much or too little thought; yet inconstancy, however dignified by its motives, is always to be avoided, because life allows us but a small time for enquiry and experiment, and he that steadily endeavours at excellence, in whatever employment, will more benefit mankind than he that hesitates in choosing his part till he is called to the performance. The traveller that resolutely follows a rough and winding path, will sooner reach the end of his journey, than he that is always changing his direction, and wastes the hours of daylight in looking for smoother ground, and shorter passages.

No. 64. Saturday, 27 October 1750.

Idem velle, et idem nolle, ea demum firma amicitia est.
SALUST.[1]

To live in friendship, is to have the same desires and the same aversions.

When Socrates was building himself a house at Athens, being asked by one that observed the littleness of the design, why a man so eminent would not have an abode more suitable to his dignity? he replied, that he should think himself sufficiently accommodated, if he could see that narrow habitation filled with real friends.[2] Such was the opinion of this great master of human life, concerning the infrequency of such an union of minds as might deserve the name of friendship, that among the multitudes whom vanity or curiosity, civility or veneration, crouded about him, he did not expect, that very spacious apartments would be necessary to contain all that should regard him with sincere kindness, or adhere to him with steady fidelity.

So many qualities are indeed requisite to the possibility of friendship, and so many accidents must concur to its rise and its continuance, that the greatest part of mankind content themselves without it, and supply its place as they can, with interest and dependance.

Multitudes are unqualified for a constant and warm reciprocation of benevolence, as they are incapacitated for any other elevated excellence, by perpetual attention to their interest, and unresisting subjection to their passions. Long habits may superinduce inability to deny any desire, or repress by superior motives, the importunities of any immediate gratification, and an inveterate selfishness will imagine all advantages diminished in proportion as they are communicated.

But not only this hateful and confirmed corruption, but many varieties of disposition, not inconsistent with common degrees of virtue, may exclude friendship from the heart. Some ardent enough in their benevolence, and defective neither in officiousness, nor liberality, are mutable and uncertain, soon attracted by new objects, disgusted without offence, and alienated without enmity. Others are soft and flexible, easily influenced by reports or whispers, ready to catch alarms from every dubious circumstance, and to listen to every suspicion which envy and flattery shall suggest, to follow the opinion of every confident adviser, and move by the impulse of the last breath. Some are impatient of contradiction, more willing to go wrong by their own judgment, than to be indebted for a better or a safer way to the sagacity of another, inclined to consider counsel as insult, and enquiry as want of confidence, and to confer their regard on no other terms than unreserved submission, and implicit compliance. Some are dark and involved, equally careful to conceal good and bad purposes; and pleased with producing effects by invisible means, and shewing their design only in its execution. Others are universally communicative, alike open to every eye, and equally profuse of their own secrets and those of others, without the necessary vigilance of caution, or the honest arts of prudent integrity, ready to accuse without malice, and to betray without treachery. Any of these may be useful to the community, and pass through the world with the reputation of good purposes and uncorrupted morals, but they are unfit for close and tender intimacies. He cannot properly be chosen for a friend, whose kindness is exhaled by its own warmth, or frozen by the first blast of slander; he cannot be a useful counsellor, who will hear no opinion but his own; he will not much invite confidence whose principal maxim is to suspect; nor can the candour and frankness of that man be much esteemed, who spreads his arms to humankind, and makes every man, without distinction, a denizon of his bosom.

That friendship may be at once fond and lasting, there must not only be equal virtue on each part, but virtue of the same kind; not only the same end must be proposed, but the same means must be approved by both. We are often, by superficial accomplishments and accidental endearments, induced to love those whom we cannot esteem; we are sometimes, by great abilities and incontestable evidences of virtue, compelled to esteem those whom we cannot love. But friendship, compounded of esteem and love, derives from one its tenderness, and its permanence from the other; and therefore requires not only that its candidates should gain the judgement, but that they should attract the affections; that they should not only be firm in the day of distress, but gay in the hour of jollity; not only useful in exigences, but pleasing in familiar life; their presence should give chearfulness as well as courage, and dispel alike the gloom of fear and of melancholy.

To this mutual complacency is generally requisite an uniformity of opinions, at least of those active and conspicuous principles which discriminate parties in government, and sects in religion, and which every day operate more or less on the common business of life. For though great tenderness has, perhaps, been sometimes known to continue between men eminent in contrary factions; yet such friends are to be shewn rather as prodigies than examples, and it is no more proper to regulate our conduct by such instances, than to leap a precipice, because some have fallen from it and escaped with life.

It cannot but be extremely difficult to preserve private kindness in the midst of publick opposition, in which will necessarily be involved a thousand incidents, extending their influence to conversation and privacy. Men engaged, by moral or religious motives, in contrary parties, will generally look with different eyes upon every man, and decide almost every question upon different principles. When such occasions of dispute happen, to comply is to betray our cause, and to maintain friendship by ceasing to deserve it; to be silent, is to lose the happiness and dignity of independence, to live in perpetual constraint, and to desert, if not to betray: and who shall determine which of two friends shall yield, where neither believes himself mistaken, and both confess the importance of the question? What then remains but contradiction and debate? and from those what can be expected, but acrimony and vehemence, the insolence of triumph, the vexation of defeat, and, in time, a weariness of contest, and an extinction of benevolence? Exchange of endearments and intercourse of civility may continue, indeed, as boughs may for a while be verdant, when the root is wounded; but the poison of discord is infused, and though the countenance may preserve its smile, the heart is hardening and contracting.

That man will not be long agreeable, whom we see only in times of seriousness and severity; and therefore, to maintain the softness and serenity of benevolence, it is necessary that friends partake each others pleasures as well as cares, and be led to the same diversions by similitude of taste. This is, however, not to be considered as equally indispensable with conformity of principles, because any man may honestly, according to the precepts of Horace,[3] resign the gratifications of taste to the humour of another, and friendship may well deserve the sacrifice of pleasure, though not of conscience.

It was once confessed to me, by a painter, that no professor of his art ever loved another. This declaration is so far justified by the knowledge of life, as to damp the hopes of warm and constant friendship, between men whom their studies have made competitors, and whom every favourer and every censurer are hourly inciting against each other. The utmost expectation that experience can warrant, is, that they should forbear open hostilities and secret machinations, and when the whole fraternity is attacked, be able to unite against a common foe. Some however, though few, may perhaps be found, in whom emulation has not been able to overpower generosity, who are distinguished from lower beings by nobler motives than the love of fame, and can preserve the sacred flame of friendship from the gusts of pride, and the rubbish of interest.

Friendship is seldom lasting but between equals, or where the superiority on one side is reduced by some equivalent advantage on the other. Benefits which cannot be repaid, and obligations which cannot be discharged, are not commonly found to increase affection; they excite gratitude indeed, and heighten veneration, but commonly take away that easy freedom, and familiarity of intercourse, without which, though there may be fidelity, and zeal, and admiration, there cannot be friendship. Thus imperfect are all earthly blessings; the great effect of friendship is beneficence, yet by the first act of uncommon kindness it is endangered, like plants that bear their fruit and die. Yet this consideration ought not to restrain bounty, or repress compassion; for duty is to be preferred before convenience, and he that loses part of the pleasures of friendship by his generosity, gains in its place the gratulation of his conscience.

No. 70. Saturday, 17 November 1750.

——————— *Argentea proles,*
Auro deterior, fulvo pretiosior ære.
                                        OVID.[1]

Succeeding times a silver age behold,
Excelling brass, but more excell'd by gold.
                                        DRYDEN.

Hesiod, in his celebrated distribution of mankind, divides them into three orders of intellect. "The first place, says he, belongs to him that can by his own powers discern what is right and fit, and penetrate to the remoter motives of action. The second is claimed by him that is willing to hear instruction, and can perceive right and wrong when they are shewn him by another; but he that has neither acuteness nor docility, who can neither find the way by himself, nor will be led by others, is a wretch without use or value."[2]

If we survey the moral world, it will be found, that the same division may be made of men, with regard to their virtue. There are some whose principles are so firmly fixed, whose conviction is so constantly present to their minds, and who have raised in themselves such ardent wishes for the approbation of God, and the happiness with which he has promised to reward obedience and perseverance, that they rise above all other cares and considerations, and uniformly examine every action and desire, by comparing it with the divine commands. There are others in a kind of equipoise between good and ill; who are moved on one part by riches or pleasure, by the gratifications of passion, and the delights of sense; and, on the other, by laws of which they own the obligation, and rewards of which they believe the reality, and whom a very small addition of weight turns either way. The third class consists of beings immersed in pleasure, or abandoned to passion, without any desire of higher good, or any effort to extend their thoughts beyond immediate and gross satisfactions.

The second class is so much the most numerous, that it may be considered as comprising the whole body of mankind. Those of the last are not very many, and those of the first are very few; and neither the one nor the other fall much under the consideration of the moralist, whose precepts are intended chiefly for those who are endeavouring to go forward up the steeps of virtue, not for those who have already reached the summit, or those who are resolved to stay for ever in their present situation.

To a man not versed in the living world, but accustomed to judge only by speculative reason, it is scarcely credible that any one should be in this state of indifference, or stand undetermined and unengaged, ready to follow the first call to either side. It seems certain, that either a man must believe that virtue will make him happy, and resolve therefore to be virtuous, or think that he may be happy without virtue, and therefore cast off all care but for his present interest. It seems impossible that conviction should be on one side, and practice on the other; and that he who has seen the right way, should voluntarily shut his eyes, that he may quit it with more tranquillity. Yet all these absurdities are every hour to be found; the wisest and best men deviate from known and acknowledged duties, by inadvertency or surprise; and most are good no longer than while temptation is away, than while their passions are without excitements, and their opinions are free from the counteraction of any other motive.

Among the sentiments which almost every man changes as he advances into years, is the expectation of uniformity of character. He that without acquaintance with the power of desire, the cogency of distress, the complications of affairs, or the force of partial influence, has filled his mind with the excellence of virtue, and having never tried his resolution in any encounters with hope or fear, believes it able to stand firm whatever shall oppose it, will be always clamorous against the smallest failure, ready to exact the utmost punctualities of right, and to consider every man that fails in any part of his duty, as without conscience and without merit; unworthy of trust, or love, of pity, or regard; as an enemy whom all should join to drive out of society, as a pest which all should avoid, or as a weed which all should trample.

It is not but by experience, that we are taught the possibility of retaining some virtues, and rejecting others, or of being good or bad to a particular degree. For it is very easy to the solitary reasoner to prove that the same arguments by which the mind is fortified against one crime are of equal force against all, and the consequence very naturally follows, that he whom they fail to move on any occasion, has either never considered them, or has by some fallacy taught himself to evade their validity; and that, therefore, when a man is known to be guilty of one crime, no farther evidence is needful of his depravity and corruption.

Yet such is the state of all mortal virtue, that it is always uncertain and variable, sometimes extending to the whole compass of duty, and sometimes shrinking into a narrow space, and fortifying only a few avenues of the heart, while all the rest is left open to the incursions of appetite, or given up to the dominion of wickedness. Nothing therefore is more unjust than to judge of man by too short an acquaintance, and too slight inspection; for it often happens, that in the loose, and thoughtless, and dissipated, there is a secret radical worth, which may shoot out by proper cultivation; that the spark of heaven, though dimmed and obstructed, is yet not extinguished, but may by the breath of counsel and exhortation be kindled into flame.

To imagine that every one who is not completely good is irrecoverably abandoned, is to suppose that all are capable of the same degrees of excellence; it is indeed to exact, from all, that perfection which none ever can attain. And since the purest virtue is consistent with some vice, and the virtue of the greatest number with almost an equal proportion of contrary qualities, let none too hastily conclude that all goodness is lost, though it may for a time be clouded and overwhelmed; for most minds are the slaves of external circumstances, and conform to any hand that undertakes to mould them, roll down any torrent of custom[3] in which they happen to be caught, or bend to any importunity that bears hard against them.

It may be particularly observed of women, that they are for the most part good or bad, as they fall among those who practise vice or virtue; and that neither education nor reason gives them much security against the influence of example. Whether it be that they have less courage to stand against opposition, or that their desire of admiration makes them sacrifice their principles to the poor pleasure of worthless praise, it is certain, whatever be the cause, that female goodness seldom keeps its ground against laughter, flattery, or fashion.

For this reason, every one should consider himself as entrusted, not only with his own conduct, but with that of others; and as accountable, not only for the duties which he neglects, or the crimes that he commits, but for that negligence and irregularity which he may encourage or inculcate. Every man, in whatever station, has, or endeavours to have his followers, admirers, and imitators, and has therefore the influence of his example to watch with care; he ought to avoid not only crimes but the appearance of crimes, and not only to practise virtue, but to applaud, countenance, and support it. For it is possible that for want of attention we may teach others faults from which ourselves are free, or by a cowardly desertion of a cause which we ourselves approve, may pervert those who fix their eyes upon us, and having no rule of their own to guide their course, are easily misled by the aberrations of that example which they chuse for their direction.

No. 71. Tuesday, 20 November 1750.

Vivere quod propero pauper, nec inutilis annis
Da veniam, properat vivere nemo satis.

MART.[1]

True, sir, to live I haste, your pardon give,
For tell me, who makes haste enough to live?

F. LEWIS.

Many words and sentences are so frequently heard in the mouths of men, that a superficial observer is inclined to believe, that they must contain some primary principle, some great rule of action, which it is proper always to have present to the attention, and by which the use of every hour is to be adjusted. Yet, if we consider the conduct of those sententious philosophers, it will often be found, that they repeat these aphorisms, merely because they have somewhere heard them, because they have nothing else to say, or because they think veneration gained by such appearances of wisdom, but that no ideas are annexed to the words, and that, according to the old blunder of the followers of Aristotle, their souls are mere pipes or organs, which transmit sounds, but do not understand them.[2]

Of this kind is the well known and well attested position, *that life is short*, which may be heard among mankind by an attentive auditor, many times a day, but which never yet within my reach of observation left any impression upon the mind; and perhaps if my readers will turn their thoughts back upon their old friends, they will find it difficult to call a single man to remembrance, who appeared to know that life was short till he was about to lose it.

It is observable that *Horace*, in his account of the characters
of men, as they are diversified by the various influence of time,
remarks, that the old man is *dilator, spe longus*,[3] given to
procrastination, and inclined to extend his hopes to a great
distance. So far are we, generally, from thinking what we often
say of the shortness of life, that at the time when it is necessarily
shortest, we form projects which we delay to execute, indulge
such expectations as nothing but a long train of events can
gratify, and suffer those passions to gain upon us, which are
only excusable in the prime of life.

These reflections were lately excited in my mind, by an
evening's conversation with my friend *Prospero*, who at the age
of fifty-five, has bought an estate, and is now contriving to
dispose and cultivate it with uncommon elegance. His great
pleasure is to walk among stately trees, and lye musing in
the heat of noon under their shade; he is therefore maturely
considering how he shall dispose his walks and his groves, and
has at last determined to send for the best plans from *Italy*, and
forbear planting till the next season.

Thus is life trifled away in preparations to do what never can
be done, if it be left unattempted till all the requisites which
imagination can suggest are gathered together. Where our
design terminates only in our own satisfaction, the mistake is of
no great importance; for the pleasure of expecting enjoyment,
is often greater than that of obtaining it, and the completion of
almost every wish is found a disappointment; but when many
others are interested in an undertaking, when any design is
formed, in which the improvement or security of mankind is
involved, nothing is more unworthy either of wisdom or benevolence, than to delay it from time to time, or to forget how much
every day that passes over us, takes away from our power, and
how soon an idle purpose to do an action, sinks into a mournful
wish that it had once been done.

We are frequently importuned, by the bacchanalian writers,
to lay hold on the present hour, to catch the pleasures within
our reach, and remember that futurity is not at our command.

Τὸ ῥόδον ἀκμάζει βαιὸν χρόνον· ἢν δὲ παρέλθῃ,
Ζητῶν εὑρήσεις οὐ ῥόδον, ἀλλά βάτον.[4]

Soon fades the rose; once past the fragrant hour,
The loiterer finds a bramble for a flow'r.

But surely these exhortations may, with equal propriety, be applied to better purposes; it may be at least inculcated, that pleasures are more safely postponed than virtues, and that greater loss is suffered by missing an opportunity of doing good, than an hour of giddy frolick and noisy merriment.

When *Baxter*[5] had lost a thousand pounds, which he had laid up for the erection of a school, he used frequently to mention the misfortune, as an incitement to be charitable while God gives the power of bestowing, and considered himself as culpable in some degree for having left a good action in the hands of chance, and suffered his benevolence to be defeated for want of quickness and diligence.

It is lamented by *Hearne*,[6] the learned antiquary of *Oxford*, that this general forgetfulness of the fragility of life, has remarkably infected the students of monuments and records; as their employment consists first in collecting and afterwards in arranging or abstracting what libraries afford them, they ought to amass no more than they can digest; but when they have undertaken a work, they go on searching and transcribing, call for new supplies, when they are already overburdened, and at last leave their work unfinished. *It is*, says he, *the business of a good antiquary, as of a good man, to have mortality always before him.*

Thus, not only in the slumber of sloth, but in the dissipation of ill directed industry, is the shortness of life generally forgotten. As some men lose their hours in laziness, because they suppose, that there is time enough for the reparation of neglect; others busy themselves in providing that no length of life may want employment; and it often happens, that sluggishness and activity are equally surprised by the last summons, and perish not more differently from each other, than the fowl that received the shot in her flight, from her that is killed upon the bush.

Among the many improvements, made by the last centuries in human knowledge, may be numbered the exact calculations of the value of life;[7] but whatever may be their use in traffick, they seem very little to have advanced morality. They have hitherto been rather applied to the acquisition of money, than of wisdom; the computer refers none of his calculations to his own tenure, but persists, in contempt of probability, to foretel old age to himself, and believes that he is marked out to reach the utmost verge of human existence, and see thousands and ten thousands fall into the grave.[8]

So deeply is this fallacy rooted in the heart, and so strongly guarded by hope and fear against the approach of reason, that neither science nor experience can shake it, and we act as if life were without end, though we see and confess its uncertainty and shortness.

Divines have, with great strength and ardour, shewn the absurdity of delaying reformation and repentance; a degree of folly indeed, which sets eternity to hazard. It is the same weakness in proportion to the importance of the neglect, to transfer any care, which now claims our attention, to a future time; we subject ourselves to needless dangers from accidents which early diligence would have obviated, or perplex our minds by vain precautions, and make provision for the execution of designs, of which the opportunity once missed never will return.

As he that lives longest lives but a little while, every man may be certain that he has no time to waste. The duties of life are commensurate to its duration, and every day brings its task, which if neglected, is doubled on the morrow. But he that has already trifled away those months and years, in which he should have laboured, must remember that he has now only a part of that of which the whole is little; and that since the few moments remaining are to be considered as the last trust of heaven, not one is to be lost.

No. 72. Saturday, 24 November 1750.

Omnis Aristippum *decuit status, et color, et res,*
Sectantem majora fere; presentibus æquum.

HOR.[1]

Yet *Aristippus* ev'ry dress became;
In ev'ry various change of life the same:
And though he aim'd at things of higher kind,
Yet to the present held an equal mind.

FRANCIS.

To the RAMBLER.

SIR,

Those who exalt themselves into the chair of instruction, without enquiring whether any will submit to their authority, have not sufficiently considered how much of human life passes in little incidents, cursory conversation, slight business, and casual amusements; and therefore they have endeavoured only to inculcate the more awful virtues, without condescending to regard those petty qualities, which grow important only by their frequency, and which though they produce no single acts of heroism, nor astonish us by great events, yet are every moment exerting their influence upon us, and make the draught of life sweet or bitter by imperceptible instillations. They operate unseen and unregarded, as change of air makes us sick or healthy, though we breathe it without attention, and only know the particles that impregnate it by their salutary or malignant effects.

You have shewn yourself not ignorant of the value of those subaltern endowments, yet have hitherto neglected to recommend good humour to the world, though a little reflection will shew you that it is the *balm of being*,[2] the quality to which all that adorns or elevates mankind must owe its power of pleasing. Without good humour, learning and bravery can only confer that superiority which swells the heart of the lion in the desart, where he roars without reply, and ravages without resistance. Without good humour, virtue may awe by its dignity, and amaze by its brightness; but must always be viewed at a distance, and will scarcely gain a friend or attract an imitator.

Good humour may be defined a habit of being pleased; a constant and perennial softness of manner, easiness of approach, and suavity of disposition; like that which every man perceives in himself, when the first transports of new felicity have subsided, and his thoughts are only kept in motion by a slow succession of soft impulses. Good humour is a state between gayety and unconcern; the act or emanation of a mind at leisure to regard the gratification of another.

It is imagined by many, that whenever they aspire to please, they are required to be merry, and to shew the gladness of their souls by flights of pleasantry, and bursts of laughter. But, though these men may be for a time heard with applause and admiration, they seldom delight us long. We enjoy them a little, and then retire to easiness and good humour, as the eye gazes a while on eminences glittering with the sun, but soon turns aching away to verdure and to flowers.

Gayety is to good humour as animal perfumes to vegetable fragrance; the one overpowers weak spirits, and the other recreates and revives them. Gayety seldom fails to give some pain; the hearers either strain their faculties to accompany its towerings, or are left behind in envy and despair. Good humour boasts no faculties which every one does not believe in his own power, and pleases principally by not offending.

It is well known that the most certain way to give any man pleasure, is to persuade him that you receive pleasure from him, to encourage him to freedom and confidence, and to avoid any such appearance of superiority as may overbear and depress him. We see many that by this art only, spend their days in the midst of caresses, invitations, and civilities; and without any extraordinary qualities or attainments, are the universal favourites of both sexes, and certainly find a friend in every place. The darlings of the world will, indeed, be generally found such as excite neither jealousy nor fear, and are not considered as candidates for any eminent degree of reputation, but content themselves with common accomplishments, and endeavour rather to solicit kindness than to raise esteem; therefore in assemblies and places of resort it seldom fails to happen, that though at the entrance of some particular person every face brightens with gladness, and every hand is extended in salutation, yet if you persue him beyond the first exchange of civilities, you will find him of very small importance, and only welcome to the company, as one by whom all conceive themselves admired, and with whom any one is at liberty to amuse himself when he can find no other auditor or companion, as one with whom all are at ease, who will hear a jest without criticism, and a narrative without contradiction, who laughs with every wit, and yields to every disputer.

There are many whose vanity always inclines them to associate with those from whom they have no reason to fear mortification; and there are times in which the wise and the knowing are willing to receive praise without the labour of deserving it, in which the most elevated mind is willing to descend, and the most active to be at rest. All therefore are at some hour or another fond of companions whom they can entertain upon easy terms, and who will relieve them from solitude, without condemning them to vigilance and caution. We are most inclined to love when we have nothing to fear, and he that encourages us to please ourselves, will not be long without preference in our affection to those whose learning holds us at the distance of pupils, or whose wit calls all attention from us, and leaves us without importance and without regard.

It is remarked by prince *Henry*, when he sees Falstaff lying on the ground, that *he could have better spared a better man.*[3] He was well acquainted with the vices and follies of him whom he lamented, but while his conviction compelled him to do justice to superior qualities, his tenderness still broke out at the remembrance of *Falstaff*, of the chearful companion, the loud buffoon, with whom he had passed his time in all the luxury of idleness, who had gladded him with unenvied merriment, and whom he could at once enjoy and despise.

You may perhaps think this account of those who are distinguished for their good humour, not very consistent with the praises which I have bestowed upon it. But surely nothing can more evidently shew the value of this quality, than that it recommends those who are destitute of all other excellencies, and procures regard to the trifling, friendship to the worthless, and affection to the dull.

Good humour is indeed generally degraded by the characters in which it is found; for being considered as a cheap and vulgar quality, we find it often neglected by those that having excellencies of higher reputation and brighter splendor, perhaps imagine that they have some right to gratify themselves at the expense of others, and are to demand compliance, rather than to practise it. It is by some unfortunate mistake that almost all those who have any claim to esteem or love, press their pretensions with too little consideration of others. This mistake my own interest as well as my zeal for general happiness makes me desirous to rectify, for I have a friend, who because he knows his own fidelity, and usefulness, is never willing to sink into a companion. I have a wife whose beauty first subdued me, and whose wit confirmed her conquest, but whose beauty now serves no other purpose than to entitle her to tyranny, and whose wit is only used to justify perverseness.

Surely nothing can be more unreasonable than to lose the will to please, when we are conscious of the power, or show more cruelty than to chuse any kind of influence before that of kindness. He that regards the welfare of others, should make his virtue approachable, that it may be loved and copied; and he that considers the wants which every man feels, or will feel of external assistance, must rather wish to be surrounded by those that love him, than by those that admire his excellencies, or sollicit his favours; for admiration ceases with novelty, and interest gains its end and retires. A man whose great qualities want the ornament of superficial attractions, is like a naked mountain with mines of gold, which will be frequented only till the treasure is exhausted.

I am, &c.
PHILOMIDES.

No. 73. Tuesday, 27 November 1750.

Stulte quid heu votis frustra puerilibus optas
Quæ non ulla tulit, fertve, feretve dies.

OVID.[1]

Why thinks the fool with childish hope to see
What neither is, nor was, nor e'er shall be?

ELPHINSTON.

To the RAMBLER.

SIR,

If you feel any of that compassion, which you recommend to others, you will not disregard a case which I have reason from observation to believe very common, and which I know by experience to be very miserable. And though the querulous are seldom received with great ardour of kindness, I hope to escape the mortification of finding that my lamentations spread the contagion of impatience, and produce anger rather than tenderness. I write not merely to vent the swelling of my heart, but to enquire by what means I may recover my tranquillity; and shall endeavour at brevity in my narrative, having long known that complaint quickly tires, however elegant, or however just.

I was born in a remote county, of a family that boasts alliances with the greatest names in *English* history, and extends its claims of affinity to the *Tudors* and *Plantagenets*.[2] My ancestors, by little and little, wasted their patrimony, till my father had not enough left for the support of a family, without descending to the cultivation of his own grounds, being condemned to pay three sisters the fortunes allotted them by my grandfather, who is suspected to have made his will when he was incapable of adjusting properly the claims of his children, and who, perhaps without design, enriched his daughters by beggaring his son. My aunts being, at the death of their father, neither young nor beautiful, nor very eminent for softness of behaviour, were suffered to live unsolicited, and by accumulating the interest of their portions grew every day richer and prouder. My father pleased himself with foreseeing that the possessions of those ladies must revert at last to the hereditary estate, and, that his family might lose none of its dignity, resolved to keep me untainted with a lucrative employment; whenever therefore I discovered any inclination to the improvement of my condition, my mother never failed to put me in mind of my birth, and charged me to do nothing with which I might be reproached, when I should come to my aunts' estate.

In all the perplexities or vexations which want of money brought upon us, it was our constant practice to have recourse to futurity. If any of our neighbours surpassed us in appearance, we went home and contrived an equipage, with which the death of my aunts was to supply us. If any purse-proud upstart was deficient in respect, vengeance was referred to the time in which our estate was to be repaired. We registered every act of civility and rudeness, enquired the number of dishes at every feast, and minuted the furniture of every house, that we might, when the hour of affluence should come, be able to eclipse all their splendor, and surpass all their magnificence.

Upon plans of elegance and schemes of pleasure the day rose and set, and the year went round unregarded, while we were busied in laying out plantations on ground not yet our own, and deliberating whether the manor-house should be rebuilt or repaired. This was the amusement of our leisure, and the solace of our exigencies; we met together only to contrive how our approaching fortune should be enjoyed; for in this our conversation always ended, on whatever subject it began. We had none of the collateral interests, which diversify the life of others with joys and hopes, but had turned our whole attention on one event, which we could neither hasten nor retard, and had no other object of curiosity, than the health or sickness of my aunts, of which we were careful to procure very exact and early intelligence.

This visionary opulence for a while soothed our imagination, but afterwards fired our wishes, and exasperated our necessities, and my father could not always restrain himself from exclaiming, that *no creature had so many lives as a cat and an old maid*. At last upon the recovery of his sister from an ague, which she was supposed to have caught by sparing fire, he began to lose his stomach, and four months afterwards sunk into the grave.

My mother, who loved her husband, survived him but a little while, and left me the sole heir of their lands, their schemes, and their wishes. As I had not enlarged my conceptions either by books or conversation, I differed only from my father by the freshness of my cheeks, and the vigour of my step; and, like him, gave way to no thoughts but of enjoying the wealth which my aunts were hoarding.

At length the eldest fell ill. I paid the civilities and compliments which sickness requires with the utmost punctuality. I dreamed every night of escutcheons and white gloves,[3] and enquired every morning at an early hour, whether there were any news of my dear aunt. At last a messenger was sent to inform me that I must come to her without the delay of a moment. I went and heard her last advice, but opening her will found that she had left her fortune to her second sister.

I hung my head; the younger sister threatned to be married, and every thing was disappointment and discontent. I was in danger of losing irreparably one third of my hopes, and was condemned still to wait for the rest. Of part of my terror I was soon eased; for the youth, whom his relations would have compelled to marry the old lady, after innumerable stipulations, articles, and settlements, ran away with the daughter of his father's groom; and my aunt, upon this conviction of the perfidy of man, resolved never to listen more to amorous addresses.

Ten years longer I dragged the shackles of expectation, without ever suffering a day to pass, in which I did not compute how much my chance was improved of being rich tomorrow. At last the second lady died, after a short illness, which yet was long enough to afford her time for the disposal of her estate, which she gave to me after the death of her sister.

I was now relieved from part of my misery; a larger fortune, though not in my power, was certain and unalienable; nor was there now any danger, that I might at last be frustrated of my hopes by a fret of dotage, the flatteries of a chambermaid, the whispers of a tale-bearer, or the officiousness of a nurse. But my wealth was yet in reversion, my aunt was to be buried before I could emerge to grandeur and pleasure; and there were yet, according to my father's observation, nine lives between me and happiness.

I however lived on, without any clamours of discontent, and comforted myself with considering, that all are mortal, and they who are continually decaying, must at last be destroyed.

But let no man from this time suffer his felicity to depend on the death of his aunt. The good gentlewoman was very regular in her hours, and simple in her diet, and in walking or sitting still, waking or sleeping, had always in view the preservation of her health. She was subject to no disorder but hypochondriac dejection; by which, without intention, she encreased my miseries, for whenever the weather was cloudy, she would take her bed and send me notice that her time was come. I went with all the haste of eagerness, and sometimes received passionate injunctions to be kind to her maid, and directions how the last offices should be performed; but if before my arrival the sun happened to break out, or the wind to change, I met her at the door, or found her in the garden, bustling and vigilant, with all the tokens of long life.

Sometimes however she fell into distempers, and was thrice given over by the doctor, yet she found means of slipping through the gripe of death, and after having tortured me three months at each time with violent alternations of hope and fear, came out of her chamber without any other hurt than the loss of flesh, which in a few weeks she recovered by broths and jellies.

As most have sagacity sufficient to guess at the desires of an heir, it was the constant practice of those who were hoping at second hand, and endeavoured to secure my favour against the time when I should be rich, to pay their court, by informing me that my aunt began to droop, that she had lately a bad night, that she coughed feebly, and that she could never climb *May* hill; or at least, that the autumn would carry her off. Thus was I flattered in the winter with the piercing winds of *March*, and in summer, with the fogs of *September*. But she lived through spring and fall, and set heat and cold at defiance, till after near half a century, I buried her on the fourteenth of last June, aged ninety-three years, five months, and six days.

For two months after her death I was rich, and was pleased with that obsequiousness and reverence which wealth instantaneously procures. But this joy is now past, and I have returned again to my old habit of wishing. Being accustomed to give the future full power over my mind, and to start away from the scene before me to some expected enjoyment, I deliver up myself to the tyranny of every desire which fancy suggests, and long for a thousand things which I am unable to procure. Money has much less power, than is ascribed to it by those that want it. I had formed schemes which I cannot execute, I had supposed events which do not come to pass, and the rest of my life must pass in craving solicitude, unless you can find some remedy for a mind, corrupted with an inveterate disease of wishing, and unable to think on any thing but wants, which reason tells me will never be supplied.

I am, &c.
CUPIDUS.

No. 76. Saturday, 8 December 1750.

———— *Silvis ubi passim*
Palantes error certo de tramite pellit,
Ille sinistrorsum, hic dextrorsum abit, unus utrique
Error, sed variis illudit partibus.

HOR.[1]

While mazy error draws mankind astray
From truth's sure path, each takes his devious way:
One to the right, one to the left recedes,
Alike deluded, as each fancy leads.

ELPHINSTON.

It is easy for every man, whatever be his character with others, to find reasons for esteeming himself, and therefore censure, contempt, or conviction of crimes, seldom deprive him of his own favour. Those, indeed, who can see only external facts, may look upon him with abhorrence, but when he calls himself to his own tribunal, he finds every fault, if not absolutely effaced, yet so much palliated by the goodness of his intention, and the cogency of the motive, that very little guilt or turpitude remains; and when he takes a survey of the whole complication of his character, he discovers so many latent excellencies, so many virtues that want but an opportunity to exert themselves in act, and so many kind wishes for universal happiness, that he looks on himself as suffering unjustly under the infamy of single failings, while the general temper of his mind is unknown or unregarded.

It is natural to mean well, when only abstracted ideas of virtue are proposed to the mind, and no particular passion turns us aside from rectitude; and so willing is every man to flatter himself, that the difference between approving laws, and obeying them, is frequently forgotten; he that acknowledges the obligations of morality, and pleases his vanity with enforcing them to others, concludes himself zealous in the cause of virtue, though he has no longer any regard to her precepts, than they conform to his own desires; and counts himself among her warmest lovers, because he praises her beauty, though every rival steals away his heart.

There are, however, great numbers who have little recourse to the refinements of speculation, but who yet live at peace with themselves, by means which require less understanding, or less attention. When their hearts are burthened with the conscious-ness of a crime, instead of seeking for some remedy within themselves, they look round upon the rest of mankind, to find others tainted with the same guilt: they please themselves with observing, that they have numbers on their side; and that though they are hunted out from the society of good men, they are not likely to be condemned to solitude.

It may be observed, perhaps without exception, that none are so industrious to detect wickedness, or so ready to impute it, as they whose crimes are apparent and confessed. They envy an unblemished reputation, and what they envy they are busy to destroy: they are unwilling to suppose themselves meaner, and more corrupt than others, and therefore willingly pull down from their elevations those with whom they cannot rise to an equality. No man yet was ever wicked without secret discontent, and according to the different degrees of remaining virtue, or unextinguished reason, he either endeavours to reform himself, or corrupt others; either to regain the station which he has quitted, or prevail on others to imitate his defection.

It has been always considered as an alleviation of misery not to suffer alone, even when union and society can contribute nothing to resistance or escape; some comfort of the same kind seems to incite wickedness to seek associates, though indeed another reason may be given, for as guilt is propagated the power of reproach is diminished, and among numbers equally detestable every individual may be sheltered from shame, though not from conscience.

Another lenitive[2] by which the throbs of the breast are assuaged, is, the contemplation, not of the same, but of different crimes. He that cannot justify himself by his resemblance to others, is ready to try some other expedient, and to enquire what will rise to his advantage from opposition and dissimilitude. He easily finds some faults in every human being, which he weighs against his own, and easily makes them preponderate while he keeps the balance in his own hand, and throws in or takes out at his pleasure circumstances that make them heavier or lighter. He then triumphs in his comparative purity, and sets himself at ease, not because he can refute the charges advanced against him, but because he can censure his accusers with equal justice, and no longer fears the arrows of reproach, when he has stored his magazine of malice with weapons equally sharp and equally envenomed.

This practice, though never just, is yet specious and artful, when the censure is directed against deviations to the contrary extreme. The man who is branded with cowardice, may, with some appearance of propriety, turn all his force of argument against a stupid contempt of life, and rash precipitation into unnecessary danger. Every recession from temerity is an approach towards cowardice, and though it be confessed that bravery, like other virtues, stands between faults on either hand, yet the place of the middle point may always be disputed; he may therefore often impose upon careless understandings, by turning the attention wholly from himself, and keeping it fixed invariably on the opposite fault; and by shewing how many evils are avoided by his behaviour, he may conceal for a time those which are incurred.

But vice has not always opportunities or address for such artful subterfuges; men often extenuate their own guilt, only by vague and general charges upon others, or endeavour to gain rest to themselves, by pointing some other prey to the persuit of censure.

Every whisper of infamy is industriously circulated, every hint of suspicion eagerly improved, and every failure of conduct joyfully published, by those whose interest it is, that the eye and voice of the publick should be employed on any rather than on themselves.

All these artifices, and a thousand others equally vain and equally despicable, are incited by that conviction of the deformity of wickedness, from which none can set himself free, and by an absurd desire to separate the cause from the effects, and to enjoy the profit of crimes without suffering the shame. Men are willing to try all methods of reconciling guilt and quiet, and when their understandings are stubborn and uncomplying, raise their passions against them, and hope to over-power their own knowledge.

It is generally not so much the desire of men, sunk into depravity, to deceive the world as themselves, for when no particular circumstances make them dependant on others, infamy disturbs them little, but as it revives their remorse, and is echoed to them from their own hearts. The sentence most dreaded is that of reason and conscience, which they would engage on their side at any price but the labours of duty, and the sorrows of repentance. For this purpose every seducement and fallacy is sought, the hopes still rest upon some new experiment till life is at an end; and the last hour steals on unperceived, while the faculties are engaged in resisting reason, and repressing the sense of the divine disapprobation.

No. 77. Tuesday, 11 December 1750.

Os dignum æterno nitidum quod fulgeat Auro,
Si mallet laudare Deum, cui sordida Monstra
Prætulit, et liquidam temeravit Crimine vocem.

PRUDENT.[1]

A golden statue such a wit might claim,
Had God and virtue rais'd the noble flame;
But ah! how lewd a subject has he sung,
What vile obscenity profanes his tongue.

F. LEWIS.

Among those, whose hopes of distinction or riches, arise from an opinion of their intellectual attainments, it has been, from age to age, an established custom to complain of the ingratitude of mankind to their instructors, and the discouragement which men of genius and study suffer from avarice and ignorance, from the prevalence of false taste, and the encroachment of barbarity.

Men are most powerfully affected by those evils which themselves feel, or which appear before their own eyes; and as there has never been a time of such general felicity, but that many have failed to obtain the rewards to which they had, in their own judgment, a just claim, some offended writer has always declaimed in the rage of disappointment, against his age or nation; nor is there one who has not fallen upon times more unfavourable to learning than any former century, or who does not wish, that he had been reserved in the insensibility of non-existence to some happier hour, when literary merit shall no longer be despis'd, and the gifts and caresses of mankind shall recompence the toils of study, and add lustre to the charms of wit.

Many of these clamours are undoubtedly to be considered only as the bursts of pride never to be satisfied, as the prattle of affectation mimicking distresses unfelt, or as the commonplaces of vanity solicitous for splendour of sentences, and acuteness of remark. Yet it cannot be denied that frequent discontent must proceed from frequent hardships, and tho' it is evident, that not more than one age or people can deserve the censure of being more averse from learning than any other, yet at all times knowledge must have encountered impediments, and wit been mortified with contempt, or harrassed with persecution.

It is not necessary, however, to join immediately in the outcry, or to condemn mankind as pleased with ignorance, or always envious of superior abilities. The miseries of the learned have been related by themselves; and since they have not been found exempt from that partiality with which men look upon their own actions and sufferings, we may conclude that they have not forgotten to deck their cause with the brightest ornaments, and strongest colours. The logician collected all his subtilties when they were to be employed in his own defence; and the master of rhetoric exerted against his adversary all the arts by which hatred is embittered, and indignation inflamed.

To believe no man in his own cause, is the standing and perpetual rule of distributive justice. Since therefore, in the controversy between the learned and their enemies, we have only the pleas of one party, of the party more able to delude our understandings, and engage our passions, we must determine our opinion by facts uncontested, and evidences on each side allowed to be genuine.

By this procedure, I know not whether the students will find their cause promoted, or the compassion which they expect much increased. Let their conduct be impartially surveyed; let them be allowed no longer to direct attention at their pleasure, by expatiating on their own deserts; let neither the dignity of knowledge over-awe the judgment, nor the graces of elegance seduce it. It will then, perhaps, be found, that they were not able to produce claims to kinder treatment, but provoked the calamities which they suffered, and seldom wanted friends, but when they wanted virtue.

That few men, celebrated for theoretic wisdom, live with conformity to their precepts, must be readily confessed; and we cannot wonder that the indignation of mankind rises with great vehemence against those, who neglect the duties which they appear to know with so strong conviction the necessity of performing. Yet since no man has power of acting equal to that of thinking, I know not whether the speculatist may not sometimes incur censures too severe, and by those, who form ideas of his life from their knowledge of his books, be considered as worse than others, only because he was expected to be better.

He, by whose writings the heart is rectified, the appetites counter-acted, and the passions repressed, may be considered as not unprofitable to the great republick of humanity, even though his behaviour should not always exemplify his rules. His instructions may diffuse their influence to regions, in which it will not be inquired, whether the author be *albus an ater*,[2] good or bad; to times, when all his faults and all his follies shall be lost in forgetfulness, among things of no concern or importance to the world; and he may kindle in thousands and ten thousands that flame which burnt but dimly in himself, through the fumes of passion, or the damps of cowardice. The vicious moralist may be considered as a taper, by which we are lighted through the labyrinth of complicated passions; he extends his radiance farther than his heat, and guides all that are within view, but burns only those who make too near approaches.

Yet, since good or harm must be received for the most part from those to whom we are familiarly known, he whose vices over-power his virtues, in the compass to which his vices can extend, has no reason to complain that he meets not with affection or veneration, when those with whom he passes his life are more corrupted by his practice than enlightened by his ideas. Admiration begins where acquaintance ceases; and his favourers are distant, but his enemies at hand.

Yet many have dared to boast of neglected merit, and to challenge their age for cruelty and folly, of whom it cannot be alleged that they have endeavoured to increase the wisdom or virtue of their readers. They have been at once profligate in their lives, and licentious in their compositions; have not only forsaken the paths of virtue, but attempted to lure others after them. They have smoothed the road of perdition, covered with flowers the thorns of guilt, and taught temptation sweeter notes, softer blandishments, and stronger allurements.

It has been apparently the settled purpose of some writers, whose powers and acquisitions place them high in the ranks of literature, to set fashion on the side of wickedness; to recommend debauchery, and lewdness, by associating them with qualities most likely to dazzle the discernment, and attract the affections; and to show innocence and goodness with such attendant weaknesses as necessarily expose them to contempt and derision.

Such naturally found intimates among the corrupt, the thoughtless, and the intemperate; passed their lives amidst the levities of sportive idleness, or the warm professions of drunken friendship; and fed their hopes with the promises of wretches, whom their precepts had taught to scoff at truth. But when fools had laughed away their sprightliness, and the languors of excess could no longer be relieved, they saw their protectors hourly drop away, and wondered and stormed to find themselves abandoned. Whether their companions persisted in wickedness, or returned to virtue, they were left equally without assistance; for debauchery is selfish and negligent, and from virtue the virtuous only can expect regard.

It is said by *Florus* of *Catiline*, who died in the midst of slaughtered enemies, that *his death had been illustrious, had it been suffered for his country*.[3] Of the wits, who have languished away life under the pressures of poverty, or in the restlessness of suspense, caressed and rejected, flattered and despised, as they were of more or less use to those who stiled themselves their patrons, it might be observed, that their miseries would enforce compassion, had they been brought upon them by honesty and religion.

The wickedness of a loose or profane author is more atrocious than that of the giddy libertine, or drunken ravisher, not only because it extends its effects wider; as a pestilence that taints the air is more destructive than poison infused in a draught, but because it is committed with cool deliberation. By the instantaneous violence of desire a good man may sometimes be surprised before reflection can come to his rescue; when the appetites have strengthened their influence by habit, they are not easily resisted or suppress'd; but for the frigid villainy of studious lewdness, for the calm malignity of laboured impiety, what apology can be invented? What punishment can be adequate to the crime of him who retires to solitudes for the refinement of debauchery; who tortures his fancy, and ransacks his memory, only that he may leave the world less virtuous than he found it; that he may intercept the hopes of the rising generation; and spread snares for the soul with more dexterity?

What were their motives, or what their excuses, is below the dignity of reason to examine. If having extinguished in themselves the distinction of right and wrong, they were insensible of the mischief which they promoted, they deserved to be hunted down by the general compact, as no longer partaking of social nature; if influenced by the corruption of patrons, or readers, they sacrificed their own convictions to vanity or interest, they were to be abhorred with more acrimony than he that murders for pay; since they committed greater crimes without greater temptations.

Of him, to whom much is given, much shall be required.[4] Those, whom God has favoured with superior faculties, and made eminent for quickness of intuition, and accuracy of distinctions, will certainly be regarded as culpable in his eye, for defects and deviations which, in souls less enlightened, may be guiltless. But, surely, none can think without horror on that man's condition, who has been more wicked in proportion as he had more means of excelling in virtue, and used the light imparted from heaven only to embellish folly, and shed lustre upon crimes.

No. 79. Tuesday, 18 December 1750.

Tam sæpe nostrum decipi Fabullum, quid
Miraris, Aule? Semper bonus homo tiro est.
                                                MART.[1]

You wonder I've so little wit,
Friend *John*, so often to be bit,—
None better guard against a cheat
Than he who is a knave compleat.
                                                F. LEWIS.

Suspicion, however necessary it may be to our safe passage through ways beset on all sides by fraud and malice, has been always considered, when it exceeds the common measures, as a token of depravity and corruption; and a *Greek* writer of sentences has laid down as a standing maxim, that *he who believes not another on his oath, knows himself to be perjured.*[2]

We can form our opinions of that which we know not, only by placing it in comparison with something that we know: whoever therefore is over-run with suspicion, and detects artifice and stratagem in every proposal, must either have learned by experience or observation the wickedness of mankind, and been taught to avoid fraud by having often suffered or seen treachery, or he must derive his judgment from the consciousness of his own disposition, and impute to others the same inclinations which he feels predominant in himself.

To learn caution by turning our eyes upon life, and observing the arts by which negligence is surprised, timidity overborne, and credulity amused, requires either great latitude of converse and long acquaintance with business, or uncommon activity of vigilance, and acuteness of penetration. When therefore a young man, not distinguished by vigour of intellect, comes into the world full of scruples and diffidence; makes a bargain with many provisional limitations; hesitates in his answer to a common question, lest more should be intended than he can immediately discover; has a long reach in detecting the projects of his acquaintance; considers every caress as an act of hypocrisy, and feels neither gratitude nor affection from the tenderness of his friends, because he believes no one to have any real tenderness but for himself; whatever expectations this early sagacity may raise of his future eminence or riches, I can seldom forbear to consider him as a wretch incapable of generosity or benevolence, as a villain early completed beyond the need of common opportunities and gradual temptations.

Upon men of this class instruction and admonition are generally thrown away, because they consider artifice and deceit as proofs of understanding; they are misled at the same time by the two great seducers of the world, vanity and interest, and not only look upon those who act with openness and confidence, as condemned by their principles to obscurity and want, but as contemptible for narrowness of comprehension, shortness of views, and slowness of contrivance.

The world has been long amused with the mention of policy in publick transactions, and of art in private affairs; they have been considered as the effects of great qualities, and as unattainable by men of the common level: yet I have not found many performances either of art, or policy, that required such stupendous efforts of intellect, or might not have been effected by falshood and impudence, without the assistance of any other powers. To profess what he does not mean, to promise what he cannot perform, to flatter ambition with prospects of promotion, and misery with hopes of relief, to sooth pride with appearances of submission, and appease enmity by blandishments and bribes, can surely imply nothing more or greater than a mind devoted wholly to its own purposes, a face that cannot blush, and a heart that cannot feel.

These practices are so mean and base, that he who finds in himself no tendency to use them, cannot easily believe that they are considered by others with less detestation; he therefore suffers himself to slumber in false security, and becomes a prey to those who applaud their own subtilty, because they know how to steal upon his sleep, and exult in the success which they could never have obtained, had they not attempted a man better than themselves, who was hindered from obviating their stratagems, not by folly, but by innocence.

Suspicion is, indeed, a temper so uneasy and restless, that it is very justly appointed the concomitant of guilt. It is said, that no torture is equal to the inhibition of sleep long continued; a pain, to which the state of that man bears a very exact analogy, who dares never give rest to his vigilance and circumspection, but considers himself as surrounded by secret foes, and fears to entrust his children, or his friend, with the secret that throbs in his breast, and the anxieties that break into his face. To avoid, at this expence, those evils to which easiness and friendship might have exposed him, is surely to buy safety at too dear a rate, and, in the language of the *Roman* satirist, to save life by losing all for which a wise man would live.[3]

When in the diet of the *German* empire, as *Camerarius*[4] relates, the princes were once displaying their felicity, and each boasting the advantages of his own dominions, one who possessed a country not remarkable for the grandeur of its cities, or the fertility of its soil, rose to speak, and the rest listened between pity and contempt, till he declared, in honour of his territories, that he could travel through them without a guard, and if he was weary, sleep in safety upon the lap of the first man whom he should meet; a commendation which would have been ill exchanged for the boast of palaces, pastures, or streams.

Suspicion is not less an enemy to virtue than to happiness: he that is already corrupt is naturally suspicious, and he that becomes suspicious will quickly be corrupt. It is too common for us to learn the frauds by which ourselves have suffered; men who are once persuaded that deceit will be employed against them, sometimes think the same arts justified by the necessity of defence. Even they whose virtue is too well established to give way to example, or be shaken by sophistry, must yet feel their love of mankind diminished with their esteem, and grow less zealous for the happiness of those by whom they imagine their own happiness endangered.

Thus we find old age, upon which suspicion has been strongly impressed by long intercourse with the world, inflexible and severe, not easily softened by submission, melted by complaint, or subdued by supplication. Frequent experience of counterfeited miseries, and dissembled virtue, in time overcomes that disposition to tenderness and sympathy, which is so powerful in our younger years, and they that happen to petition the old for compassion or assistance, are doomed to languish without regard, and suffer for the crimes of men who have formerly been found undeserving or ungrateful.

Historians are certainly chargeable with the depravation of mankind, when they relate without censure those stratagems of war by which the virtues of an enemy are engaged to his destruction. A ship comes before a port, weather-beaten and shattered, and the crew implore the liberty of repairing their breaches, supplying themselves with necessaries, or burying their dead. The humanity of the inhabitants inclines them to consent, the strangers enter the town with weapons concealed, fall suddenly upon their benefactors, destroy those that make resistance, and become masters of the place; they return home rich with plunder, and their success is recorded to encourage imitation.

But surely war has its laws, and ought to be conducted with some regard to the universal interest of man. Those may justly be pursued as enemies to the community of nature, who suffer hostility to vacate the unalterable laws of right, and pursue their private advantage by means, which, if once established, must destroy kindness, cut off from every man all hopes of assistance from another, and fill the world with perpetual suspicion and implacable malevolence. Whatever is thus gained ought to be restored, and those who have conquered by such treachery may be justly denied the protection of their native country.

Whoever commits a fraud is guilty not only of the particular injury to him whom he deceives, but of the diminution of that confidence which constitutes not only the ease but the existence of society. He that suffers by imposture has too often his virtue more impaired than his fortune. But as it is necessary not to invite robbery by supineness, so it is our duty not to suppress tenderness by suspicion; it is better to suffer wrong than to do it, and happier to be sometimes cheated than not to trust.

No. 85. Tuesday, 8 January 1751.

Otia si tollas periere Cupidinis *arcus*
Contemptæque jacent, et sine luce faces.
OVID.[1]

At busy hearts in vain love's arrows fly;
Dim, scorn'd, and impotent, his torches lie.

Many writers of eminence in physick have laid out their diligence upon the consideration of those distempers to which men are exposed by particular states of life, and very learned treatises have been produced upon the maladies of the camp, the sea, and the mines. There are, indeed, few employments which a man accustomed to anatomical enquiries, and medical refinements, would not find reasons for declining as dangerous to health, did not his learning or experience inform him, that almost every occupation, however inconvenient or formidable, is happier and safer than a life of sloth.

The necessity of action is not only demonstrable from the fabrick of the body, but evident from observation of the universal practice of mankind, who for the preservation of health, in those whose rank or wealth exempts them from the necessity of lucrative labour, have invented sports and diversions, though not of equal use to the world with manual trades, yet of equal fatigue to those that practise them, and differing only from the drudgery of the husbandman or manufacturer, as they are acts of choice, and therefore performed without the painful sense of compulsion. The huntsman rises early, persues his game through all the dangers and obstructions of the chase, swims rivers, and scales precipices, till he returns home no less harrassed than the soldier, and has, perhaps, sometimes incurred as great hazard of wounds or death: Yet he has no motive to incite his ardour; he is neither subject to the commands of a general, nor dreads any penalties for neglect and disobedience; he has neither profit or honour to expect from his perils and his conquests, but toils without the hope of mural or civick garlands,[2] and must content himself with the praise of his tenants and companions.

But such is the constitution of man, that labour may be stiled its own reward; nor will any external incitements be requisite, if it be considered how much happiness is gained, and how much misery escaped by frequent and violent agitation of the body.

Ease is the utmost that can be hoped from a sedentary and unactive habit; ease, a neutral state between pain and pleasure. The dance of spirits, the bound of vigour, readiness of enterprize, and defiance of fatigue, are reserved for him that braces his nerves, and hardens his fibres, that keeps his limbs pliant with motion, and by frequent exposure fortifies his frame against the common accidents of cold and heat.

With ease, however, if it could be secured, many would be content; but nothing terrestrial can be kept at a stand. Ease, if it is not rising into pleasure, will be falling towards pain; and whatever hope the dreams of speculation may suggest of observing the proportion between nutriment and labour, and keeping the body in a healthy state by supplies exactly equal to its waste, we know that, in effect, the vital powers unexcited by motion, grow gradually languid; that as their vigour fails, obstructions are generated; and that from obstructions proceed most of those pains which wear us away slowly with periodical tortures, and which, though they sometimes suffer life to be long, condemn it to be useless, chain us down to the couch of misery, and mock us with the hopes of death.

Exercise cannot secure us from that dissolution to which we are decreed; but while the soul and body continue united, it can make the association pleasing, and give probable hopes that they shall be disjoined by an easy separation. It was a principle among the ancients, that acute diseases are from heaven, and chronical from ourselves; the dart of death indeed falls from heaven, but we poison it by our own misconduct; to die is the fate of man, but to die with lingering anguish is generally his folly.

It is necessary to that perfection of which our present state is capable, that the mind and body should both be kept in action; that neither the faculties of the one nor of the other be suffered to grow lax or torpid for want of use; that neither health be purchased by voluntary submission to ignorance, nor knowledge cultivated at the expence of that health, which must enable it either to give pleasure to its possessor or assistance to others. It is too frequently the pride of students to despise those amusements and recreations which give to the rest of mankind strength of limbs and cheerfulness of heart. Solitude and contemplation are indeed seldom consistent with such skill in common exercises or sports as is necessary to make them practised with delight, and no man is willing to do that of which the necessity is not pressing and immediate, when he knows that his aukwardness must make him ridiculous.

Ludere qui nescit, campestribus abstinet armis,
Indoctusque Pilæ, Discive, Trochive quiescit,
Ne spissæ risum tollant impunè Coronæ.[3]

He that's unskilful will not toss a ball,
Nor run, nor wrestle, for he fears the fall;
He justly fears to meet deserv'd disgrace,
And that the *ring* will hiss the baffled ass.

CREECH.

Thus the man of learning is often resigned, almost by his own consent, to languor and pain; and while in the prosecution of his studies he suffers the weariness of labour, is subject by his course of life to the maladies of idleness.

It was, perhaps, from the observation of this mischievous omission in those who are employed about intellectual objects, that *Locke* has, in his *System of Education*,[4] urged the necessity of a trade to men of all ranks and professions, that when the mind is weary with its proper task, it may be relaxed by a slighter attention to some mechanical operation; and that while the vital functions are resuscitated and awakened by vigorous motion, the understanding may be restrained from that vagrance and dissipation by which it relieves itself after a long intenseness of thought, unless some allurement be presented that may engage application without anxiety.

There is so little reason for expecting frequent conformity to *Locke*'s precept, that it is not necessary to enquire whether the practice of mechanical arts might not give occasion to petty emulation, and degenerate ambition; and whether, if our divines and physicians were taught the lathe and the chizzel, they would not think more of their tools than their books; as *Nero*[5] neglected the care of his empire for his chariot and his fiddle. It is certainly dangerous to be too much pleased with little things; but what is there which may not be perverted? Let us remember how much worse employment might have been found for those hours, which a manual occupation appears to engross; let us compute the profit with the loss, and when we reflect how often a genius is allured from his studies, consider likewise that perhaps by the same attractions he is sometimes withheld from debauchery, or recalled from malice, from ambition, from envy, and from lust.

I have always admired the wisdom of those by whom our female education was instituted, for having contrived, that every woman of whatever condition should be taught some arts of manufacture, by which the vacuities of recluse and domestick leisure may be filled up. These arts are more necessary as the weakness of their sex and the general system of life debar ladies from many employments which by diversifying the circumstances of men, preserve them from being cankered by the rust of their own thoughts. I know not how much of the virtue and happiness of the world may be the consequence of this judicious regulation. Perhaps, the most powerful fancy might be unable to figure the confusion and slaughter that would be produced by so many piercing eyes and vivid understandings, turned loose at once upon mankind, with no other business than to sparkle and intrigue, to perplex and to destroy.

For my part, whenever chance brings within my observation a knot of misses busy at their needles, I consider myself as in the school of virtue; and though I have no extraordinary skill in plain work or embroidery, look upon their operations with as much satisfaction as their governess, because I regard them as providing a security against the most dangerous ensnarers of the soul, by enabling themselves to exclude idleness from their solitary moments, and with idleness her attendant train of passions, fancies, and chimeras, fears, sorrows and desires. *Ovid* and *Cervantes* will inform them that love has no power but over those whom he catches unemployed; and *Hector*, in the *Iliad*, when he sees *Andromache* overwhelmed with terrors, sends her for consolation to the loom and the distaff.[6]

It is certain that any wild wish or vain imagination never takes such firm possession of the mind, as when it is found empty and unoccupied. The old peripatetick[7] principle, that *Nature abhors a Vacuum*, may be properly applied to the intellect, which will embrace any thing, however absurd or criminal, rather than be wholly without an object. Perhaps every man may date the predominance of those desires that disturb his life and contaminate his conscience, from some unhappy hour when too much leisure exposed him to their incursions; for he has lived with little observation either on himself or others, who does not know that to be idle is to be vicious.

No. 87. Tuesday, 15 January 1751.

Invidus, iracundus, iners, vinosus, amator,
Nemo adeo ferus est, ut non mitescere possit,
Si modo culturæ patientem commodet aurem.

HOR.[1]

The slave to envy, anger, wine or love,
The wretch of sloth, its excellence shall prove:
Fierceness itself shall hear its rage away,
When list'ning calmly to th' instructive lay.

FRANCIS.

That few things are so liberally bestowed, or squandered with so little effect, as good advice, has been generally observed; and many sage positions have been advanced concerning the reasons of this complaint, and the means of removing it. It is, indeed, an important and noble enquiry, for little would be wanting to the happiness of life, if every man could conform to the right as soon as he was shown it.

This perverse neglect of the most salutary precepts, and stubborn resistance of the most pathetic persuasion, is usually imputed to him by whom the counsel is received, and we often hear it mentioned as a sign of hopeless depravity, that though good advice was given, it has wrought no reformation.

Others who imagine themselves to have quicker sagacity and deeper penetration, have found out, that the inefficacy of advice is usually the fault of the counsellor, and rules have been laid down, by which this important duty may be successfully performed: We are directed by what tokens to discover the favourable moment at which the heart is disposed for the operation of truth and reason, with what address to administer and with what vehicles to disguise *the catharticks of the soul.*[2]

But, notwithstanding this specious expedient, we find the world yet in the same state; advice is still given, but still received with disgust; nor has it appeared that the bitterness of the medicine has been yet abated, or its power encreased by any methods of preparing it.

If we consider the manner in which those who assume the office of directing the conduct of others execute their undertaking, it will not be very wonderful that their labours, however zealous or affectionate, are frequently useless. For what is the advice that is commonly given? A few general maxims, enforced with vehemence and inculcated with importunity, but failing for want of particular reference, and immediate application.

It is not often that any man can have so much knowledge of another, as is necessary to make instruction useful. We are sometimes not ourselves conscious of the original motives of our actions, and when we know them, our first care is to hide them from the sight of others, and often from those most diligently, whose superiority either of power or understanding may intitle them to inspect our lives; it is therefore very probable that he who endeavours the cure of our intellectual maladies, mistakes their cause; and that his prescriptions avail nothing, because he knows not which of the passions or desires is vitiated.

Advice, as it always gives a temporary appearance of superiority, can never be very grateful, even when it is most necessary or most judicious. But for the same reason every one is eager to instruct his neighbours. To be wise or to be virtuous, is to buy dignity and importance at a high price; but when nothing is necessary to elevation but detection of the follies or the faults of others, no man is so insensible to the voice of fame as to linger on the ground.

> —*Tentanda via est, qua me quoque possim*
> *Tollere humo, victorque virûm volitare per ora.*[3]

> New ways I must attempt, my groveling name
> To raise aloft, and wing my flight to fame.
>   DRYDEN.

Vanity is so frequently the apparent motive of advice, that we, for the most part, summon our powers to oppose it without any very accurate enquiry whether it is right. It is sufficient that another is growing great in his own eyes at our expence, and assumes authority over us without our permission; for many would contentedly suffer the consequences of their own mistakes, rather than the insolence of him who triumphs as their deliverer.

It is, indeed, seldom found that any advantages are enjoyed with that moderation which the uncertainty of all human good so powerfully enforces; and therefore the adviser may justly suspect, that he has inflamed the opposition which he laments by arrogance and superciliousness. He may suspect, but needs not hastily to condemn himself, for he can rarely be certain, that the softest language or most humble diffidence would have escaped resentment; since scarcely any degree of circumspection can prevent or obviate the rage with which the slothful, the impotent, and the unsuccessful, vent their discontent upon those that excel them. Modesty itself, if it is praised, will be envied; and there are minds so impatient of inferiority, that their gratitude is a species of revenge, and they return benefits, not because recompence is a pleasure, but because obligation is a pain.

The number of those whom the love of themselves has thus far corrupted, is perhaps not great; but there are few so free from vanity as not to dictate to those who will hear their instructions with a visible sense of their own beneficence; and few to whom it is not unpleasing to receive documents, however tenderly and cautiously delivered, or who are not willing to raise themselves from pupillage, by disputing the propositions of their teacher.

It was the maxim, I think, of *Alphonsus* of *Arragon*, that *dead counsellors are safest*.[4] The grave puts an end to flattery and artifice, and the information that we receive from books is pure from interest, fear, or ambition. Dead counsellors are likewise most instructive; because they are heard with patience and with reverence. We are not unwilling to believe that man wiser than ourselves, from whose abilities we may receive advantage, without any danger of rivalry or opposition, and who affords us the light of his experience, without hurting our eyes by flashes of insolence.

By the consultation of books, whether of dead or living authors, many temptations to petulance and opposition, which occur in oral conferences, are avoided. An author cannot obtrude his advice unasked, nor can be often suspected of any malignant intention to insult his readers with his knowledge or his wit. Yet so prevalent is the habit of comparing ourselves with others, while they remain within the reach of our passions, that books are seldom read with complete impartiality, but by those from whom the writer is placed at such a distance that his life or death is indifferent.

We see that volumes may be perused, and perused with attention, to little effect; and that maxims of prudence, or principles of virtue, may be treasured in the memory without influencing the conduct. Of the numbers that pass their lives among books, very few read to be made wiser or better, apply any general reproof of vice to themselves, or try their own manners by axioms of justice. They purpose either to consume those hours for which they can find no other amusement; to gain or preserve that respect which learning has always obtained; or to gratify their curiosity with knowledge, which, like treasures buried and forgotten, is of no use to others or themselves.

"The preacher, (says a *French* author) may spend an hour in explaining and enforcing a precept of religion, without feeling any impression from his own performance, because he may have no further design than to fill up his hour."[5] A student may easily exhaust his life in comparing divines and moralists, without any practical regard to morality or religion; he may be learning not to live, but to reason; he may regard only the elegance of stile, justness of argument, and accuracy of method; and may enable himself to criticise with judgment, and dispute with subtilty, while the chief use of his volumes is unthought of, his mind is unaffected, and his life is unreformed.

But though truth and virtue are thus frequently defeated by pride, obstinacy, or folly, we are not allowed to desert them; for whoever can furnish arms which they have not hitherto employed, may enable them to gain some hearts which would have resisted any other method of attack. Every man of genius has some arts of fixing the attention peculiar to himself, by

which, honestly exerted, he may benefit mankind; for the arguments for purity of life fail of their due influence, not because
they have been considered and confuted, but because they have
been passed over without consideration. To the position of
Tully,[6] that if Virtue could be seen, she must be loved, may be
added, that if Truth could be heard, she must be obeyed.

No. 90. Saturday, 26 January 1751.

In tenui labor.
VIRG.[1]

What toil in slender things!

It is very difficult to write on the minuter parts of literature
without failing either to please or instruct. Too much nicety of
detail disgusts the greatest part of readers, and to throw a
multitude of particulars under general heads, and lay down
rules of extensive comprehension, is to common understandings
of little use. They who undertake these subjects are therefore
always in danger, as one or other inconvenience arises to their
imagination, of frighting us with rugged science, or amusing us
with empty sound.

In criticising the work of *Milton*, there is, indeed, opportunity
to intersperse passages that can hardly fail to relieve the languors
of attention; and since, in examining the variety and choice of
the pauses with which he has diversified his numbers, it will be
necessary to exhibit the lines in which they are to be found,
perhaps the remarks may be well compensated by the examples,
and the irksomeness of grammatical disquisitions somewhat
alleviated.

MILTON formed his scheme of versification by the poets of
Greece and *Rome*, whom he proposed to himself for his models
so far as the difference of his language from theirs would permit
the imitation. There are indeed many inconveniencies inseparable from our heroick measure compared with that of *Homer*
and *Virgil*; inconveniencies, which it is no reproach to *Milton*

not to have overcome, because they are in their own nature insuperable; but against which he has struggled with so much art and diligence, that he may at least be said to have deserved success.

The hexameter of the ancients may be considered as consisting of fifteen syllables, so melodiously disposed, that, as every one knows who has examined the poetical authors, very pleasing and sonorous lyrick measures are formed from the fragments of the heroick. It is, indeed, scarce possible to break them in such a manner but that *invenias etiam disjecti membra poetæ*,[2] some harmony will still remain, and the due proportions of sound will always be discovered. This measure therefore allowed great variety of pauses, and great liberties of connecting one verse with another, because wherever the line was interrupted, either part singly was musical. But the ancients seem to have confined this privilege to hexameters; for in their other measures, though longer than the *English* heroick, those who wrote after the refinements of versification venture so seldom to change their pauses, that every variation may be supposed rather a compliance with necessity than the choice of judgment.

MILTON was constrained within the narrow limits of a measure not very harmonious in the utmost perfection; the single parts, therefore, into which it was to be sometimes broken by pauses, were in danger of losing the very form of verse. This has, perhaps, notwithstanding all his care, sometimes happened.

As harmony is the end of poetical measures, no part of a verse ought to be so separated from the rest as not to remain still more harmonious than prose, or to shew, by the disposition of the tones, that it is part of a verse. This rule in the old hexameter might be easily observed, but in *English* will very frequently be in danger of violation; for the order and regularity of accents cannot well be perceived in a succession of fewer than three syllables, which will confine the *English* poet to only five pauses; it being supposed, that, when he connects one line with another, he should never make a full pause at less distance than that of three syllables from the beginning or end of a verse.

That this rule should be universally and indispensably established, perhaps cannot be granted; something may be allowed to variety, and something to the adaptation of the numbers to the subject; but it will be found generally necessary, and the ear will seldom fail to suffer by its neglect.

Thus when a single syllable is cut off from the rest, it must either be united to the line with which the sense connects it, or be sounded alone. If it be united to the other line, it corrupts its harmony; if disjoined, it must stand alone and with regard to musick, be superfluous; for there is no harmony in a single sound, because it has no proportion to another.

> Hypocrites austerely talk,
> Defaming as impure what God declares
> *Pure*; and commands to some, leaves free to all.[3]

When two syllables likewise are abscinded from the rest, they evidently want some associate sounds to make them harmonious.

> ———Eyes———
> ———more wakeful than to drouze,
> Charm'd with arcadian pipe, the past'ral reed
> Of *Hermes*, or his opiate rod. *Meanwhile*
> To re-salute the world with sacred light
> *Leucothea* wak'd.[4]

> He ended, and the Son gave signal high
> To the bright minister that watch'd: *he blew*
> His trumpet[5]

> First in his east the glorious lamp was seen,
> Regent of day; and all th' horizon round
> Invested with bright rays, jocund to run
> His longitude through heav'n's high road; *the gray*
> Dawn, and the pleiades, before him danc'd,
> Shedding sweet influence.[6]

The same defect is perceived in the following lines, where the pause is at the second syllable from the beginning.

> The race
> Of that wild rout that tore the *Thracian* bard
> In *Rhodope*, where woods and rocks had ears,
> To rapture, 'till the savage clamour drown'd
> Both harp and voice; nor could the muse defend
> *Her son.* So fail not thou, who thee implores.[7]

When the pause falls upon the third syllable or the seventh, the harmony is better preserved; but as the third and seventh are weak syllables, the period leaves the ear unsatisfied, and in expectation of the remaining part of the verse.

> He, with his horrid crew,
> Lay vanquish'd, rolling in the fiery gulph,
> Confounded though immor*tal*. But his doom
> Reserv'd him to more wrath; for now the thought
> Both of lost happiness and lasting pain
> Torments *him*.[8]

> God,——with frequent intercourse,
> Thither will send his winged messengers
> On errands of supernal grace. So sung
> The glorious train ascend*ing*.[9]

It may be, I think, established as a rule, that a pause which concludes a period should be made for the most part upon a strong syllable, as the fourth and sixth; but those pauses which only suspend the sense may be placed upon the weaker. Thus the rest in the third line of the first passage satisfies the ear better than in the fourth, and the close of the second quotation better than of the third.

> The evil soon
> Drawn back, redounded (as a flood) on those
> From whom it *sprung*; impossible to mix
> With *blessedness*.[10]

> —— What we by day
> Lop overgrown, or prune, or prop, or bind

One night or two with wanton growth derides,
Tending to *wild*.[11]

    The paths and bow'rs doubt not but our joint hands
Will keep from wilderness with ease as wide
As we need walk, till younger hands ere long
Assist *us*.[12]

The rest in the fifth place has the same inconvenience as in
the seventh and third, that the syllable is weak.

Beast now with beast 'gan war, and fowl with fowl,
And fish with fish, to graze the herb all leaving,
Devour'd each *other*: Nor stood much in awe
Of man, but fled *him*, or with countenance grim,
Glar'd on him pass*ing*.[13]

The noblest and most majestic pauses which our versification
admits, are upon the fourth and sixth syllables, which are both
strongly sounded in a pure and regular verse, and at either of
which the line is so divided, that both members participate of
harmony.

    But now at last the sacred influence
Of light ap*pears*, and from the walls of heav'n
Shoots far into the bosom of dim night
A glimmering *dawn*: here nature first begins
Her farthest verge, and chaos to retire.[14]

But far above all others, if I can give any credit to my own
ear, is the rest upon the sixth syllable, which taking in a complete
compass of sound, such as is sufficient to constitute one of our
lyrick measures, makes a full and solemn close. Some passages
which conclude at this stop, I could never read without some
strong emotions of delight or admiration.

Before the hills appear'd, or fountain flow'd,
Thou with the eternal wisdom didst converse,

> Wisdom thy sister; and with her didst play
> In presence of the almighty father, pleas'd
> With thy celestial *song*.[15]
>
> Or other worlds they seem'd, or happy isles,
> Like those *Hesperian* gardens fam'd of old,
> Fortunate fields, and groves, and flow'ry vales,
> Thrice happy isles! But who dwelt happy there,
> He staid not to in*quire*.[16]
>
>   He blew
> His trumpet, heard in *Oreb* since, perhaps
> When God descended; and, perhaps, once more
> To sound at general *doom*.[17]

If the poetry of *Milton* be examined, with regard to the pauses and flow of his verses into each other, it will appear, that he has performed all that our language would admit; and the comparison of his numbers with those who have cultivated the same manner of writing, will show that he excelled as much in the lower as the higher parts of his art, and that his skill in harmony was not less than his invention or his learning.

No. 93. Tuesday, 5 February 1751.

> —— *Experiar quid concedatur in illos*
> *Quorum Flaminiâ tegitur cinis atque Latinâ.*
>   Juv.[1]

> More safely truth to urge her claim presumes,
> On names now found alone on books and tombs.

There are few books on which more time is spent by young students, than on treatises which deliver the characters of authors; nor any which oftener deceive the expectation of the reader, or fill his mind with more opinions which the progress of his studies and the encrease of his knowledge oblige him to resign.

Baillet[2] has introduced his collection of the decisions of the learned, by an enumeration of the prejudices which mislead the critick, and raise the passions in rebellion against the judgment. His catalogue, though large, is imperfect; and who can hope to complete it? The beauties of writing have been observed to be often such as cannot in the present state of human knowledge be evinced by evidence, or drawn out into demonstrations; they are therefore wholly subject to the imagination, and do not force their effects upon a mind preoccupied by unfavourable sentiments, nor overcome the counteraction of a false principle or of stubborn partiality.

To convince any man against his will is hard, but to please him against his will is justly pronounced by *Dryden* to be above the reach of human abilities.[3] Interest and passion will hold out long against the closest siege of diagrams and syllogisms, but they are absolutely impregnable to imagery and sentiment; and will for ever bid defiance to the most powerful strains of *Virgil* or *Homer*, though they may give way in time to the batteries of *Euclid* or *Archimedes*.[4]

In trusting therefore to the sentence of a critick, we are in danger not only from that vanity which exalts writers too often to the dignity of teaching what they are yet to learn, from that negligence which sometimes steals upon the most vigilant caution, and that fallibility to which the condition of nature has subjected every human understanding; but from a thousand extrinsick and accidental causes, from every thing which can excite kindness or malevolence, veneration or contempt.

Many of those who have determined with great boldness, upon the various degrees of literary merit, may be justly suspected of having passed sentence, as *Seneca* remarks of *Claudius*,

> *Una tantum Parte audita,*
> *Sæpe et nulla,*[5]

without much knowledge of the cause before them; for it will not easily be imagined of *Langbaine, Borrichius* or *Rapin*,[6] that they had very accurately perused all the books which they praise or censure; or that, even if nature and learning had qualified them for judges, they could read for ever with the attention necessary to just criticism. Such performances, however, are not wholly without their use; for they are commonly just echoes to the voice of fame, and transmit the general suffrage of mankind when they have no particular motives to suppress it.

Criticks, like all the rest of mankind, are very frequently misled by interest. The bigotry with which editors regard the authors whom they illustrate or correct, has been generally remarked. *Dryden* was known to have written most of his critical dissertations only to recommend the work upon which he then happened to be employed; and *Addison* is suspected to have denied the expediency of poetical justice, because his own *Cato* was condemned to perish in a good cause.[7]

There are prejudices which authors, not otherwise weak or corrupt, have indulged without scruple; and perhaps some of them are so complicated with our natural affections, that they cannot easily be disintangled from the heart. Scarce any can hear with impartiality a comparison between the writers of his own and another country; and though it cannot, I think, be charged equally on all nations, that they are blinded with this literary patriotism, yet there are none that do not look upon their authors with the fondness of affinity, and esteem them as well for the place of their birth, as for their knowledge or their wit. There is, therefore, seldom much respect due to comparative criticism, when the competitors are of different countries, unless the judge is of a nation equally indifferent to both. The *Italians* could not for a long time believe, that there was any learning beyond the mountains; and the *French* seem generally persuaded, that there are no wits or reasoners equal to their own. I can scarcely conceive that if *Scaliger*[8] had not considered himself as allied to *Virgil*, by being born in the same country, he would have found his works so much superior to those of *Homer*, or have thought the controversy worthy of so much zeal, vehemence, and acrimony.

There is, indeed, one prejudice, and only one, by which it may be doubted whether it is any dishonour to be sometimes misguided. Criticism has so often given occasion to the envious and ill-natured of gratifying their malignity, that some have thought it necessary to recommend the virtue of candour without restriction, and to preclude all future liberty of censure. Writers possessed with this opinion are continually enforcing civility and decency, recommending to criticks the proper diffidence of themselves, and inculcating the veneration due to celebrated names.

I am not of opinion that these professed enemies of arrogance and severity, have much more benevolence or modesty than the rest of mankind; or that they feel in their own hearts, any other intention than to distinguish themselves by their softness and delicacy. Some are modest because they are timorous, and some are lavish of praise because they hope to be repaid.

There is indeed some tenderness due to living writers, when they attack none of those truths which are of importance to the happiness of mankind, and have committed no other offence than that of betraying their own ignorance or dulness. I should think it cruelty to crush an insect who had provoked me only by buzzing in my ear; and would not willingly interrupt the dream of harmless stupidity, or destroy the jest which makes its author laugh. Yet I am far from thinking this tenderness universally necessary; for he that writes may be considered as a kind of general challenger, whom every one has a right to attack; since he quits the common rank of life, steps forward beyond the lists, and offers his merit to the publick judgment. To commence author is to claim praise, and no man can justly aspire to honour, but at the hazard of disgrace.

But whatever be decided concerning contemporaries, whom he that knows the treachery of the human heart, and considers how often we gratify our own pride or envy under the appearance of contending for elegance and propriety, will find himself not much inclined to disturb; there can surely be no exemptions pleaded to secure them from criticism, who can no longer suffer by reproach, and of whom nothing now remains but their writings and their names. Upon these authors the critick is, undoubtedly, at full liberty to exercise the strictest severity, since he endangers only his own fame, and, like *Æneas* when he drew his sword in the infernal regions, encounters phantoms which cannot be wounded.[9] He may indeed pay some regard to established reputation; but he can by that shew of reverence consult only his own security, for all other motives are now at an end.

The faults of a writer of acknowledged excellence are more dangerous, because the influence of his example is more extensive; and the interest of learning requires that they should be discovered and stigmatized, before they have the sanction of antiquity conferred upon them, and become precedents of indisputable authority.

It has, indeed, been advanced by *Addison*, as one of the characteristicks of a true critick, that he points out beauties rather than faults.[10] But it is rather natural to a man of learning and genius, to apply himself chiefly to the study of writers who have more beauties than faults to be displayed: for the duty of criticism is neither to depreciate, nor dignify by partial representations, but to hold out the light of reason, whatever it may discover; and to promulgate the determinations of truth, whatever she shall dictate.

No. 101. Tuesday, 5 March 1751.

Mella jubes Hyblæa tibi vel Hymettia nasci,
Et thyma Cecropiæ Corsica ponis api.
MART.[1]

Alas! dear Sir, you try in vain,
Impossibilities to gain;
No bee from *Corsica's* rank juice,
Hyblæan honey can produce.
F. LEWIS.

To the RAMBLER.

SIR,
Having by several years of continual study treasured in my mind a great number of principles and ideas, and obtained by frequent exercise the power of applying them with propriety, and combining them with readiness, I resolved to quit the university, where I considered myself as a gem hidden in the mine, and

to mingle in the croud of publick life. I was naturally attracted by the company of those who were of the same age with myself, and finding that my academical gravity contributed very little to my reputation, applied my faculties to jocularity and burlesque. Thus, in a short time, I had heated my imagination to such a state of activity and ebullition, that upon every occasion it fumed away in bursts of wit, and evaporations of gaiety. I became on a sudden the idol of the coffee-house, was in one winter sollicited to accept the presidentship of five clubs, was dragged by violence to every new play, and quoted in every controversy upon theatrical merit; was in every publick place surrounded by a multitude of humble auditors, who retailed in other places of resort my maxims and my jests, and was boasted as their intimate and companion by many, who had no other pretensions to my acquaintance, than that they had drank chocolate in the same room.

You will not wonder, Mr. RAMBLER, that I mention my success with some appearance of triumph and elevation. Perhaps no kind of superiority is more flattering or alluring than that which is conferred by the powers of conversation, by extemporaneous sprightliness of fancy, copiousness of language, and fertility of sentiment. In other exertions of genius, the greater part of the praise is unknown and unenjoyed; the writer, indeed, spreads his reputation to a wider extent, but receives little pleasure or advantage from the diffusion of his name, and only obtains a kind of nominal sovereignty over regions which pay no tribute. The colloquial wit has always his own radiance reflected on himself, and enjoys all the pleasure which he bestows; he finds his power confessed by every one that approaches him, sees friendship kindling with rapture, and attention swelling into praise.

The desire which every man feels of importance and esteem, is so much gratified by finding an assembly, at his entrance, brightened with gladness and hushed with expectation, that the recollection of such distinctions can scarcely fail to be pleasing whensoever it is innocent. And my conscience does not reproach me with any mean or criminal effects of vanity; since I always employed my influence on the side of virtue, and never sacrificed my understanding or my religion to the pleasure of applause.

There were many whom either the desire of enjoying my pleasantry, or the pride of being thought to enjoy it, brought often into my company; but I was caressed in a particular manner by *Demochares*, a gentleman of a large estate, and a liberal disposition. My fortune being by no means exuberant, enclined me to be pleased with a friend who was willing to be entertained at his own charge. I became by daily invitations habituated to his table, and, as he believed my acquaintance necessary to the character of elegance, which he was desirous of establishing, I lived in all the luxury of affluence, without expence or dependence, and passed my life in a perpetual reciprocation of pleasure with men brought together by similitude of accomplishments, or desire of improvement.

But all power has its sphere of activity, beyond which it produces no effect. *Demochares* being called by his affairs into the country, imagined that he should encrease his popularity by coming among his neighbours accompanied by a man whose abilities were so generally allowed. The report presently spread thro' half the county that *Demochares* was arrived, and had brought with him the celebrated *Hilarius*, by whom such merriment would be excited, as had never been enjoyed or conceived before. I knew, indeed, the purpose for which I was invited, and, as men do not look diligently out for possible miscarriages, was pleased to find myself courted upon principles of interest, and considered as capable of reconciling factions, composing feuds, and uniting a whole province in social happiness.

After a few days spent in adjusting his domestick regulations, *Demochares* invited all the gentlemen of his neighbourhood to dinner, and did not forget to hint how much my presence was expected to heighten the pleasure of the feast. He informed me what prejudices my reputation had raised in my favour, and represented the satisfaction with which he should see me kindle up the blaze of merriment, and should remark the various effects that my fire would have upon such diversity of matter.

This declaration, by which he intended to quicken my vivacity, filled me with solicitude. I felt an ambition of shining, which

I never knew before; and was therefore embarrassed with an unusual fear of disgrace. I passed the night in planning out to myself the conversation of the coming day; recollected all my topicks of raillery, proposed proper subjects of ridicule, prepared smart replies to a thousand questions, accommodated answers to imaginary repartees, and formed a magazine of remarks, apophthegms, tales, and illustrations.

The morning broke at last in the midst of these busy meditations. I rose with the palpitations of a champion on the day of combat; and, notwithstanding all my efforts, found my spirits sunk under the weight of expectation. The company soon after began to drop in, and every one, at his entrance was introduced to *Hilarius*. What conception the inhabitants of this region had formed of a wit, I cannot yet discover; but observed that they all seemed, after the regular exchange of compliments, to turn away disappointed, and that while we waited for dinner, they cast their eyes first upon me, and then upon each other, like a theatrical assembly waiting for a shew.

From the uneasiness of this situation, I was relieved by the dinner, and as every attention was taken up by the business of the hour, I sunk quietly to a level with the rest of the company. But no sooner were the dishes removed, than instead of chearful confidence and familiar prattle, an universal silence again shewed their expectation of some unusual performance. My friend endeavoured to rouse them by healths and questions, but they answered him with great brevity, and immediately relapsed into their former taciturnity.

I had waited in hope of some opportunity to divert them, but could find no pass opened for a single sally; and who can be merry without an object of mirth? After a few faint efforts, which produced neither applause nor opposition, I was content to mingle with the mass, to put round the glass in silence, and solace myself with my own contemplations.

My friend looked round him; the guests stared at one another; and if now and then a few syllables were uttered with timidity and hesitation, there was none ready to make any reply. All our faculties were frozen, and every minute took away from our capacity of pleasing, and disposition to be pleased. Thus passed the hours to which so much happiness was decreed; the hours which had, by a kind of open proclamation, been devoted to wit, to mirth, and to *Hilarius*.

At last the night came on, and the necessity of parting freed us from the persecutions of each other. I heard them as they walked along the court murmuring at the loss of the day, and enquiring whether any man would pay a second visit to a house haunted by a wit.

Demochares, whose benevolence is greater than his penetration, having flattered his hopes with the secondary honour which he was to gain by my sprightliness and elegance, and the affection with which he should be followed for a perpetual banquet of gaiety, was not able to conceal his vexation and resentment, nor would easily be convinced, that I had not sacrificed his interest to sullenness and caprice, had studiously endeavoured to disgust his guests, and suppressed my powers of delighting, in obstinate and premeditated silence. I am informed that the reproach of their ill reception is divided by the gentlemen of the country between us; some being of opinion that my friend is deluded by an impostor, who, though he has found some art of gaining his favour, is afraid to speak before men of more penetration; and others concluding, that I think only *London* the proper theatre of my abilities, and disdain to exert my genius for the praise of rusticks.

I believe, Mr. RAMBLER, that it has sometimes happened to others, who have the good or ill fortune to be celebrated for wits, to fall under the same censures upon the like occasions. I hope therefore that you will prevent any misrepresentations of such failures, by remarking that invention is not wholly at the command of its possessor; that the power of pleasing is very often obstructed by the desire; that all expectation lessens surprize, yet some surprize is necessary to gaiety; and that those who desire to partake of the pleasure of wit must contribute to its production, since the mind stagnates without external ventilation, and that effervescence of the fancy, which flashes into transport, can be raised only by the infusion of dissimilar ideas.

No. 106. Saturday, 23 March 1751.

Opinionum commenta delet dies, naturæ judicia confirmat.
                                                                Cic.[1]

Time obliterates the fictions of opinion, and confirms the
    decisions of nature.

It is necessary to the success of flattery, that it be accommodated
to particular circumstances or characters, and enter the heart
on that side where the passions stand ready to receive it. A lady
seldom listens with attention to any praise but that of her beauty;
a merchant always expects to hear of his influence at the bank,
his importance on the exchange, the height of his credit, and the
extent of his traffick: and the author will scarcely be pleased
without lamentations of the neglect of learning, the conspiracies
against genius, and the slow progress of merit, or some praises
of the magnanimity of those who encounter poverty and contempt in the cause of knowledge, and trust for the reward of
their labours to the judgment and gratitude of posterity.

An assurance of unfading laurels, and immortal reputation,
is the settled reciprocation of civility between amicable writers.
To raise *monuments more durable than brass, and more conspicuous than pyramids*,[2] has been long the common boast
of literature; but among the innumerable architects that erect
columns to themselves, far the greater part, either for want of
durable materials, or of art to dispose them, see their edifices
perish as they are towering to completion, and those few that
for a while attract the eye of mankind, are generally weak in the
foundation, and soon sink by the saps of time.

No place affords a more striking conviction of the vanity of
human hopes, than a publick library; for who can see the wall
crouded on every side by mighty volumes, the works of laborious
meditation, and accurate enquiry, now scarcely known but by
the catalogue, and preserved only to encrease the pomp of
learning, without considering how many hours have been
wasted in vain endeavours, how often imagination has antici-

pated the praises of futurity, how many statues have risen to the eye of vanity, how many ideal converts have elevated zeal, how often wit has exulted in the eternal infamy of his antagonists, and dogmatism has delighted in the gradual advances of his authority, the immutability of his decrees, and the perpetuity of his power?

> —— Non unquam dedit
> Documenta fors majora, quàm fragili loco
> Starent superbi. ——[3]

> Insulting chance ne'er call'd with louder voice,
> On swelling mortals to be proud no more.

Of the innumerable authors whose performances are thus treasured up in magnificent obscurity, most are forgotten, because they never deserved to be remembered, and owed the honours which they once obtained, not to judgment or to genius, to labour or to art, but to the prejudice of faction, the stratagem of intrigue, or the servility of adulation.

Nothing is more common than to find men whose works are now totally neglected, mentioned with praises by their contemporaries, as the oracles of their age, and the legislators of science. Curiosity is naturally excited, their volumes after long enquiry are found, but seldom reward the labour of the search. Every period of time has produced these bubbles of artificial fame, which are kept up a while by the breath of fashion, and then break at once and are annihilated. The learned often bewail the loss of ancient writers whose characters have survived their works; but, perhaps, if we could now retrieve them, we should find them only the *Granvilles*, *Montagues*, *Stepneys*, and *Sheffields*[4] of their time, and wonder by what infatuation or caprice they could be raised to notice.

It cannot, however, be denied, that many have sunk into oblivion, whom it were unjust to number with this despicable class. Various kinds of literary fame seem destined to various measures of duration. Some spread into exuberance with a very speedy growth, but soon wither and decay; some rise more slowly, but last long. *Parnassus*[5] has its flowers of transient fragrance, as well as its oaks of towering height, and its laurels of eternal verdure.

Among those whose reputation is exhausted in a short time by its own luxuriance, are the writers who take advantage of present incidents or characters which strongly interest the passions, and engage universal attention. It is not difficult to obtain readers, when we discuss a question which every one is desirous to understand, which is debated in every assembly, and has divided the nation into parties; or when we display the faults or virtues of him whose public conduct has made almost every man his enemy or his friend. To the quick circulation of such productions all the motives of interest and vanity concur; the disputant enlarges his knowledge, the zealot animates his passion, and every man is desirous to inform himself concerning affairs so vehemently agitated and variously represented.

It is scarcely to be imagined, through how many subordinations of interest, the ardour of party is diffused; and what multitudes fancy themselves affected by every satire or panegyrick on a man of eminence. Whoever has, at any time, taken occasion to mention him with praise or blame, whoever happens to love or hate any of his adherents, as he wishes to confirm his opinion, and to strengthen his party, will diligently peruse every paper from which he can hope for sentiments like his own. An object, however small in itself, if placed near to the eye, will engross all the rays of light; and a transaction, however trivial, swells into importance, when it presses immediately on our attention. He that shall peruse the political pamphlets of any past reign, will wonder why they were so eagerly read, or so loudly praised. Many of the performances which had power to inflame factions, and fill a kingdom with confusion, have now very little effect upon a frigid critick, and the time is coming, when the compositions of later hirelings shall lie equally despised. In proportion, as those who write on temporary subjects, are exalted above their merit at first, they are afterwards depressed below it; nor can the brightest elegance of diction, or most artful subtilty of reasoning, hope for much esteem from those whose regard is no longer quickened by curiosity or pride.

It is, indeed, the fate of controvertists, even when they contend for philosophical or theological truth, to be soon laid aside and slighted. Either the question is decided, and there is no more place for doubt and opposition; or mankind despair of understanding it, and grow weary of disturbance, content themselves with quiet ignorance, and refuse to be harrassed with labours which they have no hopes of recompensing with knowledge.

The authors of new discoveries may surely expect to be reckoned among those, whose writings are secure of veneration: yet it often happens that the general reception of a doctrine obscures the books in which it was delivered. When any tenet is generally received and adopted as an incontrovertible principle, we seldom look back to the arguments upon which it was first established, or can bear that tediousness of deduction, and multiplicity of evidence, by which its author was forced to reconcile it to prejudice, and fortify it in the weakness of novelty against obstinacy and envy.

It is well known how much of our philosophy is derived from *Boyle*'s discovery of the qualities of the air;[6] yet of those who now adopt or enlarge his theory, very few have read the detail of his experiments. His name is, indeed, reverenced; but his works are neglected; we are contented to know, that he conquered his opponents, without enquiring what cavils were produced against him, or by what proofs they were confuted.

Some writers apply themselves to studies boundless and inexhaustible, as experiments and natural philosophy. These are always lost in successive compilations, as new advances are made, and former observations become more familiar. Others spend their lives in remarks on language, or explanations of antiquities, and only afford materials for lexicographers and commentators, who are themselves overwhelmed by subsequent collectors, that equally destroy the memory of their predecessors by amplification, transposition, or contraction. Every new system of nature gives birth to a swarm of expositors, whose business is to explain and illustrate it, and who can hope to exist no longer than the founder of their sect preserves his reputation.

There are, indeed, few kinds of composition from which

an author, however learned or ingenious, can hope a long continuance of fame. He who has carefully studied human nature,
and can well describe it, may with most reason flatter his
ambition. *Bacon*, among all his pretensions to the regard of
posterity, seems to have pleased himself chiefly with his essays,
which come home to mens business and bosoms, and of which,
therefore, he declares his expectation, that they *will live as long
as books last*.[7] It may, however, satisfy an honest and benevolent
mind to have been useful, though less conspicuous; nor will he
that extends his hope to higher rewards, be so much anxious to
obtain praise, as to discharge the duty which Providence assigns
him.

No. 108. Saturday, 30 March 1751.

> *Sapere aude,*
> *Incipe. Vivendi recte qui prorogat horam,*
> *Rusticus expectat dum defluat amnis: at ille*
> *Labitur, & labetur in omne volubilis ævum.*
> HOR.[1]

Begin, be bold, and venture to be wise;
He who defers this work from day to day,
Does on a river's bank expecting stay,
Till the whole stream, which stop'd him, should be gone,
That runs, and as it runs, for ever will run on.
COWLEY.[2]

An ancient poet, unreasonably discontented at the present state
of things, which his system of opinions obliged him to represent
in its worst form, has observed of the earth, "that its greater
part is covered by the uninhabitable ocean; that of the rest some
is encumbered with naked mountains, and some lost under
barren sands; some scorched with unintermitted heat, and some
petrified with perpetual frost; so that only a few regions remain
for the production of fruits, the pasture of cattle, and the accommodation of man."[3]

The same observation may be transferred to the time allotted us in our present state. When we have deducted all that is absorbed in sleep, all that is inevitably appropriated to the demands of nature, or irresistibly engrossed by the tyranny of custom; all that passes in regulating the superficial decorations of life, or is given up in the reciprocations of civility to the disposal of others; all that is torn from us by the violence of disease, or stolen imperceptibly away by lassitude and languor; we shall find that part of our duration very small of which we can truly call ourselves masters, or which we can spend wholly at our own choice. Many of our hours are lost in a rotation of petty cares, in a constant recurrence of the same employments; many of our provisions for ease or happiness are always exhausted by the present day; and a great part of our existence serves no other purpose, than that of enabling us to enjoy the rest.

Of the few moments which are left in our disposal, it may reasonably be expected, that we should be so frugal, as to let none of them slip from us without some equivalent; and perhaps it might be found, that as the earth, however streightened by rocks and waters, is capable of producing more than all its inhabitants are able to consume, our lives, though much contracted by incidental distraction, would yet afford us a large space vacant to the exercise of reason and virtue; that we want not time, but diligence, for great performances; and that we squander much of our allowance, even while we think it sparing and insufficient.

This natural and necessary comminution of our lives, perhaps, often makes us insensible of the negligence with which we suffer them to slide away. We never consider ourselves as possessed at once of time sufficient for any great design, and therefore indulge ourselves in fortuitous amusements. We think it unnecessary to take an account of a few supernumerary moments, which, however employed, could have produced little advantage, and which were exposed to a thousand chances of disturbance and interruption.

It is observable, that either by nature or by habit, our faculties are fitted to images of a certain extent, to which we adjust great things by division, and little things by accumulation. Of extensive surfaces we can only take a survey, as the parts succeed one another; and atoms we cannot perceive, till they are united into masses. Thus we break the vast periods of time into centuries and years; and thus, if we would know the amount of moments, we must agglomerate them into days and weeks.

The proverbial oracles of our parsimonious ancestors have informed us, that the fatal waste of fortune is by small expences, by the profusion of sums too little singly to alarm our caution, and which we never suffer ourselves to consider together. Of the same kind is the prodigality of life; he that hopes to look back hereafter with satisfaction upon past years, must learn to know the present value of single minutes, and endeavour to let no particle of time fall useless to the ground.

It is usual for those who are advised to the attainment of any new qualification, to look upon themselves as required to change the general course of their conduct, to dismiss business, and exclude pleasure, and to devote their days and nights to a particular attention. But all common degrees of excellence are attainable at a lower price; he that should steadily and resolutely assign to any science or language those interstitial vacancies which intervene in the most crouded variety of diversion or employment, would find every day new irradiations of knowledge, and discover how much more is to be hoped from frequency and perseverance, than from violent efforts, and sudden desires; efforts which are soon remitted when they encounter difficulty, and desires which, if they are indulged too often, will shake off the authority of reason, and range capriciously from one object to another.

The disposition to defer every important design to a time of leisure, and a state of settled uniformity, proceeds generally from a false estimate of the human powers. If we except those gigantick and stupendous intelligences who are said to grasp a system by intuition, and bound forward from one series of conclusions to another, without regular steps through intermediate propositions, the most successful students make their advances in knowledge by short flights between each of which the mind may lie at rest. For every single act of progression a short time is sufficient; and it is only necessary, that whenever that time is afforded, it be well employed.

Few minds will be long confined to severe and laborious meditation; and when a successful attack on knowledge has been made, the student recreates himself with the contemplation of his conquest, and forbears another incursion, till the new-acquired truth has become familiar, and his curiosity calls upon him for fresh gratifications. Whether the time of intermission is spent in company, or in solitude, in necessary business, or in voluntary levities, the understanding is equally abstracted from the object of enquiry; but, perhaps, if it be detained by occupations less pleasing, it returns again to study with greater alacrity, than when it is glutted with ideal pleasures, and surfeited with intemperance of application. He that will not suffer himself to be discouraged by fancied impossibilities, may sometimes find his abilities invigorated by the necessity of exerting them in short intervals, as the force of a current is encreased by the contraction of its channel.

From some cause like this, it has probably proceeded, that among those who have contributed to the advancement of learning, many have risen to eminence in opposition to all the obstacles which external circumstances could place in their way, amidst the tumult of business, the distresses of poverty, or the dissipations of a wandering and unsettled state. A great part of the life of *Erasmus*[4] was one continual peregrination; ill supplied with the gifts of fortune, and led from city to city, and from kingdom to kingdom, by the hopes of patrons and preferment, hopes which always flattered and always deceived him; he yet found means by unshaken constancy, and a vigilant improvement of those hours, which, in the midst of the most restless activity, will remain unengaged, to write more than another in the same condition would have hoped to read. Compelled by want to attendance and solicitation, and so much versed in common life, that he has transmitted to us the most perfect delineation of the manners of his age, he joined to his knowledge of the world, such application to books, that he will stand for ever in the first rank of literary heroes. How this proficiency was obtained he sufficiently discovers, by informing us, that the

Praise of Folly, one of his most celebrated performances, was composed by him on the road to *Italy*; *ne totum illud tempus quo equo fuit insidendum, illiteratis fabulis terreretur*, lest the hours which he was obliged to spend on horseback, should be tattled away without regard to literature.[5]

An *Italian* philosopher expressed in his motto, that *time was his estate*;[6] an estate, indeed, which will produce nothing without cultivation, but will always abundantly repay the labours of industry, and satisfy the most extensive desires, if no part of it be suffered to lie waste by negligence, to be overrun with noxious plants, or laid out for shew rather than for use.

No. 113. Tuesday, 16 April 1751.

——— *Uxorem, Posthume, ducis?*
Dic, quâ Tisiphone, quibus exagitare colubris?
JUVENAL.[1]

A sober man like thee to change his life!
What fury wou'd possess thee with a wife?
DRYDEN.

To the RAMBLER.

SIR,

I know not whether it is always a proof of innocence to treat censure with contempt. We owe so much reverence to the wisdom of mankind, as justly to wish, that our own opinion of our merit may be ratified by the concurrence of other suffrages; and since guilt and infamy must have the same effect upon intelligences unable to pierce beyond external appearance, and influenced often rather by example than precept, we are obliged to refute a false charge, lest we should countenance the crime which we have never committed. To turn away from an accusation with supercilious silence, is equally in the power of him that is hardened by villainy, and inspirited by innocence. The wall of brass which *Horace*[2] erects upon a clear conscience, may be sometimes raised by impudence or power; and we should always wish to preserve the dignity of virtue by adorning her with graces which wickedness cannot assume.

For this reason I have determined no longer to endure, with either patient or sullen resignation, a reproach, which is, at least in my opinion, unjust; but will lay my case honestly before you, that you or your readers may at length decide it.

Whether you will be able to preserve your boasted impartiality, when you hear, that I am considered as an adversary by half the female world, you may surely pardon me for doubting, notwithstanding the veneration to which you may imagine yourself entitled by your age, your learning, your abstraction, or your virtue. Beauty, Mr. RAMBLER, has often overpowered the resolutions of the firm, and the reasonings of the wise, roused the old to sensibility, and subdued the rigorous to softness.

I am one of those unhappy beings, who have been marked out as husbands for many different women, and deliberated a hundred times on the brink of matrimony. I have discussed all the nuptial preliminaries so often, that I can repeat the forms in which jointures are settled, pin-money secured, and provisions for younger children ascertained; but am at last doomed by general consent to everlasting solitude, and excluded by an irreversible decree from all hopes of connubial felicity. I am pointed out by every mother, as a man whose visits cannot be admitted without reproach; who raises hopes only to embitter disappointment, and makes offers only to seduce girls into a waste of that part of life, in which they might gain advantageous matches, and become mistresses and mothers.

I hope you will think, that some part of this penal severity may justly be remitted, when I inform you, that I never yet professed love to a woman without sincere intentions of marriage; that I have never continued an appearance of intimacy from the hour that my inclination changed, but to preserve her whom I was leaving from the shock of abruptness, or the ignominy of contempt; that I always endeavoured to give the ladies an opportunity of seeming to discard me; and that I never forsook a mistress for larger fortune, or brighter beauty, but because I discovered some irregularity in her conduct, or some depravity in her mind; not because I was charmed by another, but because I was offended by herself.

I was very early tired of that succession of amusements by which the thoughts of most young men are dissipated, and had not long glittered in the splendour of an ample patrimony before I wished for the calm of domestick happiness. Youth is naturally delighted with sprightliness and ardour, and therefore I breathed out the sighs of my first affection at the feet of the gay, the sparkling, the vivacious *Ferocula*. I fancied to myself a perpetual source of happiness in wit never exhausted, and spirit never depressed; looked with veneration on her readiness of expedients, contempt of difficulty, assurance of address, and promptitude of reply; considered her as exempt by some prerogative of nature from the weakness and timidity of female minds; and congratulated myself upon a companion superior to all common troubles and embarrassments. I was, indeed, somewhat disturbed by the unshaken perseverance with which she enforced her demands of an unreasonable settlement; yet I should have consented to pass my life in union with her, had not my curiosity led me to a croud gathered in the street, where I found *Ferocula*, in the presence of hundreds, disputing for six-pence with a chairman. I saw her in so little need of assistance, that it was no breach of the laws of chivalry to forbear interposition, and I spared myself the shame of owning her acquaintance. I forgot some point of ceremony at our next interview, and soon provoked her to forbid me her presence.

My next attempt was upon a lady of great eminence for learning and philosophy. I had frequently observed the barrenness and uniformity of connubial conversation, and therefore thought highly of my own prudence and discernment when I selected from a multitude of wealthy beauties, the deep-read *Misothea*, who declared herself the inexorable enemy of ignorant pertness, and puerile levity; and scarcely condescended to make tea, but for the linguist, the geometrician, the astronomer, or the poet. The queen of the *Amazons* was only to be gained by the hero who could conquer her in single combat; and *Misothea*'s heart was only to bless the scholar who could overpower her by disputation. Amidst the fondest transports of courtship she could call for a definition of terms, and treated every argument with contempt that could not be reduced to regular syllogism. You may easily imagine, that I wished this courtship at an end; but when I desired her to shorten my torments, and fix the day of my felicity, we were led into a long conversation, in which *Misothea* endeavoured to demonstrate the folly of attributing choice and self-direction to any human being. It was not difficult to discover the danger of committing myself for ever to the arms of one who might at any time mistake the dictates of passion, or the calls of appetite, for the decree of fate; or consider cuckoldom as necessary to the general system, as a link in the everlasting chain of successive causes. I therefore told her, that destiny had ordained us to part; and that nothing should have torn me from her but the talons of necessity.

I then solicited the regard of the calm, the prudent, the œconomical *Sophronia*, a lady who considered wit as dangerous, and learning as superfluous; and thought that the woman who kept her house clean, and her accounts exact, took receipts for every payment, and could find them at a sudden call, enquired nicely after the condition of the tenants, read the price of stocks once a week, and purchased every thing at the best market, could want no accomplishments necessary to the happiness of a wise man. She discoursed with great solemnity on the care and vigilance which the superintendence of a family demands; observed how many were ruined by confidence in servants; and told me, that she never expected honesty but from a strong chest, and that the best storekeeper was the mistress's eye. Many such oracles of generosity she uttered, and made every day new improvements in her schemes for the regulation of her servants, and the distribution of her time. I was convinced, that whatever I might suffer from *Sophronia*, I should escape poverty; and we therefore proceeded to adjust the settlements according to her own rule, *fair and softly*. But one morning her maid came to me in tears to intreat my interest for a reconciliation to her mistress, who had turned her out at night for breaking six teeth in a tortoise-shell comb: she had attended her lady from a distant province, and having not lived long enough to save much money, was destitute among strangers, and though

of a good family, in danger of perishing in the streets, or of
being compelled by hunger to prostitution. I made no scruple
of promising to restore her; but upon my first application to
Sophronia was answered with an air which called for approbation, that if she neglected her own affairs, I might suspect her
of neglecting mine; that the comb stood her in three half-crowns;
that no servant should wrong her twice; and that indeed, she
took the first opportunity of parting with *Phyllida*, because,
though she was honest, her constitution was bad, and she
thought her very likely to fall sick. Of our conference I need not
tell you the effect; it surely may be forgiven me, if on this
occasion I forgot the decency of common forms.

From two more ladies I was disengaged by finding, that they
entertained my rivals at the same time, and determined their
choice by the liberality of our settlements. Another I thought
myself justified in forsaking, because she gave my attorney a
bribe to favour her in the bargain; another, because I could
never soften her to tenderness, till she heard that most of my
family had died young; and another, because to encrease her
fortune by expectations, she represented her sister as languishing
and consumptive.

I shall in another letter[3] give the remaining part of my history
of courtship. I presume that I should hitherto have injured the
majesty of female virtue, had I not hoped to transfer my affection
to higher merit.

I am, &c.
HYMENÆUS.

No. 114. Saturday, 20 April 1751.

——————————— *Audi,*
Nulla unquam de morte hominis cunctatio longa est.
JUV.[1]

——————— When man's life is in debate,
The judge can ne'er too long deliberate.
DRYDEN.

Power and superiority are so flattering and delightful, that, fraught with temptation and exposed to danger as they are, scarcely any virtue is so cautious, or any prudence so timorous, as to decline them. Even those that have most reverence for the laws of right, are pleased with shewing that not fear, but choice, regulates their behaviour; and would be thought to comply, rather than obey. We love to overlook the boundaries which we do not wish to pass; and, as the *Roman* satirist remarks, he that has no design to take the life of another, is yet glad to have it in his hands.[2]

From the same principle, tending yet more to degeneracy and corruption, proceeds the desire of investing lawful authority with terror, and governing by force rather than persuasion. Pride is unwilling to believe the necessity of assigning any other reason than her own will; and would rather maintain the most equitable claims by violence and penalties, than descend from the dignity of command to dispute and expostulation.

It may, I think, be suspected, that this political arrogance has sometimes found its way into legislative assemblies, and mingled with deliberations upon property and life. A slight perusal of the laws by which the measures of vindictive and coercive justice are established, will discover so many disproportions between crimes and punishments, such capricious distinctions of guilt, and such confusion of remissness and severity, as can scarcely be believed to have been produced by publick wisdom, sincerely and calmly studious of publick happiness.

The learned, the judicious, the pious *Boerhaave*[3] relates, that he never saw a criminal dragged to execution without asking himself, "Who knows whether this man is not less culpable than me?" On the days when the prisons of this city are emptied into the grave, let every spectator of the dreadful procession put the same question to his own heart. Few among those that croud in thousands to the legal massacre, and look with carelessness, perhaps with triumph, on the utmost exacerbations of human misery, would then be able to return without horror and dejection. For, who can congratulate himself upon a life passed without some act more mischievous to the peace or prosperity of others, than the theft of a piece of money?

It has been always the practice, when any particular species of robbery becomes prevalent and common, to endeavour its suppression by capital denunciations. Thus, one generation of malefactors is commonly cut off, and their successors are frighted into new expedients; the art of thievery is augmented with greater variety of fraud, and subtilized to higher degrees of dexterity, and more occult methods of conveyance. The law then renews the persuit in the heat of anger, and overtakes the offender again with death. By this practice, capital inflictions are multiplied, and crimes very different in their degrees of enormity are equally subjected to the severest punishment that man has the power of exercising upon man.

The lawgiver is undoubtedly allowed to estimate the malignity of an offence, not merely by the loss or pain which single acts may produce, but by the general alarm and anxiety arising from the fear of mischief, and insecurity of possession: he therefore exercises the right which societies are supposed to have over the lives of those that compose them, not simply to punish a transgression, but to maintain order, and preserve quiet; he enforces those laws with severity that are most in danger of violation, as the commander of a garrison doubles the guard on that side which is threatned by the enemy.

This method has been long tried, but tried with so little success, that rapine and violence are hourly encreasing; yet few seem willing to despair of its efficacy, and of those who employ their speculations upon the present corruption of the people, some propose the introduction of more horrid, lingering and terrifick punishments; some are inclined to accelerate the executions; some to discourage pardons; and all seem to think that lenity has given confidence to wickedness, and that we can only be rescued from the talons of robbery by inflexible rigour, and sanguinary justice.

Yet since the right of setting an uncertain and arbitrary value upon life has been disputed, and since experience of past times gives us little reason to hope that any reformation will be effected by a periodical havock of our fellow-beings, perhaps it will not be useless to consider what consequences might arise from relaxations of the law, and a more rational and equitable adaptation of penalties to offences.

Death is, as one of the ancients observes, τὸ τῶν φοβερῶν φοβερώτατον,[4] *of dreadful things the most dreadful;* an evil, beyond which nothing can be threatened by sublunary power, or feared from human enmity or vengeance. This terror should, therefore, be reserved as the last resort of authority, as the strongest and most operative of prohibitory sanctions, and placed before the treasure of life, to guard from invasion what cannot be restored. To equal robbery with murder is to reduce murder to robbery, to confound in common minds the gradations of iniquity, and incite the commission of a greater crime to prevent the detection of a less. If only murder were punished with death, very few robbers would stain their hands in blood; but when, by the last act of cruelty no new danger is incurred, and greater security may be obtained, upon what principle shall we bid them forbear?

It may be urged, that the sentence is often mitigated to simple robbery; but surely this is to confess, that our laws are unreasonable in our own opinion; and, indeed, it may be observed, that all but murderers have, at their last hour, the common sensations of mankind pleading in their favour.

From this conviction of the inequality of the punishment to the offence proceeds the frequent solicitation of pardons. They who would rejoice at the correction of a thief, are yet shocked at the thought of destroying him. His crime shrinks to nothing, compared with his misery; and severity defeats itself by exciting pity.

The gibbet, indeed, certainly disables those who die upon it from infesting the community; but their death seems not to contribute more to the reformation of their associates than any other method of separation. A thief seldom passes much of his time in recollection or anticipation, but from robbery hastens to riot, and from riot to robbery; nor, when the grave closes upon his companion, has any other care than to find another.

The frequency of capital punishments therefore rarely hinders the commission of a crime, but naturally and commonly prevents its detection, and is, if we proceed only upon prudential principles, chiefly for that reason to be avoided. Whatever may be urged by casuists or politicians, the greater part of mankind, as they can never think that to pick the pocket and to pierce the heart is equally criminal, will scarcely believe that two malefactors so different in guilt can be justly doomed to the same punishment; nor is the necessity of submitting the conscience to human laws so plainly evinced, so clearly stated, or so generally allowed, but that the pious, the tender, and the just, will always scruple to concur with the community in an act which their private judgment cannot approve.

He who knows not how often rigorous laws produce total impunity, and how many crimes are concealed and forgotten for fear of hurrying the offender to that state in which there is no repentance, has conversed very little with mankind. And whatever epithets of reproach or contempt this compassion may incur from those who confound cruelty with firmness, I know not whether any wise man would wish it less powerful, or less extensive.

If those whom the wisdom of our laws has condemned to die, had been detected in their rudiments of robbery, they might by proper discipline and useful labour, have been disentangled from their habits, they might have escaped all the temptations to subsequent crimes, and passed their days in reparation and penitence; and detected they might all have been, had the prosecutors been certain, that their lives would have been spared. I believe, every thief will confess, that he has been more than once seized and dismissed; and that he has sometimes ventured upon capital crimes, because he knew, that those whom he injured would rather connive at his escape, than cloud their minds with the horrors of his death.

All laws against wickedness are ineffectual, unless some will inform, and some will prosecute; but till we mitigate the penalties for mere violations of property, information will always be hated, and prosecution dreaded. The heart of a good man cannot but recoil at the thought of punishing a slight injury with death; especially when he remembers, that the thief might have procured safety by another crime, from which he was restrained only by his remaining virtue.

The obligations to assist the exercise of publick justice are indeed strong; but they will certainly be overpowered by tenderness for life. What is punished with severity contrary to our ideas of adequate retribution, will be seldom discovered; and multitudes will be suffered to advance from crime to crime, till they deserve death, because if they had been sooner prosecuted, they would have suffered death before they deserved it.

This scheme of invigorating the laws by relaxation, and extirpating wickedness by lenity, is so remote from common practice, that I might reasonably fear to expose it to the publick, could it be supported only by my own observations: I shall, therefore, by ascribing it to its author, Sir *Thomas More*,[5] endeavour to procure it that attention, which I wish always paid to prudence, to justice, and to mercy.

No. 115. Tuesday, 23 April 1751.

Quædam parva quidem, sed non toleranda maritis.
                                                    JUV.[1]

Some faults, tho' small, intolerable grow.
                                                    DRYDEN.

To the RAMBLER.

SIR,

I sit down in pursuance of my late engagement to recount the remaining part of the adventures that befel me in my long quest of conjugal felicity, which, though I have not yet been so happy as to obtain it, I have at least endeavoured to deserve by unwearied diligence, without suffering from repeated disappointments any abatement of my hope or repression of my activity.

You must have observed in the world a species of mortals who employ themselves in promoting matrimony, and without any visible motive of interest or vanity, without any discoverable impulse of malice or benevolence, without any reason, but that they want objects of attention, and topicks of conversation, are incessantly busy in procuring wives and husbands. They fill the ears of every single man and woman with some convenient match, and when they are informed of your age and fortune, offer a partner of life with the same readiness, and the same indifference, as a salesman, when he has taken measure by his eye, fits his customer with a coat.

It might be expected that they should soon be discouraged from this officious interposition by resentment or contempt; and that every man should determine the choice on which so much of his happiness must depend, by his own judgment and observation: yet it happens, that as these proposals are generally made with a shew of kindness, they seldom provoke anger, but are at worst heard with patience, and forgotten. They influence weak minds to approbation; for many are sure to find in a new acquaintance, whatever qualities report has taught them to expect; and in more powerful and active understandings they excite curiosity, and sometimes by a lucky chance bring persons of similar tempers within the attraction of each other.

I was known to possess a fortune, and to want a wife; and therefore was frequently attended by these hymeneal solicitors, with whose importunity I was sometimes diverted, and sometimes perplexed; for they contended for me as vulturs for a carcase; each employed all his eloquence, and all his artifices, to enforce and promote his own scheme, from the success of which he was to receive no other advantage than the pleasure of defeating others equally eager, and equally industrious.

An invitation to sup with one of those busy friends, made me by a concerted chance acquainted with *Camilla*, by whom it was expected, that I should be suddenly and irresistibly enslaved. The lady, whom the same kindness had brought without her own concurrence into the lists of love, seemed to think me at least worthy of the honour of captivity; and exerted the power, both of her eyes and wit, with so much art and spirit, that though I had been too often deceived by appearances to devote myself irrevocably at the first interview, yet I could not suppress some raptures of admiration, and flutters of desire. I was easily persuaded to make nearer approaches; but soon discovered, that an union with *Camilla* was not much to be wished. *Camilla* professed a boundless contempt for the folly, levity, ignorance, and impertinence of her own sex; and very frequently expressed her wonder, that men of learning or experience could submit to trifle away life, with beings incapable of solid thought. In mixed companies, she always associated with the men, and declared her satisfaction when the ladies retired. If any short excursion into the country was proposed, she commonly insisted upon the exclusion of women from the party; because, where they were admitted, the time was wasted in frothy compliments, weak indulgencies, and idle ceremonies. To shew the greatness of her mind, she avoided all compliance with the fashion; and to boast the profundity of her knowledge, mistook the various textures of silk, confounded tabbies with damasks, and sent for ribbands by wrong names. She despised the commerce of stated visits, a farce of empty form without instruction; and congratulated herself, that she never learned to write message-cards. She often applauded the noble sentiment of *Plato*, who rejoiced that he was born a man rather than a woman;[2] proclaimed her approbation of *Swift*'s opinion, that women are only a higher species of monkies;[3] and confessed, that when she considered the behaviour, or heard the conversation, of her sex, she could not but forgive the *Turks* for suspecting them to want souls.

It was the joy and pride of *Camilla* to have provoked, by this insolence, all the rage of hatred, and all the persecutions of calumny; nor was she ever more elevated with her own superiority, than when she talked of female anger, and female cunning. Well, says she, has nature provided that such virulence should be disabled by folly, and such cruelty be restrained by impotence.

CAMILLA doubtless expected, that what she lost on one side, she should gain on the other; and imagined that every male heart would be open to a lady, who made such generous advances to the borders of virility. But man, ungrateful man, instead of springing forward to meet her, shrunk back at her approach. She was persecuted by the ladies as a deserter, and at best received by the men only as a fugitive. I, for my part, amused myself a while with her fopperies, but novelty soon gave way to detestation, for nothing out of the common order of nature can be long borne. I had no inclination to a wife who had the ruggedness of man without his force, and the ignorance of woman without her softness; nor could I think my quiet and honour to be entrusted to such audacious virtue as was hourly courting danger, and soliciting assault.

My next mistress was *Nitella*, a lady of gentle mien, and soft voice, always speaking to approve, and ready to receive direction from those with whom chance had brought her into company. In *Nitella* I promised myself an easy friend, with whom I might loiter away the day without disturbance or altercation. I therefore soon resolved to address her, but was discouraged from prosecuting my courtship by observing, that her apartments were superstitiously regular; and that, unless she had notice of my visit, she was never to be seen. There is a kind of anxious cleanliness which I have always noted as the characteristick of a slattern; it is the superfluous scrupulosity of guilt, dreading discovery, and shunning suspicion: it is the violence of an effort against habit, which, being impelled by external motives, cannot stop at the middle point.

NITELLA was always tricked out rather with nicety than elegance; and seldom could forbear to discover by her uneasiness and constraint, that her attention was burdened, and her imagination engrossed: I therefore concluded, that being only occasionally and ambitiously dressed, she was not familiarized to her own ornaments. There are so many competitors for the fame of cleanliness, that it is not hard to gain information of those that fail, from those that desire to excel: I quickly found, that *Nitella* passed her time between finery and dirt; and was always in a wrapper, night-cap, and slippers, when she was not decorated for immediate shew.

I was then led by my evil destiny to *Charybdis*, who never neglected an opportunity of seizing a new prey when it came within her reach. I thought myself quickly made happy by a permission to attend her to publick places; and pleased my own vanity with imagining the envy which I should raise in a thousand hearts, by appearing as the acknowledged favourite of *Charybdis*. She soon after hinted her intention to take a ramble for a fortnight, into a part of the kingdom which she had never seen. I solicited the happiness of accompanying her, which, after a short reluctance, was indulged me. She had no other curiosity in her journey, than after all possible means of expence; and was every moment taking occasion to mention some delicacy, which I knew it my duty upon such notices to procure.

After our return, being now more familiar, she told me, whenever we met, of some new diversion; at night she had notice of a charming company that would breakfast in the gardens; and in the morning had been informed of some new song in the opera, some new dress at the play-house, or some performer at a concert whom she longed to hear. Her intelligence was such, that there never was a shew, to which she did not summon me on the second day; and as she hated a croud, and could not go alone, I was obliged to attend at some intermediate hour, and pay the price of a whole company. When we passed the streets, she was often charmed with some trinket in the toy-shops; and from moderate desires of seals and snuff-boxes, rose, by degrees, to gold and diamonds. I now began to find the smile of *Charybdis* too costly for a private purse, and added one more to six and forty lovers, whose fortune and patience her rapacity had exhausted.

IMPERIA then took possession of my affections; but kept them only for a short time. She had newly inherited a large fortune, and, having spent the early part of her life in the perusal of romances, brought with her into the gay world all the pride of *Cleopatra*; expected nothing less than vows, altars, and sacrifices; and thought her charms dishonoured, and her power infringed, by the softest opposition to her sentiments, or the smallest transgression of her commands. Time might indeed cure this species of pride in a mind not naturally undiscerning, and vitiated only by false representations; but the operations of time are slow; and I therefore left her to grow wise at leisure, or to continue in error at her own expence.

Thus I have hitherto, in spite of myself, passed my life in frozen celibacy. My friends, indeed, often tell me, that I flatter my imagination with higher hopes than human nature can gratify; that I dress up an ideal charmer in all the radiance of perfection, and then enter the world to look for the same

excellence in corporeal beauty. But surely, Mr. RAMBLER, it is
not madness to hope for some terrestrial lady unstained with
the spots which I have been describing; at least, I am resolved
to pursue my search; for I am so far from thinking meanly of
marriage, that I believe it able to afford the highest happiness
decreed to our present state; and if after all these miscarriages I
find a woman that fills up my expectation, you shall hear once
more from

Yours, &c.
HYMENÆUS.

No. 121. Tuesday, 14 May 1751.

O imitatores, servum pecus!
HOR.[1]

Away, ye imitators, servile herd!
ELPHINSTON.

I have been informed by a letter, from one of the universities,
that among the youth from whom the next swarm of reasoners
is to learn philosophy, and the next flight of beauties to hear
elegies and sonnets, there are many, who, instead of endeavouring by books and meditation to form their own opinions,
content themselves with the secondary knowledge, which a
convenient bench in a coffee-house can supply; and, without any
examination or distinction, adopt the criticisms and remarks,
which happen to drop from those, who have risen, by merit or
fortune, to reputation and authority.

These humble retailers of knowledge my correspondent stig-
matizes with the name of *Echoes*; and seems desirous, that they
should be made ashamed of lazy submission, and animated to
attempts after new discoveries, and original sentiments.

It is very natural for young men to be vehement, acrimonious,
and severe. For, as they seldom comprehend at once all the
consequences of a position, or perceive the difficulties by which
cooler and more experienced reasoners are restrained from

confidence, they form their conclusions with great precipitance. Seeing nothing that can darken or embarrass the question, they expect to find their own opinion universally prevalent, and are inclined to impute uncertainty and hesitation to want of honesty, rather than of knowledge. I may, perhaps, therefore be reproached by my lively correspondent, when it shall be found, that I have no inclination to persecute these collectors of fortuitous knowledge with the severity required; yet, as I am now too old to be much pained by hasty censure, I shall not be afraid of taking into protection those whom I think condemned without a sufficient knowledge of their cause.

He that adopts the sentiments of another, whom he has reason to believe wiser than himself, is only to be blamed, when he claims the honours which are not due but to the author, and endeavours to deceive the world into praise and veneration; for, to learn, is the proper business of youth; and whether we encrease our knowledge by books, or by conversation, we are equally indebted to foreign assistance.

The greater part of students are not born with abilities to construct systems, or advance knowledge; nor can have any hope beyond that of becoming intelligent hearers in the schools of art, of being able to comprehend what others discover, and to remember what others teach. Even those to whom Providence has allotted greater strength of understanding, can expect only to improve a single science. In every other part of learning, they must be content to follow opinions, which they are not able to examine; and, even in that which they claim as peculiarly their own, can seldom add more than some small particle of knowledge, to the hereditary stock devolved to them from ancient times, the collective labour of a thousand intellects.

In science, which being fixed and limited, admits of no other variety than such as arises from new methods of distribution, or new arts of illustration, the necessity of following the traces of our predecessors is indisputably evident; but there appears no reason, why imagination should be subject to the same restraint. It might be conceived, that of those who profess to forsake the narrow paths of truth every one may deviate towards a different point, since though rectitude is uniform and fixed, obliquity may be infinitely diversified. The roads of science are narrow, so that they who travel them, must either follow or meet one another; but in the boundless regions of possibility, which fiction claims for her dominion, there are surely a thousand recesses unexplored, a thousand flowers unplucked, a thousand fountains unexhausted, combinations of imagery yet unobserved, and races of ideal inhabitants not hitherto described.

Yet, whatever hope may persuade, or reason evince, experience can boast of very few additions to ancient fable. The wars of *Troy*, and the travels of *Ulysses*, have furnished almost all succeeding poets with incidents, characters, and sentiments. The *Romans* are confessed to have attempted little more than to display in their own tongue the inventions of the *Greeks*. There is, in all their writings, such a perpetual recurrence of allusions to the tales of the fabulous age, that they must be confessed often to want that power of giving pleasure which novelty supplies; nor can we wonder, that they excelled so much in the graces of diction, when we consider how rarely they were employed in search of new thoughts.

The warmest admirers of the great *Mantuan* poet[2] can extol him for little more than the skill with which he has, by making his hero both a traveller and a warrior, united the beauties of the *Iliad* and *Odyssey* in one composition: yet his judgment was perhaps sometimes overborn by his avarice of the *Homeric* treasures; and, for fear of suffering a sparkling ornament to be lost, he has inserted it where it cannot shine with its original splendor.

When *Ulysses* visited the infernal regions,[3] he found, among the heroes that perished at *Troy*, his competitor *Ajax*, who, when the arms of *Achilles* were adjudged to *Ulysses*, died by his own hand in the madness of disappointment. He still appeared to resent, as on earth, his loss and disgrace. *Ulysses* endeavoured to pacify him with praises and submission; but *Ajax* walked away without reply. This passage has always been considered as eminently beautiful; because *Ajax*, the haughty chief, the unlettered soldier, of unshaken courage, of immoveable constancy, but without the power of recommending his own virtues by eloquence, or enforcing his assertions by any other argument than the sword, had no way of making his anger known, but by gloomy sullenness, and dumb ferocity. His hatred of a man whom he conceived to have defeated him only by volubility of tongue, was therefore naturally shewn by silence more contemptuous and piercing than any words that so rude an orator could have found, and by which he gave his enemy no opportunity of exerting the only power in which he was superior.

When *Æneas* is sent by *Virgil* to the shades,[4] he meets *Dido* the queen of *Carthage*, whom his perfidy had hurried to the grave; he accosts her with tenderness and excuses; but the lady turns away like *Ajax* in mute disdain. She turns away like *Ajax*, but she resembles him in none of those qualities which give either dignity or propriety to silence. She might, without any departure from the tenour of her conduct, have burst out like other injured women into clamour, reproach, and denunciation; but *Virgil* had his imagination full of *Ajax*, and therefore could not prevail on himself to teach *Dido* any other mode of resentment.

If *Virgil* could be thus seduced by imitation, there will be little hope, that common wits should escape; and accordingly we find, that besides the universal and acknowledged practice of copying the ancients, there has prevailed in every age a particular species of fiction. At one time all truth was conveyed in allegory; at another, nothing was seen but in a vision; at one period, all the poets followed sheep, and every event produced a pastoral; at another they busied themselves wholly in giving directions to a painter.[5]

It is indeed easy to conceive why any fashion should become popular, by which idleness is favoured, and imbecillity assisted; but surely no man of genius can much applaud himself for repeating a tale with which the audience is already tired, and which could bring no honour to any but its inventor.

There are, I think, two schemes of writing, on which the laborious wits of the present time employ their faculties. One is the adaptation of sense to all the rhymes which our language can supply to some word, that makes the burden of the stanza; but this, as it has been only used in a kind of amorous burlesque, can scarcely be censured with much acrimony. The other is the imitation of *Spenser*, which, by the influence of some men of learning and genius, seems likely to gain upon the age, and therefore deserves to be more attentively considered.

To imitate the fictions and sentiments of *Spenser* can incur no reproach, for allegory is perhaps one of the most pleasing vehicles of instruction. But I am very far from extending the same respect to his diction or his stanza. His stile was in his own time allowed to be vicious, so darkened with old words and peculiarities of phrase, and so remote from common use, that *Johnson* boldly pronounces him *to have written no language.*[6] His stanza is at once difficult and unpleasing; tiresome to the ear by its uniformity, and to the attention by its length. It was at first formed in imitation of the *Italian* poets, without due regard to the genius of our language. The *Italians* have little variety of termination, and were forced to contrive such a stanza as might admit the greatest number of similar rhymes; but our words end with so much diversity,[7] that it is seldom convenient for us to bring more than two of the same sound together. If it be justly observed by *Milton*,[8] that rhyme obliges poets to express their thoughts in improper terms, these improprieties must always be multiplied, as the difficulty of rhyme is encreased by long concatenations.

The imitators of *Spenser*[9] are indeed not very rigid censors of themselves, for they seem to conclude, that when they have disfigured their lines with a few obsolete syllables, they have accomplished their design, without considering that they ought not only to admit old words, but to avoid new. The laws of imitation are broken by every word introduced since the time of *Spenser*, as the character of *Hector* is violated by quoting *Aristotle* in the play.[10] It would indeed be difficult to exclude from a long poem all modern phrases, though it is easy to sprinkle it with gleanings of antiquity. Perhaps, however, the stile of *Spenser* might by long labour be justly copied; but life is surely given us for higher purposes than to gather what our ancestors have wisely thrown away, and to learn what is of no value, but because it has been forgotten.

No. 129. Tuesday, 11 June 1751.

—— *Nunc, o nunc, Dædale, dixit,*
Materiam, qua sis ingeniosus, habes.
Possidet en terras, et possidet æquora Minos:
Nec tellus nostræ, nec patet unda fugæ.
Restat iter cælo: cælo tentabimus ire.
Da veniam cæpto, Jupiter alte, meo.

OVID.[1]

Now, *Dædalus*, behold, by fate assign'd,
A task proportion'd to thy mighty mind!
Unconquer'd bars on earth and sea withstand;
Thine, *Minos*, is the main, and thine the land.
The skies are open —— let us try the skies:
Forgive, great *Jove*, the daring enterprize.

Moralists, like other writers, instead of casting their eyes abroad in the living world, and endeavouring to form maxims of practice and new hints of theory, content their curiosity with that secondary knowledge which books afford, and think themselves entitled to reverence by a new arrangement of an ancient system, or new illustration of established principles. The sage precepts of the first instructors of the world are transmitted from age to age with little variation, and echoed from one author to another, not perhaps without some loss of their original force at every repercussion.

I know not whether any other reason than this idleness of imitation can be assigned for that uniform and constant partiality, by which some vices have hitherto escaped censure, and some virtues wanted recommendation; nor can I discover why else we have been warned only against part of our enemies, while the rest have been suffered to steal upon us without notice; why the heart has on one side been doubly fortified, and laid open on the other to the incursions of error, and the ravages of vice.

Among the favourite topicks of moral declamation, may be

numbered the miscarriages of imprudent boldness, and the folly of attempts beyond our power. Every page of every philosopher is crouded with examples of temerity that sunk under burthens which she laid upon herself, and called out enemies to battle by whom she was destroyed.

Their remarks are too just to be disputed, and too salutary to be rejected; but there is likewise some danger lest timorous prudence should be inculcated, till courage and enterprize are wholly repressed, and the mind congealed in perpetual inactivity by the fatal influence of frigorifick[2] wisdom.

Every man should, indeed, carefully compare his force with his undertaking; for though we ought not to live only for our own sakes, and though therefore danger or difficulty should not be avoided merely because we may expose ourselves to misery or disgrace; yet it may be justly required of us, not to throw away our lives, upon inadequate and hopeless designs, since we might by a just estimate of our abilities become more useful to mankind.

There is an irrational contempt of danger which approaches nearly to the folly, if not the guilt, of suicide; there is a ridiculous perseverance in impracticable schemes, which is justly punished with ignominy and reproach. But in the wide regions of probability which are the proper province of prudence and election, there is always room to deviate on either side of rectitude without rushing against apparent absurdity; and according to the inclinations of nature, or the impressions of precept, the daring and the cautious may move in different directions without touching upon rashness or cowardice.

That there is a middle path which it is every man's duty to find, and to keep, is unanimously confessed; but it is likewise acknowledged that this middle path is so narrow, that it cannot easily be discovered, and so little beaten that there are no certain marks by which it can be followed; the care therefore of all those who conduct others has been, that whenever they decline into obliquities, they should tend towards the side of safety.

It can, indeed, raise no wonder that temerity has been generally censured; for it is one of the vices with which few can be charged, and which therefore great numbers are ready to condemn. It is the vice of noble and generous minds, the exuberance of magnanimity, and the ebullition of genius; and is therefore not regarded with much tenderness, because it never flatters us by that appearance of softness and imbecillity which is commonly necessary to conciliate compassion. But if the same attention had been applied to the search of arguments against the folly of presupposing impossibilities, and anticipating frustration, I know not whether many would not have been roused to usefulness, who, having been taught to confound prudence with timidity, never ventured to excel, lest they should unfortunately fail.

It is necessary to distinguish our own interest from that of others, and that distinction will perhaps assist us in fixing the just limits of caution and adventurousness. In an undertaking that involves the happiness, or the safety of many, we have certainly no right to hazard more than is allowed by those who partake the danger; but where only ourselves can suffer by miscarriage, we are not confined within such narrow limits; and still less is the reproach of temerity, when numbers will receive advantage by success, and only one be incommoded by failure.

Men are generally willing to hear precepts by which ease is favoured; and as no resentment is raised by general representations of human folly, even in those who are most eminently jealous of comparative reputation, we confess, without reluctance, that vain man is ignorant of his own weakness, and therefore frequently presumes to attempt what he can never accomplish; but it ought likewise to be remembered, that man is no less ignorant of his own powers, and might perhaps have accomplished a thousand designs, which the prejudices of cowardice restrained him from attempting.

It is observed in the golden verses of *Pythagoras*, that *Power is never far from necessity*.[3] The vigour of the human mind quickly appears, when there is no longer any place for doubt and hesitation, when diffidence is absorbed in the sense of danger, or overwhelmed by some resistless passion. We then soon discover, that difficulty is, for the most part, the daughter of idleness, that the obstacles with which our way seemed to be obstructed were only phantoms, which we believed real because we durst not advance to a close examination; and we learn that it is impossible to determine without experience how much constancy may endure, or perseverance perform.

But whatever pleasure may be found in the review of distresses when art or courage has surmounted them, few will be persuaded to wish that they may be awakened by want or terror to the conviction of their own abilities. Every one should therefore endeavour to invigorate himself by reason and reflection, and determine to exert the latent force that nature may have reposited in him before the hour of exigence comes upon him, and compulsion shall torture him to diligence. It is below the dignity of a reasonable being to owe that strength to necessity which ought always to act at the call of choice, or to need any other motive to industry than the desire of performing his duty.

Reflections that may drive away despair, cannot be wanting to him who considers how much life is now advanced beyond the state of naked, undisciplined, uninstructed nature. Whatever has been effected for convenience or elegance, while it was yet unknown, was believed impossible; and therefore would never have been attempted, had not some, more daring than the rest, adventured to bid defiance to prejudice and censure. Nor is there yet any reason to doubt that the same labour would be rewarded with the same success. There are qualities in the products of nature yet undiscovered, and combinations in the powers of art yet untried. It is the duty of every man to endeavour that something may be added by his industry to the hereditary aggregate of knowledge and happiness. To add much can indeed be the lot of few, but to add something, however little, every one may hope; and of every honest endeavour it is certain, that, however unsuccessful, it will be at last rewarded.

No. 134. Saturday, 29 June 1751.

Quis scit, an adjiciant hodiernæ crastina summæ
Tempora Dî superi!

HOR.[1]

Who knows if Heav'n, with ever-bounteous pow'r,
Shall add to-morrow to the present hour?

FRANCIS.

I sat yesterday morning employed in deliberating on which, among the various subjects that occurred to my imagination, I should bestow the paper of to-day. After a short effort of meditation by which nothing was determined, I grew every moment more irresolute, my ideas wandered from the first intention, and I rather wished to think, than thought, upon any settled subject; till at last I was awakened from this dream of study by a summons from the press: the time was come for which I had been thus negligently purposing to provide, and, however dubious or sluggish, I was now necessitated to write.

Though to a writer whose design is so comprehensive and miscellaneous, that he may accommodate himself with a topick from every scene of life, or view of nature, it is no great aggravation of his task to be obliged to a sudden composition, yet I could not forbear to reproach myself for having so long neglected what was unavoidably to be done, and of which every moment's idleness increased the difficulty. There was however some pleasure in reflecting that I, who had only trifled till diligence was necessary, might still congratulate myself upon my superiority to multitudes, who have trifled till diligence is vain; who can by no degree of activity or resolution recover the opportunities which have slipped away; and who are condemned by their own carelesness to hopeless calamity and barren sorrow.

The folly of allowing ourselves to delay what we know cannot be finally escaped, is one of the general weaknesses, which, in spite of the instruction of moralists, and the remonstrances of reason, prevail to a greater or less degree in every mind: even they who most steadily withstand it, find it, if not the most violent, the most pertinacious of their passions, always renewing its attacks, and though often vanquished, never destroyed.

It is indeed natural to have particular regard to the time present, and to be most solicitous for that which is by its nearness enabled to make the strongest impressions. When therefore any sharp pain is to be suffered, or any formidable danger to be incurred, we can scarcely exempt ourselves wholly from the seducements of imagination; we readily believe that another day will bring some support or advantage which we now want; and are easily persuaded, that the moment of necessity which we desire never to arrive, is at a great distance from us.

Thus life is languished away in the gloom of anxiety, and consumed in collecting resolution which the next morning dissipates; in forming purposes which we scarcely hope to keep, and reconciling ourselves to our own cowardice by excuses, which, while we admit them, we know to be absurd. Our firmness is by the continual contemplation of misery hourly impaired; every submission to our fear enlarges its dominion; we not only waste that time in which the evil we dread might have been suffered and surmounted, but even where procrastination produces no absolute encrease of our difficulties, make them less superable to ourselves by habitual terrors. When evils cannot be avoided, it is wise to contract the interval of expectation; to meet the mischiefs which will overtake us if we fly; and suffer only their real malignity without the conflicts of doubt and anguish of anticipation.

To act is far easier than to suffer, yet we every day see the progress of life retarded by the *vis inertiae*, the mere repugnance to motion, and find multitudes repining at the want of that which nothing but idleness hinders them from enjoying. The case of *Tantalus*,[2] in the region of poetick punishment, was somewhat to be pitied, because the fruits that hung about him retired from his hand; but what tenderness can be claimed by those who though perhaps they suffer the pains of *Tantalus* will never lift their hands for their own relief?

There is nothing more common among this torpid generation than murmurs and complaints; murmurs at uneasiness which only vacancy and suspicion expose them to feel, and complaints of distresses which it is in their own power to remove. Laziness is commonly associated with timidity. Either fear originally prohibits endeavours by infusing despair of success; or the frequent failure of irresolute struggles, and the constant desire of avoiding labour, impress by degrees false terrors on the mind. But fear, whether natural or acquired, when once it has full possession of the fancy, never fails to employ it upon visions of calamity, such as if they are not dissipated by useful employment, will soon overcast it with horrors, and imbitter life not only with those miseries by which all earthly beings are really more or less tormented, but with those which do not yet exist, and which can only be discerned by the perspicacity of cowardice.

Among all who sacrifice future advantage to present inclination, scarcely any gain so little as those that suffer themselves to freeze in idleness. Others are corrupted by some enjoyment of more or less power to gratify the passions; but to neglect our duties, merely to avoid the labour of performing them, a labour which is always punctually rewarded, is surely to sink under weak temptations. Idleness never can secure tranquillity; the call of reason and of conscience will pierce the closest pavilion of the sluggard, and, though it may not have force to drive him from his down, will be loud enough to hinder him from sleep. Those moments which he cannot resolve to make useful by devoting them to the great business of his being, will still be usurped by powers that will not leave them to his disposal; remorse and vexation will seize upon them, and forbid him to enjoy what he is so desirous to appropriate.

There are other causes of inactivity incident to more active faculties and more acute discernment. He to whom many objects of persuit arise at the same time, will frequently hesitate between different desires, till a rival has precluded him, or change his course as new attractions prevail, and harrass himself without advancing. He who sees different ways to the same end, will, unless he watches carefully over his own conduct, lay out too much of his attention upon the comparison of probabilities, and the adjustment of expedients, and pause in the choice of his road, till some accident intercepts his journey. He whose penetration extends to remote consequences, and who, whenever he applies his attention to any design, discovers new prospects of advantage, and possibilities of improvement, will not easily be persuaded that his project is ripe for execution; but will superadd one contrivance to another, endeavour to unite various purposes in one operation, multiply complications, and refine niceties, till he is entangled in his own scheme, and bewildered in the perplexity of various intentions. He that resolves to unite all the beauties of situation in a new purchase, must waste his life in roving to no purpose from province to province. He that hopes in the same house to obtain every convenience, may draw plans and study *Palladio*,[3] but will never lay a stone. He will attempt a treatise on some important subject, and amass materials, consult authors, and study all the dependent and collateral parts of learning, but never conclude himself qualified to write. He that has abilities to conceive perfection, will not easily be content without it; and since perfection cannot be reached, will lose the opportunity of doing well in the vain hope of unattainable excellence.

The certainty that life cannot be long, and the probability that it will be much shorter than nature allows, ought to awaken every man to the active prosecution of whatever he is desirous to perform. It is true that no diligence can ascertain success; death may intercept the swiftest career; but he who is cut off in the execution of an honest undertaking, has at least the honour of falling in his rank, and has fought the battle, though he missed the victory.

No. 135. Tuesday, 2 July 1751.

Cœlum, non animum mutant.
HOR.[1]

Place may be chang'd; but who can change his mind?

It is impossible to take a view on any side, or observe any of the various classes that form the great community of the world, without discovering the influence of example; and admitting with new conviction the observation of *Aristotle*, that *man is an imitative being*.[2] The greater, far the greater, number follow the track which others have beaten, without any curiosity after new discoveries, or ambition of trusting themselves to their own conduct. And, of those who break the ranks and disorder the uniformity of the march, most return in a short time from their deviation, and prefer the equal and steady satisfaction of security before the frolicks of caprice and the honours of adventure.

In questions difficult or dangerous it is indeed natural to repose upon authority, and, when fear happens to predominate, upon the authority of those whom we do not in general think wiser than ourselves. Very few have abilities requisite for the discovery of abstruse truth; and of those few some want leisure and some resolution. But it is not so easy to find the reason of the universal submission to precedent where every man might safely judge for himself; where no irreparable loss can be hazarded, nor any mischief of long continuance incurred. Vanity might be expected to operate where the more powerful passions are not awakened; the mere pleasure of acknowledging no superior might produce slight singularities, or the hope of gaining some new degree of happiness awaken the mind to invention or experiment.

If in any case the shackles of prescription could be wholly shaken off, and the imagination left to act without controul, on what occasion should it be expected, but in the selection of lawful pleasure? Pleasure, of which the essence is choice; which compulsion dissociates from every thing to which nature has united it; and which owes not only its vigour but its being to the smiles of liberty. Yet we see that the senses, as well as the reason, are regulated by credulity; and that most will feel, or say that they feel, the gratifications which others have taught them to expect.

At this time of universal migration, when almost every one, considerable enough to attract regard, has retired, or is preparing with all the earnestness of distress to retire, into the country; when nothing is to be heard but the hopes of speedy departure, or the complaints of involuntary delay; I have often been tempted to enquire what happiness is to be gained, or what inconvenience to be avoided, by this stated recession. Of the birds of passage, some follow the summer, and some the winter, because they live upon sustenance which only summer or winter can supply; but of the annual flight of human rovers it is much harder to assign the reason, because they do not appear either to find or seek any thing which is not equally afforded by the town and country.

I believe, that many of these fugitives may have heard of men whose continual wish was for the quiet of retirement, who watched every opportunity to steal away from observation, to forsake the croud, and delight themselves with *the society of solitude*.[3] There is indeed scarcely any writer who has not celebrated the happiness of rural privacy, and delighted himself and his reader with the melody of birds, the whisper of groves, and the murmur of rivulets; nor any man eminent for extent of capacity, or greatness of exploits, that has not left behind him some memorials of lonely wisdom, and silent dignity.

But almost all absurdity of conduct arises from the imitation of those whom we cannot resemble. Those who thus testified their weariness of tumult and hurry, and hasted with so much eagerness to the leisure of retreat, were either men overwhelmed with the pressure of difficult employments, harrassed with importunities, and distracted with multiplicity; or men wholly engrossed by speculative sciences, who having no other end of life but to learn and teach, found their searches interrupted by the common commerce of civility, and their reasonings disjointed by frequent interruptions. Such men might reasonably fly to that ease and convenience which their condition allowed them to find only in the country. The statesman who devoted the greater part of his time to the publick, was desirous of keeping the remainder in his own power. The general ruffled with dangers, wearied with labours, and stunned with acclamations, gladly snatched an interval of silence and relaxation. The naturalist was unhappy where the works of providence were not always before him. The reasoner could adjust his systems only where his mind was free from the intrusion of outward objects.

Such examples of solitude very few of those who are now hastening from the town, have any pretensions to plead in their own justification, since they cannot pretend either weariness of labour, or desire of knowledge. They purpose nothing more than to quit one scene of idleness for another, and after having trifled in publick, to sleep in secrecy. The utmost that they can hope to gain is the change of ridiculousness to obscurity, and the privilege of having fewer witnesses to a life of folly. He who is not sufficiently important to be disturbed in his pursuits, but spends all his hours according to his own inclination, and has more hours than his mental faculties enable him to fill either with enjoyment or desires, can have nothing to demand of shades and valleys. As bravery is said to be a panoply, insignificancy is always a shelter.

There are however pleasures and advantages in a rural situation, which are not confined to philosophers and heroes. The freshness of the air, the verdure of the woods, the paint of the meadows, and the unexhausted variety which summer scatters upon the earth, may easily give delight to an unlearned spectator. It is not necessary that he who looks with pleasure on the colours of a flower should study the principles of vegetation, or that the *Ptolemaick* and *Copernican* system[4] should be compared before the light of the sun can gladden, or its warmth invigorate. Novelty is itself a source of gratification, and *Milton* justly observes,[5] that to him who has been long pent up in cities no rural object can be presented, which will not delight or refresh some of his senses.

Yet even these easy pleasures are missed by the greater part of those who waste their summer in the country. Should any man pursue his acquaintances to their retreats, he would find few of them listening to *Philomel*, loitering in woods, or plucking daisies, catching the healthy gale of the morning, or watching the gentle coruscations of declining day. Some will be discovered at a window by the road side, rejoicing when a new cloud of dust gathers towards them, as at the approach of a momentary supply of conversation, and a short relief from the tediousness of unideal vacancy. Others are placed in the adjacent villages, where they look only upon houses as in the rest of the year, with no change of objects but what a remove to any new street in *London* might have given them. The same set of acquaintances

still settle together, and the form of life is not otherwise diversified than by doing the same things in a different place. They pay
and receive visits in the usual form, they frequent the walks in
the morning, they deal cards at night, they attend to the same
tattle, and dance with the same partners; nor can they at their
return to their former habitation congratulate themselves on
any other advantage, than that they have passed their time like
others of the same rank; and have the same right to talk of the
happiness and beauty of the country, of happiness which they
never felt, and beauty which they never regarded.

To be able to procure its own entertainments, and to subsist
upon its own stock, is not the prerogative of every mind. There
are indeed understandings so fertile and comprehensive, that
they can always feed reflection with new supplies, and suffer
nothing from the preclusion of adventitious amusements; as
some cities have within their own walls enclosed ground enough
to feed their inhabitants in a siege. But others live only from day
to day, and must be constantly enabled, by foreign supplies, to
keep out the encroachments of languor and stupidity. Such
could not indeed be blamed for hovering within reach of their
usual pleasures, more than any other animal for not quitting its
native element, were not their faculties contracted by their own
fault. But let not those who go into the country, merely because
they dare not be left alone at home, boast their love of nature,
or their qualifications for solitude; nor pretend that they receive
instantaneous infusions of wisdom from the *Dryads*,[6] and are
able, when they leave smoke and noise behind, to act, or think,
or reason for themselves.

No. 137. Tuesday, 9 July 1751.

Dum vitant stulti vitia, in contraria currunt.
HOR.[1]

———— Whilst fools one vice condemn,
They run into the opposite extreme.
CREECH.

That wonder is the effect of ignorance, has been often observed. The awful stillness of attention, with which the mind is overspread at the first view of an unexpected effect, ceases when we have leisure to disentangle complications and investigate causes. Wonder is a pause of reason, a sudden cessation of the mental progress, which lasts only while the understanding is fixed upon some single idea, and is at an end when it recovers force enough to divide the object into its parts, or mark the intermediate gradations from the first agent to the last consequence.

It may be remarked with equal truth, that ignorance is often the effect of wonder. It is common for those who have never accustomed themselves to the labour of enquiry, nor invigorated their confidence by conquests over difficulty, to sleep in the gloomy quiescence of astonishment, without any effort to animate enquiry or dispel obscurity. What they cannot immediately conceive, they consider as too high to be reached, or too extensive to be comprehended; they therefore content themselves with the gaze of folly, forbear to attempt what they have no hopes of performing, and resign the pleasure of rational contemplation to more pertinacious study or more active faculties.

Among the productions of mechanic art, many are of a form so different from that of their first materials, and many consist of parts so numerous and so nicely adapted to each other, that it is not possible to view them without amazement. But when we enter the shops of artificers, observe the various tools by which every operation is facilitated, and trace the progress of a manufacture thro' the different hands that, in succession to each other, contribute to its perfection, we soon discover that every single man has an easy task, and that the extremes however remote of natural rudeness and artificial elegance, are joined by a regular concatenation of effects, of which every one is introduced by that which precedes it, and equally introduces that which is to follow.

The same is the state of intellectual and manual performances. Long calculations or complex diagrams affright the timorous and unexperienced from a second view; but if we have skill sufficient to analise them into simple principles, it will be discovered that our fear was groundless. *Divide and conquer*,[2] is a principle equally just in science as in policy. Complication is a species of confederacy, which, while it continues united, bids defiance to the most active and vigorous intellect; but of which every member is separately weak, and which may therefore be quickly subdued if it can once be broken.

The chief art of learning, as *Locke* has observed,[3] is to attempt but little at a time. The widest excursions of the mind are made by short flights frequently repeated; the most lofty fabricks of science are formed by the continued accumulation of single propositions.

It often happens, whatever be the cause, that impatience of labour or dread of miscarriage, seizes those who are most distinguished for quickness of apprehension; and that they who might with greatest reason promise themselves victory, are least willing to hazard the encounter. This diffidence, where the attention is not laid asleep by laziness or dissipated by pleasures, can arise only from confused and general views, such as negligence snatches in haste, or from the disappointment of the first hopes formed by arrogance without reflection. To expect that the intricacies of science will be pierced by a careless glance, or the eminences of fame ascended without labour, is to expect a peculiar privilege, a power denied to the rest of mankind; but to suppose that the maze is inscrutable to diligence, or the heights inaccessible to perseverance, is to submit tamely to the tyranny of fancy, and enchain the mind in voluntary shackles.

It is the proper ambition of the heroes in literature to enlarge the boundaries of knowledge by discovering and conquering new regions of the intellectual world. To the success of such undertakings perhaps some degree of fortuitous happiness is necessary, which no man can promise or procure to himself; and therefore doubt and irresolution may be forgiven in him that ventures into the unexplored abysses of truth, and attempts to find his way through the fluctuations of uncertainty, and the conflicts of contradiction. But when nothing more is required, than to pursue a path already beaten, and to trample obstacles which others have demolished, why should any man so much distrust his own intellect as to imagine himself unequal to the attempt?

It were to be wished that they who devote their lives to study would at once believe nothing too great for their attainment, and consider nothing as too little for their regard; that they would extend their notice alike to science and to life, and unite some knowledge of the present world to their acquaintance with past ages and remote events.

Nothing has so much exposed men of learning to contempt and ridicule, as their ignorance of things which are known to all but themselves. Those who have been taught to consider the institutions of the schools, as giving the last perfection to human abilities, are surprised to see men wrinkled with study, yet wanting to be instructed in the minute circumstances of propriety, or the necessary forms of daily transaction; and quickly shake off their reverence for modes of education, which they find to produce no ability above the rest of mankind.

BOOKS, says Bacon, *can never teach the use of books.*[4] The student must learn by commerce with mankind to reduce his speculations to practice, and accommodate his knowledge to the purposes of life.

It is too common for those who have been bred to scholastic professions, and passed much of their time in academies where nothing but learning confers honours, to disregard every other qualification, and to imagine that they shall find mankind ready to pay homage to their knowledge, and to crowd about them for instruction. They, therefore, step out from their cells into the open world, with all the confidence of authority and dignity of importance; they look round about them at once with ignorance and scorn on a race of beings to whom they are equally unknown and equally contemptible, but whose manners they must imitate, and with whose opinions they must comply, if they desire to pass their time happily among them.

To lessen that disdain with which scholars are inclined to look on the common business of the world, and the unwillingness with which they condescend to learn what is not to be found in any system of philosophy, it may be necessary to consider that though admiration is excited by abstruse researches and remote discoveries, yet pleasure is not given, nor affection conciliated, but by softer accomplishments, and qualities more easily communicable to those about us. He that can only converse upon questions, about which only a small part of mankind has knowledge sufficient to make them curious, must lose his days in unsocial silence, and live in the crowd of life without a companion. He that can only be useful in great occasions, may die without exerting his abilities, and stand a helpless spectator of a thousand vexations which fret away happiness, and which nothing is required to remove but a little dexterity of conduct and readiness of expedients.

No degree of knowledge attainable by man is able to set him above the want of hourly assistance, or to extinguish the desire of fond endearments, and tender officiousness; and therefore, no one should think it unnecessary to learn those arts by which friendship may be gained. Kindness is preserved by a constant reciprocation of benefits or interchange of pleasures; but such benefits only can be bestowed, as others are capable to receive, and such pleasures only imparted, as others are qualified to enjoy.

By this descent from the pinacles of art no honour will be lost; for the condescensions of learning are always overpaid by gratitude. An elevated genius employed in little things, appears, to use the simile of *Longinus*,[5] like the sun in his evening declination, he remits his splendor but retains his magnitude, and pleases more, though he dazzles less.

No. 142. Saturday, 27 July 1751.

> Ἔνθα δ' ἀνὴρ ἐνίαυε πελώριος—
>
> —οὐδὲ, μετ' ἄλλούς
> Πωλεῖτ', ἀλλ' ἀπάνευθεν ἐὼν ἀθεμίστια ᾔδη·
> Καὶ γὰρ θαῦμ' ἐτέτυκτο πελώριον, οὐδὲ ἐῴκει
> Ἀνδρί σιτοφάγῳ·
>
> Hom.[1]

A giant shepherd here his flock maintains
Far from the rest, and solitary reigns,
In shelter thick of horrid shade reclin'd;
And gloomy mischiefs labour in his mind.

> A form enormous! far unlike the race
> Of human birth, in stature or in face.
> POPE.

To the RAMBLER.

SIR,

Having been accustomed to retire annually from the town, I lately accepted the invitation of *Eugenio*, who has an estate and seat in a distant county. As we were unwilling to travel without improvement, we turned often from the direct road to please ourselves with the view of nature or of art; we examined every wild mountain and medicinal spring, criticised every edifice, contemplated every ruin, and compared every scene of action with the narratives of historians. By this succession of amusements we enjoyed the exercise of a journey without suffering the fatigue, and had nothing to regret but that by a progress so leisurely and gentle, we missed the adventures of a post chaise, and the pleasure of alarming villages with the tumult of our passage, and of disguising our insignificancy by the dignity of hurry.

The first week after our arrival at *Eugenio*'s house was passed in receiving visits from his neighbours, who crowded about him with all the eagerness of benevolence; some impatient to learn the news of the court and town, that they might be qualified by authentick information to dictate to the rural politicians on the next bowling day; others desirous of his interest to accommodate disputes, or of his advice in the settlement of their fortunes and the marriage of their children.

The civilities which we had received were soon to be returned; and I passed some time with great satisfaction in roving through the country, and viewing the seats, gardens and plantations which are scattered over it. My pleasure would indeed have been greater had I been sometimes allowed to wander in a park or wilderness alone, but to appear as the friend of *Eugenio* was an honour not to be enjoyed without some inconveniences; so much was every one solicitous for my regard, that I could seldom escape to solitude, or steal a moment from the emulation of complaisance, and the vigilance of officiousness.

In these rambles of good neighbourhood, we frequently passed by a house of unusual magnificence. While I had my curiosity yet distracted among many novelties, it did not much attract my observation; but in a short time I could not forbear surveying it with particular notice; for the length of the wall which enclosed the gardens, the disposition of the shades that waved over it, and the canals, of which I could obtain some glimpses through the trees from our own windows, gave me reason to expect more grandeur and beauty than I had yet seen in that province. I therefore enquired, as we rode by it, why we never amongst our excursions spent an hour where there was such appearance of splendor and affluence. *Eugenio* told me that the seat which I so much admired, was commonly called in the country the *haunted house*, and that no visits were paid there by any of the gentlemen whom I had yet seen. As the haunts of incorporeal beings are generally ruinous, neglected and desolate, I easily conceived that there was something to be explained, and told him that I supposed it only fairy ground, on which we might venture by day-light without danger. The danger, says he, is indeed only that of appearing to solicit the acquaintance of a man, with whom it is not possible to converse without infamy, and who has driven from him, by his insolence or malignity, every human being who can live without him.

Our conversation was then accidentally interrupted; but my inquisitive humour being now in motion, could not rest without a full account of this newly discovered prodigy. I was soon informed that the fine house and spacious gardens were haunted by squire *Bluster*, of whom it was very easy to learn the character, since nobody had regard for him sufficient to hinder them from telling whatever they could discover.

Squire *Bluster* is descended of an ancient family. The estate which his ancestors had immemorially possessed was much augmented by Captain *Bluster*, who served under *Drake*[2] in the reign of *Elizabeth*; and the *Blusters*, who were before only petty gentlemen, have from that time frequently represented the shire in parliament, been chosen to present addresses, and given laws at hunting-matches and races. They were eminently hospitable and popular, till the father of this gentleman died of an election.

His lady went to the grave soon after him, and left the heir, then only ten years old, to the care of his grandmother, who would not suffer him to be controlled, because she could not bear to hear him cry; and never sent him to school, because she was not able to live without his company. She taught him however very early to inspect the steward's accounts, to dog the butler from the cellar, and to catch the servants at a junket; so that he was at the age of eighteen a complete master of all the lower arts of domestick policy, had often on the road detected combinations between the coachman and the ostler, and procured the discharge of nineteen maids for illicit correspondence with cottagers and charwomen.

By the opportunities of parsimony which minority affords, and which the probity of his guardians had diligently improved, a very large sum of money was accumulated, and he found himself, when he took his affairs into his own hands, the richest man in the county. It has been long the custom of this family to celebrate the heir's completion of his twenty-first year, by an entertainment, at which the house is thrown open to all that are inclined to enter it, and the whole province flocks together as to a general festivity. On this occasion young *Bluster* exhibited the first tokens of his future eminence, by shaking his purse at an old gentleman, who had been the intimate friend of his father, and offering to wager a greater sum than he could afford to venture; a practice with which he has at one time or other insulted every freeholder within ten miles round him.

His next acts of offence were committed in a contentious and spiteful vindication of the privileges of his manors, and a rigorous and relentless prosecution of every man that presumed to violate his game. As he happens to have no estate adjoining equal to his own, his oppressions are often borne without resistance, for fear of a long suit, of which he delights to count the expences without the least solicitude about the event; for he knows, that where nothing but an honorary right is contested, the poorer antagonist must always suffer, whatever shall be the last decision of the law.

By the success of some of these disputes, he has so elated his insolence, and by reflection upon the general hatred which they have brought upon him, so irritated his virulence, that his whole life is spent in meditating or executing mischief. It is his common practice to procure his hedges to be broken in the night, and then to demand satisfaction for damages which his grounds have suffered from his neighbour's cattle. An old widow was yesterday soliciting *Eugenio* to enable her to replevin[3] her only cow then in the pound by squire *Bluster*'s order, who had sent one of his agents to take advantage of her calamity, and persuade her to sell the cow at an under rate. He has driven a day-labourer from his cottage, for gathering blackberries in a hedge for his children; and has now an old woman in the county-jail for a trespass which she committed, by coming into his grounds to pick up acorns for her hog.

Money, in whatever hands, will confer power. Distress will fly to immediate refuge, without much consideration of remote consequences. *Bluster* has therefore a despotick authority in many families, whom he has assisted, on pressing occasions, with larger sums than they can easily repay. The only visits that he makes are to these houses of misfortune, where he enters with the insolence of absolute command, enjoys the terrors of the family, exacts their obedience, riots at their charge, and in the height of his joy insults the father with menaces, and the daughters with obscenity.

He is of late somewhat less offensive; for one of his debtors, after gentle expostulations, by which he was only irritated to grosser outrage, seized him by the sleeve, led him trembling into the court-yard, and closed the door upon him in a stormy night. He took his usual revenge next morning by a writ, but the debt was discharged by the assistance of *Eugenio*.

It is his rule to suffer his tenants to owe him rent, because by this indulgence, he secures to himself the power of seizure whenever he has an inclination to amuse himself with calamity, and feast his ears with entreaties and lamentations. Yet as he is sometimes capriciously liberal to those whom he happens to adopt as favourites, and lets his lands at a cheap rate, his farms are never long unoccupied; and when one is ruined by oppression, the possibility of better fortune quickly lures another to supply his place.

Such is the life of squire *Bluster*; a man in whose power fortune has liberally placed the means of happiness, but who has defeated all her gifts of their end by the depravity of his mind. He is wealthy without followers; he is magnificent without witnesses; he has birth without alliance, and influence without dignity. His neighbours scorn him as a brute; his dependents dread him as an oppressor; and he has only the gloomy comfort of reflecting, that if he is hated, he is likewise feared.[4]

I am, Sir, &c.
VAGULUS.

No. 145. Tuesday, 6 August 1751.

Non si priores Mæonius tenet
Sedes Homerus, Pindaricæ latent,
Ceæque & Alcæi minaces
Stesichorique graves Camœnæ.

HOR.[1]

What though the muse her *Homer* thrones
High above all th' immortal quire;
Nor *Pindar*'s rapture she disowns,
Nor hides the plaintive *Cæan* lyre:
Alcæus strikes the tyrant's soul with dread,
Nor yet is grave *Stesichorus* unread.

FRANCIS.

It is allowed, that vocations and employments of least dignity are of the most apparent use; that the meanest artisan or manufacturer contributes more to the accommodation of life, than the profound scholar and argumentative theorist; and that the publick would suffer less present inconvenience from the banishment of philosophers than from the extinction of any common trade.

Some have been so forcibly struck with this observation, that they have, in the first warmth of their discovery, thought it reasonable to alter the common distribution of dignity, and ventured to condemn mankind of universal ingratitude. For justice exacts that those by whom we are most benefited should be most honoured. And what labour can be more useful than that which procures to families and communities those necessaries which supply the wants of nature, or those conveniencies by which ease, security, and elegance are conferred?

This is one of the innumerable theories which the first attempt to reduce them into practice certainly destroys. If we estimate dignity by immediate usefulness, agriculture is undoubtedly the first and noblest science; yet we see the plow driven, the clod broken, the manure spread, the seeds scattered, and the harvest reaped, by men whom those that feed upon their industry will never be persuaded to admit into the same rank with heroes, or with sages; and who, after all the confessions which truth may extort in favour of their occupation, must be content to fill up the lowest class of the commonwealth, to form the base of the pyramid of subordination, and lie buried in obscurity themselves, while they support all that is splendid, conspicuous, or exalted.

It will be found, upon a closer inspection, that this part of the conduct of mankind is by no means contrary to reason or equity. Remuneratory honours are proportioned at once to the usefulness and difficulty of performances, and are properly adjusted by comparison of the mental and corporeal abilities, which they appear to employ. That work, however necessary, which is carried on only by muscular strength and manual dexterity, is not of equal esteem, in the consideration of rational beings, with the tasks that exercise the intellectual powers, and require the active vigour of imagination, or the gradual and laborious investigations of reason.

The merit of all manual occupations seems to terminate in the inventor; and surely the first ages cannot be charged with ingratitude; since those who civilized barbarians, and taught them how to secure themselves from cold and hunger were numbered amongst their deities. But these arts once discovered by philosophy, and facilitated by experience, are afterwards practised with very little assistance from the faculties of the soul; nor is any thing necessary to the regular discharge of these inferior duties, beyond that rude observation which the most sluggish intellect may practise, and that industry which the stimulations of necessity naturally enforce.

Yet, though the refusal of statues and panegyrics to those who employ only their hands and feet in the service of mankind may be easily justified, I am far from intending to incite the petulance of pride, to justify the superciliousness of grandeur, or to intercept any part of that tenderness and benevolence which by the privilege of their common nature one man may claim from another.

That it would be neither wise nor equitable to discourage the husbandman, the labourer, the miner, or the smith, is generally granted; but there is another race of beings equally obscure and equally indigent, who because their usefulness is less obvious to vulgar apprehensions, live unrewarded and die unpitied, and who have been long exposed to insult without a defender, and to censure without an apologist.

The authors of *London* were formerly computed by *Swift* at several thousands,[2] and there is not any reason for suspecting that their number has decreased. Of these only a very few can be said to produce, or endeavour to produce new ideas, to extend any principle of science, or gratify the imagination with any uncommon train of images or contexture of events; the rest, however laborious, however arrogant, can only be considered as the drudges of the pen, the manufacturers of literature, who have set up for authors, either with or without a regular initiation, and like other artificers, have no other care than to deliver their tale of wares at the stated time.

It has been formerly imagined, that he who intends the entertainment or instruction of others, must feel in himself some peculiar impulse of genius; that he must watch the happy minute in which his natural fire is excited, in which his mind is elevated with nobler sentiments, enlightened with clearer views, and invigorated with stronger comprehension; that he must carefully select his thoughts and polish his expressions; and animate his efforts with the hope of raising a monument of learning, which neither time nor envy shall be able to destroy.

But the authors whom I am now endeavouring to recommend have been too long *hackneyed in the ways of men*[3] to indulge the chimerical ambition of immortality; they have seldom any claim to the trade of writing, but that they have tried some other without success; they perceive no particular summons to composition, except the sound of the clock; they have no other rule than the law or the fashion for admitting their thoughts or rejecting them; and about the opinion of posterity they have little solicitude, for their productions are seldom intended to remain in the world longer than a week.

That such authors are not to be rewarded with praise is evident, since nothing can be admired when it ceases to exist; but surely though they cannot aspire to honour, they may be exempted from ignominy, and adopted into that order of men which deserves our kindness though not our reverence. These papers of the day, the *Ephemeræ*[4] of learning, have uses more adequate to the purposes of common life than more pompous and durable volumes. If it is necessary for every man to be more acquainted with his contemporaries than with past generations, and to rather know the events which may immediately affect his fortune or quiet, than the revolutions of antient kingdoms, in which he has neither possessions nor expectations; if it be pleasing to hear of the preferment and dismission of statesmen, the birth of heirs, and the marriage of beauties, the humble author of journals and gazettes must be considered as a liberal dispenser of beneficial knowledge.

Even the abridger, compiler and translator, though their labours cannot be ranked with those of the diurnal historiographer, yet must not be rashly doomed to annihilation. Every size of readers requires a genius of correspondent capacity; some delight in abstracts and epitomes because they want room in their memory for long details, and content themselves with effects, without enquiry after causes; some minds are overpowered by splendor of sentiment, as some eyes are offended by a glaring light; such will gladly contemplate an author in an humble imitation, as we look without pain upon the sun in the water.

As every writer has his use, every writer ought to have his

patrons; and since no man, however high he may now stand, can be certain that he shall not be soon thrown down from his elevation by criticism or caprice, the common interest of learning requires that her sons should cease from intestine hostilities, and instead of sacrificing each other to malice and contempt, endeavour to avert persecution from the meanest of their fraternity.

No. 146. Saturday, 10 August 1751.

Sunt illic duo, tresve, qui revolvant
Nostrarum tineas ineptiarum:
Sed cum sponsio, fabulæque lassæ
De scorpo fuerint et Incitato.

MART.[1]

'Tis possible that one or two
These fooleries of mine may view;
But then the bettings must be o'er,
Nor *Crab* or *Childers*[2] talk'd of more.

F. LEWIS.

None of the projects or designs which exercise the mind of man, are equally subject to obstructions and disappointments with the pursuit of fame. Riches cannot easily be denied to them who have something of greater value to offer in exchange; he whose fortune is endangered by litigation, will not refuse to augment the wealth of the lawyer; he whose days are darkened by languor, or whose nerves are excruciated by pain, is compelled to pay tribute to the science of healing. But praise may be always omitted without inconvenience. When once a man has made celebrity necessary to his happiness, he has put it in the power of the weakest and most timorous malignity, if not to take away his satisfaction, at least to withhold it. His enemies may indulge their pride by airy negligence, and gratify their malice by quiet neutrality. They that could never have injured a character by invectives may combine to annihilate it by silence; as the women of *Rome* threatened to put an end to conquest and dominion, by supplying no children to the commonwealth.[3]

When a writer has with long toil produced a work intended to burst upon mankind with unexpected lustre, and withdraw the attention of the learned world from every other controversy or enquiry, he is seldom contented to wait long without the enjoyment of his new praises. With an imagination full of his own importance, he walks out like a monarch in disguise, to learn the various opinions of his readers. Prepared to feast upon admiration; composed to encounter censures without emotion; and determined not to suffer his quiet to be injured by a sensibility too exquisite of praise or blame, but to laugh with equal contempt at vain objections and injudicious commendations, he enters the places of mingled conversation, sits down to his tea in an obscure corner, and while he appears to examine a file of antiquated journals, catches the conversation of the whole room. He listens, but hears no mention of his book, and therefore supposes that he has disappointed his curiosity by delay, and that as men of learning would naturally begin their conversation with such a wonderful novelty, they had digressed to other subjects before his arrival. The company disperses, and their places are supplied by others equally ignorant, or equally careless. The same expectation hurries him to another place, from which the same disappointment drives him soon away. His impatience then grows violent and tumultuous; he ranges over the town with restless curiosity, and hears in one quarter of a cricket-match, in another of a pick-pocket; is told by some of an unexpected bankrupcy, by others of a turtle feast;[4] is sometimes provoked by importunate enquiries after the white bear, and sometimes with praises of the dancing dog; he is afterwards entreated to give his judgment upon a wager about the height of the monument;[5] invited to see a foot race in the adjacent villages; desired to read a ludicrous advertisement; or consulted about the most effectual method of making enquiry after a favourite cat. The whole world is busied in affairs, which he thinks below the notice of reasonable creatures, and which are nevertheless sufficient to withdraw all regard from his labours and his merits.

He resolves at last to violate his own modesty, and to recal the talkers from their folly by an enquiry after himself. He finds every one provided with an answer; one has seen the work advertised, but never met with any that had read it; another has been so often imposed upon by specious titles, that he never buys a book till its character is established; a third wonders what any man can hope to produce after so many writers of greater eminence; the next has enquired after the author, but can hear no account of him, and therefore suspects the name to be fictitious; and another knows him to be a man condemned by indigence to write too frequently what he does not understand.

Many are the consolations with which the unhappy author endeavours to allay his vexation, and fortify his patience. He has written with too little indulgence to the understanding of common readers; he has fallen upon an age in which solid knowledge, and delicate refinement, have given way to low merriment and idle buffoonry, and therefore no writer can hope for distinction, who has any higher purpose than to raise laughter. He finds that his enemies, such as superiority will always raise, have been industrious, while his performance was in the press, to vilify and blast it; and that the bookseller, whom he had resolved to enrich, has rivals that obstruct the circulation of his copies. He at last reposes upon the consideration, that the noblest works of learning and genius have always made their way slowly against ignorance and prejudice; and that reputation which is never to be lost, must be gradually obtained, as animals of longest life are observed not soon to attain their full stature and strength.

By such arts of voluntary delusion does every man endeavour to conceal his own unimportance from himself. It is long before we are convinced of the small proportion which every individual bears to the collective body of mankind; or learn how few can be interested in the fortune of any single man; how little vacancy is left in the world for any new object of attention; to how small extent the brightest blaze of merit can be spread amidst the mists of business and of folly; and how soon it is clouded by the intervention of other novelties. Not only the writer of books, but the commander of armies, and the deliverer of nations, will easily outlive all noisy and popular reputation: he may be celebrated for a time by the public voice, but his actions and his name will soon be considered as remote and unaffecting, and be rarely mentioned but by those whose alliance gives them some vanity to gratify by frequent commemoration.

It seems not to be sufficiently considered how little renown can be admitted in the world. Mankind are kept perpetually busy by their fears or desires, and have not more leisure from their own affairs, than to acquaint themselves with the accidents of the current day. Engaged in contriving some refuge from calamity, or in shortening the way to some new possession, they seldom suffer their thoughts to wander to the past or future; none but a few solitary students have leisure to enquire into the claims of antient heroes or sages, and names which hoped to range over kingdoms and continents shrink at last into cloisters or colleges.

Nor is it certain, that even of these dark and narrow habitations, these last retreats of fame, the possession will be long kept. Of men devoted to literature very few extend their views beyond some particular science, and the greater part seldom enquire, even in their own profession, for any authors but those whom the present mode of study happens to force upon their notice; they desire not to fill their minds with unfashionable knowledge, but contentedly resign to oblivion those books which they now find censured or neglected.

The hope of fame is necessarily connected with such considerations as must abate the ardour of confidence, and repress the vigour of pursuit. Whoever claims renown from any kind of excellence, expects to fill the place which is now possessed by another, for there are already names of every class sufficient to employ all that will desire to remember them; and surely he that is pushing his predecessors into the gulph of obscurity, cannot but sometimes suspect, that he must himself sink in like manner, and as he stands upon the same precipice, be swept away with the same violence.

It sometimes happens, that fame begins when life is at an end; but far the greater number of candidates for applause have owed their reception in the world to some favourable casualties, and have therefore immediately sunk into neglect, when death stripped them of their casual influence, and neither fortune nor patronage operated in their favour. Among those who have better claims to regard, the honour paid to their memory is commonly proportionate to the reputation which they enjoyed in their lives, though still growing fainter, as it is at a greater distance from the first emission; and since it is so difficult to obtain the notice of contemporaries, how little is to be hoped from future times? What can merit effect by its own force, when the help of art or friendship can scarcely support it?

No. 148. Saturday, 17 August 1751.

Me pater sævis oneret catenis
Quod viro clemens misero peperci,
Me vel extremis Numidarum in oris
Classe releget.
HOR.[1]

Me let my father load with chains,
Or banish to *Numidia*'s farthest plains;
My crime, that I a loyal wife,
In kind compassion spar'd my husband's life.
FRANCIS.

Politicians remark that no oppression is so heavy or lasting as that which is inflicted by the perversion and exorbitance of legal authority. The robber may be seized, and the invader repelled whenever they are found; they who pretend no right but that of force, may by force be punished or suppressed. But when plunder bears the name of impost, and murder is perpetrated by a judicial sentence, fortitude is intimidated and wisdom confounded; resistance shrinks from an alliance with rebellion, and the villain remains secure in the robes of the magistrate.

Equally dangerous and equally detestable are the cruelties often exercised in private families, under the venerable sanction of parental authority; the power which we are taught to honour from the first moments of reason; which is guarded from insult and violation by all that can impress awe upon the mind of man; and which therefore may wanton in cruelty without controul, and trample the bounds of right with innumerable transgressions, before duty and piety will dare to seek redress, or think themselves at liberty to recur to any other means of deliverance than supplications by which insolence is elated, and tears by which cruelty is gratified.

It was for a long time imagined by the *Romans*, that no son could be the murderer of his father, and they had therefore no punishment appropriated to parricide. They seem likewise to have believed with equal confidence that no father could be cruel to his child, and therefore they allowed every man the supreme judicature in his own house, and put the lives of his offspring into his hands. But experience informed them by degrees, that they had determined too hastily in favour of human nature; they found that instinct and habit were not able to contend with avarice or malice; that the nearest relation might be violated; and that power, to whomsoever entrusted, might be ill employed. They were therefore obliged to supply and to change their institutions; to deter the parricide by a new law, and to transfer capital punishments from the parent to the magistrate.[2]

There are indeed many houses which it is impossible to enter familiarly, without discovering that parents are by no means exempt from the intoxications of dominion; and that he who is in no danger of hearing remonstrances but from his own conscience, will seldom be long without the art of controlling his convictions, and modifying justice by his own will.

If in any situation the heart were inaccessible to malignity, it might be supposed to be sufficiently secured by parental relation. To have voluntarily become to any being the occasion of its existence, produces an obligation to make that existence happy. To see helpless infancy stretching out her hands and pouring out her cries in testimony of dependance, without any powers to alarm jealousy, or any guilt to alienate affection, must surely awaken tenderness in every human mind; and tenderness once excited will be hourly encreased by the natural contagion of felicity, by the repercussion of communicated pleasure, and the consciousness of the dignity of benefaction. I believe no generous or benevolent man can see the vilest animal courting his regard, and shrinking at his anger, playing his gambols of delight before him, calling on him in distress, and flying to him in danger, without more kindness than he can persuade himself to feel for the wild and unsocial inhabitants of the air and water. We naturally endear to ourselves those to whom we impart any kind of pleasure, because we imagine their affection and esteem secured to us by the benefits which they receive.

There is indeed another method by which the pride of superiority may be likewise gratified. He that has extinguished all the sensations of humanity, and has no longer any satisfaction in the reflection that he is loved as the distributor of happiness, may please himself with exciting terror as the inflicter of pain; he may delight his solitude with contemplating the extent of his power and the force of his commands, in imagining the desires that flutter on the tongue which is forbidden to utter them, or the discontent which preys on the heart in which fear confines it; he may amuse himself with new contrivances of detection, multiplications of prohibition, and varieties of punishment; and swell with exultation when he considers how little of the homage that he receives he owes to choice.

That princes of this character have been known, the history of all absolute kingdoms will inform us; and since, as *Aristotle* observes, ἡ ὀικονομικὴ μοναρχία, *the government of a family is naturally monarchical*,[3] it is like other monarchies too often arbitrarily administered. The regal and parental tyrant differ only in the extent of their dominions, and the number of their slaves. The same passions cause the same miseries; except that seldom any prince, however despotick, has so far shaken off all awe of the publick eye as to venture upon those freaks of injustice, which are sometimes indulged under the secrecy of a private dwelling. Capricious injunctions, partial decisions, unequal allotments, distributions of reward not by merit but by fancy, and punishments regulated not by the degree of the offence, but by the humour of the judge, are too frequent where no power is known but that of a father.

That he delights in the misery of others no man will confess, and yet what other motive can make a father cruel? The king may be instigated by one man to the destruction of another; he may sometimes think himself endangered by the virtues of a subject; he may dread the successful general or the popular orator; his avarice may point out golden confiscations; and his guilt may whisper that he can only be secure, by cutting off all power of revenge.

But what can a parent hope from the oppression of those who were born to his protection, of those who can disturb him with no competition, who can enrich him with no spoils? Why cowards are cruel may be easily discovered; but for what reason not more infamous than cowardice can that man delight in oppression who has nothing to fear?

The unjustifiable severity of a parent is loaded with this aggravation, that those whom he injures are always in his sight. The injustice of a prince is often exercised upon those of whom he never had any personal or particular knowledge; and the sentence which he pronounces, whether of banishment, imprisonment, or death, removes from his view the man whom he condemns. But the domestick oppressor dooms himself to gaze upon those faces which he clouds with terror and with sorrow; and beholds every moment the effects of his own barbarities. He that can bear to give continual pain to those who surround him, and can walk with satisfaction in the gloom of his own presence; he that can see submissive misery without relenting, and meet without emotion the eye that implores mercy, or demands justice, will scarcely be amended by remonstrance or admonition; he has found means of stopping the avenues of tenderness, and arming his heart against the force of reason.

Even though no consideration should be paid to the great law of social beings, by which every individual is commanded to consult the happiness of others, yet the harsh parent is less to be vindicated than any other criminal, because he less provides for the happiness of himself. Every man, however little he loves others, would willingly be loved; every man hopes to live long, and therefore hopes for that time at which he shall sink back to imbecillity, and must depend for ease and chearfulness upon the

officiousness of others. But how has he obviated the inconveniences of old age, who alienates from him the assistance of
his children, and whose bed must be surrounded in his last
hours, in the hours of languor and dejection, of impatience and
of pain, by strangers to whom his life is indifferent, or by enemies
to whom his death is desirable?

Piety will indeed in good minds overcome provocation, and
those who have been harrassed by brutality will forget the
injuries which they have suffered so far as to perform the last
duties with alacrity and zeal. But surely no resentment can be
equally painful with kindness thus undeserved, nor can severer
punishment be imprecated upon a man not wholly lost in meanness and stupidity, than through the tediousness of decrepitude,
to be reproached by the kindness of his own children, to receive
not the tribute but the alms of attendance, and to owe every
relief of his miseries not to gratitude but to mercy.

No. 151. Tuesday, 27 August 1751.

'Αμφὶ δ'ἀνθρώ—
πων φρεσὶν ἀμπλακίαι
ἀναρίθμητοι κρέμανται.
τοῦτο δ'ἀμήχανον εὑρεῖν
Ὅτι νῦν, καὶ ἐν τελευ—
τᾷ φέρτατον ἀνδρὶ τυχεῖν.
PIND.[1]

But wrapt in error is the human mind,
    And human bliss is ever insecure:
Know we what fortune yet remains behind?
    Know we how long the present shall endure?
WEST.[2]

The writers of medicine and physiology have traced with great
appearance of accuracy, the effects of time upon the human
body, by marking the various periods of the constitution, and
the several stages by which animal life makes its progress from

infancy to decrepitude. Though their observations have not enabled them to discover how manhood may be accelerated, or old age retarded, yet surely if they be considered only as the amusements of curiosity, they are of equal importance with conjectures on things more remote, with catalogues of the fixed stars, and calculations of the bulk of planets.

It had been a task worthy of the moral philosophers to have considered with equal care the climactericks[3] of the mind; to have pointed out the time at which every passion begins and ceases to predominate, and noted the regular variations of desire, and the succession of one appetite to another.

The periods of mental change are not to be stated with equal certainty: Our bodies grow up under the care of nature, and depend so little on our own management, that something more than negligence is necessary to discompose their structure, or impede their vigour. But our minds are committed in a great measure first to the direction of others, and afterwards of ourselves. It would be difficult to protract the weakness of infancy beyond the usual time, but the mind may be very easily hindered from its share of improvement, and the bulk and strength of manhood must, without the assistance of education and instruction, be informed only with the understanding of a child.

Yet amidst all the disorder and inequality which variety of discipline, example, conversation, and employment produce in the intellectual advances of different men, there is still discovered by a vigilant spectator such a general and remote similitude as may be expected in the same common nature affected by external circumstances indefinitely varied. We all enter the world in equal ignorance, gaze round about us on the same objects, and have our first pains and pleasures, our first hopes and fears, our first aversions and desires from the same causes; and though, as we proceed farther, life opens wider prospects to our view, and accidental impulses determine us to different paths, yet as every mind, however vigorous or abstracted, is necessitated in its present state of union, to receive its informations, and execute its purposes by the intervention of the body, the uniformity of our corporeal nature communicates itself to our intellectual operations; and those whose abilities or knowledge incline them most to deviate from the general round of life, are recalled from excentricity by the laws of their existence.

If we consider the exercises of the mind, it will be found that in each part of life some particular faculty is more eminently employed. When the treasures of knowledge are first opened before us, while novelty blooms alike on either hand, and every thing equally unknown and unexamined seems of equal value, the power of the soul is principally exerted in a vivacious and desultory curiosity. She applies by turns to every object, enjoys it for a short time, and flies with equal ardour to another. She delights to catch up loose and unconnected ideas, but starts away from systems and complications which would obstruct the rapidity of her transitions, and detain her long in the same pursuit.

When a number of distinct images are collected by these erratick and hasty surveys, the fancy is busied in arranging them; and combines them into pleasing pictures with more resemblance to the realities of life as experience advances, and new observations rectify the former. While the judgment is yet uninformed and unable to compare the draughts of fiction with their originals, we are delighted with improbable adventures, impracticable virtues, and inimitable characters: But, in proportion as we have more opportunities of acquainting ourselves with living nature, we are sooner disgusted with copies in which there appears no resemblance. We first discard absurdity and impossibility, then exact greater and greater degrees of probability, but at last become cold and insensible to the charms of falshood, however specious, and from the imitations of truth, which are never perfect, transfer our affection to truth itself.

Now commences the reign of judgment or reason; we begin to find little pleasure, but in comparing arguments, stating propositions, disentangling perplexities, clearing ambiguities, and deducing consequences. The painted vales of imagination are deserted, and our intellectual activity is exercised in winding through the labyrinths of fallacy, and toiling with firm and cautious steps up the narrow tracks of demonstration. Whatever may lull vigilance, or mislead attention, is contemptuously rejected, and every disguise in which error may be concealed, is

carefully observed, till by degrees a certain number of incontestable or unsuspected propositions are established, and at last
concatenated into arguments, or compacted into systems.

At length weariness succeeds to labour, and the mind lies at
ease in the contemplation of her own attainments, without
any desire of new conquests or excursions. This is the age of
recollection and narrative; the opinions are settled, and the
avenues of apprehension shut against any new intelligence; the
days that are to follow must pass in the inculcation of precepts
already collected, and assertion of tenets already received; nothing is henceforward so odious as opposition, so insolent as
doubt, or so dangerous as novelty.

In like manner the passions usurp the separate command of
the successive periods of life. To the happiness of our first years
nothing more seems necessary than freedom from restraint:
Every man may remember that if he was left to himself, and
indulged in the disposal of his own time, he was once content
without the superaddition of any actual pleasure. The new
world is itself a banquet, and till we have exhausted the freshness
of life, we have always about us sufficient gratifications: The
sunshine quickens us to play, and the shade invites us to sleep.

But we soon become unsatisfied with negative felicity, and
are solicited by our senses and appetites to more powerful
delights, as the taste of him who has satisfied his hunger must
be excited by artificial stimulations. The simplicity of natural
amusement is now past, and art and contrivance must improve
our pleasures; but in time art, like nature, is exhausted, and the
senses can no longer supply the cravings of the intellect.

The attention is then transferred from pleasure to interest, in
which pleasure is perhaps included, though diffused to a wider
extent, and protracted through new gradations. Nothing now
dances before the eyes but wealth and power, nor rings in the
ear but the voice of fame; wealth, to which, however variously
denominated, every man at some time or other aspires; power,
which all wish to obtain within their circle of action; and fame,
which no man, however high or mean, however wise or ignorant, was yet able to despise. Now prudence and foresight exert
their influence: no hour is devoted wholly to any present enjoy-

ment, no act or purpose terminates in itself, but every motion is referred to some distant end; the accomplishment of one design begins another, and the ultimate wish is always pushed off to its former distance.

At length fame is observed to be uncertain, and power to be dangerous; the man whose vigour and alacrity begin to forsake him, by degrees contracts his designs, remits his former multiplicity of persuits, and extends no longer his regard to any other honour than the reputation of wealth, or any other influence than its power. Avarice is generally the last passion of those lives of which the first part has been squandered in pleasure, and the second devoted to ambition. He that sinks under the fatigue of getting wealth, lulls his age with the milder business of saving it.

I have in this view of life considered men as actuated only by natural desires, and yielding to their own inclinations without regard to superior principles by which the force of external agents may be counteracted, and the temporary prevalence of passions restrained. Nature will indeed always operate, human desires will be always ranging; but these motions, though very powerful, are not resistless; nature may be regulated, and desires governed; and to contend with the predominance of successive passions, to be endangered first by one affection, and then by another, is the condition upon which we are to pass our time, the time of our preparation for that state which shall put an end to experiment, to disappointment, and to change.

No. 156. Saturday, 14 September 1751.

Nunquam aliud natura, aliud sapientia dicit.
Juv.[1]

For wisdom ever echoes nature's voice.

Every government, say the politicians, is perpetually degenerating towards corruption, from which it must be rescued at certain periods by the resuscitation of its first principles, and the re-establishment of its original constitution.[2] Every animal body, according to the methodick physicians, is, by the predominance of some exuberant quality, continually declining towards disease and death, which must be obviated by a seasonable reduction of the peccant humour to the just equipoise which health requires.

In the same manner the studies of mankind, all at least which, not being subject to rigorous demonstration, admit the influence of fancy and caprice, are perpetually tending to error and confusion. Of the great principles of truth which the first speculatists discovered, the simplicity is embarrassed by ambitious additions, or the evidence obscured by inaccurate argumentation; and as they descend from one succession of writers to another, like light transmitted from room to room, they lose their strength and splendour, and fade at last in total evanescence.

The systems of learning therefore must be sometimes reviewed, complications analised into principles, and knowledge disentangled from opinion. It is not always possible, without a close inspection, to separate the genuine shoots of consequential reasoning, which grow out of some radical postulate, from the branches which art has engrafted on it. The accidental prescriptions of authority, when time has procured them veneration, are often confounded with the laws of nature, and those rules are supposed coeval with reason, of which the first rise cannot be discovered.

Criticism has sometimes permitted fancy to dictate the laws by which fancy ought to be restrained, and fallacy to perplex the principles by which fallacy is to be detected; her superintendence of others has betrayed her to negligence of herself; and, like the antient *Scythians*, by extending her conquests over distant regions, she has left her throne vacant to her slaves.[3]

Among the laws of which the desire of extending authority, or ardour of promoting knowledge has prompted the prescription, all which writers have received, had not the same original right to our regard. Some are to be considered as fundamental and indispensable, others only as useful and convenient; some as dictated by reason and necessity, others as enacted by despotick antiquity; some as invincibly supported by their conformity to the order of nature and operations of the intellect; others as formed by accident, or instituted by example, and therefore always liable to dispute and alteration.

That many rules have been advanced without consulting nature or reason, we cannot but suspect, when we find it peremptorily decreed by the antient masters, that *only three speaking personages should appear at once upon the stage*;[4] a law which, as the variety and intricacy of modern plays has made it impossible to be observed, we now violate without scruple, and, as experience proves, without inconvenience.

The original of this precept was merely accidental. Tragedy was a monody or solitary song in honour of *Bacchus*,[5] improved afterwards into a dialogue by the addition of another speaker; but the antients, remembering that the tragedy was at first pronounced only by one, durst not for some time venture beyond two; at last when custom and impunity had made them daring, they extended their liberty to the admission of three, but restrained themselves by a critical edict from further exorbitance.

By what accident the number of acts was limited to five, I know not that any author has informed us; but certainly it is not determined by any necessity arising either from the nature of action or propriety of exhibition. An act is only the representation of such a part of the business of the play as proceeds in an unbroken tenor, or without any intermediate pause. Nothing is more evident than that of every real, and by consequence of every dramatick action, the intervals may be more or fewer than five; and indeed the rule is upon the *English* stage every day broken in effect, without any other mischief than that which arises from an absurd endeavour to observe it in appearance. Whenever the scene is shifted the act ceases, since some time is necessarily supposed to elapse while the personages of the drama change their place.

With no greater right to our obedience have the criticks confined the dramatic action to a certain number of hours. Probability requires that the time of action should approach somewhat nearly to that of exhibition, and those plays will always be thought most happily conducted which croud the greatest variety into the least space. But since it will frequently happen that some delusion must be admitted, I know not where the limits of imagination can be fixed. It is rarely observed that minds not prepossessed by mechanical criticism feel any offence from the extension of the intervals between the acts; nor can I conceive it absurd or impossible, that he who can multiply three hours into twelve or twenty-four, might image with equal ease a greater number.

I know not whether he that professes to regard no other laws than those of nature, will not be inclined to receive tragi-comedy to his protection, whom, however generally condemned, her own laurels have hitherto shaded from the fulminations of criticism. For what is there in the mingled drama which impartial reason can condemn? The connexion of important with trivial incidents, since it is not only common but perpetual in the world, may surely be allowed upon the stage, which pretends only to be the mirrour of life. The impropriety of suppressing passions before we have raised them to the intended agitation, and of diverting the expectation from an event which we keep suspended only to raise it, may be speciously urged. But will not experience shew this objection to be rather subtle than just? is it not certain that the tragic and comic affections have been moved alternately with equal force, and that no plays have oftner filled the eye with tears, and the breast with palpitation, than those which are variegated with interludes of mirth?

I do not however think it safe to judge of works of genius merely by the event. These resistless vicissitudes of the heart, this alternate prevalence of merriment and solemnity, may sometimes be more properly ascribed to the vigour of the writer than the justness of the design: and instead of vindicating tragi-comedy by the success of *Shakespear*, we ought perhaps to pay new honours to that transcendent and unbounded genius that could preside over the passions in sport; who, to actuate the affections, needed not the slow gradation of common means, but could fill the heart with instantaneous jollity or sorrow, and vary our disposition as he changed his scenes. Perhaps the effects even of *Shakespeare*'s poetry might have been yet greater, had he not counter-acted himself; and we might have been more interested in the distresses of his heroes had we not been so frequently diverted by the jokes of his buffoons.

There are other rules more fixed and obligatory. It is necessary that of every play the chief action should be single; for since a play represents some transaction, through its regular maturation to its final event, two actions equally important must evidently constitute two plays.

As the design of tragedy is to instruct by moving the passions, it must always have a hero, a personage apparently and incontestably superior to the rest, upon whom the attention may be fixed, and the anxiety suspended. For though of two persons opposing each other with equal abilities and equal virtue, the auditor will inevitably in time choose his favourite, yet as that choice must be without any cogency of conviction, the hopes or fears which it raises will be faint and languid. Of two heroes acting in confederacy against a common enemy, the virtues or dangers will give little emotion, because each claims our concern with the same right, and the heart lies at rest between equal motives.

It ought to be the first endeavour of a writer to distinguish nature from custom, or that which is established because it is right, from that which is right only because it is established; that he may neither violate essential principles by a desire of novelty, nor debar himself from the attainment of beauties within his view by a needless fear of breaking rules which no literary dictator had authority to enact.

No. 158. Saturday, 21 September 1751.

Grammatici certant, et adhuc sub Judice lis est.
HOR.[1]

——— Criticks yet contend,
And of their vain disputings find no end.
FRANCIS.

Criticism, though dignified from the earliest ages by the labours of men eminent for knowledge and sagacity; and, since the revival of polite literature, the favourite study of *European* scholars, has not yet attained the certainty and stability of science. The rules hitherto received, are seldom drawn from any settled principle or self-evident postulate, or adapted to the natural and invariable constitution of things; but will be found upon examination the arbitrary edicts of legislators, authorised only by themselves, who, out of various means by which the same end may be attained, selected such as happened to occur to their own reflexion, and then by a law which idleness and timidity were too willing to obey, prohibited new experiments of wit, restrained fancy from the indulgence of her innate inclination to hazard and adventure, and condemned all future flights of genius to pursue the path of the *Meonian* eagle.[2]

This authority may be more justly opposed, as it is apparently derived from them whom they endeavour to controul; for we owe few of the rules of writing to the acuteness of criticks, who have generally no other merit than that having read the works of great authors with attention, they have observed the arrangement of their matter, or the graces of their expression, and then expected honour and reverence for precepts which they never could have invented: so that practice has introduced rules, rather than rules have directed practice.

For this reason the laws of every species of writing have been settled by the ideas of him who first raised it to reputation, without enquiry whether his performances were not yet susceptible of improvement. The excellencies and faults of celebrated writers have been equally recommended to posterity; and so far has blind reverence prevailed, that even the number of their books has been thought worthy of imitation.

The imagination of the first authors of lyrick poetry was vehement and rapid, and their knowledge various and extensive. Living in an age when science had been little cultivated, and when the minds of their auditors, not being accustomed to accurate inspection, were easily dazzled by glaring ideas, they applied themselves to instruct, rather by short sentences and striking thoughts, than by regular argumentation; and finding attention more successfully excited by sudden sallies and unexpected exclamations, than by the more artful and placid beauties of methodical deduction, they loosed their genius to its own course, passed from one sentiment to another without expressing the intermediate ideas, and roved at large over the ideal world with such lightness and agility that their footsteps are scarcely to be traced.

From this accidental peculiarity of the ancient writers the criticks deduce the rules of lyrick poetry, which they have set free from all the laws by which other compositions are confined, and allow to neglect the niceties of transition, to start into remote digressions, and to wander without restraint from one scene of imagery to another.

A writer of later times has, by the vivacity of his essays, reconciled mankind to the same licentiousness in short dissertations; and he therefore who wants skill to form a plan, or diligence to pursue it, needs only entitle his performance an essay, to acquire the right of heaping together the collections of half his life, without order, coherence, or propriety.

In writing, as in life, faults are endured without disgust when they are associated with transcendent merit, and may be sometimes recommended to weak judgments by the lustre which they obtain from their union with excellence; but it is the business of those who presume to superintend the taste or morals of mankind, to separate delusive combinations, and distinguish that which may be praised from that which can only be excused. As vices never promote happiness, though when overpowered by more active and more numerous virtues, they cannot totally destroy it; so confusion and irregularity produce no beauty, though they cannot always obstruct the brightness of genius and learning. To proceed from one truth to another, and connect distant propositions by regular consequences, is the great prerogative of man. Independent and unconnected sentiments flashing upon the mind in quick succession, may, for a time, delight by their novelty, but they differ from systematical reasoning, as single notes from harmony, as glances of lightening from the radiance of the sun.

When rules are thus drawn, rather from precedents than reason, there is danger not only from the faults of an author, but from the errors of those who criticise his works; since they may often mislead their pupils by false representations, as the *Ciceronians* of the sixteenth century[3] were betrayed into barbarisms by corrupt copies of their darling writer.

It is established at present, that the proemial lines of a poem, in which the general subject is proposed, must be void of glitter and embellishment. "The first lines of *Paradise Lost*," says *Addison*, "are perhaps as plain, simple, and unadorned as any of the whole poem, in which particular the author has conformed himself to the example of *Homer* and the precept of *Horace*."[4]

This observation seems to have been made by an implicit adoption of the common opinion, without consideration either of the precept or example. Had *Horace* been consulted, he would have been found to direct only what should be comprised in the proposition, not how it should be expressed, and to have commended *Homer* in opposition to a meaner poet, not for the gradual elevation of his diction, but the judicious expansion of his plan; for displaying unpromised events, not for producing unexpected elegancies.

> —— *Speciosa dehinc miracula promit,*
> *Antiphaten Scyllamque, & cum Cyclope Charybdim.*[5]

> But from a cloud of smoke he breaks to light,
> And pours his specious miracles to sight;
> *Antiphates* his hideous feast devours,
> *Charybdis* barks, and *Polyphemus* roars.
>
> FRANCIS.

If the exordial verses of *Homer* be compared with the rest of the poem, they will not appear remarkable for plainness or simplicity, but rather eminently adorned and illuminated.

> Ἄνδρα μοι ἔννεπε Μοῦσα πολύτροπον, ὅς μάλα πολλὰ
> Πλάγχθη, ἐπεὶ Τροίης ἱερὸν πτολίεθρον ἔπερσε·
> Πολλῶν δ' ἀνθρώπων ἴδεν ἄστεα, καὶ νόον ἔγνω.
> Πολλὰ δ' ὅγ' ἐν πόντῳ πάθεν ἄλγεα ὅν κατὰ θυμόν,
> Ἀρνύμενος ἥν τε ψυχὴν καὶ νόστον ἑταίρων·
> Ἀλλ' οὐδ' ὣς ἑτάρους ἐρρύσατο ἱέμενός περ·

Αὐτῶν γὰρ σφετέρῃσιν ἀτασθαλίῃσιν ὄλοντο,
Νήπιοι οἵ κατὰ βοῦς ὑπερίονος ἠελίοιο
Ἤσθιον· αὐτὰρ ὅ τοῖσιν ἀφείλετο νόστιμον ἦμαρ·
Τῶν ἁμόθεν γε, θεά, θύγατερ Διός, εἰπὲ καὶ ἡμῖν.[6]

The man, for wisdom's various arts renown'd,
Long exercis'd in woes, O muse! resound.
Who, when his arms had wrought the destin'd fall
Of sacred *Troy*, and raz'd her heav'n-built wall,
Wand'ring from clime to clime, observant stray'd,
Their manners noted, and their states survey'd.
On stormy seas unnumber'd toils he bore,
Safe with his friends to gain his natal shore:
Vain toils! their impious folly dar'd to prey
On herds devoted to the god of day;
The god vindictive doom'd them never more
(Ah men unbless'd) to touch that natal shore.
O snatch some portion of these acts from fate,
Celestial muse! and to our world relate.

                                        POPE.

The first verses of the *Iliad* are in like manner particularly splendid, and the proposition of the *Eneid* closes with dignity and magnificence not often to be found even in the poetry of *Virgil*.

The intent of the introduction is to raise expectation, and suspend it; something therefore must be discovered, and something concealed; and the poet, while the fertility of his invention is yet unknown, may properly recommend himself by the grace of his language.

He that reveals too much, or promises too little; he that never irritates the intellectual appetite, or that immediately satiates it, equally defeats his own purpose. It is necessary to the pleasure of the reader, that the events should not be anticipated, and how then can his attention be invited, but by grandeur of expression?

No. 159. Tuesday, 24 September 1751.

Sunt verba et voces, quibus hunc lenire dolorem
Possis, et magnam morbi deponere partem.

HOR.[1]

The pow'r of words, and soothing sounds appease
The raging pain, and lessen the disease.

FRANCIS.

The imbecillity with which *Verecundulus*[2] complains that the presence of a numerous assembly freezes his faculties, is particularly incident to the studious part of mankind, whose education necessarily secludes them in their earlier years from mingled converse, till at their dismission from schools and academies they plunge at once into the tumult of the world, and coming forth from the gloom of solitude are overpowered by the blaze of publick life.

It is perhaps kindly provided by nature that, as the feathers and strength of a bird grow together, and her wings are not completed till she is able to fly, so some proportion should be preserved in the human kind between judgment and courage; the precipitation of inexperience is therefore restrained by shame, and we remain shackled by timidity, till we have learned to speak and act with propriety.

I believe few can review the days of their youth, without recollecting temptations, which shame, rather than virtue, enabled them to resist; and opinions which, however erroneous in their principles, and dangerous in their consequences, they have panted to advance at the hazard of contempt and hatred, when they found themselves irresistibly depressed by a languid anxiety, which seized them at the moment of utterance, and still gathered strength from their endeavours to resist it.

It generally happens that assurance keeps an even pace with ability, and the fear of miscarriage, which hinders our first attempts, is gradually dissipated as our skill advances towards certainty of success. That bashfulness therefore which prevents disgrace, that short and temporary shame, which secures us from the danger of lasting reproach, cannot be properly counted among our misfortunes.

Bashfulness, however it may incommode for a moment, scarcely ever produces evils of long continuance; it may flush the cheek, flutter in the heart, deject the eyes, and enchain the tongue, but its mischiefs soon pass off without remembrance. It may sometimes exclude pleasure, but seldom opens any avenue to sorrow or remorse. It is observed somewhere, that *few have repented of having forborn to speak.*[3]

To excite opposition and inflame malevolence is the unhappy privilege of courage made arrogant by consciousness of strength. No man finds in himself any inclination to attack or oppose him who confesses his superiority by blushing in his presence. Qualities exerted with apparent fearfulness, receive applause from every voice, and support from every hand. Diffidence may check resolution and obstruct performance, but compensates its embarrassments by more important advantages; it conciliates the proud, and softens the severe, averts envy from excellence, and censure from miscarriage.

It may indeed happen that knowledge and virtue remain too long congealed by this frigorifick[4] power, as the principles of vegetation are sometimes obstructed by lingering frosts. He that enters late into a publick station, though with all the abilities requisite to the discharge of his duty, will find his powers at first impeded by a timidity which he himself knows to be vitious, and must struggle long against dejection and reluctance, before he obtains the full command of his own attention, and adds the gracefulness of ease to the dignity of merit.

For this disease of the mind, I know not whether any remedies of much efficacy can be found. To advise a man unaccustomed to the eyes of multitudes to mount a tribunal without perturbation, to tell him whose life has passed in the shades of contemplation, that he must not be disconcerted or perplexed in receiving and returning the compliments of a splendid assembly, is to advise an inhabitant of *Brasil* or *Sumatra*, not to shiver at an *English* winter, or him who has always lived upon a plain to look from a precipice without emotion. It is to suppose custom instantaneously controlable by reason, and to endeavour to communicate by precept that which only time and habit can bestow.

He that hopes by philosophy and contemplation alone to fortify himself against that awe which all, at their first appearance on the stage of life, must feel from the spectators, will, at the hour of need, be mocked by his resolution; and I doubt whether the preservatives which *Plato* relates *Alcibiades* to have received from *Socrates*, when he was about to speak in publick, proved sufficient to secure him from the powerful fascination.[5]

Yet as the effects of time may by art and industry be accelerated or retarded, it cannot be improper to consider how this troublesome instinct may be opposed when it exceeds its just proportion, and instead of repressing petulance and temerity, silences eloquence, and debilitates force; since, though it cannot be hoped that anxiety should be immediately dissipated, it may be at least somewhat abated; and the passions will operate with less violence, when reason rises against them, than while she either slumbers in neutrality, or, mistaking her interest, lends them her assistance.

No cause more frequently produces bashfulness than too high an opinion of our own importance. He that imagines an assembly filled with his merit, panting with expectation, and hushed with attention, easily terrifies himself with the dread of disappointing them, and strains his imagination in pursuit of something that may vindicate the veracity of fame, and shew that his reputation was not gained by chance. He considers, that what he shall say or do will never be forgotten; that renown or infamy are suspended upon every syllable, and that nothing ought to fall from him which will not bear the test of time. Under such solicitude, who can wonder that the mind is overwhelmed, and by struggling with attempts above her strength, quickly sinks into languishment and despondency.

The most useful medicines are often unpleasing to the taste. Those who are oppressed by their own reputation, will perhaps not be comforted by hearing that their cares are unnecessary. But the truth is, that no man is much regarded by the rest of the world. He that considers how little he dwells upon the condition of others, will learn how little the attention of others is attracted by himself. While we see multitudes passing before us, of whom perhaps not one appears to deserve our notice, or excites our sympathy, we should remember, that we likewise are lost in the same throng, that the eye which happens to glance upon us is turned in a moment on him that follows us, and that the utmost which we can reasonably hope or fear is to fill a vacant hour with prattle, and be forgotten.

No. 161. Tuesday, 1 October 1751.

Οἵη γὰρ φύλλων γενέη, τοίηδε καὶ Ἀνδρῶν.

Hom.[1]

Frail as the leaves that quiver on the sprays,
Like them man flourishes, like them decays.

Mr. Rambler,

SIR,

You have formerly observed that curiosity often terminates in barren knowledge, and that the mind is prompted to study and enquiry rather by the uneasiness of ignorance, than the hope of profit. Nothing can be of less importance to any present interest than the fortune of those who have been long lost in the grave, and from whom nothing now can be hoped or feared. Yet to rouse the zeal of a true antiquary little more is necessary than to mention a name which mankind have conspired to forget; he will make his way to remote scenes of action thro' obscurity and contradiction, as *Tully* sought amidst bushes and brambles the tomb of *Archimedes*.[2]

It is not easy to discover how it concerns him that gathers the produce or receives the rent of an estate, to know through what families the land has passed, who is registered in the Conqueror's survey[3] as its possessor, how often it has been forfeited by treason, or how often sold by prodigality. The power or wealth of the present inhabitants of a country cannot be much encreased by an enquiry after the names of those barbarians, who destroyed one another twenty centuries ago, in contests for the shelter of woods or convenience of pasturage. Yet we see that no man can be at rest in the enjoyment of a new purchase till he has learned the history of his grounds from the antient inhabitants of the parish, and that no nation omits to record the actions of their ancestors, however bloody, savage and rapacious.

The same disposition, as different opportunities call it forth, discovers itself in great or little things. I have always thought it unworthy of a wise man to slumber in total inactivity only because he happens to have no employment equal to his ambition or genius; it is therefore my custom to apply my attention to the objects before me, and as I cannot think any place wholly unworthy of notice that affords a habitation to a man of letters, I have collected the history and antiquities of the several garrets in which I have resided.

> *Quantulacunque estis, vos ego magna voco.*[4]
>
> How small to others, but how great to me!

Many of these narratives my industry has been able to extend to a considerable length; but the woman with whom I now lodge has lived only eighteen months in the house, and can give no account of its ancient revolutions; the plaisterer, having, at her entrance, obliterated by his white-wash, all the smoky memorials which former tenants had left upon the cieling, and perhaps drawn the veil of oblivion over politicians, philosophers, and poets.

When I first cheapened my lodgings, the landlady told me, that she hoped I was not an author, for the lodgers on the first floor had stipulated that the upper rooms should not be occupied by a noisy trade. I very readily promised to give no disturbance to her family, and soon dispatched a bargain on the usual terms.

I had not slept many nights in my new apartment before I began to enquire after my predecessors, and found my landlady, whose imagination is filled chiefly with her own affairs, very ready to give me information.

Curiosity, like all other desires, produces pain as well as

pleasure. Before she began her narrative, I had heated my head with expectations of adventures and discoveries, of elegance in disguise, and learning in distress; and was somewhat mortified when I heard, that the first tenant was a taylor, of whom nothing was remembered but that he complained of his room for want of light; and, after having lodged in it a month, and paid only a week's rent, pawned a piece of cloth which he was trusted to cut out, and was forced to make a precipitate retreat from this quarter of the town.

The next was a young woman newly arrived from the country, who lived for five weeks with great regularity, and became by frequent treats very much the favourite of the family, but at last received visits so frequently from a cousin in *Cheapside*,[5] that she brought the reputation of the house into danger, and was therefore dismissed with good advice.

The room then stood empty for a fortnight; my landlady began to think that she had judged hardly, and often wished for such another lodger. At last an elderly man of a grave aspect, read the bill, and bargained for the room, at the very first price that was asked. He lived in close retirement, seldom went out till evening, and then returned early, sometimes chearful, and at other times dejected. It was remarkable, that whatever he purchased, he never had small money in his pocket, and tho' cool and temperate on other occasions, was always vehement and stormy till he received his change. He paid his rent with great exactness, and seldom failed once a week to requite my landlady's civility with a supper. At last, such is the fate of human felicity, the house was alarm'd at midnight by the constable, who demanded to search the garrets. My landlady assuring him that he had mistaken the door, conducted him up stairs, where he found the tools of a coiner; but the tenant had crawled along the roof to an empty house, and escaped; much to the joy of my landlady, who declares him a very honest man, and wonders why any body should be hanged for making money when such numbers are in want of it. She however confesses that she shall for the future always question the character of those who take her garret without beating down the price.

The bill was then placed again in the window, and the poor

woman was teazed for seven weeks by innumerable passengers, who obliged her to climb with them every hour up five stories, and then disliked the prospect, hated the noise of a publick street, thought the stairs narrow, objected to a low cieling, required the walls to be hung with fresher paper, asked questions about the neighbourhood, could not think of living so far from their acquaintance, wished the window had looked to the south rather than the west, told how the door and chimney might have been better disposed, bid her half the price that she asked, or promised to give her earnest the next day, and came no more.

At last, a short meagre man, in a tarnish'd waistcoat, desired to see the garret, and when he had stipulated for two long shelves and a larger table, hired it at a low rate. When the affair was completed, he looked round him with great satisfaction, and repeated some words which the woman did not understand. In two days he brought a great box of books, took possession of his room, and lived very inoffensively, except that he frequently disturbed the inhabitants of the next floor by unseasonable noises. He was generally in bed at noon, but from evening to midnight he sometimes talked aloud with great vehemence, sometimes stamped as in rage, sometimes threw down his poker, then clattered his chairs, then sat down in deep thought, and again burst out into loud vociferations; sometimes he would sigh as oppressed with misery, and sometimes shake with convulsive laughter. When he encountered any of the family he gave way or bowed, but rarely spoke, except that as he went up stairs he often repeated,

—— Ὅς ὑπέρτατα δώματα ναίει.[6]

This habitant th' aerial regions boast.

hard words, to which his neighbours listened so often, that they learned them without understanding them. What was his employment she did not venture to ask him, but at last heard a printer's boy enquire for the author.

My landlady was very often advised to beware of this strange man, who, tho' he was quiet for the present, might perhaps become outrageous in the hot months; but as she was punctually paid, she could not find any sufficient reason for dismissing him, till one night he convinced her by setting fire to his curtains, that it was not safe to have an author for her inmate.

She had then for six weeks a succession of tenants, who left the house on Saturday, and instead of paying their rent, stormed at their landlady. At last she took in two sisters, one of whom had spent her little fortune in procuring remedies for a lingering disease, and was now supported and attended by the other: she climbed with difficulty to the apartment, where she languished eight weeks, without impatience or lamentation, except for the expence and fatigue which her sister suffered, and then calmly and contentedly expired. The sister followed her to the grave, paid the few debts which they had contracted, wiped away the tears of useless sorrow, and returning to the business of common life, resigned to me the vacant habitation.

Such, Mr. *Rambler*, are the changes which have happened in the narrow space where my present fortune has fixed my residence. So true is it that amusement and instruction are always at hand for those who have skill and willingness to find them; and so just is the observation of *Juvenal*,[7] that a single house will shew whatever is done or suffered in the world.

I am, Sir, &c.

No. 165. Tuesday, 15 October 1751.

Ἦν νέος, ἀλλὰ πένης· νῦν γηρῶν, πλούσιός εἰμι.
Ὦ μόνος ἐκ πάντων οἰκτρὸς ἐν ἀμφοτέροις,
Ὃς τότε μὲν χρῆσθαι δυνάμην, ὁπότ' οὐδὲ ἐν εἶχον.
Νῦν δ' ὁπότε χρῆσθαι μή δύναμαι, τότ' ἔχω.
                                        ANTIPHILUS.[1]

Young was I once and poor, now rich and old;
A harder case than mine was never told;
Blest with the pow'r to use them — I had none;
Loaded with *riches* now, the pow'r is gone.
                                        F. LEWIS.

To the RAMBLER.

SIR,

The writers who have undertaken the unpromising task of moderating desire, exert all the power of their eloquence, to shew that happiness is not the lot of man, and have by many arguments and examples proved the instability of every condition by which envy or ambition are excited. They have set before our eyes all the calamities to which we are exposed from the frailty of nature, the influence of accident, or the stratagems of malice; they have terrified greatness with conspiracies, and riches with anxieties, wit with criticism, and beauty with disease.

All the force of reason and all the charms of language are indeed necessary to support positions which every man hears with a wish to confute them. Truth finds an easy entrance into the mind when she is introduced by desire, and attended by pleasure; but when she intrudes uncalled, and brings only fear and sorrow in her train, the passes of the intellect are barred against her by prejudice and passion; if she sometimes forces her way by the batteries of argument, she seldom long keeps possession of her conquests, but is ejected by some favoured enemy, or at best obtains only a nominal sovereignty, without influence and without authority.

That life is short we are all convinced, and yet suffer not that conviction to repress our projects or limit our expectations; that life is miserable we all feel, and yet we believe that the time is near when we shall feel it no longer. But to hope happiness and immortality is equally vain. Our state may indeed be more or less imbittered, as our duration may be more or less contracted; yet the utmost felicity which we can ever attain, will be little better than alleviation of misery, and we shall always feel more pain from our wants than pleasure from our enjoyments. The incident which I am going to relate will shew, that to destroy the effect of all our success, it is not necessary that any signal calamity should fall upon us, that we should be harrassed by implacable persecution, or excruciated by irremediable pains; the brightest hours of prosperity have their clouds, and the stream of life, if it is not ruffled by obstructions, will grow putrid by stagnation.

My father resolving not to imitate the folly of his ancestors, who had hitherto left the younger sons encumbrances on the eldest, destined me to a lucrative profession, and I being careful to lose no opportunity of improvement, was at the usual time in which young men enter the world, well qualified for the exercise of the business which I had chosen.

My eagerness to distinguish myself in publick, and my impatience of the narrow scheme of life to which my indigence confined me, did not suffer me to continue long in the town where I was born. I went away as from a place of confinement, with a resolution to return no more, till I should be able to dazzle with my splendor those who now looked upon me with contempt, to reward those who had paid honours to my dawning merit, and to show all who had suffered me to glide by them unknown and neglected, how much they mistook their interest in omitting to propitiate a genius like mine.

Such were my intentions when I sallied forth into the unknown world, in quest of riches and honours, which I expected to procure in a very short time; for what could withold them from industry and knowledge? He that indulges hope will always be disappointed. Reputation I very soon obtained, but as merit is much more cheaply acknowledged than rewarded, I did not find myself yet enriched in proportion to my celebrity.

I had however in time surmounted the obstacles by which envy and competition obstruct the first attempts of a new claimant, and saw my opponents and censurers tacitly confessing their despair of success, by courting my friendship and yielding to my influence. They who once persued me, were now satisfied to escape from me; and they who had before thought me presumptuous in hoping to overtake them, had now their utmost wish, if they were permitted at no great distance quietly to follow me.

My wants were not madly multiplied as my acquisitions encreased, and the time came at length when I thought myself enabled to gratify all reasonable desires, and when, therefore, I resolved to enjoy that plenty and serenity which I had been hitherto labouring to procure, to enjoy them while I was yet neither crushed by age into infirmity, nor so habituated to a particular manner of life as to be unqualified for new studies or entertainments.

I now quitted my profession, and to set myself at once free from all importunities to resume it, changed my residence, and devoted the remaining part of my time to quiet and amusement. Amidst innumerable projects of pleasure which restless idleness incited me to form, and of which most, when they came to the moment of execution, were rejected for others of no longer continuance, some accident revived in my imagination the pleasing ideas of my native place. It was now in my power to visit those from whom I had been so long absent, in such a manner as was consistent with my former resolution, and I wondered how it could happen that I had so long delayed my own happiness.

Full of the admiration which I should excite, and the homage which I should receive, I dressed my servants in a more ostentatious livery, purchased a magnificent chariot, and resolved to dazzle the inhabitants of the little town with an unexpected blaze of greatness.

While the preparations that vanity required were made for my departure, which, as workmen will not easily be hurried beyond their ordinary rate, I thought very tedious, I solaced my impatience with imaging the various censures that my appearance would produce, the hopes which some would feel from my bounty, the terror which my power would strike on others; the aukward respect with which I should be accosted by timorous officiousness; and the distant reverence with which others less familiar to splendour and dignity would be contented to gaze upon me. I deliberated a long time, whether I should immediately descend to a level with my former acquaintances, or make my condescension more grateful by a gentle transition from haughtiness and reserve. At length I determined to forget some of my companions, till they discovered themselves by some indubitable token, and to receive the congratulations of others upon my good fortune with indifference, to show that I always expected what I had now obtained. The acclamations of the populace I purposed to reward with six hogsheads of ale, and a roasted ox, and then recommend to them to return to their work.

At last all the trappings of grandeur were fitted, and I began the journey of triumph, which I could have wished to have ended in the same moment, but my horses felt none of their master's ardour, and I was shaken four days upon rugged roads. I then entered the town, and having graciously let fall the glasses, that my person might be seen, passed slowly through the street. The noise of the wheels brought the inhabitants to their doors, but I could not perceive that I was known by them. At last I alighted, and my name, I suppose, was told by my servants, for the barber stept from the opposite house, and seized me by the hand with honest joy in his countenance, which, according to the rule that I had prescribed to myself, I repressed with a frigid graciousness. The fellow, instead of sinking into dejection, turned away with contempt, and left me to consider how the second salutation should be received. The next friend was better treated, for I soon found that I must purchase by civility that regard which I had expected to enforce by insolence.

There was yet no smoak of bonfires, no harmony of bells, no shout of crouds, nor riot of joy; the business of the day went forward as before, and after having ordered a splendid supper, which no man came to partake, and which my chagrin hindered me from tasting, I went to bed, where the vexation of disappointment overpowered the fatigue of my journey, and kept me from sleep.

I rose so much humbled by those mortifications, as to enquire after the present state of the town, and found that I had been absent too long to obtain the triumph which had flattered my expectation. Of the friends whose compliments I expected, some had long ago moved to distant provinces, some had lost in the maladies of age all sense of another's prosperity, and some had forgotten our former intimacy amidst care and distresses. Of three whom I had resolved to punish for their former offences by a longer continuance of neglect, one was, by his own industry, raised above my scorn, and two were sheltered from it in the grave. All those whom I loved, feared, or hated, all whose envy or whose kindness I had hopes of contemplating with pleasure,

were swept away, and their place was filled by a new generation
with other views and other competitions; and among many
proofs of the impotence of wealth, I found that it conferred
upon me very few distinctions in my native place.

> *I am, Sir,* &c.
> SEROTINUS.

No. 167. Tuesday, 22 October 1751.

Candida perpetuo reside concordia lecto,
  Tamque pari semper sit Venus æqua jugo.
Diligat ipsa senem quondam, sed et ipsa marito
  Tum quoque cum fuerit, non videatur anus.

> MART.[1]

Their nuptial bed may smiling concord dress,
And *Venus* still the happy union bless!
Wrinkled with age, may mutual love and truth
To their dim eyes recall the bloom of youth.

> F. LEWIS.

To the RAMBLER.

SIR,

It is not common to envy those with whom we cannot easily
be placed in comparison. Every man sees without malevolence
the progress of another in the tracks of life, which he has himself
no desire to tread, and hears without inclination to cavils or
contradiction the renown of those whose distance will not suffer
them to draw the attention of mankind from his own merit. The
sailor never thinks it necessary to contest the lawyer's abilities;
nor would the *Rambler*, however jealous of his reputation, be
much disturbed by the success of rival wits at *Agra* or *Ispahan*.

We do not therefore ascribe to you any superlative degree of
virtue, when we believe that we may inform you of our change
of condition without danger of malignant fascination; and that
when you read of the marriage of your correspondents
Hymenæus and *Tranquilla*, you will join your wishes to those

of their other friends for the happy event of an union in which caprice and selfishness had so little part.

There is at least this reason why we should be less deceived in our connubial hopes than many who enter into the same state, that we have allowed our minds to form no unreasonable expectations, nor vitiated our fancies in the soft hours of courtship, with visions of felicity which human power cannot bestow, or of perfection which human virtue cannot attain. That impartiality with which we endeavoured to inspect the manners of all whom we have known was never so much overpowered by our passion, but that we discovered some faults and weaknesses in each other; and joined our hands in conviction, that as there are advantages to be enjoyed in marriage, there are inconveniencies likewise to be endured; and that, together with confederate intellects and auxiliar virtues, we must find different opinions and opposite inclinations.

We however flatter ourselves, for who is not flattered by himself as well as by others on the day of marriage, that we are eminently qualified to give mutual pleasure. Our birth is without any such remarkable disparity as can give either an opportunity of insulting the other with pompous names and splendid alliances, or of calling in upon any domestick controversy the overbearing assistance of powerful relations. Our fortune was equally suitable, so that we meet without any of those obligations which always produce reproach or suspicion of reproach, which, though they may be forgotten in the gaieties of the first month, no delicacy will always suppress, or of which the suppression must be considered as a new favour, to be repaid by tameness and submission, till gratitude takes the place of love, and the desire of pleasing degenerates by degrees into the fear of offending.

The settlements caused no delay; for we did not trust our affairs to the negotiation of wretches who would have paid their court by multiplying stipulations. *Tranquilla* scorned to detain any part of her fortune from him into whose hands she delivered up her person; and *Hymenæus* thought no act of baseness more criminal than his who enslaves his wife by her own generosity, who by marrying without a jointure condemns her to all the dangers of accident and caprice, and at last boasts his liberality by granting what only the indiscretion of her kindness enabled him to withhold. He therefore received on the common terms the portion which any other woman might have brought him, and reserved all the exuberance of acknowledgment for those excellencies which he has yet been able to discover only in *Tranquilla*.

We did not pass the weeks of courtship like those who consider themselves as taking the last draught of pleasure, and resolve not to quit the bowl without a surfeit, or who know themselves about to set happiness to hazard, and endeavour to lose their sense of danger in the ebriety of perpetual amusement, and whirl round the gulph before they sink. *Hymenæus* often repeated a medical axiom, that *the succours of sickness ought not to be wasted in health*. We know that however our eyes may yet sparkle, and our hearts bound at the presence of each other, the time of listlessness and satiety, of peevishness and discontent must come at last, in which we shall be driven for relief to shews and recreations; that the uniformity of life must be sometimes diversified, and the vacuities of conversation sometimes supplied. We rejoice in the reflection that we have stores of novelty yet unexhausted, which may be opened when repletion shall call for change, and gratifications yet untasted, by which life when it shall become vapid or bitter may be restored to its former sweetness and sprightliness, and again irritate the appetite, and again sparkle in the cup.

Our time will probably be less tasteless than that of those whom the authority and avarice of parents unites almost without their consent in their early years, before they have accumulated any fund of reflection, or collected materials for mutual entertainment. Such we have often seen rising in the morning to cards, and retiring in the afternoon to dose, whose happiness was celebrated by their neighbours, because they happened to grow rich by parsimony, and to be kept quiet by insensibility, and agreed to eat and to sleep together.

We have both mingled with the world, and are therefore no strangers to the faults and virtues, the designs and competitions, the hopes and fears of our contemporaries. We have both amused our leisure with books, and can therefore recount the events of former times, or cite the dictates of antient wisdom. Every occurrence furnishes us with some hint which one or the other can improve, and if it should happen that memory or imagination fail us, we can retire to no idle or unimproving solitude.

Tho' our characters beheld at a distance, exhibit this general resemblance, yet a nearer inspection discovers such a dissimilitude of our habitudes and sentiments, as leaves each some peculiar advantages, and affords that *concordia discors*,[2] that suitable disagreement which is always necessary to intellectual harmony. There may be a total diversity of ideas which admits no participation of the same delight, and there may likewise be such a conformity of notions, as leaves neither any thing to add to the decisions of the other. With such contrariety there can be no peace, with such similarity there can be no pleasure. Our reasonings, though often formed upon different views, terminate generally in the same conclusion. Our thoughts like rivulets issuing from distant springs, are each impregnated in its course with various mixtures, and tinged by infusions unknown to the other, yet at last easily unite into one stream, and purify themselves by the gentle effervescence of contrary qualities.

These benefits we receive in a greater degree as we converse without reserve, because we have nothing to conceal. We have no debts to be paid by imperceptible deductions from avowed expences, no habits to be indulged by the private subserviency of a favoured servant, no private interviews with needy relations, no intelligence with spies placed upon each other. We considered marriage as the most solemn league of perpetual friendship, a state from which artifice and concealment are to be banished for ever, and in which every act of dissimulation is a breach of faith.

The impetuous vivacity of youth, and that ardor of desire, which the first sight of pleasure naturally produces, have long ceased to hurry us into irregularity and vehemence; and experience has shewn us that few gratifications are too valuable to be sacrificed to complaisance. We have thought it convenient to rest from the fatigue of pleasure, and now only continue that course of life into which we had before entered, confirmed in our choice by mutual approbation, supported in our resolution by mutual encouragement, and assisted in our efforts by mutual exhortation.

Such, Mr. *Rambler*, is our prospect of life, a prospect which as it is beheld with more attention, seems to open more extensive happiness, and spreads by degrees into the boundless regions of eternity. But if all our prudence has been vain, and we are doomed to give one instance more of the uncertainty of human discernment, we shall comfort ourselves amidst our disappointments, that we were not betrayed but by such delusions as caution could not escape, since we sought happiness only in the arms of virtue. We are,

SIR,

Your humble Servants,

HYMENÆUS,

TRANQUILLA.

No. 168. Saturday, 26 October 1751.

------------------------ *Decipit*
Frons prima multos, rara mens intelligit
Quod interiore condidit cura angulo.
                                        PHÆDRUS.[1]

The tinsel glitter, and the specious mein,[2]
Delude the most; few pry behind the scene.

It has been observed by *Boileau*, that "a mean or common thought expressed in pompous diction, generally pleases more than a new or noble sentiment delivered in low and vulgar language; because the number is greater of those whom custom has enabled to judge of words, than whom study has qualified to examine things."[3]

This solution might satisfy, if such only were offended with meanness of expression as are unable to distinguish propriety of thought, and to separate propositions or images from the vehicles by which they are conveyed to the understanding. But this kind of disgust is by no means confined to the ignorant or superficial; it operates uniformly and universally upon readers of all classes; every man, however profound or abstracted, perceives himself irresistibly alienated by low terms; they who profess the most zealous adherence to truth are forced to admit that she owes part of her charms to her ornaments, and loses much of her power over the soul, when she appears disgraced by a dress uncouth or ill-adjusted.

We are all offended by low terms, but are not disgusted alike by the same compositions, because we do not all agree to censure the same terms as low. No word is naturally or intrinsically meaner than another; our opinion therefore of words, as of other things arbitrarily and capriciously established, depends wholly upon accident and custom. The cottager thinks those apartments splendid and spacious, which an inhabitant of palaces will despise for their inelegance; and to him who has passed most of his hours with the delicate and polite, many expressions will seem sordid, which another, equally acute, may hear without offence; but a mean term never fails to displease him to whom it appears mean, as poverty is certainly and invariably despised, though he who is poor in the eyes of some, may by others be envied for his wealth.

Words become low by the occasions to which they are applied, or the general character of them who use them; and the disgust which they produce, arises from the revival of those images with which they are commonly united. Thus if, in the most solemn discourse, a phrase happens to occur which has been successfully employed in some ludicrous narrative, the gravest auditor finds it difficult to refrain from laughter, when they who are not prepossessed by the same accidental association, are utterly unable to guess the reason of his merriment. Words which convey ideas of dignity in one age, are banished from elegant writing or conversation in another, because they are in time debased by vulgar mouths, and can be no longer heard without the involuntary recollection of unpleasing images.

When *Mackbeth* is confirming himself in the horrid purpose

of stabbing his king, he breaks out amidst his emotions into a
wish natural to a murderer,

> —— —— Come, thick night!
> And pall thee in the dunnest smoke of hell,
> That my keen knife see not the wound it makes;
> Nor heav'n peep through the blanket of the dark,
> To cry, hold, hold! —— ——[4]

In this passage is exerted all the force of poetry, that force which
calls new powers into being, which embodies sentiment, and
animates matter; yet perhaps scarce any man now peruses it
without some disturbance of his attention from the counteraction of the words to the ideas. What can be more dreadful
than to implore the presence of night, invested not in common
obscurity, but in the smoke of hell? Yet the efficacy of this
invocation is destroyed by the insertion of an epithet now seldom
heard but in the stable, and *dun* night may come or go without
any other notice than contempt.

If we start into raptures when some hero of the Iliad tells us
that δόρυ μάινεται,[5] his lance rages with eagerness to destroy; if
we are alarmed at the terror of the soldiers commanded by
Cæsar to hew down the sacred grove, who dreaded, says *Lucan*,
lest the axe aimed at the oak should fly back upon the striker,

> —————— *Si robora sacra ferirent,*
> *In sua credebant redituras membra secures,*[6]
>
> None dares with impious steel the grove to rend,
> Lest on himself the destin'd stroke descend.

we cannot surely but sympathise with the horrors of a wretch
about to murder his master, his friend, his benefactor, who
suspects that the weapon will refuse its office, and start back
from the breast which he is preparing to violate. Yet this sentiment is weakened by the name of an instrument used by butchers
and cooks in the meanest employments; we do not immediately
conceive that any crime of importance is to be committed with a

knife; or who does not, at last, from the long habit of connecting a knife with sordid offices, feel aversion rather than terror?

Mackbeth proceeds to wish, in the madness of guilt, that the inspection of heaven may be intercepted, and that he may in the involutions of infernal darkness escape the eye of providence. This is the utmost extravagance of determined wickedness; yet this is so debased by two unfortunate words, that while I endeavour to impress on my reader the energy of the senti-ment, I can scarce check my risibility, when the expression forces itself upon my mind; for who, without some relaxation of his gravity, can hear of the avengers of guilt *peeping through a blanket*?

These imperfections of diction are less obvious to the reader, as he is less acquainted with common usages; they are therefore wholly imperceptible to a foreigner, who learns our language from books, and will strike a solitary academick less forcibly than a modish lady.

Among the numerous requisites that must concur to complete an author, few are of more importance than an early entrance into the living world. The seeds of knowledge may be planted in solitude, but must be cultivated in publick. Argumentation may be taught in colleges, and theories formed in retirement, but the artifice of embellishment, and the powers of attraction, can be gained only by general converse.

An acquaintance with prevailing customs and fashionable elegance is necessary likewise for other purposes. The injury that grand imagery suffers from unsuitable language, personal merit may fear from rudeness and indelicacy. When the success of Æneas depended on the favour of the queen upon whose coasts he was driven, his celestial protectress thought him not sufficiently secured against rejection by his piety or bravery, but decorated him for the interview with preternatural beauty.[7] Whoever desires, for his writings or himself, what none can reasonably contemn, the favour of mankind, must add grace to strength, and make his thoughts agreeable as well as useful. Many complain of neglect who never tried to attract regard. It cannot be expected that the patrons of science or virtue should be solicitous to discover excellencies which they who possess them shade and disguise. Few have abilities so much needed by the rest of the world as to be caressed on their own terms; and he that will not condescend to recommend himself by external embellishments, must submit to the fate of just sentiments meanly expressed, and be ridiculed and forgotten before he is understood.

No. 170. Saturday, 2 November 1751.

Confiteor; si quid prodest delicta fateri.

OVID.[1]

I grant the charge; forgive the fault confess'd.

To the RAMBLER.

SIR,

I am one of those beings, from whom many, that melt at the sight of all other misery, think it meritorious to withhold relief; one whom the rigour of virtuous indignation dooms to suffer without complaint, and perish without regard; and whom I myself have formerly insulted in the pride of reputation and security of innocence.

I am of a good family, but my father was burthened with more children than he could decently support. A wealthy relation, as he travelled from *London* to his country seat, condescending to make him a visit, was touched with compassion of his narrow fortune, and resolved to ease him of part of his charge, by taking the care of a child upon himself. Distress on one side and ambition on the other, were too powerful for parental fondness, and the little family passed in review before him, that he might make his choice. I was then ten years old, and without knowing for what purpose, I was called to my great cousin, endeavoured to recommend myself by my best courtesy, sung him my prettiest song, told the last story that I had read, and so much endeared myself by my innocence, that he declared his resolution to adopt me, and to educate me with his own daughters.

My parents felt the common struggles at the thought of

parting, and *some natural tears they dropp'd, but wip'd them soon.*[2] They considered, not without that false estimation of the value of wealth which poverty long continued always produces, that I was raised to higher rank than they could give me, and to hopes of more ample fortune than they could bequeath. My mother sold some of her ornaments to dress me in such a manner as might secure me from contempt at my first arrival; and when she dismissed me, pressed me to her bosom with an embrace that I still feel, gave me some precepts of piety which, however neglected, I have not forgotten, and uttered prayers for my final happiness, of which I have not yet ceased to hope, that they will at last be granted.

My sisters envied my new finery, and seemed not much to regret our separation; my father conducted me to the stagecoach with a kind of chearful tenderness; and in a very short time, I was transported to splendid apartments, and a luxurious table, and grew familiar to show, noise and gaiety.

In three years my mother died, having implored a blessing on her family with her last breath. I had little opportunity to indulge a sorrow, which there was none to partake with me, and therefore soon ceased to reflect much upon my loss. My father turned all his care upon his other children, whom some fortunate adventures and unexpected legacies enabled him, when he died four years after my mother, to leave in a condition above their expectations.

I should have shared the encrease of his fortune, and had once a portion assigned me in his will; but my cousin assuring him that all care for me was needless, since he had resolved to place me happily in the world, directed him to divide my part amongst my sisters.

Thus I was thrown upon dependance without resource. Being now at an age in which young women are initiated in company, I was no longer to be supported in my former character but at considerable expence; so that partly lest I should waste money, and partly lest my appearance might draw too many compliments and assiduities, I was insensibly degraded from my equality, and enjoyed few privileges above the head servant, but that of receiving no wages.

I felt every indignity, but knew that resentment would precipitate my fall. I therefore endeavoured to continue my importance by little services and active officiousness, and for a time preserved myself from neglect, by withdrawing all pretences to competition, and studying to please rather than to shine. But my interest, notwithstanding this expedient, hourly declined, and my cousin's favourite maid began to exchange repartees with me, and consult me about the alterations of a cast gown.

I was now completely depressed, and though I had seen mankind enough to know the necessity of outward chearfulness, I often withdrew to my chamber to vent my grief, or turn my condition in my mind, and examine by what means I might escape from perpetual mortification. At last, my schemes and sorrows were interrupted by a sudden change of my relation's behaviour, who one day took an occasion when we were left together in a room, to bid me suffer myself no longer to be insulted, but assume the place which he always intended me to hold in the family. He assured me, that his wife's preference of her own daughters should never hurt me; and, accompanying his professions with a purse of gold, ordered me to bespeak a rich suit at the mercer's,[3] and to apply privately to him for money when I wanted it, and insinuate that my other friends supplied me, which he would take care to confirm.

By this stratagem, which I did not then understand, he filled me with tenderness and gratitude, compelled me to repose on him as my only support, and produced a necessity of private conversation. He often appointed interviews at the house of an acquaintance, and sometimes called on me with a coach, and carried me abroad. My sense of his favour, and the desire of retaining it, disposed me to unlimited complaisance, and though I saw his kindness grow every day more fond, I did not suffer any suspicion to enter my thoughts. At last the wretch took advantage of the familiarity which he enjoyed as my relation, and the submission which he exacted as my benefactor, to complete the ruin of an orphan whom his own promises had made indigent, whom his indulgence had melted, and his authority subdued.

I know not why it should afford subject of exultation, to overpower on any terms the resolution, or surprise the caution of a girl; but of all the boasters that deck themselves in the spoils of innocence and beauty, they surely have the least pretensions to triumph, who submit to owe their success to some casual influence. They neither employ the graces of fancy, nor the force of understanding, in their attempts; they cannot please their vanity with the art of their approaches, the delicacy of their adulations, the elegance of their address, or the efficacy of their eloquence; nor applaud themselves as possessed of any qualities, by which affection is attracted. They surmount no obstacles, they defeat no rivals, but attack only those who cannot resist, and are often content to possess the body without any solicitude to gain the heart.

Many of these despicable wretches does my present acquaintance with infamy and wickedness enable me to number among the heroes of debauchery. Reptiles whom their own servants would have despised, had they not been their servants, and with whom beggary would have disdained intercourse, had she not been allured by hopes of relief. Many of the beings which are now rioting in taverns, or shivering in the streets, have been corrupted not by arts of gallantry which stole gradually upon the affections and laid prudence asleep, but by the fear of losing benefits which were never intended, or of incurring resentment which they could not escape; some have been frighted by masters, and some awed by guardians into ruin.

Our crime had its usual consequence, and he soon perceived that I could not long continue in his family. I was distracted at the thought of the reproach which I now believed inevitable. He comforted me with hopes of eluding all discovery, and often upbraided me with the anxiety, which perhaps none but himself saw in my countenance; but at last mingled his assurances of protection and maintenance with menaces of total desertion, if in the moments of perturbation I should suffer his secret to escape, or endeavour to throw on him any part of my infamy.

Thus passed the dismal hours till my retreat could no longer be delayed. It was pretended that my relations had sent for me

to a distant country, and I entered upon a state which shall be
described in my next letter.

I am, SIR, &c.

MISELLA.

No. 171. Tuesday, 5 November 1751.

Tædet cœli convexa tueri.
VIRG.[1]

Dark is the sun, and loathsome is the day.

To the RAMBLER.

SIR,

Misella now sits down to continue her narrative. I am convinced that nothing would more powerfully preserve youth from
irregularity, or guard inexperience from seduction, than a just
description of the condition into which the wanton plunges
herself, and therefore hope that my letter may be a sufficient
antidote to my example.

After the distraction, hesitation and delays which the timidity
of guilt naturally produces, I was removed to lodgings in a
distant part of the town, under one of the characters commonly
assumed upon such occasions. Here being, by my circumstances,
condemned to solitude, I passed most of my hours in bitterness
and anguish. The conversation of the people with whom I was
placed, was not at all capable of engaging my attention or
dispossessing the reigning ideas. The books which I carried to
my retreat were such as heightened my abhorrence of myself;
for I was not so far abandoned as to sink voluntarily into
corruption, or endeavour to conceal from my own mind the
enormity of my crime.

My relation remitted none of his fondness, but visited me so
often that I was sometimes afraid lest his assiduity should expose
him to suspicion. Whenever he came he found me weeping, and
was therefore less delightfully entertained than he expected.
After frequent expostulations upon the unreasonableness of my

sorrow, and innumerable protestations of everlasting regard, he at last found that I was more affected with the loss of my innocence, than the danger of my fame, and that he might not be disturbed by my remorse, began to lull my conscience with the opiates of irreligion. His arguments were such as my course of life has since exposed me often to the necessity of hearing, vulgar, empty and fallacious; yet they at first confounded me by their novelty, filled me with doubt and perplexity, and interrupted that peace which I began to feel from the sincerity of my repentance, without substituting any other support. I listened a while to his impious gabble, but its influence was soon overpowered by natural reason and early education, and the convictions which this new attempt gave me of his baseness completed my abhorrence. I have heard of barbarians, who, when tempests drive ships upon their coast, decoy them to the rocks that they may plunder their lading, and have always thought that wretches thus merciless in their depredations, ought to be destroyed by a general insurrection of all social beings; yet how light is this guilt to the crime of him, who in the agitations of remorse cuts away the anchor of piety, and when he has drawn aside credulity from the paths of virtue, hides the light of heaven which would direct her to return. I had hitherto considered him as a man equally betrayed with myself by the concurrence of appetite and opportunity; but I now saw with horror that he was contriving to perpetuate his gratification, and was desirous to fit me to his purpose by complete and radical corruption.

To escape, however, was not yet in my power. I could support the expences of my condition, only by the continuance of his favour. He provided all that was necessary, and in a few weeks, congratulated me upon my escape from the danger which we had both expected with so much anxiety. I then began to remind him of his promise to restore me with my fame uninjured to the world. He promised me in general terms, that nothing should be wanting which his power could add to my happiness, but forbore to release me from my confinement. I knew how much my reception in the world depended upon my speedy return, and was therefore outragiously impatient of his delays, which I now perceived to be only artifices of lewdness. He told me, at

last, with an appearance of sorrow, that all hopes of restoration
to my former state were for ever precluded; that chance had
discovered my secret, and malice divulged it; and that nothing
now remained, but to seek a retreat more private, where curiosity or hatred could never find us.

The rage, anguish, and resentment, which I felt at this
account, are not to be expressed. I was in so much dread of
reproach and infamy, which he represented as pursuing me with
full cry, that I yielded myself implicitly to his disposal, and was
removed with a thousand studied precautions through by-ways
and dark passages, to another house, where I harrassed him
with perpetual solicitations for a small annuity, that might
enable me to live in the country with obscurity and innocence.

This demand he at first evaded with ardent professions, but
in time appeared offended at my importunity and distrust; and
having one day endeavoured to sooth me with uncommon
expressions of tenderness, when he found my discontent
immoveable, left me with some inarticulate murmurs of anger.
I was pleased that he was at last roused to sensibility, and
expecting that at his next visit, he would comply with my
request, lived with great tranquility upon the money in my
hands, and was so much pleased with this pause of persecution,
that I did not reflect how much his absence had exceeded the
usual intervals, till I was alarmed with the danger of wanting
subsistence. I then suddenly contracted my expences, but was
unwilling to supplicate for assistance. Necessity, however, soon
overcame my modesty or my pride, and I applied to him by a
letter, but had no answer. I writ in terms more pressing, but
without effect. I then sent an agent to enquire after him, who
informed me, that he had quitted his house, and was gone with
his family to reside for some time upon his estate in *Ireland*.

However shocked at this abrupt departure, I was yet unwilling to believe that he could wholly abandon me, and therefore
by the sale of my cloaths I supported myself, expecting that
every post would bring me relief. Thus I passed seven months
between hope and dejection, in a gradual approach to poverty
and distress, emaciated with discontent and bewildered with
uncertainty. At last, my landlady, after many hints of the neces-

sity of a new lover, took the opportunity of my absence to search my boxes, and missing some of my apparel, seized the remainder for rent, and led me to the door.

To remonstrate against legal cruelty, was vain; to supplicate obdurate brutality, was hopeless. I went away I knew not whither, and wandered about without any settled purpose, unacquainted with the usual expedients of misery, unqualified for laborious offices, afraid to meet an eye that had seen me before, and hopeless of relief from those who were strangers to my former condition. Night came on in the midst of my distraction, and I still continued to wander till the menaces of the watch obliged me to shelter myself in a covered passage.

Next day, I procured a lodging in the backward garret of a mean house, and employed my landlady to enquire for a service. My applications were generally rejected for want of a character. At length, I was received at a draper's; but when it was known to my mistress that I had only one gown, and that of silk, she was of opinion, that I looked like a thief, and without warning, hurried me away. I then tried to support myself by my needle, and by my landlady's recommendation, obtained a little work from a shop, and for three weeks lived without repining; but when my punctuality had gained me so much reputation, that I was trusted to make up a head[2] of some value, one of my fellow-lodgers stole the lace, and I was obliged to fly from a prosecution.

Thus driven again into the streets, I lived upon the least that could support me, and at night accommodated myself under pent-houses[3] as well as I could. At length I became absolutely pennyless; and having strolled all day without sustenance, was at the close of evening accosted by an elderly man, with an invitation to a tavern. I refused him with hesitation; he seized me by the hand, and drew me into a neighbouring house, where when he saw my face pale with hunger, and my eyes swelling with tears, he spurned me from him, and bad me cant and whine in some other place; he for his part would take care of his pockets.

I still continued to stand in the way, having scarcely strength to walk farther, when another soon addressed me in the same manner. When he saw the same tokens of calamity, he considered that I might be obtained at a cheap rate, and therefore quickly made overtures, which I had no longer firmness to reject. By this man I was maintained four months in penurious wickedness, and then abandoned to my former condition, from which I was delivered by another keeper.

In this abject state I have now passed four years, the drudge of extortion and the sport of drunkenness; sometimes the property of one man, and sometimes the common prey of accidental lewdness; at one time tricked up for sale by the mistress of a brothel, at another begging in the streets to be relieved from hunger by wickedness; without any hope in the day but of finding some whom folly or excess may expose to my allurements, and without any reflections at night, but such as guilt and terror impress upon me.

If those who pass their days in plenty and security, could visit for an hour the dismal receptacles to which the prostitute retires from her nocturnal excursions, and see the wretches that lie crowded together, mad with intemperance, ghastly with famine, nauseous with filth, and noisome with disease; it would not be easy for any degree of abhorrence to harden them against compassion, or to repress the desire which they must immediately feel to rescue such numbers of human beings from a state so dreadful.

It is said that in *France* they annually evacuate their streets, and ship their prostitutes and vagabonds to their colonies. If the women that infest this city had the same opportunity of escaping from their miseries, I believe very little force would be necessary; for who among them can dread any change? Many of us indeed are wholly unqualified for any but the most servile employments, and those perhaps would require the care of a magistrate to hinder them from following the same practices in another country; but others are only precluded by infamy from reformation, and would gladly be delivered on any terms from the necessity of guilt and the tyranny of chance. No place but a populous city can afford opportunities for open prostitution, and where the eye of justice can attend to individuals, those who cannot be made good may be restrained from mischief. For my part I should exult at the privilege of banishment, and think myself happy in any region that should restore me once again to honesty and peace.

I am, Sir, &c.
MISELLA.

No. 176. Saturday, 23 November 1751.

—— *Naso suspendere adunco.*
HOR.[1]

On me you turn the nose ——

There are many vexatious accidents and uneasy situations which raise little compassion for the sufferer, and which no man but those whom they immediately distress, can regard with seriousness. Petty mischiefs, that have no influence on futurity, nor extend their effects to the rest of life, are always seen with a kind of malicious pleasure. A mistake or embarrasment, which for the present moment fills the face with blushes, and the mind with confusion, will have no other effect upon those who observe it than that of convulsing them with irresistible laughter. Some circumstances of misery are so powerfully ridiculous, that neither kindness nor duty can withstand them; they bear down love, interest, and reverence, and force the friend, the dependent, or the child, to give way to instantaneous motions of merriment.

Among the principal of comick calamities, may be reckoned the pain which an author, not yet hardened into insensibility, feels at the onset of a furious critick, whose age, rank or fortune gives him confidence to speak without reserve; who heaps one objection upon another, and obtrudes his remarks, and enforces his corrections without tenderness or awe.

The author, full of the importance of his work, and anxious for the justification of every syllable, starts and kindles at the slightest attack; the critick, eager to establish his superiority, triumphing in every discovery of failure, and zealous to impress the cogency of his arguments, pursues him from line to line without cessation or remorse. The critick, who hazards little, proceeds with vehemence, impetuosity and fearlessness; the author, whose quiet and fame, and life and immortality are involved in the controversy, tries every art of subterfuge and defence; maintains modestly what he resolves never to yield, and yields unwillingly what cannot be maintained. The critick's purpose is to conquer, the author only hopes to escape; the critick therefore knits his brow, and raises his voice, and rejoices whenever he perceives any tokens of pain excited by the pressure of his assertions, or the point of his sarcasms. The author, whose endeavour is at once to mollify and elude his persecutor, composes his features, and softens his accent, breaks the force of assault by retreat, and rather steps aside than flies or advances.

As it very seldom happens that the rage of extemporary criticism inflicts fatal or lasting wounds, I know not that the laws of benevolence entitle this distress to much sympathy. The diversion of baiting an author has the sanction of all ages and nations, and is more lawful than the sport of teizing other animals, because for the most part he comes voluntarily to the stake, furnished, as he imagines, by the patron powers of literature, with resistless weapons, and impenetrable armour, with the mail of the boar of *Erymanth*, and the paws of the lion of *Nemea*.[2]

But the works of genius are sometimes produced by other motives than vanity; and he whom necessity or duty enforces to write, is not always so well satisfied with himself, as not to be discouraged by censorious impudence. It may therefore be necessary to consider how they, whom publication lays open to the insults of such as their obscurity secures against reprisals, may extricate themselves from unexpected encounters.

Vida, a man of considerable skill in the politicks of literature, directs his pupil wholly to abandon his defence, and even when he can irrefragably refute all objections, to suffer tamely the exultations of his antagonist.[3]

This rule may perhaps be just, when advice is asked, and severity solicited, because no man tells his opinion so freely as when he imagines it received with implicit veneration; and critics ought never to be consulted but while errors may yet be rectified or insipidity suppressed. But when the book has once been dismissed into the world, and can be no more retouched, I know not whether a very different conduct should not be prescribed, and whether firmness and spirit may not sometimes be of use to overpower arrogance and repel brutality. Softness, diffidence and moderation will often be mistaken for imbecility and dejection; they lure cowardice to the attack by the hopes of easy victory, and it will soon be found that he whom every man thinks he can conquer, shall never be at peace.

The animadversions of criticks are commonly such as may easily provoke the sedatest writer to some quickness of resentment and asperity of reply. A man who by long consideration has familiarised a subject to his own mind, carefully surveyed the series of his thoughts, and planned all the parts of his composition into a regular dependance on each other, will often start at the sinistrous[4] interpretations, or absurd remarks of haste and ignorance, and wonder by what infatuation they have been led away from the obvious sense, and upon what peculiar principles of judgment they decide against him.

The eye of the intellect, like that of the body, is not equally perfect in all, nor equally adapted in any to all objects; the end of criticism is to supply its defects; rules are the instruments of mental vision, which may indeed assist our faculties when properly used, but produce confusion and obscurity by unskilful application.

Some seem always to read with the microscope of criticism, and employ their whole attention upon minute elegance, or faults scarcely visible to common observation. The dissonance of a syllable, the recurrence of the same sound, the repetition of a particle, the smallest deviation from propriety, the slightest defect in construction or arrangement, swell before their eyes into enormities. As they discern with great exactness, they comprehend but a narrow compass, and know nothing of the justness of the design, the general spirit of the performance, the artifice of connection, or the harmony of the parts; they never conceive how small a proportion that which they are busy in contemplating bears to the whole, or how the petty inaccuracies with which they are offended, are absorbed and lost in general excellence.

Others are furnished by criticism with a telescope. They see with great clearness whatever is too remote to be discovered by the rest of mankind, but are totally blind to all that lies immediately before them. They discover in every passage some secret meaning, some remote allusion, some artful allegory, or some occult imitation which no other reader ever suspected, but they have no perception of the cogency of arguments, the force of pathetick sentiments, the various colours of diction, or the flowery embellishments of fancy; of all that engages the attention of others, they are totally insensible, while they pry into worlds of conjecture, and amuse themselves with phantoms in the clouds.

In criticism, as in every other art, we fail sometimes by our weakness, but more frequently by our fault. We are sometimes bewildered by ignorance, and sometimes by prejudice, but we seldom deviate far from the right, but when we deliver ourselves up to the direction of vanity.

No. 181. Tuesday, 10 December 1751.

———— *Neu fluitem dubiæ spe pendulus horæ.*
                                                        HOR.[1]

Nor let me float in fortune's pow'r,
Dependant on the future hour.
                                    FRANCIS.

To the RAMBLER.

SIR,

As I have passed much of my life in disquiet and suspense, and lost many opportunities of advantage by a passion which I have reason to believe prevalent in different degrees over a great part of mankind, I cannot but think myself well qualified to warn those who are yet uncaptivated, of the danger which they incur by placing themselves within its influence.

I served an apprenticeship to a linen-draper with uncommon

reputation for diligence and fidelity; and at the age of three and twenty opened a shop for myself, with a large stock, and such credit among all the merchants who were acquainted with my master, that I could command whatever was imported curious or valuable. For five years I proceeded with success proportionate to close application and untainted integrity; was a daring bidder at every sale; always paid my notes before they were due; and advanced so fast in commercial reputation, that I was proverbially marked out as the model of young traders, and every one expected that a few years would make me an alderman.

In this course of even prosperity, I was one day persuaded to buy a ticket in the lottery. The sum was inconsiderable, part was to be repaid though fortune might fail to favour me, and therefore my established maxims of frugality did not restrain me from so trifling an experiment. The ticket lay almost forgotten till the time at which every man's fate was to be determined; nor did the affair even then seem of any importance, till I discovered by the publick papers that the number next to mine had conferred the great prize.

My heart leaped at the thought of such an approach to sudden riches, which I considered myself, however contrarily to the laws of computation, as having missed by a single chance; and I could not forbear to revolve the consequences which such a bounteous allotment would have produced, if it had happened to me. This dream of felicity, by degrees took possession of my imagination. The great delight of my solitary hours was to purchase an estate, and form plantations with money which once might have been mine, and I never met my friends but I spoiled all their merriment by perpetual complaints of my ill luck.

At length another lottery was opened, and I had now so heated my imagination with the prospect of a prize, that I should have pressed among the first purchasers, had not my ardour been with-held by deliberation upon the probability of success from one ticket rather than another. I hesitated long between even and odd; considered the square and cubick numbers through the lottery; examined all those to which good luck had been hitherto annexed; and at last fixed upon one which by some secret relation to the events of my life I thought predestined to make me happy. Delay in great affairs is often mischievous; the ticket was sold, and its possessor could not be found.

I returned to my conjectures, and after many arts of prognostication, fixed upon another chance, but with less confidence. Never did captive, heir, or lover feel so much vexation from the slow pace of time, as I suffered between the purchase of my ticket and the distribution of the prizes. I solaced my uneasiness as well as I could, by frequent contemplations of approaching happiness; when the sun rose I knew it would set, and congratulated myself at night that I was so much nearer to my wishes. At last the day came, my ticket appeared, and rewarded all my care and sagacity with a despicable prize of fifty pounds.

My friends, who honestly rejoiced upon my success, were very coldly received; I hid myself a fortnight in the country, that my chagrine might fume away without observation, and then returning to my shop, began to listen after another lottery.

With the news of a lottery I was soon gratified, and having now found the vanity of conjecture and inefficacy of computation, I resolved to take the prize by violence, and therefore bought forty tickets, not omitting however to divide them between the even and odd numbers, that I might not miss the lucky class. Many conclusions did I form, and many experiments did I try to determine from which of those tickets I might most reasonably expect riches. At last, being unable to satisfy myself by any modes of reasoning, I wrote the numbers upon dice, and allotted five hours every day to the amusement of throwing them in a garret; and, examining the event by an exact register, found, on the evening before the lottery was drawn, that one of my numbers had been turned up five times more than any of the rest in three hundred and thirty thousand throws.

This experiment was fallacious; the first day presented the hopeful ticket, a detestable blank. The rest came out with different fortune, and in conclusion I lost thirty pounds by this great adventure.

I had now wholly changed the cast of my behaviour and the conduct of my life. The shop was for the most part abandoned to my servants, and, if I entered it, my thoughts were so engrossed by my tickets, that I scarcely heard or answered a question, but considered every customer as an intruder upon my meditations, whom I was in haste to dispatch. I mistook the price of my goods, committed blunders in my bills, forgot to file my receipts, and neglected to regulate my books. My acquaintances by degrees began to fall away, but I perceived the decline of my business with little emotion, because whatever deficiency there might be in my gains I expected the next lottery to supply.

Miscarriage naturally produces diffidence; I began now to seek assistance against ill luck, by an alliance with those that had been more successful. I enquired diligently, at what office any prize had been sold, that I might purchase of a propitious vender; solicited those who had been fortunate in former lotteries, to partake with me in my new tickets; and, whenever I met with one that had in any event of his life been eminently prosperous, I invited him to take a larger share. I had, by this rule of conduct, so diffused my interest, that I had a fourth part of fifteen tickets, an eighth of forty and a sixteenth of ninety.

I waited for the decision of my fate with my former palpitations, and looked upon the business of my trade with the usual neglect. The wheel at last was turned, and its revolutions brought me a long succession of sorrows and disappointments. I indeed often partook of a small prize, and the loss of one day was generally balanced by the gain of the next; but my desires yet remained unsatisfied, and when one of my chances had failed, all my expectation was suspended on those which remained yet undetermined. At last a prize of five thousand pounds was proclaimed; I caught fire at the cry, and enquiring the number found it to be one of my own tickets, which I had divided among those on whose luck I depended, and of which I had retained only a sixteenth part.

You will easily judge, with what detestation of himself, a man thus intent upon gain reflected that he had sold a prize which was once in his possession. It was to no purpose, that I represented to my mind, the impossibility of recalling the past, or the folly of condemning an act, which only its event, an event which no human intelligence could foresee, proved to be wrong.

The prize which, though put in my hands, had been suffered to slip from me, filled me with anguish; and knowing that complaint would only expose me to ridicule, I gave myself up silently to grief, and lost by degrees my appetite and my rest.

My indisposition soon became visible; I was visited by my friends, and among them by *Eumathes*, a clergyman, whose piety and learning gave him such an ascendant over me, that I could not refuse to open my heart. There are, said he, few minds sufficiently firm to be trusted in the hands of chance. Whoever finds himself inclined to anticipate futurity, and exalt possibility to certainty, should avoid every kind of casual adventure, since his grief must be always proportionate to his hope. You have long wasted that time which, by a proper application, would have certainly, though moderately, encreased your fortune, in a laborious and anxious persuit of a species of gain, which no labour or anxiety, no art or expedient can secure or promote. You are now fretting away your life in repentance of an act, against which repentance can give no caution, but to avoid the occasion of committing it. Rouse from this lazy dream of fortuitous riches, which, if obtained you could scarcely have enjoyed, because they could confer no consciousness of desert; return to rational and manly industry, and consider the meer gift of luck as below the care of a wise man.

No. 183. Tuesday, 17 December 1751.

Nulla fides regni sociis, omnisque potestas
Impatiens consortis erat.

                                                           LUCAN.[1]

No faith of partnership dominion owns;
Still discord hovers o'er divided thrones.

The hostility perpetually exercised between one man and another, is caused by the desire of many for that which only few can possess. Every man would be rich, powerful, and famous; yet fame, power, and riches, are only the names of relative conditions, which imply the obscurity, dependance, and poverty of greater numbers.

This universal and incessant competition, produces injury and malice by two motives, interest, and envy; the prospect of adding to our possessions what we can take from others, and the hope of alleviating the sense of our disparity by lessening others, though we gain nothing to ourselves.

Of these two malignant and destructive powers, it seems probable at the first view, that interest has the strongest and most extensive influence. It is easy to conceive that opportunities to seize what has been long wanted, may excite desires almost irresistible; but surely, the same eagerness cannot be kindled by an accidental power of destroying that which gives happiness to another. It must be more natural to rob for gain, than to ravage only for mischief.

Yet I am inclined to believe, that the great law of mutual benevolence is oftner violated by envy than by interest, and that most of the misery which the defamation of blameless actions, or the obstruction of honest endeavours brings upon the world, is inflicted by men that propose no advantage to themselves but the satisfaction of poisoning the banquet which they cannot taste, and blasting the harvest which they have no right to reap.

Interest can diffuse itself but to a narrow compass. The number is never large of those who can hope to fill the posts of degraded power, catch the fragments of shattered fortune, or succeed to the honours of depreciated beauty. But the empire of envy has no limits, as it requires to its influence very little help from external circumstances. Envy may always be produced by idleness and pride, and in what place will not they be found?

Interest requires some qualities not universally bestowed. The ruin of another will produce no profit to him, who has not discernment to mark his advantage, courage to seize, and activity to pursue it; but the cold malignity of envy may be exerted in a torpid and quiescent state, amidst the gloom of stupidity, in the coverts of cowardice. He that falls by the attacks of interest, is torn by hungry tigers; he may discover and resist his enemies. He that perishes in the ambushes of envy, is destroyed by unknown and invisible assailants, and dies like a man suffocated by a poisonous vapour, without knowledge of his danger, or possibility of contest.

Interest is seldom pursued but at some hazard. He that hopes to gain much, has commonly something to lose, and when he ventures to attack superiority, if he fails to conquer, is irrecoverably crushed. But envy may act without expence, or danger. To spread suspicion, to invent calumnies, to propagate scandal, requires neither labour nor courage. It is easy for the author of a lye, however malignant, to escape detection, and infamy needs very little industry to assist its circulation.

Envy is almost the only vice which is practicable at all times, and in every place; the only passion which can never lie quiet for want of irritation; its effects therefore are every where discoverable, and its attempts always to be dreaded.

It is impossible to mention a name which any advantageous distinction has made eminent, but some latent animosity will burst out. The wealthy trader, however he may abstract himself from publick affairs, will never want those who hint, with *Shylock*, that ships are but boards.[2] The beauty, adorned only with the unambitious graces of innocence and modesty, provokes, whenever she appears, a thousand murmurs of detraction. The genius, even when he endeavours only to entertain or instruct, yet suffers persecution from innumerable criticks, whose acrimony is excited merely by the pain of seeing others pleased, and of hearing applauses which another enjoys.

The frequency of envy makes it so familiar, that it escapes our notice; nor do we often reflect upon its turpitude or malignity, till we happen to feel its influence. When he that has given no provocation to malice, but by attempting to excel, finds himself pursued by multitudes whom he never saw with all the implacability of personal resentment; when he perceives clamour and malice let loose upon him as a publick enemy, and incited by every stratagem of defamation; when he hears the misfortunes of his family, or the follies of his youth exposed to the world; and every failure of conduct, or defect of nature aggravated and ridiculed; he then learns to abhor those artifices at which he only laughed before, and discovers how much the happiness of life would be advanced by the eradication of envy from the human heart.

Envy is, indeed, a stubborn weed of the mind, and seldom yields to the culture of philosophy. There are, however, considerations, which if carefully implanted and diligently propagated, might in time overpower and repress it, since no one can nurse it for the sake of pleasure, as its effects are only shame, anguish, and perturbation.

It is above all other vices inconsistent with the character of a social being, because it sacrifices truth and kindness to very weak temptations. He that plunders a wealthy neighbour, gains as much as he takes away, and may improve his own condition in the same proportion as he impairs another's; but he that blasts a flourishing reputation, must be content with a small dividend of additional fame, so small as can afford very little consolation to balance the guilt by which it is obtained.

I have hitherto avoided that dangerous and empirical morality, which cures one vice by means of another. But envy is so base and detestable, so vile in its original, and so pernicious in its effects, that the predominance of almost any other quality is to be preferred. It is one of those lawless enemies of society, against which poisoned arrows may honestly be used. Let it, therefore, be constantly remembered, that whoever envies another, confesses his superiority, and let those be reformed by their pride who have lost their virtue.

It is no slight aggravation of the injuries which envy incites, that they are committed against those who have given no intentional provocation; and that the sufferer is often marked out for ruin, not because he has failed in any duty, but because he has dared to do more than was required.

Almost every other crime is practised by the help of some quality which might have produced esteem or love, if it had been well employed; but envy is mere unmixed and genuine evil; it pursues a hateful end by despicable means, and desires not so much its own happiness as another's misery. To avoid depravity like this, it is not necessary that any one should aspire to heroism or sanctity, but only, that he should resolve not to quit the rank which nature assigns him, and wish to maintain the dignity of a human being.

No. 184. Saturday, 21 December 1751.

Permittes ipsis expendere numinibus, quid
Conveniat nobis, rebusque sit utile nostris.
                                                                JUV.[1]

Intrust thy fortune to the pow'rs above:
Leave them to manage for thee, and to grant
What their unerring wisdom sees thee want.
                                                                DRYDEN.

As every scheme of life, so every form of writing has its advantages and inconveniencies, though not mingled in the same
proportions. The writer of essays, escapes many embarrassments to which a large work would have exposed him; he seldom
harrasses his reason with long trains of consequence, dims his
eyes with the perusal of antiquated volumes, or burthens his
memory with great accumulations of preparatory knowledge.
A careless glance upon a favourite author, or transient survey
of the varieties of life, is sufficient to supply the first hint or
seminal idea, which enlarged by the gradual accretion of matter
stored in the mind, is by the warmth of fancy easily expanded
into flowers, and sometimes ripened into fruit.

The most frequent difficulty, by which the authors of these
petty compositions are distressed, arises from the perpetual
demand of novelty and change. The compiler of a system of
science lays his invention at rest, and employs only his judgment,
the faculty exerted with least fatigue. Even the relator of feigned
adventures, when once the principal characters are established,
and the great events regularly connected, finds incidents and
episodes crouding upon his mind; every change opens new
views, and the latter part of the story grows without labour out
of the former. But he that attempts to entertain his reader with
unconnected pieces, finds the irksomeness of his task rather
encreased than lessened by every production. The day calls
afresh upon him for a new topick, and he is again obliged to
choose, without any principle to regulate his choice.

It is indeed true, that there is seldom any necessity of looking far, or enquiring long for a proper subject. Every diversity of art or nature, every public blessing or calamity, every domestick pain or gratification, every sally of caprice, blunder of absurdity, or stratagem of affectation may supply matter to him whose only rule is to avoid uniformity. But it often happens, that the judgment is distracted with boundless multiplicity, the imagination ranges from one design to another, and the hours pass imperceptibly away till the composition can be no longer delayed, and necessity enforces the use of those thoughts which then happen to be at hand. The mind rejoicing at deliverance on any terms from perplexity and suspense, applies herself vigorously to the work before her, collects embellishments and illustrations, and sometimes finishes with great elegance and happiness what in a state of ease and leisure she never had begun.

It is not commonly observed, how much, even of actions considered as particularly subject to choice, is to be attributed to accident, or some cause out of our own power, by whatever name it be distinguished. To close tedious deliberations with hasty resolves, and after long consultations with reason to refer the question to caprice, is by no means peculiar to the essayist. Let him that peruses this paper, review the series of his life, and enquire how he was placed in his present condition. He will find that of the good or ill which he has experienced, a great part came unexpected, without any visible gradations of approach; that every event has been influenced by causes acting without his intervention; and that whenever he pretended to the prerogative of foresight, he was mortified with new conviction of the shortness of his views.

The busy, the ambitious, the inconstant, and the adventurous, may be said to throw themselves by design into the arms of fortune, and voluntarily to quit the power of governing themselves; they engage in a course of life in which little can be ascertained by previous measures; nor is it any wonder that their time is past between elation and despondency, hope and disappointment.

Some there are who appear to walk the road of life with more circumspection, and make no step till they think themselves secure from the hazard of a precipice; when neither pleasure nor profit can tempt them from the beaten path; who refuse to climb lest they should fall, or to run lest they should stumble, and move slowly forward without any compliance with those passions by which the heady and vehement are seduced and betrayed.

Yet even the timorous prudence of this judicious class is far from exempting them from the dominion of chance, a subtle and insidious power, who will intrude upon privacy and embarrass caution. No course of life is so prescribed and limited, but that many actions must result from arbitrary election. Every one must form the general plan of his conduct by his own reflections; he must resolve whether he will endeavour at riches or at content; whether he will exercise private or publick virtues; whether he will labour for the general benefit of mankind, or contract his beneficence to his family and dependents.

This question has long exercised the schools of philosophy, but remains yet undecided; and what hope is there that a young man, unacquainted with the arguments on either side, should determine his own destiny otherwise than by chance?

When chance has given him a partner of his bed, whom he prefers to all other women, without any proof of superior desert, chance must again direct him in the education of his children; for, who was ever able to convince himself by arguments, that he had chosen for his son that mode of instruction to which his understanding was best adapted, or by which he would most easily be made wise or virtuous?

Whoever shall enquire by what motives he was determined on these important occasions, will find them such, as his pride will scarcely suffer him to confess; some sudden ardour of desire, some uncertain glimpse of advantage, some petty competition, some inaccurate conclusion, or some example implicitly reverenced. Such are often the first causes of our resolves; for it is necessary to act, but impossible to know the consequences of action, or to discuss all the reasons which offer themselves on every part to inquisitiveness and solicitude.

Since life itself is uncertain, nothing which has life for its basis, can boast much stability. Yet this is but a small part of our perplexity. We set out on a tempestuous sea, in quest of some port, where we expect to find rest, but where we are not sure of admission; we are not only in danger of sinking in the way, but of being misled by meteors mistaken for stars, of being driven from our course by the changes of the wind, and of losing it by unskilful steerage; yet it sometimes happens, that cross winds blow us to a safer coast, that meteors draw us aside from whirlpools, and that negligence or error contributes to our escape from mischiefs to which a direct course would have exposed us. Of those that by precipitate conclusions, involve themselves in calamities without guilt, very few, however they may reproach themselves, can be certain that other measures would have been more successful.

In this state of universal uncertainty, where a thousand dangers hover about us, and none can tell whether the good that he persues is not evil in disguise, or whether the next step will lead him to safety or destruction, nothing can afford any rational tranquillity, but the conviction that, however we amuse ourselves with unideal sounds, nothing in reality is governed by chance, but that the universe is under the perpetual super-intendence of him who created it; that our being is in the hands of omnipotent goodness, by whom what appears casual to us is directed for ends ultimately kind and merciful; and that nothing can finally hurt him who debars not himself from the divine favour.

No. 188. Saturday, 4 January 1752.

───── *Si te colo,* Sexte, *non amabo.*
                              MART.[1]

The more I honour thee, the less I love.

None of the desires dictated by vanity is more general, or less blameable, than that of being distinguished for the arts of con-versation. Other accomplishments may be possessed without opportunity of exerting them, or wanted without danger that

the defect can often be remarked; but as no man can live otherwise than in an hermitage, without hourly pleasure or vexation,
from the fondness or neglect of those about him, the faculty of
giving pleasure is of continual use. Few are more frequently
envied than those who have the power of forcing attention
wherever they come, whose entrance is considered as a promise
of felicity, and whose departure is lamented, like the recess of
the sun from northern climates, as a privation of all that enlivens
fancy, or inspirits gaiety.

It is apparent, that to excellence in this valuable art, some
peculiar qualifications are necessary; for every one's experience
will inform him, that the pleasure which men are able to give in
conversation, holds no stated proportion to their knowledge or
their virtue. Many find their way to the tables and the parties of
those who never consider them as of the least importance in any
other place; we have all, at one time or other, been content to
love those whom we could not esteem, and been persuaded to
try the dangerous experiment of admitting him for a companion
whom we knew to be too ignorant for a counsellor, and too
treacherous for a friend.

I question whether some abatement of character is not necessary to general acceptance. Few spend their time with much
satisfaction under the eye of uncontestable superiority; and
therefore, among those whose presence is courted at assemblies
of jollity, there are seldom found men eminently distinguished
for powers or acquisitions. The wit whose vivacity condemns
slower tongues to silence, the scholar whose knowledge allows
no man to fancy that he instructs him, the critick who suffers
no fallacy to pass undetected, and the reasoner who condemns
the idle to thought, and the negligent to attention, are generally
praised and feared, reverenced and avoided.

He that would please must rarely aim at such excellence as
depresses his hearers in their own opinion, or debars them from
the hope of contributing reciprocally to the entertainment of
the company. Merriment, extorted by sallies of imagination,
sprightliness of remark, or quickness of reply, is too often what
the *Latins* call, the *Sardinian Laughter*,[2] a distortion of the face
without gladness of heart.

For this reason, no stile of conversation is more extensively acceptable than the narrative. He who has stored his memory with slight anecdotes, private incidents, and personal particularities, seldom fails to find his audience favourable. Almost every man listens with eagerness to contemporary history; for almost every man has some real or imaginary connection with a celebrated character, some desire to advance, or oppose a rising name. Vanity often co-operates with curiosity. He that is a hearer in one place qualifies himself to become a speaker in another; for though he cannot comprehend a series of argument, or transport the volatile spirit of wit without evaporation, he yet thinks himself able to treasure up the various incidents of a story, and pleases his hopes with the information which he shall give to some inferior society.

Narratives are for the most part heard without envy, because they are not supposed to imply any intellectual qualities above the common rate. To be acquainted with facts not yet echoed by plebeian mouths, may happen to one man as well as to another, and to relate them when they are known, has in appearance so little difficulty, that every one concludes himself equal to the task.

But it is not easy, and in some situations of life not possible, to accumulate such a stock of materials as may support the expence of continual narration; and it frequently happens, that they who attempt this method of ingratiating themselves, please only at the first interview; and, for want of new supplies of intelligence, wear out their stories by continual repetition.

There would be, therefore, little hope of obtaining the praise of a good companion, were it not to be gained by more compendious methods; but such is the kindness of mankind to all, except those who aspire to real merit and rational dignity, that every understanding may find some way to excite benevolence; and whoever is not envied, may learn the art of procuring love. We are willing to be pleased, but are not willing to admire; we favour the mirth or officiousness that solicits our regard, but oppose the worth or spirit that enforces it.

The first place among those that please, because they desire only to please, is due to the *merry fellow*, whose laugh is loud, and whose voice is strong; who is ready to echo every jest with obstreperous approbation, and countenance every frolick with vociferations of applause. It is not necessary to a merry fellow to have in himself any fund of jocularity, or force of conception; it is sufficient that he always appears in the highest exaltation of gladness, for the greater part of mankind are gay or serious by infection, and follow without resistance the attraction of example.

Next to the merry fellow is the *good-natured man*, a being generally without benevolence, or any other virtue, than such as indolence and insensibility confer. The characteristick of a good-natured man is to bear a joke; to sit unmoved and unaffected amidst noise and turbulence, profaneness and obscenity; to hear every tale without contradiction; to endure insult without reply; and to follow the stream of folly, whatever course it shall happen to take. The good-natured man is commonly the darling of the petty wits, with whom they exercise themselves in the rudiments of raillery; for he never takes advantage of failings, nor disconcerts a puny satirist with unexpected sarcasms; but while the glass continues to circulate, contentedly bears the expence of uninterrupted laughter, and retires rejoicing at his own importance.

The *modest man* is a companion of a yet lower rank, whose only power of giving pleasure is not to interrupt it. The modest man satisfies himself with peaceful silence, which all his companions are candid enough to consider as proceeding not from inability to speak, but willingness to hear.

Many, without being able to attain any general character of excellence, have some single art of entertainment which serves them as a passport through the world. One I have known for fifteen years the darling of a weekly club, because every night, precisely at eleven, he begins his favourite song, and during the vocal performance by correspondent motions of his hand, chalks out a giant upon the wall. Another has endeared himself to a long succession of acquaintances by sitting among them with his wig reversed; another by contriving to smut the nose of any stranger who was to be initiated in the club; another by purring like a cat, and then pretending to be frighted; and another by yelping like a hound, and calling to the drawers to drive out the dog.

Such are the arts by which cheerfulness is promoted, and sometimes friendship established; arts, which those who despise them should not rigorously blame, except when they are practised at the expence of innocence; for it is always necessary to be loved, but not always necessary to be reverenced.[3]

No. 191. Tuesday, 14 January 1752.

Cereus in Vitium flecti, Monitoribus asper.

HOR.[1]

The youth ——
Yielding like wax, th' impressive folly bears;
Rough to reproof, and slow to future cares.

FRANCIS.

To *the* RAMBLER.

Dear Mr. RAMBLER,

I have been four days confined to my chamber by a cold, which has already kept me from three plays, nine sales, five shows, and six card-tables, and put me seventeen visits behindhand; and the doctor tells my mamma, that if I fret and cry, it will settle in my head, and I shall not be fit to be seen these six weeks. But, dear Mr. *Rambler*, how can I help it? at this very time *Melissa* is dancing with the prettiest gentleman;—she will breakfast with him to-morrow, and then run to two auctions, and hear compliments, and have presents; then she will be drest, and visit, and get a ticket to the play; then go to cards, and win, and come home with two flambeaus[2] before her chair. Dear Mr. *Rambler*, who can bear it?

My aunt has just brought me a bundle of your papers for my amusement. She says, you are a philosopher, and will teach me to moderate my desires, and look upon the world with indifference. But, dear sir, I do not wish, nor intend to moderate my desires, nor can I think it proper to look upon the world with indifference, till the world looks with indifference on me. I have been forced, however, to sit this morning a whole quarter of an hour with your paper before my face; but just as my aunt came in, *Phyllida* had brought me a letter from Mr. *Trip*, which I put within the leaves, and read about *absence* and *inconsolableness*, and *ardour*, and *irresistible passion*, and *eternal constancy*, while my aunt imagined, that I was puzzling myself with your philosophy, and often cried out, when she saw me look confused, "If there is any word that you do not understand, child, I will explain it."

Dear soul! how old people that think themselves wise may be imposed upon! But it is fit that they should take their turn, for I am sure, while they can keep poor girls close in the nursery, they tyrannize over us in a very shameful manner, and fill our imaginations with tales of terror, only to make us live in quiet subjection, and fancy that we can never be safe but by their protection.

I have a mamma and two aunts, who have all been formerly celebrated for wit and beauty, and are still generally admired by those that value themselves upon their understanding, and love to talk of vice and virtue, nature and simplicity, and beauty, and propriety; but if there was not some hope of meeting me, scarcely a creature would come near them that wears a fashionable coat. These ladies, Mr. *Rambler*, have had me under their government fifteen years and a half, and have all that time been endeavouring to deceive me by such representations of life as I now find not to be true; but I knew not whether I ought to impute them to ignorance or malice, as it is possible the world may be much changed since they mingled in general conversation.

Being desirous that I should love books, they told me, that nothing but knowledge could make me an agreeable companion to men of sense, or qualify me to distinguish the superficial glitter of vanity from the solid merit of understanding; and that a habit of reading would enable me to fill up the vacuities of life without the help of silly or dangerous amusements, and preserve me from the snares of idleness and the inroads of temptation.

But their principal intention was to make me afraid of men, in which they succeeded so well for a time, that I durst not look in their faces, or be left alone with them in a parlour; for they made me fancy, that no man ever spoke but to deceive, or looked but to allure; that the girl who suffered him that had once squeezed her hand, to approach her a second time was on the brink of ruin; and that she who answered a billet, without consulting her relations, gave love such power over her, that she would certainly become either poor or infamous.

From the time that my leading-strings[3] were taken off, I scarce heard any mention of my beauty but from the milliner, the mantua-maker, and my own maid; for my mamma never said more, when she heard me commended, but "The girl is very well," and then endeavoured to divert my attention by some enquiry after my needle, or my book.

It is now three months since I have been suffered to pay and receive visits, to dance at publick assemblies, to have a place kept for me in the boxes, and to play at Lady *Racket*'s rout; and you may easily imagine what I think of those who have so long cheated me with false expectations, disturbed me with fictitious terrors, and concealed from me all that I have found to make the happiness of woman.

I am so far from perceiving the usefulness or necessity of books, that if I had not dropped all pretensions to learning, I should have lost Mr. *Trip*, whom I once frighted into another box, by retailing some of *Dryden*'s remarks upon a tragedy; for Mr. *Trip* declares, that he hates nothing like hard words, and I am sure, there is not a better partner to be found; his very walk is a dance. I have talked once or twice among ladies about principles and ideas, but they put their fans before their faces, and told me, I was too wise for them, who for their part, never pretended to read any thing but the play-bill, and then asked me the price of my best head.[4]

Those vacancies of time which are to be filled up with books, I have never yet obtained; for, consider, Mr. *Rambler*, I go to bed late, and therefore cannot rise early; as soon as I am up, I dress for the gardens; then walk in the park; then always go to some sale or show, or entertainment at the little theatre; then must be dressed for dinner; then must pay my visits; then walk in the park; then hurry to the play; and from thence to the card-table. This is the general course of the day, when there happens nothing extraordinary; but sometimes I ramble into the country and come back again to a ball; sometimes I am engaged for a whole day and part of the night. If, at any time, I can gain an hour by not being at home, I have so many things to do, so many orders to give to the milliner, so many alterations to make in my cloaths, so many visitants names to read over, so many invitations to accept or refuse, so many cards to write, and so many fashions to consider, that I am lost in confusion, forced at last to let in company or step into my chair, and leave half my affairs to the direction of my maid.

This is the round of my day; and when shall I either stop my course, or so change it as to want a book? I suppose it cannot be imagined, that any of these diversions will be soon at an end. There will always be gardens, and a park, and auctions, and shows, and play-houses, and cards; visits will always be paid, and cloaths always be worn; and how can I have time unemployed upon my hands?

But I am most at a loss to guess for what purpose they related such tragick stories of the cruelty, perfidy, and artifices of men, who, if they ever were so malicious and destructive, have certainly now reformed their manners. I have not, since my entrance into the world, found one who does not profess himself devoted to my service, and ready to live or die, as I shall command him. They are so far from intending to hurt me, that their only contention is, who shall be allowed most closely to attend, and most frequently to treat me; when different places of entertainment, or schemes of pleasure are mentioned, I can see the eyes sparkle and the cheeks glow of him whose proposals obtain my approbation; he then leads me off in triumph, adores my condescension, and congratulates himself that he has lived to the hour of felicity. Are these, Mr. *Rambler*, creatures to be feared? Is it likely that any injury will be done me by those who can enjoy life only while I favour them with my presence?

As little reason can I yet find to suspect them of stratagems and fraud. When I play at cards, they never take advantage of my mistakes, nor exact from me a rigorous observation of the game. Even Mr. *Shuffle*, a grave gentleman, who has daughters older than myself, plays with me so negligently, that I am sometimes inclined to believe he loses his money by design, and yet he is so fond of play, that he says, he will one day take me to his house in the country; that we may try by ourselves who can conquer. I have not yet promised him; but when the town grows a little empty, I shall think upon it, for I want some trinkets, like *Letitia*'s, to my watch. I do not doubt my luck, but must study some means of amusing my relations.

For all these distinctions I find myself indebted to that beauty which I was never suffered to hear praised, and of which, therefore, I did not before know the full value. This concealment was certainly an intentional fraud, for my aunts have eyes like other people, and I am every day told, that nothing but blindness can escape the influence of my charms. Their whole account of that world which they pretend to know so well, has been only one fiction entangled with another; and though the modes of life oblige me to continue some appearances of respect, I cannot think that they, who have been so clearly detected in ignorance or imposture, have any right to the esteem, veneration, or obedience of,

SIR, Yours,

BELLARIA.

No. 196. Saturday, 1 February 1752.

Multa ferunt anni venientes commoda secum
Multa recedentes adimunt. ——

HOR.[1]

The blessings flowing in with life's full tide,
Down with our ebb of life decreasing glide.

FRANCIS.

Baxter, in the narrative of his own life, has enumerated several opinions, which, though he thought them evident and incontestable at his first entrance into the world, time and experience disposed him to change.[2]

Whoever reviews the state of his own mind from the dawn of manhood to its decline, and considers what he pursued or dreaded, slighted or esteemed at different periods of his age, will have no reason to imagine such changes of sentiment peculiar to any station or character. Every man, however careless and inattentive, has conviction forced upon him; the lectures of time obtrude themselves upon the most unwilling or dissipated auditor; and, by comparing our past with our present thoughts, we perceive that we have changed our minds, though perhaps we cannot discover when the alteration happened, or by what causes it was produced.

This revolution of sentiments occasions a perpetual contest between the old and young. They who imagine themselves entitled to veneration by the prerogative of longer life, are inclined to treat the notions of those whose conduct they superintend with superciliousness and contempt, for want of considering that the future and the past have different appearances; that the disproportion will always be great between expectation and enjoyment, between new possession and satiety; that the truth of many maxims of age, gives too little pleasure to be allowed till it is felt; and that the miseries of life would be encreased beyond all human power of endurance, if we were to enter the world with the same opinions as we carry from it.

We naturally indulge those ideas that please us. Hope will predominate in every mind, till it has been suppressed by frequent disappointments. The youth has not yet discovered how many evils are continually hovering about us, and when he is set free from the shackles of discipline, looks abroad into the world with rapture; he sees an elysian region open before him, so variegated with beauty, and so stored with pleasure, that his care is rather to accumulate good, than to shun evil; he stands distracted by different forms of delight, and has no other doubt than which path to follow of those which all lead equally to the bowers of happiness.

He who has seen only the superficies of life believes every thing to be what it appears, and rarely suspects that external splendor conceals any latent sorrow or vexation. He never imagines that there may be greatness without safety, affluence without content, jollity without friendship, and solitude without peace. He fancies himself permitted to cull the blessings of every condition, and to leave its inconveniencies to the idle and the ignorant. He is inclined to believe no man miserable but by his own fault, and seldom looks with much pity upon failings or miscarriages, because he thinks them willingly admitted, or negligently incurred.

It is impossible, without pity and contempt, to hear a youth of generous sentiments and warm imagination, declaring in the moment of openness and confidence his designs and expectations; because long life is possible, he considers it as certain, and therefore promises himself all the changes of happiness, and provides gratifications for every desire. He is, for a time, to give himself wholly to frolick and diversion, to range the world in search of pleasure, to delight every eye, to gain every heart, and to be celebrated equally for his pleasing levities and solid attainments, his deep reflections, and his sparkling repartees. He then elevates his views to nobler enjoyments, and finds all the scattered excellencies of the female world united in a woman, who prefers his addresses to wealth and titles; he is afterwards to engage in business, to dissipate difficulty, and over-power opposition; to climb by the mere force of merit to fame and greatness; and reward all those who countenanced his rise, or paid due regard to his early excellence. At last he will retire in peace and honour; contract his views to domestick pleasures; form the manners of children like himself; observe how every year expands the beauty of his daughters, and how his sons catch ardour from their father's history; he will give laws to the neighbourhood; dictate axioms to posterity; and leave the world an example of wisdom and of happiness.

With hopes like these, he sallies jocund into life; to little purpose is he told, that the condition of humanity admits no pure and unmingled happiness; that the exuberant gaiety of youth ends in poverty or disease; that uncommon qualifications and contrarieties of excellence, produce envy equally with applause; that whatever admiration and fondness may promise him, he must marry a wife like the wives of others, with some virtues and some faults, and be as often disgusted by her vices, as delighted by her elegance; that if he adventures into the circle of action, he must expect to encounter men as artful, as daring, as resolute as himself; that of his children, some may be deformed, and others vicious; some may disgrace him by their follies, some offend him by their insolence, and some exhaust him by their profusion. He hears all this with obstinate incredulity, and wonders by what malignity old age is influenced, that it cannot forbear to fill his ears with predictions of misery.

Among other pleasing errors of young minds, is the opinion of their own importance. He that has not yet remarked, how little attention his contemporaries can spare from their own affairs, conceives all eyes turned upon himself, and imagines every one that approaches him to be an enemy or a follower, an admirer or a spy. He therefore considers his fame as involved in the event of every action. Many of the virtues and vices of youth proceed from this quick sense of reputation. This it is that gives firmness and constancy, fidelity and disinterestedness, and it is this that kindles resentment for slight injuries, and dictates all the principles of sanguinary honour.

But as time brings him forward into the world, he soon discovers that he only shares fame or reproach with innumerable partners; that he is left unmarked in the obscurity of the croud; and that what he does, whether good or bad, soon gives way to new objects of regard. He then easily sets himself free from the anxieties of reputation, and considers praise or censure as a transient breath, which, while he hears it, is passing away, without any lasting mischief or advantage.

In youth, it is common to measure right and wrong by the opinion of the world, and in age to act without any measure but interest, and to lose shame without substituting virtue.

Such is the condition of life, that something is always wanting to happiness. In youth we have warm hopes, which are soon blasted by rashness and negligence, and great designs which are defeated by inexperience. In age we have knowledge and prudence without spirit to exert, or motives to prompt them; we are able to plan schemes and regulate measures, but have not time remaining to bring them to completion.

No. 207. Tuesday, 10 March 1752.

Solve senescentem mature sanus equum, ne
Peccet ad extremum ridendus.

HOR.[1]

The voice of reason cries with winning force,
Loose from the rapid car your aged horse,
Lest, in the race derided, left behind,
He drag his jaded limbs and burst his wind.

FRANCIS.

Such is the emptiness of human enjoyment, that we are always impatient of the present. Attainment is followed by neglect, and possession by disgust; and the malicious remark of the *Greek* epigrammatist on marriage may be applied to every other course of life, that its two days of happiness are the first and the last.[2]

Few moments are more pleasing than those in which the mind is concerting measures for a new undertaking. From the first hint that wakens the fancy, till the hour of actual execution, all is improvement and progress, triumph and felicity. Every hour brings additions to the original scheme, suggests some new expedient to secure success, or discovers consequential advantages not hitherto foreseen. While preparations are made, and materials accumulated, day glides after day through elysian prospects, and the heart dances to the song of hope.

Such is the pleasure of projecting, that many content themselves with a succession of visionary schemes, and wear out their allotted time in the calm amusement of contriving what they never attempt or hope to execute.

Others, not able to feast their imagination with pure ideas, advance somewhat nearer to the grossness of action, with great diligence collect whatever is requisite to their design, and, after a thousand researches and consultations, are snatched away by death, as they stand *in procinctu*[3] waiting for a proper opportunity to begin.

If there were no other end of life, than to find some adequate solace for every day, I know not whether any condition could be preferred to that of the man who involves himself in his own thoughts, and never suffers experience to shew him the vanity of speculation; for no sooner are notions reduced to practice, than tranquillity and confidence forsake the breast; every day brings its task, and often without bringing abilities to perform it: Difficulties embarrass, uncertainty perplexes, opposition retards, censure exasperates, or neglect depresses. We proceed, because we have begun; we complete our design, that the labour already spent may not be vain: but as expectation gradually dies away, the gay smile of alacrity disappears, we are compelled to implore severer powers, and trust the event to patience and constancy.

When once our labour has begun, the comfort that enables us to endure it is the prospect of its end; for though in every long work there are some joyous intervals of self-applause, when the attention is recreated by unexpected facility, and the imagination soothed by incidental excellencies; yet the toil with which performance struggles after idea, is so irksome and disgusting, and so frequent is the necessity of resting below that perfection which we imagined within our reach, that seldom any man obtains more from his endeavours than a painful conviction of his defects, and a continual resuscitation of desires which he feels himself unable to gratify.

So certainly is weariness the concomitant of our undertakings, that every man, in whatever he is engaged, consoles himself with the hope of change; if he has made his way by assiduity to publick employment, he talks among his friends of the delight of retreat; if by the necessity of solitary application he is secluded from the world, he listens with a beating heart to distant noises, longs to mingle with living beings, and resolves to take hereafter his fill of diversions, or display his abilities on the universal theatre, and enjoy the pleasure of distinction and applause.

Every desire, however innocent, grows dangerous, as by long indulgence it becomes ascendent in the mind. When we have been much accustomed to consider any thing as capable of giving happiness, it is not easy to restrain our ardour, or to forbear some precipitation in our advances, and irregularity in our persuits. He that has cultivated the tree, watched the swelling bud and opening blossom, and pleased himself with computing how much every sun and shower add to its growth, scarcely stays till the fruit has obtained its maturity, but defeats his own cares by eagerness to reward them. When we have diligently laboured for any purpose, we are willing to believe that we have attained it, and, because we have already done much, too suddenly conclude that no more is to be done.

All attraction is encreased by the approach of the attracting body. We never find ourselves so desirous to finish, as in the latter part of our work, or so impatient of delay, as when we know that delay cannot be long. This unseasonable importunity of discontent may be partly imputed to languor and weariness, which must always oppress those more whose toil has been longer continued; but the greater part usually proceeds from frequent contemplation of that ease which is now considered as within reach, and which, when it has once flattered our hopes, we cannot suffer to be withheld.

In some of the noblest compositions of wit, the conclusion falls below the vigour and spirit of the first books; and as a genius is not to be degraded by the imputation of human failings, the cause of this declension is commonly sought in the structure of the work, and plausible reasons are given why in the defective part less ornament was necessary, or less could be admitted. But, perhaps, the author would have confessed, that his fancy was tired, and his perseverance broken; that he knew his design to be unfinished, but that, when he saw the end so near, he could no longer refuse to be at rest.

Against the instillations of this frigid opiate, the heart should be secured by all the considerations which once concurred to kindle the ardour of enterprize. Whatever motive first incited action, has still greater force to stimulate perseverance; since he that might have lain still at first in blameless obscurity, cannot afterwards desist but with infamy and reproach. He, whom a doubtful promise of distant good, could encourage to set difficulties at defiance, ought not to remit his vigour, when he has almost obtained his recompence. To faint or loiter, when only the last efforts are required, is to steer the ship through tempests, and abandon it to the winds in sight of land; it is to break the ground and scatter the seed, and at last to neglect the harvest.

The masters of rhetorick direct, that the most forcible arguments be produced in the latter part of an oration, lest they should be effaced or perplexed by supervenient[4] images. This precept may be justly extended to the series of life: Nothing is ended with honour, which does not conclude better than it begun. It is not sufficient to maintain the first vigour; for excellence loses its effect upon the mind by custom, as light after a time ceases to dazzle. Admiration must be continued by that novelty which first produced it, and how much soever is given, there must always be reason to imagine that more remains.

We not only are most sensible of the last impressions, but such is the unwillingness of mankind to admit transcendent merit, that, though it be difficult to obliterate the reproach of miscarriages by any subsequent atchievement, however illustrious, yet the reputation raised by a long train of success, may be finally ruined by a single failure, for weakness or error will be always remembered by that malice and envy which it gratifies.

For the prevention of that disgrace, which lassitude and negligence may bring at last upon the greatest performances, it is necessary to proportion carefully our labour to our strength. If the design comprises many parts, equally essential, and therefore not to be separated, the only time for caution is before we engage; the powers of the mind must be then impartially estimated, and it must be remembered, that not to complete the plan, is not to have begun it; and, that nothing is done, while any thing is omitted.

But, if the task consists in the repetition of single acts, no one of which derives its efficacy from the rest, it may be attempted with less scruple, because there is always opportunity to retreat with honour. The danger is only lest we expect from the world the indulgence with which most are disposed to treat themselves; and in the hour of listlessness imagine, that the diligence of one day will atone for the idleness of another, and that applause begun by approbation will be continued by habit.

He that is himself weary will soon weary the public. Let him therefore lay down his employment, whatever it be, who can no longer exert his former activity or attention; let him not endeavour to struggle with censure, or obstinately infest the stage till a general hiss commands him to depart.

No. 208. Saturday, 14 March 1752.

'Ηράκλειτος ἐγώ· τί μεῶ κάτω ἕλκετ' ἄμουσοι;
Οὐχ' ὑμῖν ἐπόνουν, τοῖς δέ μ' ἐπισταμένοις.
Εἶς ἐμοὶ ἄνθρωπος τρισμύριοι οἱ δ' ἀνάριθμοι
Οὐδείς· ταῦτ' αὐδῶ καὶ παρὰ Περσεφόνῃ.

DIOG. LAERT.[1]

Be gone, ye blockheads, *Heraclitus* cries,
And leave my labours to the learn'd and wise:
By wit, by knowledge, studious to be read,
I scorn the multitude, alive and dead.

Time, which puts an end to all human pleasures and sorrows, has likewise concluded the labours of the RAMBLER. Having supported, for two years, the anxious employment of a periodical writer, and multiplied my essays to four volumes, I have now determined to desist.

The reasons of this resolution it is of little importance to declare, since justification is unnecessary when no objection is made. I am far from supposing, that the cessation of my performances will raise any inquiry, for I have never been much a favourite of the publick, nor can boast that, in the progress of my undertaking, I have been animated by the rewards of the liberal, the caresses of the great, or the praises of the eminent.

But I have no design to gratify pride by submission, or malice by lamentation; nor think it reasonable to complain of neglect from those whose regard I never solicited. If I have not been distinguished by the distributers of literary honours, I have seldom descended to the arts by which favour is obtained. I have seen the meteors of fashion rise and fall, without any attempt to add a moment to their duration. I have never complied with temporary curiosity, nor enabled my readers to discuss the topick of the day; I have rarely exemplified my assertions by living characters; in my papers, no man could look for censures of his enemies, or praises of himself; and they only were expected to peruse them, whose passions left them leisure for abstracted truth, and whom virtue could please by its naked dignity.

To some, however, I am indebted for encouragement, and to others for assistance. The number of my friends was never great, but they have been such as would not suffer me to think that I was writing in vain, and I did not feel much dejection from the want of popularity.

My obligations having not been frequent, my acknowledgements may be soon dispatched. I can restore to all my correspondents their productions, with little diminution of the bulk of my volumes, though not without the loss of some pieces to which particular honours have been paid.

The parts from which I claim no other praise than that of having given them an opportunity of appearing, are the four billets in the tenth paper, the second letter in the fifteenth, the thirtieth, the forty-fourth, the ninety-seventh, and the hundredth papers, and the second letter in the hundred and seventh.

Having thus deprived myself of many excuses which candor might have admitted for the inequality of my compositions, being no longer able to alledge the necessity of gratifying correspondents, the importunity with which publication was solicited, or obstinacy with which correction was rejected, I must remain accountable for all my faults, and submit, without subterfuge, to the censures of criticism, which, however, I shall not endeavour to soften by a formal deprecation, or to overbear by the influence of a patron. The supplications of an author never yet reprieved him a moment from oblivion; and, though greatness has sometimes sheltered guilt, it can afford no protection to ignorance or dulness. Having hitherto attempted only the propagation of truth, I will not at last violate it by the confession of terrors which I do not feel: Having laboured to maintain the dignity of virtue, I will not now degrade it by the meanness of dedication.

The seeming vanity with which I have sometimes spoken of myself, would perhaps require an apology, were it not extenuated by the example of those who have published essays before me, and by the privilege which every nameless writer has been hitherto allowed. "A mask," says *Castiglione*, "confers a right of acting and speaking with less restraint, even when the wearer happens to be known."[2] He that is discovered without his own consent, may claim some indulgence, and cannot be rigorously called to justify those sallies or frolicks which his disguise must prove him desirous to conceal.

But I have been cautious lest this offence should be frequently or grossly committed; for, as one of the philosophers directs us to live with a friend, as with one that is some time to become an enemy, I have always thought it the duty of an anonymous author to write, as if he expected to be hereafter known.

I am willing to flatter myself with hopes, that, by collecting these papers, I am not preparing for my future life, either shame or repentance. That all are happily imagined, or accurately polished, that the same sentiments have not sometimes recurred, or the same expressions been too frequently repeated, I have not confidence in my abilities sufficient to warrant. He that condemns himself to compose on a stated day, will often bring to his task an attention dissipated, a memory embarrassed, an imagination overwhelmed, a mind distracted with anxieties, a body languishing with disease: He will labour on a barren topick, till it is too late to change it; or in the ardour of invention, diffuse his thoughts into wild exuberance, which the pressing hour of publication cannot suffer judgment to examine or reduce.

Whatever shall be the final sentence of mankind, I have at least endeavoured to deserve their kindness. I have laboured to refine our language to grammatical purity, and to clear it from colloquial barbarisms, licentious idioms, and irregular combinations.[3] Something, perhaps, I have added to the elegance of its construction, and something to the harmony of its cadence. When common words were less pleasing to the ear, or less distinct in their signification, I have familiarized the terms of philosophy by applying them to popular ideas, but have rarely admitted any word not authorized by former writers; for I believe that whoever knows the *English* tongue in its present extent, will be able to express his thoughts without further help from other nations.

As it has been my principal design to inculcate wisdom or piety, I have allotted few papers to the idle sports of imagination. Some, perhaps, may be found, of which the highest excellence is harmless merriment, but scarcely any man is so steadily serious, as not to complain, that the severity of dictatorial instruction has been too seldom relieved, and that he is driven by the sternness of the Rambler's philosophy to more chearful and airy companions.

Next to the excursions of fancy are the disquisitions of criticism, which, in my opinion, is only to be ranked among the subordinate and instrumental arts. Arbitrary decision and general exclamation I have carefully avoided, by asserting nothing without a reason, and establishing all my principles of judgment on unalterable and evident truth.

In the pictures of life I have never been so studious of novelty or surprize, as to depart wholly from all resemblance; a fault which writers deservedly celebrated frequently commit, that they may raise, as the occasion requires, either mirth or abhorrence. Some enlargement may be allowed to declamation, and some exaggeration to burlesque; but as they deviate farther from reality, they become less useful, because their lessons will fail of application. The mind of the reader is carried away from the contemplation of his own manners; he finds in himself no likeness to the phantom before him; and though he laughs or rages, is not reformed.

The essays professedly serious, if I have been able to execute my own intentions, will be found exactly conformable to the precepts of Christianity, without any accommodation to the licentiousness and levity of the present age. I therefore look back on this part of my work with pleasure, which no blame or praise of man shall diminish or augment. I shall never envy the honours which wit and learning obtain in any other cause, if I can be numbered among the writers who have given ardour to virtue, and confidence to truth.

Αὐτῶν ἐκ μακάρων ἀντάξιος εἴη ἀμοιβή.[4]

Celestial pow'rs! that piety regard,
From you my labours wait their last reward.

THE ADVENTURER
(1753-4)

No. 39. Tuesday, 20 March 1753.

——'Οδυσεὺς φύλλοισι καλύψατο. τῷ δ' ἄρ' 'Αθήνη
῞Υπνον ἐπ' ὄμμασι χεῦ, ἵνα μιν παύσειε τάχιστα
Δυσπονέος καμάτοιο.

Hom.[1]

——Pallas pour'd sweet slumbers on his soul;
And balmy dreams, the gift of soft repose,
Calm'd all his pains and banish'd all his woes.

Pope.[2]

If every day did not produce fresh instances of the ingratitude of mankind, we might perhaps be at a loss, why so liberal and impartial a benefactor as Sleep, should meet with so few historians or panegyrists. Writers are so totally absorbed by the business of the day, as never to turn their attention to that power, whose officious hand so seasonably suspends the burthen of life; and without whose interposition, man would not be able to endure the fatigue of labour however rewarded, or the struggle with opposition however successful.

Night, though she divides to many the longest part of life, and to almost all the most innocent and happy, is yet unthankfully neglected, except by those who pervert her gifts.

The astronomers, indeed, expect her with impatience, and felicitate themselves upon her arrival: Fontenelle[3] has not failed to celebrate her praises; and to chide the sun for hiding from his view, the worlds which he imagines to appear in every constellation. Nor have the poets been always deficient in her praises: Milton has observed of the Night, that it is "the pleasant time, the cool, the silent."[4]

These men may, indeed, well be expected to pay particular homage to night; since they are indebted to her, not only for cessation of pain, but increase of pleasure; not only for slumber, but for knowledge. But the greater part of her avowed votaries are the sons of luxury; who appropriate to festivity the hours designed for rest; who consider the reign of pleasure as commencing, when day begins to withdraw her busy multitudes, and ceases to dissipate attention by intrusive and unwelcome variety; who begin to awake to joy, when the rest of the world sinks into insensibility; and revel in the soft effluence of flattering and artificial lights, which "more shadowy set off the face of things."[5]

Without touching upon the fatal consequences of a custom, which, as RAMAZZINI[6] observes, will be for ever condemned, and for ever retained; it may be observed, that however Sleep may be put off from time to time, yet the demand is of so importunate a nature, as not to remain long unsatisfied; and if, as some have done, we consider it as the tax of life, we cannot but observe it is a tax that must be paid, unless we could cease to be men; for Alexander declared, that nothing convinced him that he was not a Divinity, but his not being able to live without Sleep.[7]

To live without Sleep in our present fluctuating state, however desirable it might seem to the lady in CLELIA,[8] can surely be the wish only of the young or the ignorant; to every one else, a perpetual vigil will appear to be a state of wretchedness, second only to that of the miserable beings, whom SWIFT has in his travels so elegantly described, as "supremely cursed with immortality."[9]

Sleep is necessary to the happy, to prevent satiety and to endear life by a short absence; and to the miserable, to relieve them by intervals of quiet. Life is to most, such as could not be endured without frequent intermissions of existence: HOMER, therefore, has thought it an office worthy of the goddess of wisdom, to lay Ulysses asleep when landed on Phæacia.[10]

It is related of BARRETIER,[11] whose early advances in literature scarce any human mind has equalled, that he spent twelve hours of the four and twenty in sleep: yet this appears, from the bad state of his health, and the shortness of his life, to have been too small a respite for a mind so vigorously and intensely employed: it is to be regretted, therefore, that he did not exercise his mind less, and his body more; since by this means it is highly probable, that though he would not then have astonished with the blaze of a comet, he would yet have shone with the permanent radiance of a fixed star.

Nor should it be objected, that there have been many men who daily spent fifteen or sixteen hours in study; for by some of whom this is reported, it has never been done; others have done it for a short time only; and of the rest it appears, that they employed their minds in such operations, as required neither celerity nor strength; in the low drudgery of collating copies, comparing authorities, digesting dictionaries, or accumulating compilations.

Men of study and imagination are frequently upbraided by the industrious and plodding sons of care, with passing too great a part of their life in a state of inaction. But these defiers of Sleep seem not to remember, that though it must be granted them that they are crawling about before the break of day, it can seldom be said that they are perfectly awake; they exhaust no spirits, and require no repairs; but lie torpid as a toad in marble, or at least are known to live only by an inert and sluggish loco-motive faculty, and may be said, like a wounded snake, to "dragg their slow length along."[12]

Man has been long known among philosophers, by the appellation of the microcosm, or epitome of the world: the resemblance between the great and little world, might by a rational observer be detailed to many particulars; and to many more by a fanciful speculatist. I know not in which of these two classes I shall be ranged for observing, that as the total quantity of light and darkness, allotted in the course of the year to every region of the earth, is the same, though distributed at various times and in different portions; so, perhaps, to each individual of the human species, nature has ordained the same quantity of wakefulness and sleep; though divided by some into a total quiescence and vigorous exertion of their faculties, and blended by others in a kind of twilight of existence, in a state between dreaming and reasoning, in which they either think without action, or act without thought.

The poets are generally well affected to sleep: as men who think with vigour, they require respite from thought; and gladly resign themselves to that gentle power, who not only bestows rest, but frequently leads them to happier regions, where patrons are always kind, and audiences are always candid, where they are feasted in the bowers of imagination, and crowned with flowers divested of their prickles, and laurels of unfading verdure.

The more refined and penetrating part of mankind, who take wide surveys of the wilds of life, who see the innumerable terrors and distresses that are perpetually preying on the heart of man, and discern with unhappy perspicuity calamities yet latent in their causes, are glad to close their eyes upon the gloomy prospect, and lose in a short insensibility the remembrance of others miseries and their own. The hero has no higher hope, than that after having routed legions after legions, and added kingdom to kingdom, he shall retire to milder happiness, and close his days in social festivity. The wit or the sage can expect no greater happiness, than that after having harrassed his reason in deep researches, and fatigued his fancy in boundless excursions, he shall sink at night in the tranquillity of Sleep.

The poets among all those that enjoy the blessings of Sleep, have been least ashamed to acknowledge their benefactor. How much STATIUS considered the evils of life as asswaged and softened by the balm of slumber, we may discover by that pathetic invocation, which he poured out in his waking nights:[13] and that COWLEY,[14] among the other felicities of his darling solitude, did not forget to number the privilege of sleeping without disturbance, we may learn from the rank that he assigns among the gifts of nature to the poppy; "which is scattered," says he, "over the fields of corn, that all the needs of man may be easily satisfied, and that bread and sleep may be found together."

> *Si quis invisum Cereri benignæ*
> *Me putat germen, vehementer errat;*
> *Illa me in partem recipit libenter*
> > *Fertilis agri.*
>
> *Meque frumentumque simul per omnes*
> *Consulens mundo Dea spargit oras;*
> *Crescite, O! dixit, duo magna susten-*
> > *tacula vitæ.*
>
> *Carpe, mortalis, mea dona lætus,*
> *Carpe, nec plantas alias require,*

Sed satur panis, satur et soporis,
                    Cætera sperne.

He widely errs who thinks I yield
Precedence in the well cloth'd field,
   Tho' mix'd with wheat I grow:
Indulgent Ceres knew my worth,
And to adorn the teeming earth,
She bade the POPPY blow.

Nor vainly gay the sight to please,
But blest with power mankind to ease,
   The Goddess saw me rise:
"Thrive with the life-supporting grain,"
She cry'd, "the solace of the swain,
The cordial of his eyes."

"Seize, happy mortal, seize the good;
My hand supplies thy sleep and food,
   And makes thee truly blest:
With plenteous meals enjoy the day,
In slumbers pass the night away,
And leave to fate the rest."

                         C. B.[15]

Sleep, therefore, as the chief of all earthly blessings, is justly
appropriated to industry and temperance; the refreshing rest,
and the peaceful night, are the portion only of him, who lies
down weary with honest labour, and free from the fumes of
indigested luxury: it is the just doom of laziness and gluttony,
to be inactive without ease, and drowsy without tranquillity.

Sleep has been often mentioned as the image of death; "so
like it," says Sir THOMAS BROWN, "that I dare not trust it
without my prayers:"[16] their resemblance is, indeed, apparent
and striking; they both, when they seize the body, leave the soul
at liberty; and wise is he that remembers of both, that they can
be made safe and happy only by VIRTUE.

T

No. 45. Tuesday, 10 April 1753.

Nulla fides regni sociis, omnisque potestas
Impatiens consortis erit.

LUCAN.[1]

No faith of partnership dominion owns;
Still discord hovers o'er divided thrones.

It is well known, that many things appear plausible in speculation, which can never be reduced to practice; and that of the
numberless projects that have flattered mankind with theoretical
speciousness, few have served any other purpose than to shew
the ingenuity of their contrivers. A voyage to the moon, however
romantic and absurd the scheme may now appear, since the
properties of air have been better understood, seemed highly
probable to many of the aspiring wits in the last century, who
began to doat upon their glossy plumes, and fluttered with
impatience for the hour of their departure:

——*Pereant vestigia mille*
Ante fugam, absentemque ferit gravis ungula campum.[2]

Hills, vales, and floods appear already crost;
And, e'er he starts, a thousand steps are lost.

POPE.[3]

Among the fallacies which only experience can detect, there
are some of which scarcely experience itself can destroy the
influence; some which, by a captivating shew of indubitable
certainty, are perpetually gaining upon the human mind; and
which, though every trial ends in disappointment, obtain new
credit as the sense of miscarriage wears gradually away, persuade us to try again what we have tried already, and expose us
by the same failure to double vexation.

Of this tempting, this delusive kind, is the expectation of
great performances by confederated strength. The speculatist,
when he has carefully observed how much may be performed

by a single hand, calculates by a very easy operation the force of thousands, and goes on accumulating power till resistance vanishes before it; then rejoices in the success of his new scheme, and wonders at the folly or idleness of former ages, who have lived in want of what might so readily be procured, and suffered themselves to be debarred from happiness by obstacles which one united effort would have so easily surmounted.

But this gigantic phantom of collective power vanishes at once into air and emptiness, at the first attempt to put it into action. The different apprehensions, the discordant passions, the jarring interests of men, will scarcely permit that many should unite in one undertaking.

Of a great and complicated design, some will never be brought to discern the end; and of the several means by which it may be accomplished, the choice will be a perpetual subject of debate, as every man is swayed in his determination by his own knowledge or convenience. In a long series of action, some will languish with fatigue, and some be drawn off by present gratifications; some will loiter because others labour, and some will cease to labour because others loiter; and if once they come within prospect of success and profit, some will be greedy and others envious; some will undertake more than they can perform, to enlarge their claims of advantage; some will perform less than they undertake, lest their labours should turn chiefly to the benefit of others.

The history of mankind informs us, that a single power is very seldom broken by a confederacy. States of different interests, and aspects malevolent to each other, may be united for a time by common distress; and in the ardour of self-preservation fall unanimously upon an enemy by whom they are all equally endangered. But if their first attack can be withstood, time will never fail to dissolve their union: success and miscarriage will be equally destructive: after the conquest of a province, they will quarrel in the division; after the loss of a battle, all will be endeavouring to secure themselves by abandoning the rest.

From the impossibility of confining numbers to the constant and uniform prosecution of a common interest, arises the difficulty of securing subjects against the incroachment of governors.

Power is always gradually stealing away from the many to the few, because the few are more vigilant and consistent; it still contracts to a smaller number, till in time it centers in a single person.

Thus all the forms of government instituted among mankind, perpetually tend towards monarchy; and power, however diffused through the whole community, is by negligence or corruption, commotion or distress, reposed at last in the chief magistrate.

"There never appear," says SWIFT, "more than five or six men of genius in an age; but if they were united, the world could not stand before them."[4] It is happy, therefore, for mankind, that of this union there is no probability. As men take in a wider compass of intellectual survey, they are more likely to chuse different objects of persuit; as they see more ways to the same end, they will be less easily persuaded to travel together; as each is better qualified to form an independent scheme of private greatness, he will reject with greater obstinacy the project of another; as each is more able to distinguish himself as the head of a party, he will less readily be made a follower or an associate.

The reigning philosophy informs us, that the vast bodies which constitute the universe, are regulated in their progress through the etherial spaces, by the perpetual agency of contrary forces; by one of which they are restrained from deserting their orbits, and losing themselves in the immensity of heaven; and held off by the other from rushing together, and clustering round their centre with everlasting cohesion.

The same contrariety of impulse may be perhaps discovered in the motions of men: we are formed for society, not for combination; we are equally unqualified to live in a close connection with our fellow beings, and in total separation from them: we are attracted towards each other by general sympathy, but kept back from contact by private interests.

Some philosophers have been foolish enough to imagine, that improvements might be made in the system of the universe, by a different arrangement of the orbs of heaven; and politicians, equally ignorant and equally presumptuous, may easily be led to suppose, that the happiness of our world would be promoted by a different tendency of the human mind. It appears, indeed, to a slight and superficial observer, that many things impracticable in our present state, might be easily effected, if mankind were better disposed to union and co-operation: but a little reflection will discover, that if confederacies were easily formed, they would lose their efficacy, since numbers would be opposed to numbers, and unanimity to unanimity; and instead of the present petty competitions of individuals or single families, multitudes would be supplanting multitudes, and thousands plotting against thousands.

There is no class of the human species, of which the union seems to have been more expected, than of the learned: the rest of the world have almost always agreed, to shut scholars up together in colleges and cloisters; surely not without hope, that they would look for that happiness in concord, which they were debarred from finding in variety; and that such conjunctions of intellect would recompense the munificence of founders and patrons, by performances above the reach of any single mind.

But DISCORD, who found means to roll her apple into the banquetting chamber of the Goddesses, has had the address to scatter her laurels in the seminaries of learning. The friendship of students and of beauties is for the most part equally sincere, and equally durable: as both depend for happiness on the regard of others, on that of which the value arises merely from comparison, they are both exposed to perpetual jealousies, and both incessantly employed in schemes to intercept the praises of each other.

I am, however, far from intending to inculcate, that this confinement of the studious to studious companions, has been wholly without advantage to the public: neighbourhood, where it does not conciliate friendship, incites competition; and he that would contentedly rest in a lower degree of excellence, where he had no rival to dread, will be urged by his impatience of inferiority to incessant endeavours after great attainments.

These stimulations of honest rivalry, are, perhaps, the chief effects of academies and societies; for whatever be the bulk of their joint labours, every single piece is always the production of an individual, that owes nothing to his collegues but the contagion of diligence, a resolution to write because the rest are writing, and the scorn of obscurity while the rest are illustrious.

T

No. 50. Saturday, 28 April 1753.

Quicunque turpi fraude semel innotuit,
Etiamsi vera dicit, amittit fidem.

PHÆD.[1]

The wretch that often has deceiv'd,
Though truth he speaks, is ne'er believ'd.

When ARISTOTLE was once asked, what a man could gain by uttering falsehoods; he replied, "not to be credited when he shall tell the truth."[2]

The character of a liar is at once so hateful and contemptible, that even of those who have lost their virtue it might be expected, that from the violation of truth they should be restrained by their pride. Almost every other vice that disgraces human nature, may be kept in countenance by applause and association: the corrupter of virgin innocence sees himself envied by the men, and at least not detested by the women: the drunkard may easily unite with beings, devoted like himself to noisy merriment or silent insensibility, who will celebrate his victories over the novices of intemperance, boast themselves the companions of his prowess, and tell with rapture of the multitudes whom unsuccessful emulation has hurried to the grave: even the robber and the cut-throat have their followers, who admire their address and intrepidity, their stratagems of rapine, and their fidelity to the gang.

The liar, and only the liar, is invariably and universally despised, abandoned, and disowned; he has no domestic consolations, which he can oppose to the censure of mankind; he can retire to no fraternity where his crimes may stand in the place of virtues; but is given up to the hisses of the multitude, without friend and without apologist. It is the peculiar condition of falsehood, to be equally detested by the good and bad: "The devils," says Sir THOMAS BROWN, "do not tell lies to one another; for truth is necessary to all societies; nor can the society of hell subsist without it."[3]

It is natural to expect, that a crime thus generally detested, should be generally avoided; at least, that none should expose himself to unabated and unpitied infamy, without an adequate temptation; and that to guilt so easily detected, and so severely punished, an adequate temptation would not readily be found.

Yet so it is, that in defiance of censure and contempt, truth is frequently violated; and scarcely the most vigilant and unremitted circumspection will secure him that mixes with mankind, from being hourly deceived by men of whom it can scarcely be imagined, that they mean any injury to him, or profit to themselves; even where the subject of conversation could not have been expected to put the passions in motion, or to have excited either hope or fear, or zeal or malignity, sufficient to induce any man to put his reputation in hazard, however little he might value it, or to overpower the love of truth, however weak might be its influence.

The casuists have very diligently distinguished lyes into their several classes, according to their various degrees of malignity: but they have, I think, generally omitted that which is most common, and, perhaps, not least mischievous; which, since the moralists have not given it a name, I shall distinguish as the LYE of VANITY.

To vanity may justly be imputed most of the falsehoods, which every man perceives hourly playing upon his ear, and, perhaps, most of those that are propagated with success. To the lye of commerce, and the lye of malice, the motive is so apparent, that they are seldom negligently or implicitly received: suspicion is always watchful over the practices of interest; and whatever the hope of gain, or desire of mischief, can prompt one man to assert, another is by reasons equally cogent incited to refute. But vanity pleases herself with such slight gratifications, and looks forward to pleasure so remotely consequential, that her practices raise no alarm, and her stratagems are not easily discovered.

Vanity is, indeed, often suffered to pass unpersued by suspicion; because he that would watch her motions, can never be at rest: fraud and malice are bounded in their influence; some opportunity of time and place is necessary to their agency; but scarce any man is abstracted one moment from his vanity; and he, to whom truth affords no gratifications, is generally inclined to seek them in falsehood.

It is remarked by Sir KENELM DIGBY, "that every man has a desire to appear superior to others, though it were only in having seen what they have not seen."[4] Such an accidental advantage, since it neither implies merit, nor confers dignity, one would think should not be desired so much as to be counterfeited: yet even this vanity, trifling as it is, produces innumerable narratives, all equally false; but more or less credible, in proportion to the skill or confidence of the relator. How many may a man of diffusive conversation count among his acquaintances, whose lives have been signalised by numberless escapes; who never cross the river but in a storm, or take a journey into the country without more adventures than befel the knight-errants of antient times, in pathless forests or enchanted castles! How many must he know to whom portents and prodigies are of daily occurrence; and for whom nature is hourly working wonders invisible to every other eye, only to supply them with subjects of conversation!

Others there are that amuse themselves with the dissemination of falsehood, at greater hazard of detection and disgrace; men marked out by some lucky planet for universal confidence and friendship, who have been consulted in every difficulty, entrusted with every secret, and summoned to every transaction: it is the supreme felicity of these men, to stun all companies with noisy information; to still doubt, and overbear opposition, with certain knowledge or authentic intelligence. A liar of this kind, with a strong memory or brisk imagination, is often the oracle of an obscure club, and till time discovers his impostures, dictates to his hearers with uncontrouled authority; for if a public question be started, he was present at the debate; if a new fashion be mentioned, he was at court the first day of its appearance; if a new performance of literature draws the attention of the public, he has patronised the author, and seen his work in manuscript; if a criminal of eminence be condemned to die, he often predicted his fate, and endeavoured his reformation: and who that lives at a distance from the scene of action, will dare to contradict a man, who reports from his own eyes and ears, and to whom all persons and affairs are thus intimately known?

This kind of falsehood is generally successful for a time, because it is practised at first with timidity and caution: but the prosperity of the liar is of short duration; the reception of one story, is always an incitement to the forgery of another less probable; and he goes on to triumph over tacit credulity, till pride or reason rises up against him, and his companions will no longer endure to see him wiser than themselves.

It is apparent, that the inventors of all these fictions intend some exaltation of themselves, and are led off by the persuit of honour from their attendance upon truth: their narratives always imply some consequence in favour of their courage, their sagacity or their activity, their familiarity with the learned, or their reception among the great; they are always bribed by the present pleasure of seeing themselves superior to those that surround them, and receiving the homage of silent attention and envious admiration.

But vanity is sometimes incited to fiction, by less visible gratifications: the present age abounds with a race of liars, who are content with the consciousness of falsehood, and whose pride is to deceive others without any gain or glory to themselves. Of this tribe it is the supreme pleasure to remark a lady in the play-house or the park, and to publish, under the character of a man suddenly enamoured, an advertisement in the news of the next day, containing a minute description of her person and her dress. From this artifice, indeed, no other effect can be expected than perturbations which the writer can never see, and conjectures of which he can never be informed: some mischief, however, he hopes he has done; and to have done mischief, is of some importance. He sets his invention to work again, and produces a narrative of a robbery, or a murder, with all the circumstances of time and place accurately adjusted: this is a jest of greater effect and longer duration: if he fixes his scene at a proper distance, he may for several days keep a wife in terror for her husband, or a mother for her son; and please himself with reflecting, that by his abilities and address, some addition is made to the miseries of life.

There is, I think, an antient law in Scotland, by which LEAS-ING-MAKING was capitally punished. I am, indeed, far from desiring to increase in this kingdom the number of executions: yet I cannot but think, that they who destroy the confidence of society, weaken the credit of intelligence, and interrupt the security of life; harrass the delicate with shame, and perplex the timorous with alarms; might very properly be awakened to a sense of their crimes, by denunciations of a whipping post or pillory: since many are so insensible of right and wrong, that they have no standard of action but the law; nor feel guilt, but as they dread punishment.

T

No. 67. Tuesday, 26 June 1753.

Inventas—vitam excoluere per artes.
                                                                   VIRG.[1]

They polish life by useful arts.

That familiarity produces neglect, has been long observed. The effect of all external objects, however great or splendid, ceases with their novelty: the courtier stands without emotion in the royal presence; the rustic tramples under his foot the beauties of the spring, with little attention to their colour or their fragrance; and the inhabitant of the coast darts his eye upon the immense diffusion of waters, without awe, wonder, or terror.

Those who have past much of their lives in this great city, look upon its opulence and its multitudes, its extent and variety, with cold indifference; but an inhabitant of the remoter parts of the kingdom is immediately distinguished by a kind of dissipated curiosity, a busy endeavour to divide his attention amongst a thousand objects, and a wild confusion of astonishment and alarm.

The attention of a new-comer is generally first struck by the multiplicity of cries that stun him in the streets, and the variety of merchandise and manufactures which the shopkeepers expose on every hand; and he is apt, by unwary bursts of admiration, to excite the merriment and contempt of those, who mistake the use of their eyes for effects of their understanding, and confound accidental knowledge with just reasoning.

But, surely, these are subjects on which any man may without reproach employ his meditations: the innumerable occupations, among which the thousands that swarm in the streets of London are distributed, may furnish employment to minds of every cast, and capacities of every degree. He that contemplates the extent of this wonderful city, finds it difficult to conceive, by what method plenty is maintained in our markets, and how the inhabitants are regularly supplied with the necessaries of life; but when he examines the shops and warehouses, sees the immense stores of every kind of merchandise piled up for sale, and runs over all the manufactures of art and products of nature, which are every where attracting his eye and solliciting his purse, he will be inclined to conclude, that such quantities cannot easily be exhausted, and that part of mankind must soon stand still for want of employment, till the wares already provided shall be worn out and destroyed.

As SOCRATES was passing through the fair at Athens, and casting his eyes over the shops and customers, "how many things are here," says he, "that I do not want!"[2] The same sentiment is every moment rising in the mind of him that walks the streets of London, however inferior in philosophy to SOCRATES: he beholds a thousand shops crouded with goods, of which he can scarcely tell the use, and which, therefore, he is apt to consider as of no value; and, indeed, many of the arts by which families are supported, and wealth is heaped together, are of that minute and superfluous kind, which nothing but experience could evince possible to be prosecuted with advantage, and which, as the world might easily want, it could scarcely be expected to encourage.

But so it is, that custom, curiosity, or wantonness, supplies every art with patrons, and finds purchasers for every manufacture; the world is so adjusted, that not only bread, but riches may be obtained without great abilities, or arduous performances: the most unskilful hand and unenlightened mind have sufficient incitements to industry; for he that is resolutely busy, can scarcely be in want. There is, indeed, no employment, however despicable, from which a man may not promise himself more than competence, when he sees thousands and myriads raised to dignity, by no other merit than that of contributing to supply their neighbours with the means of sucking smoke through a tube of clay; and others raising contributions upon those, whose elegance disdains the grossness of smoky luxury, by grinding the same materials into a powder, that may at once gratify and impair the smell.

Not only by these popular and modish trifles, but by a thousand unheeded and evanescent kinds of business, are the multitudes of this city preserved from idleness, and consequently from want. In the endless variety of tastes and circumstances that diversify mankind, nothing is so superfluous, but that some one desires it; or so common, but that some one is compelled to buy it. As nothing is useless but because it is in improper hands, what is thrown away by one is gathered up by another; and the refuse of part of mankind furnishes a subordinate class with the materials necessary to their support.

When I look round upon those who are thus variously exerting their qualifications, I cannot but admire the secret concatenation of society, that links together the great and the mean, the illustrious and the obscure; and consider with benevolent satisfaction, that no man, unless his body or mind be totally disabled, has need to suffer the mortification of seeing himself useless or burdensome to the community: he that will diligently labour, in whatever occupation, will deserve the sustenance which he obtains, and the protection which he enjoys; and may lie down every night with the pleasing consciousness, of having contributed something to the happiness of life.

Contempt and admiration are equally incident to narrow minds: he whose comprehension can take in the whole subordination of mankind, and whose perspicacity can pierce to the real state of things through the thin veils of fortune or of fashion, will discover meanness in the highest stations, and dignity in the meanest; and find that no man can become venerable but by virtue, or contemptible but by wickedness.

In the midst of this universal hurry, no man ought to be so little influenced by example, or so void of honest emulation, as to stand a lazy spectator of incessant labour; or please himself with the mean happiness of a drone, while the active swarms are buzzing about him: no man is without some quality, by the due application of which he might deserve well of the world; and whoever he be that has but little in his power, should be in haste to do that little, lest he be confounded with him that can do nothing.

By this general concurrence of endeavours, arts of every kind have been so long cultivated, that all the wants of man may be immediately supplied; idleness can scarcely form a wish which she may not gratify by the toil of others, or curiosity dream of a toy which the shops are not ready to afford her.

Happiness is enjoyed only in proportion as it is known; and such is the state or folly of man, that it is known only by experience of its contrary: we who have long lived amidst the conveniences of a town immensely populous, have scarce an idea of a place where desire cannot be gratified by money. In order to have a just sense of this artificial plenty, it is necessary to have passed some time in a distant colony, or those parts of our island which are thinly inhabited: he that has once known how many trades every man in such situations is compelled to exercise, with how much labour the products of nature must be accommodated to human use, how long the loss or defect of any common utensil must be endured, or by what aukward expedients it must be supplied, how far men may wander with money in their hands before any can sell them what they wish to buy, will know how to rate at its proper value the plenty and ease of a great city.

But that the happiness of man may still remain imperfect, as wants in this place are easily supplied, new wants likewise are easily created: every man, in surveying the shops of London, sees numberless instruments and conveniences, of which, while he did not know them, he never felt the need; and yet, when use has made them familiar, wonders how life could be supported without them. Thus it comes to pass, that our desires always increase with our possessions; the knowledge that something remains yet unenjoyed, impairs our enjoyment of the good before us.

They who have been accustomed to the refinements of science, and multiplications of contrivance, soon lose their confidence in the unassisted powers of nature, forget the paucity of our real necessities, and overlook the easy methods by which they may be supplied. It were a speculation worthy of a philosophical mind, to examine how much is taken away from our native abilities, as well as added to them by artificial expedients. We are so accustomed to give and receive assistance, that each of us singly can do little for himself; and there is scarce any one amongst us, however contracted may be his form of life, who does not enjoy the labour of a thousand artists.

But a survey of the various nations that inhabit the earth will inform us, that life may be supported with less assistance, and that the dexterity, which practice enforced by necessity produces, is able to effect much by very scanty means. The nations of Mexico and Peru erected cities and temples without the use of iron; and at this day the rude Indian supplies himself with all the necessaries of life: sent like the rest of mankind naked into the world, as soon as his parents have nursed him up to strength, he is to provide by his own labour for his own support. His first care is to find a sharp flint among the rocks; with this he undertakes to fell the trees of the forest; he shapes his bow, heads his arrows, builds his cottage, and hollows his canoe, and from that time lives in a state of plenty and prosperity; he is sheltered from the storms, he is fortified against beasts of prey, he is enabled to persue the fish of the sea, and the deer of the mountains; and as he does not know, does not envy the happiness of polished nations, where gold can supply the want of fortitude and skill, and he whose laborious ancestors have made him rich, may lie stretched upon a couch, and see all the treasures of all the elements poured down before him.

This picture of a savage life, if it shews how much individuals may perform, shews likewise how much society is to be desired.

Though the perseverance and address of the Indian excite our admiration, they nevertheless cannot procure him the conveniences which are enjoyed by the vagrant begger of a civilized country: he hunts like a wild beast to satisfy his hunger; and when he lies down to rest after a successful chace, cannot pronounce himself secure against the danger of perishing in a few days; he is, perhaps, content with his condition, because he knows not that a better is attainable by man; as he that is born blind does not long for the perception of light, because he cannot conceive the advantages which light would afford him: but hunger, wounds and weariness are real evils, though he believes them equally incident to all his fellow creatures; and when a tempest compels him to lie starving in his hut, he cannot justly be concluded equally happy with those whom art has exempted from the power of chance, and who make the foregoing year provide for the following.

To receive and to communicate assistance, constitutes the happiness of human life: man may indeed preserve his existence in solitude, but can enjoy it only in society: the greatest understanding of an individual, doomed to procure food and cloathing for himself, will barely supply him with expedients to keep off death from day to day; but as one of a large community performing only his share of the common business, he gains leisure for intellectual pleasures, and enjoys the happiness of reason and reflection.

T

No. 69. Tuesday, 3 July 1753.

Ferè libenter homines id quod volunt credunt.

CÆSAR.[1]

Men willingly believe what they wish to be true.

Tully has long ago observed, that no man, however weakened by long life, is so conscious of his own decrepitude, as not to imagine that he may yet hold his station in the world for another year.[2]

Of the truth of this remark every day furnishes new confirmation: there is no time of life, in which men for the most part seem less to expect the stroke of death, than when every other eye sees it impending; or are more busy in providing for another year, than when it is plain to all but themselves, that at another year they cannot arrive. Though every funeral that passes before their eyes, evinces the deceitfulness of such expectations, since every man who is borne to the grave thought himself equally certain of living at least to the next year, the survivor still continues to flatter himself, and is never at a loss for some reason why his life should be protracted, and the voracity of death continue to be pacified with some other prey.

But this is only one of the innumerable artifices practised in the universal conspiracy of mankind against themselves: every age and every condition indulges some darling fallacy; every man amuses himself with projects which he knows to be improbable, and which, therefore, he resolves to persue without daring to examine them. Whatever any man ardently desires, he very readily believes that he shall some time attain: he whose intemperance has overwhelmed him with diseases, while he languishes in the spring, expects vigour and recovery from the summer sun; and while he melts away in the summer, transfers his hopes to the frosts of winter: he that gazes upon elegance or pleasure, which want of money hinders him from imitating or partaking, comforts himself that the time of distress will soon be at an end, and that every day brings him nearer to a state of happiness; though he knows it has passed not only without acquisition of advantage, but perhaps without endeavours after it, in the formation of schemes that cannot be executed, and in the contemplation of prospects which cannot be approached.

Such is the general dream in which we all slumber out our time; every man thinks the day coming, in which he shall be gratified with all his wishes, in which he shall leave all those competitors behind, who are now rejoicing like himself in the expectation of victory; the day is always coming to the servile in which they shall be powerful, to the obscure in which they shall be eminent, and to the deformed in which they shall be beautiful.

If any of my readers has looked with so little attention on the world about him, as to imagine this representation exaggerated beyond probability, let him reflect a little upon his own life; let him consider what were his hopes and prospects ten years ago, and what additions he then expected to be made by ten years to his happiness: those years are now elapsed; have they made good the promise that was extorted from them, have they advanced his fortune, enlarged his knowledge, or reformed his conduct to the degree that was once expected? I am afraid, every man that recollects his hopes, must confess his disappointment; and own, that day has glided unprofitably after day, and that he is still at the same distance from the point of happiness.

With what consolations can those who have thus miscarried in their chief design, elude the memory of their ill success? with what amusements can they pacify their discontent, after the loss of so large a portion of life? they can give themselves up again to the same delusions, they can form new schemes of airy gratifications, and fix another period of felicity; they can again resolve to trust the promise which they know will be broken, they can walk in a circle with their eyes shut, and persuade themselves to think that they go forward.

Of every great and complicated event, part depends upon causes out of our power, and part must be effected by vigour and perseverance. With regard to that which is stiled in common language the work of chance, men will always find reasons for confidence or distrust, according to their different tempers or inclinations; and he that has been long accustomed to please himself with possibilities of fortuitous happiness, will not easily or willingly be reclaimed from his mistake. But the effects of human industry and skill are more easily subjected to calculation; whatever can be completed in a year, is divisible into parts, of which each may be performed in the compass of a day; he, therefore, that has passed the day without attention to the task assigned him, may be certain that the lapse of life has brought him no nearer to his object; for whatever idleness may expect from time, its produce will be only in proportion to the diligence with which it has been used. He that floats lazily down the stream,[3] in persuit of something borne along by the same current, will find himself indeed move forward; but unless he lays his hand to the oar, and increases his speed by his own labour, must be always at the same distance from that which he is following.

There have happened in every age some contingencies of unexpected and undeserved success, by which those who are determined to believe whatever favours their inclinations, have been encouraged to delight themselves with future advantages; they support confidence by considerations, of which the only proper use is to chace away despair: it is equally absurd to sit down in idleness, because some have been enriched without labour; as to leap a precipice because some have fallen and escaped with life, or to put to sea in a storm because some have been driven from a wreck upon the coast to which they were bound.

We are all ready to confess, that belief ought to be proportioned to evidence or probability: let any man, therefore, compare the number of those who have been thus favoured by fortune, and of those who have failed of their expectations; and he will easily determine, with what justness he has registered himself in the lucky catalogue.

But there is no need on these occasions for deep inquiries or laborious calculations; there is a far easier method of distinguishing the hopes of folly from those of reason, of finding the difference between prospects that exist before the eyes, and those that are only painted on a fond imagination. TOM DROWSY had accustomed himself to compute the profit of a darling project, till he had no longer any doubt of its success; it was at last matured by close consideration, all the measures were accurately adjusted, and he wanted only five hundred pounds to become master of a fortune that might be envied by a director of a trading company. TOM was generous and grateful, and was resolved to recompence this small assistance with an ample fortune: he, therefore, deliberated for a time, to whom amongst his friends he should declare his necessities; not that he suspected a refusal, but because he could not suddenly determine which of them would make the best use of riches, and was, therefore, most worthy of his favour. At last his choice was settled; and knowing that in order to borrow he must shew the probability of repayment, he prepared for a minute and copious explanation of his project. But here the golden dream was at an end: he soon discovered the impossibility of imposing upon others the notions by which he had so long imposed upon himself; which way soever he turned his thoughts, impossibility and absurdity rose in opposition on every side; even credulity and prejudice were at last forced to give way, and he grew ashamed of crediting himself what shame would not suffer him to communicate to another.

To this test let every man bring his imaginations, before they have been too long predominant in his mind. Whatever is true will bear to be related, whatever is rational will endure to be explained: but when we delight to brood in secret over future happiness, and silently to employ our meditations upon schemes of which we are conscious that the bare mention would expose us to derision and contempt; we should then remember, that we are cheating ourselves by voluntary delusions; and giving up to the unreal mockeries of fancy, those hours in which solid advantages might be attained by sober thought and rational assiduity.

There is, indeed, so little certainty in human affairs, that the most cautious and severe examiner may be allowed to indulge some hopes, which he cannot prove to be much favoured by probability; since after his utmost endeavours to ascertain events, he must often leave the issue in the hands of chance. And so scanty is our present allowance of happiness, that in many situations life could scarcely be supported, if hope were not allowed to relieve the present hour by pleasures borrowed from futurity; and reanimate the languor of dejection to new efforts, by pointing to distant regions of felicity, which yet no resolution or perseverance shall ever reach.

But these, like all other cordials, though they may invigorate in a small quantity, intoxicate in a greater; these pleasures, like the rest, are lawful only in certain circumstances, and to certain degrees; they may be useful in a due subserviency to nobler purposes, but become dangerous and destructive, when once they gain the ascendant in the heart: to sooth the mind to tranquillity by hope, even when that hope is likely to deceive us, may be sometimes useful; but to lull our faculties in a lethargy, is poor and despicable.

Vices and errors are differently modified, according to the state of the minds to which they are incident: to indulge hope beyond the warrant of reason, is the failure alike of mean and elevated understandings; but its foundation and its effects are totally different: the man of high courage and great abilities, is apt to place too much confidence in himself, and to expect from a vigorous exertion of his powers more than spirit or diligence can attain; between him and his wish he sees obstacles indeed, but he expects to overleap or break them; his mistaken ardour hurries him forward; and though perhaps he misses his end, he nevertheless obtains some collateral good, and performs something useful to mankind and honourable to himself.

The drone of timidity presumes likewise to hope, but without ground and without consequence; the bliss with which he solaces his hours, he always expects from others, though very often he knows not from whom; he folds his arms about him, and sits in expectation of some revolution in the state that shall raise him to greatness, or some golden shower that shall load him with wealth; he dozes away the day in musing upon the morrow; and at the end of life is rouzed from his dream only to discover, that the time of action is past, and that he can now shew his wisdom only by repentance.

T

No. 84. Saturday, 25 August 1753.

——Tolle periclum,
Jam vaga prosiliet frænis natura remotis.

HOR.[1]

But take the danger and the shame away,
And vagrant nature bounds upon her prey.

FRANCIS.

To the ADVENTURER.

SIR,

It has been observed, I think, by Sir WILLIAM TEMPLE, and after him by almost every other writer, that England affords a greater variety of characters, than the rest of the world.[2] This is ascribed to the liberty prevailing amongst us, which gives every man the privilege of being wise or foolish his own way, and preserves him from the necessity of hypocrisy, or the servility of imitation.

That the position itself is true, I am not completely satisfied. To be nearly acquainted with the people of different countries can happen to very few; and in life, as in every thing else beheld at a distance, there appears an even uniformity; the petty discriminations which diversify the natural character, are not discoverable but by a close inspection; we, therefore, find them most at home, because there we have most opportunities of remarking them. Much less am I convinced, that this peculiar diversification, if it be real, is the consequence of peculiar liberty: for where is the government to be found, that superintends individuals with so much vigilance, as not to leave their private conduct without restraint? Can it enter into a reasonable mind to imagine, that men of every other nation are not equally masters of their own time or houses with ourselves, and equally at liberty to be parsimonious or profuse, frolic or sullen, abstinent or luxurious? Liberty is certainly necessary to the full play of predominant humours; but such liberty is to be found alike under the government of the many or the few, in monarchies or in commonwealths.

How readily the predominant passion snatches an interval of liberty, and how fast it expands itself when the weight of restraint is taken away, I had lately an opportunity to discover, as I took a journey into the country in a stage coach; which, as every journey is a kind of adventure, may be very properly related to you, though I can display no such extraordinary assembly as CERVANTES has collected at DON QUIXOTE's inn.[3]

In a stage coach the passengers are for the most part wholly unknown to one another, and without expectation of ever meeting again when their journey is at an end; one should therefore imagine, that it was of little importance to any of them, what conjectures the rest should form concerning him. Yet so it is, that as all think themselves secure from detection, all assume that character of which they are most desirous, and on no occasion is the general ambition of superiority more apparently indulged.

On the day of our departure, in the twilight of the morning, I ascended the vehicle, with three men and two women my fellow travellers. It was easy to observe the affected elevation of mien with which every one entered, and the supercilious civility with which they paid their compliments to each other. When the first ceremony was dispatched, we sat silent for a long time, all employed in collecting importance into our faces, and endeavouring to strike reverence and submission into our companions.

It is always observable that silence propagates itself, and that the longer talk has been suspended, the more difficult it is to find any thing to say. We began now to wish for conversation; but no one seemed inclined to descend from his dignity, or first to propose a topic of discourse. At last a corpulent gentleman, who had equipped himself for this expedition with a scarlet surtout,[4] and a large hat with a broad lace, drew out his watch, looked on it in silence, and then held it dangling at his finger. This was, I suppose, understood by all the company as an invitation to ask the time of the day; but no body appeared to heed his overture; and his desire to be talking so far overcame his resentment, that he let us know of his own accord that it was past five, and that in two hours we should be at breakfast.

His condescension was thrown away; we continued all obdurate; the ladies held up their heads; I amused myself with watching their behaviour; and of the other two, one seemed to employ himself in counting the trees as we drove by them, the other drew his hat over his eyes, and counterfeited a slumber. The man of benevolence, to shew that he was not depressed by our neglect, hummed a tune and beat time upon his snuff-box.

Thus universally displeased with one another, and not much delighted with ourselves, we came at last to the little inn appointed for our repast, and all began at once to recompence themselves for the constraint of silence, by innumerable questions and orders to the people that attended us. At last, what every one had called for was got, or declared impossible to be got at that time, and we were persuaded to sit round the same table; when the gentleman in the red surtout looked again upon his watch, told us that we had half an hour to spare, but he was sorry to see so little merriment among us; that all fellow travellers were for the time upon the level, and that it was always his way to make himself one of the company. "I remember," says he, "it was on just such a morning as this that I and my lord Mumble and the duke of Tenterden were out upon a ramble; we called at a little house as it might be this; and my landlady, I warrant you, not suspecting to whom she was talking, was so jocular and facetious, and made so many merry answers to our questions, that we were all ready to burst with laughter. At last the good woman happening to overhear me whisper the duke and call him by his title, was so surprised and confounded that we could scarcely get a word from her: and the duke never met me from that day to this, but he talks of the little house, and quarrels with me for terrifying the landlady."

He had scarcely had time to congratulate himself on the veneration which this narrative must have procured him from the company, when one of the ladies having reached out for a plate on a distant part of the table, began to remark "the inconveniences of travelling, and the difficulty which they who never sat at home without a great number of attendants found in performing for themselves such offices as the road required; but that people of quality often travelled in disguise, and might be generally known from the vulgar by their condescension to poor inn-keepers, and the allowance which they made for any defect in their entertainment: that for her part, while people were civil and meant well, it was never her custom to find fault; for one was not to expect upon a journey all that one enjoyed at one's own house."

A general emulation seemed now to be excited. One of the men, who had hitherto said nothing, called for the last news paper; and having perused it a while with deep pensiveness, "It is impossible," says he, "for any man to guess how to act with regard to the stocks; last week it was the general opinion that they would fall; and I sold out twenty thousand pounds in order to a purchase: they have now risen unexpectedly; and I make no doubt but at my return to London I shall risk thirty thousand pounds amongst them again."

A young man, who had hitherto distinguished himself only by the vivacity of his look, and a frequent diversion of his eyes from one object to another, upon this closed his snuff-box, and told us that "he had a hundred times talked with the chancellor and the judges on the subject of the stocks; that for his part he did not pretend to be well acquainted with the principles on which they were established, but had always heard them reckoned pernicious to trade, uncertain in their produce, and unsolid in their foundation; and that he had been advised by three judges, his most intimate friends, never to venture his money in the funds, but to put it out upon land security, till he could light upon an estate in his own country."

It might be expected that, upon these glimpses of latent dignity, we should all have began to look around us with veneration, and have behaved like the princes of romance, when the enchantment that disguises them is dissolved, and they discover the dignity of each other: yet it happened, that none of these hints made much impression on the company; every one was apparently suspected of endeavouring to impose false appearances upon the rest; all continued their haughtiness, in hopes to enforce their claims; and all grew every hour more sullen, because they found their representations of themselves without effect.

Thus we travelled on four days with malevolence perpetually increasing, and without any endeavour but to outvie each other in superciliousness and neglect; and when any two of us could separate ourselves for a moment, we vented our indignation at the sauciness of the rest.

At length the journey was at an end, and time and chance, that strip off all disguises, have discovered that the intimate of lords and dukes is a nobleman's butler, who has furnished a shop with the money he has saved; the man who deals so largely in the funds, is the clerk of a broker in 'Change-alley; the lady who so carefully concealed her quality, keeps a cookshop behind the Exchange; and the young man, who is so happy in the friendship of the judges, engrosses and transcribes for bread in a garret of the Temple. Of one of the women only I could make no disadvantageous detection, because she had assumed no character, but accommodated herself to the scene before her, without any struggle for distinction or superiority.

I could not forbear to reflect on the folly of practising a fraud, which, as the event shewed, had been already practised too often to succeed, and by the success of which no advantage could have been obtained; of assuming a character, which was to end with the day; and of claiming upon false pretences honours which must perish with the breath that paid them.

But MR. ADVENTURER, let not those who laugh at me and my companions, think this folly confined to a stage coach. Every man in the journey of life takes the same advantage of the ignorance of his fellow travellers, disguises himself in counter-feited merit, and hears those praises with complacency which his conscience reproaches him for accepting. Every man deceives himself, while he thinks he is deceiving others; and forgets that the time is at hand when every illusion shall cease, when fictitious excellence shall be torn away, and ALL must be shown to ALL in their real state.

I am, SIR,

Your humble Servant,

VIATOR.[5]

T

No. 85. Tuesday, 28 August 1753.

Qui cupit optatam cursu contingere metam,
Multa tulit fecitque puer.

HOR.[1]

The youth, who hopes th' Olympic prize to gain,
All arts must try, and every toil sustain.

FRANCIS.

It is observed by BACON,[2] that "reading makes a full man, conversation a ready man, and writing an exact man."

As BACON attained to degrees of knowledge scarcely ever reached by any other man, the directions which he gives for study, have certainly a just claim to our regard; for who can teach an art with so great authority, as he that has practised it with undisputed success?

Under the protection of so great a name, I shall, therefore, venture to inculcate to my ingenious contemporaries, the necessity of reading, the fitness of consulting other understandings than their own, and of considering the sentiments and opinions of those who, however neglected in the present age, had in their own times, and many of them a long time afterwards, such reputation for knowledge and acuteness, as will scarcely ever be attained by those that despise them.

An opinion has of late been,[3] I know not how, propagated among us, that libraries are filled only with useless lumber; that men of parts stand in need of no assistance; and that to spend life in poring upon books, is only to imbibe prejudices, to obstruct and embarrass the powers of nature, to cultivate memory at the expence of judgement, and to bury reason under a chaos of indigested learning.

Such is the talk of many who think themselves wise, and of some who are thought wise by others; of whom part probably believe their own tenets, and part may be justly suspected of endeavouring to shelter their ignorance in multitudes, and of wishing to destroy that reputation which they have no hopes to share. It will, I believe, be found invariably true, that learning was never decried by any learned man; and what credit can be given to those, who venture to condemn that which they do not know?

If reason has the power ascribed to it by its advocates, if so much is to be discovered by attention and meditation, it is hard to believe, that so many millions, equally participating of the bounties of nature with ourselves, have been for ages upon ages meditating in vain: if the wits of the present time expect the regard of posterity, which will then inherit the reason which is now thought superior to instruction, surely they may allow themselves to be instructed by the reason of former generations. When, therefore, an author declares, that he has been able to learn nothing from the writings of his predecessors, and such a declaration has been lately made, nothing but a degree of arrogance unpardonable in the greatest human understanding, can hinder him from perceiving, that he is raising prejudices against his own performance; for with what hopes of success can he attempt that in which greater abilities have hitherto miscarried? or with what peculiar force does he suppose himself invigorated, that difficulties hitherto invincible should give way before him?

Of those whom PROVIDENCE has qualified to make any additions to human knowledge, the number is extremely small; and what can be added by each single mind, even of this superior class, is very little: the greatest part of mankind must owe all their knowledge, and all must owe far the larger part of it, to the information of others. To understand the works of celebrated authors, to comprehend their systems, and retain their reasonings, is a task more than equal to common intellects; and he is by no means to be accounted useless or idle, who has stored his mind with acquired knowledge, and can detail it occasionally to others who have less leisure or weaker abilities.

PERSIUS has justly observed, that knowledge is nothing to him who is not known by others to possess it:[4] to the scholar himself it is nothing with respect either to honour or advantage, for the world cannot reward those qualities which are concealed from it; with respect to others it is nothing, because it affords no help to ignorance or error.

It is with justice, therefore, that in an accomplished character, HORACE unites just sentiments with the power of expressing them; and he that has once accumulated learning, is next to consider, how he shall most widely diffuse and most agreeably impart it.

A ready man is made by conversation. He that buries himself among his manuscripts "besprent," as POPE expresses it,[5] "with learned dust," and wears out his days and nights in perpetual research and solitary meditation, is too apt to lose in his elocution what he adds to his wisdom, and when he comes into the world, to appear overloaded with his own notions, like a man armed with weapons which he cannot wield. He has no facility of inculcating his speculations, of adapting himself to the various degrees of intellect which the accidents of conversation will present; but will talk to most unintelligibly, and to all unpleasantly.

I was once present at the lectures of a profound philosopher, a man really skilled in the science which he professed, who having occasion to explain the terms OPACUM and PEL-LUCIDUM, told us, after some hesitation, that OPACUM was as one might say OPAKE, and that PELLUCIDUM signified PEL-LUCID. Such was the dexterity, with which this learned reader facilitated to his auditors the intricacies of science; and so true is it, that a man may know what he cannot teach.

BOERHAAVE complains,[6] that the writers who have treated of chemistry before him, are useless to the greater part of students; because they presuppose their readers to have such degrees of skill as are not often to be found. Into the same error are all men apt to fall, who have familiarized any subject to themselves in solitude: they discourse, as if they thought every other man had been employed in the same inquiries; and expect that short hints and obscure allusions will produce in others, the same train of ideas which they excite in themselves.

Nor is this the only inconvenience which the man of study suffers from a recluse life. When he meets with an opinion that pleases him, he catches it up with eagerness; looks only after such arguments as tend to his confirmation; or spares himself the trouble of discussion, and adopts it with very little proof; indulges it long without suspicion, and in time unites it to the general body of his knowledge, and treasures it up among incontestible truths: but when he comes into the world among men who, arguing upon dissimilar principles, have been led to different conclusions, and being placed in various situations view the same object on many sides; he finds his darling position attacked, and himself in no condition to defend it: having thought always in one train, he is in the state of a man who having fenced always with the same master, is perplexed and amazed by a new posture of his antagonist; he is entangled in unexpected difficulties, he is harrassed by sudden objections, he is unprovided with solutions or replies, his surprize impedes his natural powers of reasoning, his thoughts are scattered and confounded, and he gratifies the pride of airy petulance with an easy victory.

It is difficult to imagine, with what obstinacy truths which one mind perceives almost by intuition, will be rejected by another; and how many artifices must be practised, to procure admission for the most evident propositions into understandings frighted by their novelty, or hardened against them by accidental prejudice: it can scarcely be conceived, how frequently in these extemporaneous controversies, the dull will be subtle, and the acute absurd; how often stupidity will elude the force of argument, by involving itself in its own gloom; and mistaken ingenuity will weave artful fallacies, which reason can scarcely find means to disentangle.

In these encounters the learning of the recluse usually fails him: nothing but long habit and frequent experiments can confer the power of changing a position into various forms, presenting it in different points of view, connecting it with known and granted truths, fortifying it with intelligible arguments, and illustrating it by apt similitudes; and he, therefore, that has collected his knowledge in solitude, must learn its application by mixing with mankind.

But while the various opportunities of conversation invite us to try every mode of argument, and every art of recommending our sentiments, we are frequently betrayed to the use of such as are not in themselves strictly defensible: a man heated in talk, and eager of victory, takes advantage of the mistakes or ignorance of his adversary, lays hold of concessions to which he knows he has no right, and urges proofs likely to prevail on his opponent, though he knows himself that they have no force: thus the severity of reason is relaxed; many topics are accumulated, but without just arrangement or distinction; we learn to satisfy ourselves with such ratiocination as silences others; and seldom recall to a close examination, that discourse which has gratified our vanity with victory and applause.

Some caution, therefore, must be used, lest copiousness and facility be made less valuable by inaccuracy and confusion.

To fix the thoughts by writing, and subject them to frequent examinations and reviews, is the best method of enabling the mind to detect its own sophisms, and keep it on guard against the fallacies which it practices on others: in conversation we naturally diffuse our thoughts, and in writing we contract them; method is the excellence of writing, and unconstraint the grace of conversation.

To read, write, and converse in due proportions, is, therefore, the business of a man of letters. For all these there is not often equal opportunity; excellence, therefore, is not often attainable; and most men fail in one or other of the ends proposed, and are full without readiness, or ready without exactness. Some deficiency must be forgiven all, because all are men; and more must be allowed to pass uncensured in the greater part of the world, because none can confer upon himself abilities, and few have the choice of situations proper for the improvement of those which nature has bestowed: it is, however, reasonable, to have PERFECTION in our eye; that we may always advance towards it, though we know it never can be reached.

T

No. 95. Tuesday, 2 October 1753.

—— *Dulcique animos novitate tenebo.*
OVID.[1]

And with sweet novelty your soul detain.

It is often charged upon writers, that with all their pretensions to genius and discoveries, they do little more than copy one another; and that compositions obtruded upon the world with the pomp of novelty, contain only tedious repetitions of common sentiments, or at best exhibit a transposition of known images, and give a new appearance to truth only by some slight difference of dress and decoration.

The allegation of resemblance between authors, is indisputably true; but the charge of plagiarism, which is raised upon it, is not to be allowed with equal readiness.[2] A coincidence of sentiment may easily happen without any communication, since there are many occasions in which all reasonable men will nearly think alike. Writers of all ages have had the same sentiments, because they have in all ages had the same objects of speculation; the interests and passions, the virtues and vices of mankind, have been diversified in different times, only by unessential and casual varieties; and we must, therefore, expect in the works of all those who attempt to describe them, such a likeness as we find in the pictures of the same person drawn in different periods of his life.

It is necessary, therefore, that before an author be charged with plagiarism, one of the most reproachful, though, perhaps, not the most atrocious of literary crimes, the subject on which he treats should be carefully considered. We do not wonder, that historians, relating the same facts, agree in their narration; or that authors, delivering the elements of science, advance the same theorems, and lay down the same definitions: yet it is not wholly without use to mankind, that books are multiplied, and that different authors lay out their labours on the same subject; for there will always be some reason why one should on particular occasions, or to particular persons, be preferable to another; some will be clear where others are obscure, some will please by their stile and others by their method, some by their embellishments and others by their simplicity, some by closeness and others by diffusion.

The same indulgence is to be shewn to the writers of morality: right and wrong are immutable; and those, therefore, who teach us to distinguish them, if they all teach us right, must agree with one another. The relations of social life, and the duties resulting from them, must be the same at all times and in all nations: some petty differences may be, indeed, produced, by forms of government or arbitrary customs; but the general doctrine can receive no alteration.

Yet it is not to be desired, that morality should be considered as interdicted to all future writers: men will always be tempted to deviate from their duty, and will, therefore, always want a monitor to recall them; and a new book often seizes the attention of the public, without any other claim than that it is new.

There is likewise in composition, as in other things, a perpetual vicissitude of fashion; and truth is recommended at one time to regard, by appearances which at another would expose it to neglect; the author, therefore, who has judgement to discern the taste of his contemporaries, and skill to gratify it, will have always an opportunity to deserve well of mankind, by conveying instruction to them in a grateful vehicle.

There are likewise many modes of composition, by which a moralist may deserve the name of an original writer: he may familiarise his system by dialogues after the manner of the ancients, or subtilize it into a series of syllogistic arguments; he may enforce his doctrine by seriousness and solemnity, or enliven it by sprightliness and gayety; he may deliver his sentiments in naked precepts, or illustrate them by historical examples; he may detain the studious by the artful concatenation of a continued discourse, or relieve the busy by short strictures and unconnected essays.

To excel in any of these forms of writing, will require a particular cultivation of the genius; whoever can attain to excellence, will be certain to engage a set of readers, whom no other method would have equally allured; and he that communicates truth with success, must be numbered among the first benefactors to mankind.

The same observation may be extended likewise to the passions: their influence is uniform, and their effects nearly the same in every human breast: a man loves and hates, desires and avoids, exactly like his neighbour; resentment and ambition, avarice and indolence, discover themselves by the same symptoms, in minds distant a thousand years from one another.

Nothing, therefore, can be more unjust, than to charge an author with plagiarism, merely because he assigns to every cause its natural effect; and makes his personages act, as others in like circumstances have always done. There are conceptions in which all men will agree, though each derives them from his own observation: whoever has been in love, will represent a lover impatient of every idea that interrupts his meditations on his mistress, retiring to shades and solitude that he may muse without disturbance on his approaching happiness, or associating himself with some friend that flatters his passion, and talking away the hours of absence upon his darling subject. Whoever has been so unhappy as to have felt the miseries of long continued hatred, will, without any assistance from antient volumes, be able to relate how the passions are kept in perpetual agitation, by the recollection of injury and meditations of revenge; how the blood boils at the name of the enemy, and life is worn away in contrivances of mischief.

Every other passion is alike simple and limited, if it be considered only with regard to the breast which it inhabits: the anatomy of the mind, as that of the body, must perpetually exhibit the same appearances; and though by the continued industry of successive inquirers, new movements will be from time to time discovered, they can affect only the minuter parts, and are commonly of more curiosity than importance.

It will now be natural to inquire, by what arts are the writers of the present and future ages to attract the notice and favour of mankind. They are to observe the alterations which time is always making in the modes of life, that they may gratify every generation with a picture of themselves. Thus love is uniform, but courtship is perpetually varying: the different arts of gallantry, which beauty has inspired, would of themselves be sufficient to fill a volume; sometimes balls and serenades, sometimes tournaments and adventures have been employed to melt the hearts of ladies, who in another century have been sensible of scarce any other merit than that of riches, and listened only to jointures and pin-money. Thus the ambitious man has at all times been eager of wealth and power; but these hopes have been gratified in some countries by supplicating the people, and in others by flattering the prince: honour in some states has been only the reward of military achievements, in others it has been gained by noisy turbulence and popular clamours. Avarice has worn a different form, as she actuated the usurer of Rome, and the stock-jobber of England; and idleness itself, how little soever inclined to the trouble of invention, has been forced from time to time to change its amusements, and contrive different methods of wearing out the day.

Here then is the fund, from which those who study mankind

may fill their compositions with an inexhaustible variety of
images and allusions; and he must be confessed to look with
little attention upon scenes thus perpetually changing, who
cannot catch some of the figures before they are made vulgar by
reiterated descriptions.

It has been discovered by Sir ISAAC NEWTON,[3] that the
distinct and primogenial colours are only seven; but every eye
can witness, that from various mixtures in various proportions,
infinite diversifications of tints may be produced. In like manner,
the passions of the mind, which put the world in motion, and
produce all the bustle and eagerness of the busy crouds that
swarm upon the earth; the passions, from whence arise all the
pleasures and pains that we see and hear of, if we analyze the
mind of man, are very few; but those few agitated and combined,
as external causes shall happen to operate, and modified by
prevailing opinions and accidental caprices, make such frequent
alterations on the surface of life, that the show while we are
busied in delineating it, vanishes from the view, and a new set
of objects succeeds, doomed to the same shortness of duration
with the former: thus curiosity may always find employment,
and the busy part of mankind will furnish the contemplative
with the materials of speculation to the end of time.

The complaint, therefore, that all topics are preoccupied, is
nothing more than the murmur of ignorance or idleness, by
which some discourage others and some themselves: the mutability of mankind will always furnish writers with new images,
and the luxuriance of fancy may always embellish them with
new decorations.

T

No. 99. Tuesday, 16 October 1753.

——*Magnis tamen excidit ausis.*

OVID.[1]

But in the glorious enterprize he dy'd.

ADDISON.

It has always been the practice of mankind, to judge of actions by the event. The same attempts, conducted in the same manner, but terminated by different success, produce different judgments: they who attain their wishes, never want celebrators of their wisdom and their virtue; and they that miscarry, are quickly discovered to have been defective not only in mental but in moral qualities. The world will never be long without some good reason to hate the unhappy; their real faults are immediately detected, and if those are not sufficient to sink them into infamy, an additional weight of calumny will be superadded: he that fails in his endeavours after wealth or power, will not long retain either honesty or courage.

This species of injustice has so long prevailed in universal practice, that it seems likewise to have infected speculation: so few minds are able to separate the ideas of greatness and prosperity, that even Sir WILLIAM TEMPLE has determined, that "he who can deserve the name of a hero, must not only be virtuous but fortunate."[2]

By this unreasonable distribution of praise and blame, none have suffered oftener than PROJECTORS, whose rapidity of imagination and vastness of design, raise such envy in their fellow mortals, that every eye watches for their fall, and every heart exults at their distresses: yet even a PROJECTOR may gain favour by success; and the tongue that was prepared to hiss, then endeavours to excell others in loudness of applause.

When CORIOLANUS, in SHAKESPEARE, deserted to AUFIDIUS, the Volscian servants at first insulted him, even while he stood under the protection of the houshold Gods: but when they saw that the PROJECT took effect, and the stranger was seated at the head of the table, one of them very judiciously observes, "that he always thought there was more in him than he could think."[3]

MACHIAVEL has justly animadverted on the different notice taken by all succeeding times, of the two great projectors CATILINE and CÆSAR. Both formed the same PROJECT, and intended to raise themselves to power, by subverting the commonwealth: they persued their design, perhaps, with equal abilities, and with equal virtue; but CATILINE perished in the field, and CÆSAR returned from Pharsalia with unlimited authority: and from that time, every monarch of the earth has thought himself honoured by a comparison with CÆSAR; and CATILINE has been never mentioned, but that his name might be applied to traitors and incendiaries.[4]

In an age more remote, XERXES projected the conquest of Greece, and brought down the power of Asia against it: but after the world had been filled with expectation and terror, his army was beaten, his fleet was destroyed, and XERXES has been never mentioned without contempt.

A few years afterwards, Greece likewise had her turn of giving birth to a PROJECTOR; who invading Asia with a small army, went forward in search of adventures, and by his escape from one danger gained only more rashness to rush into another: he stormed city after city, over-ran kingdom after kingdom, fought battles only for barren victory, and invaded nations only that he might make his way through them to new invasions: but having been fortunate in the execution of his projects, he died with the name of ALEXANDER the GREAT.[5]

These are, indeed, events of ancient time; but human nature is always the same, and every age will afford us instances of public censures influenced by events. The great business of the middle centuries, was the holy war; which undoubtedly was a noble PROJECT, and was for a long time prosecuted with a spirit equal to that with which it had been contrived: but the ardour of the European heroes only hurried them to destruction; for a long time they could not gain the territories for which they fought, and, when at last gained, they could not keep them: their expeditions, therefore, have been the scoff of idleness and ignorance, their understanding and their virtue have been equally vilified, their conduct has been ridiculed, and their cause has been defamed.

When COLUMBUS had engaged King Ferdinand in the discovery of the other hemisphere, the sailors with whom he embarked in the expedition had so little confidence in their commander, that after having been long at sea looking for coasts which they expected never to find, they raised a general mutiny, and demanded to return. He found means to sooth them into a permission to continue the same course three days longer, and on the evening of the third day descried land. Had the impatience of his crew denied him a few hours of the time requested, what had been his fate but to have come back with the infamy of a vain PROJECTOR, who had betrayed the king's credulity to useless expences, and risked his life in seeking countries that had no existence? how would those that had rejected his proposals, have triumphed in their acuteness? and when would his name have been mentioned, but with the makers of potable gold and malleable glass?

The last royal PROJECTORS with whom the world has been troubled, were CHARLES of SWEDEN and the CZAR of MUSCOVY. CHARLES, if any judgement may be formed of his designs by his measures and his enquiries, had purposed first to dethrone the CZAR, then to lead his army through pathless desarts into China, thence to make his way by the sword through the whole circuit of Asia, and by the conquest of Turkey to unite Sweden with his new dominions: but this mighty PROJECT was crushed at Pultowa,[6] and CHARLES has since been considered as a madman by those powers, who sent their embassadors to sollicit his friendship, and their generals "to learn under him the art of war."[7]

The CZAR found employment sufficient in his own dominions, and amused himself in digging canals, and building cities; murdering his subjects with insufferable fatigues, and transplanting nations from one corner of his dominions to another, without regretting the thousands that perished on the way: but he attained his end, he made his people formidable, and is numbered by fame among the Demi-gods.

I am far from intending to vindicate the sanguinary projects of heroes and conquerors, and would wish rather to diminish the reputation of their success, than the infamy of their miscarriages: for I cannot conceive, why he that has burnt cities, and wasted nations, and filled the world with horror and desolation, should be more kindly regarded by mankind, than he that died in the rudiments of wickedness; why he that accomplished mischief should be glorious, and he that only endeavoured it should be criminal: I would wish CÆSAR and CATILINE,

XERXES and ALEXANDER, CHARLES and PETER,[8] huddled together in obscurity or detestation.

But there is another species of PROJECTORS, to whom I would willingly conciliate mankind; whose ends are generally laudable, and whose labours are innocent; who are searching out new powers of nature, or contriving new works of art; but who are yet persecuted with incessant obloquy, and whom the universal contempt with which they are treated, often debars from that success which their industry would obtain, if it were permitted to act without opposition.

They who find themselves inclined to censure new undertakings, only because they are new, should consider, that the folly of PROJECTION is very seldom the folly of a fool; it is commonly the ebullition of a capacious mind, crouded with variety of knowledge, and heated with intenseness of thought; it proceeds often from the consciousness of uncommon powers, from the confidence of those, who having already done much, are easily persuaded that they can do more: when ROWLEY had completed the Orrery,[9] he attempted the perpetual motion; when BOYLE[10] had exhausted the secrets of vulgar chemistry, he turned his thoughts to the work of transmutation.

A PROJECTOR generally unites those qualities which have the fairest claim to veneration, extent of knowledge and greatness of design: it was said of CATILINE, "immoderata, incredibilia, nimis alta semper cupiebat."[11] Projectors of all kinds agree in their intellects, though they differ in their morals; they all fail by attempting things beyond their power, by despising vulgar attainments, and aspiring to performances, to which, perhaps, nature has not proportioned the force of man: when they fail, therefore, they fail not by idleness or timidity, but by rash adventure and fruitless diligence.

That the attempts of such men will often miscarry, we may reasonably expect; yet from such men, and such only, are we to hope for the cultivation of those parts of nature which lie yet waste, and the invention of those arts which are yet wanting to the felicity of life. If they are, therefore, universally discouraged, art and discovery can make no advances. Whatever is attempted without previous certainty of success, may be considered as a

PROJECT, and amongst narrow minds may, therefore, expose its author to censure and contempt; and if the liberty of laughing be once indulged, every man will laugh at what he does not understand, every PROJECT will be considered as madness, and every great or new design will be censured as a PROJECT. Men, unaccustomed to reason and researches, think every enterprise impracticable, which is extended beyond common effects, or comprises many intermediate operations. Many that presume to laugh at PROJECTORS, would consider a flight through the air in a winged chariot, and the movement of a mighty engine by the steam of water, as equally the dreams of mechanic lunacy; and would hear, with equal negligence, of the union of the Thames and Severn by a canal,[12] and the scheme of Albuquerque the viceroy of the Indies, who in the rage of hostility had contrived to make Egypt a barren desart, by turning the Nile into the Red Sea.[13]

Those who have attempted much, have seldom failed to perform more than those who never deviated from the common roads of action: many valuable preparations of chemistry, are supposed to have risen from unsuccessful enquiries after the grand elixir; it is, therefore, just to encourage those who endeavour to enlarge the power of art, since they often succeed beyond expectation; and when they fail, may sometimes benefit the world even by their miscarriages.

T

No. 102. Saturday, 27 October 1753.

——Quid tam dextro pede concipis, ut te
Conatus non pœniteat votique peracti?

JUV.[1]

What in the conduct of our life appears
So well design'd, so luckily begun,
But, when we have our wish, we wish undone.

DRYDEN.

To the ADVENTURER.

SIR,

I have been for many years a trader in London. My beginning
was narrow, and my stock small; I was, therefore, a long time
brow-beaten and despised by those, who having more money
thought they had more merit than myself. I did not, however,
suffer my resentment to instigate me to any mean arts of supplantation, nor my eagerness of riches to betray me to any
indirect methods of gain; I persued my business with incessant
assiduity, supported by the hope of being one day richer than
those who contemned me; and had upon every annual review
of my books, the satisfaction of finding my fortune increased
beyond my expectation.

In a few years my industry and probity were fully recompensed, my wealth was really great, and my reputation for
wealth still greater. I had large warehouses crouded with goods,
and considerable sums in the public funds; I was caressed upon
the Exchange by the most eminent merchants; became the oracle
of the common council; was sollicited to engage in all commercial undertakings; was flattered with the hopes of becoming in
a short time one of the directors of a wealthy company; and to
complete my mercantile honours enjoyed the expensive happiness of fining for Sheriff.[2]

Riches, you know, easily produce riches: when I had arrived
to this degree of wealth, I had no longer any obstruction or
opposition to fear; new acquisitions were hourly brought within
my reach, and I continued for some years longer to heap thousands upon thousands.

At last I resolved to complete the circle of a citizen's prosperity
by the purchase of an estate in the country, and to close my
life in retirement. From the hour that this design entered my
imagination, I found the fatigues of my employment every day
more oppressive, and persuaded myself that I was no longer
equal to perpetual attention, and that my health would soon be
destroyed by the torment and distraction of extensive business.
I could image to myself no happiness, but in vacant jollity, and
uninterrupted leisure; nor entertain my friends with any other

topic, than the vexation and uncertainty of trade, and the happiness of rural privacy.

But notwithstanding these declarations, I could not at once reconcile myself to the thoughts of ceasing to get money; and though I was every day enquiring for a purchase, I found some reason for rejecting all that were offered me; and, indeed, had accumulated so many beauties and conveniencies in my idea of the spot, where I was finally to be happy, that, perhaps, the world might have been travelled over, without discovery of a place which would not have been defective in some particular.

Thus I went on still talking of retirement, and still refusing to retire; my friends began to laugh at my delays, and I grew ashamed to trifle longer with my own inclinations: an estate was at length purchased, I transferred my stock to a prudent young man who had married my daughter, went down into the country, and commenced lord of a spacious manor.

Here for some time I found happiness equal to my expectation. I reformed the old house according to the advice of the best architects, I threw down the walls of the garden and inclosed it with palisades, planted long avenues of trees, filled a greenhouse with exotic plants, dug a new canal, and threw the earth into the old moat.

The fame of these expensive improvements brought in all the country to see the show. I entertained my visitors with great liberality, led them round my gardens, shewed them my apartments, laid before them plans for new decorations, and was gratified by the wonder of some and the envy of others.

I was envied; but how little can one man judge of the condition of another? The time was now coming, in which affluence and splendor could no longer make me pleased with myself. I had built till the imagination of the architect was exhausted; I had added one convenience to another till I knew not what more to wish or to design; I had laid out my gardens, planted my park, and compleated my water-works; and what now remained to be done? what, but to look up to turrets of which when they were once raised I had no farther use, to range over apartments where time was tarnishing the furniture, to stand by the cascade of which I scarcely now perceived the sound, and to watch the growth of woods that must give their shade to a distant generation.

In this gloomy inactivity, is every day begun and ended; the happiness that I have been so long procuring is now at an end, because it has been procured; I wander from room to room till I am weary of myself; I ride out to a neighbouring hill in the centre of my estate, from whence all my lands lie in prospect round me; I see nothing that I have not seen before, and return home disappointed, though I knew that I had nothing to expect.

In my happy days of business I had been accustomed to rise early in the morning, and remember the time when I grieved that the night came so soon upon me, and obliged me for a few hours to shut out affluence and prosperity. I now seldom see the rising sun, but "to tell him," with the fallen angel, "how I hate his beams."[3] I awake from sleep as to languor or imprisonment, and have no employment for the first hour but to consider by what art I shall rid myself of the second. I protract the breakfast as long as I can, because when it is ended I have no call for my attention, till I can with some degree of decency grow impatient for my dinner. If I could dine all my life, I should be happy: I eat not because I am hungry, but because I am idle: but alas! the time quickly comes when I can eat no longer; and so ill does my constitution second my inclination, that I cannot bear strong liquors: seven hours must then be endured before I shall sup; but supper comes at last, the more welcome as it is in a short time succeeded by sleep.

Such, MR. ADVENTURER, is the happiness, the hope of which seduced me from the duties and pleasures of a mercantile life. I shall be told by those who read my narrative, that there are many means of innocent amusement, and many schemes of useful employment which I do not appear ever to have known; and that nature and art have provided pleasures, by which, without the drudgery of settled business, the active may be engaged, the solitary soothed, and the social entertained.

These arts, Sir, I have tried. When first I took possession of my estate, in conformity to the taste of my neighbours, I bought guns and nets, filled my kennel with dogs and my stable with horses; but a little experience shewed me, that these instruments of rural felicity would afford me few gratifications. I never shot but to miss the mark, and, to confess the truth, was afraid of the fire of my own gun. I could discover no music in the cry of the dogs, nor could divest myself of pity for the animal whose peaceful and inoffensive life was sacrificed to our sport: I was not, indeed, always at leisure to reflect upon her danger; for my horse, who had been bred to the chace, did not always regard my choice either of speed or way, but leaped hedges and ditches at his own discretion, and hurried me along with the dogs, to the great diversion of my brother sportsmen: his eagerness of persuit once incited him to swim a river; and I had leisure to resolve in the water, that I would never hazard my life again for the destruction of a hare.

I then ordered books to be procured, and by the direction of the vicar had in a few weeks a closet elegantly furnished. You will, perhaps, be surprized when I shall tell you, that when once I had ranged them according to their sizes, and piled them up in regular gradations, I had received all the pleasure which they could give me. I am not able to excite in myself any curiosity after events which have been long passed, and in which I can, therefore, have no interest: I am utterly unconcerned to know whether TULLY or DEMOSTHENES excelled in oratory, whether HANNIBAL lost Italy by his own negligence or the corruption of his countrymen.[4] I have no skill in controversial learning, nor can conceive why so many volumes should have been written upon questions, which I have lived so long and so happily without understanding. I once resolved to go through the volumes relating to the office of justice of the peace, but found them so crabbed and intricate, that in less than a month I desisted in despair, and resolved to supply my deficiencies by paying a competent salary to a skillful clerk.

I am naturally inclined to hospitality, and for some time kept up a constant intercourse of visits with the neighbouring gentlemen; but though they are easily brought about me by better wine than they can find at any other house, I am not much relieved by their conversation; they have no skill in commerce or the stocks, and I have no knowledge of the history of families

or the factions of the county; so that when the first civilities are
over, they usually talk to one another, and I am left alone in the
midst of the company. Though I cannot drink myself, I am
obliged to encourage the circulation of the glass; their mirth
grows more turbulent and obstreperous, and before their merriment is at an end, I am sick with disgust, and, perhaps,
reproached with my sobriety, or by some sly insinuations
insulted as a cit.[5]

Such, MR. ADVENTURER, is the life to which I am condemned by a foolish endeavour to be happy by imitation; such
is the happiness to which I pleased myself with approaching,
and which I considered as the chief end of my cares and my
labours. I toiled year after year with chearfulness, in expectation
of the happy hour in which I might be idle; the privilege of
idleness is attained, but has not brought with it the blessing of
tranquillity.

                                    I am,
                                    Yours, &c.
                                    MERCATOR.[6]
    T

No. 107. Tuesday, 13 November 1753.

————*Sub judice lis est.*
                HOR.[1]

And of their vain disputings find no end.
                FRANCIS.

It has been sometimes asked by those, who find the appearance
of wisdom more easily attained by questions than solutions,
how it comes to pass, that the world is divided by such difference
of opinion; and why men, equally reasonable, and equally lovers
of truth, do not always think in the same manner.

With regard to simple propositions, where the terms are
understood, and the whole subject is comprehended at once,
there is such an uniformity of sentiment among all human

beings, that, for many ages, a very numerous set of notions were supposed to be innate, or necessarily coexistent with the faculty of reason; it being imagined, that universal agreement could proceed only from the invariable dictates of the universal parent.

In questions diffuse and compounded, this similarity of determination is no longer to be expected. At our first sally into the intellectual world, we all march together along one strait and open road; but as we proceed further, and wider prospects open to our view, every eye fixes upon a different scene; we divide into various paths, and, as we move forward, are still at a greater distance from each other. As a question becomes more complicated and involved, and extends to a greater number of relations, disagreement of opinion will always be multiplied; not because we are irrational, but because we are finite beings, furnished with different kinds of knowledge, exerting different degrees of attention, one discovering consequences which escape another, none taking in the whole concatenation of causes and effects, and most comprehending but a very small part, each comparing what he observes with a different criterion, and each referring it to a different purpose.

Where, then, is the wonder, that they, who see only a small part, should judge erroneously of the whole? or that they, who see different and dissimilar parts, should judge differently from each other?

Whatever has various respects, must have various appearances of good and evil, beauty or deformity: thus, the gardener tears up as a weed, the plant which the physician gathers as a medicine; and "a general," says Sir KENELM DIGBY, "will look with pleasure over a plain, as a fit place on which the fate of empires might be decided in battle; which the farmer will despise as bleak and barren, neither fruitful of pasturage, nor fit for tillage."[2]

Two men examining the same question, proceed commonly like the physician and gardener in selecting herbs, or the farmer and hero looking on the plain; they bring minds impressed with different notions, and direct their inquiries to different ends; they form, therefore, contrary conclusions, and each wonders at the other's absurdity.

We have less reason to be surprised or offended when we find others differ from us in opinion, because we very often differ from ourselves: how often we alter our minds, we do not always remark; because the change is sometimes made imperceptibly and gradually, and the last conviction effaces all memory of the former: yet every man, accustomed from time to time to take a survey of his own notions, will by a slight retrospection be able to discover, that his mind has suffered many revolutions, that the same things have in the several parts of his life been condemned and approved, persued and shunned; and that on many occasions, even when his practice has been steddy, his mind has been wavering, and he has persisted in a scheme of action, rather because he feared the censure of inconstancy, than because he was always pleased with his own choice.

Of the different faces shewn by the same objects as they are viewed on opposite sides, and of the different inclinations which they must constantly raise in him that contemplates them, a more striking example cannot easily be found than two Greek Epigrammatists will afford us in their accounts of human life, which I shall lay before the reader in English prose.

POSIDIPPUS, a comic poet, utters this complaint; "Through which of the paths of life is it eligible to pass? In public assemblies are debates and troublesome affairs; domestic privacies are haunted with anxieties; in the country is labour; on the sea is terror; in a foreign land, he that has money must live in fear, he that wants it must pine in distress; are you married? you are troubled with suspicions; are you single? you languish in solitude; children occasion toil, and a childless life is a state of destitution; the time of youth is a time of folly, and grey hairs are loaded with infirmity. This choice only, therefore, can be made, either never to receive being, or immediately to lose it."[3]

Such and so gloomy is the prospect, which POSIDIPPUS has laid before us. But we are not to acquiesce too hastily in his determination against the value of existence, for METRODORUS, a philosopher of Athens, has shewn, that life has pleasures as well as pains; and having exhibited the present state of man in brighter colours, draws, with equal appearance of reason, a contrary conclusion:

"You may pass well through any of the paths of life. In public assemblies are honours, and transactions of wisdom; in domestic privacy, is stilness and quiet; in the country are the beauties of nature; on the sea is the hope of gain; in a foreign land, he that is rich is honoured, he that is poor may keep his poverty secret; are you married? you have a chearful house; are you single? you are unincumbered; children are objects of affection; to be without children is to be without care; the time of youth is the time of vigour; and grey hairs are made venerable by piety. It will, therefore, never be a wise man's choice, either not to obtain existence, or to lose it; for every state of life has its felicity."[4]

In these epigrams are included most of the questions, which have engaged the speculations of the enquirers after happiness; and though they will not much assist our determinations, they may, perhaps, equally promote our quiet, by shewing that no absolute determination ever can be formed.

Whether a public station, or private life be desirable, has always been debated. We see here both the allurements and discouragements of civil employments; on one side there is trouble, on the other honour; the management of affairs is vexatious and difficult, but it is the only duty in which wisdom can be conspicuously displayed: it must then still be left to every man to chuse either ease or glory; nor can any general precept be given, since no man can be happy by the prescription of another.

Thus what is said of children by POSIDIPPUS, "that they are occasions of fatigue," and by METRODORUS, "that they are objects of affection," is equally certain; but whether they will give most pain or pleasure, must depend on their future conduct and dispositions, on many causes over which the parent can have little influence: there is, therefore, room for all the caprices of imagination, and desire must be proportioned to the hope or fear that shall happen to predominate.

Such is the uncertainty, in which we are always likely to remain with regard to questions, wherein we have most interest, and which every day affords us fresh opportunity to examine: we may examine, indeed, but we never can decide, because our faculties are unequal to the subject: we see a little, and form an opinion; we see more, and change it.

This inconstancy and unsteadiness, to which we must so often find ourselves liable, ought certainly to teach us moderation and forbearance towards those, who cannot accommodate themselves to our sentiments: if they are deceived, we have no right to attribute their mistake to obstinacy or negligence, because we likewise have been mistaken: we may, perhaps, again change our own opinion; and what excuse shall we be able to find for aversion and malignity conceived against him, whom we shall then find to have committed no fault, and who offended us only by refusing to follow us into error.

It may likewise contribute to soften that resentment, which pride naturally raises against opposition, if we consider, that he, who differs from us, does not always contradict us; he has one view of an object, and we have another; each describes what he sees with equal fidelity, and each regulates his steps by his own eyes: one man, with POSIDIPPUS, looks on celibacy as a state of gloomy solitude, without a partner in joy or a comforter in sorrow; the other considers it, with METRODORUS, as a state free from incumbrances, in which a man is at liberty to chuse his own gratifications, to remove from place to place in quest of pleasure, and to think of nothing but merriment and diversion; full of these notions, one hastens to chuse a wife, and the other laughs at his rashness, or pities his ignorance; yet it is possible that each is right, but that each is right only for himself.

Life is not the object of science: we see a little, very little; and what is beyond we only can conjecture. If we enquire of those who have gone before us, we receive small satisfaction; some have travelled life without observation, and some willingly mislead us. The only thought, therefore, on which we can repose with comfort, is that which presents to us the care of PROVIDENCE, whose eye takes in the whole of things, and under whose direction all involuntary errors will terminate in happiness.

T

No. 111. Tuesday, 27 November 1753.

——Quæ non fecimus ipsi,
Vix ea nostra voco.
                    OVID.[1]

The deeds of long descended ancestors
Are but by grace of imputation ours.
                    DRYDEN.

The evils inseparably annexed to the present condition of man, are so numerous and afflictive, that it has been, from age to age, the task of some to bewail, and of others to solace them: and he, therefore, will be in danger of seeming a common enemy, who shall attempt to depreciate the few pleasures and felicities which nature has allowed us.

Yet I will confess, that I have sometimes employed my thoughts in examining the pretensions that are made to happiness, by the splendid and envied conditions of life; and have not thought the hour unprofitably spent, when I have detected the imposture of counterfeit advantages, and found disquiet lurking under false appearances of gayety and greatness.

It is asserted by a tragic poet,[2] that "est miser nemo nisi comparatus," "no man is miserable, but as he is compared with others happier than himself:" this position is not strictly and philosophically true. He might have said, with rigorous propriety, that no man is happy, but as he is compared with the miserable; for such is the state of this world, that we find in it absolute misery, but happiness only comparative; we may incur as much pain as we can possibly endure, though we can never obtain as much happiness as we might possibly enjoy.

Yet it is certain likewise, that many of our miseries are merely comparative: we are often made unhappy, not by the presence of any real evil, but by the absence of some fictitious good; of something which is not required by any real want of nature, which has not in itself any power of gratification, and which neither reason nor fancy would have prompted us to wish, did we not see it in the possession of others.

For a mind diseased with vain longings after unattainable advantages, no medicine can be prescribed, but an impartial enquiry into the real worth of that which is so ardently desired. It is well known, how much the mind, as well as the eye, is deceived by distance; and, perhaps, it will be found, that of many imagined blessings it may be doubted, whether he that wants or possesses them has more reason to be satisfied with his lot.

The dignity of high birth and long extraction, no man, to whom nature has denied it, can confer upon himself; and, therefore, it deserves to be considered, whether the want of that which can never be gained, may not easily be endured. It is true, that if we consider the triumph and delight with which most of those recount their ancestors who have ancestors to recount, and the artifices by which some who have risen to unexpected fortune endeavour to insert themselves into an honourable stem, we shall be inclined to fancy, that wisdom or virtue may be had by inheritance, or that all the excellencies of a line of progenitors are accumulated on their descendant. Reason, indeed, will soon inform us, that our estimation of birth is arbitrary and capricious, and that dead ancestors can have no influence but upon imagination: let it then be examined, whether one dream may not operate in the place of another; whether he that owes nothing to fore-fathers, may not receive equal pleasure from the consciousness of owing all to himself; whether he may not, with a little meditation, find it more honourable to found than to continue a family, and to gain dignity than transmit it; whether, if he receives no dignity from the virtues of his family, he does not likewise escape the danger of being disgraced by their crimes; and whether he that brings a new name into the world, has not the convenience of playing the game of life without a stake, an opportunity of winning much though he has nothing to lose.

There is another opinion concerning happiness, which approaches much more nearly to universality, but which may, perhaps, with equal reason, be disputed. The pretensions to ancestral honours many of the sons of earth easily see to be ill grounded; but all agree to celebrate the advantage of hereditary riches, and to consider those as the minions of fortune, who are wealthy from their cradles; whose estate is "res non parta labore sed relicta," "the acquisition of another, not of themselves;"[3] and whom a father's industry has dispensed from a laborious attention to arts or commerce, and left at liberty to dispose of life as fancy shall direct them.

If every man were wise and virtuous, capable to discern the best use of time, and resolute to practise it; it might be granted, I think, without hesitation, that total liberty would be a blessing; and that it would be desirable to be left at large to the exercise of religious and social duties, without the interruption of importunate avocations.

But since felicity is relative, and that which is the means of happiness to one man may be to another the cause of misery, we are to consider, what state is best adapted to human nature in its present degeneracy and frailty. And, surely, to far the greater number it is highly expedient, that they should by some settled scheme of duties be rescued from the tyranny of caprice, that they should be driven on by necessity through the paths of life, with their attention confined to a stated task, that they may be less at leisure to deviate into mischief at the call of folly.

When we observe the lives of those whom an ample inheritance has let loose to their own direction, what do we discover that can excite our envy? Their time seems not to pass with much applause from others, or satisfaction to themselves; many squander their exuberance of fortune in luxury and debauchery, and have no other use of money than to inflame their passions, and riot in a wider range of licentiousness; others, less criminal indeed, but, surely, not much to be praised, lie down to sleep and rise up to trifle, are employed every morning in finding expedients to rid themselves of the day, chase pleasure through all the places of public resort, fly from London to Bath and from Bath to London, without any other reason for changing place, but that they go in quest of company as idle and as vagrant as themselves, always endeavouring to raise some new desire that they may have something to persue, to rekindle some hope which they know will be disappointed, changing one amusement for another which a few months will make equally insipid, or sinking into languor and disease for want of something to actuate their bodies or exhilarate their minds.

Whoever has frequented those places, where idlers assemble to escape from solitude, knows that this is generally the state of the wealthy; and from this state it is no great hardship to be debarred. No man can be happy in total idleness: he that should be condemned to lie torpid and motionless, "would fly for recreation," says SOUTH,[4] "to the mines and the gallies;" and it is well, when nature or fortune find employment for those, who would not have known how to procure it for themselves.

He, whose mind is engaged by the acquisition or improvement of a fortune, not only escapes the insipidity of indifference, and the tediousness of inactivity; but gains enjoyments wholly unknown to those, who live lazily on the toil of others; for life affords no higher pleasure, than that of surmounting difficulties, passing from one step of success to another, forming new wishes and seeing them gratified. He that labours in any great or laudable undertaking, has his fatigues first supported by hope, and afterwards rewarded by joy; he is always moving to a certain end, and when he has attained it, an end more distant invites him to a new persuit.

It does not, indeed, always happen, that diligence is fortunate; the wisest schemes are broken by unexpected accidents; the most constant perseverance sometimes toils through life without a recompence; but labour, though unsuccessful, is more eligible than idleness: he that prosecutes a lawful purpose by lawful means, acts always with the approbation of his own reason; he is animated through the course of his endeavours by an expectation which though not certain, he knows to be just; and is at last comforted in his disappointment, by the consciousness that he has not failed by his own fault.

That kind of life is most happy which affords us most opportunities of gaining our own esteem; and what can any man infer in his own favour from a condition to which, however prosperous, he contributed nothing, and which the vilest and weakest of the species would have obtained by the same right, had he happened to be the son of the same father?

To strive with difficulties, and to conquer them, is the highest human felicity; the next, is to strive, and deserve to conquer: but he whose life has passed without a contest, and who can boast neither success nor merit, can survey himself only as a useless filler of existence; and if he is content with his own character, must owe his satisfaction to insensibility.

Thus it appears that the satyrist advised rightly, when he directed us to resign ourselves to the hands of HEAVEN, and to leave to superior powers the determination of our lot:

> *Permittes ipsis expendere Numinibus, quid*
> *Conveniat nobis, rebusque sit utile nostris,*
> *Carior est illis homo quam sibi.*[5]

> Intrust thy fortune to the pow'rs above:
> Leave them to manage for thee, and to grant
> What their unerring wisdom sees thee want.
> In goodness as in greatness they excell.
> Ah! that we lov'd ourselves but half so well.
>   DRYDEN.

What state of life admits most happiness is uncertain; but that uncertainty ought to repress the petulance of comparison, and silence the murmurs of discontent.

T

No. 119. Tuesday, 25 December 1753.

> *Latiùs regnes avidum domando*
> *Spiritum, quàm si Lybiam remotis*
> *Gadibus jungas, et uterque Pœnus*
>   *Serviat uni.*
>   HOR.[1]

> By virtue's precepts to controul
> The thirsty cravings of the soul,

Is over wider realms to reign
Unenvied monarch, than if Spain
You could to distant Lybia join,
And both the Carthages were thine.
                                        FRANCIS.

When SOCRATES was asked, "which of mortal men was to be accounted nearest to the GODS in happiness?" he answered, "that man, who is in want of the fewest things."[2]

In this answer, SOCRATES left it to be guessed by his auditors, whether, by the exemption from want which was to constitute happiness, he meant amplitude of possessions or contraction of desire. And, indeed, there is so little difference between them, that ALEXANDER the great confessed the inhabitant of a tub the next man to the master of the world; and left a declaration to future ages, that if he were not ALEXANDER, he should wish to be DIOGENES.[3]

These two states, however, though they resemble each other in their consequence, differ widely with respect to the facility with which they may be attained. To make great acquisitions, can happen to very few; and in the uncertainty of human affairs, to many it will be incident to labour without reward, and to lose what they already possess by endeavours to make it more; some will always want abilities, and others opportunities to accumulate wealth. It is, therefore, happy, that nature has allowed us a more certain and easy road to plenty; every man may grow rich by contracting his wishes, and by quiet acquiescence in what has been given him supply the absence of more.

Yet so far is almost every man from emulating the happiness of the Gods, by any other means than grasping at their power; that it seems to be the great business of life to create wants as fast as they are satisfied. It has been long observed by moralists, that every man squanders or loses a great part of that life, of which every man knows and deplores the shortness; and it may be remarked with equal justness, that though every man laments his own insufficiency to his happiness, and knows himself a necessitous and precarious being, incessantly solliciting the assistance of others, and feeling wants which his own art or strength cannot supply; yet there is no man, who does not, by the superaddition of unnatural cares, render himself still more dependant; who does not create an artificial poverty, and suffer himself to feel pain for the want of that, of which, when it is gained, he can have no enjoyment.

It must, indeed, be allowed, that as we lose part of our time because it steals away silent and invisible, and many an hour is passed before we recollect that it is passing; so unnatural desires insinuate themselves unobserved into the mind, and we do not perceive that they are gaining upon us, till the pain which they give us awakens us to notice. No man is sufficiently vigilant to take account of every minute of his life, or to watch every motion of his heart. Much of our time likewise is sacrificed to custom; we trifle, because we see others trifle: in the same manner we catch from example the contagion of desire; we see all about us busied in persuit of imaginary good, and begin to bustle in the same chace, lest greater activity should triumph over us.

It is true, that to man, as a member of society, many things become necessary, which, perhaps, in a state of nature are superfluous; and that many things, not absolutely necessary, are yet so useful and convenient, that they cannot easily be spared. I will make yet a more ample and liberal concession. In opulent states and regular governments, the temptations to wealth and rank, and to the distinctions that follow them, are such as no force of understanding finds it easy to resist.

If, therefore, I saw the quiet of life disturbed only by endeavours after wealth and honour; by sollicitude, which the world, whether justly or not, considered as important; I should scarcely have had courage to inculcate any precepts of moderation and forbearance. He that is engaged in a persuit, in which all mankind profess to be his rivals, is supported by the authority of all mankind in the prosecution of his design, and will, therefore, scarcely stop to hear the lectures of a solitary philosopher. Nor am I certain, that the accumulation of honest gain ought to be hindered, or the ambition of just honours always to be repressed. Whatever can enable the possessor to confer any benefit upon others, may be desired upon virtuous principles; and we ought not too rashly to accuse any man of intending to confine the influence of his acquisitions to himself.

But if we look round upon mankind, whom shall we find among those that fortune permits to form their own manners, that is not tormenting himself with a wish for something, of which all the pleasure and all the benefit will cease at the moment of attainment? One man is beggering his posterity to build a house, which when finished he never will inhabit; another is levelling mountains to open a prospect, which, when he has once enjoyed it, he can enjoy no more; another is painting cielings, carving wainscot, and filling his apartments with costly furniture, only that some neighbouring house may not be richer or finer than his own.

That splendor and elegance are not desireable, I am not so abstracted from life as to inculcate; but if we enquire closely into the reason for which they are esteemed, we shall find them valued principally as evidences of wealth. Nothing, therefore, can shew greater depravity of understanding, than to delight in the shew when the reality is wanting; or voluntarily to become poor, that strangers may for a time imagine us to be rich.

But there are yet minuter objects and more trifling anxieties. Men may be found, who are kept from sleep by the want of a shell particularly variegated; who are wasting their lives, in stratagems to obtain a book in a language which they do not understand; who pine with envy at the flowers of another man's parterre; who hover like vultures round the owner of a fossil, in hopes to plunder his cabinet at his death; and who would not much regret to see a street in flames, if a box of medals might be scattered in the tumult.

He that imagines me to speak of these sages in terms exaggerated and hyperbolical, has conversed but little with the race of virtuosos.[4] A slight acquaintance with their studies, and a few visits to their assemblies, would inform him, that nothing is so worthless, but that prejudice and caprice can give it value; nor any thing of so little use, but that by indulging an idle competition or unreasonable pride, a man may make it to himself one of the necessaries of life.

Desires like these, I may surely, without incurring the censure of moroseness, advise every man to repel when they invade his mind; or if he admits them, never to allow them any greater influence, than is necessary to give petty employments the power of pleasing, and diversify the day with slight amusements.

An ardent wish, whatever be its object, will always be able to interrupt tranquillity. What we believe ourselves to want, torments us not in proportion to its real value, but according to the estimation by which we have rated it in our own minds: in some diseases, the patient has been observed to long for food, which scarce any extremity of hunger would in health have compelled him to swallow; but while his organs were thus depraved the craving was irresistible, nor could any rest be obtained till it was appeased by compliance. Of the same nature are the irregular appetites of the mind; though they are often excited by trifles, they are equally disquieting with real wants: the Roman, who wept at the death of his lamprey, felt the same degree of sorrow that extorts tears on other occasions.[5]

Inordinate desires, of whatever kind, ought to be repressed upon yet a higher consideration; they must be considered as enemies not only to HAPPINESS but to VIRTUE. There are men among those commonly reckoned the learned and the wise, who spare no stratagems to remove a competitor at an auction, who will sink the price of a rarity at the expence of truth, and whom it is not safe to trust alone in a library or cabinet. These are faults, which the fraternity seem to look upon as jocular mischiefs, or to think excused by the violence of the temptation: but I shall always fear that he, who accustoms himself to fraud in little things, wants only opportunity to practise it in greater: "he that has hardened himself by killing a sheep," says PYTHAGORAS, "will with less reluctance shed the blood of a man."[6]

To prize every thing according to its REAL use, ought to be the aim of a rational being. There are few things which can much conduce to HAPPINESS, and, therefore, few things to be ardently desired. He that looks upon the business and bustle of the world, with the philosophy with which SOCRATES surveyed the fair at Athens, will turn away at last with his exclamation, "How many things are here which I do not want!"[7]

T

No. 126. Saturday, 19 January 1754.

——Steriles nec legit arenas
Ut caneret paucis, mersitque hoc pulvere verum.
                                                LUCAN.[1]

Canst thou believe the vast eternal mind
Was e'er to Syrts and Libyan sands confin'd?
That he would chuse this waste, this barren ground,
To teach the thin inhabitants around,
And leave his truth in wilds and desarts drown'd?

There has always prevailed among that part of mankind that
addict their minds to speculation, a propensity to talk much
of the delights of retirement; and some of the most pleasing
compositions produced in every age, contain descriptions of the
peace and happiness of a country life.

I know not whether those who thus ambitiously repeat the
praises of solitude, have always considered, how much they
depreciate mankind by declaring, that whatever is excellent or
desirable is to be obtained by departing from them; that the
assistance which we may derive from one another, is not equivalent to the evils which we have to fear; that the kindness of a few
is overbalanced by the malice of many; and that the protection of
society is too dearly purchased, by encountering its dangers and
enduring its oppressions.

These specious representations of solitary happiness, however opprobrious to human nature, have so far spread their
influence over the world, that almost every man delights his
imagination with the hopes of obtaining some time an opportunity of retreat. Many indeed, who enjoy retreat only in imagination, content themselves with believing, that another year will
transport them to rural tranquillity, and die while they talk of
doing what if they had lived longer they would never have done.
But many likewise there are, either of greater resolution or more
credulity, who in earnest try the state which they have been
taught to think thus secure from cares and dangers; and retire

to privacy, either that they may improve their happiness, increase their knowledge, or exalt their virtue.

The greater part of the admirers of solitude, as of all other classes of mankind, have no higher or remoter view, than the present gratification of their passions. Of these some, haughty and impetuous, fly from society only because they cannot bear to repay to others the regard which themselves exact, and think no state of life eligible, but that which places them out of the reach of censure or controul, and affords them opportunities of living in a perpetual compliance with their own inclinations, without the necessity of regulating their actions by any other man's convenience or opinion.

There are others of minds more delicate and tender, easily offended by every deviation from rectitude, soon disgusted by ignorance or impertinence, and always expecting from the conversation of mankind, more elegance, purity and truth than the mingled mass of life will easily afford. Such men are in haste to retire from grossness, falshood and brutality; and hope to find in private habitations at least a negative felicity, and exemption from the shocks and perturbations with which public scenes are continually distressing them.

To neither of these votaries will solitude afford that content, which she has been taught so lavishly to promise. The man of arrogance will quickly discover, that by escaping from his opponents he has lost his flatterers, that greatness is nothing where it is not seen, and power nothing where it cannot be felt: and he, whose faculties are employed in too close an observation of failings and defects, will find his condition very little mended by transferring his attention from others to himself; he will probably soon come back in quest of new objects, and be glad to keep his captiousness employed on any character rather than his own.

Others are seduced into solitude merely by the authority of great names, and expect to find those charms in tranquillity which have allured statesmen and conquerors to the shades: these likewise are apt to wonder at their disappointment, from want of considering, that those whom they aspire to imitate carried with them to their country seats minds full fraught with subjects of reflection, the consciousness of great merit, the memory of illustrious actions, the knowledge of important events, and the seeds of mighty designs to be ripened by future meditation. Solitude was to such men a release from fatigue, and an opportunity of usefulness. But what can retirement confer upon him, who having done nothing can receive no support from his own importance, who having known nothing can find no entertainment in reviewing the past, and who intending nothing can form no hopes from prospects of the future: he can, surely, take no wiser course, than that of losing himself again in the croud, and filling the vacuities of his mind with the news of the day.

Others consider solitude as the parent of philosophy, and retire in expectation of greater intimacies with science, as NUMA repaired to the groves when he conferred with EGERIA.[2] These men have not always reason to repent. Some studies require a continued prosecution of the same train of thought, such as is too often interrupted by the petty avocations of common life: sometimes, likewise, it is necessary, that a multiplicity of objects be at once present to the mind; and every thing, therefore, must be kept at a distance, which may perplex the memory, or dissipate the attention.

But though learning may be conferred by solitude, its application must be attained by general converse. He has learned to no purpose, that is not able to teach; and he will always teach unsuccessfully, who cannot recommend his sentiments by his diction or address.

Even the acquisition of knowledge is often much facilitated by the advantages of society: he that never compares his notions with those of others, readily acquiesces in his first thoughts, and very seldom discovers the objections which may be raised against his opinions; he, therefore, often thinks himself in possession of truth, when he is only fondling an error long since exploded. He that has neither companions nor rivals in his studies, will always applaud his own progress, and think highly of his performances, because he knows not that others have equalled or excelled him. And I am afraid it may be added, that the student who withdraws himself from the world, will soon feel that ardour extinguished which praise or emulation had enkindled, and take the advantage of secrecy to sleep rather than to labour.

There remains yet another set of recluses, whose intention intitles them to higher respect, and whose motives deserve a more serious consideration. These retire from the world, not merely to bask in ease or gratify curiosity, but that being disengaged from common cares, they may employ more time in the duties of religion, that they may regulate their actions with stricter vigilance, and purify their thoughts by more frequent meditation.

To men thus elevated above the mists of mortality, I am far from presuming myself qualified to give directions. On him that appears "to pass through things temporary," with no other care than "not to lose finally the things eternal,"[3] I look with such veneration as inclines me to approve his conduct in the whole, without a minute examination of its parts; yet I could never forbear to wish, that while vice is every day multiplying seducements, and stalking forth with more hardened effrontry, virtue would not withdraw the influence of her presence, or forbear to assert her natural dignity by open and undaunted perseverance in the right. Piety practised in solitude, like the flower that blooms in the desart, may give its fragrance to the winds of heaven, and delight those unbodied spirits that survey the works of GOD and the actions of men; but it bestows no assistance upon earthly beings, and however free from taints of impurity, yet wants the sacred splendor of beneficence.

Our MAKER, who, though he gave us such varieties of temper and such difference of powers yet designed us all for happiness, undoubtedly intended, that we should obtain that happiness by different means. Some are unable to resist the temptations of importunity, or the impetuosity of their own passions incited by the force of present temptations: of these it is undoubtedly the duty, to fly from enemies which they cannot conquer, and to cultivate, in the calm of solitude, that virtue which is too tender to endure the tempests of public life. But there are others, whose passions grow more strong and irregular in privacy; and who cannot maintain an uniform tenor of virtue,

but by exposing their manners to the public eye, and assisting
the admonitions of conscience with the fear of infamy: for such
it is dangerous to exclude all witnesses of their conduct, till
they have formed strong habits of virtue, and weakened their
passions by frequent victories. But there is a higher order of men
so inspirited with ardour, and so fortified with resolution, that
the world passes before them without influence or regard: these
ought to consider themselves as appointed the guardians of
mankind; they are placed in an evil world, to exhibit public
examples of good life; and may be said, when they withdraw to
solitude, to desert the station which PROVIDENCE assigned
them.

T

No. 137. Tuesday, 26 February 1754.

Τί δ'ἔρεξα,
PYTH.[1]

What have I been doing?

As man is a being very sparingly furnished with the power of
prescience, he can provide for the future only by considering the
past; and as futurity is all in which he has any real interest, he
ought very diligently to use the only means by which he can be
enabled to enjoy it, and frequently to revolve the experiments
which he has hitherto made upon life, that he may gain wisdom
from his mistakes and caution from his miscarriages.

Though I do not so exactly conform to the precepts of
PYTHAGORAS, as to practise every night this solemn recollection, yet I am not so lost in dissipation as wholly to omit it;
nor can I forbear sometimes to enquire of myself, in what
employments my life has passed away. Much of my time has
sunk into nothing, and left no trace by which it can be distinguished, and of this I now only know, that it was once in my
power and might once have been improved.

Of other parts of life memory can give some account: at some hours I have been gay, and at others serious; I have sometimes mingled in conversation, and sometimes meditated in solitude; one day has been spent in consulting the antient sages, and another in writing ADVENTURERS.

At the conclusion of any undertaking, it is usual to compute the loss and profit. As I shall soon cease to write ADVENTURERS, I could not forbear lately to consider what has been the consequence of my labours; and whether I am to reckon the hours laid out in these compositions, as applied to a good and laudable purpose, or suffered to fume away in useless evaporations.

That I have intended well, I have the attestation of my own heart; but good intentions may be frustrated, when they are executed without suitable skill, or directed to an end unattainable in itself.

Some there are, who leave writers very little room for self congratulation; some who affirm, that books have no influence upon the public, that no age was ever made better by its authors, and that to call upon mankind to correct their manners, is, like XERXES, to scourge the wind or shackle the torrent.[2]

This opinion they pretend to support by unfailing experience. The world is full of fraud and corruption, rapine and malignity; interest is the ruling motive of mankind, and every one is endeavouring to increase his own stores of happiness by perpetual accumulation, without reflecting upon the numbers whom his superfluity condemns to want: in this state of things a book of morality is published, in which charity and benevolence are strongly enforced; and it is proved beyond opposition, that men are happy in proportion as they are virtuous, and rich as they are liberal. The book is applauded, and the author is preferred; he imagines his applause deserved, and receives less pleasure from the acquisition of reward, than the consciousness of merit. Let us look again upon mankind: interest is still the ruling motive, and the world is yet full of fraud and corruption, malevolence and rapine.

The difficulty of confuting this assertion, arises merely from its generality and comprehension: to overthrow it by a detail of distinct facts, requires a wider survey of the world than human eyes can take; the progress of reformation is gradual and silent, as the extension of evening shadows; we know that they were short at noon, and are long at sun-set, but our senses were not able to discern their increase; we know of every civil nation that it was once savage, and how was it reclaimed but by precept and admonition?

Mankind are universally corrupt, but corrupt in different degrees; as they are universally ignorant, yet with greater or less irradiations of knowledge. How has knowledge or virtue been increased and preserved in one place beyond another, but by diligent inculcation and rational inforcement.

Books of morality are daily written, yet its influence is still little in the world; so the ground is annually ploughed, and yet multitudes are in want of bread. But, surely, neither the labours of the moralist nor of the husbandman are vain: let them for a while neglect their tasks, and their usefulness will be known; the wickedness that is now frequent would become universal, the bread that is now scarce would wholly fail.

The power, indeed, of every individual is small, and the consequence of his endeavours imperceptible in a general prospect of the world. PROVIDENCE has given no man ability to do much, that something might be left for every man to do. The business of life is carried on by a general co-operation; in which the part of any single man can be no more distinguished, than the effect of a particular drop when the meadows are floated by a summer shower: yet every drop increases the inundation, and every hand adds to the happiness or misery of mankind.

That a writer, however zealous or eloquent, seldom works a visible effect upon cities or nations, will readily be granted. The book which is read most, is read by few, compared with those that read it not; and of those few, the greater part peruse it with dispositions that very little favour their own improvement.

It is difficult to enumerate the several motives, which procure to books the honour of perusal: spite, vanity, and curiosity, hope and fear, love and hatred, every passion which incites to any other action, serves at one time or other to stimulate a reader.

Some are fond to take a celebrated volume into their hands, because they hope to distinguish their penetration, by finding faults which have escaped the public; others eagerly buy it in the first bloom of reputation, that they may join the chorus of praise, and not lag, as FALSTAFF terms it, in "the rearward of the fashion."[3]

Some read for stile, and some for argument: one has little care about the sentiment, he observes only how it is expressed; another regards not the conclusion, but is diligent to mark how it is inferred: they read for other purposes, than the attainment of practical knowledge; and are no more likely to grow wise by an examination of a treatise of moral prudence, than an architect to inflame his devotion by considering attentively the proportions of a temple.

Some read that they may embellish their conversation, or shine in dispute; some that they may not be detected in ignorance, or want the reputation of literary accomplishments: but the most general and prevalent reason of study, is the impossibility of finding another amusement equally cheap or constant, equally independent on the hour or the weather. He that wants money to follow the chace of pleasure through her yearly circuit, and is left at home when the gay world rolls to Bath or Tunbridge; he whose gout compells him to hear from his chamber, the rattle of chariots transporting happier beings to plays and assemblies, will be forced to seek in books a refuge from himself.

The author is not wholly useless, who provides innocent amusements for minds like these. There are in the present state of things so many more instigations to evil, than incitements to good, that he who keeps men in a neutral state, may be justly considered as a benefactor to life.

But, perhaps, it seldom happens, that study terminates in mere pastime. Books have always a secret influence on the understanding; we cannot at pleasure obliterate ideas; he that reads books of science, though without any fixed desire of improvement, will grow more knowing; he that entertains himself with moral or religious treatises, will imperceptibly advance in goodness; the ideas which are often offered to the mind, will at last find a lucky moment when it is disposed to receive them.

It is, therefore, urged without reason, as a discouragement to writers, that there are already books sufficient in the world; that all the topics of persuasion have been discussed, and every important question clearly stated and justly decided; and that, therefore, there is no room to hope, that pigmies should conquer where heroes have been defeated, or that the petty copiers of the present time should advance the great work of reformation, which their predecessors were forced to leave unfinished.

Whatever be the present extent of human knowledge, it is not only finite, and therefore in its own nature capable of increase; but so narrow, that almost every understanding may by a diligent application of its powers hope to enlarge it. It is, however, not necessary, that a man should forbear to write, till he has discovered some truth unknown before; he may be sufficiently useful, by only diversifying the surface of knowledge, and luring the mind by a new appearance to a second view of those beauties which it had passed over inattentively before. Every writer may find intellects correspondent to his own, to whom his expressions are familiar, and his thoughts congenial; and, perhaps, truth is often more successfully propagated by men of moderate abilities, who, adopting the opinions of others, have no care but to explain them clearly, than by subtile specula-tists and curious searchers, who exact from their readers powers equal to their own, and if their fabrics of science be strong take no care to render them accessible.

For my part, I do not regret the hours which I have laid out on these little compositions. That the world has grown apparently better, since the publication of the ADVENTURER, I have not observed; but am willing to think, that many have been affected by single sentiments, of which it is their business to renew the impression; that many have caught hints of truth, which it is now their duty to persue; and that those who have received no improvement, have wanted not opportunity but intention to improve.

T

No. 138. Saturday, 2 March 1754.

Quid purè tranquillet? honos, an dulce lucellum,
An secretum iter et fallentis semita vitæ?

HOR.[1]

Whether the tranquil mind and pure,
Honours or wealth our bliss insure;
Or down through life unknown to stray,
Where lonely leads the silent way.

FRANCIS.

Having considered the importance of authors to the welfare of
the public, I am led by a natural train of thought, to reflect on
their condition with regard to themselves; and to enquire, what
degree of happiness or vexation is annexed to the difficult and
laborious employment, of providing instruction or entertainment for mankind.

In estimating the pain or pleasure of any particular state,
every man, indeed, draws his decisions from his own breast,
and cannot with certainty determine, whether other minds are
affected by the same causes in the same manner. Yet by this
criterion we must be content to judge, because no other can
be obtained; and, indeed, we have no reason to think it very
fallacious, for excepting here and there an anomalous mind,
which either does not feel like others, or dissembles its sensibility, we find men unanimously concur in attributing happiness
or misery to particular conditions, as they agree in acknowledging the cold of winter and the heat of autumn.

If we apply to authors themselves for an account of their
state, it will appear very little to deserve envy; for they have in
all ages been addicted to complaint. The neglect of learning, the
ingratitude of the present age, and the absurd preference by
which ignorance and dulness often obtain favour and rewards,
have been from age to age topics of invective; and few have left
their names to posterity, without some appeal to future candour
from the perverseness and malice of their own times.

I have, nevertheless, been often inclined to doubt, whether authors, however querulous, are in reality more miserable than their fellow mortals. The present life is to all a state of infelicity; every man, like an author, believes himself to merit more than he obtains, and solaces the present with the prospect of the future: others, indeed, suffer those disappointments in silence, of which the writer complains, to shew how well he has learned the art of lamentation.

There is at least one gleam of felicity, of which few writers have missed the enjoyment: he whose hopes have so far over-powered his fears, as that he has resolved to stand forth a candidate for fame, seldom fails to amuse himself, before his appearance, with pleasing scenes of affluence or honour; while his fortune is yet under the regulation of fancy, he easily models it to his wish, suffers no thoughts of critics or rivals to intrude upon his mind, but counts over the bounties of patronage or listens to the voice of praise.

Some there are, that talk very luxuriously of the second period of an author's happiness, and tell of the tumultuous raptures of invention, when the mind riots in imagery, and the choice stands suspended between different sentiments.

These pleasures, I believe, may sometimes be indulged to those, who come to a subject of disquisition with minds full of ideas, and with fancies so vigorous, as easily to excite, select, and arrange them. To write, is, indeed, no unpleasing employment, when one sentiment readily produces another, and both ideas and expressions present themselves at the first summons: but such happiness, the greatest genius does not always obtain; and common writers know it only to such a degree, as to credit its possibility. Composition is, for the most part, an effort of slow diligence and steady perseverance, to which the mind is dragged by necessity or resolution, and from which the attention is every moment starting to more delightful amusements.

It frequently happens, that a design which, when considered at a distance, gave flattering hopes of facility, mocks us in the execution with unexpected difficulties; the mind which, while it considered it in the gross, imagined itself amply furnished with materials, finds sometimes an unexpected barrenness and vacuity, and wonders whither all those ideas are vanished, which a little before seemed struggling for emission.

Sometimes many thoughts present themselves; but so confused and unconnected, that they are not without difficulty reduced to method, or concatenated in a regular and dependent series: the mind falls at once into a labyrinth, of which neither the beginning nor end can be discovered, and toils and struggles without progress or extrication.

It is asserted by HORACE,[2] that "if matter be once got together, words will be found with very little difficulty;" a position which, though sufficiently plausible to be inserted in poetical precepts, is by no means strictly and philosophically true. If words were naturally and necessarily consequential to sentiments, it would always follow, that he who has most knowledge must have most eloquence, and that every man would clearly express what he fully understood: yet we find, that to think, and to discourse, are often the qualities of different persons; and many books might surely be produced, where just and noble sentiments are degraded and obscured by unsuitable diction.

Words, therefore, as well as things, claim the care of an author. Indeed, of many authors, and those not useless or contemptible, words are almost the only care: many make it their study, not so much to strike out new sentiments, as to recommend those which are already known to more favourable notice by fairer decorations; but every man, whether he copies or invents, whether he delivers his own thoughts or those of another, has often found himself deficient in the power of expression, big with ideas which he could not utter, obliged to ransack his memory for terms adequate to his conceptions, and at last unable to impress upon his reader the image existing in his own mind.

It is one of the common distresses of a writer, to be within a word of a happy period, to want only a single epithet to give amplification its full force, to require only a correspondent term in order to finish a paragraph with elegance and make one of its members answer to the other: but these deficiencies cannot always be supplied; and after long study and vexation, the passage is turned anew, and the web unwoven that was so nearly finished.

But when thoughts and words are collected and adjusted, and the whole composition at last concluded, it seldom gratifies the author, when he comes coolly and deliberately to review it, with the hopes which had been excited in the fury of the performance: novelty always captivates the mind; as our thoughts rise fresh upon us, we readily believe them just and original, which, when the pleasure of production is over, we find to be mean and common, or borrowed from the works of others, and supplied by memory rather than invention.

But though it should happen, that the writer finds no such faults in his performance, he is still to remember, that he looks upon it with partial eyes; and when he considers, how much men who could judge of others with great exactness, have often failed in judging of themselves, he will be afraid of deciding too hastily in his own favour, or of allowing himself to contemplate with too much complacence, treasure that has not yet been brought to the test, nor passed the only trial that can stamp its value.

From the public, and only from the public, is he to await a confirmation of his claim, and a final justification of self esteem; but the public is not easily persuaded to favour an author. If mankind were left to judge for themselves, it is reasonable to imagine, that of such writings, at least, as describe the movements of the human passions, and of which every man carries the arche-type within him, a just opinion would be formed; but whoever has remarked the fate of books, must have found it governed by other causes, than general consent arising from general conviction. If a new performance happens not to fall into the hands of some, who have courage to tell, and authority to propagate their opinion, it often remains long in obscurity, and perhaps perishes unknown and unexamined. A few, a very few, commonly constitute the taste of the time; the judgment which they have once pronounced, some are too lazy to discuss, and some too timorous to contradict: it may, however, be I think observed, that their power is greater to depress than exalt, as mankind are more credulous of censure than of praise.

This perversion of the public judgment, is not to be rashly numbered amongst the miseries of an author; since it commonly serves, after miscarriage, to reconcile him to himself. Because the world has sometimes passed an unjust sentence, he readily concludes the sentence unjust by which his performance is condemned; because some have been exalted above their merits by partiality, he is sure to ascribe the success of a rival, not to the merit of his work, but the zeal of his patrons. Upon the whole, as the author seems to share all the common miseries of life, he appears to partake likewise of its lenitives and abatements.

T

THE IDLER
(1758–60)

No. 1. Saturday, 15 April 1758.

Vacui sub umbra
Lusimus.
HOR.[1]

Those who attempt periodical Essays seem to be often stopped in the beginning, by the difficulty of finding a proper Title. Two Writers, since the time of the Spectator, have assumed his Name, without any pretensions to lawful inheritance; an effort was once made to revive the Tatler; and the strange appellations, by which other Papers have been called, show that the Authours were distressed, like the Natives of *America*, who come to the *Europeans* to beg a Name.[2]

It will be easily believed of the *Idler*, that if his Title had required any search, he never would have found it. Every mode of life has its conveniencies. The *Idler*, who habituates himself to be satisfied with what he can most easily obtain, not only escapes labours which are often fruitless, but sometimes succeeds better than those who despise all that is within their reach, and think every thing more valuable as it is harder to be acquired.

If similitude of manners be a motive to kindness, the *Idler* may flatter himself with universal Patronage. There is no single character under which such numbers are comprised. Every man is, or hopes to be, an *Idler*. Even those who seem to differ most from us are hastening to encrease our Fraternity; as peace is the end of war, so to be idle is the ultimate purpose of the busy.

There is perhaps no Appellation by which a Writer can better denote his Kindred to the human Species. It has been found hard to describe Man by an adequate Definition. Some Philosophers have called him a reasonable Animal, but others have considered Reason as a Quality of which many creatures partake. He has been termed likewise a laughing Animal; but it is said that some Men have never laughed. Perhaps Man may be more properly distinguished as an Idle Animal; for there is no Man who is not sometimes Idle. It is at least a Definition from which none that shall find it in this Paper can be excepted; for who can be more idle than the Reader of the *Idler?*

That the Definition may be complete, Idleness must be not only the general, but the peculiar characteristic of Man; and perhaps Man is the only Being that can properly be called Idle, that does by others what he might do himself, or sacrifices Duty or Pleasure to the Love of Ease.

Scarcely any Name can be imagined from which less envy or competition is to be dreaded. The *Idler* has no Rivals or Enemies. The Man of Business forgets him; the Man of Enterprize despises him; and though such as tread the same track of Life, fall commonly into jealousy and discord, *Idlers* are always found to associate in Peace, and he who is most famed for doing Nothing, is glad to meet another as idle as himself.

What is to be expected from this Paper, whether it will be uniform or various, learned or familiar, serious or gay, political or moral, continued or interrupted, it is hoped that no Reader will enquire. That the *Idler* has some scheme, cannot be doubted; for to form schemes is the *Idler*'s privilege. But tho' he has many projects in his head, he is now grown sparing of communication, having observed, that his hearers are apt to remember what he forgets himself; that his tardiness of execution exposes him to the encroachments of those who catch a hint and fall to work; and that very specious plans, after long contrivance and pompous displays, have subsided in weariness without a trial, and without miscarriage have been blasted by derision.

Something the *Idler's* Character may be supposed to promise. Those that are curious after diminutive History, who watch the Revolutions of Families, and the Rise and Fall of Characters either Male or Female, will hope to be gratified by this Paper; for the *Idler* is always inquisitive and seldom retentive. He that delights in Obloquy and Satire, and wishes to see Clouds gathering over any Reputation that dazzles him with its Brightness, will snatch up the *Idler*'s Essays with a beating Heart. The *Idler* is naturally censorious; those who attempt nothing themselves think every thing easily performed, and consider the unsuccessful always as criminal.

I think it necessary to give notice, that I make no contract, nor incur any obligation. If those who depend on the *Idler* for intelligence and entertainment, should suffer the disappointment which commonly follows ill-placed expectations, they are to lay the blame only on themselves.

Yet Hope is not wholly to be cast away. The *Idler*, tho' sluggish, is yet alive, and may sometimes be stimulated to vigour and activity. He may descend into profoundness, or tower into sublimity; for the diligence of an *Idler* is rapid and impetuous, as ponderous bodies forced into velocity move with violence proportionate to their weight.

But these vehement exertions of intellect cannot be frequent, and he will therefore gladly receive help from any Correspondent, who shall enable him to please without his own labour. He excludes no style, he prohibits no subject; only let him that writes to the *Idler* remember, that his letters must not be long; no words are to be squandered in declarations of esteem, or confessions of inability; conscious Dulness has little right to be prolix, and Praise is not so welcome to the *Idler* as Quiet.

No. 5. Saturday, 13 May 1758.

Κάλλος,
ἀντ' ἀσπίδων ἁπασῶν,
ἀντ' ἐγχέων ἁπάντων
ANAC.[1]

Our Military Operations are at last begun; our troops are marching in all the pomp of war, and a camp is marked out on the Isle of Wight; the heart of every Englishman now swells with confidence, though somewhat softened by generous compassion for the consternation and distresses of our enemies.

This formidable armament and splendid march produce different effects upon different minds, according to the boundless diversities of temper, occupation, and habits of thought.

Many a tender Maiden considers her Lover as already lost, because he cannot reach the camp but by crossing the sea; Men, of a more political understanding, are persuaded that we shall now see, in a few days, the Ambassadors of France supplicating for pity. Some are hoping for a bloody battle, because a bloody battle makes a vendible[2] narrative; some are composing songs of victory; some planning arches of triumph; and some are mixing fireworks for the celebration of a peace.

Of all extensive and complicated objects different parts are selected by different eyes; and minds are variously affected, as they vary their attention. The care of the publick is now fixed upon our Soldiers, who are leaving their native country to wander, none can tell how long, in the pathless desarts of the *Isle of Wight*. The Tender sigh for their sufferings, and the Gay drink to their success. I, who look, or believe myself to look, with more philosophick eyes, on human affairs, must confess, that I saw the troops march with little emotion; my thoughts were fixed upon other scenes, and the tear stole into my eyes, not for those who were going away, but for those who were left behind.

We have no reason to doubt but our troops will proceed with proper caution; there are men among them who can take care of themselves. But how shall the Ladies endure without them? By what arts can they, who have long had no joy, but from the civilities of a Soldier, now amuse their hours, and solace their separation?

Of fifty thousand men, now destined to different stations, if we allow each to have been occasionally necessary only to four women, a short computation will inform us, that two hundred thousand Ladies are left to languish in distress; two hundred thousand Ladies, who must run to Sales and Auctions without an attendant; sit at the Play, without a Critick to direct their opinion; buy their Fans by their own judgment; dispose Shells by their own invention; walk in the Mall without a Gallant; go to the Gardens without a Protector; and shuffle Cards with vain impatience for want of a fourth to complete the party.

Of these Ladies, some, I hope, have lapdogs, and some monkeys, but they are unsatisfactory companions. Many useful offices are performed by men of scarlet, to which neither dog nor monkey has adequate abilities: A parrot, indeed, is as fine as a Colonel, and if he has been much used to good company, is not wholly without conversation; but a parrot, after all, is a poor little creature, and has neither sword nor shoulder-knot, can neither dance nor play at cards.

Since the soldiers must obey the call of their duty, and go to that side of the kingdom which faces *France*, I know not why the Ladies, who cannot live without them, should not follow them. The prejudices and pride of man have long presumed the sword and spindle made for different hands, and denied the other sex, to partake the grandeur of military glory. This notion may be consistently enough received in *France*, where the Salic law[3] excludes females from the Throne; but we, who allow them to be Sovereigns, may surely suppose them capable to be soldiers.

It were to be wished that some man, whose experience and authority might enforce regard, would propose that our encampments for the present year should comprise an equal number of men and women, who should march and fight in mingled bodies. If proper Colonels were once appointed, and the drums ordered to beat for female volunteers, our regiments would soon be filled without the reproach or cruelty of an impress.

Of these Heroines, some might serve on foot, under the denomination of the *Female Buffs*, and some on horseback, with the title of *Lady Hussars*.

What objections can be made to this scheme I have endeavoured maturely to consider; and cannot find that a modern soldier has any duties, except that of obedience, which a Lady cannot perform. If the hair has lost its powder, a Lady has a puff. If a coat be spotted, a Lady has a brush. Strength is of less importance since fire-arms have been used; blows of the hand are now seldom exchanged; and what is there to be done in the charge or the retreat beyond the powers of a sprightly maiden?

Our masculine squadrons will not suppose themselves disgraced by their auxiliaries, till they have done something which women could not have done. The troops of *Braddock* never saw their enemies, and perhaps were defeated by women.[4] If our *American* General had headed an army of girls, he might still have built a fort, and taken it. Had *Minorca*[5] been defended by a female garrison, it might have been surrendered, as it was, without a breach; and I cannot but think, that seven thousand women might have ventured to look at *Rochfort*, sack a village, rob a vineyard, and return in safety.[6]

No. 10. Saturday, 17 June 1758.

Credulity, or Confidence of opinion too great for the evidence from which opinion is derived, we find to be a general weakness imputed by every sect and party to all others, and indeed by every man to every other man.

Of all kinds of Credulity, the most obstinate and wonderful is that of political zealots; of men, who, being numbered, they know not how nor why, in any of the parties that divide a state, resign the use of their own eyes and ears, and resolve to believe nothing that does not favour those whom they profess to follow.[1]

The Bigot of Philosophy is seduced by authorities which he has not always opportunities to examine, is intangled in systems by which truth and falshood are inextricably complicated, or undertakes to talk on subjects, which Nature did not form him able to comprehend.

The Cartesian,[2] who denies that his horse feels the spur, or that the hare is afraid when the hounds approach her; the Disciple of *Malbranche*,[3] who maintains that the man was not hurt by the bullet, which, according to vulgar apprehensions, swept away his legs; the Follower of *Berkley*,[4] who, while he sits writing at his table, declares that he has neither table, paper, nor fingers; have all the honour at least of being deceived by fallacies not easily detected, and may plead that they did not forsake truth, but for appearances which they were not able to distinguish from it.

But the man who engages in a party has seldom to do with any thing remote or abstruse. The present state of things is before his eyes; and, if he cannot be satisfied without retrospection, yet he seldom extends his views beyond the historical events of the last century. All the knowledge that he can want is within his attainment, and most of the arguments which he can hear are within his capacity.

Yet so it is that an *Idler* meets every hour of his life with men who have different opinions upon every thing past, present, and future; who deny the most notorious facts, contradict the most cogent truths, and persist in asserting to-day what they asserted yesterday, in defiance of evidence, and contempt of confutation.

Two of my companions, who are grown old in Idleness, are *Tom Tempest* and *Jack Sneaker*. Both of them consider themselves as neglected by their parties, and therefore intitled to credit, for why should they favour ingratitude? They are both men of integrity where no factious interest is to be promoted, and both lovers of truth, when they are not heated with political debate.

Tom Tempest is a steady friend to the House of *Stuart*. He can recount the prodigies that have appeared in the sky, and the calamities that have afflicted the nation every year from the Revolution, and is of opinion, that if the exiled family had continued to reign, there would have neither been worms in our ships nor caterpillars on our trees. He wonders that the nation was not awakened by the hard frost to a revocation of the true King, and is hourly afraid that the whole island will be lost in the sea. He believes that King *William* burned *Whitehall* that he might steal the furniture, and that *Tillotson*⁵ died an Atheist. Of Queen *Anne* he speaks with more tenderness, owns that she meant well, and can tell by whom and why she was poisoned. In the succeeding reigns all has been corruption, malice, and design. He believes that nothing ill has ever happened for these forty years by chance or error; he holds that the battle of *Dettingen*⁶ was won by mistake, and that of *Fontenoy*⁷ lost by contract; that the *Victory* was sunk by a private order; that *Cornhill*⁸ was fired by emissaries from the Council; and the arch of *Westminster-Bridge* was so contrived as to sink on purpose that the nation might be put to charge. He considers the new road to *Islington* as an encroachment on liberty, and often asserts that *broad wheels* will be the ruin of *England*.⁹

Tom is generally vehement and noisy, but nevertheless has some secrets which he always communicates in a whisper. Many and many a time has *Tom* told me, in a corner, that our miseries were almost at an end, and that we should see, in a month, another Monarch on the Throne; the time elapses without a Revolution; *Tom* meets me again with new intelligence, the whole scheme is now settled, and we shall see great events in another month.

Jack Sneaker is a hearty adherent to the present establishment; he has known those who saw the bed into which the Pretender was conveyed in a warming-pan. He often rejoices that the nation was not enslaved by the *Irish*. He believes that King *William* never lost a battle, and that if he had lived one year longer he would have conquered *France*. He holds that *Charles* the First was a Papist. He allows there were some good men in the reign of Queen *Anne*, but the Peace of *Utrecht*[10] brought a blast upon the nation, and has been the cause of all the evil that we have suffered to the present hour. He believes that the scheme of the *South Sea*[11] was well intended, but that it miscarried by the influence of *France*. He considers a standing army as the bulwark of liberty, thinks us secured from corruption by septennial Parliaments, relates how we are enriched and strengthened by the Electoral Dominions,[12] and declares that the public debt is a blessing to the nation.

Yet amidst all this prosperity, poor *Jack* is hourly disturbed by the dread of Popery. He wonders that some stricter laws are not made against Papists, and is sometimes afraid that they are busy with *French* gold among the Bishops and Judges.

He cannot believe that the Nonjurors are so quiet for nothing, they must certainly be forming some plot for the establishment of Popery; he does not think the present Oaths sufficiently binding, and wishes that some better security could be found for the succession of *Hanover*. He is zealous for the naturalization of foreign Protestants, and rejoiced at the admission of the *Jews* to the *English* privileges, because he thought a *Jew* would never be a Papist.[13]

No. 17. Saturday, 5 August 1758.

The rainy weather which has continued the last month, is said to have given great disturbance to the inspectors of barometers. The oraculous glasses have deceived their votaries; shower has succeeded shower, though they predicted sunshine and dry skies; and by fatal confidence in these fallacious promises, many coats have lost their gloss, and many curls been moistened to flaccidity.

This is one of the distresses to which mortals subject themselves by the pride of speculation. I had no part in this learned disappointment, who am content to credit my senses, and to believe that rain will fall when the air blackens, and that the weather will be dry when the sun is bright. My caution indeed does not always preserve me from a shower. To be wet may happen to the genuine *Idler*, but to be wet in opposition to Theory, can befall only the *Idler* that pretends to be busy. Of those that spin out life in trifles, and die without a memorial, many flatter themselves with high opinions of their own importance, and imagine that they are every day adding some improvement to human life. To be idle and to be poor have always been reproaches, and therefore every man endeavours with his utmost care, to hide his poverty from others, and his *Idleness* from himself.

Among those whom I never could persuade to rank themselves with *Idlers*, and who speak with indignation of my morning sleeps and nocturnal rambles; one passes the day in catching spiders that he may count their eyes with a microscope; another erects his head, and exhibits the dust of a marigold separated from the flower with dexterity worthy of *Leeuwenhoeck*[1] himself. Some turn the wheel of Electricity, some suspend rings to a loadstone, and find that what they did yesterday they can do again to-day. Some register the changes of the wind, and die fully convinced that the wind is changeable.

There are men yet more profound, who have heard that two colourless liquors may produce a colour by union, and that two cold bodies will grow hot if they are mingled: they mingle them, and produce the effect expected, say it is strange, and mingle them again.

The *Idlers* that sport only with inanimate nature may claim some indulgence; if they are useless they are still innocent: but there are others, whom I know not how to mention without more emotion than my love of quiet willingly admits. Among the inferiour Professors of medical knowledge, is a race of wretches, whose lives are only varied by varieties of cruelty; whose favourite amusement is to nail dogs to tables and open them alive; to try how long life may be continued in various degrees of mutilation, or with the excision or laceration of the vital parts; to examine whether burning irons are felt more acutely by the bone or tendon; and whether the more lasting agonies are produced by poison forced into the mouth or injected into the veins.

It is not without reluctance that I offend the sensibility of the tender mind with images like these. If such cruelties were not practised it were to be desired that they should not be conceived, but since they are published every day with ostentation, let me be allowed once to mention them, since I mention them with abhorrence.

Mead has invidiously remarked of *Woodward* that he gathered shells and stones, and would pass for a Philosopher.[2] With pretensions much less reasonable, the anatomical novice tears out the living bowels of an animal, and stiles himself Physician, prepares himself by familiar cruelty for that profession which he is to exercise upon the tender and the helpless, upon feeble bodies and broken minds, and by which he has opportunities to extend his arts of torture, and continue those experiments upon infancy and age, which he has hitherto tried upon cats and dogs.

What is alleged in defence of these hateful practices, every one knows; but the truth is, that by knives, fire, and poison, knowledge is not always sought, and is very seldom attained. The experiments that have been tried, are tried again; he that burned an animal with irons yesterday, will be willing to amuse himself with burning another to-morrow. I know not, that by living dissections any discovery has been made by which a single malady is more easily cured. And if the knowledge of Physiology has been somewhat encreased, he surely buys knowledge dear, who learns the use of the lacteals at the expence of his humanity. It is time that universal resentment should arise against these horrid operations, which tend to harden the heart, extinguish those sensations which give man confidence in man, and make the Physician more dreadful than the gout or stone.

No. [22]. Saturday, 9 September 1758.[1]

Many Naturalists are of opinion, that the Animals which we commonly consider as mute, have the power of imparting their thoughts to one another. That they can express general sensations is very certain; every Being that can utter sounds, has a different voice for pleasure and for pain. The Hound informs his fellows when he scents his game; the Hen calls her chickens to their food by her cluck, and drives them from danger by her scream.

Birds have the greatest variety of notes; they have indeed a variety, which seems almost sufficient to make a speech adequate to the purposes of a life, which is regulated by instinct, and can admit little change or improvement. To the cries of Birds, curiosity or superstition has been always attentive, many have studied the language of the feathered tribes, and some have boasted that they understood it.

The most skilful or most confident interpreters of the Silvan Dialogues have been commonly found among the Philosophers of the East, in a country where the calmness of the air, and the mildness of the seasons, allow the Student to pass a great part of the year in groves and bowers. But what may be done in one place by peculiar opportunities, may be performed in another by peculiar diligence. A Shepherd of Bohemia has, by long abode in the forests, enabled himself to understand the voice of Birds, at least he relates with great confidence a story of which the credibility may be considered by the learned.

As I was sitting, (said he) within a hollow rock, and watching my Sheep that fed in the valley, I heard two Vultures interchangeably crying on the summit of the cliff. Both voices were earnest and deliberate. My curiosity prevailed over my care of the flock; I climbed slowly and silently from crag to crag, concealed among the shrubs, till I found a cavity where I might sit and listen without suffering, or giving disturbance.

I soon perceived, that my labour would be well repaid; for an old Vulture was sitting on a naked prominence, with her young about her, whom she was instructing in the arts of a Vulture's life, and preparing, by the last Lecture, for their final dismission to the mountains and the skies.

My children, said the old Vulture, you will the less want my instructions because you have had my practice before your eyes; you have seen me snatch from the Farm the Houshold Fowl, you have seen me seize the Leveret in the Bush, and the Kid in the Pasture, you know how to fix your talons, and how to balance your flight when you are laden with your prey. But you remember the taste of more delicious food; I have often regaled you with the flesh of man. Tell us, said the young Vultures, where man may be found, and how he may be known; his flesh is surely the natural food of a Vulture. Why have you never brought a Man in your talons to the Nest? He is too bulky, said the Mother; when we find a Man, we can only tear away his flesh and leave his bones upon the ground. Since man is so big, said the young ones, how do you kill him. You are afraid of the Wolf and of the Bear, by what power are Vultures superior to Man, is Man more defenseless than a Sheep? We have not the strength of Man, returned the Mother, and I am sometimes in doubt whether we have the subtilty; and the Vultures would seldom feast upon his flesh, had not nature, that devoted him to our uses, infused into him a strange ferocity, which I have never observed in any other Being that feeds upon the Earth. Two herds of Men will often meet and shake the Earth with noise, and fill the Air with fire. When you hear noise and see fire which flashes along the ground, hasten to the place with your swiftest wing, for men are surely destroying one another; you will then find the ground smoking with blood and covered with carcasses, of which many are dismembered and mangled for the convenience of the Vulture. But when Men have killed their prey, said the Pupil, Why do they not eat it? When the Wolf has killed a Sheep he suffers not the Vulture to touch it till he has satisfied himself. Is not Man another kind of Wolf? Man, said the Mother, is the only Beast who kills that which he does not devour, and this quality makes him so much a benefactor to our species. If Men kill our prey and lay it in our way, said the young one, what need shall we have of labouring for ourselves? Because Man will, sometimes, replied the Mother, remain for a long time quiet in his den. The old Vultures will tell you when you are to watch his motions. When you see men in great numbers moving close together, like a flight of Storks, you may conclude that they are hunting, and that you will soon revel in human blood. But still, said the young one, I would gladly know the reason of this mutual slaughter. I could never kill what I could not eat. My Child, said the Mother, this is a question which I cannot answer, tho' I am reckoned the most subtile Bird of the mountain. When I was young I used frequently to visit the ayry of an old Vulture who dwelt upon the Carpathian rocks; he had made many observations; he knew the places that afforded prey round his habitation, as far in every direction as the strongest wing can fly between the rising and setting of the Summer Sun; he had fed year after year on the entrails of Men. His opinion was, That Men had only the appearance of Animal Life, being really Vegetables with a power of motion; and that as the boughs of an Oak are dashed together by the storm, that Swine may fatten upon the falling Acorns, so Men are by some unaccountable power driven one against another, till they lose their motion, that Vultures may be fed. Others think they have observed something of contrivance and policy among these mischievous Beings, and those that hover more closely round them, pretend, that there is, in every herd, one that gives directions to the rest, and seems to be more eminently delighted with a wide carnage. What it is that intitles him to such pre-eminence we know not; he is seldom the biggest or the swiftest, but he shews by his eagerness and diligence that he is, more than any of the others, a friend to Vultures.

No. 22. Saturday, 16 September 1758.

To the IDLER,

SIR,

As I was passing lately under one of the gates of this city, I was struck with horror by a rueful cry, which summoned me *to remember the poor Debtors*.

The wisdom and justice of the *English* laws are, by *Englishmen* at least, loudly celebrated; but scarcely the most zealous admirers of our Institutions can think that law wise, which when men are capable of work, obliges them to beg; or just, which exposes the liberty of one to the passions of another.

The prosperity of a people is proportionate to the number of hands and minds usefully employed. To the community sedition is a fever, corruption is a gangrene, and idleness an atrophy. Whatever body, and whatever society, wastes more than it acquires, must gradually decay; and every being that continues to be fed, and ceases to labour, takes away something from the public stock.

The confinement, therefore, of any man in the sloth and darkness of a prison, is a loss to the nation, and no gain to the Creditor. For of the multitudes who are pining in those cells of misery, a very small part is suspected of any fraudulent act by which they retain what belongs to others. The rest are imprisoned by the wantonness of pride, the malignity of revenge, or the acrimony of disappointed expectation.

If those, who thus rigorously exercise the power which the law has put into their hands, be asked, why they continue to imprison those whom they know to be unable to pay them: One will answer, that his Debtor once lived better than himself; another, that his wife looked above her neighbours, and his children went in silk cloaths to the dancing school; and another, that he pretended to be a joker and a wit. Some will reply, that if they were in debt they should meet with the same treatment; some, that they owe no more than they can pay, and need therefore give no account of their actions. Some will confess their resolution, that their Debtors shall rot in jail; and some will discover, that they hope, by cruelty, to wring the payment from their friends.

The end of all civil regulations is to secure private happiness from private malignity; to keep individuals from the power of one another; but this end is apparently neglected, when a man, irritated with loss, is allowed to be the judge of his own cause, and to assign the punishment of his own pain; when the distinction between guilt and unhappiness, between casualty and design, is intrusted to eyes blind with interest, to understandings depraved by resentment.

Since Poverty is punished among us as a crime, it ought at least to be treated with the same lenity as other crimes; the offender ought not to languish, at the will of him whom he has offended, but to be allowed some appeal to the justice of his country. There can be no reason, why any Debtor should be imprisoned, but that he may be compelled to payment; and a term should therefore be fixed, in which the Creditor should exhibit his accusation of concealed property. If such property can be discovered, let it be given to the Creditor; if the charge is not offered, or cannot be proved, let the prisoner be dismissed.

Those who made the laws, have apparently supposed, that every deficiency of payment is the crime of the Debtor. But the truth is, that the Creditor always shares the act, and often more than shares the guilt of improper trust. It seldom happens that any man imprisons another but for debts which he suffered to be contracted, in hope of advantage to himself, and for bargains in which he proportioned his profit to his own opinion of the hazard; and there is no reason, why one should punish the other, for a contract in which both concurred.

Many of the inhabitants of prisons may justly complain of harder treatment. He that once owes more than he can pay, is often obliged to bribe his Creditor to patience, by encreasing his debt. Worse and worse commodities, at a higher and higher price, are forced upon him; he is impoverished by compulsive traffick, and at last overwhelmed, in the common receptacles of misery, by debts, which, without his own consent, were accumulated on his head. To the relief of this distress, no other objection can be made, but that by an easy dissolution of debts, fraud will be left without punishment, and imprudence without awe, and that when insolvency shall be no longer punishable, credit will cease.

The motive to credit, is the hope of advantage. Commerce can never be at a stop, while one man wants what another can supply; and credit will never be denied, while it is likely to be repaid with profit. He that trusts one whom he designs to sue, is criminal by the act of trust; the cessation of such insidious traffick is to be desired, and no reason can be given why a change of the law should impair any other.

We see nation trade with nation, where no payment can be compelled. Mutual convenience produces mutual confidence, and the Merchants continue to satisfy the demands of each other, though they have nothing to dread but the loss of trade.

It is vain to continue an institution, which experience shews to be ineffectual. We have now imprisoned one generation of Debtors after another, but we do not find that their numbers lessen. We have now learned, that rashness and imprudence will not be deterred from taking credit; let us try whether fraud and avarice may be more easily restrained from giving it.

I am, Sir, &c.

No. 23. Saturday, 23 September 1758.

Life has no pleasure higher or nobler than that of Friendship. It is painful to consider, that this sublime enjoyment may be impaired or destroyed by innumerable causes, and that there is no human possession of which the duration is less certain.

Many have talked, in very exalted language, of the perpetuity of Friendship, of invincible Constancy, and unalienable Kindness; and some examples have been seen of men who have continued faithful to their earliest choice, and whose affection has predominated over changes of fortune, and contrariety of opinion.

But these instances are memorable, because they are rare. The Friendship which is to be practised or expected by common mortals, must take its rise from mutual pleasure, and must end when the power ceases of delighting each other.

Many accidents therefore may happen, by which the ardour of kindness will be abated, without criminal baseness or contemptible inconstancy on either part. To give pleasure is not always in our power; and little does he know himself, who believes that he can be always able to receive it.

Those who would gladly pass their days together may be separated by the different course of their affairs; and Friendship, like Love, is destroyed by long absence, though it may be encreased by short intermissions. What we have missed long enough to want it, we value more when it is regained; but that which has been lost till it is forgotten, will be found at last with little gladness, and with still less, if a substitute has supplied the place. A man deprived of the companion to whom he used to open his bosom, and with whom he shared the hours of leisure and merriment, feels the day at first hanging heavy on him; his difficulties oppress, and his doubts distract him; he sees time come and go without his wonted gratification, and all is sadness within and solitude about him. But this uneasiness never lasts long, necessity produces expedients, new amusements are discovered, and new conversation is admitted.

No expectation is more frequently disappointed, than that which naturally arises in the mind, from the prospect of meeting an old Friend, after long separation. We expect the attraction to be revived, and the coalition to be renewed; no man considers how much alteration time has made in himself, and very few enquire what effect it has had upon others. The first hour convinces them, that the pleasure, which they have formerly enjoyed, is for ever at an end; different scenes have made different impressions, the opinions of both are changed, and that similitude of manners and sentiment is lost, which confirmed them both in the approbation of themselves.

Friendship is often destroyed by opposition of interest, not only by the ponderous and visible interest, which the desire of wealth and greatness forms and maintains, but by a thousand secret and slight competitions, scarcely known to the mind upon which they operate. There is scarcely any man without some favourite trifle which he values above greater attainments, some desire of petty praise which he cannot patiently suffer to be frustrated. This minute ambition is sometimes crossed before it is known, and sometimes defeated by wanton petulance; but such attacks are seldom made without the loss of Friendship; for whoever has once found the vulnerable part will always be feared, and the resentment will burn on in secret of which shame hinders the discovery.

This, however, is a slow malignity, which a wise man will obviate as inconsistent with quiet, and a good man will repress as contrary to virtue; but human happiness is sometimes violated by some more sudden strokes.

A dispute begun in jest, upon a subject which a moment before was on both parts regarded with careless indifference, is continued by the desire of conquest, till vanity kindles into rage, and opposition rankles into enmity. Against this hasty mischief I know not what security can be obtained; men will be sometimes surprized into quarrels, and though they might both hasten to reconciliation, as soon as their tumult has subsided, yet two minds will seldom be found together, which can at once subdue their discontent, or immediately enjoy the sweets of peace, without remembring the wounds of the conflict.

Friendship has other enemies. Suspicion is always hardening the cautious, and Disgust repelling the delicate. Very slender differences will sometimes part those whom long reciprocation of civility or beneficence has united. *Lonelove* and *Ranger* retired into the country to enjoy the company of each other, and returned in six weeks cold and petulant; *Ranger's* pleasure was to walk in the fields, and *Lonelove's* to sit in a bower; each had complied with the other in his turn, and each was angry that compliance had been exacted.

The most fatal disease of Friendship is gradual decay, or dislike hourly encreased by causes too slender for complaint, and too numerous for removal. Those who are angry may be reconciled; those who have been injured may receive a recompence; but when the desire of pleasing and willingness to be pleased is silently diminished, the renovation of Friendship is hopeless; as, when the vital powers sink into languor, there is no longer any use of the Physician.

No. 27. Saturday, 21 October 1758.

It has been the endeavour of all those whom the world has reverenced for superior wisdom, to persuade man to be acquainted with himself,[1] to learn his own powers and his own weakness, to observe by what evils he is most dangerously beset, and by what temptations most easily overcome.

This counsel has been often given with serious dignity, and often received with appearance of conviction; but, as very few can search deep into their own minds without meeting what they wish to hide from themselves, scarce any man persists in cultivating such disagreeable acquaintance, but draws the veil again between his eyes and his heart, leaves his passions and appetites as he found them, and advises others to look into themselves.

This is the common result of enquiry even among those that endeavour to grow wiser or better, but this endeavour is far enough from frequency; the greater part of the multitudes that swarm upon the earth, have never been disturbed by such uneasy curiosity, but deliver themselves up to business or to pleasure, plunge into the current of life, whether placid or turbulent, and pass on from one point of prospect to another, attentive rather to any thing than the state of their minds; satisfied, at an easy rate, with an opinion that they are no worse than others, that every man must mind his own interest, or that their pleasures hurt only themselves, and are therefore no proper subjects of censure.

Some, however, there are, whom the intrusion of scruples, the recollection of better notions, or the latent reprehension of good examples, will not suffer to live entirely contented with their own conduct; these are forced to pacify the mutiny of reason with fair promises, and quiet their thoughts with designs of calling all their actions to review, and planning a new scheme for the time to come.

There is nothing which we estimate so fallaciously as the force of our own resolutions, nor any fallacy which we so unwillingly and tardily detect. He that has resolved a thousand times, and a thousand times deserted his own purpose, yet suffers no abatement of his confidence, but still believes himself his own master, and able, by innate vigour of soul, to press forward to his end, through all the obstructions that inconveniences or delights can put in his way.

That this mistake should prevail for a time is very natural. When conviction is present, and temptation out of sight, we do not easily conceive how any reasonable being can deviate from his true interest. What ought to be done while it yet hangs only in speculation, is so plain and certain, that there is no place for doubt; the whole soul yields itself to the predominance of truth, and readily determines to do what, when the time of action comes, will be at last omitted.

I believe most men may review all the lives that have passed within their observation, without remembring one efficacious resolution, or being able to tell a single instance of a course of practice suddenly changed in consequence of a change of opinion, or an establishment of determination. Many indeed alter their conduct, and are not at fifty what they were at thirty, but they commonly varied imperceptibly from themselves, followed the train of external causes, and rather suffered reformation than made it.

It is not uncommon to charge the difference between promise and performance, between profession and reality, upon deep design and studied deceit; but the truth is, that there is very little hypocrisy in the world; we do not so often endeavour or wish to impose on others as on ourselves; we resolve to do right, we hope to keep our resolutions, we declare them to confirm our own hope, and fix our own inconstancy by calling witnesses of our actions; but at last habit prevails, and those whom we invited to our triumph, laugh at our defeat.

Custom is commonly too strong for the most resolute resolver though furnished for the assault with all the weapons of philosophy. "He that endeavours to free himself from an ill habit, says *Bacon*, must not change too much at a time lest he should be discouraged by difficulty; nor too little, for then he will make but slow advances."[2] This is a precept which may be applauded in a book, but will fail in the trial, in which every change will be found too great or too little. Those who have been able to conquer habit, are like those that are fabled to have returned from the realms of *Pluto*:

> *Pauci, quos æquus amavit*
> *Jupiter, atque ardens evexit ad æthera virtus.*[3]

They are sufficient to give hope but not security, to animate the contest but not to promise victory.

Those who are in the power of evil habits, must conquer them as they can, and conquered they must be, or neither wisdom nor happiness can be attained; but those who are not yet subject to their influence, may, by timely caution, preserve their freedom, they may effectually resolve to escape the tyrant, whom they will very vainly resolve to conquer.

No. 30. Saturday, 11 November 1758.

The desires of man encrease with his acquisitions; every step which he advances brings something within his view, which he did not see before, and which, as soon as he sees it, he begins to want. Where necessity ends curiosity begins, and no sooner are we supplied with every thing that nature can demand, than we sit down to contrive artificial appetites.

By this restlessness of mind, every populous and wealthy city is filled with innumerable employments, for which the greater part of mankind is without a name; with artificers whose labour is exerted in producing such petty conveniences, that many shops are furnished with instruments, of which the use can hardly be found without enquiry, but which he that once knows them, quickly learns to number among necessary things.

Such is the diligence, with which, in countries completely civilized, one part of mankind labours for another, that wants are supplied faster than they can be formed, and the idle and luxurious find life stagnate, for want of some desire to keep it in motion.[1] This species of distress furnishes a new set of occupations, and multitudes are busied, from day to day, in finding the rich and the fortunate something to do.

It is very common to reproach those artists as useless, who produce only such superfluities as neither accommodate the body nor improve the mind; and of which no other effect can be imagined, than that they are the occasions of spending money, and consuming time.

But this censure will be mitigated, when it is seriously considered, that money and time are the heaviest burthens of life, and that the unhappiest of all mortals are those who have more of either than they know how to use. To set himself free from these incumbrances, one hurries to *New-market*; another travels over *Europe*; one pulls down his house and calls architects about him; another buys a seat in the country, and follows his hounds over hedges and through rivers; one makes collections of shells, and another searches the world for tulips and carnations.

He is surely a public benefactor who finds employment for those to whom it is thus difficult to find it for themselves. It is true that this is seldom done merely from generosity or compassion, almost every man seeks his own advantage in helping others, and therefore it is too common for mercenary officiousness, to consider rather what is grateful than what is right.

We all know that it is more profitable to be loved than esteemed, and ministers of pleasure will always be found, who study to make themselves necessary, and to supplant those who are practising the same arts.

One of the amusements of idleness is reading without the fatigue of close attention, and the world therefore swarms with writers whose wish is not to be studied but to be read.

No species of literary men has lately been so much multiplied as the writers of news. Not many years ago the nation was content with one Gazette; but now we have not only in the metropolis papers for every morning and every evening, but almost every large town has its weekly historian, who regularly circulates his periodical intelligence, and fills the villages of his district with conjectures on the events of war, and with debates on the true interest of *Europe*.

To write news in its perfection requires such a combination of qualities, that a man completely fitted for the task is not always to be found. In Sir *Henry Wotton's*[2] jocular definition, *An*

Ambassador is said to be *a man of virtue sent abroad to tell lies for the advantage of his country*; a News-writer is *a man without virtue, who writes lies at home for his own profit*. To these compositions is required neither genius nor knowledge, neither industry nor sprightliness, but contempt of shame, and indifference to truth are absolutely necessary. He who by a long familiarity with infamy has obtained these qualities, may confidently tell to-day what he intends to contradict to-morrow; he may affirm fearlessly what he knows that he shall be obliged to recant, and may write letters from *Amsterdam* or *Dresden* to himself.

In a time of war the nation is always of one mind, eager to hear something good of themselves and ill of the enemy. At this time the task of News-writers is easy, they have nothing to do but to tell that a battle is expected, and afterwards that a battle has been fought, in which we and our friends, whether conquering or conquered, did all, and our enemies did nothing.

Scarce any thing awakens attention like a tale of cruelty. The Writer of news never fails in the intermission of action to tell how the enemies murdered children and ravished virgins; and if the scene of action be somewhat distant, scalps half the inhabitants of a province.

Among the calamities of War may be justly numbered the diminution of the love of truth, by the falshoods which interest dictates and credulity encourages. A Peace will equally leave the Warriour and Relator of Wars destitute of employment; and I know not whether more is to be dreaded from streets filled with Soldiers accustomed to plunder, or from garrets filled with Scribblers accustomed to lie.

No. 31. Saturday, 18 November 1758.

Many moralists have remarked, that Pride has of all human vices the widest dominion, appears in the greatest multiplicity of forms, and lies hid under the greatest variety of disguises; of disguises, which, like the moon's *veil of brightness*, are both its *lustre and its shade*,[1] and betray it to others, tho' they hide it from ourselves.

It is not my intention to degrade Pride from this pre-eminence of mischief, yet I know not whether Idleness may not maintain a very doubtful and obstinate competition.

There are some that profess Idleness in its full dignity, who call themselves the *Idle*, as *Busiris* in the play *calls himself the Proud*;[2] who boast that they do nothing, and thank their stars that they have nothing to do; who sleep every night till they can sleep no longer, and rise only that exercise may enable them to sleep again; who prolong the reign of darkness by double curtains, and never see the sun but to *tell him how they hate his beams*;[3] whose whole labour is to vary the postures of indulgence, and whose day differs from their night but as a couch or chair differs from a bed.

These are the true and open votaries of Idleness, for whom she weaves the garlands of poppies, and into whose cup she pours the waters of oblivion; who exist in a state of unruffled stupidity, forgetting and forgotten; who have long ceased to live, and at whose death the survivors can only say, that they have ceased to breathe.

But Idleness predominates in many lives where it is not suspected, for being a vice which terminates in itself, it may be enjoyed without injury to others, and is therefore not watched like Fraud, which endangers property, or like Pride which naturally seeks its gratifications in another's inferiority. Idleness is a silent and peaceful quality, that neither raises envy by ostentation, nor hatred by opposition; and therefore no body is busy to censure or detect it.

As Pride sometimes is hid under humility, Idleness is often covered by turbulence and hurry. He that neglects his known duty and real employment, naturally endeavours to croud his mind with something that may bar out the remembrance of his own folly, and does any thing but what he ought to do with eager diligence, that he may keep himself in his own favour.

Some are always in a state of preparation, occupied in previous measures, forming plans, accumulating materials, and providing for the main affair. These are certainly under the secret power of Idleness. Nothing is to be expected from the workman whose tools are for ever to be sought. I was once told by a great master, that no man ever excelled in painting, who was eminently curious about pencils and colours.

There are others to whom Idleness dictates another expedient, by which life may be passed unprofitably away without the tediousness of many vacant hours. The art is, to fill the day with petty business, to have always something in hand which may raise curiosity, but not solicitude, and keep the mind in a state of action, but not of labour.

This art has for many years been practised by my old friend *Sober*, with wonderful success. *Sober* is a man of strong desires and quick imagination, so exactly ballanced by the love of ease, that they can seldom stimulate him to any difficult undertaking; they have, however, so much power, that they will not suffer him to lie quite at rest, and though they do not make him sufficiently useful to others, they make him at least weary of himself.

Mr. *Sober's* chief pleasure is conversation; there is no end of his talk or his attention; to speak or to hear is equally pleasing; for he still fancies that he is teaching or learning something, and is free for the time from his own reproaches.

But there is one time at night when he must go home, that his friends may sleep; and another time in the morning, when all the world agrees to shut out interruption. These are the moments of which poor *Sober* trembles at the thought. But the misery of these tiresome intervals, he has many means of alleviating. He has persuaded himself that the manual arts are undeservedly overlooked; he has observed in many trades the effects of close thought, and just ratiocination. From speculation he proceeded to practice, and supplied himself with the tools of a carpenter, with which he mended his coal-box very successfully, and which he still continues to employ, as he finds occasion.

He has attempted at other times the crafts of the Shoe-maker, Tinman, Plumber, and Potter; in all these arts he has failed, and resolves to qualify himself for them by better information. But his daily amusement is Chemistry. He has a small furnace, which he employs in distillation, and which has long been the solace of his life. He draws oils and waters, and essences and spirits, which he knows to be of no use; sits and counts the drops as they come from his retort, and forgets that, while a drop is falling, a moment flies away.

Poor *Sober!* I have often teaz'd him with reproof, and he has often promised reformation; for no man is so much open to conviction as the *Idler*, but there is none on whom it operates so little. What will be the effect of this paper I know not; perhaps he will read it and laugh, and light the fire in his furnace; but my hope is that he will quit his trifles, and betake himself to rational and useful diligence.

No. 32. Saturday, 25 November 1758.

Among the innumerable mortifications that waylay human arrogance on every side may well be reckoned our ignorance of the most common objects and effects, a defect of which we become more sensible by every attempt to supply it. Vulgar and inactive minds confound familiarity with knowledge, and conceive themselves informed of the whole nature of things when they are shewn their form or told their use; but the Speculatist, who is not content with superficial views, harrasses himself with fruitless curiosity, and still as he enquires more perceives only that he knows less.

Sleep is a state in which a great part of every life is passed. No animal has been yet discovered, whose existence is not varied with intervals of insensibility; and some late Philosophers have extended the Empire of Sleep over the vegetable world.

Yet of this change so frequent, so great, so general, and so necessary, no searcher has yet found either the efficient or final cause; or can tell by what power the mind and body are thus chained down in irresistible stupefaction; or what benefits the animal receives from this alternate suspension of its active powers.

Whatever may be the multiplicity or contrariety of opinions upon this subject, Nature has taken sufficient care that Theory shall have little influence on Practice. The most diligent enquirer is not able long to keep his eyes open; the most eager disputant will begin about midnight to desert his argument, and once in four and twenty hours, the gay and the gloomy, the witty and the dull, the clamorous and the silent, the busy and the idle, are all overpowered by the gentle tyrant, and all lie down in the equality of Sleep.

Philosophy has often attempted to repress insolence by asserting that all conditions are levelled by Death;[1] a position which, however it may deject the happy, will seldom afford much comfort to the wretched. It is far more pleasing to consider that Sleep is equally a leveller with Death; that the time is never at a great distance, when the balm of rest shall be effused alike upon every head, when the diversities of life shall stop their operation, and the high and the low shall lie down together.

It is somewhere recorded of *Alexander*, that in the pride of conquests, and intoxication of flattery, he declared that he only perceived himself to be a man by the necessity of Sleep.[2] Whether he considered Sleep as necessary to his mind or body it was indeed a sufficient evidence of human infirmity; the body which required such frequency of renovation gave but faint promises of immortality; and the mind which, from time to time, sunk gladly into insensibility, had made no very near approaches to the felicity of the supreme and self-sufficient Nature.

I know not what can tend more to repress all the passions that disturb the peace of the world, than the consideration that there is no height of happiness or honour, from which man does not eagerly descend to a state of unconscious repose; that the best condition of life is such, that we contentedly quit its good to be disentangled from its evils; that in a few hours splendour fades before the eye, and praise itself deadens in the ear; the senses withdraw from their objects, and reason favours the retreat.

What then are the hopes and prospects of covetousness, ambition and rapacity? Let him that desires most have all his desires gratified, he never shall attain a state, which he can, for a day and a night, contemplate with satisfaction, or from which, if he had the power of perpetual vigilance, he would not long for periodical separations.

All envy would be extinguished if it were universally known that there are none to be envied, and surely none can be much envied who are not pleased with themselves. There is reason to suspect that the distinctions of mankind have more shew than value, when it is found that all agree to be weary alike of pleasures and of cares, that the powerful and the weak, the celebrated and obscure, join in one common wish, and implore from Nature's hand the nectar of oblivion.

Such is our desire of abstraction from ourselves, that very few are satisfied with the quantity of stupefaction which the needs of the body force upon the mind. *Alexander* himself added intemperance to sleep, and solaced with the fumes of wine the sovereignty of the world. And almost every man has some art, by which he steals his thoughts away from his present state.

It is not much of life that is spent in close attention to any important duty. Many hours of every day are suffered to fly away without any traces left upon the intellects. We suffer phantoms to rise up before us, and amuse ourselves with the dance of airy images, which after a time we dismiss for ever, and know not how we have been busied.

Many have no happier moments than those that they pass in solitude, abandoned to their own imagination, which sometimes puts sceptres in their hands or mitres on their heads, shifts the scene of pleasure with endless variety, bids all the forms of beauty sparkle before them, and gluts them with every change of visionary luxury.

It is easy in these semi-slumbers to collect all the possibilities of happiness, to alter the course of the Sun, to bring back the past, and anticipate the future, to unite all the beauties of all seasons, and all the blessings of all climates, to receive and bestow felicity, and forget that misery is the lot of man. All this is a voluntary dream, a temporary recession from the realities of life to airy fictions; and habitual subjection of reason to fancy.

Others are afraid to be alone, and amuse themselves by a perpetual succession of companions, but the difference is not great, in solitude we have our dreams to ourselves, and in company we agree to dream in concert. The end sought in both is forgetfulness of ourselves.

No. 36. Saturday, 23 December 1758.

The great differences that disturb the peace of mankind, are not about ends but means. We have all the same general desires, but how those desires shall be accomplished will for ever be disputed. The ultimate purpose of government is temporal, and that of religion is eternal happiness. Hitherto we agree; but here we must part, to try, according to the endless varieties of passion and understanding combined with one another, every possible form of Government, and every imaginable tenet of Religion.

We are told by *Cumberland*, that *Rectitude*, applied to action or contemplation, is merely metaphorical; and that as a *right* line describes the shortest passage from point to point, so a *right* action effects a good design by the fewest means; and so likewise a *right* opinion is that which connects distant truths by the shortest train of intermediate propositions.[1]

To find the nearest way from truth to truth, or from purpose to effect, not to use more instruments where fewer will be sufficient, not to move by wheels and levers what will give way to the naked hand, is the great proof of a healthful and vigorous mind, neither feeble with helpless ignorance, nor overburdened with unwieldy knowledge.

But there are men who seem to think nothing so much the characteristick of a genius, as to do common things in an uncommon manner; like *Hudibras* to *tell the clock by Algebra*, or like the Lady in Dr. *Young's* Satires, *to drink Tea by stratagem*.[2] To quit the beaten track only because it is known, and take a new path, however crooked or rough, because the strait was found out before.

Every man speaks and writes with intent to be understood, and it can seldom happen but he that understands himself might convey his notions to another, if, content to be understood, he did not seek to be admired; but when once he begins to contrive how his sentiments may be received, not with most ease to his reader, but with most advantage to himself, he then transfers his consideration from words to sounds, from sentences to periods, and as he grows more elegant becomes less intelligible.

It is difficult to enumerate every species of Authors whose labours counteract themselves. The man of exuberance and copiousness, who diffuses every thought thro' so many diversities of expression, that it is lost like water in a mist. The ponderous dictator of sentences, whose notions are delivered in the lump, and are, like uncoined bullion, of more weight than use. The liberal illustrator, who shews by examples and comparisons what was clearly seen when it was first proposed; and the stately son of demonstration, who proves with mathematical formality what no man has yet pretended to doubt.

There is a mode of style for which I know not that the Masters of Oratory have yet found a name, a style by which the most evident truths are so obscured that they can no longer be perceived, and the most familiar propositions so disguised that they cannot be known. Every other kind of eloquence is the dress of sense, but this is the mask, by which a true Master of his art will so effectually conceal it, that a man will as easily mistake his own positions if he meets them thus transformed, as he may pass in a masquerade his nearest acquaintance.

This style may be called the *terrifick*, for its chief intention is to terrify and amaze; it may be termed the *repulsive*, for its natural effect is to drive away the reader; or it may be distinguished, in plain *English*, by the denomination of the *bugbear style*, for it has more terror than danger, and will appear less formidable, as it is more nearly approached.

A mother tells her infant, that *two and two make four*, the child remembers the proposition, and is able to count four to all the purposes of life, till the course of his education brings him among philosophers, who fright him from his former knowledge, by telling him that four is a certain aggregate of unites; that all numbers being only the repetition of an unite, which, though not a number itself, is the parent, root, or original of all number, *four* is the denomination assigned to a certain number of such repetitions. The only danger is, lest, when he first hears these dreadful sounds, the pupil should run away; if he has but the courage to stay till the conclusion, he will find that, when speculation has done its worst, two and two still make four.

An illustrious example of this species of eloquence, may

be found in *Letters concerning Mind*. The author begins by declaring, that *the sorts of things are things that now are, have been, and shall be, and the things that strictly* ARE. In this position, except the last clause, in which he uses something of the scholastick language, there is nothing but what every man has heard and imagines himself to know. But who would not believe that some wonderful novelty is presented to his intellect, when he is afterwards told, in the true *bugbear* style, that *the* Ares, *in the former sense, are things that lie between the* Have-beens *and* Shall-bes. *The* Have-beens *are things that are past; the* Shall-bes *are things that are to come; and the things that* ARE, in the latter sense, *are things that have not been, nor shall be, nor stand in the midst of such as are before them or shall be after them. The things that have been, and shall be, have respect to present, past, and future. Those likewise that now* ARE *have moreover place; that, for instance, which is here, that which is to the east, that which is to the west.*[3]

All this, my dear reader, is very strange; but though it be strange, it is not new; survey these wonderful sentences again, and they will be found to contain nothing more than very plain truths, which till this Author arose had always been delivered in plain language.

No. 38. Saturday, 6 January 1759.

Since the publication of the letter, concerning the condition of those who are confined in Gaols by their Creditors, an enquiry is said to have been made, by which it appears that more than* twenty thousand are at this time prisoners for debt.

We often look with indifference on the successive parts of that, which, if the whole were seen together, would shake us with emotion. A Debtor is dragged to prison, pitied for a moment, and then forgotten; another follows him, and is lost alike in the caverns of oblivion; but when the whole mass of

---

* This number was at that time confidently published, but the authour has since found reason to question the calculation.

calamity rises up at once, when twenty thousand reasonable Beings are heard all groaning in unnecessary misery, not by the infirmity of nature, but the mistake or negligence of policy, who can forbear to pity and lament, to wonder and abhor.

There is here no need of declamatory vehemence; we live in an age of Commerce and Computation; let us therefore coolly enquire what is the sum of evil which the imprisonment of Debtors brings upon our country.

It seems to be the opinion of the later computists, that the inhabitants of *England* do not exceed six millions, of which twenty thousand is the three-hundredth part. What shall we say of the humanity or the wisdom of a nation, that voluntarily sacrifices one in every three hundred to lingering destruction!

The misfortunes of an individual do not extend their influence to many; yet, if we consider the effects of consanguinity and friendship, and the general reciprocation of wants and benefits, which make one man dear or necessary to another, it may reasonably be supposed, that every man languishing in prison gives trouble of some kind to two others who love or need him. By this multiplication of misery we see distress extended to the hundredth part of the whole society.

If we estimate at a shilling a day what is lost by the inaction and consumed in the support of each man thus chained down to involuntary idleness, the publick loss will rise in one year to three hundred thousand pounds; in ten years to more than a sixth part of our circulating coin.

I am afraid that those who are best acquainted with the state of our prisons, will confess that my conjecture is too near the truth, when I suppose that the corrosion of resentment, the heaviness of sorrow, the corruption of confined air, the want of exercise, and sometimes of food, the contagion of diseases from which there is no retreat, and the severity of tyrants against whom there can be no resistance, and all the complicated horrors of a prison, put an end every year to the life of one in four of those that are shut up from the common comforts of human life.

Thus perish yearly five thousand men, overborne with sorrow, consumed by famine, or putrified by filth; many of them in the most vigorous and useful part of life; for the thoughtless and imprudent are commonly young, and the active and busy are seldom old.

According to the rule generally received, which supposes that one in thirty dies yearly, the race of man may be said to be renewed at the end of thirty years. Who would have believed till now, that of every *English* generation an hundred and fifty thousand perish in our gaols! That in every century, a nation eminent for science, studious of commerce, ambitious of empire, should willingly lose, in noisome dungeons, five hundred thousand of its inhabitants: A number greater than has ever been destroyed in the same time by the Pestilence and Sword!

A very late occurrence may shew us the value of the number which we thus condemn to be useless; in the re-establishment of the Trained Bands, thirty thousand are considered as a force sufficient against all exigencies: While, therefore, we detain twenty thousand in prison, we shut up in darkness and uselessness two thirds of an army which ourselves judge equal to the defence of our country.

The monastick institutions have been often blamed, as tending to retard the increase of mankind. And perhaps retirement ought rarely to be permitted, except to those whose employment is consistent with abstraction, and who, tho' solitary, will not be idle; to those whom infirmity makes useless to the commonwealth, or to those who have paid their due proportion to Society, and who, having lived for others, may be honourably dismissed to live for themselves. But whatever be the evil or the folly of these retreats, those have no right to censure them whose prisons contain greater numbers than the Monasteries of other countries. It is, surely, less foolish and less criminal to permit inaction than compel it; to comply with doubtful opinions of happiness, than condemn to certain and apparent misery; to indulge the extravagancies of erroneous piety, than to multiply and enforce temptations to wickedness.

The misery of gaols is not half their evil; they are filled with every corruption which poverty and wickedness can generate between them; with all the shameless and profligate enormities

that can be produced by the impudence of ignominy, the rage
of want, and the malignity of despair. In a prison the awe of the
publick eye is lost, and the power of the law is spent; there are
few fears, there are no blushes. The lewd inflame the lewd, the
audacious harden the audacious. Every one fortifies himself as
he can against his own sensibility, endeavours to practise on
others the arts which are practised on himself; and gains the
kindness of his associates by similitude of manners.

Thus some sink amidst their misery, and others survive only
to propagate villainy. It may be hoped that our Lawgivers will
at length take away from us this power of starving and depraving
one another: but, if there be any reason why this inveterate
evil should not be removed in our age, which true policy has
enlightened beyond any former time, let those, whose writings
form the opinions and the practices of their contemporaries,
endeavour to transfer the reproach of such imprisonment from
the Debtor to the Creditor, till universal infamy shall pursue the
wretch, whose wantonness of power, or revenge of disappointment, condemns another to torture and to ruin; till he shall be
hunted through the world as an enemy to man, and find in riches
no shelter from contempt.

Surely, he whose Debtor has perished in prison, though he
may acquit himself of deliberate murder, must at least have his
mind clouded with discontent, when he considers how much
another has suffered from him; when he thinks on the wife
bewailing her husband, or the children begging the bread which
their father would have earned. If there are any made so obdurate by avarice or cruelty, as to revolve these consequences
without dread or pity, I must leave them to be awakened by
some other power, for I write only to human Beings.

No. 40. Saturday, 20 January 1759.

The practice of appending to the narratives of public transactions, more minute and domestic intelligence, and filling the
News-papers with advertisements, has grown up by slow
degrees to its present state.

Genius is shewn only by Invention. The man who first took advantage of the general curiosity that was excited by a siege or battle, to betray the Readers of News into the knowledge of the shop where the best Puffs and Powder were to be sold, was undoubtedly a man of great sagacity, and profound skill in the nature of Man. But when he had once shewn the way, it was easy to follow him; and every man now knows a ready method of informing the Publick of all that he desires to buy or sell, whether his wares be material or intellectual; whether he makes Cloaths, or teaches the Mathematics; whether he be a Tutor that wants a Pupil, or a Pupil that wants a Tutor.

Whatever is common is despised. Advertisements are now so numerous that they are very negligently perused, and it is therefore become necessary to gain attention by magnificence of promises, and by eloquence sometimes sublime and sometimes pathetic.

Promise, large Promise, is the soul of an Advertisement. I remember a *wash-ball* that had a quality truly wonderful, it gave *an exquisite edge to the razor*. And there are now to be sold *for ready money only*, some *Duvets for bed-coverings, of down, beyond comparison superior to what is called Otter Down*, and indeed such, that its *many excellencies cannot be here set forth*. With one excellence we are made acquainted, *It is warmer than four or five blankets, and lighter than one.*

There are some, however, that know the prejudice of mankind in favour of modest sincerity. The Vender of the *Beautifying Fluid* sells a lotion that repels pimples, washes away freckles, smooths the skin, and plumps the flesh; and yet, with a generous abhorrence of ostentation, confesses, that it will not *restore the bloom of fifteen to a Lady of fifty*.

The true pathos of Advertisements must have sunk deep into the heart of every man that remembers the zeal shewn by the Seller of the Anodyne Necklace, for the ease and safety *of poor toothing infants*, and the affection with which he warned every mother, that *she would never forgive herself* if her infant should perish without a Necklace.

I cannot but remark to the celebrated Author who gave, in his notifications of the Camel and Dromedary, so many specimens of the genuine sublime, that there is now arrived another subject yet more worthy of his pen. *A famous Mohawk Indian warrior, who took* Dieskaw[1] *the French General prisoner, dressed in the same manner with the native Indians when they go to war, with his face and body painted, with his scalping knife, Tom-ax, and all other implements of war: A sight worthy the curiosity of every true Briton!* This is a very powerful description; but a Critic of great refinement would say that it conveys rather *horror* than *terror.* An *Indian,* dressed as he goes to war, may bring company together; but if he carries the scalping knife and tom ax, there are many true Britons that will never be persuaded to see him but through a grate.

It has been remarked by the severer judges, that the salutary sorrow of tragick scenes is too soon effaced by the merriment of the Epilogue; the same inconvenience arises from the improper disposition of Advertisements. The noblest objects may be so associated as to be made ridiculous. The Camel and Dromedary themselves might have lost much of their dignity between *The true Flower of Mustard* and *The Original Daffy's Elixir*; and I could not but feel some indignation when I found this illustrious *Indian* warrior immediately succeeded by *A fresh Parcel of Dublin Butter.*

The trade of advertising is now so near to perfection, that it is not easy to propose any improvement. But as every art ought to be exercised in due subordination to the publick good, I cannot but propose it as a moral question to these masters of the publick ear, Whether they do not sometimes play too wantonly with our passions, as when the Register of Lottery Tickets invites us to his shop by an account of the prize which he sold last year; and whether the advertising Controvertists do not indulge asperity of language without any adequate provocation; as in the dispute about *Straps for Razors,* now happily subsided, and in the altercation which at present subsists concerning *Eau de Luce.*[2]

In an Advertisement it is allowed to every man to speak well of himself, but I know not why he should assume the privilege of censuring his neighbour. He may proclaim his own virtue or skill, but ought not to exclude others from the same pretensions.

Every man that advertises his own excellence, should write with some consciousness of a character which dares to call the attention of the Publick. He should remember that his name is to stand in the same paper with those of the King of *Prussia*, and the Emperor of *Germany*, and endeavour to make himself worthy of such association.

Some regard is likewise to be paid to posterity. There are men of diligence and curiosity who treasure up the Papers of the Day merely because others neglect them, and in time they will be scarce. When these collections shall be read in another century, how will numberless contradictions be reconciled, and how shall Fame be possibly distributed among the Tailors and Boddice-makers of the present age?

Surely these things deserve consideration. It is enough for me to have hinted my desire that these abuses may be rectified; but such is the state of nature, that what all have the right of doing, many will attempt without sufficient care or due qualifications.

No. 41. Saturday, 27 January 1759.

The following Letter relates to an affliction perhaps not necessary to be imparted to the Publick, but I could not persuade myself to suppress it, because I think I know the sentiments to be sincere, and I feel no disposition to provide for this day any other entertainment.

> *At tu quisquis eris, miseri qui cruda poetæ*
> *Credideris fletu funera digna tuo,*
> *Hæc postrema tibi sit flendi causa, fluatque*
> *Lenis inoffenso vitaque morsque gradu.*[1]

Mr. IDLER,

Notwithstanding the warnings of Philosophers, and the daily examples of losses and misfortunes which life forces upon our observation, such is the absorption of our thoughts in the business of the present day, such the resignation of our reason to empty hopes of future felicity, or such our unwillingness to foresee what we dread, that every calamity comes suddenly upon us, and not only presses us as a burthen, but crushes as a blow.

There are evils which happen out of the common course of nature, against which it is no reproach not to be provided. A flash of lightning intercepts the traveller in his way. The concussion of an earthquake heaps the ruins of cities upon their inhabitants. But other miseries time brings, though silently yet visibly forward by its even lapse, which yet approach us unseen because we turn our eyes away, and seize us unresisted because we could not arm ourselves against them, but by setting them before us.

That it is vain to shrink from what cannot be avoided, and to hide that from ourselves which must some time be found, is a truth which we all know, but which all neglect, and perhaps none more than the speculative reasoner, whose thoughts are always from home, whose eye wanders over life, whose fancy dances after meteors of happiness kindled by itself, and who examines every thing rather than his own state.

Nothing is more evident than that the decays of age must terminate in death; yet there is no man, says *Tully*,[2] who does not believe that he may yet live another year; and there is none who does not, upon the same principle, hope another year for his parent or his friend; but the fallacy will be in time detected; the last year, the last day must come. It has come and is past. The life which made my own life pleasant is at an end, and the gates of death are shut upon my prospects.

The loss of a friend upon whom the heart was fixed, to whom every wish and endeavour tended, is a state of dreary desolation in which the mind looks abroad impatient of itself, and finds nothing but emptiness and horror. The blameless life, the artless tenderness, the pious simplicity, the modest resignation, the patient sickness, and the quiet death, are remembered only to add value to the loss, to aggravate regret for what cannot be amended, to deepen sorrow for what cannot be recalled.

These are the calamities by which Providence gradually disengages us from the love of life. Other evils fortitude may repel, or hope may mitigate; but irreparable privation leaves nothing to exercise resolution or flatter expectation. The dead cannot return, and nothing is left us here but languishment and grief.

Yet such is the course of nature, that whoever lives long must outlive those whom he loves and honours. Such is the condition of our present existence, that life must one time lose its associations, and every inhabitant of the earth must walk downward to the grave alone and unregarded, without any partner of his joy or grief, without any interested witness of his misfortunes or success.

Misfortune, indeed, he may yet feel, for where is the bottom of the misery of man? But what is success to him that has none to enjoy it. Happiness is not found in self-contemplation; it is perceived only when it is reflected from another.

We know little of the state of departed souls, because such knowledge is not necessary to a good life. Reason deserts us at the brink of the grave, and can give no further intelligence. Revelation is not wholly silent. *There is joy in the Angels of Heaven over one sinner that repenteth*;[3] and surely this joy is not incommunicable to souls disentangled from the body, and made like Angels.

Let Hope therefore dictate, what Revelation does not confute, that the union of souls may still remain; and that we who are struggling with sin, sorrow, and infirmities, may have our part in the attention and kindness of those who have finished their course and are now receiving their reward.

These are the great occasions which force the mind to take refuge in Religion: when we have no help in ourselves, what can remain but that we look up to a higher and a greater Power; and to what hope may we not raise our eyes and hearts, when we consider that the Greatest POWER is the BEST.

Surely there is no man who, thus afflicted, does not seek succour in the *Gospel*, which has brought *Life and Immortality to light*.[4] The Precepts of *Epicurus*, who teaches us to endure what the Laws of the Universe make necessary, may silence but not content us. The dictates of *Zeno*, who commands us to look with indifference on external things, may dispose us to conceal our sorrow, but cannot assuage it.[5] Real alleviation of the loss of friends, and rational tranquillity in the prospect of our own dissolution, can be received only from the promises of him in whose hands are life and death, and from the assurance of another and better state, in which all tears will be wiped from the eyes,[6] and the whole soul shall be filled with joy. Philosophy may infuse stubbornness, but Religion only can give Patience.

　　　　　　　　　　　　　　　　　I am, &c.

No. 44. Saturday, 17 February 1759.

Memory is, among the faculties of the human mind, that of which we make the most frequent use, or rather that of which the agency is incessant or perpetual. Memory is the primary and fundamental power, without which there could be no other intellectual operation. Judgment and Ratiocination suppose something already known, and draw their decisions only from experience. Imagination selects ideas from the treasures of Remembrance, and produces novelty only by varied combinations. We do not even form conjectures of distant, or anticipations of future events, but by concluding what is possible from what is past.

The two offices of Memory are Collection and Distribution; by one images are accumulated, and by the other produced for use. Collection is always the employment of our first years, and Distribution commonly that of our advanced age.

To collect and reposite the various forms of things, is far the most pleasing part of mental occupation. We are naturally delighted with novelty, and there is a time when all that we see is new. When first we enter into the world, whithersoever we turn our eyes, they meet Knowledge with Pleasure at her side; every diversity of Nature pours ideas in upon the soul; neither search nor labour are necessary; we have nothing more to do than to open our eyes, and curiosity is gratified.

Much of the pleasure which the first survey of the world affords, is exhausted before we are conscious of our own felicity, or able to compare our condition with some other possible state. We have therefore few traces of the joy of our earliest discoveries; yet we all remember a time when Nature had so many untasted gratifications, that every excursion gave delight which can now be found no longer, when the noise of a torrent, the rustle of a wood, the song of birds, or the play of lambs, had power to fill the attention, and suspend all perception of the course of time.

But these easy pleasures are soon at an end; we have seen in a very little time so much, that we call out for new objects of observation, and endeavour to find variety in books and life. But study is laborious, and not always satisfactory; and Conversation has its pains as well as pleasures; we are willing to learn, but not willing to be taught; we are pained by ignorance, but pained yet more by another's knowledge.

From the vexation of pupillage men commonly set themselves free about the middle of life, by shutting up the avenues of intelligence, and resolving to rest in their present state; and they, whose ardour of enquiry continues longer, find themselves insensibly forsaken by their instructors. As every man advances in life, the proportion between those that are younger, and that are older than himself, is continually changing; and he that has lived half a century, finds few that do not require from him that information which he once expected from those that went before him.

Then it is that the magazines of memory are opened, and the stores of accumulated knowledge are displayed by vanity or benevolence, or in honest commerce of mutual interest. Every man wants others, and is therefore glad when he is wanted by them. And as few men will endure the labour of intense meditation without necessity, he that has learned enough for his profit or his honour, seldom endeavours after further acquisitions.

The pleasure of recollecting speculative notions would not be much less than that of gaining them, if they could be kept pure and unmingled with the passages of life; but such is the necessary concatenation of our thoughts, that good and evil are linked together, and no pleasure recurs but associated with pain. Every revived idea reminds us of a time when something was enjoyed that is now lost, when some hope was yet not blasted, when some purpose had yet not languished into sluggishness or indifference.

Whether it be that life has more vexations than comforts, or, what is in the event just the same, that evil makes deeper impression than good, it is certain that few can review the time past without heaviness of heart. He remembers many calamities incurred by folly, many opportunities lost by negligence. The shades of the dead rise up before him, and he laments the companions of his youth, the partners of his amusements, the assistants of his labours, whom the hand of death has snatched away.

When an offer was made to *Themistocles* of teaching him the art of Memory, he answered, that he would rather wish for the art of Forgetfulness.[1] He felt his imagination haunted by phantoms of misery which he was unable to suppress, and would gladly have calmed his thoughts with some *oblivious antidote*. In this we all resemble one another; the hero and the sage are, like vulgar mortals, overburthened by the weight of life, all shrink from recollection, and all wish for an art of Forgetfulness.

No. 48. Saturday, 17 March 1759.

There is no kind of idleness, by which we are so easily seduced, as that which dignifies itself by the appearance of business, and by making the loiterer imagine that he has something to do which must not be neglected, keeps him in perpetual agitation, and hurries him rapidly from place to place.

He that sits still, or reposes himself upon a couch, no more deceives himself than he deceives others; he knows that he is doing nothing, and has no other solace of his insignificance than the resolution which the lazy hourly make, of changing his mode of life.

To do nothing every man is ashamed, and to do much almost every man is unwilling or afraid. Innumerable expedients have therefore been invented to produce motion without labour, and employment without solicitude. The greater part of those whom the kindness of fortune has left to their own direction, and whom want does not keep chained to the counter or the plow, play throughout life with the shadows of business, and know not at last what they have been doing.

These imitators of action are of all denominations. Some are seen at every Auction without intention to purchase; others appear punctually at the *Exchange*, though they are known there only by their faces. Some are always making parties, to visit Collections for which they have no taste, and some neglect every pleasure and every duty to hear questions in which they have no interest, debated in Parliament.

These men never appear more ridiculous, than in the distress which they imagine themselves to feel, from some accidental interruption of those empty pursuits. A Tiger newly imprisoned is indeed more formidable, but not more angry than *Jack Tulip* with-held from a Florist's feast, or *Tom Distich*[1] hindered from seeing the first representation of a Play.

As political affairs are the highest and most extensive of temporal concerns; the mimick of a Politician is more busy and important than any other trifler. Monsieur *le Noir*, a man who, without property or importance in any corner of the earth, has, in the present confusion of the world, declared himself a steady adherent to the *French*, is made miserable by a wind that keeps back the packet-boat, and still more miserable, by every account of a *Malouin* privateer[2] caught in his cruize; he knows well that nothing can be done or said by him which can produce any effect but that of laughter, that he can neither hasten nor retard good or evil, that his joys and sorrows have scarcely any partakers; yet such is his zeal, and such his curiosity, that he would run barefooted to *Gravesend*, for the sake of knowing first that the *English* had lost a tender, and would ride out to meet every mail from the Continent if he might be permitted to open it.

Learning is generally confessed to be desirable, and there are some who fancy themselves always busy in acquiring it. Of these ambulatory Students, one of the most busy is my friend *Tom Restless*.

Tom has long had a mind to be a man of knowledge, but he does not care to spend much time among Authors, for he is of opinion that few books deserve the labour of perusal, that they give the mind an unfashionable cast, and destroy that freedom of thought and easiness of manners indispensibly requisite to acceptance in the world. *Tom* has therefore found another way to wisdom. When he rises he goes into a Coffee-house, where he creeps so near to men whom he takes to be reasoners as to hear their discourse, and endeavours to remember something which, when it has been strained thro' *Tom's* head, is so near to nothing that what it once was cannot be discovered. This he carries round from friend to friend thro' a circle of visits, till hearing what each says upon the question he becomes able at dinner to say a little himself, and as every great genius relaxes himself among his inferiors, meets with some who wonder how so young a man can talk so wisely.

At night he has a new feast prepared for his intellects; he always runs to a disputing society, or a speaking club, where he half hears what, if he had heard the whole, he would but half understand; goes home pleased with the consciousness of a day well spent, lies down full of ideas, and rises in the morning empty as before.

No. 49. Saturday, 24 March 1759.

I supped three nights ago with my friend *Will Marvel*. His affairs obliged him lately to take a journey into *Devonshire*, from which he has just returned. He knows me to be a very patient hearer, and was glad of my company, as it gave him an opportunity of disburthening himself by a minute relation of the casualties of his expedition.

Will is not one of those who go out and return with nothing to tell. He has a story of his travels, which will strike a home-bred citizen with horror, and has in ten days suffered so often the extremes of terror and joy, that he is in doubt whether he shall ever again expose either his body or mind to such danger and fatigue.

When he left *London* the morning was bright, and a fair day was promised. But *Will* is born to struggle with difficulties. That happened to him, which has sometimes, perhaps, happened to others. Before he had gone more than ten miles it began to rain.

What course was to be taken! His soul disdained to turn back. He did what the king of *Prussia*[1] might have done, he flapped his hat, buttoned up his cape, and went forwards, fortifying his mind, by the stoical consolation, that whatever is violent will be short.

His constancy was not long tried; at the distance of about half a mile he saw an inn, which he entered wet and weary, and found civil treatment and proper refreshment. After a respite of about two hours he looked abroad, and seeing the sky clear, called for his horse and passed the first stage without any other memorable accident.

Will considered, that labour must be relieved by pleasure, and that the strength which great undertakings require must be maintained by copious nutriment; he therefore ordered himself an elegant supper, drank two bottles of claret, and passed the beginning of the night in sound sleep; but waking before light, was forewarned of the troubles of the next day, by a shower beating against his windows with such violence as to threaten the dissolution of nature. When he arose he found what he expected, that the country was under water. He joined himself, however, to a company that was travelling the same way, and came safely to the place of dinner, tho' every step of his horse dashed the mud into the air.

In the afternoon, having parted from his company, he set forward alone, and passed many collections of water of which it was impossible to guess the depth, and which he now cannot review without some censure of his own rashness; but what a man undertakes he must perform, and *Marvel* hates a coward at his heart.

Few that lie warm in their beds, think what others undergo, who have perhaps been as tenderly educated, and have as acute sensations as themselves. My friend was now to lodge the second night almost fifty miles from home, in a house which he never had seen before, among people to whom he was totally a stranger, not knowing whether the next man he should meet would prove good or bad; but seeing an inn of a good appearance, he rode resolutely into the yard, and knowing that respect is often paid in proportion as it is claimed, delivered his injunction to the hostler with spirit, and entering the house, called vigorously about him.

On the third day up rose the sun and Mr. *Marvel*. His troubles and his dangers were now such, as he wishes no other man ever to encounter. The ways were less frequented, and the country more thinly inhabited. He rode many a lonely hour thro' mire and water, and met not a single soul for two miles together with whom he could exchange a word. He cannot deny that, looking round upon the dreary region, and seeing nothing but bleak fields and naked trees, hills obscured by fogs, and flats covered with inundations, he did for some time suffer melancholy to prevail upon him, and wished himself again safe at home. One comfort he had, which was to consider, that none of his friends were in the same distress, for whom, if they had been with him, he should have suffered more than for himself; he could not forbear sometimes to consider how happily the *Idler* is settled in an easier condition, who, surrounded like him with terrors, could have done nothing but lie down and die.

Amidst these reflections he came to a town and found a dinner, which disposed him to more chearful sentiments: but the joys of life are short, and its miseries are long; he mounted and travelled fifteen miles more thro' dirt and desolation.

At last the sun set, and all the horrors of darkness came upon him. He then repented the weak indulgence by which he had gratified himself at noon with too long an interval of rest: yet he went forward along a path which he could no longer see, sometimes rushing suddenly into water, and sometimes incumbered with stiff clay, ignorant whither he was going, and uncertain whether his next step might not be the last.

In this dismal gloom of nocturnal peregrination his horse unexpectedly stood still. *Marvel* had heard many relations of the instinct of horses, and was in doubt what danger might be at hand. Sometimes he fancied that he was on the bank of a river still and deep, and sometimes that a dead body lay across the track. He sat still awhile to recollect his thoughts; and as he was about to alight and explore the darkness, out stepped a man with a lantern, and opened the turnpike. He hired a guide to the town, arrived in safety, and slept in quiet.

The rest of his journey was nothing but danger. He climbed and descended precipices on which vulgar mortals tremble to look; he passed marshes like the *Serbonian bog, where armies whole have sunk*;[2] he forded rivers where the current roared like the *Egre* of the *Severn*;[3] or ventured himself on bridges that trembled under him, from which he looked down on foaming whirlpools, or dreadful abysses; he wandered over houseless heaths, amidst all the rage of the Elements, with the snow driving in his face, and the tempest howling in his ears.

Such are the colours in which *Marvel* paints his adventures. He has accustomed himself to sounding words and hyperbolical images, till he has lost the power of true description. In a road through which the heaviest carriages pass without difficulty, and the post-boy every day and night goes and returns, he meets with hardships like those which are endured in *Siberian* deserts, and misses nothing of romantic danger but a giant and a dragon. When his dreadful story is told in proper terms, it is only, that the way was dirty in winter, and that he experienced the common vicissitudes of rain and sunshine.

No. 50. Saturday, 31 March 1759.

The character of Mr. *Marvel* has raised the merriment of some and the contempt of others, who do not sufficiently consider how often they hear and practise the same arts of exaggerated narration.

There is not, perhaps, among the multitudes of all conditions that swarm upon the earth, a single man who does not believe that he has something extraordinary to relate of himself; and who does not, at one time or other, summon the attention of his friends to the casualties of his adventures and the vicissitudes of his fortune; casualties and vicissitudes that happen alike in lives uniform and diversified; to the Commander of armies, and the Writer at a desk; to the Sailor who resigns himself to the wind and water, and the Farmer whose longest journey is to the market.

In the present state of the world man may pass thro' *Shakespear*'s seven stages of life,[1] and meet nothing singular or wonderful. But such is every man's attention to himself, that what is common and unheeded when it is only seen, becomes remarkable and peculiar when we happen to feel it.

It is well enough known to be according to the usual process of Nature, that men should sicken and recover, that some designs should succeed and others miscarry, that friends should be separated and meet again, that some should be made angry by endeavours to please them, and some be pleased when no care has been used to gain their approbation; that men and women should at first come together by chance, like each other so well as to commence acquaintance, improve acquaintance into fondness, increase or extinguish fondness by marriage, and have children of different degrees of intellects and virtue, some of whom die before their parents, and others survive them.

Yet let any man tell his own story, and nothing of all this has ever befallen him according to the common order of things; something has always discriminated his case; some unusual concurrence of events has appeared which made him more happy or more miserable than other mortals; for in pleasures or calamities, however common, every one has comforts and afflictions of his own.

It is certain that without some artificial augmentations, many of the pleasures of life, and almost all its embellishments, would fall to the ground. If no man was to express more delight than he felt, those who felt most would raise little envy. If travellers were to describe the most laboured performances of art with the same coldness as they survey them, all expectations of happiness from change of place would cease. The Pictures of *Raphael* would hang without spectators, and the Gardens of *Versailles* might be inhabited by hermits.[2] All the pleasure that is received ends in an opportunity of splendid falshood, in the power of gaining notice by the display of beauties which the eye was weary of beholding, and a history of happy moments, of which, in reality, the most happy was the last.

The ambition of superior sensibility and superior eloquence disposes the lovers of arts to receive rapture at one time, and communicate it at another; and each labours first to impose upon himself, and then to propagate the imposture.

Pain is less subject than pleasure to caprices of expression. The torments of disease, and the grief for irremediable misfortunes, sometimes are such as no words can declare, and can only be signified by groans, or sobs, or inarticulate ejulations.[3] Man has from nature a mode of utterance peculiar to pain, but he has none peculiar to pleasure, because he never has pleasure but in such degrees as the ordinary use of language may equal or surpass.

It is nevertheless certain, that many pains as well as pleasures are heightened by rhetorical affectation, and that the picture is, for the most part, bigger than the life.

When we describe our sensations of another's sorrows, either in friendly or ceremonious condolence, the customs of the world scarcely admit of rigid veracity. Perhaps the fondest friendship would enrage oftner than comfort, were the tongue on such occasions faithfully to represent the sentiments of the heart; and I think the strictest moralists allow forms of address to be used without much regard to their literal acceptation, when either respect or tenderness requires them, because they are universally known to denote not the degree but the species of our sentiments.

But the same indulgence cannot be allowed to him who aggravates dangers incurred or sorrow endured by himself, because he darkens the prospect of futurity, and multiplies the pains of our condition by useless terror. Those who magnify their delights are less criminal deceivers, yet they raise hopes which are sure to be disappointed. It would be undoubtedly best, if we could see and hear every thing as it is, that nothing might be too anxiously dreaded, or too ardently pursued.

No. 51. Saturday, 7 April 1759.

It has been commonly remarked, that eminent men are least eminent at home, that bright characters lose much of their splendor at a nearer view, and many who fill the world with

their fame, excite very little reverence among those that surround them in their domestick privacies.

To blame or to suspect is easy and natural. When the fact is
evident, and the cause doubtful, some accusation is always
engendered between idleness and malignity. This disparity of
general and familiar esteem is therefore imputed to hidden vices,
and to practices indulged in secret, but carefully covered from
the publick eye.

Vice will indeed always produce contempt. The Dignity of
Alexander, tho' nations fell prostrate before him, was certainly
held in little veneration by the partakers of his midnight revels,
who had seen him, in the madness of wine, murder his friend,
or set fire to the *Persian* palace at the instigation of a harlot;[1]
and it is well remembered among us, that the Avarice of *Marlborough* kept him in subjection to his wife,[2] while he was
dreaded by *France* as her Conqueror, and honoured by the
Emperor as his Deliverer.

But though where there is vice there must be want of reverence, it is not reciprocally true, that when there is want of
reverence there is always vice. That awe which great actions or
abilities impress will be inevitably diminished by acquaintance,
tho' nothing either mean or criminal should be found.

Of men, as of every thing else, we must judge according to
our knowledge. When we see of a Hero only his Battles, or of a
Writer only his Books, we have nothing to allay our ideas of
their Greatness. We consider the one only as the Guardian of
his country, and the other only as the Instructor of mankind.
We have neither opportunity nor motive to examine the minuter
parts of their lives, or the less apparent peculiarities of their
characters; we name them with habitual respect, and forget,
what we still continue to know, that they are men like other
mortals.

But such is the constitution of the world, that much of life
must be spent in the same manner by the wise and the ignorant,
the exalted and the low. Men, however distinguished by external
accidents or intrinsick qualities, have all the same wants, the
same pains, and, as far as the senses are consulted, the same
pleasures. The petty cares and petty duties are the same in every

station to every understanding, and every hour brings some occasion on which we all sink to the common level. We are all naked till we are dressed, and hungry till we are fed; and the General's Triumph, and Sage's Disputation, end, like the humble labours of the Smith or Plowman, in a dinner or in sleep.

Those notions which are to be collected by reason in opposition to the senses, will seldom stand forward in the mind, but lie treasured in the remoter repositories of memory, to be found only when they are sought. Whatever any man may have written or done, his precepts or his valour will scarcely over-ballance the unimportant uniformity which runs thro' his time. We do not easily consider him as great, whom our own eyes shew us to be little; nor labour to keep present to our thoughts the latent excellencies of him who shares with us all our weaknesses and many of our follies; who like us is delighted with slight amusements, busied with trifling employments, and disturbed by little vexations.

Great powers cannot be exerted, but when great exigencies make them necessary. Great exigencies can happen but seldom, and therefore those qualities which have a claim to the veneration of mankind, lie hid, for the most part, like subterranean treasures, over which the foot passes as on common ground, till necessity breaks open the golden cavern.

In the ancient celebrations of victory, a slave was placed on the triumphal car, by the side of the General, who reminded him by a short sentence, that he was a Man.[3] Whatever danger there might be lest a Leader, in his passage to the Capitol, should forget the frailties of his nature, there was surely no need of such an admonition; the intoxication could not have continued long; he would have been at home but a few hours before some of his dependents would have forgot his greatness, and shewn him, that notwithstanding his laurels he was yet a man.

There are some who try to escape this domestic degradation, by labouring to appear always wise or always great; but he that strives against nature, will for ever strive in vain. To be grave of mien and slow of utterance; to look with solicitude and speak with hesitation, is attainable at will; but the shew of Wisdom is ridiculous when there is nothing to cause doubt, as that of Valour where there is nothing to be feared.

A man who has duly considered the condition of his being, will contentedly yield to the course of things: he will not pant for distinction where distinction would imply no merit, but tho' on great occasions he may wish to be greater than others, he will be satisfied in common occurrences not to be less.

No. 57. Saturday, 19 May 1759.

Prudence is of more frequent use than any other intellectual quality; it is exerted on slight occasions, and called into act by the cursory business of common life.

Whatever is universally necessary, has been granted to mankind on easy terms. Prudence, as it is always wanted, is without great difficulty obtained. It requires neither extensive view nor profound search, but forces itself, by spontaneous impulse, upon a mind neither great nor busy, neither ingrossed by vast designs nor distracted by multiplicity of attention.

Prudence operates on life in the same manner as rules on composition; it produces vigilance rather than elevation, rather prevents loss than procures advantages; and often escapes miscarriages, but seldom reaches either power or honour. It quenches that ardour of enterprize, by which every thing is done that can claim praise or admiration, and represses that generous temerity which often fails and often succeeds. Rules may obviate faults, but can never confer beauties; and Prudence keeps life safe, but does not often make it happy. The world is not amazed with prodigies of excellence, but when Wit tramples upon Rules, and Magnanimity breaks the chains of Prudence.

One of the most prudent of all that have fallen within my observation, is my old companion *Sophron*, who has passed through the world in quiet, by perpetual adherence to a few plain maxims, and wonders how contention and distress can so often happen.

The first principle of *Sophron* is to *run no hazards*. Tho' he loves money, he is of opinion, that frugality is a more certain source of riches than industry. It is to no purpose that any prospect of large profit is set before him; he believes little about futurity, and does not love to trust his money out of his sight, for nobody knows what may happen. He has a small estate which he lets at the old rent, because *it is better to have a little than nothing*; but he rigorously demands payment on the stated day, for *he that cannot pay one quarter cannot pay two*. If he is told of any improvements in Agriculture, he likes the old way, has observed that changes very seldom answer expectation, is of opinion that our forefathers knew how to till the ground as well as we; and concludes with an argument that nothing can overpower, that the expence of planting and fencing is immediate, and the advantage distant, and that *he is no wise man who will quit a certainty for an uncertainty*.

Another of *Sophron*'s rules is, *to mind no business but his own*. In the State he is of no party; but hears and speaks of publick affairs with the same coldness as of the administration of some ancient republick. If any flagrant act of Fraud or Oppression is mentioned, he hopes that *all is not true that is told*: if Misconduct or Corruption puts the nation in a flame, he hopes that *every man means well*. At Elections he leaves his dependents to their own choice, and declines to vote himself, for every Candidate is a good man, whom he is unwilling to oppose or offend.

If disputes happen among his neighbours he observes an invariable and cold neutrality. His punctuality has gained him the reputation of honesty, and his caution that of wisdom, and few would refuse to refer their claims to his award. He might have prevented many expensive law-suits, and quenched many a feud in its first smoke, but always refuses the office of Arbitration, because he must decide against one or the other.

With the affairs of other families he is always unacquainted. He sees estates bought and sold, squandered and increased, without praising the economist or censuring the spendthrift. He never courts the rising lest they should fall, nor insults the fallen lest they should rise again. His caution has the appearance of virtue, and all who do not want his help praise his benevolence; but if any man solicits his assistance, he has just sent away all his money; and when the petitioner is gone declares to his family that he is sorry for his misfortunes, has always looked upon him with particular kindness, and therefore could not lend him money, lest he should destroy their friendship by the necessity of enforcing payment.

Of domestic misfortunes he has never heard. When he is told the hundredth time of a Gentleman's daughter who has married the coachman, he lifts up his hands with astonishment, for he always thought her a very sober girl. When nuptial quarrels, after having filled the country with talk and laughter, at last end in separation, he never can conceive how it happened, for he looked upon them as a happy couple.

If his advice is asked, he never gives any particular direction, because events are uncertain, and he will bring no blame upon himself; but he takes the consulter tenderly by the hand, tells him he makes his case his own, and advises him not to act rashly, but to weigh the reasons on both sides; observes that a man may be as easily too hasty as too slow, and that as many fail by doing too much as too little; that *a wise man has two ears and one tongue*; and *that little said is soon amended*; that he could tell him this and that, but that after all every man is the best judge of his own affairs.

With this some are satisfied, and go home with great reverence of *Sophron*'s wisdom, and none are offended, because every one is left in full possession of his own opinion.

Sophron gives no characters. It is equally vain to tell him of Vice and Virtue, for he has remarked that no man likes to be censured, and that very few are delighted with the praises of another. He has a few terms which he uses to all alike. With respect to fortune, he believes every family to be in good circumstances; he never exalts any understanding by lavish praise, yet he meets with none but very sensible people. Every man is honest and hearty, and every woman is a good creature.

Thus *Sophron* creeps along, neither loved nor hated, neither favoured nor opposed; he has never attempted to grow rich for fear of growing poor, and has raised no friends for fear of making enemies.

No. 58. Saturday, 26 May 1759.

Pleasure is very seldom found where it is sought. Our brightest blazes of gladness are commonly kindled by unexpected sparks. The flowers which scatter their odours from time to time in the paths of life, grow up without culture from seeds scattered by chance.

Nothing is more hopeless than a scheme of merriment. Wits and humorists are brought together from distant quarters by preconcerted invitations; they come attended by their admirers prepared to laugh and to applaud: They gaze a-while on each other, ashamed to be silent, and afraid to speak; every man is discontented with himself, grows angry with those that give him pain, and resolves that he will contribute nothing to the merriment of such worthless company. Wine inflames the general malignity, and changes sullenness to petulance, till at last none can bear any longer the presence of the rest. They retire to vent their indignation in safer places, where they are heard with attention; their importance is restored, they recover their good humour, and gladden the night with wit and jocularity.

Merriment is always the effect of a sudden impression. The jest which is expected is already destroyed. The most active imagination will be sometimes torpid, under the frigid influence of melancholy, and sometimes occasions will be wanting to tempt the mind, however volatile, to sallies and excursions. Nothing was ever said with uncommon felicity, but by the co-operation of chance; and therefore, wit as well as valour must be content to share its honours with fortune.

All other pleasures are equally uncertain; the general remedy of uneasiness is change of place; almost every one has some journey of Pleasure in his mind, with which he flatters his expectation. He that travels in theory has no inconveniences; he has shade and sunshine at his disposal, and wherever he alights finds tables of plenty and looks of gaiety. These ideas are indulged till the day of departure arrives, the chaise is called, and the progress of happiness begins.

A few miles teach him the fallacies of imagination. The road is dusty, the air is sultry, the horses are sluggish, and the postilion brutal. He longs for the time of dinner that he may eat and rest. The inn is crouded, his orders are neglected, and nothing remains but that he devour in haste what the cook has spoiled, and drive on in quest of better entertainment. He finds at night a more commodious house, but the best is always worse than he expected.

He at last enters his native province, and resolves to feast his mind with the conversation of his old friends, and the recollection of juvenile frolicks. He stops at the house of his friend whom he designs to overpower with pleasure by the unexpected interview. He is not known till he tells his name, and revives the memory of himself by a gradual explanation. He is then coldly received, and ceremoniously feasted. He hastes away to another whom his affairs have called to a distant place, and having seen the empty house, goes away disgusted, by a disappointment which could not be intended because it could not be foreseen. At the next house he finds every face clouded with misfortune, and is regarded with malevolence as an unreasonable intruder, who comes not to visit but to insult them.

It is seldom that we find either men or places such as we expect them. He that has pictured a prospect upon his fancy, will receive little pleasure from his eyes; he that has anticipated the conversation of a wit, will wonder to what prejudice he owes his reputation. Yet it is necessary to hope, tho' hope should always be deluded, for hope itself is happiness, and its frustrations, however frequent, are yet less dreadful than its extinction.

No. 59. Saturday, 2 June 1759.

In the common enjoyments of life, we cannot very liberally indulge the present hour, but by anticipating part of the pleasure which might have relieved the tediousness of another day; and any uncommon exertion of strength, or perseverance in labour, is succeeded by a long interval of languor and weariness. Whatever advantage we snatch beyond the certain portion allotted us by nature, is like money spent before it is due, which at the time of regular payment will be missed and regretted.

Fame, like all other things which are supposed to give or to encrease happiness, is dispensed with the same equality of distribution. He that is loudly praised will be clamorously censured; he that rises hastily into fame will be in danger of sinking suddenly into oblivion.

Of many writers who filled their age with wonder, and whose names we find celebrated in the books of their cotemporaries, the works are now no longer to be seen, or are seen only amidst the lumber of libraries which are seldom visited, where they lie only to shew the deceitfulness of hope, and the uncertainty of honour.

Of the decline of reputation many causes may be assigned. It is commonly lost because it never was deserved, and was conferred at first, not by the suffrage of criticism, but by the fondness of friendship, or servility of flattery. The great and popular are very freely applauded, but all soon grow weary of echoing to each other a name which has no other claim to notice, but that many mouths are pronouncing it at once.

But many have lost the final reward of their labours, because they were too hasty to enjoy it. They have laid hold on recent occurrences, and eminent names, and delighted their readers with allusions and remarks, in which all were interested, and to which all therefore were attentive. But the effect ceased with its cause; the time quickly came when new events drove the former from memory, when the vicissitudes of the world brought new hopes and fears, transferred the love and hatred of the public to other agents, and the writer whose works were no longer assisted by gratitude or resentment, was left to the cold regard of idle curiosity.

He that writes upon general principles, or delivers universal truths, may hope to be often read, because his work will be equally useful at all times and in every country, but he cannot expect it to be received with eagerness, or to spread with rapidity, because desire can have no particular stimulation; that which is to be loved long must be loved with reason rather than with passion. He that lays out his labours upon temporary subjects, easily finds readers, and quickly loses them; for what should make the book valued when its subject is no more.

These observations will shew the reason why the Poem of *Hudibras*[1] is almost forgotten however embellished with sentiments and diversified with allusions, however bright with wit, and however solid with truth. The hypocrisy which it detected, and the folly which it ridiculed, have long vanished from public notice. Those who had felt the mischiefs of discord, and the tyranny of usurpation, read it with rapture, for every line brought back to memory something known, and gratified resentment, by the just censure of something hated. But the book which was once quoted by princes, and which supplied conversation to all the assemblies of the gay and witty, is now seldom mentioned, and even by those that affect to mention it, is seldom read. So vainly is wit lavished upon fugitive topics, so little can architecture secure duration when the ground is false.

No. 60. Saturday, 9 June 1759.

Criticism is a study by which men grow important and formidable at very small expence. The power of invention has been conferred by Nature upon few, and the labour of learning those sciences which may, by mere labour, be obtained, is too great to be willingly endured; but every man can exert such judgment as he has upon the works of others; and he whom Nature has made weak, and Idleness keeps ignorant, may yet support his vanity by the name of a Critick.

I hope it will give comfort to great numbers who are passing thro' the world in obscurity, when I inform them how easily distinction may be obtained. All the other powers of literature are coy and haughty, they must be long courted, and at last are not always gained; but Criticism is a goddess easy of access and forward of advance, who will meet the slow and encourage the timorous; the want of meaning she supplies with words, and the want of spirit she recompenses with malignity.

This profession has one recommendation peculiar to itself, that it gives vent to malignity without real mischief. No genius was ever blasted by the breath of Criticks. The poison which, if confined, would have burst the heart, fumes away in empty hisses, and malice is set at ease with very little danger to merit. The Critick is the only man whose triumph is without another's pain, and whose greatness does not rise upon another's ruin.

To a study at once so easy and so reputable, so malicious and so harmless, it cannot be necessary to invite my readers by a long or laboured exhortation; it is sufficient, since all would be Criticks if they could, to shew by one eminent example that all can be Criticks if they will.

Dick Minim, after the common course of puerile studies, in which he was no great proficient, was put apprentice to a Brewer, with whom he had lived two years, when his uncle died in the city, and left him a large fortune in the stocks. *Dick* had for six months before used the company of the lower players, of whom he had learned to scorn a trade, and being now at liberty to follow his genius, he resolved to be a man of wit and humour. That he might be properly initiated in his new character, he frequented the coffee-houses near the theatres, where he listened very diligently day, after day, to those who talked of language and sentiments, and unities and catastrophes, till by slow degrees he began to think that he understood something of the Stage, and hoped in time to talk himself.

But he did not trust so much to natural sagacity, as wholly to neglect the help of books. When the theatres were shut, he retired to *Richmond* with a few select writers, whose opinions he impressed upon his memory by unwearied diligence; and when he returned with other wits to the town, was able to tell, in very proper phrases, that the chief business of art is to copy nature; that a perfect writer is not to be expected, because genius decays as judgment increases; that the great art is the art of blotting, and that according to the rule of *Horace* every piece should be kept nine years.[1]

Of the great Authors he now began to display the Characters, laying down as an universal position that all had beauties and defects. His opinion was,[2] that *Shakespear*, committing himself wholly to the impulse of Nature, wanted that correctness which learning would have given him; and that *Johnson*,[3] trusting to learning, did not sufficiently cast his eye on Nature. He blamed the *Stanza* of *Spenser*, and could not bear the *Hexameters* of *Sidney*. *Denham* and *Waller* he held the first reformers of *English* Numbers, and thought that if *Waller* could have obtained the strength of *Denham*, or *Denham* the sweetness of *Waller*, there had been nothing wanting to complete a Poet. He often expressed his commiseration of *Dryden*'s poverty, and his indignation at the age which suffered him to write for bread; he repeated with rapture the first lines of *All for Love*, but wondered at the corruption of taste which could bear any thing so unnatural as rhyming Tragedies. In *Otway*[4] he found uncommon powers of moving the passions, but was disgusted by his general negligence, and blamed him for making a Conspirator his Hero; and never concluded his disquisition, without remarking how happily the sound of the clock is made to alarm the audience. *Southern*[5] would have been his favourite, but that he mixes comick with tragick scenes, intercepts the natural course of the passions, and fills the mind with a wild confusion of mirth and melancholy. The versification of *Rowe*[6] he thought too melodious for the stage, and too little varied in different passions. He made it the great fault of *Congreve*,[7] that all his persons were wits, and that he always wrote with more art than nature. He considered *Cato* rather as a poem than a play, and allowed *Addison*[8] to be the complete master of Allegory and grave humour, but paid no great deference to him as a Critick. He thought the chief merit of *Prior*[9] was in his easy tales and lighter poems, tho' he allowed that his *Solomon* had many noble sentiments elegantly expressed. In *Swift*[10] he discovered an inimitable vein of irony, and an easiness which all would hope and few would attain. *Pope*[11] he was inclined to degrade from a Poet to a Versifier, and thought his Numbers rather luscious than sweet. He often lamented the neglect of *Phædra and Hippolitus*,[12] and wished to see the stage under better regulations.

These assertions passed commonly uncontradicted; and if now and then an opponent started up, he was quickly repressed by the suffrages of the company, and *Minim* went away from every dispute with elation of heart and increase of confidence.

He now grew conscious of his abilities, and began to talk of the present state of dramatick Poetry; wondered what was become of the comick genius which supplied our ancestors with wit and pleasantry, and why no writer could be found that durst now venture beyond a Farce. He saw no reason for thinking that the vein of humour was exhausted, since we live in a country where liberty suffers every character to spread itself to its utmost bulk, and which therefore produces more originals than all the rest of the world together.[13] Of Tragedy he concluded business to be the soul, and yet often hinted that love predominates too much upon the modern stage.

He was now an acknowledged Critick, and had his own seat in the coffee-house, and headed a party in the pit. *Minim* has more vanity than ill-nature, and seldom desires to do much mischief; he will perhaps murmur a little in the ear of him that sits next him, but endeavours to influence the audience to favour, by clapping when an actor exclaims *ye Gods*, or laments the misery of his country.

By degrees he was admitted to Rehearsals, and many of his friends are of opinion, that our present Poets are indebted to him for their happiest thoughts; by his contrivance the bell was rung twice in *Barbarossa*,[14] and by his persuasion the author of *Cleone*[15] concluded his Play without a couplet; for what can be more absurd, said *Minim*, than that part of a play should be rhymed, and part written in blank verse? and by what acquisition of faculties is the Speaker who never could find rhymes before, enabled to rhyme at the conclusion of an Act!

He is the great investigator of hidden beauties, and is particularly delighted when he finds *the Sound an Echo to the Sense*.[16] He has read all our Poets with particular attention to this delicacy of Versification, and wonders at the supineness with which their Works have been hitherto perused, so that no man has found the sound of a Drum in this distich,

> When Pulpit, Drum ecclesiastic,
> Was beat with fist instead of a stick;[17]

and that the wonderful lines upon Honour and a Bubble have hitherto passed without notice.

> Honour is like the glassy Bubble,
> Which costs Philosophers such trouble,
> Where one part crack'd, the whole does fly,
> And Wits are crack'd to find out why.[18]

In these Verses, says *Minim*, we have two striking accommodations of the Sound to the Sense. It is impossible to utter the two lines emphatically without an act like that which they describe; *Bubble* and *Trouble* causing a momentary inflation of the Cheeks by the retention of the breath, which is afterwards forcibly emitted, as in the practice of *blowing bubbles*. But the greatest excellence is in the third line, which is *crack'd* in the middle to express a crack, and then shivers into monosyllables. Yet has this diamond lain neglected with common stones, and among the innumerable admirers of *Hudibras* the observation of this superlative passage has been reserved for the sagacity of *Minim*.

No. 61. Saturday, 16 June 1759.

Mr. *Minim* had now advanced himself to the zenith of critical reputation; when he was in the Pit, every eye in the Boxes was fixed upon him, when he entered his Coffee-house, he was surrounded by circles of candidates, who passed their noviciate of literature under his tuition; his opinion was asked by all who had no opinion of their own, and yet loved to debate and decide; and no composition was supposed to pass in safety to posterity, till it had been secured by *Minim*'s approbation.

Minim professes great admiration of the wisdom and munificence by which the Academies of the Continent were raised, and often wishes for some standard of taste, for some tribunal,[1] to which merit may appeal from caprice, prejudice, and malignity. He has formed a plan for an Academy of Criticism, where every work of Imagination may be read before it is printed, and which shall authoritatively direct the Theatres what pieces to receive or reject, to exclude or to revive.

Such an institution would, in *Dick*'s opinion, spread the fame of *English* literature over *Europe*, and make *London* the metropolis of elegance and politeness, the place to which the learned and ingenious of all countries would repair for instruction and improvement, and where nothing would any longer be applauded or endured that was not conformed to the nicest rules, and finished with the highest elegance.

Till some happy conjunction of the planets shall dispose our Princes or Ministers to make themselves immortal by such an Academy, *Minim* contents himself to preside four nights in a week in a Critical Society selected by himself, where he is heard without contradiction, and whence his judgment is disseminated through the great vulgar and the small.

When he is placed in the chair of Criticism, he declares loudly for the noble simplicity of our ancestors, in opposition to the petty refinements, and ornamental luxuriance.[2] Sometimes he is sunk in despair, and perceives false delicacy daily gaining ground, and sometimes brightens his countenance with a gleam of hope, and predicts the revival of the true sublime. He then fulminates his loudest censures against the monkish barbarity of rhyme;[3] wonders how beings that pretend to reason can be pleased with one line always ending like another; tells how unjustly and unnaturally sense is sacrificed to sound; how often the best thoughts are mangled by the necessity of confining or extending them to the dimensions of a couplet; and rejoices that genius has, in our days, shaken off the shackles which had encumbered it so long. Yet he allows that rhyme may sometimes be borne, if the lines be often broken, and the pauses judiciously diversified.

From Blank Verse he makes an easy transition to *Milton*, whom he produces as an example of the slow advance of lasting reputation. *Milton* is the only writer whose books *Minim* can read for ever without weariness. What cause it is that exempts this pleasure from satiety he has long and diligently enquired, and believes it to consist in the perpetual variation of the numbers,[4] by which the ear is gratified and the attention awakened. The lines that are commonly thought rugged and unmusical, he conceives to have been written to temper the melodious luxury of the rest, or to express things by a proper cadence: for he scarcely finds a verse that has not this favourite beauty; he declares that he could shiver in a hot-house when he reads that

> the ground
> Burns frore, and cold performs th' effect of fire.[5]

And that when *Milton* bewails his blindness, the verse

> So thick a drop serene has quench'd these orbs,[6]

has, he knows not how, something that strikes him with an obscure sensation like that which he fancies would be felt from the sound of Darkness.

Minim is not so confident of his rules of Judgment as not very eagerly to catch new light from the name of the author. He is commonly so prudent as to spare those whom he cannot resist, unless, as will sometimes happen, he finds the publick combined against them. But a fresh pretender to fame he is strongly inclined to censure, 'till his own honour requires that he commend him. 'Till he knows the success of a composition, he intrenches himself in general terms; there are some new thoughts and beautiful passages, but there is likewise much which he would have advised the author to expunge. He has several favourite epithets, of which he has never settled the meaning, but which are very commodiously applied to books which he has not read, or cannot understand. One is *manly*, another is *dry*, another *stiff*, and another *flimzy*; sometimes he discovers delicacy of style, and sometimes meets with *strange expressions*.

He is never so great, or so happy, as when a youth of promising parts is brought to receive his directions for the prosecution of his studies. He then puts on a very serious air; he advises the pupil to read none but the best Authors, and, when he finds one congenial to his own mind, to study his beauties, but avoid his faults, and, when he sits down to write, to consider how his favourite Author would think at the present time on the present occasion. He exhorts him to catch those moments when he finds his thoughts expanded and his genius exalted, but to take care lest imagination hurry him beyond the bounds of Nature. He holds Diligence the mother of Success, yet enjoins him, with great earnestness, not to read more than he can digest, and not to confuse his mind by pursuing studies of contrary tendencies. He tells him, that every man has his genius, and that *Cicero* could never be a Poet. The boy retires illuminated, resolves to follow his genius, and to think how *Milton* would have thought; and *Minim* feasts upon his own beneficence till another day brings another Pupil.

No. 65. Saturday, 14 July 1759.

The Sequel of *Clarendon*'s History,[1] at last happily published, is an accession to *English* Literature equally agreeable to the admirers of elegance and the lovers of truth; many doubtful facts may now be ascertained, and many questions, after long debate, may be determined by decisive authority. He that records transactions in which himself was engaged, has not only an opportunity of knowing innumerable particulars which escape spectators, but has his natural powers exalted by that ardour which always rises at the remembrance of our own importance, and by which every man is enabled to relate his own actions better than another's.

The difficulties thro' which this Work has struggled into light, and the delays with which our hopes have been long mocked, naturally lead the mind to the consideration of the common fate of posthumous compositions.

He who sees himself surrounded by admirers, and whose vanity is hourly feasted with all the luxuries of studied praise, is easily persuaded that his influence will be extended beyond his life; that they who cringe in his presence will reverence his memory, and that those who are proud to be numbered among his friends, will endeavour to vindicate his choice by zeal for his reputation.

With hopes like these, to the Executors of *Swift* was committed the History of the last years of Queen *Anne*, and to those of *Pope* the Works which remained unprinted in his closet. The performances of *Pope* were burnt by those whom he had perhaps selected from all mankind as most likely to publish them; and the History had likewise perished, had not a straggling transcript fallen into busy hands.

The Papers left in the closet of *Peiresc* supplied his heirs with a whole winter's fuel,[2] and many of the labours of the learned Bishop *Lloyd*[3] were consumed in the kitchen of his descendants.

Some Works, indeed, have escaped total destruction, but yet have had reason to lament the fate of Orphans exposed to the frauds of unfaithful Guardians. How *Hale* would have borne the mutilations which his *Pleas of the Crown* have suffered from the Editor, they who know his character will easily conceive.[4]

The original Copy of *Burnet*'s History, tho' promised to some publick* Library, has been never given;[5] and who then can prove the fidelity of the publication, when the authenticity of *Clarendon*'s History, tho' printed with the sanction of one of the first Universities of the World, had not an unexpected manuscript been happily discovered, would, with the help of factious credulity, have been brought into question by the two lowest of all human beings,[6] a Scribbler for a Party, and a Commissioner of Excise?

Vanity is often no less mischievous than negligence or dishonesty. He that possesses a valuable Manuscript, hopes to raise its esteem by concealment, and delights in the distinction which he imagines himself to obtain by keeping the key of a treasure which he neither uses nor imparts. From him it falls to some other owner, less vain but more negligent, who considers it as useless lumber, and rids himself of the incumbrance.

Yet there are some works which the Authors must consign unpublished to posterity, however uncertain be the event, however hopeless be the trust. He that writes the history of his own times, if he adheres steadily to truth, will write that which his

---

* It would be proper to reposite, in some publick Place, the Manuscript of *Clarendon*, which has not escaped all suspicion of unfaithful publication.

own times will not easily endure. He must be content to reposite his book till all private passions shall cease, and love and hatred give way to curiosity.

But many leave the labour of half their life to their executors and to chance, because they will not send them abroad unfinished, and are unable to finish them, having prescribed to themselves such a degree of exactness as human diligence scarcely can attain. *Lloyd*, says *Burnet*, *did not lay out his learning with the same diligence as he laid it in*.[7] He was always hesitating and enquiring, raising objections and removing them, and waiting for clearer light and fuller discovery. *Baker*, after many years past in Biography, left his manuscripts to be buried in a library, because that was imperfect which could never be perfected.[8]

Of these learned men let those who aspire to the same praise, imitate the diligence and avoid the scrupulosity. Let it be always remembered that life is short, that knowledge is endless, and that many doubts deserve not to be cleared. Let those whom nature and study have qualified to teach mankind, tell us what they have learned while they are yet able to tell it, and trust their reputation only to themselves.

No. 66. Saturday, 21 July 1759.

No complaint is more frequently repeated among the learned, than that of the waste made by time among the labours of Antiquity. Of those who once filled the civilized world with their renown nothing is now left but their names, which are left only to raise desires that never can be satisfied, and sorrow which never can be comforted.

Had all the writings of the ancients been faithfully delivered down from age to age, had the *Alexandrian* library been spared, and the *Palatine* repositories[1] remained unimpaired, how much might we have known of which we are now doomed to be ignorant; how many laborious enquiries, and dark conjectures, how many collations of broken hints and mutilated passages might have been spared. We should have known the Successions of Princes, the Revolutions of Empire, the Actions of the Great, and Opinions of the Wise, the Laws and Constitutions of every State, and the Arts by which public Grandeur and Happiness are acquired and preserved. We should have traced the progress of Life, seen Colonies from distant regions take possession of *European* deserts, and troops of Savages settled into Communities by the desire of keeping what they had acquired; we should have traced the gradations of civility, and travelled upward to the original of things by the light of History, till in remoter times it had glimmered in fable, and at last sunk into darkness.

If the works of imagination had been less diminished, it is likely that all future times might have been supplied with inexhaustible amusement by the fictions of Antiquity. The Tragedies of *Sophocles* and *Euripides* would have shewn all the stronger passions in all their diversities, and the Comedies of *Menander*[2] would have furnished all the maxims of domestic life. Nothing would have been necessary to moral wisdom but to have studied these great Masters, whose knowledge would have guided doubt, and whose authority would have silenced cavils.

Such are the thoughts that rise in every Student, when his curiosity is eluded, and his searches are frustrated; yet it may perhaps be doubted, whether our complaints are not sometimes inconsiderate, and whether we do not imagine more evil than we feel. Of the Ancients, enough remains to excite our emulation, and direct our endeavours.[3] Many of the works which time has left us, we know to have been those that were most esteemed, and which Antiquity itself considered as Models; so that having the Originals, we may without much regret lose the imitations. The obscurity which the want of contemporary writers often produces, only darkens single passages, and those commonly of slight importance. The general tendency of every piece may be known, and tho' that diligence deserves praise which leaves nothing unexamined, yet its miscarriages are not much to be lamented; for the most useful truths are always universal, and unconnected with accidents and customs.

Such is the general conspiracy of human nature against contemporary merit, that if we had inherited from Antiquity enough to afford employment for the laborious, and amusement for the idle, I know not what room would have been left for modern genius or modern industry; almost every subject would have been preoccupied, and every style would have been fixed by a precedent from which few would have ventured to depart. Every writer would have had a rival, whose superiority was already acknowledged, and to whose fame his work would, even before it was seen, be marked out for a sacrifice.

We see how little the united experience of mankind have been able to add to the heroic characters displayed by *Homer*, and how few incidents the fertile imagination of modern *Italy* has yet produced, which may not be found in the *Iliad* and *Odyssey*. It is likely, that if all the works of the *Athenian* Philosophers had been extant, *Malbranche* and *Locke*[4] would have been condemned to be silent readers of the ancient Metaphysicians; and it is apparent, that if the old writers had all remained, the *Idler* could not have written a disquisition on the loss.

No. 72. Saturday, 1 September 1759.

Men complain of nothing more frequently than of deficient Memory; and indeed, every one finds that many of the ideas which he desired to retain have slipped irretrievably away; that the acquisitions of the mind are sometimes equally fugitive with the gifts of fortune; and that a short intermission of attention more certainly lessens knowledge than impairs an estate.

To assist this weakness of our nature many methods have been proposed, all of which may be justly suspected of being ineffectual; for no art of memory, however its effects have been boasted or admired, has been ever adopted into general use, nor have those who possessed it, appeared to excel others in readiness of recollection or multiplicity of attainments.

There is another art of which all have felt the want, tho' *Themistocles*[1] only confessed it. We suffer equal pain from the pertinacious adhesion of unwelcome images, as from the evanescence of those which are pleasing and useful; and it may be doubted whether we should be more benefited by the art of Memory or the art of Forgetfulness.[2]

Forgetfulness is necessary to Remembrance. Ideas are retained by renovation of that impression which time is always wearing away, and which new images are striving to obliterate. If useless thoughts could be expelled from the mind, all the valuable parts of our knowledge would more frequently recur, and every recurrence would reinstate them in their former place.

It is impossible to consider, without some regret, how much might have been learned, or how much might have been invented by a rational and vigorous application of time, uselessly or painfully passed in the revocation of events, which have left neither good nor evil behind them, in grief for misfortunes either repaired or irreparable, in resentment of injuries known only to ourselves, of which death has put the authors beyond our power.

Philosophy has accumulated precept upon precept, to warn us against the anticipation of future calamities. All useless misery is certainly folly, and he that feels evils before they come may be deservedly censured; yet surely to dread the future is more reasonable than to lament the past. The business of life is to go forwards; he who sees evil in prospect meets it in his way, but he who catches it by retrospection turns back to find it. That which is feared may sometimes be avoided, but that which is regretted to-day may be regretted again to-morrow.

Regret is indeed useful and virtuous, and not only allowable but necessary, when it tends to the amendment of life, or to admonition of error which we may be again in danger of committing. But a very small part of the moments spent in meditation on the past, produce any reasonable caution or salutary sorrow. Most of the mortifications that we have suffered, arose from the concurrence of local and temporary circumstances, which can never meet again; and most of our disappointments have succeeded those expectations, which life allows not to be formed a second time.

It would add much to human happiness, if an art could be taught of forgetting all of which the remembrance is at once useless and afflictive, if that pain which never can end in pleasure could be driven totally away, that the mind might perform its functions without incumbrance, and the past might no longer encroach upon the present.

Little can be done well to which the whole mind is not applied; the business of every day calls for the day to which it is assigned, and he will have no leisure to regret yesterday's vexations who resolves not to have a new subject of regret tomorrow.

But to forget or to remember at pleasure, are equally beyond the power of man. Yet as memory may be assisted by method, and the decays of knowledge repaired by stated times of recollection, so the power of forgetting is capable of improvement. Reason will, by a resolute contest, prevail over imagination, and the power may be obtained of transferring the attention as judgment shall direct.

The incursions of troublesome thoughts are often violent and importunate; and it is not easy to a mind accustomed to their inroads to expel them immediately by putting better images into motion; but this enemy of quiet is above all others weakened by every defeat; the reflection which has been once overpowered and ejected, seldom returns with any formidable vehemence.

Employment is the great instrument of intellectual dominion. The mind cannot retire from its enemy into total vacancy, or turn aside from one object but by passing to another. The gloomy and the resentful are always found among those who have nothing to do, or who do nothing. We must be busy about good or evil, and he to whom the present offers nothing will often be looking backward on the past.

No. 81. Saturday, 3 November 1759.

As the *English* army was passing towards *Quebec*[1] along a soft savanna between a mountain and a lake, one of the petty Chiefs of the inland regions stood upon a rock surrounded by his clan, and from behind the shelter of the bushes contemplated the art and regularity of *European* war. It was evening, the tents were pitched, he observed the security with which the troops rested in the night, and the order with which the march was renewed in the morning. He continued to pursue them with his eye till they could be seen no longer, and then stood for some time silent and pensive.

Then turning to his followers, "My children (said he) I have often heard from men hoary with long life, that there was a time when our ancestors were absolute lords of the woods, the meadows, and the lakes, wherever the eye can reach or the foot can pass. They fished and hunted, feasted and danced, and when they were weary lay down under the first thicket, without danger and without fear. They changed their habitations as the seasons required, convenience prompted, or curiosity allured them, and sometimes gathered the fruits of the mountain, and sometimes sported in canoes along the coast.

"Many years and ages are supposed to have been thus passed in plenty and security; when at last, a new race of men entered our country from the great Ocean. They inclosed themselves in habitations of stone, which our ancestors could neither enter by violence, nor destroy by fire. They issued from those fastnesses, sometimes covered like the armadillo with shells, from which the lance rebounded on the striker, and sometimes carried by mighty beasts which had never been seen in our vales or forests, of such strength and swiftness, that flight and opposition were vain alike. Those invaders ranged over the continent, slaughtering in their rage those that resisted, and those that submitted, in their mirth. Of those that remained, some were buried in caverns, and condemned to dig metals for their masters; some were employed in tilling the ground, of which foreign tyrants devour the produce; and when the sword and the mines have destroyed the natives, they supply their place by human beings of another colour, brought from some distant country to perish here under toil and torture.

"Some there are who boast their humanity, and content themselves to seize our chaces and fisheries, who drive us from every track of ground where fertility and pleasantness invite them to settle, and make no war upon us except when we intrude upon our own lands.

"Others pretend to have purchased a right of residence and tyranny; but surely the insolence of such bargains is more offensive than the avowed and open dominion of force. What reward can induce the possessor of a country to admit a stranger more powerful than himself? Fraud or terror must operate in such contracts; either they promised protection which they never have afforded, or instruction which they never imparted. We hoped to be secured by their favour from some other evil, or to learn the arts of *Europe*, by which we might be able to secure ourselves. Their power they have never exerted in our defence, and their arts they have studiously concealed from us. Their treaties are only to deceive, and their traffick only to defraud us. They have a written Law among them, of which they boast as derived from him who made the Earth and Sea, and by which they profess to believe that man will be made happy when life shall forsake him. Why is not this Law communicated to us? It is concealed because it is violated. For how can they preach it to an *Indian* nation, when I am told that one of its first precepts forbids them to do to others what they would not that others should do to them.

"But the time perhaps is now approaching when the pride of usurpation shall be crushed, and the cruelties of invasion shall be revenged. The Sons of Rapacity have now drawn their swords upon each other, and referred their claims to the decision of war; let us look unconcerned upon the slaughter, and remember that the death of every *European* delivers the country from a tyrant and a robber; for what is the claim of either nation, but the claim of the vultur to the leveret, of the tiger to the faun? Let them then continue to dispute their title to regions which they cannot people, to purchase by danger and blood the empty dignity of dominion over mountains which they will never climb, and rivers which they will never pass. Let us endeavour, in the mean time, to learn their discipline, and to forge their weapons; and when they shall be weakened with mutual slaughter, let us rush down upon them, force their remains to take shelter in their ships, and reign once more in our native country."

No. 84. Saturday, 24 November 1759.

Biography is, of the various kinds of narrative writing, that which is most eagerly read, and most easily applied to the purposes of life.

In Romances, when the wild field of Possibility lies open to invention, the incidents may easily be made more numerous, the vicissitudes more sudden, and the events more wonderful; but from the time of life when Fancy begins to be over-ruled by Reason and corrected by Experience, the most artful tale raises little curiosity when it is known to be false; tho' it may, perhaps, be sometimes read as a model of a neat or elegant stile, not for the sake of knowing what it contains, but how it is written; or those that are weary of themselves, may have recourse to it as a pleasing dream, of which, when they awake, they voluntarily dismiss the images from their minds.

The examples and events of History press, indeed, upon the mind with the weight of truth; but when they are reposited in the memory, they are oftener employed for shew than use, and rather diversify conversation than regulate life. Few are engaged in such scenes as give them opportunities of growing wiser by the downfal of Statesmen or the defeat of Generals. The stratagems of War, and the intrigues of Courts, are read by far the greater part of mankind with the same indifference as the adventures of fabled Heroes, or the revolutions of a Fairy Region. Between falsehood and useless truth there is little difference. As gold which he cannot spend will make no man rich, so knowledge which he cannot apply will make no man wise.

The mischievous consequences of vice and folly, of irregular desires and predominant passions, are best discovered by those relations which are levelled with the general surface of life, which tell not how any man became great, but how he was made happy; not how he lost the favour of his Prince, but how he became discontented with himself.

Those relations are therefore commonly of most value in which the writer tells his own story. He that recounts the life of another, commonly dwells most upon conspicuous events, lessens the familiarity of his tale to increase its dignity, shews his favourite at a distance decorated and magnified like the ancient actors in their tragick dress, and endeavours to hide the man that he may produce a hero.

But if it be true which was said by a *French* Prince, *That no man was a Hero to the servants of his chamber*,[1] it is equally true that every man is yet less a Hero to himself. He that is most elevated above the croud by the importance of his employments or the reputation of his genius, feels himself affected by fame or business but as they influence his domestick life. The high and low, as they have the same faculties and the same senses, have no less similitude in their pains and pleasures. The sensations are the same in all, tho' produced by very different occasions. The Prince feels the same pain when an invader seizes a province, as the Farmer when a thief drives away his cow. Men thus equal in themselves will appear equal in honest and impartial Biography; and those whom Fortune or Nature place at the greatest distance may afford instruction to each other.

The writer of his own life has at least the first qualification of an Historian, the knowledge of the truth; and though it may be plausibly objected that his temptations to disguise it are equal to his opportunities of knowing it, yet I cannot but think that impartiality may be expected with equal confidence from him that relates the passages of his own life, as from him that delivers the transactions of another.

Certainty of knowledge not only excludes mistake but fortifies veracity. What we collect by conjecture, and by conjecture only can one man judge of another's motives or sentiments, is easily modified by fancy or by desire; as objects imperfectly discerned, take forms from the hope or fear of the beholder. But that which is fully known cannot be falsified but with reluctance of understanding, and alarm of conscience; of Understanding, the lover of Truth; of Conscience, the sentinel of Virtue.

He that writes the Life of another is either his friend or his enemy, and wishes either to exalt his praise or aggravate his infamy; many temptations to falsehood will occur in the disguise of passions, too specious to fear much resistance. Love of Virtue will animate Panegyrick, and hatred of Wickedness imbitter

Censure. The Zeal of Gratitude, the Ardour of Patriotism, Fondness for an Opinion, or Fidelity to a Party, may easily overpower the vigilance of a mind habitually well disposed, and prevail over unassisted and unfriended Veracity.

But he that speaks of himself has no motive to Falshood or Partiality except Self-love, by which all have so often been betrayed, that all are on the watch against its artifices. He that writes an Apology for a single Action, to confute an Accusation, or recommend himself to Favour, is indeed always to be suspected of favouring his own cause; but he that sits down calmly and voluntarily to review his Life for the admonition of Posterity, or to amuse himself, and leaves this account unpublished, may be commonly presumed to tell Truth, since Falshood cannot appease his own Mind, and Fame will not be heard beneath the Tomb.

No. 88. Saturday, 22 December 1759.

When the Philosophers of the last Age were first congregated into the Royal Society, great expectations were raised of the sudden progress of useful Arts; the time was supposed to be near when Engines should turn by a perpetual Motion, and Health be secured by the universal Medicine; when Learning should be facilitated by a real Character,[1] and Commerce extended by ships which could reach their Ports in defiance of the Tempest.

But Improvement is naturally slow. The Society met and parted without any visible diminution of the miseries of life. The Gout and Stone were still painful, the Ground that was not plowed brought no Harvest, and neither Oranges nor Grapes would grow upon the Hawthorn. At last, those who were disappointed began to be angry; those likewise who hated innovation were glad to gain an opportunity of ridiculing men who had depreciated, perhaps with too much arrogance, the Knowledge of Antiquity. And it appears from some of their earliest Apologies, that the Philosophers felt with great sensibility the unwelcome importunities of those who were daily asking, "What have ye done?"

The truth is, that little had been done compared with what Fame had been suffered to promise; and the question could only be answered by general apologies and by new hopes, which, when they were frustrated, gave a new occasion to the same vexatious enquiry.

This fatal question has disturbed the quiet of many other minds. He that in the latter part of his life too strictly enquires what he has done, can very seldom receive from his own heart such an account as will give him satisfaction.

We do not indeed so often disappoint others as ourselves. We not only think more highly than others of our own abilities, but allow ourselves to form hopes which we never communicate, and please our thoughts with employments which none ever will allot us, and with elevations to which we are never expected to rise; and when our days and years have passed away in common business or common amusements, and we find at last that we have suffered our purposes to sleep till the time of action is past, we are reproached only by our own reflections; neither our friends nor our enemies wonder that we live and die like the rest of mankind, that we live without notice and die without memorial; they know not what task we had proposed, and therefore cannot discern whether it is finished.

He that compares what he has done with what he has left undone, will feel the effect which must always follow the comparison of imagination with reality; he will look with contempt on his own unimportance, and wonder to what purpose he came into the world; he will repine that he shall leave behind him no evidence of his having been, that he has added nothing to the system of life, but has glided from Youth to Age among the crowd, without any effort for distinction.

Man is seldom willing to let fall the opinion of his own dignity, or to believe that he does little only because every individual is a very little being. He is better content to want Diligence than Power, and sooner confesses the Depravity of his Will than the Imbecillity of his Nature.

From this mistaken notion of human Greatness it proceeds, that many who pretend to have made great Advances in Wisdom so loudly declare that they despise themselves. If I had ever

found any of the Self-contemners much irritated or pained by
the consciousness of their meanness, I should have given them
consolation by observing, that a little more than nothing is as
much as can be expected from a being who with respect to the
multitudes about him is himself little more than nothing. Every
man is obliged by the supreme Master of the Universe to improve
all the opportunities of Good which are afforded him, and to
keep in continual activity such Abilities as are bestowed upon
him. But he has no reason to repine though his Abilities are
small and his Opportunities few. He that has improved the
Virtue or advanced the Happiness of one Fellow-creature, he
that has ascertained a single moral Proposition, or added one
useful Experiment to natural Knowledge, may be contented
with his own Performance, and, with respect to mortals like
himself, may demand, like *Augustus*, to be dismissed at his
departure with Applause.[2]

No. 94. Saturday, 2 February 1760.

It is common to find young men ardent and diligent in the pursuit
of knowledge, but the progress of life very often produces laxity
and indifference; and not only those who are at liberty to chuse
their business and amusements, but those likewise whose professions engage them in literary enquiries pass the latter part of
their time without improvement, and spend the day rather in
any other entertainment than that which they might find among
their books.

This abatement of the vigour of curiosity is sometimes
imputed to the insufficiency of Learning. Men are supposed to
remit their labours, because they find their labours to have been
vain; and to search no longer after Truth and Wisdom, because
they at last despair of finding them.

But this reason is for the most part very falsely assigned. Of
Learning, as of Virtue, it may be affirmed, that it is at once
honoured and neglected. Whoever forsakes it will for ever look
after it with longing, lament the loss which he does not endeavour to repair, and desire the good which he wants resolution to

seize and keep. The Idler never applauds his own Idleness, nor does any man repent of the diligence of his youth.

So many hindrances may obstruct the acquisition of Knowledge, that there is little reason for wondering that it is in a few hands. To the greater part of mankind the duties of life are inconsistent with much study, and the hours which they would spend upon letters must be stolen from their occupations and their families. Many suffer themselves to be lured by more spritely and luxurious pleasures from the shades of Contemplation, where they find seldom more than a calm delight, such as, though greater than all others, if its certainty and its duration be reckoned with its power of gratification, is yet easily quitted for some extemporary joy, which the present moment offers, and another perhaps will put out of reach.

It is the great excellence of Learning that it borrows very little from time or place; it is not confined to season or to climate, to cities or to the country, but may be cultivated and enjoyed where no other pleasure can be obtained. But this quality, which constitutes much of its value, is one occasion of neglect; what may be done at all times with equal propriety, is deferred from day to day, till the mind is gradually reconciled to the omission, and the attention is turned to other objects. Thus habitual idleness gains too much power to be conquered, and the soul shrinks from the idea of intellectual labour and intenseness of meditation.

That those who profess to advance Learning sometimes obstruct it, cannot be denied; the continual multiplication of books not only distracts choice but disappoints enquiry. To him that has moderately stored his mind with images, few writers afford any novelty; or what little they have to add to the common stock of Learning is so buried in the mass of general notions, that, like silver mingled with the oar of lead, it is too little to pay for the labour of separation; and he that has often been deceived by the promise of a title, at last grows weary of examining, and is tempted to consider all as equally fallacious.

There are indeed some repetitions always lawful, because they never deceive. He that writes the History of past times, undertakes only to decorate known facts by new beauties of method or of style, or at most to illustrate them by his own reflections. The Author of a system, whether moral or physical, is obliged to nothing beyond care of selection and regularity of disposition. But there are others who claim the name of Authors merely to disgrace it, and fill the world with volumes only to bury letters in their own rubbish. The Traveller who tells, in a pompous Folio, that he saw the *Pantheon* at *Rome*, and the *Medicean Venus* at *Florence*; the Natural Historian who, describing the productions of a narrow Island, recounts all that it has in common with every other part of the world; the Collector of Antiquities, that accounts every thing a curiosity which the Ruins of *Herculaneum* happen to emit, though an instrument already shewn in a thousand repositories, or a cup common to the ancients, the moderns, and all mankind, may be justly censured as the Persecutors of Students, and the Thieves of that Time which never can be restored.

No. 100. Saturday, 15 March 1760.

To the IDLER.

SIR,

The uncertainty and defects of Language have produced very frequent complaints among the Learned; yet there still remain many words among us undefined, which are very necessary to be rightly understood, and which produce very mischievous mistakes when they are erroneously interpreted.

I lived in a state of celibacy beyond the usual time. In the hurry first of pleasure and afterwards of business, I felt no want of a domestick companion; but becoming weary of labour I soon grew more weary of idleness, and thought it reasonable to follow the custom of life, and to seek some solace of my cares in female tenderness, and some amusement of my leisure in female chearfulness.

The choice which has been long delayed is commonly made at last with great caution. My resolution was to keep my passions neutral, and to marry only in compliance with my reason. I drew upon a page of my pocket book a scheme of all female virtues and vices, with the vices which border upon every virtue, and the virtues which are allied to every vice. I considered that wit was sarcastick, and magnanimity imperious; that avarice was economical, and ignorance obsequious; and having estimated the good and evil of every quality, employed my own diligence and that of my friends to find the lady in whom nature and reason had reached that happy mediocrity which is equally remote from exuberance and deficience.

Every woman had her admirers and her censurers, and the expectations which one raised were by another quickly depressed: yet there was one in whose favour almost all suffrages concurred. Miss *Gentle* was universally allowed to be a good sort of woman. Her fortune was not large, but so prudently managed, that she wore finer cloaths and saw more company than many who were known to be twice as rich. Miss *Gentle*'s visits were every where welcome, and whatever family she favoured with her company, she always left behind her such a degree of kindness as recommended her to others; every day extended her acquaintance, and all who knew her declared that they never met with a better sort of woman.

To Miss *Gentle* I made my addresses, and was received with great equality of temper. She did not in the days of courtship assume the privilege of imposing rigorous commands, or resenting slight offences. If I forgot any of her injunctions I was gently reminded, if I missed the minute of appointment I was easily forgiven. I foresaw nothing in marriage but a halcyon calm, and longed for the happiness which was to be found in the inseparable society of a good sort of woman.

The jointure was soon settled by the intervention of friends, and the day came in which Miss *Gentle* was made mine for ever. The first month was passed easily enough in receiving and repaying the civilities of our friends. The bride practised with great exactness all the niceties of ceremony, and distributed her notice in the most punctilious proportions to the friends who surrounded us with their happy auguries.

But the time soon came when we were left to ourselves, and were to receive our pleasures from each other, and I then began to perceive that I was not formed to be much delighted by a good sort of woman. Her great principle is, that the orders of a family must not be broken. Every hour of the day has its employment inviolably appropriated, nor will any importunity persuade her to walk in the garden, at the time which she has devoted to her needlework, or to sit up stairs in that part of the forenoon, which she has accustomed herself to spend in the back parlour. She allows herself to sit half an hour after breakfast, and an hour after dinner; while I am talking or reading to her, she keeps her eye upon her watch, and when the minute of departure comes, will leave an argument unfinished, or the intrigue of a play unravelled. She once called me to supper when I was watching an eclipse, and summoned me at another time to bed when I was going to give directions at a fire.

Her conversation is so habitually cautious, that she never talks to me but in general terms, as to one whom it is dangerous to trust. For discriminations of character she has no names; all whom she mentions are honest men and agreeable women. She smiles not by sensation but by practice. Her laughter is never excited but by a joke, and her notion of a joke is not very delicate. The repetition of a good joke does not weaken its effect; if she has laughed once, she will laugh again.

She is an enemy to nothing but ill nature and pride, but she has frequent reason to lament that they are so frequent in the world. All who are not equally pleased with the good and bad, with the elegant and gross, with the witty and the dull, all who distinguish excellence from defect she considers as ill-natured; and she condemns as proud all who repress impertinence or quell presumption, or expect respect from any other eminence than that of fortune, to which she is always willing to pay homage.

There are none whom she openly hates; for if once she suffers, or believes herself to suffer, any contempt or insult, she never dismisses it from her mind but takes all opportunities to tell how easily she can forgive. There are none whom she loves much better than others; for when any of her acquaintance decline in the opinion of the world she always finds it inconvenient to visit them; her affection continues unaltered but it is impossible to be intimate with the whole town.

She daily exercises her benevolence by pitying every misfortune that happens to every family within her circle of notice; she is in hourly terrors lest one should catch cold in the rain, and another be frighted by the high wind. Her charity she shews by lamenting that so many poor wretches should languish in the streets, and by wondering what the great can think on that they do so little good with such large estates.

Her house is elegant and her table dainty though she has little taste of elegance, and is wholly free from vicious luxury; but she comforts herself that nobody can say that her house is dirty, or that her dishes are not well drest.

This, Mr. *Idler*, I have found by long experience to be the character of a good sort of woman, which I have sent you for the information of those by whom *a good sort of woman* and *a good woman* may happen to be used as equivalent terms, and who may suffer by the mistake like

Your humble servant,
TIM WARNER.

No. 103. Saturday, 5 April 1760.

Respicere ad longæ jussit spatia ultima vitæ.[1]

JUV.

Much of the Pain and Pleasure of mankind arises from the conjectures which every one makes of the thoughts of others; we all enjoy praise which we do not hear, and resent contempt which we do not see. The *Idler* may therefore be forgiven, if he suffers his Imagination to represent to him what his readers will say or think when they are informed that they have now his last paper in their hands.

Value is more frequently raised by scarcity than by use. That which lay neglected when it was common, rises in estimation as its quantity becomes less. We seldom learn the true want of what we have till it is discovered that we can have no more.

This essay will, perhaps, be read with care even by those who have not yet attended to any other; and he that finds this late attention recompensed, will not forbear to wish that he had bestowed it sooner.

Though the *Idler* and his readers have contracted no close friendship they are perhaps both unwilling to part. There are few things not purely evil, of which we can say, without some emotion of uneasiness, *this is the last*. Those who never could agree together, shed tears when mutual discontent has determined them to final separation; of a place which has been frequently visited, tho' without pleasure, the last look is taken with heaviness of heart; and the *Idler*, with all his chilness of tranquillity, is not wholly unaffected by the thought that his last essay is now before him.

This secret horrour of the last is inseparable from a thinking being whose life is limited, and to whom death is dreadful. We always make a secret comparison between a part and the whole; the termination of any period of life reminds us that life itself has likewise its termination; when we have done any thing for the last time, we involuntarily reflect that a part of the days allotted us is past, and that as more is past there is less remaining.

It is very happily and kindly provided, that in every life there are certain pauses and interruptions, which force consideration upon the careless, and seriousness upon the light; points of time where one course of action ends and another begins; and by vicissitude of fortune, or alteration of employment, by change of place, or loss of friendship, we are forced to say of something, *this is the last*.

An even and unvaried tenour of life always hides from our apprehension the approach of its end. Succession is not perceived but by variation; he that lives to-day as he lived yesterday, and expects that, as the present day is, such will be the morrow, easily conceives time as running in a circle and returning to itself. The uncertainty of our duration is impressed commonly by dissimilitude of condition; it is only by finding life changeable that we are reminded of its shortness.

This conviction, however forcible at every new impression, is every moment fading from the mind; and partly by the inevitable incursion of new images, and partly by voluntary exclusion of unwelcome thoughts, we are again exposed to the universal fallacy; and we must do another thing for the last time, before we consider that the time is nigh when we shall do no more.

As the last *Idler* is published in that solemn week[2] which the Christian world has always set apart for the examination of the conscience, the review of life, the extinction of earthly desires and the renovation of holy purposes, I hope that my readers are already disposed to view every incident with seriousness, and improve it by meditation; and that when they see this series of trifles brought to a conclusion, they will consider that by outliving the *Idler*, they have past weeks, months, and years which are now no longer in their power; that an end must in time be put to every thing great as to every thing little; that to life must come its last hour, and to this system of being its last day, the hour at which probation ceases, and repentance will be vain; the day in which every work of the hand, and imagination of the heart shall be brought to judgment, and an everlasting futurity shall be determined by the past.

MISCELLANEOUS ESSAYS

A Compleat Vindication of the Licensers of the Stage,
FROM THE MALICIOUS AND SCANDALOUS ASPERSIONS OF MR *BROOKE*, AUTHOR OF *Gustavus Vasa* WITH A PROPOSAL FOR MAKING THE OFFICE OF LICENSER MORE EXTENSIVE AND EFFECTUAL. BY AN IMPARTIAL HAND.[1]

It is generally agreed by the Writers of all Parties, that few Crimes are equal, in their Degree of Guilt, to that of calumniating a good and gentle, or defending a wicked and oppressive Administration.

It is therefore with the utmost Satisfaction of Mind, that I reflect how often I have employed my Pen in Vindication of the present Ministry, and their Dependents and Adherents, how often I have detected the specious Fallacies of the Advocates for Independence, how often I have softened the Obstinacy of Patriotism, and how often triumphed over the Clamour of Opposition.

I have, indeed, observed but one Set of Men upon whom all my Arguments have been thrown away, which neither Flattery can draw to Compliance, nor Threats reduce to Submission, and who have, notwithstanding all Expedients that either Invention or Experience could suggest, continued to exert their Abilities in a vigorous and constant Opposition of all our Measures.

The unaccountable Behaviour of these Men, the enthusiastick Resolution with which, after a hundred successive Defeats, they still renewed their Attacks, the Spirit with which they continued to repeat their Arguments in the Senate, though they found a Majority determined to condemn them, and the Inflexibility with which they rejected all Offers of Places and Preferments at last excited my Curiosity so far that I applied myself to enquire with great Diligence into the real Motives of their Conduct, and to discover what Principle it was that had Force to inspire such unextinguishable Zeal, and to animate such unwearied Efforts.

For this Reason I attempted to cultivate a nearer Acquaintance with some of the Chiefs of that Party, and imagined that it would be necessary for some Time to dissemble my Sentiments that I might learn theirs.

Dissimulation to a true Politician is not difficult, and therefore I readily assumed the Character of a Proselyte, but found that their Principle of Action was no other, than that which they make no Scruple of avowing in the most publick Manner, notwithstanding the Contempt and Ridicule to which it every Day exposes them, and the Loss of those Honours and Profits from which it excludes them.

This wild Passion, or Principle, is a kind of Fanaticism by which they distinguish those of their own Party, and which they look upon as a certain Indication of a great Mind. We have no name for it *at Court*,[2] but among themselves, they term it by a kind of *Cant-phrase*, A REGARD FOR POSTERITY.

This Passion seems to predominate in all their Conduct, to regulate every Action of their Lives, and Sentiment of their Minds; I have heard *L*— and *P*—,[3] when they have made a vigorous Opposition, or blasted the Blossom of some ministerial Scheme, cry out, in the Height of their Exultations, *This will deserve the Thanks of Posterity!*

And when their Adversaries, as it much more frequently falls out, have out-number'd and overthrown them, they will say with an Air of Revenge, and a kind of gloomy Triumph, *Posterity will curse you for this*.

It is common among Men under the Influence of any kind of Frenzy, to believe that all the World has the same odd Notions that disorder their own Imaginations. Did these unhappy Men, these deluded Patriots, know how little we are concerned about Posterity, they would never attempt to fright us with their Curses, or tempt us to a Neglect of our own Interest by a Prospect of their Gratitude.

But so strong is their Infatuation, that they seem to have forgotten even the primary Law of Self-preservation, for they sacrifice without scruple every flattering Hope, every darling Enjoyment, and every Satisfaction of Life to this *ruling Passion*, and appear in every Step to consult not so much their own Advantage as that of *Posterity*.

Strange Delusion! that can confine all their Thoughts to a
Race of Men whom they neither know, nor can know; from
whom nothing is to be feared, nor any Thing expected; who
cannot even bribe a special Jury,[4] nor have so much as a single
Riband to bestow.

This Fondness for Posterity is a kind of Madness which at
Rome was once almost epidemical, and infected even the
Women and the Children. It reigned there till the entire Destruction of *Carthage*, after which it began to be less general, and in
a few Years afterwards a Remedy was discovered, by which it
was almost entirely extinguished.

In *England* it never prevailed in any such Degree; some few
of the ancient Barons seem indeed to have been disorder'd by it,
but the Contagion has been for the most part timely checked,
and our Ladies have been generally free.

But there has been in every Age a Set of Men much admired
and reverenced, who have affected to be always talking of
Posterity, and have laid out their Lives upon the Composition
of Poems for the Sake of being applauded by this imaginary
Generation.

The present Poets I reckon amongst the most inexorable
Enemies[5] of our most excellent Ministry, and much doubt
whether any Method will effect the Cure of a Distemper which
in this Class of Men may be termed not an accidental Disease,
but a Defect in their original Frame and Constitution.

Mr. *Brooke*, a Name I mention with all the Detestation
suitable to my Character, could not forbear discovering this
Depravity of his Mind in his very Prologue, which is filled with
Sentiments so wild, and so much unheard of among those who
frequent Levees and Courts, that I much doubt, whether the
zealous Licenser proceeded any further in his Examination of
his Performance.

He might easily perceive that a Man,

Who bade his moral Beam through every Age,[6]

was too much a Bigot to exploded Notions, to compose a Play
which he could license without manifest Hazard of his Office, a

Hazard which no Man would incur untainted with the Love of Posterity.

We cannot therefore wonder that an Author, wholly possessed by this Passion, should vent his Resentment for the Licenser's just Refusal, in virulent Advertisements, insolent Complaints, and scurrilous Assertions of his Rights and Privileges, and proceed in Defiance of Authority to solicite a Subscription.

This Temper which I have been describing is almost always complicated with Ideas of the high Prerogatives of human Nature, of a sacred unalienable Birthright, which no Man has conferr'd upon us, and which neither Kings can take, nor Senates give away, which we may justly assert whenever and by whomsoever it is attacked, and which, if ever it should happen to be lost, we may take the first Opportunity to recover.

The natural Consequence of these Chimeras is Contempt of Authority, and an Irreverence for any Superiority but what is founded upon Merit, and their Notions of Merit are very peculiar, for it is among them no great Proof of Merit to be wealthy and powerful, to wear a Garter or a Star, to command a Regiment or a Senate, to have the Ear of the Minister or of the King, or to possess any of those Virtues and Excellencies which among us entitle a Man to little less than Worship and Prostration.

We may therefore easily conceive that Mr. *Brooke* thought himself entitled to be importunate for a License, because, in his own Opinion, he deserved one, and to complain thus loudly at the Repulse he met with.

His Complaints will have, I hope, but little Weight with the Publick, since the Opinions of the Sect in which he is enlisted are exposed and shown to be evidently and demonstrably opposite to that System of Subordination and Dependence to which we are indebted for the present Tranquillity of the Nation, and that Chearfulness and Readiness with which the two Houses[7] concur in all our Designs.

I shall however, to silence him intirely, or at least to shew those of our Party, that he ought to be silent, consider singly every Instance of Hardship and Oppression which he has dared to publish in the Papers, and to publish in such a Manner that I hope no Man will condemn me for Want of Candour in becoming an Advocate for the Ministry, if I can consider his Advertisements as nothing less than AN APPEAL TO HIS COUNTRY.

Let me be forgiven if I cannot speak with Temper of such Insolence as this: Is a Man without Title, Pension, or Place, to suspect the Impartiality or the Judgment of those who are intrusted with the Administration of publick Affairs? Is he, when the Law is not strictly observed in Regard to him, to think himself *aggrieved*, to tell his Sentiments in Print, assert his Claim to better Usage, and fly for Redress to another Tribunal?

If such Practices are permitted, I will not venture to foretell the Effects of them, the Ministry may soon be convinced that such Sufferers will find Compassion, and that it is safer not to bear hard upon them than to allow them to complain.

The Power of Licensing in general, being firmly established by an Act of Parliament, our Poet has not attempted to call in Question, but contents himself with censuring the Manner in which it has been executed, so that I am not now engaged to assert the Licenser's Authority, but to defend his Conduct.

The Poet seems to think himself aggrieved, because the Licenser kept his Tragedy in his Hands one and twenty Days, whereas the Law allows him to detain it only fourteen.

Where will the Insolence of the Malcontents end? Or how are such unreasonable Expectations possibly to be satisfied? Was it ever known that a Man exalted into a high Station dismissed a Suppliant in the Time limited by Law? Ought not Mr. *Brooke* to think himself happy that his Play was not detained longer? If he had been kept a Year in Suspense, what Redress could he have obtained? Let the Poets remember when they appear before the Licenser, or his Deputy, that they stand at the Tribunal from which there is no Appeal permitted, and where nothing will so well become them as Reverence and Submission.

Mr. *Brooke* mentions in his Preface his Knowledge of the Laws of his own Country; had he extended his Enquiries to the Civil Law, he could have found a full Justification of the Licenser's Conduct, *Boni Judicis est ampliare suam auctoritatem.*[8]

If then it be *the Business of a good Judge to enlarge his*

Authority, was it not in the Licenser the utmost Clemency and Forbearance, to extend fourteen Days only to twenty-one.

I suppose this great Man's Inclination to perform at least this Duty of a good Judge, is not questioned by any, either of his Friends or Enemies, I may therefore venture to hope that he will extend his Power by proper Degrees, and that I shall live to see a Malecontent Writer earnestly soliciting for the Copy of a Play, which he had delivered to the Licenser twenty Years before.

I waited, says he, *often on the Licenser, and with the utmost Importunity entreated an Answer.* Let Mr. *Brooke* consider whether that Importunity was not a sufficient Reason for the Disappointment. Let him reflect how much more decent it had been to have waited the Leisure of a great Man, than to have pressed upon him with repeated Petitions, and to have intruded upon those precious Moments which he has dedicated to the Service of his Country.

Mr. *Brooke* was doubtless led into this improper Manner of acting, by an erroneous Notion that the Grant of a License was not an Act of Favour but of Justice, a Mistake into which he could not have fallen, but from a supine Inattention to the Design of the Statute, which was only to bring Poets into Subjection and Dependence, not to encourage good Writers, but to discourage all.

There lies no Obligation upon the Licenser to grant his Sanction to a Play, however excellent, nor can Mr. *Brooke* demand any Reparation, whatever Applause his Performance may meet with.

Another Grievance is, that the Licenser assigned no Reason for his Refusal. This is a higher Strain of Insolence than any of the former. Is it for a Poet to demand a Licenser's Reason for his Proceedings? Is he not rather to acquiesce in the Decision of Authority, and conclude that there are Reasons which he cannot comprehend?

Unhappy would it be for Men in Power, were they always obliged to publish the Motives of their Conduct. What is Power but the Liberty of acting without being accountable? The Advocates for the Licensing Act have alledged, that the Lord

Chamberlain has always had Authority to prohibit the Representation of a Play for just Reasons. Why then did we call in all our Force to procure an Act of Parliament? Was it to enable him to do what he has always done, to confirm an Authority which no Man attempted to impair, or pretended to dispute; no, certainly: Our Intention was to invest him with new Privileges, and to empower him to do that *without* Reason, which *with* Reason he could do before.

We have found by long Experience, that to lie under a Necessity of assigning Reasons, is very troublesome, and that many an excellent Design has miscarried by the Loss of Time spent unnecessarily in examining Reasons.

Always to call for Reasons, and always to reject them, shews a strange Degree of Perverseness; yet such is the daily Behaviour of our Adversaries, who have never yet been satisfied with any Reasons that have been offered by us.

They have made it their Practice to demand once a Year the Reasons for which we maintain a Standing Army.[9]

One Year we told them that it was necessary, because all the Nations round us were involved in War; this had no Effect upon them, and therefore resolving to do our utmost for their Satisfaction, we told them the next Year that it was necessary because all the Nations round us were at Peace.

This Reason finding no better Reception than the other, we had Recourse to our Apprehensions of an Invasion from the Pretender, of an Insurrection in Favour of *Gin*, and of a general Disaffection among the People.

But as they continue still impenetrable, and oblige us still to assign our annual Reasons, we shall spare no Endeavours to procure such as may be more satisfactory than any of the former.

The Reason we once gave for building Barracks was for Fear of the Plague, and we intend next Year to propose the Augmentation of our Troops for fear of a Famine.

The Committee, by which the Act for Licensing the Stage was drawn up, had too long known the Inconvenience of giving Reasons, and were too well acquainted with the Characters of great Men, to lay the Lord Chamberlain, or his deputy, under any such tormenting Obligation.

Yet lest Mr. *Brooke* should imagine that a License was refused him without just Reasons, I shall condescend to treat him with more Regard than he can reasonably expect, and point out such Sentiments as not only justly exposed him to that Refusal, but would have provoked any Ministry less merciful than the present to have inflicted some heavier Penalties upon him.

His Prologue is filled with such Insinuations as no Friend of our excellent Government can read without Indignation and Abhorrence, and cannot but be owned to be a proper Introduction to such Scenes as seem designed to kindle in the Audience a Flame of Opposition, Patriotism, Publick Spirit, and Independency, that Spirit which we have so long endeavoured to suppress, and which cannot be revived without the entire Subversion of all our Schemes.

This seditious Poet not content with making an open Attack upon us, by declaring in plain Terms, that he looks upon Freedom as the only Source of publick Happiness and national Security, has endeavoured with Subtlety, equal to his Malice, to make us suspicious of our firmest Friends, to infect our Consultations with Distrust, and to ruin us by disuniting us.

This indeed will not be easily effected, an Union founded upon Interest and cemented by Dependance is naturally lasting: But Confederacies which owe their Rise to Virtue or mere Conformity of Sentiments are quickly dissolved, since no Individual has any Thing either to hope or fear for himself, and publick Spirit is generally too weak to combat with private Passions.

The Poet has, however, attempted to weaken our Combination by an artful and sly Assertion, which, if suffered to remain unconfuted, may operate by Degrees upon our Minds in the Days of Leisure and Retirement which are now approaching, and perhaps fill us with such Surmises as may at least very much embarrass our Affairs.

The Law by which the *Swedes* justified their Opposition to the incroachments of the King of *Denmark* he not only calls

Great Nature's Law, the Law within the Breast

But proceeds to tell us that it is

——Stamp'd by Heav'n upon th' unletter'd Mind.[10]

By which he evidently intends to insinuate a Maxim which is, I hope, as false as it is pernicious, that Men are naturally fond of Liberty till those unborn Ideas and Desires are effaced by Literature.

The Author, if he be not a Man mew'd up in his solitary Study and entirely unacquainted with the Conduct of the present Ministry, must know that we have hitherto acted upon different Principles. We have always regarded *Letters* as great Obstructions to our Scheme of Subordination, and have therefore, when we have heard of any Man remarkably *unletter'd*, carefully noted him down as the most proper Person for any Employments of Trust or Honour, and considered him as a Man in whom we could safely repose our most important Secrets.

From among the uneducated and *unletter'd* we have chosen not only our Embassadors and other Negotiators, but even our Journalists and Pamphleteers, nor have we had any Reason to change our Measures or to repent of the Confidence which we have placed in Ignorance.

Are we now therefore to be told that this Law is

Stamp'd upon th' unletter'd Mind?

Are we to suspect our Place-men, our Pensioners, our Generals, our Lawyers, our best Friends in both Houses, all our Adherents among the Atheists and Infidels, and our very Gazetteers, Clerks, and Court-pages, as Friends to Independency? Doubtless this is the Tendency of his Assertion, but we have known them too long to be thus imposed upon, the *unletter'd* have been our warmest and most constant Defenders, nor have we omitted any Thing to deserve their Favour, but have always endeavoured to raise their Reputation, extend their Influence, and encrease their Number.

In his first Act he abounds with Sentiments very inconsistent with the Ends for which the Power of Licensing was granted; to enumerate them all would be to transcribe a great Part of his Play, a Task which I shall very willingly leave to others, who, tho' true Friends to the Government, are not inflamed with Zeal so fiery and impatient as mine, and therefore do not feel the same Emotions of Rage and Resentment at the Sight of those infamous Passages, in which Venality and Dependence are presented as mean in themselves, and productive of Remorse and Infelicity.

One Line which ought, in my Opinion, to be erased from every Copy by a special Act of Parliament, is mentioned by *Anderson*,[11] as pronounced by the Hero in his Sleep,

O Sweden, O my Country, yet I'll save thee.[12]

This Line I have Reason to believe thrown out as a kind of Watch-word for the opposing Faction, who, when they meet in their seditious Assemblies, have been observed to lay their Hands upon their Breasts, and cry out with great Vehemence of Accent,

O B——, O my Country, yet I'll save thee.

In the second Scene he endeavours to fix Epithets of Contempt upon those Passions and Desires which have been always found most useful to the Ministry, and most opposite to the Spirit of Independency.

> *Base Fear, the Laziness of Lust, gross Appetites,*
> *These are the Ladders and the grov'ling Foot-stool*
> *From whence the Tyrant rises——*
> *Secure and scepter'd in the Soul's Servility*
> *He has debauched the Genius of our Country*
> *And rides triumphant, while her captive Sons*
> *Await his Nod, the silken Slaves of Pleasure,*
> *Or fettered in their Fears.——*[13]

Thus is that decent Submission to our Superiors, and that proper Awe of Authority which we are taught in Courts, termed *base*

Fear and the *Servility of the Soul*. Thus are those Gayeties and Enjoyments, those elegant Amusements, and lulling Pleasures which the Followers of a Court are blessed with, as the just Rewards of their Attendance and Submission, degraded to *Lust, Grossness*, and *Debauchery*. The Author ought to be told, that Courts are not to be mentioned with so little Ceremony, and that though Gallantries and Amours are admitted there, it is almost Treason to suppose them infected with Debauchery or Lust.

It is observable that when this hateful Writer has conceived any Thought of an uncommon Malignity, a Thought which tends in a more particular Manner to excite the Love of Liberty, animate the Heat of Patriotism, or degrade the Majesty of Kings, he takes Care to put it in the Mouth of his Hero, that it may be more forcibly impressed upon his Reader. Thus *Gustavus*, speaking of his Tatters, cries out,

> ——*Yes, my* Arvida,
> *Beyond the Sweeping of the proudest Train*
> *That shades a Monarch's Heel, I prize these Weeds,*
> *For they are sacred to my Country's Freedom.*[14]

Here this abandoned Son of Liberty makes a full Discovery of his execrable Principles, the Tatters of *Gustavus*, the usual Dress of the Assertors of these Doctrines, are of more Divinity, because they are sacred to Freedom than the sumptuous and magnificent Robes of Regality itself. Such Sentiments are truly detestable, nor could any Thing be an Aggravation of the Author's Guilt, except his ludicrous Manner of mentioning a Monarch.

The *Heel of a Monarch*, or even the Print of his *Heel* is a Thing too venerable and sacred to be treated with such Levity, and placed in Contrast with Rags and Poverty. He that will speak contemptuously of the *Heel* of a *Monarch* will, whenever he can with Security, speak contemptuously of his Head.

These are the most glaring Passages which have occurr'd, in the Perusal of the first Pages; my Indignation will not suffer me to proceed farther, and I think much better of the Licenser, than to believe he went so far.

In the few Remarks which I have set down, the Reader will

easily observe that I have strained no Expression beyond its natural Import, and have divested myself of all Heat, Partiality, and Prejudice.

So far therefore is Mr. *Brooke* from having received any hard or unwarrantable Treatment, that the Licenser has only acted in Pursuance of that Law to which he owes his Power, a Law which every Admirer of the Administration must own to be very necessary, and to have produced very salutary Effects.

I am indeed surprised that this great Office is not drawn out into a longer series of Deputations, since it might afford a gainful and reputable Employment to a great Number of the Friends of the Government; and I should think instead of having immediate Recourse to the Deputy-licenser himself, it might be sufficient Honour for any Poet, except the Laureat, to stand bare-headed in the Presence of the Deputy of the Deputy's Deputy in the nineteenth Subordination.

Such a Number cannot but be thought necessary if we take into Consideration the great Work of drawing up an *Index Expurgatorius* to all the old Plays; which is, I hope, already undertaken, or if it has been hitherto unhappily neglected, I take this Opportunity to recommend.

The Productions of our old Poets are crouded with Passages very unfit for the Ears of an *English* Audience, and which cannot be pronounced without irritating the Minds of the People.

This Censure I do not confine to those Lines in which Liberty, natural Equality, wicked Ministers, deluded Kings, mean Arts of Negotiation, venal Senates, mercenary Troops, oppressive Officers, servile and exorbitant Taxes, universal Corruption, the Luxuries of a Court, the Miseries of the People, the Decline of Trade, or the Happiness of Independency are directly mentioned. These are such glaring Passages as cannot be suffered to pass without the most supine and criminal Negligence. I hope the Vigilance of the Licensers will extend to all such Speeches and Soliloquies as tend to recommend the Pleasures of Virtue, the Tranquillity of an uncorrupted Head, and the Satisfactions of conscious Innocence; for though such Strokes as these do not appear to a common Eye to threaten any Danger to the Government, yet it is well known to more penetrating Observers that they have such Consequences as cannot be too diligently obviated, or too cautiously avoided.

A Man who becomes once enamour'd of the Charms of Virtue is apt to be very little concerned about the Acquisition of Wealth or Titles, and is therefore not easily induced to act in a Manner contrary to his real Sentiments, or to vote at theWord of Command; by contracting his Desires, and regulating his Appetites, he wants much less than other Men, and every one versed in the Arts of Government can tell, that Men are more easily influenced in Proportion as they are more necessitous.

This is not the only Reason why Virtue should not receive too much Countenance from a licensed Stage; her Admirers and Followers are not only naturally independent, but learn such a uniform and consistent Manner of speaking and acting, that they frequently by the mere Force of artless Honesty surmount all the Obstacles which Subtlety and Politicks can throw in their way, and obtain their Ends in spite of the most profound and sagacious Ministry.

Such then are the Passages to be expunged by the Licensers: In many Parts indeed the Speeches will be imperfect, and the Action appear not regularly conducted, but the Poet Laureat[15] may easily supply these Vacuities by inserting some of his own Verses in praise of Wealth, Luxury, and Venality.

But alas! all those pernicious Sentiments which we shall banish from the Stage, will be vented from the Press, and more studiously read because they are prohibited.

I cannot but earnestly implore the Friends of the Government to leave no Art untry'd by which we may hope to succeed in our Design of extending the Power of the Licenser to the Press, and of making it criminal to publish any Thing without an *Imprimatur*.[16]

How much would this single Law lighten the mighty Burden of State Affairs? With how much Security might our Ministers enjoy their Honours, their Places, their Reputations, and their Admirers, could they once suppress those malicious Invectives which are at present so industriously propagated, and so eagerly read, could they hinder any Arguments but their own from coming to the Ears of the People, and stop effectually the Voice of Cavil and Enquiry.

I cannot but indulge myself a little while by dwelling on this pleasing Scene, and imagining those *Halcyon-days* in which no Politicks shall be read but those of the *Gazetteer*,[17] nor any Poetry but that of the Laureat; when we shall hear of nothing but the successful Negotiations of our Ministers, and the great Actions of ——.

How much happier would this State be, than those perpetual Jealousies and Contentions which are inseparable from Knowledge and Liberty, and which have for many Years kept this Nation in perpetual Commotions.

But these are Times rather to be wished for than expected, for such is the Nature of our unquiet Countrymen, that if they are not admitted to the Knowledge of Affairs, they are always suspecting their Governors of Designs prejudicial to their Interest; they have not the least Notion of the pleasing Tranquillity of Ignorance, nor can be brought to imagine that they are kept in the Dark, lest too much Light should hurt their Eyes. They have long claimed a Right of directing their Superiors, and are exasperated at the least Mention of Secrets of State.

This Temper makes them very readily encourage any Writer or Printer, who, at the Hazard of his Life or Fortune, will give them any Information; and while this Humour prevails there never will be wanting some daring Adventurer who will write in Defence of Liberty, and some zealous or avaricious Printer who will disperse his Papers.

It has never yet been found that any Power, however vigilant or despotick, has been able to prevent the Publication of seditious Journals, Ballads, Essays and Dissertations, *Considerations on the present State of Affairs,* and *Enquiries into the Conduct of the Administration.*

Yet I must confess, that considering the Success with which the present Ministry has hitherto proceeded in their Attempts to drive out of the World the old Prejudices of Patriotism and publick Spirit, I cannot but entertain some Hopes that what has been so often attempted by their Predecessors, is reserved to be accomplished by their superior Abilities.

If I might presume to advise them upon this great Affair, I should dissuade them from any direct Attempt upon the Liberty of the Press, which is the Darling of the common People, and therefore cannot be attacked without immediate Danger. They may proceed by a more sure and silent Way, and attain the desired End without Noise, Detraction, or Opposition.

There are scatter'd over this Kingdom several little Seminaries in which the lower Ranks of People, and the younger Sons of our Nobility and Gentry are taught, from their earliest infancy, the pernicious Arts of Spelling and Reading, which they afterwards continue to practise very much to the Disturbance of their own Quiet, and the Interruption of ministerial Measures.

These Seminaries may, by an Act of Parliament, be at once suppressed, and that our Posterity be deprived of all Means of reviving this corrupt Method of Education, it may be made Felony to teach to read, without a License from the Lord Chamberlain.

This Expedient, which I hope will be carefully concealed from the Vulgar, must infallibly answer the great End proposed by it, and set the Power of the Court not only above the Insults of the Poets, but in a short Time above the Necessity of providing against them. The Licenser having his Authority thus extended will in Time enjoy the Title and the Salary without the Trouble of exercising his Power, and the Nation will rest at length in Ignorance and Peace.

An Essay on EPITAPHS.[1]

Tho' Criticism has been cultivated in every Age of Learning, by Men of great Abilities and extensive Knowledge, till the Rules of Writing are become rather burdensome than instructive to the Mind; tho' almost every Species of Composition has been the Subject of particular Treatises, and given Birth to Definitions, Distinctions, Precepts and Illustrations; yet no Critic of Note, that has fallen within my Observation, has hitherto thought *Sepulchral Inscriptions* worthy of a minute Examination, or ed out with proper Accuracy their Beauties and Defects.

The Reasons of this Neglect it is useless to enquire, and perhaps impossible to discover; it might be justly expected that this Kind of Writing would have been the favourite Topic of Criticism, and that Self-Love might have produced some Regard for it, in those Authors that have crowded Libraries with elaborate Dissertations upon *Homer*; since to afford a Subject for heroick Poems is the Privilege of very few, but every Man may expect to be recorded in an Epitaph, and, therefore, finds some Interest in providing that his Memory may not suffer by an unskilful Panegyrick.

If our Prejudices in favour of Antiquity deserve to have any Part in the Regulation of our Studies, EPITAPHS seem entitled to more than common Regard, as they are probably of the same Age with the Art of Writing. The most ancient Structures in the World, the Pyramids, are supposed to be Sepulchral Monuments, which either Pride or Gratitude erected, and the same Passions which incited Men to such laborious and expensive Methods of preserving their own Memory, or that of their Benefactors, would doubtless incline them not to neglect any easier Means by which ye same Ends might be obtained. Nature and Reason have dictated to every Nation, that to preserve good Actions from Oblivion, is both the Interest and Duty of Mankind; and therefore we find no People acquainted with the Use of Letters that omitted to grace the Tombs of their Heroes and wise Men with panegyrical Inscriptions.

To examine, therefore, in what the Perfection of EPITAPHS consists, and what Rules are to be observed in composing them, will be at least of as much use as other critical Enquiries; and for assigning a few Hours to such Disquisitions, great Examples at least, if not strong Reasons, may be pleaded.

An EPITAPH, as the word itself implies, is an *Inscription on a Tomb*, and in its most extensive Import may admit indiscriminately Satire or Praise. But as Malice has seldom produced Monuments of Defamation, and the Tombs hitherto raised have been the Work of Friendship and Benevolence, Custom has contracted the Original Latitude of the *Word*, so that it signifies in the general Acceptation an *Inscription engraven on a Tomb in Honour of the Person deceased*.

As Honours are paid to the Dead in order to incite others to the Imitation of their Excellencies, the principal Intention of EPITAPHS is to perpetuate the examples of Virtue, that the Tomb of a good Man may supply the Want of his Presence, and Veneration for his Memory produce the same Effect as the Observation of his Life. Those EPITAPHS are, therefore, the most perfect, which set Virtue in the strongest Light, and are best adapted to exalt the Reader's Ideas, and rouse his Emulation.

To this End it is not always necessary to recount the Actions of a Hero, or enumerate the Writings of a Philosopher; to imagine such Informations necessary, is to detract from their Characters, or to suppose their Works mortal, or their Atchievements in danger of being forgotten. The bare Name of such Men answers every Purpose of a long Inscription.

Had only the Name of Sir ISAAC NEWTON[2] been subjoined to the Design upon his Monument, instead of a long Detail of his Discoveries, which no Philosopher can want, and which none but a Philosopher can understand, those by whose Direction it was raised, had done more Honour both to him and to themselves.

This indeed is a Commendation which it requires no Genius to bestow, but which can never become vulgar or contemptible, if bestow'd with Judgment; because no single Age produces many Men of Merit superior to Panegyrick. None but the first Names can stand unassisted against the Attacks of Time, and if Men raised to Reputation by Accident or Caprice have nothing but their Names engraved on their Tombs, there is Danger lest in a few Years the Inscription require an Interpreter. Thus have their Expectations been disappointed who honoured *Picus* of *Mirandola*, with this pompous Epitaph,

Hic situs est PICUS MIRANDOLA, *cætera norunt*
Et Tagus *et* Ganges, *forsan et* Antipodes.[3]

His Name then celebrated in the remotest Corners of the Earth is now almost forgotten, and his Works, then studied, admired, and applauded, are now mouldering in Obscurity.

Next in Dignity to the bare Name is a short Character simple and unadorned, without Exaggeration, Superlatives, or Rhetoric. Such were the Inscriptions in Use among the *Romans*, in which the Victories gained by their Emperors were commemorated by a single Epithet; as Cæsar *Germanicus*, Cæsar *Dacicus*, *Germanicus*, *Illyricus*.[4] Such would be this Epitaph, ISAACUS NEWTONUS, *Naturæ Legibus investigatis, hic quiescit.*[5]

But to far the greatest Part of Mankind a longer Encomium is necessary for the Publication of their Virtues, and the Preservation of their Memories, and in the Composition of these it is that Art is principally required, and Precepts therefore may be useful.

In writing EPITAPHS, one circumstance is to be considered, which affects no other Composition; the Place in which they are now commonly found restrains them to a particular Air of Solemnity, and debars them from the Admission of all lighter or gayer Ornaments. In this it is that the Stile of an EPITAPH necessarily differs from that of an ELEGY. The Customs of burying our Dead either in or near our Churches, perhaps originally founded on a rational Design of fitting the Mind for religious Exercises, by laying before it the most affecting Proofs of the Uncertainty of Life, makes it proper to exclude from our EPITAPHS all such Allusions as are contrary to the Doctrines for the Propagation of which the Churches are erected, and to the End for which those who peruse the Monuments must be supposed to come thither. Nothing is, therefore, more ridiculous than to copy the *Roman* Inscriptions which were engraven on Stones by the Highway, and composed by those who generally reflected on Mortality only to excite in themselves and others a quicker Relish of Pleasure, and a more luxurious Enjoyment of Life, and whose Regard for the Dead extended no farther than a Wish that *the Earth might be light upon them.*

All Allusions to the Heathen Mythology are therefore absurd, and all Regard for the senseless Remains of a dead Man impertinent and superstitious. One of the first Distinctions of the primitive Christians was their Neglect of bestowing Garlands on the Dead, in which they are very rationally defended by their Apologist in *Minutius Felix. We lavish no Flowers nor Odours on the Dead*, says he, *because they have no Sense of Fragrance or of Beauty.*[6] We profess to Reverence the Dead not for their Sake but for our own. It is therefore always with Indignation or Contempt that I read the Epitaph on *Cowley*, a Man whose Learning and Poetry were his lowest Merits.

> *Aurea dum late volitant tua Scripta per Orbem,*
> *Et fama eternum vivis, divine Poeta,*
> *Hic placida jaceas requie, custodiat urnam*
> *Cana, Fides, vigilentque perenni Lampade Musæ!*
> *Sit sacer ille locus, nec quis temerarius ausit*
> *Sacrilega turbare manu venerabile bustum,*
> *Intacti maneant, maneant per sæcula dulces*
> Cowleii *cineres, serventq; immobile Saxum.*[7]

To pray, that ye Ashes of a Friend may lie undisturbed, and that the Divinities that favoured him in his Life, may watch for ever round him to preserve his Tomb from Violation and drive Sacrilege away, is only rational in him who believes the Soul interested in the Repose of the Body, and the Powers which he invokes for its Protection able to preserve it. To censure such Expressions as contrary to Religion, or as Remains of Heathen Superstition, would be too great a Degree of Severity. I condemn them only as uninstructive and unaffecting, as too ludicrous for Reverence or Grief, for Christianity and a Temple.

That the Designs and Decorations of Monuments, ought likewise to be formed with the same Regard to the Solemnity of the Place, cannot be denied; It is an established Principle that all Ornaments owe their Beauty to their Propriety. The same Glitter of Dress that adds Graces to Gayety and Youth, would make Age and Dignity contemptible. CHARON with his Boat is far from heightening the awful Grandeur of the universal Judgment, tho' drawn by *Angelo*[8] himself; nor is it easy to imagine a greater Absurdity than that of gracing the Walls of a Christian Temple with the Figure of *Mars* leading a Hero to Battle, or *Cupids* sporting round a Virgin. The Pope who defaced the Statues of the Deities, at the Tomb of *Sannazarius*[9] is, in my opinion, more easily to be defended than he that erected them.

It is for the same Reason improper to address the EPITAPH

to the Passenger, a Custom which in injudicious Veneration for Antiquity introduced again at the Revival of Letters, and which, among many others, *Passeratius* suffered to mislead him in his EPITAPH upon the Heart of *Henry* King of *France*, who was stabbed by *Clement* the Monk, which yet deserves to be inserted, for the Sake of showing how beautiful even Improprieties may become in the Hands of a good Writer.

> *Adsta, Viator, et dole regum vices.*
> *Cor Regis isto conditur sub marmore,*
> *Qui jura Gallis, jura Sarmatis dedit;*
> *Tectus Cucullo hunc sustulit Sicarius.*
> Abi, Viator, et dole regum vices.[10]

In the Monkish Ages, however ignorant and unpolished, the EPITAPHS were drawn up with far greater Propriety than can be shown in those, which more enlightened Times have produced.

Orate pro Anima —— miserrimi Peccatoris[11]

was an Address to the last Degree striking and solemn, as it flowed naturally from the Religion then believed, and awakened in the Reader Sentiments of Benevolence for the Deceased, and of Concern for his own Happiness. There was Nothing trifling or ludicrous, Nothing that did not tend to the noblest End, the Propagation of Piety and the Increase of Devotion.

It may seem very superfluous to lay it down as the first Rule for writing EPITAPHS, that the Name of the Deceased is not to be omitted; nor should I have thought such a Precept necessary, had not the Practice of the greatest Writers shewn, that it has not been sufficiently regarded. In most of the Poetical EPITAPHS, the Names for whom they were composed may be sought to no Purpose, being only prefixed on the Monument. To expose ye Absurdity of this Omission, it is only necessary to ask how the EPITAPHS, which have outlived the Stones on which they were inscribed, would have contributed to the Information of Posterity, had they wanted the Names of those whom they celebrated.

In drawing the Character of the Deceased, there are no Rules to be observ'd which do not equally relate to other Compositions. The Praise ought not to be general, because the Mind is lost in the Extent of any indefinite Idea, and cannot be affected with what it cannot comprehend.[12] When we hear only of a good or great Man, we know not in what Class to place him, nor have any Notion of his Character, distinct from that of a thousand others; his Example can have no Effect upon our Conduct, as we have nothing remarkable or eminent to propose to our Imitation. The EPITAPH composed by *Ennius* for his own Tomb, has both the Faults last mentioned,

> *Nemo me decoret lacrumis, nec funera, fletu*
> *Faxit. Cur?—volito vivu' per ora virum.*[13]

The Reader of this EPITAPH receives scarce any Idea from it; he neither conceives any Veneration for the Man to whom it belongs, nor is instructed by what Methods this boasted Reputation is to be obtained.

Tho' a sepulchral Inscription is professedly a Panegyric, and, therefore, not confined to historical Impartiality, yet it ought always to be written with regard to Truth. No Man ought to be commended for Virtues which he never possessed, but whoever is curious to know his Faults must enquire after them in other Places; the Monuments of the Dead are not intended to perpetuate the Memory of Crimes, but to exhibit Patterns of Virtue. On the Tomb of *Mæcenas*, his Luxury is not to be mentioned with his Munificence, nor is the Proscription to find a Place on the Monument of *Augustus*.[14]

The best Subject for EPITAPHS is private Virtue; Virtue exerted in the same Circumstances in which the Bulk of Mankind are placed, and which, therefore, may admit of many Imitators. He that has delivered his Country from Oppression, or freed the World from Ignorance and Error, can excite the Emulation of a very small Number; but he that has repelled the Temptations of Poverty, and disdained to free himself from Distress at the Expence of his Virtue, may animate Multitudes, by his Example, to the same Firmness of Heart and Steadiness of Resolution.

Of this Kind I cannot forbear the Mention of two *Greek* Inscriptions;[15] one upon a Man whose Writings are well known, the other upon a Person whose Memory is preserved only in her EPITAPH, who both lived in Slavery, the most calamitous Estate in human Life.

Ζωσιμη ἡ πριν ἐουσα μονω τω Σωματι δουλη,
  Και τω σωματι νυν εὑρεν ἐλευθεριην.

Zosima, *quæ solo fuit olim Corpore Serva,*
  Corpore nunc etiam libera facta fuit.

Zosima, *who in her Life could only have her Body enslaved, now finds her Body likewise set at Liberty.*

It is impossible to read this EPITAPH without being animated to bear the Evils of Life with Constancy, and to support the Dignity of Human Nature under the most pressing Afflictions, both by the Example of the Heroine, whose Grave we behold, and the Prospect of that State in which, to use the Language of the inspired Writers, *The Poor cease from their Labours, and the Weary be at rest.*

The other is upon *Epictetus*, the Stoic Philosopher.[16]

Δουλος ᾿Επικτητος γενομην, και Σωμ' ἀναπηρος,
  Και πενιην ᾿Ιρος, και φιλος ᾿Αθανατοις.

Servus Epictetus, *mutilatus corpore, vixi*
  Pauperieque Irus, Curaque prima Deum.

Epictetus, *who lies here, was a Slave and a Cripple, poor as the Begger in the Proverb, and the Favourite of Heaven.*

In this Distich is comprised the noblest Panegyric, and the most important Instruction. We may learn from it that Virtue is impracticable in no Condition, since *Epictetus* could recommend himself to the Regard of Heaven, amidst the Temptations of Poverty and Slavery; Slavery, which has always been found so destructive to Virtue that in many Languages a Slave and a Thief are expressed by the same Word. And we may be likewise admonished by it, not to lay any Stress on a Man's outward Circumstances in making an Estimate of his real value, since *Epictetus* the Begger, the Cripple, and the Slave, was the Favourite of Heaven.

'Introduction' to the *Harleian Miscellany*.[1]

Though the Scheme of the following *Miscellany* is so obvious, that the Title alone is sufficient to explain it; and though several Collections have been formerly attempted upon Plans, as to the Method, very little, but, as to the Capacity and Execution, very different from Ours; we, being possessed of the greatest Variety for such a Work, hope for a more general Reception than those confined Schemes had the Fortune to meet with; and, therefore, think it not wholly unnecessary to explain our Intentions, to display the Treasure of Materials, out of which this *Miscellany* is to be compiled, and to exhibit a general Idea of the Pieces which we intend to insert in it.

There is, perhaps, no Nation, in which it is so necessary, as in our own, to assemble, from Time to Time, the *small* Tracts and *fugitive* Pieces, which are occasionally published: For, besides the general Subjects of Enquiry which are cultivated by us, in common with every other learned Nation, our Constitution in Church and State naturally gives Birth to a Multitude of Performances, which would either not have been written, or could not have been made publick in any other Place.

The *Form* of our *Government*, which gives every Man, that has Leisure, or Curiosity, or Vanity the Right of enquiring into the Propriety of publick Measures, and, by consequence, obliges those, who are intrusted with the Administration of *National* Affairs, to give an Account of their Conduct, to almost every Man, who demands it, may be reasonably imagined to have occasioned *innumerable* Pamphlets, which would never have appeared under *arbitrary* Governments, where every Man lulls himself in Indolence under Calamities, of which he cannot promote the Redress, or thinks it prudent to conceal the Uneasiness of which he cannot complain without Danger.

The Multiplicity of *Religious Sects* tolerated among us, of which every one has found Opponents and Vindicators, is another Source of unexhaustible Publication, almost peculiar to ourselves; for, Controversies cannot be long continued, nor frequently revived, where an *Inquisitor* has a Right to shut up the Disputants in Dungeons, or where Silence can be imposed on either Party, by the Refusal of a *License*.

Not that it should be inferred from hence, that *Political* or *Religious* Controversies are the *only* Products of the *Liberty* of the *British Press*; the Mind once let loose to Enquiry, and suffered to operate without Restraint, necessarily deviates into peculiar Opinions, and wanders in new Tracks, where she is indeed sometimes lost in a Labyrinth, from which, tho' she cannot return, and scarce knows how to proceed; yet, sometimes, makes useful Discoveries, or finds out nearer Paths to Knowledge.

The boundless Liberty, with which every Man may write his own Thoughts, and the Opportunity of conveying new Sentiments to the Publick, without Danger of suffering either Ridicule or Censure, which every Man may enjoy, whose Vanity does not incite him too hastily to own his Performances, naturally invites those, who employ themselves in Speculation, to try how their Notions will be received by a Nation, which exempts Caution from Fear, and Modesty from Shame; and it is no Wonder, that where Reputation may be gained, but needs not be lost, Multitudes are willing to try their Fortune, and thrust their Opinions into the Light, sometimes with unsuccessful Haste, and sometimes with happy Temerity.

It is observed, that, among the Natives of *England*, is to be found a greater Variety of Humour, than in any other Country; and, doubtless, where every Man has a full Liberty to propagate his Conceptions, Variety of Humour must produce Variety of Writers; and, where the Number of Authors is so great, there cannot but be some worthy of Distinction.

All these and many other Causes, too tedious to be enumerated, have contributed to make *Pamphlets* and *small Tracts* a very *important* Part of an *English* Library; nor are there any Pieces, upon which those, who aspire to the Reputation of *judicious* Collectors of Books, bestow more Attention, or greater Expence; because many Advantages may be expected from the Perusal of these small Productions, which are scarcely to be found in that of larger Works.

If we regard *History*, it is well known, that most *Political* Treatises have for a long Time appeared in this Form, and that the first Relations of Transactions, while they are yet the Subject of Conversation, divide the Opinions, and employ the Conjectures of Mankind, are delivered by these *petty* Writers, who have Opportunities of collecting the different Sentiments of Disputants, of inquiring the Truth from living Witnesses, and of copying their Representations from the Life; and, therefore, they preserve a Multitude of particular Incidents, which are forgotten in a short Time, or omitted in formal Relations, and which are yet to be considered as Sparks of Truth, which, when united, may afford Light in some of the darkest Scenes of State, as, we doubt not, will be sufficiently proved in the Course of this *Miscellany*; and which it is, therefore, the *Interest* of the Publick to preserve unextinguished.

The same Observation may be extended to Subjects of yet more Importance. In Controversies that relate to the Truths of Religion, the first Essays of Reformation are generally timorous; and those, who have Opinions to offer, which they expect to be opposed, produce their Sentiments, by Degrees, and, for the most Part in *small Tracts*: By Degrees, that they may not shock their Readers with too many Novelties at once; and in *small Tracts*, that they may be easily dispersed, or privately printed; Almost every Controversy, therefore, has been, for a Time, carried on in Pamphlets, nor has swelled into larger Volumes, till the first Ardor of the Disputants has subsided, and they have recollected their Notions with Coolness enough to digest them into Order, consolidate them into Systems, and fortify them with Authorities.

From *Pamphlets*, consequently, are to be learned the *Progress* of every Debate; the various State, to which the Questions have been changed; the Artifices and Fallacies, which have been used; and the Subterfuges, by which Reason has been eluded: In such Writings may be seen how the Mind has been opened by Degrees, how one Truth has led to another, how Error has been disentangled, and Hints improved to Demonstration. Which Pleasure, and many others are lost by him, that only reads the *larger Writers* by whom these scattered Sentiments are collected, who will see none of the Changes of Fortune, which every Opinion has passed through, will have no Opportunity of remarking the transient Advantages, which Error may sometimes obtain, by the Artifices of its Patron, or the successful Rallies, by which Truth regains the Day, after a Repulse; but will be to him, who traces the Dispute through, into particular Gradations, as he that hears of a Victory, to him that sees the Battle.

Since the Advantages of preserving these *small Tracts* are so numerous; our Attempt to unite them in Volumes cannot be thought either *useless* or *unseasonable*; for there is *no other* Method of securing them from Accidents; and they have already been so long neglected, that this Design cannot be delayed, without hazarding the Loss of many Pieces, which deserve to be transmitted to another Age.

The Practice of publishing Pamphlets, on the most important Subjects, has now prevailed more than *two Centuries* among us; and, therefore, it cannot be doubted, but that, as no large Collections have been yet made, many curious Tracts must have perished; but it is too late to lament that Loss; nor ought we to reflect upon it, with any other View, than that of quickening our Endeavours, for the Preservation of those that yet remain, of which we have now a *greater Number*, than was, perhaps, ever amassed by any *one* Person.

The first Appearance of Pamphlets among us is generally thought to be at the new Opposition raised against the Errors and Corruptions of the Church of *Rome*. Those, who were first convinced of the Reasonableness of the *New Learning*, as it was *then* called, propagated their Opinions in small Pieces, which were cheaply printed and, what was then of great Importance, easily concealed. These Treatises were generally printed in foreign Countries, and are not, therefore, always very correct. There was not then that Opportunity of Printing in *private*, for, the Number of Printers was small, and the Presses were easily overlooked by the Clergy, who spared no Labour or Vigilance for the Suppression of *Heresy*. There is, however, Reason to suspect, that some Attempts were made to carry on the Propagation of Truth by a *secret* Press; for one of the first Treatises, in Favour of the Reformation, is said, at the End, to be printed *at Greenwich, by the Permission of the Lord of Hosts.*

In the Time of King *Edward the Sixth*, the Presses were employed in Favour of the *Reformed* Religion, and *small Tracts* were dispersed over the Nation, to reconcile them to the new Forms of Worship. In this Reign, likewise, *Political* Pamphlets may be said to have been begun, by the Address of the Rebels of *Devonshire*; all which Means of propagating the Sentiments of the People so disturbed the Court, that no sooner was Queen *Mary* resolved to reduce her Subjects to the *Romish* Superstition, but she artfully, by a *Charter** granted to certain Freemen of *London*, in whose Fidelity, no doubt, she confided, intirely prohibited *all* Presses, but what should be licensed by them; which Charter is that by which the Corporation of *Stationers*, in *London*, is at this time incorporated.

Under the Reign of Queen *Elizabeth*, when Liberty again began to flourish, the Practice of writing Pamphlets became more general; Presses were multiplied, and Books more dispersed; and, I believe, it may properly be said that the *Trade of Writing* began at this Time, and that it has ever since gradually increased in the Number, though, perhaps, not in the Stile of those that followed it.

In this Reign, was erected the first *secret* Press against the Church as now Established, of which I have found any certain Account. It was employed by the *Puritans*, and conveighed from one Part of the Nation to another, by them, as they found themselves in Danger of Discovery. From this Press issued most of the Pamphlets against *Whitgift*, and his Associates, in the Ecclesiastical Government; and, when it was at last seized at *Manchester*, it was employed upon a Pamphlet, called *MORE WORK FOR A COOPER.*[2]

In the peaceable Reign of King *James*, those Minds, which

---

* Which begins thus, KNOW YE, that WE considering, and manifestly perceiving, that several *seditious* and *heretical* Books or *Tracts*—against the Faith and sound Catholic Doctrine of holy Mother, the Church, *&c.*

might, perhaps, with less Disturbance of the World, have been engrossed by War, were employed in Controversy; and Writings of all Kinds were multiplied among us. The Press, however, was not wholly engaged in Polemical Performances, for more innocent Subjects were sometimes treated; and it deserves to be remarked, because it is not generally known, that the Treatises of *Husbandry* and *Agriculture*, which were published about that Time, are so numerous, that it can scarcely be imagined by whom they were written, or to whom they were sold.

The next Reign is too well known to have been a Time of Confusion, and Disturbance, and Disputes of every Kind; and the Writings, which were produced, bear a natural Proportion to the Number of the Questions that were discussed at that Time; each Party had its Authors, and its Presses, and no Endeavours were omitted to gain Proselytes to every Opinion. I know not whether this may not properly be called, *The Age of Pamphlets*; for, though they, perhaps, may not arise to such Multitudes as Mr. *Rawlinson*[3] imagined, they were, undoubtedly, more numerous than can be conceived by any who have not had an Opportunity of examining them.

After the Restoration, the same Differences, in Religious Opinions, are well known to have subsisted, and the same Political Struggles to have been frequently renewed; and, therefore, a great Number of Pens were employed, on different Occasions, till, at length, all other Disputes were absorbed in the *Popish* Controversy.

From the Pamphlets which these different Periods of Time produced, it is proposed, that this *Miscellany* shall be compiled; for which it cannot be supposed that Materials will be wanting, and, therefore, the only Difficulty will be in what Manner to dispose them.

Those who have gone before us, in Undertakings of this Kind, have ranged the Pamphlets, which Chance threw into their Hands, without any Regard either to the Subject on which they treated, or the Time in which they were written; a Practice, in no wise, to be imitated by us, who want for no Materials; of which we shall chuse those we think best for the *particular*

Circumstances of *Times* and *Things*, and most instructing and entertaining to the Reader.

Of the different Methods which present themselves, upon the first View of the great Heaps of Pamphlets, which the *Harleian Library* exhibits, the two which merit most Attention, are to distribute the Treatises according to their *Subjects* or their *Dates*; but neither of these Ways can be conveniently followed. By ranging our Collection in *Order of Time*, we must necessarily publish those Pieces first, which least engage the Curiosity of the Bulk of Mankind, and our Design must fall to the Ground for Want of Encouragement, before it can be so far advanced to obtain general Regard. By confining ourselves for any long Time to any *single Subject*, we shall reduce our Readers to one Class, and, as we shall lose all the Grace of Variety, shall disgust all those who read chiefly to be diverted. There is likewise one Objection of equal Force, against both these Methods, that we shall preclude ourselves from the Advantage of any future Discoveries, and we cannot hope to assemble at once all the Pamphlets which have been written in any Age, or on any Subject.

It may be added, in Vindication of our intended Practice, that it is the same with that of *Photius*,[4] whose Collections are no less Miscellaneous than ours, and who declares, that he leaves it to his Reader, to reduce his Extracts under their proper Heads.

Most of the Pieces, which shall be offered in this Collection to the Publick, will be introduced by short Prefaces, in which will be given some Account of the Reasons for which they are inserted; Notes will be sometimes adjoined for the Explanation of obscure Passages, or obsolete Expressions; and Care will be taken to mingle Use and Pleasure through the whole Collection. Notwithstanding *every Subject* may not be relished by *every Reader*, yet the Buyer may be assured that each Number will repay his generous Subscription.

Observations on the present State of Affairs.[1]

The time is now come in which every *Englishman* expects to be informed of the national affairs, and in which he has a right to have that expectation gratified. For whatever may be urged by ministers, or those whom vanity or interest make the followers of ministers, concerning the necessity of confidence in our governors, and the presumption of prying with profane eyes into the recesses of policy, it is evident, that this reverence can be claimed only by counsels yet unexecuted, and projects suspended in deliberation. But when a design has ended in miscarriage or success, when every eye and every ear is witness to general discontent, or general satisfaction, it is then a proper time to disintangle confusion and illustrate obscurity, to shew by what causes every event was produced, and in what effects it is likely to terminate: to lay down with distinct particularity what rumour always huddles in general exclamations, or perplexes by undigested narratives; to shew whence happiness or calamity is derived, and whence it may be expected, and honestly to lay before the people what inquiry can gather of the past, and conjecture can estimate of the future.

The general subject of the present war is sufficiently known. It is allowed on both sides, that hostilities began in *America*, and that the *French* and *English* quarrelled about the boundaries of their settlements, about grounds and rivers to which, I am afraid, neither can shew any other right than that of power, and which neither can occupy but by usurpation, and the dispossession of the natural lords and original inhabitants. Such is the contest that no honest man can heartily wish success to either party.

It may indeed be alleged, that the Indians have granted large tracts of land both to one and to the other; but these grants can add little to the validity of our titles, till it be experienced how they were obtained: for if they were extorted by violence, or induced by fraud; by threats, which the miseries of other nations had shewn not to be vain, or by promises of which no performance was ever intended, what are they but new modes of usurpation, but new instances of cruelty and treachery?

And indeed what but false hope, or resistless terror can prevail upon a weaker nation to invite a stronger into their country, to give their lands to strangers whom no affinity of manners, or similitude of opinion can be said to recommend, to permit them to build towns from which the natives are excluded, to raise fortresses by which they are intimidated, to settle themselves with such strength, that they cannot afterwards be expelled, but are for ever to remain the masters of the original inhabitants, the dictators of their conduct, and the arbiters of their fate?

When we see men acting thus against the precepts of reason, and the instincts of nature, we cannot hesitate to determine, that by some means or other they were debarred from choice; that they were lured or frighted into compliance; that they either granted only what they found impossible to keep, or expected advantages upon the faith of their new inmates, which there was no purpose to confer upon them. It cannot be said, that the Indians originally invited us to their coasts; we went uncalled and unexpected to nations who had no imagination that the earth contained any inhabitants so distant and so different from themselves. We astonished them with our ships, with our arms, and with our general superiority. They yielded to us as to beings of another and higher race, sent among them from some unknown regions, with power which naked Indians could not resist, and which they were therefore, by every act of humility, to propitiate, that they, who could so easily destroy, might be induced to spare.

To this influence, and to this only, are to be attributed all the cessions and submissions of the Indian princes, if indeed any such cessions were ever made, of which we have no witness but those who claim from them, and there is no great malignity in suspecting, that those who have robbed have also lied.

Some colonies indeed have been established more peaceably than others. The utmost extremity of wrong has not always been practised; but those that have settled in the new world on the fairest terms, have no other merit than that of a scrivener who ruins in silence over a plunderer that seizes by force; all have taken what had other owners, and all have had recourse to arms, rather than quit the prey on which they had fastened.

The *American* dispute between the *French* and us is therefore only the quarrel of two robbers for the spoils of a passenger, but as robbers have terms of confederacy, which they are obliged to observe as members of the gang, so the *English* and *French* may have relative rights, and do injustice to each other, while both are injuring the Indians. And such, indeed, is the present contest: they have parted the northern continent of *America* between them, and are now disputing about their boundaries, and each is endeavouring the destruction of the other by the help of the Indians, whose interest it is that both should be destroyed.

Both nations clamour with great vehemence about infraction of limits, violation of treaties, open usurpation, insidious artifices, and breach of faith. The *English* rail at the perfidious *French*, and the *French* at the encroaching *English*; they quote treaties on each side, charge each other with aspiring to universal monarchy, and complain on either part of the insecurity of possession near such turbulent neighbours.

Through this mist of controversy it can raise no wonder, that the truth is not easily discovered. When a quarrel has been long carried on between individuals, it is often very hard to tell by whom it was begun. Every fact is darkened by distance, by interest, and by multitudes. Information is not easily procured from far; those whom the truth will not favour, will not step voluntarily forth to tell it, and where there are many agents, it is easy for every single action to be concealed.

All these causes concur to the obscurity of the question, by whom were hostilities in *America* commenced? Perhaps there never can be remembered a time in which hostilities had ceased. Two powerful colonies enflamed with immemorial rivalry, and placed out of the superintendence of the mother nations, were not likely to be long at rest. Some opposition was always going forward, some mischief was every day done or meditated, and the borderers were always better pleased with what they could snatch from their neighbours, than what they had of their own.

In this disposition to reciprocal invasion a cause of dispute never could be wanting. The forests and desarts of *America* are without land-marks, and therefore cannot be particularly specified in stipulations; the appellations of those wide extended regions have in every mouth a different meaning, and are understood on either side as inclination happens to contract or extend them. Who has yet pretended to define how much of *America* is included in *Brazil*, *Mexico*, or *Peru*? It is almost as easy to divide the *Atlantic* ocean by a line as clearly to ascertain the limits of those uncultivated, uninhabitable, unmeasured regions.

It is likewise to be considered, that contracts concerning boundaries are often left vague and indefinite without necessity, by the desire of each party, to interpret the ambiguity to its own advantage when a fit opportunity shall be found. In forming stipulations, the commissaries are often ignorant, and often negligent; they are sometimes weary with debate, and contract a tedious discussion into general terms, or refer it to a former treaty, which was never understood. The weaker part is always afraid of requiring explanations, and the stronger always has an interest in leaving the question undecided: thus it will happen without great caution on either side, that after long treaties solemnly ratified, the rights that had been disputed are still equally open to controversy.

In *America* it may easily be supposed, that there are tracts of land yet claimed by neither party, and therefore mentioned in no treaties, which yet one or the other may be afterwards inclined to occupy; but to these vacant and unsettled countries each nation may pretend, as each conceives itself intitled to all that is not expressly granted to the other.

Here then is a perpetual ground of contest, every enlargement of the possessions of either will be considered as something taken from the other, and each will endeavour to regain what had never been claimed, but that the other occupied it.

Thus obscure in its original is the *American* contest. It is difficult to find the first invader, or to tell where invasion properly begins; but I suppose it is not to be doubted, that after the last war, when the *French* had made peace with such apparent superiority, they naturally began to treat us with less respect in distant parts of the world, and to consider us as a people from whom they had nothing to fear, and who could no longer presume to contravene their designs, or to check their progress.

The power of doing wrong with impunity seldom waits long for the will, and it is reasonable to believe, that in *America* the *French* would avow their purpose of aggrandising themselves with at least as little reserve as in *Europe*. We may therefore readily believe, that they were unquiet neighbours, and had no great regard to right which they believed us no longer able to enforce.

That in forming a line of forts behind our colonies, if in no other part of their attempt, they had acted against the general intention, if not against the literal terms of treaties, can scarcely be denied; for it never can be supposed, that we intended to be inclosed between the sea and the *French* garrisons, or preclude ourselves from extending our plantations backwards to any length that our convenience should require.

With dominion is conferred every thing that can secure dominion. He that has the coast has likewise the sea to a certain distance; he that possesses a fortress, has the right of prohibiting another fortress to be built within the command of its cannon. When therefore we planted the coast of *North-America* we supposed the possession of the inland region granted to an indefinite extent, and every nation that settled in that part of the world, seems, by the permission of every other nation, to have made the same supposition in its own favour.

Here then, perhaps, it will be safest to fix the justice of our cause; here we are apparently and indisputably injured, and this injury may, according to the practice of nations, be justly resented. Whether we have not in return made some incroachments upon them, must be left doubtful, till our practices on the *Ohio* shall be stated and vindicated. There are no two nations confining on each other, between whom a war may not always be kindled with plausible pretences on either part, as there is always passing between them a reciprocation of injuries and fluctuation of incroachments.

From the conclusion of the last peace perpetual complaints of the supplantations and invasions of the *French* have been sent to *Europe* from our colonies, and transmitted to our ministers at *Paris*, where good words were sometimes given us, and the practices of the *American* commanders were sometimes disowned, but no redress was ever obtained, nor is it probable that any prohibition was sent to *America*. We were still amused with such doubtful promises as those who are afraid of war are ready to interpret in their own favour, and the *French* pushed forward their line of fortresses, and seemed to resolve that before our complaints were finally dismissed, all remedy should be hopeless.

We likewise endeavour'd at the same time to form a barrier against the *Canadians* by sending a colony to *New-Scotland*,[2] a cold uncomfortable tract of ground, of which we had long the nominal possession before we really began to occupy it. To this those were invited whom the cessation of war deprived of employment, and made burdensome to their country, and settlers were allured thither by many fallacious descriptions of fertile vallies and clear skies. What effect these pictures of *American* happiness had upon my countrymen I was never informed, but I suppose very few sought provision in those frozen regions, whom guilt or poverty did not drive from their native country. About the boundaries of this new colony there were some disputes, but as there was nothing yet worth a contest, the power of the *French* was not much exerted on that side: some disturbance was however given and some skirmishes ensued. But perhaps being peopled chiefly with soldiers, who would rather live by plunder than by agriculture, and who consider war as their best trade, *New-Scotland* would be more obstinately defended than some settlements of far greater value, and the *French* are too well informed of their own interest, to provoke hostility for no advantage, or to select that country for invasion, where they must hazard much, and can win little. They therefore pressed on southward behind our ancient and wealthy settlements, and built fort after fort at such distances that they might conveniently relieve one another, invade our colonies with sudden incursions, and retire to places of safety before our people could unite to oppose them.

This design of the *French* has been long formed, and long known, both in *America* and *Europe*, and might at first have been easily repressed had force been used instead of expostulation. When the *English* attempted a settlement upon the Island of St. *Lucia*, the *French*, whether justly or not, considering it as neutral and forbidden to be occupied by either nation, immediately landed upon it, and destroyed the houses, wasted the plantations, and drove or carried away the inhabitants. This was done in the time of peace, when mutual professions of friendship were daily exchanged by the two courts, and was not considered as any violation of treaties, nor was any more than a very soft remonstrance made on our part.

The *French* therefore taught us how to act, but an *Hanoverian* quarrel with the house of *Austria* for some time induced us to court, at any expence, the alliance of a nation whose very situation makes them our enemies. We suffered them to destroy our settlements, and to advance their own, which we had an equal right to attack. The time however came at last, when we ventured to quarrel with *Spain*, and then *France* no longer suffered the appearance of peace to subsist between us, but armed in defence of her ally.

The events of the war are well known, we pleased ourselves with victory at *Dettingen*,[3] where we left our wounded men to the care of our enemies, but our army was broken at *Fontenoy* and *Val*;[4] and though after the disgrace which we suffered in the *Mediterranean* we had some naval success, and an accidental dearth made peace necessary for the *French*, yet they prescribed the conditions, obliged us to give hostages, and acted as conquerors, though as conquerors of moderation.

In this war the *Americans* distinguished themselves in a manner unknown and unexpected. The *New English* raised an army, and under the command of *Pepperel* took *Cape-Breton*,[5] with the assistance of the fleet. This is the most important fortress in *America*. We pleased ourselves so much with the acquisition, that we could not think of restoring it, and among the arguments used to inflame the people against *Charles Stuart*,[6] it was very clamorously urged, that if he gained the kingdom, he would give *Cape-Breton* back to the *French*.

The *French* however had a more easy expedient to regain *Cape-Breton* than by exalting *Charles Stuart* to the *English* throne; they took in their turn fort *St. George*, and had our *East-India* company wholly in their power, whom they restored at the peace to their former possessions, that they may continue to export our silver.

Cape-Breton therefore was restored, and the *French* were

re-established in *America*, with equal power and greater spirit, having lost nothing by the war which they had before gained.

To the general reputation of their arms, and that habitual superiority which they derive from it, they owe their power in *America*, rather than to any real strength, or circumstances of advantage. Their numbers are yet not great; their trade, though daily improved, is not very extensive; their country is barren, their fortresses, though numerous, are weak, and rather shelters from wild beasts, or savage nations, than places built for defence against bombs or cannons. *Cape-Breton* has been found not to be impregnable; nor, if we consider the state of the places possessed by the two nations in *America*, is there any reason upon which the *French* should have presumed to molest us but that they thought our spirit so broken that we durst not resist them, and in this opinion our long forbearance easily confirmed them.

We forgot, or rather avoided to think, that what we delayed to do must be done at last, and done with more difficulty, as it was delayed longer; that while we were complaining, and they were eluding, or answering our complaints, fort was rising upon fort, and one invasion made a precedent for another.

This confidence of the *French* is exalted by some real advantages. If they possess in those countries less than we, they have more to gain, and less to hazard; if they are less numerous, they are better united.

The *French* compose one body with one head. They have all the same interest, and agree to pursue it by the same means. They are subject to a governor commission'd by an absolute monarch, and participating the authority of his master. Designs are therefore formed without debate, and executed without impediment. They have yet more martial than mercantile ambition, and seldom suffer their military schemes to be entangled with collateral projects of gain: they have no wish but for conquest, of which they justly consider riches as the consequence.

Some advantages they will always have as invaders. They make war at the hazard of their enemies: the contest being carried on in our territories we must lose more by a victory than they will suffer by a defeat. They will subsist, while they stay, upon our plantations, and perhaps destroy them when they can stay no longer. If we pursue them and carry the war into their dominions, our difficulties will encrease every step as we advance, for we shall leave plenty behind us, and find nothing in *Canada*, but lakes and forests barren and trackless, our enemies will shut themselves up in their forts, against which it is difficult to bring cannon through so rough a country, and which if they are provided with good magazines will soon starve those who besiege them.

All these are the natural effects of their government, and situation; they are accidentally more formidable as they are less happy. But the favour of the Indians which they enjoy, with very few exceptions, among all the nations of the northern continent, we ought to consider with other thoughts; this favour we might have enjoyed, if we had been careful to deserve it. The *French* by having these savage nations on their side, are always supplied with spies, and guides, and with auxiliaries, like the *Tartars* to the *Turks* or the Hussars to the *Germans*, of no great use against troops ranged in order of battle, but very well qualified to maintain a war among woods and rivulets, where much mischief may be done by unexpected onsets, and safety be obtained by quick retreats. They can waste a colony by sudden inroads, surprise the straggling planters, frighten the inhabitants into towns, hinder the cultivation of lands, and starve those whom they are not able to conquer.

(*To be continued.*)[7]

Of the Duty of a JOURNALIST.[1]

It is an unpleasing consideration that Virtue cannot be inferred from Knowledge; that many can teach others those Duties which they never practise themselves; yet, tho' there may be speculative Knowledge without actual Performance, there can be no Performance without Knowledge; and the present state of many of our Papers is such that it may be doubted not only whether the Compilers know their Duty, but whether they have endeavoured or wished to know it.

A Journalist is an Historian, not indeed of the highest Class, nor of the number of those whose works bestow immortality upon others or themselves; yet, like other Historians, he distributes for a time Reputation or Infamy, regulates the opinion of the week, raises hopes and terrors, inflames or allays the violence of the people. He ought therefore to consider himself as subject at least to the first law of History, the Obligation to tell Truth. The Journalist, indeed, however honest, will frequently deceive, because he will frequently be deceived himself. He is obliged to transmit the earliest intelligence before he knows how far it may be credited; he relates transactions yet fluctuating in uncertainty; he delivers reports of which he knows not the Authors. It cannot be expected that he should know more than he is told, or that he should not sometimes be hurried down the current of a popular clamour. All that he can do is to consider attentively, and determine impartially, to admit no falsehoods by design, and to retract those which he shall have adopted by mistake.

This is not much to be required, and yet this is more than the Writers of News seem to exact from themselves. It must surely sometimes raise indignation to observe with what serenity of confidence they relate on one day, what they know not to be true, because they hope that it will please; and with what shameless tranquillity they contradict it on the next day, when they find that it will please no longer. How readily they receive any report that will disgrace our enemies, and how eagerly they accumulate praises upon a name, which caprice or accident has made a Favourite. They know, by experience, however destitute of reason, that what is desired will be credited without nice examination: they do not therefore always limit their narratives by possibility, but slaughter armies without battles, and conquer countries without invasions.

There are other violations of truth admitted only to gratify idle curiosity, which yet are mischievous in their consequences, and hateful in their contrivance. Accounts are sometimes published of robberies and murders which never were committed, men's minds are terrified with fictitious dangers, the publick indignation is raised, and the Government of our country depreciated and contemned. These Scriblers, who give false alarms, ought to be taught, by some public animadversion, that to relate crimes is to teach them, and that as most men are content to follow the herd, and to be like their neighbours, nothing contributes more to the frequency of wickedness, than the representation of it as already frequent.

There is another practice, of which the injuriousness is more apparent, and which, if the law could succour the Poor, is now punishable by law. The Advertisement of Apprentices who have left their Masters, and who are often driven away by cruelty or hunger; the minute descriptions of men whom the law has not considered as criminal, and the insinuations often published in such a manner, that, though obscure to the publick, they are well understood where they can do most mischief; and many other practices by which particular interests are injured, are to be diligently avoided by an honest Journalist, whose business is only to tell transactions of general importance, or uncontested notoriety, or by Advertisements to promote private convenience without disturbance of private quiet.

Thus far the Journalist is obliged to deviate from the common methods of his Competitors by the laws of unvariable morality. Other improvements may be expected from him as conducive to delight or information. It is common to find passages, in Papers of Intelligence, which cannot be understood: Obscure places are sometimes mentioned without any information from Geography or History. Sums of money are reckoned by coins or denominations, of which the value is not known in this country. Terms of war and navigation are inserted, which are utterly unintelligible to all who are not engaged in military or naval business. A Journalist, above most other men, ought to be acquainted with the lower orders of mankind, that he may be able to judge, what will be plain and what will be obscure; what will require a Comment, and what will be apprehended without Explanation. He is to consider himself not as writing to Students or Statesmen alone, but to Women, Shopkeepers, and Artisans, who have little time to bestow upon mental attainments, but desire, upon easy terms, to know how the world goes; who rises, and who falls; who triumphs, and who is defeated.

If the Writer of this Journal shall be able to execute his own

Plan; if he shall carefully enquire after Truth, and diligently impart it; if he shall resolutely refuse to admit into his Paper whatever is injurious to private Reputation; if he shall relate transactions with greater clearness than others, and sell more instruction at a cheaper rate, he hopes that his labours will not be overlooked. This he promises to endeavour; and, if this Promise shall obtain the Favour of an early Attention, he desires that Favour to be continued only as it is deserved.

The Bravery of the *English* Common Soldiers.[1]

By those who have compared the military genius of the English with that of the French nation, it is remarked, that *the French officers will always lead, if the soldiers will follow*; and that *the English soldiers will always follow, if their officers will lead*.

In all pointed sentences some degree of accuracy must be sacrificed to conciseness; and, in this comparison, our officers seem to lose what our soldiers gain. I know not any reason for supposing that the English officers are less willing than the French to lead; but it is, I think, universally allowed that the English soldiers are more willing to follow. Our nation may boast, beyond any other people in the world, of a kind of epidemic bravery, diffused equally through all its ranks. We can shew a peasantry of heroes, and fill our armies with clowns, whose courage may vie with that of their general.

There may be some pleasure in tracing the causes of this plebeian magnanimity. The qualities which commonly make an army formidable, are long habits of regularity, great exactness of discipline, and great confidence in the commander. Regularity may in time, produce a kind of mechanical obedience to signals and commands, like that which the perverse Cartesians[2] impute to animals: discipline may impress such an awe upon the mind, that any danger shall be less dreaded than the danger of punishment; and confidence in the wisdom or fortune of the general, may induce the soldiers to follow him blindly to the most dangerous enterprize.

What may be done by discipline and regularity, may be seen

in the troops of the Russian Empress, and Prussian Monarch.[3] We find that they may be broken without confusion, and repulsed without flight.

But the English troops have none of these requisites, in any eminent degree. Regularity is by no means part of their character: they are rarely exercised, and therefore shew very little dexterity in their evolutions as bodies of men, or in the manual use of their weapons as individuals: they neither are thought by others, nor by themselves, more active or exact than their enemies, and therefore derive none of their courage from such imaginary superiority.

The manner in which they are dispersed in quarters over the country during times of peace, naturally produces laxity of discipline: they are very little in sight of their officers; and, when they are not engaged in the slight duty of the guard, are suffered to live every man his own way.

The equality of English privileges, the impartiality of our laws, the freedom of our tenures, and the prosperity of our trade, dispose us very little to reverence of superiors. It is not to any great esteem of the officers that the English soldier is indebted for his spirit in the hour of battle: for perhaps it does not often happen that he thinks much better of his leader than of himself. The French Count,[4] who has lately published the *Art of War*, remarks how much soldiers are animated, when they see all their dangers shared by those who were born to be their masters, and whom they consider as beings of a different rank. The Englishman despises such motives of courage: he was born without a master; and looks not on any man, however dignified by lace or titles, as deriving from Nature any claims to his respect, or inheriting any qualities superior to his own.

There are some, perhaps, who would imagine that every Englishman fights better than the subjects of absolute governments, because he has more to defend. But what has the English more than the French soldier? Property they are both commonly without. Liberty is, to the lowest rank of every nation, little more than the choice of working or starving; and this choice is, I suppose, equally allowed in every country. The English soldier seldom has his head very full of the constitution; nor has there been, for more than a century, any war that put the property or liberty of a single Englishman in danger.

Whence then is the courage of the English vulgar? It proceeds, in my opinion, from that dissolution of dependance which obliges every man to regard his own character. While every man is fed by his own hands, he has no need of any servile arts: he may always have wages for his labour; and is no less necessary to his employer, than his employer is to him. While he looks for no protection from others, he is naturally roused to be his own protector; and having nothing to abate his esteem of himself, he consequently aspires to the esteem of others. Thus every man that crowds our streets is a man of honour, disdainful of obligation, impatient of reproach, and desirous of extending his reputation among those of his own rank; and as courage is in most frequent use, the fame of courage is most eagerly pursued. From this neglect of subordination I do not deny that some inconveniencies may from time to time proceed: the power of the law does not always sufficiently supply the want of reverence, or maintain the proper distinction between different ranks: but good and evil will grow up in this world together; and they who complain, in peace, of the insolence of the populace, must remember that their insolence in peace is bravery in war.

Appendix I
Johnson's prayer on beginning
The Rambler

Almighty God, the giver of all good things, without whose help all Labour is ineffectual, and without whose grace all wisdom is folly, grant, I beseech Thee, that in this my undertaking thy Holy Spirit may not be witheld from me, but that I may promote thy glory, and the Salvation both of myself and others,—Grant this O Lord for the sake of Jesus Christ. Amen. Lord bless me. So be it.

Taken from Samuel Johnson, *Diaries, Prayers, and Annals*, ed. E. L. McAdam, Jr (New Haven: Yale University Press, 1958), p. 43.

Appendix II
Parallel texts of the original and revised states of *The Rambler* No. 1

First edition (1750)	Fourth edition (1756)

*Cur tamen hoc libeat potiùs
  decurrere campo,
Per quem magnus equos
  Auruncæ flexit Alumnus,
Si vacat, et placidi rationem
  admittitis, edam.*

JUV.

*Cur tamen hoc libeat potius
  decurrere campo,
Per quem magnus equos
  Auruncæ flexit alumnus,
Si vacat, et placidi rationem
  admittitis, edam.*

JUV.

Why to expatiate in this beaten field,
Why arms, oft us'd in vain, I mean to
  wield;
If time permit, and candour will
  attend,
Some satisfaction this essay may
  lend.

ELPHINSTON.

THE Difficulty of the first
Address, on any new Occasion,
is felt by every Man in his
Transactions with the World,
and confessed by the settled and
regular Forms of Salutation,
which Necessity has introduced
into all Languages. Judgment
was wearied with the
inextricable Perplexity of being
forced upon Choice, where there
was often no Motive to
Preference; and it was found

THE difficulty of the first address
on any new occasion, is felt by
every man in his transactions
with the world, and confessed by
the settled and regular forms of
salutation which necessity has
introduced into all languages.
Judgment was wearied with the
perplexity of being forced upon
choice, where there was no
motive to preference; and it was
found convenient that some easy
method of introduction should

convenient that some easy
Method of Introduction should
be established, which, if it
wanted the Allurement of
Novelty, might enjoy in its place
the Security of Prescription.

Perhaps few Authors have
presented themselves before the
Publick, without wishing that
such ceremonial Modes of
Entrance had been anciently
established, as might have freed
us from the Dangers, which the
too ardent Desire of pleasing is
certain to produce; and
precluded the vain Expedients of
softening Censure by Apologies,
and of rousing Attention by
Abruptness.

The Epic Writers, indeed, have
found the proemial Part of the
Poem such an Addition to their
laborious Undertaking, that they
have almost unanimously
adopted the first Lines of *Homer*,
and the Reader needs only be
informed of the Subject to know
in what Manner the Scene will
open.

But this solemn Repetition has
been hitherto the peculiar
Distinction of Heroic Poetry,
and has never been legally
extended to the lower Orders of
Literature, and seems to be
considered as an hereditary
Privilege, to be enjoyed only by
those who can claim it from their
Alliance to the Genius of *Homer*.

The Rules, which long
Observation of the injudicious
Use of this Prerogative suggested

be established, which, if it
wanted the allurement of
novelty, might enjoy the security
of prescription.

PERHAPS few authors have
presented themselves before the
public, without wishing that
such ceremonial modes of
entrance had been anciently
established, as might have freed
them from those dangers which
the desire of pleasing is certain to
produce, and precluded the vain
expedients of softening censure
by apologies, or rousing
attention by abruptness.

THE epic writers have found
the proemial part of the poem
such an addition to their
undertaking, that they have
almost unanimously adopted the
first lines of Homer, and the
reader needs only be informed of
the subject to know in what
manner the poem will begin.

BUT this solemn repetition is
hitherto the peculiar distinction
of heroic poetry; it has never
been legally extended to the
lower orders of literature, but
seems to be considered as an
hereditary privilege, to be
enjoyed only by those who claim
it from their alliance to the
genius of Homer.

THE rules which the
injudicious use of this
prerogative suggested to Horace,

to *Horace*, may, indeed, be applied to the Direction of Candidates for inferior Fame; and it may be proper for all to remember, that they ought not to raise Expectation which it is not in their power to satisfy, and that it is more pleasing to see Smoke gradually brightening into Flame, than Flame sinking into Smoke.

Yet though this Precept has been long received, both from regard to the Authority of his that delivered it, and its Conformity to the general Opinion of the World, as well since as before his Time, there have been some, who have thought it no Deviation from Modesty, to recommend their own Labours, and imagined themselves entitled, by indisputable Merit, to an Exemption from general Restraints, and to Elevations not allowed in common Life. They, perhaps, believed, that when, like *Thucydides*, they bequeathed to Mankind κτημα ες αει, *an Estate for ever*, it was an additional Favour to inform them of its Value.

It may, indeed, be no less dangerous to claim, on some Occasions, too little than too much. There is something captivating in Spirit and Intrepidity, to which we often yield, as to a resistless Power; nor can he reasonably expect the Confidence of others, who, too

may indeed be applied to the direction of candidates for inferior fame; it may be proper for all to remember, that they ought not to raise expectation which it is not in their power to satisfy, and that it is more pleasing to see smoke brightening into flame, than flame sinking into smoke.

THIS precept has been long received both from regard to the authority of Horace and its conformity to the general opinion of the world, yet there have been always some, that thought it no deviation from modesty to recommend their own labours, and imagined themselves entitled by indisputable merit to an exemption from general restraints, and to elevations not allowed in common life. They, perhaps, believed that when, like Thucydides, they bequeathed to mankind κτημα ες αει, *an estate for ever*, it was an additional favour to inform them of its value.

IT may, indeed, be no less dangerous to claim, on certain occasions, too little than too much. There is something captivating in spirit and intrepidity, to which we often yield, as to a resistless power; nor can he reasonably expect the confidence of others, who too apparently, distrusts himself.

Plutarch, in his Enumeration of the various Occasions on which a Man may, without just Offence, proclaim his own Excellencies, has, I think, omitted the Case of an Author entering the World; unless it may be comprehended under his general Position, that a Man may lawfully praise himself for those Qualities which cannot be known, but from his own Mouth; as when he is among Strangers, and can probably have no Opportunity of an actual Exertion of his Powers. That the Case of an Author is parallel, will scarcely be granted, because he necessarily discovers the Degree of his Merit to the Judges, when he solicits their Suffrages. But it should be remembered, that unless his Judges be prejudiced in his Favour, they will not be persuaded to hear the Cause.

In Love, the State which fills the Heart with a Degree of Solicitude next that of an Author, it has been held a Maxim, that Success is more easily obtained by indirect and concealed Approaches; he who too soon professes himself a Lover, raises Obstacles to his own Wishes, and those whom Disappointments have taught Experience, endeavour to conceal their Passion till they believe their Mistress wishes for the Discovery. The same

apparently distrusts himself.

PLUTARCH, in his enumeration of the various occasions, on which a man may without just offence proclaim his own excellencies, has omitted the case of an author entering the world; unless it may be comprehended under his general position, that a man may lawfully praise himself for those qualities which cannot be known but from his own mouth; as when he is among strangers, and can have no opportunity of an actual exertion of his powers. That the case of an author is parallel will scarcely be granted, because he necessarily discovers the degree of his merit to his judges, when he appears at his trial. But it should be remembered, that unless his judges are inclined to favour him, they will hardly be persuaded to hear the cause.

IN love, the state which fills the heart with a degree of solicitude next that of an author, it has been held a maxim, that success is most easily obtained by indirect and unperceived approaches; he who too soon professes himself a lover, raises obstacles to his own wishes, and those whom disappointments have taught experience, endeavour to conceal their passion till they believe their mistress wishes for the discovery. The same method, if it were

Method, if it were practicable to Writers, would save many Complaints of the Partiality of the World, the Severity of the Age, and the Caprices of Criticism. If a Man could glide imperceptibly into the Favour of the Publick, and only proclaim his Pretensions to literary Honours, when he is sure of not being rejected, he might commence Author with better Hopes, as his Failings might escape Contempt, though he shall never attain Excellence sufficient to excite much regard.

But since the Publick supposes every Man that writes ambitious of Applause; as some Ladies have taught themselves to believe that every Man intends Love, who expresses Civility, the Miscarriage of any new Endeavour in Learning raises an unbounded Contempt, which is indulged by most Minds without scruple, as an honest Triumph over unjust Claims, and exorbitant Expectations. The Artifices of those who put themselves in this hazardous State, have therefore been multiplied in proportion to their Fear as well as their Ambition; and are to be looked upon with more Indulgence, as they result from complicated Passions, and are incited at once by the two great Movers of the human Mind, the Desire of Good, and the Fear of Evil. For who can wonder that, thus allured on one

practicable to writers, would save many complaints of the severity of the age, and the caprices of criticism. If a man could glide imperceptibly into the favour of the publick, and only proclaim his pretensions to literary honours when he is sure of not being rejected, he might commence author with better hopes, as his failings might escape contempt, though he shall never attain much regard.

BUT since the world supposes every man that writes ambitious of applause, as some ladies have taught themselves to believe that every man intends love, who expresses civility, the miscarriage of any endeavour in learning raises an unbounded contempt, indulged by most minds without scruple, as an honest triumph over unjust claims, and exorbitant expectations. The artifices of those who put themselves in this hazardous state, have therefore been multiplied in proportion to their fear as well as their ambition; and are to be looked upon with more indulgence, as they are incited at once by the two great movers of the human mind, the desire of good, and the fear of evil. For who can wonder that, allured on one side, and frightned on the other, some should endeavour to gain favour

Side, and frighted on the other, some Men should endeavour to gain Favour by bribing the Judge with an Appearance of Respect which they do not feel, to excite Compassion by confessing Weakness of which they are not convinced, or to attract Regard by a Shew of Openness and Magnanimity, by a daring Profession of their own Deserts, and a publick Challenge of Honours and Rewards.

The ostentatious and haughty Display of themselves has been the usual Refuge of diurnal Writers, in vindication of whose Practice it may be said, that what it wants in Prudence is supplied by Sincerity, and who, at least, may plead, that if their Boasts deceive any into the Perusal of their Performances, they defraud them of but little Time.

— *Quid enim? Concurritur* —
   Horæ
Momento cita Mors venit, aut
   Victoria læta.

The Question concerning the Merit of the Day is soon decided, and we are not condemned to toil through half a Folio, to be convinced that the Writer has broke his Promise.

It is one among many Reasons

by bribing the judge with an appearance of respect which they do not feel, to excite compassion by confessing weakness of which they are not convinced, and others to attract regard by a shew of openness and magnanimity, by a daring profession of their own deserts, and a publick challenge of honours and rewards.

THE ostentatious and haughty display of themselves has been the usual refuge of diurnal writers, in vindication of whose practice it may be said, that what it wants in prudence is supplied by sincerity, and who at least may plead, that if their boasts deceive any into the perusal of their performances, they defraud them of but little time.

— *Quid enim? Concurritur* —
   horæ
Momento cita mors venit, aut
   victoria læta.

The battle joins, and, in a moment's
   flight,
Death, or a joyful conquest, ends the
   fight.

FRANCIS.

The question concerning the merit of the day is soon decided, and we are not condemned to toil thro' half a folio, to be convinced that the writer has broke his promise.

IT is one among many reasons

for which I purpose to endeavour the Entertainment of my Countrymen, by a short Essay on *Tuesdays* and *Saturdays*, that I hope not much to tire those whom I shall not happen to please; and if I am not commended for the Beauty of my Works, to be at least pardoned for their Brevity. But whether my Expectations are most fixed on Pardon or Praise, I think it not necessary to discover; for, having accurately weighed the Reasons for Arrogance and Submission, I find them so nearly equiponderant, that my Impatience to try the Event of my first Performance will not suffer me to attend any longer the Trepidation of the Balance.

There are, indeed, many Conveniences almost peculiar to this Method of Publication, which may naturally flatter the Author, whether he be confident or timorous. The Man to whom the Extent of his Knowledge, or the Sprightliness of his Imagination, has, in his own Opinion, already secured the Praises of the World, willingly takes that Way of displaying his Abilities, which will soonest give him an Opportunity of hearing the Voice of Fame, and it heightens his Alacrity to think in how many Places he shall hear what he is now writing, read with Ecstasies to morrow. He will often please himself with reflecting, that the Author of a

for which I purpose to endeavour the entertainment of my countrymen by a short essay on Tuesday and Saturday, that I hope not much to tire those whom I shall not happen to please; and if I am not commended for the beauty of my works, to be at least pardoned for their brevity. But whether my expectations are most fixed on pardon or praise, I think it not necessary to discover; for having accurately weighed the reasons for arrogance and submission, I find them so nearly equiponderant, that my impatience to try the event of my first performance will not suffer me to attend any longer the trepidations of the balance.

THERE are, indeed, many conveniences almost peculiar to this method of publication, which may naturally flatter the author, whether he be confident or timorous. The man to whom the extent of his knowledge, or the sprightliness of his imagination, has, in his own opinion, already secured the praises of the world, willingly takes that way of displaying his abilities which will soonest give him an opportunity of hearing the voice of fame; it heightens his alacrity to think in how many places he shall hear what he is now writing, read with ecstasies to morrow. He will often please himself with reflecting, that the author of a large treatise must large Treatise must proceed with Anxiety, lest, before the Completion of his Work, the Attention of the Publick may have changed its Object; but that he who is confined to no single Subject, may follow the national Taste through all its Variations, and catch the *Aura popularis*, the Gale of Favour, from what Point soever it shall blow.

Nor is the Prospect less likely to ease the Doubts of the Cautious, and allay the Terrours of the Fearful, for to such the Shortness of every single Paper is a powerful Encouragement. He that questions his Abilities to arrange the dissimilar Parts of an extensive Plan, or fears to be lost in a complicated System, may yet hope to adjust a few Pages without Perplexity; and if, when he turns over the Repositories of his Memory, he finds his Collection too small for a Volume, he may yet have enough to furnish out an Essay. He that is afraid of laying out too much Time upon an Experiment of which he fears the Event, persuades himself that a few Days will shew him what he is to expect from his Learning and his Genius. If he thinks his own Judgment not sufficiently enlightened, he may, by attending the Remarks which every Paper will produce, inform himself of his Mistakes, rectify his Opinions, and extend his Views. If he suspects that he may

proceed with anxiety, lest, before the completion of his work, the attention of the publick may have changed its object; but that he who is confined to no single topick, may follow the national taste through all its variations, and catch the *Aura popularis*, the gale of favour, from what point soever it shall blow.

Nor is the prospect less likely to ease the doubts of the cautious, and the terrours of the fearful, for to such the shortness of every single paper is a powerful encouragement. He that questions his abilities to arrange the dissimilar parts of an extensive plan, or fears to be lost in a complicated system, may yet hope to adjust a few pages without perplexity; and if, when he turns over the repositories of his memory, he finds his collection too small for a volume, he may yet have enough to furnish out an essay. He that would fear to lay out too much time upon an experiment of which he knows not the event, persuades himself that a few days will shew him what he is to expect from his learning and his genius. If he thinks his own judgment not sufficiently enlightned, he may, by attending the remarks which every paper will produce, rectify his opinions. If he should with too little premeditation encumber himself by an unweildly subject,

with too little Premeditation
entangle himself in an unweildy
Subject, he may quit it without
confessing his Ignorance, and
pass to other Topicks less
dangerous, or more tractable.
And if he finds, with all his
Industry, and all his Artifices,
that he cannot deserve Regard,
or cannot attain it, he may let the
Design fall at once, and, without
Injury to others, or himself,
retire to Amusements of greater
Pleasure, or to Studies of better
Prospect.

he can quit it without confessing
his ignorance, and pass to other
topicks less dangerous, or more
tractable. And if he finds, with
all his industry, and all his
artifices, that he cannot deserve
regard, or cannot attain it, he
may let the design fall at once,
and, without injury to others or
himself, retire to amusements of
greater pleasure, or to studies of
better prospect.

Appendix III
Bonnell Thornton's parody of
The Rambler

*ΓΝΩΘΙ ΣΕΑΥΤΟΝ**

Expatiate free o'er all this Scene of MAN,
A might Maze, *but not without a* Plan.
POPE.

WHILE capricious CURIOSITY persuades the youth of *Great-Britain* to relish no scenes but those that are extraneous; while the fashionable practice so extensively prevails of visiting distant countries, and in short of cultivating any thing but what is truly *British* and domestic; I shall beg leave to look at home, and take a survey of what more properly may be said to be our own; accurately to delineate the topography of the human body, and enumerate it's respective inhabitants.

First of all, let us investigate the BRAIN, where the MIND sits sceptered and enthroned, and from this eminent situation, like an absolute monarch, regulates and dispenses her commands over the whole subject system of the body.

As soon as we emerge from these obscure regions, the first object that exhibits itself to the attentive examiner is ASSURANCE, high-plumed on the smooth and unembarrassed surface of the FOREHEAD. Observe with what an obstinate and immoveable gaze she stares on every thing around her, and how she glories in her brazen bulwark of countenance. Sublime on the ridgy hillocks of the EYE-BROWS is seated VANITY, and near her PRIDE contracts his face into frowns, and fiercely casts down his eye beneath with a disdainful leer.

As you descend lower, you may observe the FIELDS styled in poetical language, the LAUGHING FIELDS displaying themselves over either JAW. Here every thing wears a brighter and more joyous aspect; here LAUGHTER disports in a thousand wanton wiles, and scatters

---

* 'Know thyself.'

sleek dimples over the adjacent CHEEKS. — And yet is not this climate always cloudless and serene. ANXIETY is no stranger to these regions; he often bids the salt torrent stream from the swelling eyes, while GRIEF holds out the ready hand to rend the flowing tresses. So close is the neighbourhood between PLEASURE and PAIN!

In the middle of these plains arises a prominence, which mortals have named the NOSE. JESTS wanton on it's summit, and TAUNTS in various shapes sport around it's brow. It must not be forgot, that the top of this hill is sometimes possessed by that savage and implacable fury ANGER.

Nor far off are the roseate LIPS, where Pallas keeps her nectar, and from which distil the streams of ELOQUENCE and PERSUASION in gentle dews, or pour down in fuller and more vehement tides. But near the interior caverns of the THROAT a magnificent Queen, called LUXURY, holds her high-arched palace. And in this neighbourhood ENVY infects the TEETH with her venomous and corrosive gall.

After leaving the declivities of the HEAD, and the rugged ridges of the CHIN, we arrive at the vallies of the NECK. Here VIRTUE, the sister of LIBERTY, resides; here she maintains her unshaken inflexibility, in which she is often assisted by STRENGTH who keeps his *Herculian* fortress on the muscular vigour of the BACK and manly BREAST.

Let us now march by a narrow path down the descent of the ARMS, and we shall find SLOTH reclined on the bend of the ELBOW, while CONTEMPT stands erect and unabashed on the tip of the FORE-FINGER. Nor seldom does AVARICE and the insatiable DESIRE OF GAIN tempt the insidious hand to clandestine deeds of theft.

We will now cross over that part, where the trepidating LUNGS receive and give back the vital inspiration in alternate heavings, and where the RIBS confine the VISCERA within their concave circle. Here meek CLEMENCY has chosen her station; here she breathes sigh for sigh, and returns sorrow for sorrow. Hail, tenderest inmate of the HEART! in whatsoever BREAST thou art now compassionating human misfortunes, whatsoever BOWELS are now struggling beneath thy influence, – adieu! – we are reluctantly summoned to proceed farther, and as we descend lower, arrive at – but MODESTY turns away her blushing countenance from this detested seat, this habitation of that impure dæmon LUST.

Not far hence in a desponding condition (and indeed it may be superfluous to remark that the joys of VENUS are ever attended by a dreary train of CARES) REPENTANCE appears, whose business it is to supple the knees to adoration. Behold him prostrate, as in the monastic cloyster, or the desolate cavern, and mixing a flood of tears with a storm of sighs.

Our journey is at length almost consummated; and having now passed the perpendicular declivity of the legs, we shall find FLIGHT and SWIFTNESS situated in the FEET. Nor is every one endued with the same degree of swiftness: cast your eyes from *Pyrenæan* cliffs! Examine the nations of either side! Here you will perceive the slow *Spaniard* stalking with stiff and stately steps; there the *Frenchman* practising every art of agility, cutting everlasting capers, and leaping through life. Nay, so eminently does this volatile people excel in dancing and running away, that some philosophers imagine all that strength, which in others is proportionably diffused over the whole body, to be in them concentred in their heels.

Taken from Isaac Reed, *The Repository: A Select Collection of Fugitive Pieces of Wit and Humour, in Prose and Verse. By the Most Eminent Writers*. The Second Edition. Four volumes (London, 1790), iii, pp. 216–20.

Notes

THE RAMBLER

Johnson began composing *The Rambler* in March 1750. The first paper was published anonymously on Tuesday, 20 March, and subsequently one appeared each Saturday and Tuesday, until the final paper was published on Saturday, 14 March 1752. Something of the spirit in which Johnson approached his task is captured in the prayer he composed on beginning *The Rambler* (see Appendix I). The publishers were John Payne, Joseph Bouquet and Edward Cave. They paid Johnson two guineas per paper, and on 1 April 1751 Johnson assigned the copyright to Edward Cave. According to Arthur Murphy, the circulation of *The Rambler* never rose above five hundred copies. Nevertheless, the papers were soon reprinted in collected editions, and Johnson took advantage of the opportunity represented by these early reprintings to revise his text. Something of the scale and direction of these acts of revision is suggested by the parallel texts of *Rambler* No. 1 reprinted here in Appendix II. After the fourth collected edition of 1756, however, the incidence of revision subsides. Therefore the fourth edition has furnished the copy-text for this selection.

No. 1. Tuesday, 20 March 1750.

1. *Juv*: Juvenal, i. 19–21.
2. *Horace*: Johnson has in mind 'non fumum ex fulgore, sed ex fumo dare lucem / cogitat'; 'he aims to produce, not smoke out of light, but light from smoke' (*Ars Poetica*, ll. 143–4).
3. *an estate for ever*: Thucydides, *History*, I. xxii. 4.
4. *powers*: 'On Praising Oneself Inoffensively', Plutarch, *Moralia*, 539A–547F.
5. *læta*: Horace, *Satires*, I. i. 7–8.
6. *popularis*: Cf. Horace, *Odes*, III. ii. 20.

No. 2. Saturday, 24 March 1750.

1. *STATIUS*: 'such misery it is to be rooted to the spot – miles are lost before they begin, and their hooves re-echo across the deserted plain'; Statius, *Thebaid*, vi. 400–1.

2. *POPE*: *Windsor Forest*, ll. 151–4.

3. *hope to hope*: A sentiment with parallels in *Rasselas*, where in chapter 3 Rasselas himself regrets that 'I have already enjoyed too much; give me something to desire', and where in chapter 47 Nekayah observes that 'none are happy but by the anticipation of change: the change itself is nothing; when we have made it, the next wish is to change again. The world is not exhausted; let me see something to morrow which I never saw before' (*Rasselas and Other Tales*, ed. Gwin J. Kolb (New Haven and London: Yale University Press, 1990), pp. 16 and 164). Johnson mistrusted Hobbes, remarking to Thomas Tyers that 'when I published my Dictionary I might have quoted *Hobbes* as an authority in language, as well as many other writers of his time; but I scorned, sir, to quote him at all; because I did not like his principles' (*The Early Biographies of Samuel Johnson*, ed. O. M. Brack Jr and Robert E. Kelley (Iowa: University of Iowa Press, 1974), p. 82). But nevertheless his understanding of man as driven more by hope than by gratification is compatible with a notorious passage of *Leviathan*: 'the Felicity of this life, consisteth not in the repose of a mind satisfied. For there is no such *Finis ultimus*, (utmost ayme,) nor *Summum Bonum*, (greatest Good,) as is spoken of in the Books of the old Morall Philosophers. Nor can a man any more live, whose Desires are at an end, than he, whose Senses and Imaginations are at a stand. Felicity is a continuall progresse of the desire, from one object to another; the attaining of the former, being still but the way to the later' (chapter 11).

4. *inadequate*: Cervantes, *Don Quixote*, pt. 1, chs 7, 15 and 21.

5. *libello*: Horace, *Epistles*, I. i. 36–7.

6. *Epictetus*: 'Keep before your eyes day by day death and exile, and everything that seems terrible, but most of all death; and then you will never have any abject thought, nor will you yearn for anything immoderately' (*Enchiridion*, c. 21).

7. *canoros*: Horace, *Epistles*, II. ii. 76.

No. 4. Saturday, 31 March 1750.

1. *Vitæ*: Horace, *Ars Poetica*, l. 334.

2. *CREECH*: Thomas Creech (1659–1700), translator.

3. *fiction*: According to Arthur Murphy, Johnson had in mind Smollett's *Roderick Random* (1748) and Fielding's *Tom Jones* (1749).

4. *Pontanus*: Julius Caesar Scaliger (1484–1558) was a French polymath who pursued research in zoology, botany, grammar and literary criticism; his *Poetics* (1561) imparted a neo-classical flavour to the literary criticism of the early modern period, and was particularly important for reinforcing the authority of Aristotle. Giovanni Pontano (or Jovianus Pontanus) (1426–1503), an Italian poet, man of letters and statesman, was one of the finest Latin prose stylists of the Renaissance. See Scaliger, *Poetics*, VI. 4.

5. *minus*: Horace, *Epistles*, II. i. 170.

6. *Apelles*: Apelles (*fl.* fourth century BC) was the greatest painter of antiquity. It is said that a cobbler criticized the drawing of a sandal in a picture by Apelles. Apelles altered the sandal in deference to the cobbler's opinion, but when the next day the cobbler criticized the drawing of the leg, Apelles replied 'ne sutor supra crepidam', 'a cobbler should not judge of anything above the sole', or as we say, 'let the cobbler stick to his last'. Pliny, *Natural History*, XXXV. xxxvi. 85.

7. *chastity of thought*: 'Plurima sunt, Fuscine, et fama digna sinistra / et nitidis maculam haesuram figentia rebus, / quae monstrant ipsi pueris traduntque parentes'; 'Fuscinus, there are many infamous things – things capable of besmirching even the most brilliant lives – which parents themselves point out and pass on to their sons.' Juvenal, xiv.

8. *effects*: For another, celebrated, instance of Johnson's concern over the receptiveness of the imagination, and the consequent need for only uplifting or strengthening examples to be placed before it by literature, see his comments on the ending of *King Lear*, in *Samuel Johnson on Shakespeare*, ed. H. R. Woudhuysen (Harmondsworth: Penguin Books, 1989), pp. 221–3.

9. *resentful*: Alexander Pope and Jonathan Swift, *Miscellanies* (1727), ii. 354.

10. *but feared*: An allusion to the principle of Caligula, 'oderint, dum metuant', 'let them hate, so long as they fear' (Suetonius, 'Gaius Caligula', xxx. 1).

No. 6. Saturday, 7 April 1750.

1. *HOR*: Horace, *Epistles*, I. xi. 28–30.

2. *insaniens*: 'Crazy wisdom' (Horace, *Odes*, I. xxxiv. 2).

3. *ortum*: Boethius, *Consolatio*, III. metr.6.9.

4. *canine madness*: Rabies.

5. *philosophy*: Abraham Cowley, *Works* (1669), sig. C1ʳ (slightly misquoted and abbreviated).

6. *new persuit*: Again, there is a parallel with Rasselas's regret that 'I have already enjoyed too much; give me something to desire' (*Rasselas*

and Other Tales, ed. Gwin J. Kolb (New Haven and London: Yale University Press, 1990), p. 16).

No. 7. Tuesday, 10 April 1750.

1. *BOETHIUS*: Boethius, *Consolatio*, III. metr. 9.1–2, 25–28.
2. *master*: Plutarch, *Moralia*, 780c.
3. *geometry*: The king was Ptolemy I; see Proclus, *In primum Euclidis Elementorum librum commentarii* (1560), Book 2, ch. 4, p. 39.
4. *now especially*: I.e. at Easter.

No. 8. Saturday, 14 April 1750.

1. *JUV*: Juvenal, xiii. 208–10.
2. *vacavi*: Lucan, *Pharsalia*, X. 185–6.
3. *crime to think*: Aquinas, *Summa*, I–II, Q.74, a.8; Q.108, a.3.
4. τέρπου: Pythagoras, *Aurea Carmina*, ll. 40–4.
5. *MILTON*: John Milton, *Paradise Lost*, v. 117–19.

No. 9. Tuesday, 17 April 1750.

1. *MART*: Martial, X. xlvii. 12.
2. *upon him thus*: Joseph Addison, *Cato*, II. vi. 48–50.
3. *at sea*: A reference to actions in the War of the Austrian Succession (1740–48). In 1747 two French fleets convoying merchantmen to the colonies had been successfully attacked; these victories were a consequence of the policy of Admiral Edward Vernon, who in the 1740s had established the Western Squadron, commanded by Admiral George Anson.

No. 13. Tuesday, 1 May 1750.

1. *HOR*: Horace, *Epistles*, I. xviii. 38.
2. *not to speak*: Quintus Curtius, *History of Alexander*, IV. vi. 5–6.
3. *virtually the same*: This was said of Sarah Churchill, the Duchess of Marlborough; cf. [Nathaniel Hooke], *An Account of the Conduct of the Dowager Duchess of Marlborough* (1742), p. 222, for an expression of her friendship for Anne. In 'De l'Amitié', Montaigne describes his friendship with La Boëtie as one in which 'souls are mingled and confounded in so universal a blending that they efface the seam which joins them together so that it cannot be found' (Michel de Montaigne, *The Complete Essays*, tr. M. Screech (Harmondsworth: Penguin Books, 1991), pp. 211–12).

No. 14. Saturday, 5 May 1750.

1. *HOR*: Horace, *Satires*, I. iii. 18–19.
2. *procured him*: John Milton to Emeric Bigot, 24 March 1656/57 (*The Works of John Milton*, vol. 12 (New York: Columbia University Press, 1936), p. 84).
3. *in their work*: Diodorus Siculus, *Bibliotheca Historica*, II. 24. 4.
4. *attainable*: Francis Bacon, *Historia Naturalis*, in *Works*, ed. Spedding, Ellis and Heath (1857), ii. 38.
5. *disgrace*: 'From the first time that the Impressions of Religion setled deeply in his Mind, He used great caution to conceal it: ... for he said he was afraid, he should at some time or other, do some enormous thing, which if he were look't on as a very Religious Man, might cast a reproach on the profession of it, and give great advantages to impious Men, to blaspheme the name of God ...' (Gilbert Burnet, *Life and Death of Sir Matthew Hale, Kt.* (1682), pp. 141–2).

No. 16. Saturday, 12 May 1750.

1. *JUV*: Juvenal, X. 9–10.
2. *a late paper*: *Rambler* No. 10.
3. *Ditis*: Virgil, *Æneid*, vi. 126–7. A favourite quotation of Johnson's: cf. *Rambler* No. 155 and *Adventurer* No. 34.
4. *profit of their works*: Pope and Swift, *Miscellanies* (1727), 'Preface'.

No. 17. Tuesday, 15 May 1750.

1. *LUCAN*: Lucan, *Pharsalia*, ix. 582–3.
2. *ROWE*: N. Rowe, *Lucan's Pharsalia* (1718), ix. 1000–1003, p. 385; capitalization altered.
3. *thou shalt die*: A commonplace, but see e.g. Herodotus, ii. 78.
4. *end of life*: *Greek Anthology*, ix. 366.
5. τινός: Epictetus, *Enchiridion*, c. 21; cf. also *Rambler* No. 2, note 6.
6. *trunci*: Lucan, *Pharsalia*, ix. 14.
7. *life is short*: Hippocrates, *Aphorisms*, I. i.

No. 18. Saturday, 19 May 1750.

1. *HOR*: Horace, *Odes*, III. xxiv. 17–23.
2. *on the other*: An allusion to the celebrated sentiment 'Victrix causa deis placuit, sed victa Catoni', 'the victorious side enjoyed the favour of the gods, but the defeated enjoyed that of Cato'; Lucan, *Pharsalia*, i. 128.

No. 22. Saturday, 2 June 1750.

1. *HOR*: Horace, *Ars Poetica*, ll. 409–11.
2. *merriment*: 'And unquenchable laughter arose among the blessed gods, as they saw Hephaestus puffing through the palace'; Homer, *Iliad*, i. 599–600.

No. 23. Tuesday, 5 June 1750.

1. *HOR*: Horace, *Epistles*, II. ii. 61–2.
2. *younger Pliny*: 'Praeterea suae quisque inventioni favet, et quasi fortissimum amplectitur, cum ab alio dictum est quod ipse praevidit'; 'Moreover, everyone favours his own powers of invention, and will be most persuaded by what matches his own conclusion'; Pliny, *Epistles*, i. 20. 13.
3. *physiognomy*: See *Spectator* No. 1, 1 March 1711.

No. 24. Saturday, 9 June 1750.

1. *PERSIUS*: Persius, *Satires*, iv. 23.
2. *Lacedemon*: 'Know thyself' (*Greek Anthology*, ix. 366); cf. Johnson's poem of the same title (*Samuel Johnson: The Complete English Poems*, ed. J. D. Fleeman (Harmondsworth: Penguin Books, 1971), p. 146) which Johnson had composed on 12 December 1772, after revising and enlarging the *Dictionary*, and also the epigraph to Bonnell Thornton's imitation of *The Rambler* in Appendix III.
3. *deep researches*: Mrs Thrale states that the character of Gelidus was based on that of John Colson, the Lucasian Professor of Mathematics at Cambridge.
4. *dramatick reputation*: See Johnson, *Lives of the English Poets*, ed. G. B. Hill, 3 vols. (Oxford: The Clarendon Press, 1905), ii. 61–2 (Garth) and ii. 226 (Congreve). Congreve's alleged negligence of his achievements as a dramatist stems from Voltaire's account of his meeting with the aged playwright, then 'almost at death's door': 'he had one failing, which was that he did not rank high enough his first profession, that of a writer, which had made his reputation and his fortune. He spoke of his works as trifles beneath him, and in our first conversation he told me to think of him as a gentleman who lived very simply. I answered him that if he had had the misfortune of being just a gentleman like any other I would never have come to see him, and I was very shocked at such misplaced vanity' (Voltaire, *Letters on England*, tr. L. Tancock (Harmondsworth: Penguin Books, 1980), pp. 99–100). For sensitive and informed commentary relating to the issues raised by this celebrated anecdote, see two recent articles by

D. F. McKenzie: '*Mea Culpa*: Voltaire's Retraction of his Comments Critical of Congreve', *Review of English Studies* (*RES*), 49 (1998), pp. 461–65 and 'Richard van Bleeck's Painting of William Congreve as Contemplative' (1715), *RES*, 51 (2000), pp. 41–61.

No. 25. Tuesday, 12 June 1750.

1. *VIRGIL*: Virgil, *Æneid*, v. 231. Dryden had also used this well-known tag in a footnote to the second edition of his *Conquest of Granada*, Part I (1670), II. iii.

2. *right path*: 'Virtus est medium vitiorum et utrimque reductum', 'virtue is found between vices, and shuns extremes' (Horace, *Epistles*, I. xviii. 9). This is also, of course, an Aristotelian idea of virtue: see Aristotle, *Nicomachean Ethics*, II. 6.

3. *Infantes barbati*: The tag is ambiguous, being capable of meaning both 'bearded children' and 'dumb philosophers'.

No. 28. Saturday, 23 June 1750.

1. *SENECA*: Seneca, *Thyestes*, ll. 401–3.

2. *COWLEY*: From Abraham Cowley's 'Of Solitude'.

3. *late essay*: *Rambler* No. 24.

4. *sincerity*: Cf. Bacon, who in his essay 'Of Friendship' admires 'the wisest and most politic [princes] that ever reigned' for their practice of joining 'to themselves some of their servants, whom both themselves have called *friends*, and allowed others likewise to call them in the same manner, using the word which is received between private men' (Francis Bacon, *The Essays*, ed. John Pitcher (Harmondsworth: Penguin Books, 1985), p. 139).

5. *his death*: Alfonso de Valdés (1490–1532), Latin secretary to Charles V. Johnson probably learnt of the anecdote from Izaak Walton's life of Herbert, where the resolution is more pithily expressed as '*there ought to be a vacancy of time, betwixt fighting and dying*' (Izaak Walton, *Lives*, ed. G. Saintsbury (Oxford: Oxford University Press, 1927), pp. 312–13).

6. *ourselves*: William Chillingworth, sermon IV, sects. 12 and 15, in *Nine Sermons* (1664), pp. 52–3.

7. *and be still*: Psalm 4:4.

8. *to himself*: Johnson refers to the Senecan epigraph of this paper.

9. *Pontanus*: Giovanni Pontano (1426–1503), Italian humanist, statesman and man of letters. The quotation (which Johnson slightly misquotes) is to be found in Sir Thomas Pope Blount's *Censura Celebriorum Authorum* (1690), p. 354.

No. 29. Tuesday, 26 June 1750.

1. *HOR*: Horace, *Odes*, III. xxix. 29–32.
2. *dismission*: Act of dispersal or dismissal.
3. *never surprised*: A reference to the Horatian maxim 'nil admirari' (Horace, *Epistles*, I. vi. 1).
4. *old Cornaro*: Luigi Cornaro (*c.* 1467–1566); see his *La Vita Sobria* (1558), p. 25.
5. *send strength*: 'Be satisfied with thus much, that your present strength is sufficient for any present trial; and when a greater comes, God hath promised to give you more strength when you shall have need of more' (Jeremy Taylor, *The Worthy Communicant* (1660), ch. 2, sect. 3, p. 153).

No. 31. Tuesday, 3 July 1750.

1. *OVID*: Ovid, *Amores*, II. iv. 1–2.
2. *one of the philosophers*: Lochagus the Spartan, as reported in Plutarch, *Moralia*, 225F. Compare also *Rambler* No. 32 below, and the portrait of the affected Stoic in *Rasselas*, ch. 18 (*Rasselas and Other Tales*, ed. Gwin J. Kolb (New Haven and London: Yale University Press, 1990), pp. 74–6).
3. *were confuted*: This was said of Julius Libri, who rejected Galileo's theories out of hand.
4. *persue*: From John Dryden, *The Indian Emperor* (1665), IV. iii. 3.
5. *fugitque*: This is not in fact in Virgil, but in Ovid, *Metamorphoses*, iv. 461.
6. *to find it*: Johnson is here misquoting from memory. In the 'Preface' to *Tyrannick Love* (1670), Dryden in fact says: '*Some foole . . . had charg'd me in the* Indian Emperour *with nonsence in these words*, And follow fate which does too fast pursue; *which was borrow'd from* Virgil *in the XIth of his* Æneids, Eludit gyro inferior, sequiturque sequentem. *I quote not these to prove that I never writ Nonsence, but onely to show that they are so unfortunate as not to have found it*' (*The Works of John Dryden*, vol. X, ed. M. Novak (Los Angeles: University of California Press, 1970), p. 113).
7. *character*: Celsus, *De Medicina*, VIII. iv. 4.

No. 32. Saturday, 7 July 1750.

1. *PYTHAG*: Pythagoras, *Aurea Carmina*, ii. 17–19.
2. *Zeno*: Zeno of Citium (*c.* 335–*c.* 263 BC), founder of the school of Stoic philosophy, which taught a doctrine of detachment from the outside world.

3. *an evil*: It was said in fact of Dionysius, who suffered from ophthalmia, not gout; cf. Diogenes Laertius, *Lives*, vii. 37. c. 1.

4. *ferendum est*: Ovid, *Heroides*, v. 7.

5. *repair it*: Henri de la Tour d'Auvergne (1611–75), vicomte de Turenne and a French military commander during the reign of Louis XIV. The advice was given by the duc de Weymar, the guiding principles of whose conduct Turenne recalled in these words: 'ce Général ... ne s'enorgueillissoit point de ses succès; que, lorsqu'il avoit du malheur, il ne songeoit pas tant à se plaindre, qu'à s'en relever; qu'il aimoit mieux se laisser blâmer injustement, que de s'excuser aux dépens de ses amis qui avoient manqué dans l'action; qu'il étoit plus occupé à réparer ses fautes, qu'à perdre son tems en apologies ...; 'this general ... did not allow himself to be puffed up with pride on account of his successes; when he suffered a setback, he did not dream of complaining, but rather set about remedying the situation; he would rather bear unjust criticism, than exculpate himself at the expense of friends whose conduct had fallen short; and he was busier in remedying his defects, than in wasting his time in apologies; ...' (Andrew Ramsay, *Histoire du Vicomte de Turenne* (La Haye, 1736), i, pp. 108–9).

6. *takes away*: Job 1:21.

No. 33. Tuesday, 10 July 1750.

1. *OVID*: Ovid, *Heroides*, iv. 89.

No. 36. Saturday, 21 July 1750.

1. *HOMER*: Homer, *Iliad*, xviii. 525–6.

2. *Maker*: Milton, *Paradise Lost*, v. 153–208.

3. *without number*: Milton, *Paradise Lost*, iii. 346.

4. *Sannazarius*: Jacopo Sannazzaro (1458–1530), Neapolitan poet and celebrant of rustic life, author of a series of verse eclogues published in 1504 as *Arcadia*, and of piscatory eclogues.

5. *metrical geography of Dionysius*: The *Periegesis* of Dionysius.

No. 37. Tuesday, 24 July 1750.

1. *VIRG*: Virgil, *Eclogues*, ii. 23–4.

2. *Theocritus*: Theocritus (*fl. c.* 270 BC), Doric poet, considered to be the father of pastoral.

3. *apprehension*: Anaximander of Miletus (*fl.* early sixth century BC), scientist, philosopher, constructor of the sun dial, and alleged to have compiled a map of the world. He was said to be the first writer of Greek prose; cf. *Eclogues*, iii. 40–1. Pope, *Pastorals*, 'Spring', l. 38 and

note, where Pope claims that 'the Shepherd's hesitation at the name of
the Zodiac, imitates that in Virgil'.

4. *wretched wight*: Edmund Spenser, *Shepheardes Calendar*, 'September', ll. 1–4.

5. *edunt*: Virgil, *Eclogues*, viii. 43–5.

6. *born!*: Pope, 'Autumn', ll. 89–92.

7. *Pollio*: Gaius Asinius Pollio (76 BC – AD 5), an associate of Catullus,
Julius Caesar and Mark Antony and consul in 40 BC. Pollio was the
first to recognize the genius of Virgil, and gave practical assistance to
the poet when his farm near Mantua was seized as war booty after
Philippi. Virgil celebrates Pollio in the eighth and fourth eclogues;
Johnson here refers to the fourth. Because this poem is a vision of a
golden age inaugurated by the birth of a child, it was for many years
given a Christian interpretation, although it is more likely that Virgil
refers to the son of Pollio himself, who was born in the year of his
father's consulship.

8. *Silenus*: Silenus was a satyr, sometimes said to be the son of Pan,
and a companion of Dionysus; he was frequently depicted as elderly
and drunken, and there are often said to be many Sileni, not just one
Silenus. Johnson refers to the tenth eclogue of Virgil.

9. *Gallus*: Gaius Cornelius Gallus (69–26 BC), poet and soldier, first
prefect of Egypt under Augustus. He eventually committed suicide,
having fallen from favour; he was praised by Virgil in the sixth and
tenth eclogues, see especially *Eclogues*, x. 2–3 and 72–3.

10. *harvests*: 'Frugibus alternis, non consule computat annum: /
autumnum pomis, ver sibi flore notat'; 'For him the returning seasons,
not the consuls, mark the year: he knows autumn by her fruits, spring
by her flowers' (Claudian, 'Felix, qui propriis aevum transegit in arvis').

No. 39. Tuesday, 31 July 1750.

1. *AUSONIUS*: Untraced.

No. 41. Tuesday, 7 August 1750.

1. *MART*: Martial, X. xxiii. 5–8.

2. *pedant's pride*: Matthew Prior, *Solomon on the Vanity of the World*,
i. 236.

3. *rasure*: Erasure.

4. *treasure of the past*: Apparently a misremembering of Dryden's
Hind and the Panther, i. 258.

5. *vexit*: Horace, *Odes*, III. xxix. 45–8.

6. *longam*: Horace, *Odes*, I. iv. 15.

7. *canis*: Persius, *Satires*, v. 64–5.

No. 45. Tuesday, 21 August 1750.

1. *EURIP*: Euripides, *Medea*, ll. 14–16.
2. *dissertations*: Earlier *Rambler*s on the subject of marriage are Nos 18, 35 and 39.
3. *crouds*: Horace, *Satires*, I. i. 4–12.

No. 47. Tuesday, 28 August 1750.

1. *PLIN*: Pliny, *Epistles*, viii. 16. The translation is by Johnson's friend John Boyle, Earl of Orrery (1707–62), who in 1751 had published his *Letters of Pliny the Younger*; this text (of which the punctuation has been slightly changed) may be found at ii. 231.
2. *devotion*: Plutarch, *Lives*, 'Pyrrhus', xiv.
3. *vulnerary herbs*: Herbs said to possess the power to heal wounds, typically, arnica. See Virgil, *Aeneid*, xii. 411 ff. and Claudius Aelianus, *Varia Historia*, i. 10: 'The *Cretans* are excellent Archers; they shoot the Goats which feed on the tops of mountains, which being hurt, immediately eat of the herb Dittany, which as soon as they have tasted, the Arrow drops out' (*Claudius Aelianus his Various History*, tr. Thomas Stanley (1666), p. 5).
4. *GROTIUS*: Hugo Grotius (1583–1645), Dutch statesman and jurist. The quotation comes from his 'Consolatoria ad Patrem', in *Poemata Collecta* (1617), p. 457, where, however, the text runs: 'Non cedit Natura morae, si tempore reddi / Pax animo tranquilla potest, tu sperne morari. / Qui sapiet, sibi tempus erit . . .' It would seem that Johnson was quoting from memory.

No. 49. Tuesday, 4 September 1750.

1. *HOR*: Horace, *Odes*, III. xxx. 6–8.
2. *capital of the world*: Plutarch, *Lives*, 'Caesar', xi. 2.
3. *adscititious*: Additional or supplemental.
4. *tomb*: Anacreontica, iv.
5. *same cause*: Plutarch, *Lives*, 'Themistocles', iii. 3–4.
6. *country*: Plutarch, *Lives*, 'Caesar', xi. 3; cf. also Dio Cassius, XXXVII. lii. 2 and Suetonius, 'Divo Iulio', vii. 1.
7. 'Ρόδιος: Greek Anthology, viii. 348.

No. 60. Saturday, 13 October 1750.

1. *HOR*: Horace, *Epistles*, I. ii. 3–4.
2. *Pliny*: Pliny, *Epistles*, III. i.
3. *miraturi*: Jacques-Auguste de Thou (1533–1617), French statesman and historian. The quotation comes from 'Viri Illustris Jac. Aug.

Thuani ... Commentariorum de Vita Sua Libri Sex', in *Historiarum Sui Temporis* (1733), VII, pt. iv, p. 3 n. Johnson slightly misquotes: in the original, the final word is 'cognituri', which trims the boastfulness of the sentiment.

4. *again slow*: 'Citus modo modo tardus incessus'; Sallust, *De Coniuratione Catilinae*, xv. 5.

5. *idleness of suspense*: Joachim Camerarius, *Vita Melancthonis* (1777), ch. xvii, p. 62, where the text is: 'Usque adeo vero indiserta, confusa, vaga, indefinita, inexplicataque auersabatur, ut, quoties cum aliquibus de tempore esset constituendum, semper momentum horae iuberet nominari.'

6. *negligent of his life*: Sir William Temple, 'Essay on the Cure of the Gout by Moxa', in *Works* (1757), iii. 244.

7. *pulse*: 'Preface' to the *Works* of Joseph Addison (1721), i, p. xvi.

8. *sense of both*: Honorat de Beuil, 'Mémoires pour la vie de Malherbe'.

9. *due to the country*: I have not been able to find this text in Burnet's life of Hale: but it is perhaps a recollection of the tenth item in Hale's list of 'Things Necessary to be Continually had in Remembrance': 'X. *That I be not biassed with Compassion to the Poor, or favour to the Rich, in point of Justice*' (Gilbert Burnet, *Life and Death of Sir Matthew Hale, Kt.* (1682), p. 59).

No. 63. Tuesday, 23 October 1750.

1. *HOR*: Horace, *Satires*, I. iii. 11–15.

2. *deliberation*: Horace, *Satires*, I. i. 1–3.

3. *Hermetick philosophy*: So-called after Hermes Trismegistus, an aspect of the Egyptian god Thoth and author of all mystical doctrines, including that of alchemy, to which Johnson here refers.

No. 64. Saturday, 27 October 1750.

1. *SALUST*: Sallust, *De Coniuratione Catilinae*, xx. 4.

2. *real friends*: Phaedrus, *Fabulae Aesopiae*, iii. 9.

3. *Horace*: 'Audebit, quaecumque parum splendoris habebunt / et sine pondere erunt et honore indigna ferentur, / verba movere loco, quamvis invita rededant'; 'he will dare to revise, no matter how reluctantly, if his words are dull, or slight, or low' (Horace, *Epistles*, II. ii. 111–13).

No. 70. Saturday, 17 November 1750.

1. *OVID*: Ovid, *Metamorphoses*, i. 114–15.

2. *use or value*: Hesiod, *Works and Days*, ll. 293–7.

3. *torrent of custom*: Cf. 'Must helpless Man, in Ignorance sedate, /

Roll darkling down the Torrent of his Fate?' (Samuel Johnson, *The Vanity of Human Wishes*, ll. 345–6.

No. 71. Tuesday, 20 November 1750.

1. *MART*: Martial, II. xc. 3–4.
2. *do not understand them*: An obscure reference, but cf. Aristotle, *De Anima*, II. i. 412 b, 5–6.
3. *dilator, spe longus*: Horace, *Ars Poetica*, l. 172.
4. ἀλλὰ βάτον: *Greek Anthology*, xi. 53. The translation is Johnson's own: cf. *Samuel Johnson: The Complete English Poems*, ed. J. D. Fleeman (Harmondsworth: Penguin Books, 1971), p. 98.
5. *Baxter*: Richard Baxter (1615–91), Puritan divine, imprisoned 1685–6. Edmund Calamy, *Abridgement of Mr. Baxter's . . . Life and Times* (1702), pp. 596–7.
6. *Hearne*: Thomas Hearne (1678–1735), antiquary and non-juror. The *Reliquiae Hearnianae*, the most likely source for a judgement such as this, were only published from Hearne's notebooks by Philip Bliss in 1857, and so could not have been known to Johnson. I have not been able to trace this remark in those works of Hearne's which Johnson could have read. It may depend on oral tradition.
7. *value of life*: Actuarial science advanced significantly during the eighteenth century, particularly at the hands of Richard Price (1723–91), although his most influential writings on this subject were published after *The Rambler*.
8. *into the grave*: An egregious example of such miscalculation was Edward Gibbon, who relied on actuarial tables to claim for himself 'about fifteen years' remaining to live, less than three years before he actually died of peritonitis (*The Autobiographies of Edward Gibbon*, ed. J. Murray (London: John Murray, 1896), p. 347).

No. 72. Saturday, 24 November 1750.

1. *HOR*: Horace, *Epistles*, I. xvii. 23–4.
2. *balm of being*: Cf. Milton, *Paradise Lost*, xi. 546.
3. *better man*: William Shakespeare, *1 Henry IV*, V. iv. 103.

No. 73. Tuesday, 27 November 1750.

1. *OVID*: Ovid, *Tristia*, III. viii. 11–12.
2. *Tudors and Plantagenets*: Both royal dynasties which had occupied the throne of England.
3. *escutcheons and white gloves*: Both tokens of aristocracy.

No. 76. Saturday, 8 December 1750.

1. *HOR*: Horace, *Satires*, II. iii. 48–51.
2. *lenitive*: A palliative, or soothing, medicine.

No. 77. Tuesday, 11 December 1750.

1. *PRUDENT*: Prudentius, *Contra Symmachi Orationem*, i. 635–7.
2. *albus an ater*: Literally, white or black.
3. *for his country*: 'Catilina long a suis inter hostium cadavera repertus est, pulcherrima morte, si pro patria sic concidisset'; 'Catiline was discovered far from his comrades amidst the corpses of his enemies – a fine death, if he had fallen for his homeland' (Florus, *Epitomae Bellorum*, II. xii. 12).
4. *much shall be required*: Luke 12:48.

No. 79. Tuesday, 18 December 1750.

1. *MART*: Martial, xii. 51.
2. *himself to be perjured*: Antiphanes, fragment 241.
3. *would live*: Juvenal, viii. 84.
4. *Camerarius*: Joachim Camerarius (1500–74), German classical scholar and theologian, who sought to reconcile Catholics and Protestants. The anecdote, however, is not to be found in his works.

No. 85. Tuesday, 8 January 1751.

1. *OVID*: Ovid, *Remedia Amoris*, ll. 139–40.
2. *mural or civick garlands*: Mural honours were awarded in the Roman army to the first soldier to scale the walls of a besieged town; by extension, any military or civic honours.
3. *Coronæ*: Horace, *Ars Poetica*, ll. 379–81.
4. *System of Education*: John Locke, *Some Thoughts Concerning Education* (1693), §§ 201–6.
5. *Nero*: Nero, who was Roman emperor AD 54–68, was infamous for his affectation of artistic talent, and for singing while watching Rome burn.
6. *loom and the distaff*: Ovid, *Ars Amatoria*, i. 359–60; Homer, *Iliad*, vi. 490–91.
7. *peripatetick*: The peripatetic school of philosophy was founded by Aristotle, and was so called because of his habit of teaching his students while walking through the Lyceum; hence, Aristotelian.

No. 87. Tuesday, 15 January 1751.

1. *HOR*: Horace, *Epistles*, I. i. 38–40.
2. *catharticks of the soul*: Cf. Joseph Addison, *Spectator* No. 507 (11 October 1712): 'The Platonists have so just a Notion of the Almighty's Aversion to every thing which is false and erroneous, that they looked upon *Truth* as no less necessary than *Virtue*, to qualifie an Human Soul for the Enjoyment of a separate State. For this Reason, as they recommended Moral Duties to qualifie and season the Will for a future Life, so they prescribed several Contemplations and Sciences to rectifie the Understanding. Thus *Plato* has called Mathematical Demonstrations the Catharticks or Purgatives of the Soul, as being the most proper Means to cleanse it from Error, and to give it a Relish of Truth, which is the natural Food and Nourishment of the Understanding, as Virtue is the Perfection and Happiness of the Will.'
3. *per ora*: Virgil, *Georgics*, iii. 8–9.
4. *dead counsellors are safest*: The saying is reported in Melchior de Santa Cruz de Dueñas, *Floresta Española* (1578), i. 25, sig. C5ᵛ: 'Dezia el rey den Alonso de Aragon, que ningũo auia de to mar cõsejo cõ los viuos, sino cõ los muertos. Entendiendo por los libros, porque siu amore ni temor siempre dizen la verdad.' ('King Alonso of Aragon used to say that nobody should take advice from the living, but from the dead. By which he meant from books, because free from love or fear they always speak the truth.') I am grateful to my colleague Dr Jonathan Thacker of Merton College, Oxford, for assistance with this translation.
5. *fill up his hour*: Untraced.
6. *Tully*: I.e. Cicero.

No. 90. Saturday, 26 January 1751.

1. *VIRG*: Virgil, *Georgics*, iv. 6.
2. *membra poetæ*: Horace, *Satires*, I. iv. 62; 'you may find the limbs of a poet, albeit a dismembered one'.
3. *free to all*: Milton, *Paradise Lost*, iv. 744 and 746–7.
4. *Leucothea wak'd*: *Paradise Lost*, xi. 130 and 131–5.
5. *His trumpet*: *Paradise Lost*, xi. 72–4.
6. *sweet influence*: *Paradise Lost*, vii. 370–5.
7. *thee implores*: *Paradise Lost*, vii. 33–8.
8. *Torments him*: *Paradise Lost*, i. 51–6.
9. *train ascending*: *Paradise Lost*, vii. 569 and 571–4.
10. *With blessedness*: *Paradise Lost*, vii. 56–9.
11. *to wild*: *Paradise Lost*, ix. 209–12.

12. *Assist us*: Paradise Lost, ix. 244–7.
13. *him passing*: Paradise Lost, x. 710–14.
14. *chaos to retire*: Paradise Lost, ii. 1034–8.
15. *celestial song*: Paradise Lost, vii. 8–12.
16. *not to inquire*: Paradise Lost, iii. 567–71.
17. *general doom*: Paradise Lost, xi. 73–6.

No. 93. Tuesday, 5 February 1751.

1. *JUV*: Juvenal, i. 170–1.
2. *Baillet*: Adrien Baillet (1649–1706), French cleric, scholar and man of letters. For Baillet's indeed lengthy catalogue of the 'préjugés' which can impede the reception of criticism, see his *Jugemens des Scavans* (Amsterdam, 1725), I, i. 118–572.
3. *reach of human abilities*: Johnson may here be confusing some lines from the 'Epilogue' to Congreve's *The Way of the World* ('And sure he must have more than mortal skill / Who pleases anyone against his will') with Dryden's comment in the 'Preface' to *Absalom and Achitophel*, that 'no man can be heartily angry with him, who pleases him against his will'.
4. *Euclid or Archimedes*: Euclid (*fl. c.* 300 BC), pre-eminent Greek mathematician and geometrician. Archimedes (*c.* 287–212 BC) was the most complete scientific genius of antiquity, who made enduring advances in the fields of mathematics, mechanics, physics and astronomy.
5. *Sæpe et nulla*: Seneca, *Apocolocyntosis*, xii. 21–2.
6. *Langbaine, Borrichitus or Rapin*: Gerard Langbaine (1656–92), dramatic critic and author of *An Account of the English Dramatic Poets* (Oxford, 1691) and *Momus Triumphans: or, the Plagiaries of the English Stage* (1688), in which prodigious reading is displayed. Olaus Borch, or Borrichius (not Borrichitus) (1626–90), Danish philologist and scientist, librarian of the University of Copenhagen. René Rapin (1621–87), French poet, critic and theologian, influential in imparting a neo-classical and Aristotelian quality to literary criticism in France and elsewhere during the later seventeenth century.
7. *in a good cause*: Cf. *Spectator* No. 40 (16 April 1711).
8. *Scaliger*: Joseph Justus Scaliger (1540–1609) was the greatest literary scholar of the Renaissance. Like his father, Julius Caesar Scaliger (see above p. 542, note 3 to No. 4), he hailed from Lake Garda, and claimed descent from the noble Italian Della Scala family.
9. *cannot be wounded*: Cf. Virgil, *Æneid*, vi. 290–94.
10. *beauties rather than faults*: Cf. *Spectator* No. 291 (2 February 1712).

No. 101. Tuesday, 5 March 1751.

1. *MART*: Martial, XI. xlii. 3–4.

No. 106. Saturday, 23 March 1751.

1. *CIC*: Cicero, *De Natura Deorum*, II. ii. 5.
2. *more conspicuous than pyramids*: Horace, *Odes*, III. xxx. 1–2.
3. *Starent superbi* —.: Seneca, *Troades*, ll. 4–6.
4. *Granvilles, Montagues, Stepneys, and Sheffields*: All minor poets of the later seventeenth and early eighteenth centuries. George Granville, Lord Lansdowne (1667–1735), was a statesman, poet and dramatist, a suspected Jacobite, and an early patron of Pope. Charles Montagu, first earl of Halifax (1661–1715), was one of the signatories of the letter of invitation to William of Orange and the prime architect, with John Somers, of William III's financial policy in the 1690s. He was also founder of the Bank of England. George Stepney (1663–1707) was a poet, Whig diplomat, and an associate of Halifax and Marlborough. John Sheffield, third earl of Mulgrave and later first duke of Buckingham and Normanby (1648–1721), was a patron of Dryden and friend of Pope.
5. *Parnassus*: A mountain north of Delphi in Greece, associated with the worship of Apollo and the muses; poetically, the home of the muses.
6. *qualities of the air*: Robert Boyle (1627–91) was an experimental scientist and man of letters. Assisted by Robert Hooke he performed the experiments on the qualities of air which led to the formulation of Boyle's Law.
7. *long as books last*: Sir Francis Bacon (1561–1626), lawyer, statesman, philosopher and essayist. The quotation is taken from the 'Dedication' to the *Essays*, although there Bacon's confidence in the *Essays*' longevity seems to be based more on the fact of their existing in a Latin version ('being in the universal language') than on the perennial human centrality of their subject matter.

No. 108. Saturday, 30 March 1751.

1. *HOR*: Horace, *Epistles*, I. ii. 40–43.
2. *COWLEY*: Abraham Cowley (1618–67), poet.
3. *accommodation of man*: Lucretius, *De Rerum Natura*, v. 200–9.
4. *Erasmus*: Desiderius Erasmus (1466–1536), humanist, scholar and man of letters.
5. *without regard to literature*: Erasmus, μωρίας ενκομιον [*The Praise of Folly*] (Basel, 1515), sig. ai^v.

6. *time was his estate*: This was said of Girolamo Cardano (1501–76), Italian philosopher, doctor and mathematician.

No. 113. Tuesday, 16 April 1751.

1. *JUVENAL*: Juvenal, vi. 28–9.
2. *Horace*: 'Hic murus aeneus esto, / nil conscire sibi, nulla pallescere culpa' (Horace, *Epistles*, I. i. 60–61); 'may this be to us as a wall of bronze – to have no uneasy conscience, no sense of guilt to make us blanch'.
3. *another letter*: Rambler No. 115.

No. 114. Saturday, 20 April 1751.

1. *JUV*: Juvenal, vi. 220–21.
2. *in his hands*: Juvenal, x. 96–7.
3. *Boerhaave*: Herman Boerhaave (1668–1738), Dutch physician and professor of medicine. Cf. Johnson's 'Life of Boerhaave', *Gentleman's Magazine*, ix (1739), 37–8, 72–3, 114–16 and 172–6.
4. *φοβερώτατον*: Aristotle, *Nicomachean Ethics*, III. vi. 2.
5. *Sir Thomas More*: Sir Thomas More (1478–1535), lawyer, statesman and humanist; Lord Chancellor 1529–32; friend of Erasmus. Johnson alludes to a passage in Book One of *Utopia* (1516), in which a character, Raphael Hythlodaeus (and thus not More himself), advocates a policy of controlling crime, not by the threat of ever more savage punishments, but by mitigating the poverty which leads people to commit crimes.

No. 115. Tuesday, 23 April 1751.

1. *JUV*: Juvenal, vi. 184.
2. *rather than a woman*: Reported in Lactantius, *Divinae Institutiones*, iii. 19.
3. *higher species of monkies*: Letter to a Young Lady on Her Marriage (1723), in *The Prose Works of Jonathan Swift*, ed. H. Davis *et al.* (Oxford: Basil Blackwell, 1939–68), ix. 83–94.

No. 121. Tuesday, 14 May 1751.

1. *HOR*: Horace, *Epistles*, I. xix. 19.
2. *great Mantuan poet*: I.e. Virgil.
3. *infernal regions*: Homer, *Odyssey*, book xi.
4. *to the shades*: Virgil, *Æneid*, book vi.
5. *directions to a painter*: A reference to the seventeenth-century vogue – initiated by Edmund Waller's panegyrical 'Instructions to a Painter' and sustained in Andrew Marvell's satirical 'Last Instructions

to a Painter' – of composing poems in the form of guidance to a painter.

6. *written no language*: A reference to the comment in Ben Jonson's *Timber, or Discoveries* (1640), that '*Spencer*, in affecting the Ancients, writ no Language: Yet I would have him read for his matter; but as *Virgil* read *Ennius*' (*Ben Jonson*, ed. C. H. Herford and P. and E. Simpson, volume viii, 'The Poems. The Prose Works' (Oxford: The Clarendon Press, 1947), p. 618).

7. *so much diversity*: For an amusing late eighteenth-century attempt to provide English with the same harmonious endings enjoyed by Italian, see the scheme of John Pinkerton as described by Hugh Trevor-Roper in his 'Gibbon's Last Project', in David Womersley (ed.), *Edward Gibbon: Bicentenary Lectures* (Oxford: The Voltaire Foundation, 1997), p. 407.

8. *observed by Milton*: A reference to the 'Preface' to *Paradise Lost* and Milton's notorious justification of his own choice of 'English heroic verse without rhyme' for that poem by reference to what he calls 'the troublesome and modern bondage of rhyming'.

9. *imitators of Spenser*: A reference to eighteenth-century imitations of Edmund Spenser, of which perhaps the best-known is James Thomson's *The Castle of Indolence* (1748).

10. *in the play*: Shakespeare, *Troilus and Cressida*, II. ii. 166.

No. 129. Tuesday, 11 June 1751.

1. *OVID*: Ovid, *Ars Amatoria*, ii. 33–8.

2. *frigorifick*: Cooling.

3. *far from necessity*: Pythagoras, *Aurea Carmina*, l. 8.

No. 134. Saturday, 29 June 1751.

1. *HOR*: Horace, *Odes*, IV. vii. 17–18.

2. *Tantalus*: In Greek mythology, Tantalus was the father of Pelops and Niobe. He was punished in Hades by having the water and food he craved always just out of reach.

3. *Palladio*: Andrea Palladio (1508–80), an Italian neo-classical architect of the late Renaissance.

No. 135. Tuesday, 2 July 1751.

1. *HOR*: Horace, *Epistles*, I. xi. 27.

2. *an imitative being*: Aristotle, *Poetics*, ch. 1 (1448^{b} 4).

3. *society of solitude*: Milton, *Paradise Lost*, ix. 249.

4. *Ptolemaick and Copernican system*: Ptolemy, or Claudius Ptolemaeus (*fl.* second century AD), an Alexandrian astronomer, developed a theory of planetary motion which placed the earth in a stationary,

central position. This theory held the field until Copernicus, or Nicolas Koppernik (1473–1543), a Polish astronomer, propounded the rival theory that the planets, including the earth, move in orbits around the sun.

5. *Milton justly observes*: Milton, *Paradise Lost*, ix. 445–51.

6. *Dryads*: In classical mythology, nymphs associated with trees.

No. 137. Tuesday, 9 July 1751.

1. *HOR*: Horace, *Satires*, I. ii. 24.

2. *Divide and conquer*: A proverbial saying, dating in English from the early seventeenth century, translating the Latin tag 'divide et impera'.

3. *as Locke has observed*: John Locke, *Of the Conduct of the Understanding*, § 28.

4. *the use of books*: Johnson slightly misremembers a passage from Francis Bacon's essay 'Of Studies': 'Crafty men contemn studies, simple men admire them, and wise men use them; for they teach not their own use; but that is a wisdom without them and above them, won by observation' (Francis Bacon, *The Essays*, ed. J. Pitcher (Harmondsworth: Penguin Books, 1985), p. 209).

5. *the simile of Longinus*: 'Longinus', *On the Sublime*, ix. 13.

No. 142. Saturday, 27 July 1751.

1. *HOM*: Homer, *Odyssey*, ix. 187–91.

2. *Drake*: Sir Francis Drake (?1540–96), sailor and circumnavigator of the globe.

3. *replevin*: In law, the restoration to a person of goods taken from him, provided that he undertakes to have the matter tried in a court of law, and to return the goods should the judgment go against him.

4. *if he is hated, he is likewise feared*: An allusion to the saying of the Emperor Caligula, who was fond of quoting a line from the tragic poet Accius, 'Oderint, dum metuant' – 'Let them hate me, as long as they also fear me' (Suetonius, 'Gaius (Caligula)', xxx. 2).

No. 145. Tuesday, 6 August 1751.

1. *HOR*: Horace, *Odes*, IV. ix. 5–8. Pindar (*c.* 520–*c.* 440 BC), a major Greek lyric poet; Alcaeus (*fl.* 7–6th century BC), a Greek lyric poet; Stesichorus (*c.* 640–*c.* 555 BC), a Greek lyric poet.

2. *several thousands*: Presumably a reference to the 'Preface' to Jonathan Swift's *Tale of a Tub*, in which he proposes the erection of a 'large Academy . . . capable of containing nine thousand seven hundred forty and three Persons; which by modest Computation is reckoned to be pretty near the current Number of *Wits* in this Island' (Jonathan Swift,

A Tale of a Tub, ed. A. C. Guthkelch and D. Nichol Smith, second edition (Oxford: The Clarendon Press, 1958), p. 41).

3. *hackneyed in the ways of men*: Cf. *1 Henry IV*, III. ii. 40.

4. *Ephemeræ*: Literally, insects which live for only one day; therefore, metaphorically, transient and trifling works.

No. 146. Saturday, 10 August 1751.

1. *MART*: Martial, XI. i. 13–16.

2. *Crab or Childers*: Both the names of race horses of the time.

3. *supplying no children to the commonwealth*: Perhaps a confusion in Johnson's mind between the response of the Roman matrons to the murder of Verginia by Appius (Livy, *Ab Urbe Condita*, iii. 48), and the plot of Aristophanes' *Lysistrata*.

4. *a turtle feast*: A particularly lavish City feast, at which turtle (proverbially a favourite food of aldermen) would be served.

5. *the monument*: The monument to the Great Fire of London; cf. Pope, *Epistle to Bathurst*, ll. 339–40.

No. 148. Saturday, 17 August 1751.

1. *HOR*: Horace, *Odes*, III. xi. 45–8.

2. *from the parent to the magistrate*: Cf. the Pompeian and Cornelian laws *de sicariis* and *de parricidis*.

3. *naturally monarchical*: Aristotle, *Politics*, I. ii. 21.

No. 151. Tuesday, 27 August 1751.

1. *PIND*: Pindar, *Olympia*, vii. 44–8.

2. *WEST*: Gilbert West (1703–56), civil servant and poet.

3. *climactericks*: A critical or fatal period of life, at which the vital forces begin to decline.

No. 156. Saturday, 14 September 1751.

1. *JUV*: Juvenal, xiv. 321.

2. *original constitution*: A glance at the Machiavellian doctrine of the *ricorso*.

3. *vacant to her slaves*: Herodotus, IV. i–iv.

4. *upon the stage*: Horace, *Ars Poetica*, l. 192.

5. *Bacchus*: Another name for Dionysus. In Greek mythology the son of Zeus and Semele; his cult incorporated elements of ecstasy and mysticism, and he was closely associated with tragedy.

No. 158. Saturday, 21 September 1751.

1. *HOR*: Horace, *Ars Poetica*, l. 78.
2. *the Meonian eagle*: I.e. Homer.
3. *Ciceronians of the sixteenth century*: A reference to those, such as
Roger Ascham (1515–68), who modelled their style on that of Cicero
(106–43 BC), the Roman statesman, philosopher and man of letters.
Johnson composed an anonymous 'Life' of Ascham for the 1761
edition of his works.
4. *precept of Horace*: Joseph Addison, *Spectator* No. 303, Saturday,
16 February 1712.
5. *Cyclope Charybdim*: Horace, *Ars Poetica*, ll. 144–5.
6. *καὶ ἡμῖν*: Homer, *Odyssey*, i. 1–10.

No. 159. Tuesday, 24 September 1751.

1. *HOR*: Horace, *Epistles*, I. i. 34–5.
2. *Verecundulus*: The author of the letter in *Rambler* No. 157.
3. *forborn to speak*: Untraced.
4. *powerful fascination*: Socrates prepares Alcibiades for public life in
Alcibiades I; cf. especially 105E and 106C.

No. 161. Tuesday, 1 October 1751.

1. *HOM*: Homer, *Iliad*, vi. 146.
2. *the tomb of Archimedes*: Cicero, *Tusculan Disputations*, V. xxiii.
64.
3. *the Conqueror's survey*: The *Domesday Book*, a register of property
compiled on the order of William the Conqueror.
4. *magna voco*: Ovid, *Amores*, III. xv. 14.
5. *a cousin in Cheapside*: In other words, she was a kept woman.
6. *ναίει*: Hesiod, *Works and Days*, l. 8.
7. *the observation of Juvenal*: Juvenal, xiii. 159–60.

No. 165. Tuesday, 15 October 1751.

1. *ANTIPHILUS*: *Greek Anthology*, ix. 138.

No. 167. Tuesday, 22 October 1751.

1. *MART*: Martial, IV. xiii. 7–10.
2. *concordia discors*: 'Harmony of dissonance', Horace, *Epistles*, I. xii.
19.

No. 168. Saturday, 26 October 1751.

1. *PHÆDRUS*: Phaedrus, *Fabulae Aesopiae*, IV. ii. 5–7.
2. *mein*: Obsolete form of 'mien', meaning 'air', 'bearing' or 'manner'.
3. *to examine things*: Johnson has in mind this passage, from the opening to 'Reflexion IX' of *Reflexions critiques sur quelques passages du rheteur Longin*: 'Il n'y a rien qui avilisse davantage un discours que les mots bas. On souffrira plutost, generalement parlant, une pensée basse exprimée en termes nobles, que la pensée la plus noble exprimée en termes bas. La raison de cela est, que tout le monde ne peut pas juger de la justesse & de la force d'une pensée: mais qu'il n'y a presque personne, sur tout dans les Langues vivantes, qui ne sente la bassesse des mots' (Nicolas Boileaux Despreaux, *Oeuvres de Nicolas Boileaux Despreaux*, 'Nouvelle Edition', première partie (Paris, 1713), p. 550). 'Nothing lowers a discourse so much as base diction. In general, one can more easily tolerate a low thought dressed in noble language, than the most noble thought imaginable expressed in base diction. The reason for this is that not every one can gauge the justness and vigour of a thought, but there is hardly anyone who is not sensitive to the baseness of diction, above all in living languages.')
4. *To cry, hold, hold!*: Shakespeare, *Macbeth*, I. v. 48–52, where the lines are spoken by Lady Macbeth.
5. δόρυ μαίνεται: Homer, *Iliad*, viii. 111.
6. *membra secures*: Lucan, *Pharsalia*, iii. 430–31.
7. *preternatural beauty*: Virgil, *Æneid*, i. 586–93.

No. 170. Saturday, 2 November 1751.

1. *OVID*: Ovid, *Amores*, II. iv. 3.
2. *wip'd them soon*: Milton, *Paradise Lost*, xii. 645.
3. *mercer's*: A dealer in silks or velvets.

No. 171. Tuesday, 5 November 1751.

1. *VIRG*: Virgil, *Aeneid*, iv. 451.
2. *best head*: 'Head' here means 'head-dress', cf. *OED*.
3. *pent-houses*: This was defined by Johnson as 'a shed hanging out aslope from the main wall'.

No. 176. Saturday, 23 November 1751.

1. *HOR*: Horace, *Satires*, I. vi. 5.
2. *boar of Ergmanth .. lion of Nemea*: Two of the six labours of Hercules.
3. *exultations of his antagonist*: Marco Girolamo Vida (1485–1566),

Renaissance Latin poet; and author of *De Arte Poetica* (1527), influential in eighteenth-century England through the editions by Basil Kennett (Oxford, 1701) and Thomas Tristram (Oxford, 1723), as well as the translation by Christopher Pitt (1725; second edition, 1742). *De Arte Poetica*, iii. 469–72.

4. *sinistrous*: Malicious or prejudiced.

No. 181. Tuesday, 10 December 1751.

1. *HOR*: Horace, *Epistles*, I. xviii. 110.

No. 183. Tuesday, 17 December 1751.

1. *LUCAN*: Lucan, *Pharsalia*, i. 92–3.
2. *ships are but boards*: Shakespeare, *The Merchant of Venice*, I. iii. 20.

No. 184. Saturday, 21 December 1751.

1. *JUV*: Juvenal, x. 347–8.

No. 188. Saturday, 4 January 1752.

1. *MART*: Martial, II. lv. 3.
2. *Sardinian Laughter*: Homer, *Odyssey*, xx. 302 (where it is characterized by a mixture of wrath and scorn).
3. *not always necessary to be reverenced*: A reproof of the Machiavellian doctrine, that it is better for a prince to be feared than loved; cf. *The Prince*, ch. xvii.

No. 191. Tuesday, 14 January 1752.

1. *HOR*: Horace, *Ars Poetica*, l. 163.
2. *flambeaus*: Large torches; here by extension the bearers of such torches.
3. *leading-strings*: Strings with which children are guided and supported when learning to walk.

No. 196. Saturday, 1 February 1752.

1. *HOR*: Horace, *Ars Poetica*, ll. 175–6.
2. *disposed him to change*: Richard Baxter (1615–91), puritan divine. The reference is to his *Reliquiae Baxterianae*, ed. M. Sylvester (1696), i. 124–38, where the section begins: 'Because it is Soul-Experiments which those that urge me to this kind of Writing, do expect that I should especially communicate to others, and I have said little of God's dealing with my Soul since the time of my younger Years, I shall only give the Reader so much Satisfaction, as to acquaint him truly what

Change God hath made upon my Mind and Heart since those unriper times, and wherein I now differ in Judgment and Disposition from my self . . .'

No. 207. Tuesday, 10 March 1752.

1. *HOR*: Horace, *Epistles*, I. i. 8–9.
2. *the first and the last*: Attributed to Palladas, *Greek Anthology*, xi. 381.
3. *in procinctu*: To be in readiness.
4. *supervenient*: Occurring subsequent to something else.

No. 208. Saturday, 14 March 1752.

1. *DIOG. LAERT*: *Greek Anthology*, vii. 128.
2. *happens to be known*: Baldassare Castiglione (1478–1529), Italian humanist. *Book of the Courtier*, ii. 11.
3. *irregular combinations*: Here the congruence of *The Rambler* with the *Dictionary* is apparent.
4. ἀμοιβή: Dionysius Periegetes, l. 1186.

THE ADVENTURER

Johnson contributed twenty-nine essays to *The Adventurer*, which ran from 7 November 1752 to 9 March 1754. The publisher was again John Payne, one of the triumvirate who had published *The Rambler*. The text for this edition is based on the 'second' edition of 1754, after which Johnson seems to have made no substantive changes to the wording of the essays.

No. 39. Tuesday, 20 March 1753.

1. *HOM*: Homer, *Odyssey*, v. 491–3.
2. *POPE*: Slightly misquoted. It should read: 'Till *Pallas* pour'd soft slumbers on his eyes; / And golden dreams (the gift of sweet repose) / Lull'd all his cares, and banish'd all his woes' (v. 635–37).
3. *FONTENELLE*: Bernard le Bovier de Fontenelle (1667–1757), French man of letters. Johnson is thinking of the following conversation, from the 'Premier Soir' of the *Entretiens sur la pluralité des mondes*, in which the character of Fontenelle is speaking to 'la Marquise': 'J'ai toûjours senti ce que vous me dites, reprit-elle, j'aime les Etoiles, & je me plaindrois volontiers du Soleil qui nous les efface. Ah! m'écriai-je, je ne puis lui pardonner de me faire perdre de vûë tous ces

Mondes. . . . je me suis mis dans la tête que chaque Etoile pourroit bien être un Monde' (*Entretiens sur la Pluralité des Mondes*, 'Nouvelle Edition' (La Haye, 1733), p. 15). 'I have always felt what you say, she replied, I love the stars, and I would willingly rail at the sun which makes them invisible to us. Ah! I cried, I can never forgive it for denying me the sight of all those worlds . . . I've taken it into my head that each star could indeed be a world.'

4. *the cool, the silent*: Milton, *Paradise Lost*, v. 38–9.

5. *the face of things*: Milton, *Paradise Lost*, v. 43.

6. *RAMAZZINI*: Bernardino Ramazzini (1633–1714), Italian physician.

7. *without Sleep*: Plutarch, *Lives*, 'Alexander', xxii.

8. *CLELIA*: The romance by Madeleine de Scudéry, *Clélie* (1654–61).

9. *cursed with immortality*: A reference to the Struldbrugs, in book three of Swift's *Gulliver's Travels* (1726).

10. *Phæacia*: Cf. the motto for this paper.

11. *BARRETIER*: Perhaps Barezzi (*fl.* early seventeenth century), Italian printer and savant.

12. *slow length along*: Pope, *An Essay on Criticism*, l. 357.

13. *waking nights*: Publius Papinius Statius (*c.* 40–96 AD), Roman epic and miscellaneous poet. *Sylvae*, v. 4.

14. *COWLEY*: Abraham Cowley, *Sex Libri Plantarum*, iv. 49–60.

15. *C. B.*: It is not known whose initials these were.

16. *without my prayers*: Sir Thomas Browne (1605–82), doctor and prose writer, author of *Religio Medici* (1643). *Religio Medici*, ii. 12.

No. 45. Tuesday, 10 April 1753.

1. *LUCAN*: Lucan, *Pharsalia*, i. 92–3.

2. *ungula campum*: Statius, *Thebaid*, vi. 400–401.

3. *POPE*: Pope, *Windsor Forest*, ll. 153–4.

4. *could not stand before them*: Johnson here is misremembering the comment Swift made in a letter to Pope of 20 September 1723: 'I have often endeavoured to establish a friendship among all men of genius, and would fain have it done. They are seldom above three or four contemporaries, and if they could be united, would drive the world before them' (*The Correspondence of Jonathan Swift*, ed. F. Elrington Ball, 6 vols. (London: Bell and Sons, 1910–14), iii, p. 175).

No. 50. Saturday, 28 April 1753.

1. *PHÆD*: Phaedrus, *Fabulae Aesopiae*, I. x. 1–2.
2. *tell the truth*: Diogenes Laertius, *Lives*, 'Aristotle', xi.
3. *subsist without it*: For Browne, see *Adventurer* No. 39, note 16. *Pseudodoxia Epidemica*, I. xi. 16.
4. *they have not seen*: Sir Kenelm Digby (1603–65), author, sailor and diplomat. Quotation untraced.

No. 67. Tuesday, 26 June 1753.

1. *VIRG*: Virgil, *Æneid*, vi. 663.
2. *that I do not want*: Diogenes Laertius, *Lives*, 'Socrates', ix.

No. 69. Tuesday, 3 July 1753.

1. *CÆSAR*: Caesar, *Gallic War*, iii. 18.
2. *for another year*: I.e. Cicero, *De Senectute*, vii. 24.
3. *floats lazily down the stream*: Cf. ll. 345–6 of Johnson's *The Vanity of Human Wishes* for another, although slightly differing, use of this metaphor: 'Must helpless Man, in Ignorance sedate, / Roll darkling down the Torrent of his Fate?'

No. 84. Saturday, 25 August 1753.

1. *HOR*: Horace, *Satires*, II. vii. 73–4.
2. *the rest of the world*: Sir William Temple, 'Of Poetry', in his *Works* (1757), iii. 425.
3. *DON QUIXOTE's inn*: Cervantes, *Don Quixote*, pt. 1, chs. 32–47.
4. *surtout*: An overcoat or greatcoat.
5. *VIATOR*: I.e. traveller.

No. 85. Tuesday, 28 August 1753.

1. *HOR*: Horace, *Ars Poetica*, ll. 412–13.
2. *observed by BACON*: 'Of Studies', in Francis Bacon, *The Essays*, ed. J. Pitcher (Harmondsworth: Penguin Books, 1985), p. 209; cf. n. 4 to *The Rambler* No. 137 above for another reference by Johnson to this essay.
3. *opinion has of late been*: Johnson here caricatures and attacks some of the attitudes associated most notoriously with French philosophers such as D'Alembert, who in the 'Discours Préliminaire' to the *Encyclopédie* had recently disparaged scholarship.
4. *to possess it*: Persius, i. 27.
5. *as POPE expresses it*: Pope, *Dunciad*, iii. 182.

6. *BOERHAAVE complains*: Cf. above, *Rambler* No. 114, note 3. *Elementa Chemiæ* (1733), i, 'Propositum'.

No. 95. Tuesday, 2 October 1753.

1. *OVID*: Ovid, *Metamorphoses*, iv. 284.

2. *equal readiness*: Cf. Johnson's comment about his own *Rasselas* and Voltaire's *Candide*, 'that if they had not been published so closely one after the other that there was not time for imitation, it would have been in vain to deny that the scheme of that which came latest was taken from the other' (James Boswell, *Life of Johnson*, ed. R. W. Chapman, corr. J. D. Fleeman (Oxford: Oxford University Press, 1976), p. 241).

3. *by Sir ISAAC NEWTON*: Newton's work on colour, including the demonstration of the seven spectral colours, was the subject of experiments he performed in 1665 and 1666. These experiments later formed the basis of a paper he delivered at the Royal Society in 1672 (subsequently published in the *Philosophical Transactions* for that year), and for the first book of his *Opticks* (1704).

No. 99. Tuesday, 16 October 1753.

1. *OVID*: Ovid, *Metamorphoses*, ii. 328.

2. *not only be virtuous but fortunate*: Sir William Temple, 'Of Heroick Virtue', in his *Works* (1757), iii. 306, where Temple in fact says that the 'excellency of genius' necessary for heroic virtue 'must be assisted by fortune, to preserve it to maturity'.

3. *than he could think*: Shakespeare, *Coriolanus*, IV. v. 167–8.

4. *traitors and incendiaries*: Machiavelli, *Discorsi*, I, x.

5. *ALEXANDER the GREAT*: Cf. Samuel Johnson, *The Vanity of Human Wishes*, l. 179. For another instance of contemporary disparagement of Alexander the Great, see Alexander Pope, *An Essay on Man*, iv. 217–20.

6. *Pultowa*: Battle fought between the Russians under Peter the Great and the Swedish forces under Charles XII on 8 July 1709.

7. *the art of war*: Cf. *Vanity of Human Wishes*, l. 210.

8. *PETER*: Peter I, or the Great (1672–1725), Tsar of Russia.

9. *the Orrery*: A clockwork mechanism designed to show the movement of the planets around the sun. The actual inventor was George Graham (1673–1711), John Rowley being the instrument-maker who realized his design.

10. *BOYLE*: Robert Boyle (1627–91), experimental scientist, founder of the Boyle Lectures, of which the purpose was to demonstrate the congruence of natural and revealed religion.

11. *alta semper cupiebat*: 'His soul craved the excessive, the incredible, the gigantic'; Sallust, *Catiline*, v. 5.

12. *union of the Thames and Severn by a canal*: Such a canal was in fact constructed and opened in 1789.

13. *turning the Nile into the Red Sea*: In 1513 Afonso de Albuquerque (1453–1515), the Portuguese viceroy, proposed such a scheme for the reduction of Egypt.

No. 102. Saturday, 27 October 1753.

1. *JUV*: Juvenal, x. 5–6.

2. *fining for Sheriff*: That is, paying a fine in lieu of shouldering the office.

3. *how I hate his beams*: Milton, *Paradise Lost*, iv. 37.

4. *corruption of his countrymen*: Marcus Tullius Cicero (106–43 BC) and Demosthenes (383–322 BC), both great orators of respectively republican Rome and ancient Athens; Hannibal (247–182 BC), supreme military commander of the Carthaginians, whose audacious invasion of Italy during the Second Punic War ended in retreat, attributed by some to Hannibal's own reluctance to pursue an advantage, by others to the enervating effects of Italian luxury on the morale of his troops.

5. *cit*: Short for 'citizen' and defined by Johnson as 'A pert low townsman; A pragmatical trader'.

6. *MERCATOR*: I.e. merchant.

No. 107. Tuesday, 13 November 1753.

1. *HOR*: Horace, *Ars Poetica*, l. 78.

2. *nor fit for tillage*: For Sir Kenelm Digby, see above, *Adventurer* No. 50, note 4. Johnson is here paraphrasing the end of his *Observations upon Religio Medici* (1643).

3. *or immediately to lose it*: Greek Anthology, ix. epigr. 359.

4. *has its felicity*: Greek Anthology, ix. epigr. 360.

No. 111. Tuesday, 27 November 1753.

1. *OVID*: Ovid, *Metamorphoses*, xiii. 140–41.

2. *a tragic poet*: Seneca, *Troades*, l. 1023.

3. *not of themselves*: Martial, X. xlvii. 3.

4. *says SOUTH*: Robert South (1634–1716), court preacher favoured by Charles II, who specialized in attacking Dissenters. The reference is to South's sermon on Proverbs 3:17, 'Her Wayes are Wayes of Pleasantness', in which however Johnson has substituted idleness for South's pleasure as the thing men eventually shun: 'The most Voluptu-

ous, and loose person breathing, were he but tyed to follow his Hawks, and his Hounds, his Dice, and his Courtships every day, would find it the greatest Torment, and Calamity that could befal him; he would flie to the *Mines* and the *Gallyes* for his Recreation, and to the Spade and the Mattock for a Diversion from the misery of a Continuall un-intermitted Pleasure' (Robert South, *Sermons Preached Upon Several Occasions* (Oxford, 1679), p. 190).

5. *homo quam sibi*: Juvenal, x. 347–48, 350.

No. 119. Tuesday, 25 December 1753.

1. *HOR*: Horace, *Odes*, II. ii. 9–12.
2. *the fewest things*: Diogenes Laertius, *Lives*, 'Socrates', xi.
3. *to be DIOGENES*: Plutarch, *Lives*, 'Alexander', xiv.
4. *virtuosos*: A connoisseur or savant in the realm of the fine arts, antiquities or natural curiosities, but with overtones of dilettantism and shallowness.
5. *tears on other occasions*: Related of M. L. Crassus by Plutarch (*Moralia*, 89, 811 and 976), and of Hortensius by Pliny (*Natural History*, ix. 172).
6. *the blood of a man*: Iamblichus, *Life of Pythagoras*, xxx.
7. *which I do not want*: Diogenes Laertius, *Lives*, 'Socrates', ix.

No. 126. Saturday, 19 January 1754.

1. *LUCAN*: Lucan, *Pharsalia*, ix. 576–7.
2. *when he conferred with EGERIA*: Plutarch, *Lives*, 'Numa', IV.
3. *the things eternal*: Cf. 2 Corinthians 4:18.

No. 137. Tuesday, 26 February 1754.

1. *PYTH*: Pythagoras, *Aurea Carmina*, xlii.
2. *shackle the torrent*: Xerxes, when a bridge of ships thrown across the Hellespont to enable him to invade Greece had been destroyed by a storm, had chains thrown over the sea, as a token of his mastery; cf. Samuel Johnson, *The Vanity of Human Wishes*, l. 232.
3. *the rearward of the fashion*: Shakespeare, *2 Henry IV*, III. ii. 339.

No. 138. Saturday, 2 March 1754.

1. *HOR*: Horace, *Epistles*, I. xviii. 102–3.
2. *by HORACE*: 'Cui lecta potenter erit res, / nec facundia deseret hunc nec lucidus ordo'; Horace, *Ars Poetica*, ll. 40–41.

THE IDLER

Johnson wrote *The Idler* between 1758 and 1760. Lighter in tone and shorter in length than both *The Rambler* and *The Adventurer*, these essays were published as leading articles in the *Universal Chronicle*, a new weekly newspaper. Johnson, then occupied with his edition of Shakespeare, had been induced to contribute to the newspaper by the promise of a share in the profits. The text for this edition has been taken from the second edition of 1761 (with the exception of the original No. 22).

No. 1. Saturday, 15 April 1758.

1. *HOR*: Horace, *Odes*, I. xxxii. 1–2. Epigraph translates: 'we idly play, beneath the shade'.
2. *to beg a Name*: Johnson refers to the *Universal Spectator* (1728–46), the *Female Spectator* (1744–6), the *Spectator* (1753–4), and the *Tatler Revived* (1750).

No. 5. Saturday, 13 May 1758.

1. *ANAC*: Anacreon, *Carmina Anacreontea*, xxiv. 9–11. The whole of the short lyric from which Johnson quotes the penultimate sentence may be translated as follows: 'Nature gave horns to bulls, hooves to horses, swiftness to hares, a wide mouth full of teeth to lions, the power of swimming to fish, flight to birds, wisdom to men. But for women she had nothing left. And so? She gives them beauty, strong as any shield, strong as any sword. A beautiful woman prevails over even steel or flame.'
2. *vendible*: Saleable or marketable.
3. *the Salic law*: The alleged fundamental law of the French monarchy, which excluded females from the succession; cf. Shakespeare, *Henry V*, I. ii. 33–95.
4. *defeated by women*: On 9 July 1755, at Fort Duquesne.
5. *Minorca*: Surrendered to the French on 28 June 1756.
6. *return in safety*: The expedition against Rochefort had been launched in September 1756, and had been a fiasco.

No. 10. Saturday, 17 June 1758.

1. *whom they profess to follow*: For a different view of political association, consider this passage from Burke's *Thoughts on the Cause of the Present Discontents* (1770): 'How men can proceed without any connexion at all, is to me utterly incomprehensible. Of what sort of

materials must that man be made, how must he be tempered and put together, who can sit whole years in Parliament, with five hundred and fifty of his fellow citizens, amidst the storm of such tempestuous passions, in the sharp conflict of so many wits, and tempers, and characters, in the agitation of such mighty questions, in the discussion of such vast and ponderous interests, without seeing any one sort of men, whose character, conduct, or disposition, would lead him to associate himself with them, to aid and be aided in any one system of public utility' (Edmund Burke, *A Philosophical Enquiry into the Sublime and Beautiful*, ed. David Womersley (Harmondsworth: Penguin Books, 1998), p. 274).

2. *Cartesian*: That is, a follower of René Descartes (1596–1650), French philosopher and mathematician, whose dualistic philosophy in which mind and body were rigidly separated enabled the denial of finer sensations to animals.

3. *Disciple of Malbranche*: Nicolas Malebranche (1638–1715), French theologian and philosopher, who expounded the doctrine of Cartesian dualism.

4. *Follower of Berkley*: George Berkeley (1685–1753), notorious, because much misunderstood, immaterialist philosopher. Boswell records a famous incident when Johnson, challenged to refute Berkeley's philosophy, 'answered, striking his foot with mighty force against a large stone, till he rebounded from it, "I refute it *thus*"' (James Boswell, *Life of Johnson*, ed. R. W. Chapman, corr. J. D. Fleeman (Oxford: Oxford University Press, 1976), p. 333).

5. *Tillotson*: John Tillotson (1630–94), archbishop of Canterbury, whose pronounced latitudinarian beliefs exposed him to the suspicion of deism and even atheism, at least in the minds of Jacobites and Tories.

6. *Dettingen*: A battle fought in 1743 between Allied and French forces as part of the War of the Austrian Succession (1740–48); now chiefly remembered for the fact that George II led his troops into action.

7. *Fontenoy*: A battle of the War of the Austrian Succession, fought on 11 May 1745 between French and Allied troops and resulting in a victory for the maréchal de Saxe.

8. *Cornhill*: The allusion is to a serious fire in London in 1758, which destroyed houses in and around Change Alley in Cornhill.

9. *the ruin of England*: Tom Tempest interprets recent English history as a conspiracy carried on by the Hanoverians and their adherents against the Stuarts. His beliefs comprise a caricatured Jacobite creed.

10. *Utrecht*: The Peace of Utrecht (1713) brought to a close the War of the Spanish Succession; it was hailed by the Tories as a triumph of diplomacy, and deplored by the Whigs as a blunder.

11. *South Sea*: The South Sea Company was formed in 1711, and in 1720 its shares rose very rapidly in value, before collapsing in a classic stock-market bubble. For Tories, the South Sea Bubble embodied all that was suspicious in the financial innovations associated with the Whigs; hence Jack's willingness to attribute the failure of the company to the malign influence of the Whigs' favourite villain, France.

12. *Electoral Dominions*: Hanover.

13. *never be a Papist*: Jack Sneaker is simply the obverse of Tom Tempest, and therefore subscribes to a caricatured Whig creed.

No. 17. Saturday, 5 August 1758.

1. *Leeuwenhoeck*: Antoine van Leeuwenhoek (1632–1723), Dutch microscopist; the first man to observe bacteria.

2. *would pass for a Philosopher*: Richard Mead, *Of the Small-Pox and Measles* (1747), 'Preface', pp. v–vi. Mead is discussing '*a malevolent sort of men, who endeavour all they can to villify and depreciate other people's works, as if they added to their own reputation in proportion as they detracted from others*' (p. v), and for Mead the '*chief among them was* John Woodward, *Gresham professor, who serv'd an apprenticeship to a Linnen Draper, and afterwards from having got together an heap of shells, pebbles, and such like fossells, would pass for a Philosopher . . .*' (p. vi).

No. [22]. Saturday, 9 September 1758.

1. *9 September 1758*: This essay was not included by Johnson in the collected edition of *The Idler*, presumably on account of the sombreness of its vision.

No. 27. Saturday, 21 October 1758.

1. *acquainted with himself*: The need for self-knowledge is an emphasis so frequent in Johnson's writings that it was a natural choice of theme when Bonnell Thornton chose to parody Johnson's style; see Appendix III, and also note 2 to *The Rambler* No. 24 (9 June 1750).

2. *but slow advances.*: Francis Bacon, *Essays*, 'Of Nature in Men', where however the text reads: 'He that seeketh victory over his nature, let him not set himself too great nor too small tasks: for the first will make him dejected by often failings, and the second will make him a small proceeder, though by often prevailings' (Bacon, *Essays*, ed. J. Pitcher (Harmondsworth: Penguin Books, 1985), p. 177).

3. *æthera virtus*: Virgil, *Æneid*, vi. 129–30.

No. 30. Saturday, 11 November 1758.

1. *keep it in motion.*: Cf. note 3 to *The Rambler* No. 2 (24 March 1750).
2. *Sir Henry Wotton's*: Sir Henry Wotton (1568–1639), Provost of Eton, 1624–39, diplomat and man of letters. The definition was written by Wotton in the commonplace book of a friend; cf. Logan Pearsall Smith, *Life and Letters of Sir Henry Wotton* (1907), ii. 9–11.

No. 31. Saturday, 18 November 1758.

1. *lustre and its shade*: A slight misquotation of Samuel Butler, *Hudibras*, II. i. 905–8.
2. *calls himself the Proud*: Edward Young, *Busiris, King of Egypt. A Tragedy* (1719), I. i. 13, p. 2, where Syphaces says of Busiris: 'He calls himself the *Proud*, and Glories in it.'
3. *how they hate his beams*: Milton, *Paradise Lost*, iv. 37.

No. 32. Saturday, 25 November 1758.

1. *levelled by Death*: Claudian, *De raptu Proserpinæ*, ii. 302.
2. *necessity of Sleep*: Plutarch, *Lives*, 'Alexander', xxii. 3–4.

No. 36. Saturday, 23 December 1758.

1. *shortest train of intermediate propositions*: Richard Cumberland (1631–1718), bishop of Peterborough, adversary of Hobbes (which no doubt recommended him to Johnson). The passage Johnson has in mind is the following: 'such Acts which, in the shortest Method, produce the principal Effect as their chief End, are, in their own Nature, Acts strait and right, upon account of that natural Similitude which they bear to a right Line; which Line, between any two given Points, is always the shortest. These very same Acts, however, when they come afterwards to be compared with any Law (whether natural or instituted) as the Rule of Action; and, when such Acts are found to agree, and are conformable to such a *Law* or *Rule*, they then are called *morally good*, or exactly strait and right, *i.e.* they are well and exactly fitted to such a Rule. For, the Rule itself is called strait and right, because it directs and shews the shortest Way to the End proposed' (*Philosophical Enquiry into the Laws of Nature* (1750), 'Prolegomena', sect. xvi, pp. xlv–xlvi).
2. *by stratagem*: Samuel Butler, *Hudibras*, I. i. 125–26; Edward Young, *Satires*, vi. 188.
3. *which is to the west*: John Petvin, *Letters Concerning Mind* (1750), pp. 40–41 (with some trivial deviations from Petvin's actual words).

No. 40. Saturday, 20 January 1759.

1. *took Dieskaw*: Louis-Auguste Dieskau (1701–67), soldier, German by birth, entered into French service as the aide-de-camp of the maréchal de Saxe. He was commander of the French troops in Canada, 1755, and was taken prisoner at the Battle of Lake George, 8 September 1755.

2. *Eau de Luce*: A mixture of alcohol, ammonia and amber, which was used in India as a cure for snake-bites, and in England as smelling-salts.

No. 41. Saturday, 27 January 1759.

1. *morsque gradu*: Apparently these verses were composed by Johnson himself on the death of his mother (*Samuel Johnson: The Complete English Poems*, ed. J. D. Fleeman (Harmondsworth: Penguin Books, 1971), pp. 146 and 230–31). 'But you, whoever you may be, you who thought the untimely death of an unhappy poet worthy of your tears; may this be your last time to weep, and may life and death for you flow smoothly on with an even pace.'

2. *says Tully*: 'Nemo enim est tam senex qui se annum non putet posse vivere'; Cicero, *De Senectute*, vii. 24.

3. *one sinner that repenteth*: Luke 15:10.

4. *Immortality to light*: 2 Timothy 1:10.

5. *cannot assuage it*: Epicurus (341–270 BC) and Zeno of Citium (c.335–c.263 BC), both ancient Greek philosophers, of whose doctrines Johnson here supplies succinct accounts.

6. *wiped from the eyes*: Revelation 21:4.

No. 44. Saturday, 17 February 1759.

1. *art of Forgetfulness*: Themistocles (c. 524–c. 460 BC), Athenian statesman and commander. Cicero, *De Finibus*, II. xxxii. 104.

No. 48. Saturday, 17 March 1759.

1. *Tom Distich*: A spoof name for a follower of the theatre.

2. *Malouin privateer*: A pirate based in the port of St Malo, in Brittany.

No. 49. Saturday, 24 March 1759.

1. *king of Prussia*: Frederick II, or the Great (1712–86).

2. *where armies whole have sunk*: Milton, *Paradise Lost*, ii. 592–4.

3. *Egre of the Severn*: A tidal wave of unusual height, now more usually referred to when it occurs on the Severn as a 'bore'.

No. 50. Saturday, 31 March 1759.

1. *seven stages of life*: As related by Jaques, in Shakespeare, *As You Like It*, II. vii. 142–66.

2. *by hermits*: Raffaello Sanzio (1483–1520), Italian painter of the high Renaissance. Versailles was the lavish palace of the French monarch, built by Louis XIV just outside Paris.

3. *ejulations*: Sounds of wailing or lamentation.

No. 51. Saturday, 7 April 1759.

1. *instigation of a harlot*: Alexander is said to have burnt the palace of Xerxes at Persepolis at the suggestion of Thais, a courtesan; cf. Quintus Curtius, *History of Alexander*, V. vii. 1–7 and VIII. i. 50–52.

2. *subjection to his wife*: John Churchill (1650–1722), first duke of Marlborough, the greatest military commander of the late seventeenth and early eighteenth centuries. He was never forgiven by some for his desertion of James II in 1688, and the charges of avarice and domination by his wife Sarah (1660–1744), through whom he enjoyed the favour of Queen Anne, were in large measure the creation of his Jacobite and Tory enemies.

3. *that he was a Man*: Juvenal, x. 41–2.

No. 59. Saturday, 2 June 1759.

1. *the Poem of Hudibras*: A satire by Samuel Butler (1613–80), published in three parts between 1663 and 1680. One of its main targets was religious dissent.

No. 60. Saturday, 9 June 1759.

1. *kept nine years*: Horace, *Ars Poetica*, l. 388.

2. *His opinion was*: There follows a series of critical commonplaces.

3. *Johnson*: Ben Jonson.

4. *Otway*: Thomas Otway (1652–85), playwright.

5. *Southern*: Thomas Southern (1659–1746), playwright.

6. *Rowe*: Nicholas Rowe (1674–1718), a playwright whose translation of Lucan was praised by Johnson as 'one of the greatest productions of English poetry'.

7. *Congreve*: William Congreve (1670–1729), dramatist and Whig statesman.

8. *Addison*: Joseph Addison (1672–1719), Whig statesman, poet and man of letters; together with Richard Steele, responsible for the *Spectator* (1711–12), and hence an arbiter of taste in the early eighteenth century.

9. *Prior*: Matthew Prior (1664–1721), poet, essayist and diplomat.

10. *Swift*: Jonathan Swift (1667–1745), poet and man of letters; member of the Scriblerus Club and friend of Pope, Gay and Arbuthnot.

11. *Pope*: Alexander Pope (1688–1744), the most accomplished poet, critic and translator of the early Hanoverian period.

12. *Phædra and Hippolitus*: Edmund Smith, *Phaedra and Hippolitus* (1707).

13. *rest of the world together.* Cf. *The Adventurer* No. 84 (25 August 1753), note 2.

14. *Barbarossa*: John Brown, *Barbarossa* (1754).

15. *the author of Cleone*: Robert Dodsley (1758).

16. *an Echo to the Sense*: Pope, *Essay on Criticism*, l. 365.

17. *instead of a stick*: Butler, *Hudibras*, I. i. 11–12.

18. *find out why*: Butler, *Hudibras*, II. ii. 385–8.

No. 61. Saturday, 16 June 1759.

1. *some tribunal*: The project for a British Academy, in emulation of the French Academy established by Cardinal de Richelieu, was frequently discussed after the Restoration, although it seems never to have enjoyed the support of Johnson, who in his 'Life' of Roscommon wrote that 'such a society might perhaps without much difficulty be collected; but that it would produce what is expected from it may be doubted' (*Lives of the English Poets*, ed. G. B. Hill, 3 vols. (Oxford: The Clarendon Press, 1905), i, p. 232).

2. *ornamental luxuriance*: An echo perhaps of the critical views of John Dennis (1657–1734), whose pungently Whiggish outlook would have done little to recommend him to Johnson.

3. *monkish barbarity of rhyme*: Cf. Milton, *Paradise Lost*, 'Preface'.

4. *perpetual variation of the numbers*: Cf. *Rambler* Nos. 88 and 90, in which Johnson praises Milton's versification in similar terms.

5. *th' effect of fire*: Milton, *Paradise Lost*, ii. 594–5.

6. *quench'd these orbs*: Milton, *Paradise Lost*, iii. 25.

No. 65. Saturday, 14 July 1759.

1. *Sequel of Clarendon's History*: Johnson refers to *The Life of Edward, Earl of Clarendon ... Being a Continuation of the History of the Grand Rebellion* (1759).

2. *whole winter's fuel*: Nicolas-Claude Fabri de Pieresc (1580–1637), antiquarian, philologist, astronomer. On account of both his humane learning and his wealth, he was accounted the Maecenas of his age. The anecdote is related by Gilles Ménage, *Ménagiana* (1693).

3. *Bishop Lloyd*: William Lloyd (1627–1717), bishop of St Asaph,

Lichfield and Coventry, and Worcester. An opponent of Charles II and upholder of Revolution Principles after 1688, he was eventually driven insane by his remorseless study of the Book of Revelation.

4. *will easily conceive*: Cf. Gilbert Burnet, *Life and Death of Sir Matthew Hale, kt.* (1682).

5. *never given*: The Bodleian copy of the 1734 first edition of the second volume of this work (O.2.8 Jur.) bears the following inscription on the reverse of the title page: 'The Original Manuscript of both Volumes of this History will be deposited in the Cotton Library by T Burnett'.

6. *two lowest of all human beings*: I.e. John Oldmixon (1673–1742) and George Duckett (d. 1732).

7. *as he laid it in*: Burnet's character of Lloyd is as follows: 'He was so exact in every thing he set about, that he never gave over any part of study, till he had quite mastered it. But when that was done, he went to another subject, and did not lay out his learning with the diligence with which he laid it in' (Gilbert Burnet, *History of his Own Time*, 2 vols. (1724, 1734), i. 190).

8. *could never be perfected*: Thomas Baker (1656–1740), author and antiquary, non-juror, friend of Matthew Prior.

No. 66. Saturday, 21 July 1759.

1. *Alexandrian library... Palatine repositories*: Both great libraries of antiquity. The Alexandrian library was founded by Ptolemy I. At the time of Callimachus (b. 310 BC) it held 400,000 volumes, and by the first century AD had expanded to 700,000 volumes. Ptolemy III is said to have deposited in the library the official, Athenian, copy of the works of Aeschylus, Sophocles and Euripides. It was for long thought that the library had been burnt in 642 by Amrou, the general of the caliph Omar, but this is now discredited. The Palatine is the hill in Rome on which the imperial palace of the Caesars was constructed.

2. *Sophocles and Euripides ... Menander*: Sophocles (496–406 BC), Greek tragedian, was said to be the author of some 120 plays, only 7 of which have survived. Euripides (480–406 BC), Greek tragedian, was said to have written some 80 or 90 plays, 19 of which have survived (although one, 'Rhesus', is of doubtful authenticity). Menander (c. 342–292 BC), comic playwright, was said to have written in the region of 100 plays, of which substantial fragments of four plays, and shorter fragments of many more, have survived.

3. *direct our endeavours*: Here, for once at least, Johnson was of one mind with Gibbon, who in chapter fifty-one of *The Decline and Fall* chose also to lay the emphasis on how much of antiquity has survived,

rather than on that portion which has perished: 'I sincerely regret the more valuable libraries which have been involved in the ruin of the Roman empire; but when I seriously compute the lapse of ages, the waste of ignorance, and the calamities of war, our treasures, rather than our losses, are the object of my surprise. Many curious and interesting facts are buried in oblivion; the three great historians of Rome have been transmitted to our hands in a mutilated state, and we are deprived of many pleasing compositions of the lyric, iambic, and dramatic poetry of the Greeks. Yet we should gratefully remember, that the mischances of time and accident have spared the classic works to which the suffrage of antiquity had adjudged the first place of genius and glory: the teachers of ancient knowledge, who are still extant, had perused and compared the writings of their predecessors; nor can it fairly be presumed that any important truth, any useful discovery in art or nature, has been snatched away from the curiosity of modern ages' (Edward Gibbon, *The History of the Decline and Fall of the Roman Empire*, ed. D. J. Womersley (Harmondsworth: Penguin Books, 1994), iii. 286).

4. *Malbranche and Locke*: Nicolas Malebranche (1638–1715), French philosopher. John Locke (1632–1704), English philosopher.

No. 72. Saturday, 1 September 1759.

1. *Themistocles*: Themistocles (*c.* 524–*c.* 460 BC), Athenian politician and naval strategist; victor of the Battle of Salamis (480 BC).
2. *art of Forgetfulness*: Cf. *Idler* No. 44.

No. 81. Saturday, 3 November 1759.

1. *towards Quebec*: Quebec had been taken by the English on 13 September 1759.

No. 84. Saturday, 24 November 1759.

1. *servants of his chamber*: Usually attributed to Louis II de Bourbon, prince de Condé (1621–86), French soldier, statesman and patron of the arts.

No. 88. Saturday, 22 December 1759.

1. *a real Character*: A reference to the title of the celebrated work by John Wilkins (1614–72), whose *An Essay towards a Real Character and a Philosophical Language* (1668) was an attempt to overcome the deficiencies of natural languages.
2. *with Applause*: Suetonius, 'Divus Augustus', xcix.

No. 103. Saturday, 5 April 1760.

1. *ultima vitæ*: Juvenal, x. 275.
2. *that solemn week*: I.e. Easter.

MISCELLANEOUS ESSAYS

A Compleat Vindication of the Licensers of the Stage.

1. *BY AN IMPARTIAL HAND*: *The Compleat Vindication* was published in May 1739, in response to the refusal of the Lord Chamberlain to grant a licence to Henry Brooke's play *Gustavus Vasa*, presumably because in its depiction of a corrupt prime minister it was thought to reflect too closely upon Robert Walpole.

2. *at Court*: That is, in the administration.

3. *L—and P—*: George Lyttelton (1709–73), first baron Lyttelton, prominent politician and opponent of Sir Robert Walpole. William Pitt (1708–78), first earl of Chatham, Whig statesman and orator.

4. *special Jury*: A jury consisting of persons who occupied a comparatively elevated station in life, such as that of banker or merchant, or who owned real property above a certain rateable value; cf. Samuel Johnson, *London*, l. 252.

5. *the most inexorable Enemies*: An allusion to the notorious indifference of Walpole to literary culture. Scholarly treatments of this subject include Bertrand Goldgar, *Walpole and the Wits: The Relation of Politics to Literature, 1722–1742* (Lincoln, Nebr.: University of Nebraska Press, 1976) and Christine Gerrard, *The Patriot Opposition to Walpole: Politics, Poetry, and National Myth 1725–1742* (Oxford: The Clarendon Press, 1994).

6. *through every Age*: Henry Brooke, *Gustavus Vasa* (1739), I. i. 22.

7. *the two Houses*: I.e. the House of Commons and the House of Lords.

8. *ampliare suam auctoritatem*: 'It is the sign of a good judge that he should augment his authority'; a traditional legal maxim.

9. *a Standing Army*: The maintenance of a standing army was a frequent topic amongst those suspicious of the motives of the ministry.

10. *th' unletter'd Mind*: *Gustavus Vasa*, 'Prologue'.

11. *Anderson*: A character in *Gustavus Vasa*.

12. *save thee*: *Gustavus Vasa*, I. i. 116.

13. *fettered in their Fears.—*: *Gustavus Vasa*, I. ii. 80.

14. *my Country's Freedom*: *Gustavus Vasa*, I. iii. 31.

15. *the Poet Laureat*: At this time, Colley Cibber (1671–1757), the dramatist, actor and theatrical impresario.

16. *Imprimatur*: Literally, 'let it be published'; by extension, the permission to print something.

17. *the Gazetteer*: The *Daily Gazetteer*, the newspaper of the ministry.

An Essay on Epitaphs.

1. *ESSAY on EPITAPHS*: Published in *The Gentleman's Magazine*, September 1740, x, pp. 593–6.

2. *Sir ISAAC NEWTON*: Sir Isaac Newton (1642–1727), Master of the Royal Mint, PRS, pre-eminent mathematician and scientist, whose work on in particular optics and celestial mechanics exerted great influence over the imaginative world of the eighteenth century.

3. *forsan et Antipodes*: 'Here lies Pico della Mirandola: the Tagus, the Ganges, even the Antipodes, know the rest.'

4. *Illyricus*: The suffix '-icus' indicates 'conqueror of' or 'slayer of'.

5. *hic quiescit*: 'Having searched out the laws of nature, Isaac Newton rests here.'

6. *Fragrance or of Beauty*: Minutius (or Minucius) Felix (*fl.* second–third century AD), advocate, and early Latin Christian apologist. Johnson is thinking of the following passage from the dialogue *Octavius*, in which Christian belief and conduct are defended against the charges of the pagans: 'Nec mortuos coronamus. Ego vos in hoc magis miror, quemadmodum tribuatis exanimi aut [non] sentienti facem aut non sentienti coronam, cum et beatus non egeat et miser non gaudeat floribus'; 'Nor do we garland the dead with flowers; I'm astonished by you, when you bestow a garland on a corpse, as if we assumed they could sense it: they are as happy in not needing flowers as they are unhappy in being unable to take pleasure in them' (*Octavius*, xxxviii. 3).

7. *immobile Saxum*: Abraham Cowley (1618–67), Royalist poet. The epitaph translates as follows: 'O divine poet, while your golden writings fly far and wide throughout the globe and you live perpetually in fame, may you lie here in peaceful rest. May aged faith guard your urn, and may the muses keep watch over you with their inextinguishable torch. May this place be sacred, and let no one be so rash as to dare disturb this venerable bust with sacrilegious hand. May Cowley's dust rest undisturbed, rest through sweet ages, and may his tombstone be unmoved.'

8. *Angelo*: Michelangelo Buonarroti (1475–1564), Florentine painter, sculptor, architect and poet. Johnson refers to the ceiling of the Sistine Chapel (which he had himself not seen).

9. *Sannazarius*: Jacopo Sannazzaro (1458–1530), Neapolitan poet and celebrant of rural life. The statues of Apollo and Minerva on either side of his tomb in the church of Santa Maria del Parto in Naples were renamed David and Judith.

10. *dole regum vices*: Jean Passerat (1534–1602), French man of letters, pupil of Cujas, successor to Ramus in the chair of rhetoric at the Collège de France. The epitaph translates as follows: 'Pause, traveller, and commiserate the fate of kings. Beneath this marble is laid the heart of a king who gave laws equally to the French and to the Poles. A murderer hidden beneath a cowl killed him. Pass on, traveller, and commiserate the fate of kings.'

11. *miserrimi Peccatoris*: 'Pray for the soul of — a most miserable sinner.'

12. *what it cannot comprehend*: Contrast, however, the opinion of Burke, that the mind is most powerfully affected precisely by what it cannot comprehend (*A Philosophical Enquiry into the Origin of our Ideas of the Sublime and Beautiful*, pt. 2, sect. 3 and 4).

13. *per ora virum*: Quintus Ennius (239–169 BC), one of the greatest of the early Roman poets. The epitaph translates as follows: 'Let no one honour me with tears, nor lay me in the earth with weeping. Why? I live in the mouths of men.'

14. *Monument of Augustus*: A weakness for luxury was allegedly the failing of Gaius Maecenas (c. 74–8 BC), the chief minister of Augustus (63 BC – AD 14), whose own approach to supreme power in the Roman state had been blemished by the proscription which followed the assassination of Julius Caesar, and in which Augustus' enemies were executed without trial or other legal process.

15. *two Greek Inscriptions*: Both taken from the *Greek Anthology*. The translations into Latin and English are Johnson's own.

16. *Epictetus, the Stoic Philosopher*: Epictetus (60–140 AD), originally a slave, subsequently a philosopher, who taught that through endurance and abstention men might achieve independence of external circumstances.

'Introduction' to the *Harleian Miscellany*.

1. *Harleian Miscellany*: The *Harleian Miscellany* is a selection of tracts from the Harleian collection, the books, pamphlets and manuscripts amassed by Robert and Edward Harley, respectively the first and second earls of Oxford. On the death of Edward Harley in 1753 the collection was purchased by Parliament and placed in the British Museum. The *Miscellany* was co-edited by Johnson and the antiquary

William Oldys (1696–1761), and published in 1744–6 by the book-seller Thomas Osborne (d. 1767).

2. *MORE WORK FOR A COOPER*: One of the scurrilous pamphlets published in 1588–9 under the pseudonym of Martin Marprelate, in which the episcopalian government of the Elizabethan Church of England was subjected to presbyterian attack. The title of this particular pamphlet glances at Thomas Cooper, bishop of Winchester.

3. *Rawlinson*: Thomas Rawlinson (1681–1725), book-collector and antiquarian.

4. *Photius*: Photius (*c.* 820–91), patriarch of Byzantium, lexicographer and literary critic.

Observations on the present State of Affairs.

1. *State of Affairs*: First published in the *Literary Magazine*, iv, 15 July–15 August 1756. The conflict in question is the Seven Years' War between France and Britain (1756–63). Compare *Idler* No. 81.

2. *New-Scotland*: I.e. Nova Scotia.

3. *Dettingen*: See note 6 to *Idler* No. 10.

4. *Fontenoy and Val*: See note 7 to *Idler* No. 10. Val was another battle of the War of the Austrian Succession.

5. *Cape-Breton*: Sir William Pepperell (1696–1759), shipbuilder and soldier of Massachusetts.

6. *Charles Stuart*: I.e. the Young Pretender, who had raised rebellion in Scotland in 1745.

7. *(To be continued.)*: No continuation was in fact published.

Of the Duty of a JOURNALIST.

1. *Of the Duty of a JOURNALIST*: First published in *Payne's Universal Chronicle*, no. 1, 8 April 1758, pp. 1–2.

The Bravery of the *English* Common Soldiers.

1. *English Common Soldiers*: First published in *The British Magazine* for January 1760, pp. 37–9.

2. *perverse Cartesians*: A critical glance at the Cartesian doctrine that animals are insensate; cf. *Idler* No. 17.

3. *Russian Empires, and Prussian Monarch*: Tsarina Elizabeth (1709–62) and Frederick II, or the Great (1712–86).

4. *French Count*: Lancelot, comte Turpin de Cressé (1715–95), French soldier and tactician. *Essai sur l'Art de la Guerre* (1754).